ESSENTIALS OF BIOLOGICAL ANTHROPOLOGY

FIFTH EDITION

FIFTH EDITION

ESSENTIALS OF
BIOLOGICAL
ANTHROPOLOGY

CLARK SPENCER LARSEN

THE OHIO STATE UNIVERSITY

W. W. NORTON & COMPANY
Independent Publishers Since 1923

W. W. Norton & Company has been independent since its founding in 1923, when William Warder Norton and Mary D. Herter Norton first published lectures delivered at the People's Institute, the adult education division of New York City's Cooper Union. The firm soon expanded its program beyond the Institute, publishing books by celebrated academics from America and abroad. By midcentury, the two major pillars of Norton's publishing program—trade books and college texts—were firmly established. In the 1950s, the Norton family transferred control of the company to its employees, and today—with a staff of five hundred and hundreds of trade, college, and professional titles published each year—W. W. Norton & Company stands as the largest and oldest publishing house owned wholly by its employees.

Editor: Jake Schindel
Senior Project Editor: Jennifer Barnhardt
Editorial Assistant: Mia Davis
Managing Editor, College: Marian Johnson
Associate Director of Production, College: Benjamin Reynolds
Production Manager: Liz Marotta
Media Editor: Michael Jaoui
Associate Media Editor: Ariel Eaton
Media Project Editor: Jesse Newkirk
Media Editorial Assistant: Jesse Singh
Managing Editor, College Digital Media: Kim Yi
Ebook Production Manager: Kate Barnes
Marketing Manager, Anthropology: Kandace Starbird
Design Director: Rubina Yeh
Designer: Marisa Nakasone
Director of College Permissions: Megan Schindel
College Permissions Associate: Patricia Wong
Photo Editor: Amla Sanghvi
Photo Researchers: Lynn Gadson and Jane Sanders Miller
Composition: MPS North America LLC / MPS Project Manager: Jackie Strohl
Illustrations: Dragonfly Media Group
Manufacturing: TC Transcontinental, Interglobe

Library of Congress Cataloging-in-Publication Data

Names: Larsen, Clark Spencer, author.
Title: Essentials of biological anthropology / Clark Spencer Larsen, The
    Ohio State University.
Description: Fifth edition. | New York : W. W. Norton & Company, [2022] |
    Includes bibliographical references and index.
Identifiers: LCCN 2021011576 | **ISBN 9780393871371 (paperback)** | ISBN
    9780393876802 (epub)
Subjects: LCSH: Physical anthropology.
Classification: LCC GN50.4 .L367 2022 | DDC 599.9--dc23
LC record available at https://lccn.loc.gov/2021011576

W. W. Norton & Company, Inc., 500 Fifth Avenue, New York, N.Y. 10110
www.wwnorton.com
W. W. Norton & Company Ltd., 15 Carlisle Street, London W1D 3BS

1 2 3 4 5 6 7 8 9 0

ABOUT THE AUTHOR

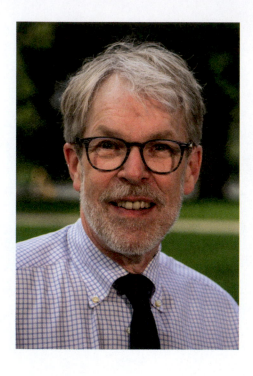

Clark Spencer Larsen is a native of Nebraska. He received his BA in anthropology from Kansas State University and his MA and PhD in biological anthropology from the University of Michigan. Clark's research is in bioarchaeology, skeletal biology, and paleoanthropology. He has worked in North America, Europe, and Asia and has taught at the University of Massachusetts Dartmouth, Northern Illinois University, Purdue University, and the University of North Carolina. Since 2001, he has been a member of the faculty at The Ohio State University, where he is Distinguished University Professor. He served as chair of the Department of Anthropology from 2001 to 2017. He teaches introductory biological anthropology, osteology, bioarchaeology, and paleoanthropology. Clark has served as president of the American Association of Physical Anthropologists and as editor-in-chief of the *American Journal of Physical Anthropology*. He is a member of the National Academy of Sciences and the American Academy of Arts and Sciences, and is a fellow of the American Association for the Advancement of Science. His research team's publication in the *Proceedings of the National Academy of Sciences* received the 2019 Cozzarelli Prize. In addition to *Essentials of Biological Anthropology*, he has authored or edited 35 books and monographs, including *Bioarchaeology: Interpreting Behavior from the Human Skeleton*, *Skeletons in Our Closet: Revealing Our Past through Bioarchaeology*, *Advances in Dental Anthropology*, and *A Companion to Biological Anthropology*.

BRIEF CONTENTS

CONTENTS

Chapter 1   What Is Biological Anthropology?   3

PART I   THE PRESENT: FOUNDATION FOR THE PAST   21

Chapter 4   Genes and Their Evolution: Population Genetics   81

PART II THE PAST: EVIDENCE FOR THE PRESENT 205

Chapter 8 Fossils and Their Place in Time and Nature 207

Chapter 9   Primate Origins and Evolution: The First 50 Million Years   243

Chapter 10   Early Hominin Origins and Evolution: The Roots of Humanity   275

Chapter 11   The Origins and Evolution of Early *Homo*   315

Chapter 12   The Origins, Evolution, and Dispersal of Modern People   349

TWO-PAGE SPREADS

TO THE INSTRUCTOR

HOW THIS BOOK CAN HELP YOUR STUDENTS DISCOVER BIOLOGICAL ANTHROPOLOGY

It Is about Engagement

Teaching is about engagement—connecting students with knowledge, making it real to them, and having them come away from the course with an understanding of core concepts. *Essentials of Biological Anthropology* seeks to engage students in the learning process. This is perhaps more of a challenge in the study of biological anthropology than in the study of other sciences, mainly because most students have never heard of the subject. The average student has probably taken a precollege course in chemistry, physics, or biology. Biological anthropology, though, is rarely mentioned or taught in precollege settings. Commonly, a student first hears of the subject when an academic advisor explains that biological anthropology is a popular course that fulfills the college's natural science requirement.

Once taking the course, however, that same student usually connects quickly with the subject because so many of the topics are familiar—fossils, evolution, race, genetics, DNA, monkeys, forensic investigations, and origins of speech, to name a few. Often, students simply do not realize that these separately engaging topics come under the umbrella of one discipline, the subject of which is the study of human evolution and human variability.

Perhaps drawn to biological anthropology because it focuses on our past and our present as a species, many young learners quickly see the fundamental importance of the discipline. In the issue of *Discover* magazine featuring the top 100 stories of 2017, two of the top 10 were from the field of biological anthropology, one of which was the featured cover story on human evolution. Moreover, biological anthropology, including most of the topics that you will teach in your course, is well represented in the popular press,

news magazines, and various media outlets. In this textbook, the discussions of topics familiar and unfamiliar will provide students with stepping-stones to science and to the centrality of biological anthropology in understanding our world. Whether your students find the material familiar or unfamiliar, they will see that the book relates the discipline to human life: real concerns about human bodies and human identity. They will see themselves from an entirely different point of view and gain new self-awareness.

In writing this book, I made no assumptions about what the reader knows, except to assume that the student attending your biological anthropology class has very little or no background in biological anthropology. As I wrote the book, I constantly reflected on the core concepts of biological anthropology and how to make them understandable. I combined this quest for both accuracy and clarity with my philosophy of teaching; namely, engage students to help them learn. Simply put, teaching is about engagement. Although most students in an introductory biological anthropology class do not intend to become professional biological anthropologists, some will become interested enough to take more courses. For that reason, this book is written for all students—those who will not continue to study biological anthropology, those who get "hooked" by this fascinating subject (a common occurrence!), and those who now or will eventually decide to become professionals in the field.

The book is unified by the subject matter of biological anthropology. But equally important is the central theme of science—what it is, how it is done, and how scientists (in our case, anthropologists) learn about the natural world. I wrote the book with the goal of creating a picture of who humans are as organisms, how we got to where we are over the past millions of years of evolution, and where we are going in the future in light of current conditions. Regarding biological anthropology specifically, your students should finish the book understanding human evolution and how it is studied, how the present helps us understand the past, the diversity of organisms living and past, the diversity of human beings, and the nature of biological change over time and across geography. Such knowledge should help them answer questions about the world. For example: How did primates emerge as a unique group of mammals? Why do people look different from place to place around the world? Why is it important to gain exposure to sunlight yet unsafe to prolong that exposure? Why is it unhealthy to be excessively overweight? Throughout human history, what have humans eaten, and why is it important to know?

I have presented such topics so that each student can come to understand the central concepts and build from them a fuller understanding of biological anthropology. Throughout, I emphasize hypothesis testing—the core of the scientific method—and focus on that process and the excitement of discovery. The narrative style is personalized. To show students how problems are addressed through fieldwork or through laboratory investigations, I often draw on my own experiences and those of scientists I know or am familiar with through their teaching and writing.

Scientists do not just collect facts. Rather, they collect data and make observations that help them answer questions about the complex natural world we all inhabit. Reflecting this practice, *Essentials of Biological Anthropology* is a collection not of facts for the student to learn but of answers to questions that help all of us understand who we are as living organisms and what our place is in the world. Science is a way of knowing, a learning process, and a means of connecting our lives with our world. In these ways, it is liberating.

HOW THE BOOK IS ORGANIZED

The book is divided into two parts. After an introductory overview of anthropology and biological anthropology (chapter 1), part I presents the key principles and concepts in biology, especially from an evolutionary perspective. This material draws largely on the study of living organisms, including humans and nonhuman primates. Because much of our understanding of the past is drawn from what we learn from the present, this part lays the foundation for the presentation in part II—the past record of primate and human evolution. In putting the record of the living up front, this book departs from the style of most other introductory biological anthropology textbooks, which start out with the earliest record and end with the living. Just as all of Charles Darwin's ideas were first derived from seeing living plants and animals, much of our understanding of function and adaptation comes from observing living organisms as models. Therefore, this book views the living as the

window onto what came before—the present contextualizes and informs our understanding of the past. The individual chapters of this book can be taught in any order, and that is partly because each chapter reinforces the central point: we understand our past via what we see in the living.

Part II presents evidence of the past, covering more than 50 million years of primate and human evolution. Most textbooks of this kind end the record of human evolution at about 25,000 years before present (yBP), when modern *Homo sapiens* evolved worldwide. But this textbook does not end there: it also provides the record since the appearance of modern humans, showing that important biological changes have occurred in the past 10,000 years, largely relating to the shift from hunting and gathering to the domestication of plants and animals. Food production was a revolutionary development in the human story, and part II presents this remarkable record, including changes in health and well-being that continue today. A new subdiscipline of biological anthropology—bioarchaeology—is contributing profound insights into the past 10,000 years, one of the most dynamic periods of human evolution. During this period, a fundamental change occurred in how humans obtained food. This change set the stage for our current environmental disruptions and modern living conditions.

CHANGES IN THE FIFTH EDITION

Reflecting the dynamic nature of biological anthropology, numerous revisions and updates have been made to this new edition of *Essentials of Biological Anthropology*. These updates serve to provide content on the new and cutting-edge developments in the discipline, to give new ways of looking at older findings, and to keep the book engaging and timely for both you and your students. Although the core principles of the book remain the same—namely, the focus on evolution—the revisions throughout the book present new insights, new discoveries, and new perspectives. Other changes are intended to give added focus and clarity and to increase the visual appeal that supports the pedagogy of engagement and learning:

- **New Anthropology at Work features.** The new edition includes five new Anthropology at Work features spotlighting former anthropology majors—three professional biological anthropologists (a primatologist, a paleoanthropologist, and a human-health scholar) and two who are applying their anthropology background to other career fields (an epidemiologist and a forensic scientist). In the features, they discuss what excites them about their work and why they decided to study biological anthropology. Three of the features have brief accompanying videos in which these individuals provide a closer look at their research and explain how they got from an introductory course to the fascinating work they do today. They also share their insights into how an anthropology background can serve students in any number of career endeavors.

- **New content on the COVID-19 virus and pandemic.** This is, in many ways, the defining event to date in so many college students' lives, and this new edition helps them understand elements of the pandemic from an anthropological perspective, including how and why viruses impact human populations in the context of evolution.

- **New content on the role of biological anthropology in addressing critical issues facing our planet.** The health of our planet and its occupants in the twenty-first century is at a crossroads. New content examines how existing and newly developing research on emerging issues such as food security, plant and animal biodiversity, and the future of our planet is being confronted by biological anthropologists.

- **New content on the genetics and genomes of hominins, both fossil and recent.** Analysis of ancient DNA from Neandertals reveals the presence of alleles for modern human disease and other health-related conditions. New analysis of ancient DNA—made possible by genomes from humans worldwide, past and present—is providing unprecedented insights into population movement and human variation. We are learning that mobility—a fundamental characteristic of humans—results in considerable gene flow, more than previously understood. The rise in paleogenetics is facilitating the testing of long-standing hypotheses regarding human variation in the modern world. While natural selection explains most of human variation and evolution, gene flow is fundamental in determining biological change.

- **New content on the origins of adaptability to high altitude.** The discovery of previously unknown human ancestors—the Denisovans—reveals a far longer history of human adaptation to life at high altitudes than previously understood. We are learning that rather than representing a relatively recent development, adaptation to high altitude extends back in time to some 160,000 yBP in a remote site in China.

- **New content on fossil hominin discoveries.** The exciting recent discoveries related to *Homo luzonensis*

in the Philippines and the Denisovan fossil in Tibet help open students' eyes to the dynamic and exciting nature of anthropological discovery. Additionally, new discoveries of *Homo naledi* in the Rising Star Cave system in South Africa have provided numerous new fossils, in addition to those discovered earlier and discussed in the fourth edition of *Essentials of Biological Anthropology*. These discoveries contribute new understanding to these enigmatic hominins and provide confirmation that the series of fossils represent not only a new genus and species but a population of hominins. Excavations on Flores Island, where the famous "hobbit" (*Homo floresiensis*) fossils were found, landed a new surprise: the ancestor of *H. floresiensis* dating to 700,000 yBP. Redating of the original fossil *H. floresiensis* shows it to have existed more than 60,000 yBP. It has always been assumed that the first producers of stone tools were early members of the genus *Homo*. New discoveries from East Africa point to *Australopithecus* as the first manufacturer and user of stone tools. To make matters more complex, yet more interesting, some authorities believe that there may be as many as 10 species of *Australopithecus*. Whatever the number, the australopithecines were remarkably successful over a time period of at least 2–3 million years.

- **New content on fossil primate discoveries.** Newly discovered early primates in East Asia are revealing complexity in the origins of primates and their later evolution.

- **New content on primate social behavior.** Anthropologists continue to learn more about social interactions between members of primate groups and just how critical social behavior is for the well-being and functioning of social units. It is becoming increasingly clear that social learning is an element of behavior in all primates. While humans are the only primates that can talk, other primates share similar communication patterns.

- **New content on dramatic changes in the world's climate today.** We are living at a time of rapidly changing climate involving global warming. New predictions reveal that the climate is changing faster than originally predicted, presenting the world with new health and lifeway challenges.

- **Continued enhancement of the art program.** The new edition contains many more new or revised figures, which add clarity as well as content related to key terms and concepts in biological anthropology.

IN-TEXT AIDS TO THE LEARNING PROCESS

Each chapter opens with a vignette telling the story of one person's discovery that relates directly to the central theme of the chapter. This vignette is intended to draw students into the excitement of the topic and to set the stage for the Big Questions addressed by the chapter.

- **Big Questions.** Appearing at the beginning of each chapter, the Big Questions are learning objectives in the form of questions; these objectives provide a framework to help students organize their reading and understand the topic.

- **Concept Checks.** These aids are scattered throughout each chapter. Each Concept Check immediately follows a major section and is intended to help students briefly revisit the key points they have been reading in that section.

- **Locator maps.** College-level instructors tend to hope that students have a good sense of geography, but like many people who do not look at places around the world on a daily basis, students often need reminders about geography. In recognition of this, locator maps in the book's margins show the names and locations of places that are likely not common knowledge.

- **Photorealistic art you can "touch."** Designed to give students a deep appreciation for the feel of the discipline, most of the illustrations of bones and skeletons in the book have an almost photorealistic feel, and most primates are drawn for a high degree of realism. In addition, hundreds of images, many specially prepared for the book, help your students visualize what they are reading about in the text. These illustrations tell the story of biological anthropology, including key processes, central players, and important concepts. As much thought went into the pedagogy behind the illustration program as into the writing of the text.

- **Definitions.** Key terms are highlighted in boldface in the text, with definitions provided in the Glossary at the end of the book. In addition, many of the definitions are presented in the text's margins, giving students ready access to what a term means and its use in the associated text. For convenient reference, defined terms are signaled with boldface page numbers in the index.

- **Answering the Big Questions.** Like a matching bookend, this end-of-chapter review aid presents a summary of the chapter's central points organized along the lines of the Big Questions presented at the beginning.

- **Study Quizzes.** Each chapter review also includes a brief quiz, consisting of a handful of key questions that I ask my own students, to help your students test their knowledge.

- **Evolution Reviews.** Because the study of evolution is the central concept of biological anthropology, an end-of-chapter Evolution Review addresses topics on evolution featured in the chapter and asks questions to help students develop a focused understanding of content and ideas.

- **Key Terms list.** A handy list provides of all the bold-face terms in the chapter in one place.

- **Additional Readings.** These suggested readings are for students who wish to explore the chapter's topics further.

Join me now in engaging your students in the excitement of discovering biological anthropology.

ONLINE TOOLS FOR LEARNING AND TEACHING

The *Essentials of Biological Anthropology* teaching and learning package provides students and instructors with all the tools they need to visualize anthropological concepts, learn key vocabulary, and test knowledge.

- **InQuizitive.** This adaptive, gamelike learning tool includes a variety of question types featuring the vibrant, detailed, and photorealistic art from the text, as well as the accompanying suite of animations and—new to the fifth edition—the Anthropology at Work and Anthropology Matters videos. Changes for the fifth edition also include a greater number of critical-thinking questions to complement those focused on core-concept mastery. Answer-specific feedback for every question helps students work through their mistakes, and InQuizitive personalizes students' quizzing experience to target the areas they need help with most.

  InQuizitive comes at no charge with all new books in any format (paperback, loose-leaf, ebook, or custom). If students need to purchase a stand-alone access code for InQuizitive, they can do so at an affordable price at digital.wwnorton.com/essanthro5.

- **Anthropology at Work features and videos.** These feature real anthropologists in both academic and nonacademic jobs, talking about their experience studying anthropology and how that led to their current work. These videos and texts help students understand the wide-ranging applicability of studying anthropology.

- **Anthropology Matters videos.** These feature real anthropologists discussing their research and how it connects to topics of interest and relevance to students' lives (including how virus epidemics spread, why race is bad biology, and what happens as human and non-human primate communities increasingly come into contact worldwide).

- **Animations.** Animations of key concepts from the text are available to instructors through the Resources for Your LMS package (see next) and on digital .wwnorton.com/essanthro5. These are brief, easy to use, and great for explaining concepts either in class or as a self-study tool.

- **Resources for Your Learning Management System (LMS).** Easily add high-quality Norton digital resources to your online, hybrid, or lecture courses. Get started on building your course with our easy-to-use integrated resources; all activities can be accessed right within your existing LMS. Graded activities can be configured to report to the LMS course grade book. The Norton resources that can be integrated into your LMS include the ebook, InQuizitive, and videos and animations. Instructors can also add customizable multiple-choice and short-answer questions to their

LMS from the Test Bank using Norton Testmaker (see next page).

- **Update PowerPoint Slides.** To help cover what is new in the discipline, each semester Norton provides a supplemental PowerPoint lecture with notes and assessment material covering current and breaking research. Prepared by Jennifer Spence (Texas State University), this material is made available for download at https://wwnorton.com/instructor-resources/9780393876857.

- **Lecture PowerPoint Slides and Art Slides.** Designed for instant classroom use, our Lecture PowerPoint Slides incorporate text and art from the book and are a great resource for your lectures. In addition, all art from the book is available separately in PowerPoint and JPEG formats. Download these resources from https://wwnorton.com/instructor-resources/9780393876857.

- **Instructor's Manual.** This resource provides lecture ideas, discussion topics, suggested reading lists for instructors and students, and suggested answers to

Evolution Review questions. This edition includes three new features: spotlight activities that highlight women anthropologists and/or anthropologists of color working in the field today; lists of tips for online and blended learning; and a teaching guide for making your pedagogy and course more inclusive.

- **Test Bank and Testmaker.** The Test Bank for the fifth edition contains multiple-choice and short-answer questions for each chapter in the book. It is available in Norton Testmaker, our new online system that allows you to quickly and easily create assessments or use premade review quizzes for your course from anywhere with an internet connection, without having to download files or install software. You can search and filter Test Bank questions by chapter, type, difficulty, and other criteria. You can also edit or create your own. Then, easily export your tests to Microsoft Word or Common Cartridge files for import into your LMS.

- **Ebook: Same great book, a fraction of the price!** An affordable and convenient alternative, the ebook retains the content and design of the print book and allows students to highlight and take notes with ease, print chapters as needed, read online or off-line, and search the text. Instructors can even take notes in their ebook that can be shared with their students.

WHO HELPED

I owe much to the many people who made this book possible, from the planning and writing of the previous four editions and now this fifth edition. First and foremost, I thank my wife, Christine, and son, Spencer, who helped in innumerable ways. They were my captive audience: without protest, they listened to my ideas at the dinner table, on family trips, and in other places where we probably should have been talking about other things. Christine read many drafts of chapters and gave great advice on when and where to cut, add, or rethink. I also bounced many of my ideas and thoughts off her. I thank my parents, the late Leon and Patricia Larsen, who introduced me to things old and sparked my interest in the human past.

Jack Repcheck first approached me about writing a textbook on introductory biological anthropology. His power of persuasion, combined with my own interest in the discipline and its presentation to college students, was instrumental in reeling me in and getting the project off the ground. Jack and others at W. W. Norton & Company made the process of writing the book a great experience in all ways, from writing to publication. On the first edition, I began work with editors John Byram and then Leo Wiegman. I am indebted to Peter Lesser, who took on the project after Leo. Peter gave direction on writing and production, provided very helpful feedback on presentation and pedagogy, and orchestrated the process of review, revision, and production—all without a hitch. Under Peter's guidance, the first edition became the most widely used textbook in biological anthropology, and it has held steady in that position. Jack Repcheck continued the project in preparation for the second edition. The preparation of the third edition was overseen by editor Eric Svendsen. The fourth and current editions were completed with the guidance, advice, and support of Jake Schindel. I also thank Rachel Goodman and Mia Davis for support, advice, and assistance throughout the entire process, especially in production of pages and overseeing a wide variety of editorial issues. The present edition of the book benefited from the editorial talents of Gwen Burda. I thank her for her diligence in editing, close attention to detail, and advice on a range of issues.

Michael Jaoui and Christopher Rapp have spearheaded the development of new media for this edition. Ariel Eaton and Jesse Singh do an excellent job developing the core supplement package for each edition. I thank Kandace Starbird, who crafted an expert marketing and promotional campaign. Ben Reynolds and Liz Marotta guided the process of production from beginning to end. Leilani Lucas and Scott Suarez augmented our InQuizitive course to make it more interactive and multimedia-focused than ever before. Lily Malekfar and Tracy Betsinger's timely and efficient revision of the Test Bank is much appreciated. Liz Soluri, Sabrina Agarwal, and Beth Roselyn provided quality work on the Instructor's Manual. Jennifer Spence produces our valuable Update PowerPoint Slides each semester. Thanks to Karen Muir for her capable work on the Lecture PowerPoint Slides.

With the input of instructors and focus-group attendees who are included in the list of reviewers and advisors at the end of these acknowledgments, we have continued to work on the development of new media and the assessment suite. However, my thanks for extensive work in developing InQuizitive go to Tracy Betsinger of the State University of New York at Oneonta, Ashley Hurst at the University of Texas at San Antonio, Kristina Killgrove of the University of North Carolina at Chapel Hill, Joanna Lambert of the University of Colorado Boulder, and Heather Worne of the University of Kentucky, with further thanks to contributors Jaime Ullinger of Quinnipiac University and Nancy Cordell of South Puget Sound Community College. And thanks to Sandra Wheeler of the University of Central Florida, Ellen Miller of Wake Forest University, Bonnie

Yoshida-Levine of Grossmont College, Jacqueline Eng of Western Michigan University, Jeremy DeSilva of Dartmouth College, K. Elizabeth Soluri of the Cabrillo College, and again, Nancy Cordell, for their important feedback and reviews of these resources.

Thanks go to former and current graduate students and faculty colleagues at Ohio State University who helped in so many ways. Virtually every one of my former PhD advisees provided opinions and advice. I offer a very special thanks to Tracy Betsinger, who assisted in a number of aspects of the book, as well as the Resources for Your LMS. For the first edition, she read drafts of chapters at various stages, helped in figure selection and glossary compilation, served as a sounding board in general for ideas that went into the book, and created the cover. She set a high bar for all future covers and for content. Over the course of preparing these chapters, Tracy, Jaime Ullinger, Jim Gosman, Dan Temple, Haagen Klaus, and Josh Sadvari read parts or all of the manuscript and offered great advice. For all five editions, I had many helpful discussions with Scott McGraw and Dawn Kitchen about primate behavior, evolution, and taxonomy. Barbara Piperata advised me on key aspects of modern human biology and nutrition science, and Dawn Kitchen provided discussion and help on the fundamentals of primate communication and how best to present it. Josh Sadvari was indispensable in the creation of the Evolution Review sections at the end of each chapter. Ellen Mosley-Thompson and John Brooke advised me on historical aspects of climate change and its importance for understanding conditions in our rapidly changing world. Likewise, Mary Beth Cole developed terrific student review questions for each chapter.

Over the years, I have had helpful conversations with my teachers, colleagues, and students about areas of their expertise, and these people have influenced the development of the book in so many ways. I am grateful to Patricia J. O'Brien and Milford H. Wolpoff, my respective undergraduate and graduate advisors. Both were instrumental in developing my interest in science and putting me on the path toward the wonderful profession I work in. I thank Barry Bogin, Kristen Hawkes, Jim O'Connell, David Thomas, Bob Kelly, Bruce Smith, Matt Cartmill, Dale Hutchinson, Chris Ruff, Simon Hillson, Michael Schultz, Sam Stout, Doug Ubelaker, Dan Sellen, Clark Howell, Rick Steckel, Phil Walker, John Relethford, Mark Weiss, Margaret Schoeninger, Karen Rosenberg, Lynne Schepartz, Fred Smith, Brian Hemphill, Bruce Winterhalder, Meg Conkey, Desmond Clark, Erik Trinkaus, Katherine Russell, Vin Steponaitis, Mark Teaford, Richard Wrangham, Jerry Rose, Mark Cohen, William Bass, Loring Brace, Stanley Garn, Frank Livingstone, Phil Gingerich, T. Dale Stewart, Larry Angel, Mike Finnegan, Harriet Ottenheimer, Marty Ottenheimer, Roberto Frisancho, Randy Susman, Leslea Hlusko, Karen Strier, Joanna Lambert, Jim Hijiya, Cecil Brown, Bill Fash, Rich Blanton, Henry Wright, James Griffin, Bill Jungers, David Frayer, Bill Pollitzer, George Armelagos, Jane Buikstra, Elwyn Simons, Steve Churchill, Neil Tubbs, Bob Bettinger, Tim White, Dean Falk, Owen Lovejoy, Scott Simpson, David Carlson, Alan Goodman, Debbie Guatelli-Steinberg, Clark Mallam, Chris Peebles, and Fabian Crespo.

The book benefited from the expertise of many anthropologists and other experts over the course of development of the present and past editions. I especially acknowledge the following reviewers and advisors for their insights, advice, and suggestions for revision of the text and creation of the support package:

Sabrina Agarwal, University of California, Berkeley
Paul Aiello, Ventura College
Lon Alterman, North Carolina State University
Tara Devi Ashok, University of Massachusetts Boston
Diana Ayers-Darling, Mohawk Valley Community College
Gerald Bacon, Coconino Community College
Philip de Barros, Palomar College
Thad Bartlett, University of Texas, San Antonio
Cynthia Beall, Case Western Reserve University
Owen Beattie, University of Alberta
Sara Becker, University of California, Riverside
Daniel Benyshek, University of Nevada, Las Vegas
Tracy Betsinger, College at Oneonta, State University of New York
Deborah Blom, University of Vermont
Amy Bogaard, Oxford University
Günter Bräuer, University of Hamburg
Juliet Brophy, Louisiana State University
Margaret Bruchez, Blinn College
Emily Brunson, University of Washington
Victoria Buresch, Glendale Community College
Susan Cachel, Rutgers University
Jessica Cade, Richland College
Maria Leonor Cadena, Fullerton College
Benjamin Campbell, University of Wisconsin, Milwaukee
Isabelle Champlin, University of Pittsburgh, Bradford
Joyce Chan, California State University, Dominguez Hills
Chi-hua Chiu, Kent State University
David Clark, Catholic University of America
Raffaella Commitante, California State University, Fullerton

Nancy Cordell, South Puget Sound Community College
Robert Corruccini, Southern Illinois University
Herbert Covert, University of Colorado
Libby Cowgill, University of Missouri, Columbia
Joseph Creason, Long Beach City College
Fabian Crespo, University of Louisville
Douglas Crews, Ohio State University
Alejandra Estrin Dashe, Northwestern Health Sciences University
Ann O'Neill Deal, Houston Community College
Eric Delson, Lehman College, City University of New York
Jeremy DeSilva, Dartmouth College
Katherine Dettwyler, University of Delaware
Joanne Devlin, University of Tennessee
Kerry M. Dore, Marist College
William Duncan, East Tennessee State University
Arthur Durband, Texas Tech University
Marta Alfonso Durruty, Kansas State University
Phyllisa Eisentraut, Santa Barbara City College
Jacqueline Eng, Western Michigan University
Paul Erickson, St. Mary's University
Becky Floyd, Cypress College
Susan Ford, Southern Illinois University
David Frayer, University of Kansas
Renee Garcia, Saddleback College
Daniel Gebo, Northern Illinois University
Victoria Giambrone, Oakton Community College
Rebecca Gibson, American University
Anne Grauer, Loyola University of Chicago
Mark Griffin, San Francisco State University
Michael Grimes, Western Washington University
Nanda B. Grow, Texas A&M University
Gregg Gunnell, Duke University
Sharon Gursky, Texas A&M University
Diane Hardgrave, College of Southern Nevada
Lesley Harrington, University of Alberta
Cory Harris, Orange County Community College, State University of New York
Ryan P. Harrod, University of Alaska Anchorage
Lauren Hasten, Las Positas College
John Hawks, University of Wisconsin, Madison
Carrie Healy, University of Arkansas
Samantha Hens, California State University, Sacramento
James Hingham, New York University
Madeline Hinkes, San Diego Mesa College
Leslea Hlusko, University of California, Berkeley
Homes Hogue, Ball State University
Brigitte Holt, University of Massachusetts Amherst
Ashley Hurst, University of Texas at San Antonio

Nina Jablonski, Pennsylvania State University
Karin Enstam Jaffe, Sonoma State University
Gabriela Jakubowska, Ohio State University
Gail Kennedy, University of California, Los Angeles
Kristina Killgrove, University of North Carolina at Chapel Hill
Alice Kingsnorth, American River College
Dawn Kitchen, Ohio State University
Haagen Klaus, George Mason University
Leslie Knapp, University of Utah
Sam Kobari, San Diego State University
Andrew Kramer, University of Tennessee
Greg Laden, University of Minnesota
Joanna Lambert, University of Colorado Boulder
Patricia Lambert, Utah State University
Cari Lange, Ventura College
Sang-Hee Lee, University of California, Riverside
Ginesse Listi, Louisiana State University
Michael Little, Binghamton University
Chris Loeffler, Irvine Valley College
Marilyn London, University of Maryland
R. Lee Lyman, University of Missouri
Sara Lynch, Queens College, City University of New York
Lorena Madrigal, University of South Florida
Ann Magennis, Colorado State University
Stephen Marshak, University of Illinois, Urbana–Champaign
Debra Martin, University of Nevada, Las Vegas
Stacey Matarazzo-Rine, Holyoke Community College
Thomas McDade, Northwestern University
Richard McFarland, University of Wisconsin–Madison
William McFarlane, Johnson County Community College
Scott McGraw, Ohio State University
Matthew McIntyre, University of Central Florida
Arion Melidonis, Oxnard College
Rachel Messinger, Moorpark College
Ellen Miller, Wake Forest University
Leonor Monreal, Fullerton College
Ellen Mosley-Thompson, Ohio State University
Michael Muehlenbein, Indiana University
Jennifer Muller, Ithaca College
Dawn Neill, California State Polytechnic University, San Luis Obispo
Elizabeth Newell, Elizabethtown College
Kimberly Nichols, Colorado State University
Wesley Niewoehner, California State University, San Bernardino
Kevin Nolan, Ball State University

Rachel Nuger, Hunter College, City University of New York
James O'Connell, University of Utah
Dennis O'Rourke, University of Kansas
John Otte, Ohlone College
Janet Padiak, McMaster University
Elizabeth Pain, Palomar Community College
Amanda Wolcott Paskey, Cosumnes River College
Sandra Peacock, University of British Columbia
Michael Pietrusewsky, University of Hawai'i
Michael Pilakowski, Butte College
Dolores Piperno, Smithsonian Institution
Deborah Poole, Austin Community College
Leila Porter, Northern Illinois University
Teresa Potter, Salt Lake Community College
Frances E. Purifoy, University of Louisville
Ryan Raaum, Lehman College, City University of New York
Mary Ann Raghanti, Kent State University
Lesley M. Rankin-Hill, University of Oklahoma
Jeffrey Ratcliffe, Pennsylvania State University, Abington
Marcia Regan, Hamline University
Laurie Reitsema, University of Georgia
Melissa Remis, Purdue University
Robert Renger, Ventura College
Erin Riley, San Diego State University
Paul Roach, Century College
Michael Robertson, Los Angeles Harbor College
Charles Roseman, University of Illinois
Karen Rosenberg, University of Delaware
John Rush, Sierra College
Joshua Sadvari, Ohio State University
Susan Saul, California State University, Los Angeles
Melissa Schaefer, University of Utah
Sarah A. Schrader, University of California, Santa Cruz
Timothy Sefczek, Henry Doorly Zoo and Aquarium
Beth Shook, California State University, Chico
Sara Shrader, University of California, Santa Cruz
Lynette Leidy Sievert, University of Massachusetts
Scott Simpson, Case Western Reserve University
Pete Sinelli, University of Central Florida
Cynthia Smith, Ohio State University
Fred Smith, Illinois State University
Richard Smith, Washington University
Sara Smith, Delta College
Sarah Kirkpatrick Smith, Kennesaw State University
Lillian Spencer, Glendale Community College

James Stewart, Columbus State Community College
Marissa Stewart, University of Maryland
Sara Stinson, Queens College, City University of New York
Christopher Stojanowski, Arizona State University
Margaret Streeter, Boise State University
Karen Strier, University of Wisconsin, Madison
Nancy Tatarek, Ohio University
Linda Taylor, University of Miami
Geoffrey Thomas, Florida State University
Lonnie Thompson, Ohio State University
Victor Thompson, University of Georgia
Christopher Tillquist, University of Louisville
Melissa Torpey, University of North Carolina, Wilmington
Sebina Trumble, Hartnell College
Lisa Valkenier, Berkeley City College
Dennis Van Gerven, University of Colorado, Boulder
Patricia Vinyard, University of Akron
Ronald Wallace, University of Central Florida
Brittany Walter, University of South Carolina
David Webb, Kutztown University
Daniel Wescott, Texas State University
Jessica Westin, Pennsylvania State University
Adam Wetsman, Rio Hondo College
Sandra Wheeler, University of Central Florida
Tim White, University of California, Berkeley
Janet Wiebold, Spokane Community College
Caleb Wild, Mira Costa College
Leslie Williams, Beloit College
Sharon Williams, Purdue University
Teresa Wilson, Louisiana State University
Milford Wolpoff, University of Michigan
Thomas Wynn, University of Colorado, Colorado Springs

Thanks, everyone, for your help! Lastly, a very special thanks goes to all of the faculty around the world who adopted the previous four editions of *Essentials of Biological Anthropology* for their introductory biological anthropology classes. I am also grateful to the thousands of students who connected with the book. This book was written for you and the many others who traveled into the wonderfully interesting world of biological anthropology and science for the first time. Please continue to send me your comments and questions (Larsen.53@osu.edu)!

Columbus, Ohio
February 22, 2021

TO THE STUDENT

BIOLOGICAL ANTHROPOLOGY IS ABOUT DISCOVERING WHO WE ARE

Thinking Like an Anthropologist

Who are we? Where do we come from? Why do we look and behave the way we do? This book is a journey that addresses these and other big questions about us, *Homo sapiens*. This journey emphasizes discovery of the fascinating record of our diversity and of our evolution, a record that serves as a collective memory of our shared biological presence on Earth. From here to the end of the book, I will share with you all kinds of ideas that add up to our current understanding of human beings as living organisms. Along the way, you will experience scientific breakthroughs such as genomics and forensics. You will gain new understandings of phenomena such as race and human diversity, global warming and its impact on our evolution and well-being, the origins of human violence, global epidemic disease, and the alarming worldwide spread of obesity, now affecting every country around the globe. Like an anthropologist tackling important questions, you will discover places on nearly every continent and come to see what life was like millions of years before the present, before the emergence and evolution of humans.

Neither your instructor nor I can expect you as an introductory student to understand all the developments in biological anthropology. Both of us can, however, present you with a clear and concise framework of the field. By the time you are finished reading this book and completing this course, you will have a solid background in the basic tenets of the discipline. This knowledge will help you understand your place in nature and the world that we—approaching 8 billion of us and growing—live in. The framework for developing your understanding of biological anthropology is the scientific method, a universal approach to understanding the complex natural world. If you haven't already, you will appreciate the importance of science at many levels of decision-making and observation in today's ever-changing, complex world. You should not assume that this book and this course are about only knowing the right answers, the "facts" of biological anthropology. Rather, the book and the course are also about seeing how biological anthropologists know what they know—understanding the scientific method. As you read, keep in mind the key questions that scientists try to answer, their processes and methods for finding the answers, and the answers themselves.

In writing this book, I have focused on the big questions in biological anthropology, how scientists have tackled them, and what key discoveries have been made. I have not shied away from identifying the scientists who made these discoveries—real people, young and old, from all over the world. Whether you need to learn all these individuals' names and what they contributed to the growth of biological anthropology and to our knowledge of human evolution and variation is up to your instructor. But in the introductory biological anthropology class that I teach, I encourage my students to learn about the people behind the ideas. By seeing the field through these people's eyes, you can start thinking like an anthropologist.

Seeing Like an Anthropologist

Thinking like an anthropologist includes seeing what anthropologists see. We anthropologists are constantly looking at things—fossilized human teeth, ancient DNA, excavated stone tools, primate skeletons, living primates, and much, much more—and using what we see to understand biology in the past and how that past laid the foundation for the present. The photos and drawn art throughout this book have been carefully chosen to help you see what anthropologists see. Fortunately, biological anthropology is a highly visual field (as you will discover in reading your textbook and in class lectures). I strongly encourage you to pay close attention to the visuals in the book and their captions, because much of our anthropological understanding is in the art program.

The Structure of the Book and Supporting Resources

The book is divided into two parts. After an overview of anthropology, its subdisciplines, and biological anthropology (chapter 1), part I provides the basic context for how we understand human biology (and the biology of our non-human primate relatives) in the present and how that helps us understand the past. From this section of the book, you should come away with an understanding of evolution and the biology associated with it. Evolution as an idea has a long history (chapter 2). You will need to fully grasp the meaning and power of this theory, which explains humans' biological variation today and in the past. Part I also has the important job of providing you with an understanding of genetics (chapters 3 and 4). This information is a central part of the evidence for evolution, from the level of the molecule to the level of the population.

Part I also looks at the biology of living people, that of the other living primates, and the variation among primate species. I am keen on debunking the common (and very wrong) notion that there are discrete categories—races—of human beings (chapter 5). In fact, nothing about the biology of people, present or past, indicates that we can be divided into distinct groups. After looking at how environment and culture help shape the way humans look and behave, I will look similarly at nonhuman primates (chapters 6 and 7). Because nonhuman primates' appearances are much more categorical than those of humans, nonhuman primate appearance lends itself to classification or taxonomy. In these chapters, we will look at what nonhuman primates do in the wild, what they are adapted to, and especially the environment's role in shaping their behavior and biology. By looking at living people and living nonhuman primates, we will be better equipped to understand the biological evidence drawn from the past.

Part II examines the processes and evidence biological anthropologists and other scientists use to understand the past (chapter 8), the evolution of prehuman primates beginning some 55 million years ago (chapter 9), and both the emergence of our humanlike ancestors and their evolution into modern humans (chapters 10, 11, and 12). Contrary to popular (and some scientific) opinion, human evolution did not stop when anatomically modern people first made their appearance in various corners of the world. Rather, even during the past 10,000 years, a considerable amount of biological change has occurred. Anthropologists have learned that agriculture, which began 10,000 yBP or so, has been a fundamental force behind population increase. The downside of this shift to new kinds of food and the resulting population increase was a general decline in health. The last chapter of part II (chapter 13) explores the nature and cause of biological change, including the changes associated with health and well-being that led to the biological and environmental conditions we face today. The challenges to health and well-being seem insurmountable at times. However, the role of discovery and science continues to address and offer solutions. These issues are many and diverse, but one thing we have learned in science is that virtually no problem, concern, or issue is unsolvable.

With this book in hand and our goals—thinking and seeing like anthropologists—in mind, let us set off on this exciting journey. Consider it a voyage of discovery, on which our shipmates include your instructor and your fellow students. If we work hard and work together, we will find perhaps the most interesting thing on Earth: ourselves.

ESSENTIALS OF BIOLOGICAL ANTHROPOLOGY

FIFTH EDITION

Searching for, carefully excavating, and studying fossil remains is one way biological anthropologists learn about our human ancestors and better understand our evolutionary history. In this aerial view of the Çatalhöyük site in Turkey, the two white-topped areas are structures covering excavation areas. The site encompasses the equivalent of 25 American football fields.

1

What Is Biological Anthropology?

BIG QUESTIONS

1. **What is anthropology?**
2. **What is biological anthropology?**
3. **What makes humans so different from other animals?**
4. **How do biological anthropologists know what they know?**

When the call came, it was a dream come true.

All through college, graduate school, and my career as a professor, I have been fascinated by what human remains from past societies tell us about the people who lived in them—the challenges they faced, their health and lifestyles, and the ways they adapted to the conditions where they lived. This interest is why I began studying biological anthropology in the first place, as this discipline focuses on how humans adapt and evolve in all times and in all places, from our earliest ancestors right up to the present, and looking ahead to our species' future. Specifically, my research, from the time I was a graduate student, has looked at the transition within the past 10,000 years from a lifestyle in which humans primarily ate wild plants and animals to one in which they primarily raised crops and domesticated animals as their main food sources. This enormous shift resulted in reduced health, poorer hygiene, the introduction of new infectious diseases, and other detrimental impacts on the human body with regard to physical activity. In short, it introduced a host of new challenges for our species, and my research has sought to uncover more about how we have evolved and adapted in response.

To study this question, I have had to explore settings in the world where our human ancestors faced these challenges. I had long known about a place called Çatalhöyük, the site of one of the earliest cities in the world, located in south-central Turkey. The people who lived in the city were among the world's first farmers. Decades of archaeological research at the site had yielded evidence of more than a 1,000-year presence of this ancient city, including scores of closely packed mudbrick houses and the skeletons of those who had had lived and worked there, and who had been buried within the floors of the houses following their death. Çatalhöyük was founded by a few families and expanded into a full-blown city, with its population peaking at some 5,000 to 8,000 women, men, and children. These people grew crops of wheat, barley, and other domesticated plants, and they herded sheep and cattle. Those resources, in addition to the wild plants they collected and animals they hunted, are what sustained the community over centuries.

Çatalhöyük's rich history made it an enormously fascinating place to me. So it was one of the happiest days of my professional life when, shortly before attending a conference in England, I was contacted by the archaeologist Ian Hodder to ask if I would be interested in heading the study of human remains being recovered at the site. We arranged a meeting at the conference, during which he described what the project was accomplishing, its goals, and its interest in understanding the people who lived there—what they ate, what their nutritional health was like, what their relationships were like, and many other unanswered questions about the community. I couldn't imagine a better setting for addressing my own research questions about the social, behavioral, and health impacts of one of the most important transitions in human history. These questions included: *How did the people change biologically over time? What caused these changes? What were the key factors underlying the experience of living in the flat plains of the region?* And, *How can we measure human resilience and change during this time?*

The other scientists and scholars Hodder had recruited for the project included specialists who study food remains of plants and animals, architecture and building history, arts, and many other areas that collectively provide the context for the study of human adaptation in a critically important period of human evolution—so important, in fact, that the setting reveals a foundation for what was to come in later human evolution, including today's complete dependence on domesticated plants and animals and the adoption of highly sedentary lifestyles. This latter transition has led to significant health outcomes for our species, including the rise of infectious diseases associated with population crowding, a trend that continues to the present day with a range of newly emerging infectious diseases.

I vividly recall my reaction to seeing Çatalhöyük for the first time. I had traveled thousands of miles from my home in Ohio to Turkey. After a sequence of long flights, we made the final trek to the site. I was the first to spot it in the distance—a gigantic mound, some 20 m (66 ft) in height, and with its base encompassing the equivalent of 25 American football fields. The mound dominated the flat landscape, covered by wheat fields, of the Konya Plain. I knew then that our team was about to engage in an incredibly exciting process of discovery, in which we would seek answers to questions that had consumed me since my days as a college student.

Over the course of nearly two decades of fieldwork and research, our team's excavations yielded hundreds of skeletons. The team comprised leading experts in the study of ancient DNA (for determining biological relatedness), stable isotopes (for dietary reconstruction), paleopathology (for the record of health and disease), skeletal biomechanics (for behavioral and lifestyle reconstruction), skeletal growth and development (for assessing heath), and many other areas of investigation. Our collective research detailed the rise of a community and the health impacts of living in a close, crowded setting where refuse from animals and food debris was discarded near homes. Our stable-isotope studies revealed that over the 1,000-year history of the city, food and other resources were depleted close to the community, resulting in its inhabitants' having to herd sheep further and further from the area. Our research group's biomechanical analysis of the human skeletons showed that all members of the community—adults and children—worked hard and became increasingly mobile over time. Importantly, the science revealed that biological changes in the community were an ongoing process that involved major adaptations, costs to health and well-being, intracommunity interactions, and biological adjustments to the increasing workload caused by moving to a diet based on domesticated plants and animals.

This research is just one example of the fascinating avenues you can pursue within biological anthropology, but there are countless others. The temporal and geographic coverage of biological anthropology is so broad and so diverse because the field addresses big-picture issues about the history and biology of the human experience—what we were in the past, who we are today, and what we may become in the future. Biological anthropologists seek answers to fundamental questions about our biology and evolution. As with any scientific pursuit, getting answers to such questions is often difficult. These questions motivate biological anthropologists to spend months in the deserts of central Ethiopia, finding and studying the remains of human ancestors who lived thousands or even millions of years ago; in the jungles of Uganda, studying our closest primate relatives; or in the high-altitude regions of the Andes Mountains, studying the living inhabitants and their responses and long-term adaptation to low oxygen levels and extreme cold—to name just a few of the settings you will learn about in this book and in your class. In this chapter, we will explore in more detail the nature of biological anthropology and its subject matter.

1.1 What Is Anthropology?

When European explorers first undertook transcontinental travel (for example, Marco Polo into Asia in the late 1200s) or transoceanic voyages to faraway lands (for example, Christopher Columbus to the Americas in the late 1400s and early 1500s), they encountered people that looked, talked, dressed, and behaved very differently from themselves. When these travelers returned to their home countries, they described the peoples and cultures they saw. Building on these accounts, early scholars speculated on the relationships between humans living in Europe and those encountered in distant places. Eventually, later scholars developed new ideas about other cultures, resulting in the development of the discipline anthropology.

(a) (b) (c) (d)

FIGURE 1.1

The Four Branches of Anthropology **(a)** Cultural anthropologists, who study living populations, often spend time living with cultural groups to gain more intimate perspectives on those cultures. The American anthropologist Margaret Mead (1901–1978; right), one of the most recognizable names in cultural anthropology, studied the peoples of the Admiralty Islands, near Papua New Guinea. **(b)** Archaeologists study past human behaviors by investigating material remains that humans leave behind, such as buildings and other structures. This archaeologist examines remnants from a pyramid in the ancient sacred city of Caral, Peru. **(c)** Linguistic anthropologists study all aspects of language and language use. Here, Leslie Moore, a linguistic anthropologist working in a Fulbe community in northern Cameroon, records as a teacher guides a boy in memorizing Koranic verses. **(d)** Biological anthropologists study human evolution and variation. Some biological anthropologists study skeletons from the past to investigate evolution and variation throughout human history, especially the past 10,000 years of human evolution. Those working in forensic anthropology, a subarea within biological anthropology, examine skeletons to identify who they were in life. Such an identification may be of a single person or of thousands. For example, the forensic anthropologist pictured here was called on to help identify the estimated 30,000 victims of Argentina's "Dirty War," which followed the country's 1976 coup.

artifacts Material objects from past cultures.

sociolinguistics The science of investigating language's social contexts.

Anthropology is the study of humankind, viewed from the perspective of all people and all times. As it is practiced in the United States, it includes four branches or subdisciplines: **cultural anthropology, archaeology, linguistic anthropology**, and **biological anthropology** (**Figure 1.1**).

Cultural anthropologists typically study present-day societies in non-Western settings, such as in Africa, South America, or Australia. **Culture**—defined as learned behavior that is transmitted from person to person—is the unifying theme of study in cultural anthropology.

Archaeologists study earlier human societies, focusing mostly on their material remains—such as animal and plant remains and places where people lived in the past. Archaeologists are best known for their study of material objects—**artifacts**—from past cultures, such as weaponry and ceramics. Archaeologists study the processes behind past human behaviors; for example, why people lived where they did, why some societies were simple and others complex, and why people shifted from hunting and gathering to agriculture beginning more than 10,000 years ago. Archaeologists are the cultural anthropologists of the past—they seek to reassemble cultures of the past as though those cultures were alive today.

Linguistic anthropologists study the construction and use of language by human societies. **Language**—defined as a set of written or spoken symbols used by humans to refer to things (people, places, concepts, etc.) other than themselves—makes possible the transfer of knowledge from one person to the next and from one generation to the next. Popular among linguistic anthropologists is a subfield called **sociolinguistics**, the investigation of language's social contexts.

Biological anthropologists study all aspects of present and past human biology. As we will explore in the next section, biological anthropology—sometimes called **physical anthropology**—deals with the evolution of and variation among human beings and their living and past relatives.

No anthropologist is expected to be an expert in all four branches of the discipline. Anthropologists in all four areas and with very different interests, however, acknowledge the diversity of humankind in all contexts. No other discipline embraces the breadth of the human condition in this manner. In fact, this remarkably diverse discipline differs from other disciplines in its commitment to the notion that, unlike other animals, humans are biocultural—both biological and cultural beings. Anthropologists are interested in the interrelationship between biology and culture. Anthropologists call this focus the **biocultural approach**. Anthropology also differs from other disciplines in emphasizing a broad comparative approach to the study of biology and culture, looking at all people (and their ancestors) and all cultures in all times and all places. Anthropologists are interested in people, their ancestors, and their living and past biological relatives, wherever or whenever they lived. Simply, you are studying a field that is holistic, unlike any you have studied before.

Anthropology is a remarkably diverse discipline and has considerable overlap between its subdisciplines. For example, a number of anthropologists pursue a biomedical path, using their knowledge of health and disease in collaboration with doctors and other health professionals to address serious issues involving new and returning epidemic diseases. In this regard, medical anthropologists are key players in addressing disease outbreaks in a range of settings worldwide, such as in remote communities in West Africa hit hard by the Ebola outbreaks over the past decade. Simply, the knowledge of health in its larger cultural context gives the discipline a unique perspective on the importance of the interlinkages between our well-being and the myriad culturally based behaviors that influence it. You will learn about health connections throughout the text, including but not limited to disease (chapters 2 and 13), growth and aging (chapter 5), diet (chapter 13), and the challenges to health associated with global warming (chapter 14).

biocultural approach The scientific study of the interrelationship between what humans have inherited genetically and culturally.

1.2 What Is Biological Anthropology?

The short answer to this question is *biological anthropology is the study of human biological evolution and human biocultural variation*. Two key concepts underlie this definition.

First, every person is a product of evolutionary history, or all the biological changes that have brought humanity to its current form. The remains of humanlike beings, or **hominins**, indicate that the earliest human ancestors, first appearing in Africa, date to sometime around 6–8 million years ago (mya). Since that time, the physical appearance of hominins and their descendants, including modern humans, has changed dramatically. Our physical appearance, our intelligence, and everything else that makes us distinctive biological organisms evolved in our predecessors, whose genes led to the species we are today. (Genes and species are among the subjects of chapters 3 and 4.)

Second, each of us is the product of his or her own individual life history. From the moment you were conceived, your biological makeup has been determined mostly by your genes. (The human **genome**—that is, all the genetic material in a person—includes some 20,000 or so genes.) Your biological makeup is also strongly influenced by your environment. *Environment* here refers not just to the obvious factors, such as climate, but to everything that has affected you—the physical activities you have engaged in (which have placed stress on your muscles and bones), the foods you have eaten and the nutrition that these foods provide, exposure to infectious diseases and the pathogenic viruses and bacteria that cause them, and many other factors that affect overall health and well-being. Environment also includes social and cultural factors. A disadvantaged social environment, such as

hominins Humans and humanlike ancestors.

genome The complete set of genetic information—chromosomal and mitochondrial DNA—for an organism or species that represents all of the inheritable traits.

WATCH THE VIDEO
ANTHROPOLOGY OF DECAY
digital.wwnorton.com/essanthro5

FRANKLIN DAMANN, PHD

Defense POW/MIA Accounting Agency

What do I do? As a forensic anthropologist, I apply my skills in human skeletal biology to identify the remains of missing US service members. In my current position, I direct the Defense POW/MIA Accounting Agency (DPAA) laboratory at Offutt Air Force Base, Nebraska. The DPAA mission is to conduct the fullest possible accounting of the some 83,000 missing US service members from World War II, the Korean War, the Cold War, and the Vietnam War. In order to recover and identify the remains of missing service members, I work with historians, researchers, forensic anthropologists, archaeologists, and molecular biologists to sort through various types of evidence recovered from the historical record, antemortem and postmortem biological profile data, DNA, and all available information on the circumstances of the loss in order to provide a recommendation of identity to the DPAA medical examiner.

What excites me most about my work? I enjoy the diverse nature of my job and the opportunity to provide answers to families of missing service members, many of whom have waited a long time. I cross-reference many types of collected data that are used to identify a missing service member, such as sex, age, ancestry, stature, and trauma collected from a skeleton by a forensic anthropologist; mitochondrial and nuclear DNA data collected by a molecular biologist; and historical information about the service member's disappearance as collected by researchers and historians from primary source documentation. The moment our team makes a solid link between the totality of

collected evidence—historical, archaeological, skeletal, dental, and DNA—and a named person is one of the greatest unifying moments of this profession. Additionally, I enjoy developing new ways of doing our work, focusing on gaining efficiencies, and thus effectiveness, in our processes. For example, by moving our data into more sophisticated computing environments, we standardize the data and improve our ability to visualize data relationships, which are defined by the methods used, among individual bone specimens in ways that were not previously possible. By operating in these new ways, we can work cases more quickly while also establishing a registry of case data that can be used to refine our methods for our specific population of missing people.

Why did I study biological anthropology? At first, biological anthropology wasn't a consideration for me as a career path. In fact, during my early undergraduate years, I wasn't even sure I wanted to be in school, but eventually I realized I was just postponing the decision about what career path to choose when so many interested me. Eventually, I decided I just needed to pick something. Following a positive experience in one Introduction to Archaeology and Physical Anthropology course, I committed to anthropology based on the simple premise that there isn't much in this world that humans do not or have not influenced. In short, I found a discipline where I could explore multiple facets of being human and see how they relate to one another. To me, this meant I could chart my own course, as long as I could maintain a passion for learning. It was this freedom as an anthropologist that allowed me the opportunity to be a forensic anthropologist, to research microbial ecology of skeletal remains, and also to promote interdisciplinary approaches among forensic scientists and data scientists for improving data analytics and visualizations.

WATCH THE VIDEO

digital.wwwnorton
.com/essanthro5

one in which infants and children receive poor-quality nutrition, can result in negative consequences such as poor health, reduced growth and height, and shortened life expectancy. The Native American child who lived after the shift from foraging to farming on the Georgia coast ate more corn than did the Native American child who lived in the same place before AD 1000. Because of the corn-rich diet, the later child's teeth had more cavities, and they were likely more susceptible to poor health outcomes relating to a sedentary lifestyle and population crowding. Each child's condition reflects, therefore, two key circumstances: namely, the millions of years of human evolution and the more immediate circumstances, such as his or her individual diet, exposure to disease, and the stresses of day-to-day living.

WHAT DO BIOLOGICAL ANTHROPOLOGISTS DO?

Biological anthropologists routinely travel to places throughout the United States and around the world to investigate populations. Some biological anthropologists study living people, while others study extinct and living species of our nearest biological relatives, **primates** such as lemurs, monkeys, and apes. I am among the biological anthropologists who travel to museum collections and archaeological localities to study human biology in past societies. When I tell people outside the field what I do for a living, they often think biological anthropology is quite odd, bizarre even. Frequently they ask, "Why would anyone want to study dead people and old bones and teeth?" A good answer to this question is provided by the American biological anthropologist Tiffiny Tung, who says, "Skeletons tell us a considerable amount about a person when they were alive. Biological anthropologists study bones and teeth because they are a time capsule, telling the story of the person's life experiences, including the age of a person when they died, their sex, their diet, their stresses, injuries, and where they were from. Biological anthropologists place that person in their larger society and living circumstances." Everyone has heard of physics, chemistry, and biology; but the average person has never heard of biological anthropology. Compared to other areas of science, biological anthropology is small. But smallness does not make it unimportant. It is practical and significant, providing answers to fundamental questions that have been asked by scholars and scientists for centuries, such as *Who are we as a species? What does it mean to be human? Where did we come from?* Moreover, biological anthropology plays a vital role in addressing questions that are central to our society, sometimes involving circumstances that all of us wish had never come about. For example, the tragedy that Americans identify as 9/11 called immediately for the assistance of specialists from a branch of biological anthropology known as **forensic anthropology**.

Biological anthropology as practiced in the United States began in the first half of the twentieth century, especially under the guidance of three key figures: German-born Franz Boas (1858–1942), who pioneered the general field of American anthropology; Czech-born Aleš Hrdlička (1869–1943), who started the professional scientific journal and professional society devoted to biological anthropology; and Earnest Hooton (1887–1954), who trained most of the first generation of biological anthropologists. While the theory and methods of biological anthropologists today have changed greatly since the early 1900s, the same basic topics first envisioned by these founders form the framework of our science today.

Biological anthropologists study all aspects of human biology, specifically looking at the evolution and variation of human beings and their living and past relatives. This focus on biology means that biological anthropologists practice a *biological science*. But they also practice a *social science,* in that they study biology within the context of culture, society, and behavior. Depending on their areas of interest, biological anthropologists might examine molecular structure, biomechanics, teeth disease, blood types, breathing capacity and lung volume, genetics and genetic history, infectious and other types of disease, origins of language and speech, nutrition, reproduction, growth and development, aging, primate origins and evolution, primate social behavior, brain biology, and many other topics dealing with variation in both the living and the dead—sometimes the bones and teeth of the very long dead (**Figure 1.2**).

primates A group of mammals in the order Primates that have complex behavior, varied forms of locomotion, and a unique suite of traits, including large brains, forward-facing eyes, fingernails, and reduced snouts.

forensic anthropology The branch of biological anthropology pertaining to the recovery, analysis, and identification of human remains.

FIGURE 1.2

A Sample of What Biological Anthropologists Do **(a)** Human remains excavated at Badia Pozzeveri, a medieval church cemetery in Tuscany, Italy, provide a window through which to view health and living conditions in Europe. **(b)** Geneticists analyze samples of human DNA for various anthropological purposes. DNA studies are used to determine how closely related humans are to other primate species, to examine human origins, and to determine individual identities. **(c)** A human biologist records the physical activities of a lactating woman (right, weaving basket) living in a rural community in the eastern Amazon, Brazil. These data will be used to calculate the woman's energy expenditure and to understand how she copes with reproduction's great energy demands. **(d)** In a lab, a forensic anthropologist measures and assesses human bones. If the bones came from a contemporary grave, this forensic information might help to identify the victim. If the bones belonged to a past population, biological anthropologists might use these data to gain insight into the population's health and lifestyle. **(e)** Laboratory investigations of human ancestors' bones help paleoanthropologists to determine where these ancestors fit in the human family tree. **(f)** Primatologists, such as the British researcher Jane Goodall (b. 1934), study our closest living relatives, nonhuman primates. The behavior and lifestyle of chimpanzees, for example, help biological anthropologists to understand our evolutionary past.

In dealing with such topics, biological anthropologists apply methods and theories developed in other disciplines, as well as in their own, as they answer questions that help us understand who we are, a point that I will raise over and over again throughout this book. The very nature of their discipline and the constant borrowing from other disciplines mean that biological anthropologists practice an *interdisciplinary science*. For example, they might draw on the work of geologists who study the landforms and layering of deposits of soil and rock that tell us when earlier humans lived. Or they might obtain information from paleontologists, who study the evolution of plants and animals in the distant past and thus provide the essential context for understanding the world in which earlier humans lived. Some biological anthropologists are trained in chemistry, so they can analyze the chemical properties of bones and teeth to determine what kinds of foods were eaten by those earlier humans. Or to learn how living humans adapt to reduced-oxygen settings, such as in the high altitudes of the Peruvian Andes, biological anthropologists might work with physiologists who study the ability of the lungs to absorb oxygen. The firm yet flexible identity of their science allows biological anthropologists to gather data from other disciplines in order to address key questions—questions drive what they do.

1.3 What Makes Humans So Different from Other Animals? The Six Steps to Humanness

Human beings clearly differ from other animals. From humanity's earliest origin (about 6–8 mya, when an apelike primate began walking on two feet) to the period beginning about 10,000 years ago (when modern climates and environments emerged after what is commonly known as the Ice Age), six key attributes developed that make us unique: bipedalism, nonhoning chewing, complex material culture and tool use, hunting, speech, and dependence on domesticated foods (**Figure 1.3**). The first development represents the most profound physical difference between humans and other animals: namely, the manner in which we get around. We are committed to **bipedalism**—that is, walking on two feet. The next development was the loss of a large, honing canine tooth, like the one that apes typically use to shred their food (mostly plants), and its replacement by the simple **nonhoning canine**, with which we process food in ways unique to humans. Some authorities argue that our ancestors' honing canine disappeared due to a changed diet. The changes involving canine reduction and loss of honing function in early hominins occurred around 5.5 mya (see chapter 10).

Today, our species completely depends on culture—and especially material culture—for its day-to-day living and its very survival. Culture is a complex human characteristic that facilitates our survival by enabling us to adapt to different settings. **Material culture** is the part of culture that is expressed as material objects that humans use to manipulate environments. For example, hammers and nails are forms of material culture that enable us to make cabinets, tables, and countless other forms of material culture. The material remains of past cultures go back hundreds of thousands of years, to the first simple tools made from rocks. The best evidence for the date of these tools is from sites dating to 2.6 mya in East Africa (**Figure 1.4**; see also chapter 10). Material culture today makes our lifestyles possible. Can you imagine your life without it? We could survive without modern additions to material culture, such as cars, computers, television sets, plumbing,

bipedalism Walking on two feet.

nonhoning canine An upper canine tooth that, as part of a nonhoning chewing mechanism, is not sharpened against the lower third premolar.

material culture The part of culture that is expressed as material objects that humans use to manipulate environments.

THE SIX BIG EVENTS OF HUMAN EVOLUTION

BIPEDALISM, NONHONING CHEWING, DEPENDENCE ON MATERIAL CULTURE, SPEECH, HUNTING, AND DOMESTICATION OF PLANTS AND ANIMALS

BIPEDALISM 6 MYA

The upright, bipedal (two-footed) gait was the first hallmark feature of our hominin ancestors.

NONHONING CHEWING 5.5 MYA

Humans' nonhoning chewing complex (below) lacks large, projecting canines in the upper jaw and a diastema, or gap, between the lower canine and the third premolar.

Human

Hyoid bone

SPEECH 2.5 MYA

In the entire animal kingdom, only humans can speak and, through speech, express complex thoughts and ideas. The shape of the hyoid bone is unique to hominins and reflects their ability to speak. Speech is part of the overall package in the human lineage of increased cognition, intelligence, and brain-size expansion.

The chewing complex of apes such as gorillas (below) has large, projecting upper canines and a diastema in the lower jaw to accommodate them.

Ape

Diastema

MATERIAL CULTURE AND TOOLS 2.6 MYA

Humans' production and use of stone tools is one example of complex material culture. The tools of our closest living relatives, the chimpanzees, do not approach the complexity and diversity of modern and ancestral humans' tools.

HUNTING 1 MYA

Humans' relatively large brains require lots of energy to develop and function. Animal protein is an ideal source of that energy, and humans obtained it for most of their evolution by eating animals they hunted. To increase their chances of success in hunting, humans employed tools they made and cooperative strategies.

DOMESTICATED FOODS 11,000 YEARS AGO

In recent evolution—within the last 10,000–11,000 years—humans domesticated a wide variety of plants and animals, controlling their life cycles and using them for food and other products, such as clothing and shelter.

FIGURE 1.4

First Tools The earliest stone tools date to 2.6 mya and are associated with early human ancestors in East Africa. The example shown here is from the Gona River area in the Afar region of Ethiopia. This tool likely had various functions, including the processing of plants and meat for food.

and electricity, as our ancestors did before the past century. But what about living without basic material culture, such as houses and clothing, especially in climates where it can be very, very cold in the winter? Without material culture, how would any of us get food? The answer to both questions is simple: we could not make it without some forms of technology—to regulate temperature, to acquire food, and so on. Some societies are much less technologically complex than others, but no society functions without any technology.

Anthropologists and animal behaviorists have shown that human beings are not, however, the only type of animal that has or can employ material culture. Primatologists have observed some chimpanzee societies in Africa, for example, making simple tools from twigs (**Figure 1.5**). In laboratories, chimpanzees have been taught to use physical symbols that approximate human communication. Still, these and other forms of material culture used by nonhuman species are nowhere near as complex as those created by humans.

The other three key attributes of humanness—hunting, speech, and dependence on domesticated foods—appeared much later in human evolution than bipedalism, nonhoning chewing, and complex material culture and tool use. *Hunting* here refers to the social behavior whereby a group of individuals, adult males in general, organize themselves to pursue animals for food. This behavior likely dates back to a million or more years ago. Some nonhuman primates—such as chimpanzees—organize to pursue prey, but they do not use tools or travel long distances as humans distinctively do when they hunt.

An equally distinctive human behavior is speech. We are the only animal that communicates by talking. Unfortunately for research purposes, recording-and-listening technology was invented only about a century ago. For information about long-past speech, anthropologists rely on indirect evidence within the skeleton. For example, the hyoid bone (located in the neck) is part of the vocal structure that helps produce words. The unique appearance of the human hyoid helps anthropologists conjecture about the origins of speech in earlier human ancestors.

The most recently developed unique human behavior is the domesticated manner in which we acquire our food. About 10,000–11,000 years before the

FIGURE 1.5

Toolmaking Once thought to be a uniquely human phenomenon, toolmaking has been observed in chimpanzees, the closest biological relatives of humans. As seen here, a chimpanzee has modified a twig to scoop termites from nests. Other chimpanzees have used two rocks as a hammer and anvil to crack open nuts. More recently, gorillas were seen using a stick to test the depth of a pool of water they wanted to cross. Tool use such as this likely preceded the first identified tools (see Figure 1.4).

present (yBP), humans began to raise animals and grow plants. This development led to our current total reliance on domesticated plants and animals for food. This reliance has had a profound impact on human biology and behavior, and it represents a fundamental part of our biological evolution and influences our health, behavior, activity, and general living conditions.

Human beings' unique behaviors and survival mechanisms, and the anatomical features related to them, arose through the complex interaction of biology and culture. Indeed, our ancestors' increasing dependence on culture for survival has made us *entirely* culture-dependent for survival. The behaviors that are unique to humans—speech, tool use, and dependence on culture—are also related to the fact that humans are very smart. Our remarkable intelligence is reflected in our abilities to think and interact in the ways we do (and usually take for granted), to communicate in complex ways, and to accomplish diverse tasks on a daily basis in order to survive. Our brains are bigger and have more complex analytical skills than the brains of other primates and of animals in general. These biological attributes enable us to solve complex problems, including how to survive in a wide range of environments and rapidly changing circumstances.

The American anthropologist Robert Boyd and his colleagues argue that while humans are the smartest animals, in no way are we individually smart enough to acquire all the complex information necessary to survive in any particular environment. Today, and through much of human evolution, our species has survived owing to our complex culture, including tool use and other technology, practices, and beliefs. For hundreds of thousands of years, humans have had a record of unique ways of learning from other humans. Retaining new knowledge, we pass this information to our offspring and other members of our societies, and this process extends over many generations (**Figure 1.6**). In other words, **social learning** makes it possible for humans to accumulate an amazing amount of information over very long time periods and over many generations. Anthropologists are finding that social learning is also present in nonhuman primates and other animals. However, the degree of knowledge transmission is more developed in humans, and the process of knowledge transmission is highly consequential for our education.

social learning The capacity to learn from other humans, enabling the accumulation of knowledge across many generations.

FIGURE 1.6
Social Learning A father teaches his son traditional wood carving in Ubud, Bali, Indonesia. Social learning provides a means of accumulating and maintaining knowledge over many generations.

In the chapters that follow, you will be looking at these processes and behaviors—the particulars of biological anthropology—from a biocultural perspective. It is the unique and phenomenal interplay between biology, culture, and behavior that makes us human. It is this interplay that has driven the success of humans. Human **evolvability** has resulted in millions of years of successful adaptation and remarkable growth in numbers, territorial expansion, and diversity.

1.4 How We Know What We Know: The Scientific Method

How do biological anthropologists and other scientists make decisions about what their subject matter means? More specifically, how do we know what we know about human evolution and human variation? Like all other scientists, biological anthropologists carefully and systematically observe and ask questions about the natural world around them. These observations and questions form the basis for identifying problems and gathering evidence—**data**—that will help answer questions and solve problems, thus filling gaps in our scientific knowledge about how the natural world operates. These data are used to test **hypotheses**, possible explanations for the processes under study. Scientists observe and then reject or accept these hypotheses. This process of determining whether ideas are right or wrong is called the **scientific method** (**Figure 1.7**). The scientific method is the foundation of science. It is the basis for all discovery of how the natural world works. The concept of the scientific method is so important that I regard it as among the most fundamental concepts in this book, in the field this book represents, and in your course of study in science generally.

Science (Latin *scientia,* meaning "knowledge"), then, is more than just knowledge of facts about the natural world. Science is also much more than technical details. Certainly, facts and technical details are important in developing answers to questions, but facts and technical skills are not science. Rather, science is a *process* that provides new discoveries that connect our lives with the world we live in—it is a way of knowing through observation of natural phenomena. This repeated acquisition results in an ever-expanding knowledge base, one built from measurable, repeatable, and highly tangible observations. In this way, science is **empirical**, or based on observation or experiment. After the systematic collection of observations, the

hypotheses Testable statements that potentially explain specific phenomena observed in the natural world.

scientific method An empirical research method in which data are gathered from observations of natural phenomena, hypotheses are formulated and tested, and conclusions are drawn that validate or modify the original hypotheses.

empirical Verified through observation and experiment.

FIGURE 1.7

The Scientific Method: How We Know What We Know Biological anthropologists use the scientific method to gain understanding about the natural world. Starting with observations of natural phenomena, they develop a hypothesis that will predict an outcome. They test the hypothesis with additional observations, which either support or reject the hypothesis.

scientist develops a **theory**—an explanation as to why a natural phenomenon takes place. For many nonscientists, a theory is simply a guess or a hunch; but for a scientist, a theory is not just some stab at an explanation. Rather, a theory is an explanation grounded in a great deal of evidence, or what a lawyer calls the "evidentiary record." A scientist builds a case by identifying incontrovertible facts. To arrive at these facts, the scientist examines and reexamines the evidence, putting it through many tests.

The scientist thus uses observation, documentation, and testing to generate hypotheses and, eventually, to construct a theory based on those hypotheses. Hypotheses *explain* observations, *predict* the results of future investigation, and *can be refuted* by new evidence.

For example, the great English naturalist Charles Robert Darwin (1809–1882) developed the hypothesis that the origin of human bipedalism was linked to the shift from life in the trees to life on the ground (**Figure 1.8**). Darwin's hypothesis was based on his own observations of humans walking, other scientists' then-limited observations of nonhuman primate behavior, and other scientists' **anatomical** evidence, or information about structural makeup drawn from dissections, in this case of apes. Darwin's hypothesis led to an additional hypothesis—itself based on evidence accumulated over decades, and widely believed for the subsequent century and a half—that the first hominins arose in the open grasslands of Africa from some ape-like animal that was formerly **arboreal**; that is, had once lived in trees (**Figure 1.9**).

Support for Darwin's hypothesis about human origins—and in particular the origin of bipedal locomotion—began to erode in 2001, when a group of scientists discovered early hominins, dating from 5.8 to 5.2 mya, in the modern country of Ethiopia. Contrary to expectation and accepted wisdom, these hominins had lived not in grasslands but in woodlands (**Figure 1.10**). Moreover, unlike modern humans, whose fingers and toes are straight because we are fully **terrestrial**—we live

FIGURE 1.8

Charles Darwin George Richmond painted this portrait of Darwin in 1840.

anatomical Pertaining to an organism's physical structure.

terrestrial Life-forms, including humans, that live on land versus living in water or in trees.

FIGURE 1.9

Grasslands Darwin hypothesized that the earliest hominins originated in open grasslands similar to this one (Serengeti Plain, Tanzania, East Africa). Recent studies refute the notion that hominins originated in open grassland habitats.

FIGURE 1.10

Forests Scientific findings have revealed that, in fact, the earliest hominins lived in wooded settings, perhaps like this locality in East Africa (Great Rift Valley, Lake Manyara National Park, Tanzania).

morphology Physical shape and appearance.

scientific law A statement of fact describing natural phenomena.

on the ground (**Figure 1.11**)—the early hominins had slightly curved fingers and toes. The physical shape and appearance (what biological anthropologists call **morphology**) of the hominins' finger and toe bones indicate a lot of time spent in trees, holding on to branches and moving from limb to limb. These findings forced scientists to reject Darwin's hypothesis, to toss out what had been a fundamental tenet of biological anthropology.

This story does not end, however, with the understanding that the earliest hominins lived in forests. Instead, this new hypothesis generated new questions. For example, why did the earliest hominins arise in a wooded setting, and why did they "come out of the woods" as time went on? Later in this book, we will consider these questions. For now, the point is that science is a *self-correcting* approach to knowledge acquisition. Scientists develop new hypotheses as new findings are made. Scientists use these hypotheses to build theories. And like the hypotheses that underlie them, theories can be modified or even replaced by better theories, depending on findings made through meticulous observation. As new observations are made and hypotheses and theories are subjected to the test of time, science revises its own errors.

A **scientific law** is a statement of irrefutable truth of some action or actions occurring in the natural world. Among the few scientific laws, the well-known ones are the laws of gravity, thermodynamics, and motion. But scientific truth seldom gets finalized into law. Rather, truth is continually developed—new facts are discovered and new understandings about natural phenomena are made. Unlike theories, scientific laws do not address the larger questions as to why a natural action or actions take place.

As my crew and I traveled to St. Catherines Island, we were intent on discovering new facts and forming new understandings about the prehistoric farmers' descendants who were first encountered by Spaniards in the early 1500s. These facts and understandings would enable us to test hypotheses about human evolution and human variation. Once we completed the months of arduous fieldwork and the years of laboratory investigations on the remains that fieldwork uncovered, we would have some answers. The scientific method would guide us in providing insights into this part of the human lineage—human beings' most recent evolution—and how our species came to be what it is in the early twenty-first century.

FIGURE 1.11

Bipedalism These 1887 photographs by Eadweard Muybridge capture the habitual upright stance of humans. Other animals, such as chimpanzees, occasionally walk on two feet, but humans alone make bipedalism their main form of locomotion. As Darwin observed, this stance frees the hands to hold objects. What are some other advantages of bipedalism?

ANSWERING THE BIG QUESTIONS

1. **What is anthropology?**
   - Anthropology is the study of humankind. In two major ways, it differs from other sciences that study humankind. First, anthropology views humans as both biological and cultural beings. Second, anthropology emphasizes a holistic, comparative approach, encompassing all people at all times and all places.
   - The four branches of anthropology are cultural anthropology (study of living cultures), archaeology (study of past cultures), linguistic anthropology (study of language), and biological anthropology.

2. **What is biological anthropology?**
   - Biological anthropology (sometimes called physical anthropology) is the study of human biology, specifically of the evolution and variation of humans (and their relatives, past and present).
   - Biological anthropology is an eclectic field, deriving theory and method both from within the discipline and from other sciences that address important questions about human evolution and human variation.

3. **What makes humans so different from other animals?**
   - Humans living today are the product of millions of years of evolutionary history and their own personal life histories.
   - Humans have six unique physical and behavioral characteristics: bipedalism, nonhoning chewing, complex material culture and tool use, hunting, speech, and dependence on domesticated foods.

4. **How do biological anthropologists know what they know?**
   - Biological anthropologists derive knowledge via the scientific method. This method involves observations, the development of questions, and the answering of those questions. Scientists formulate and test hypotheses that they hope will lead to theories about the natural world.

STUDY QUIZ

1. **A biological anthropologist would be most likely to study**
   a. learned and shared behaviors in a current human society.
   b. material remains from a past human society.
   c. the evolution of humans or other primates.
   d. the construction and cultural context of human language.

2. **What is influenced both by genes and by environmental factors?**
   a. Cultural behavior
   b. Biological makeup
   c. Spoken language
   d. Individual genome

3. **Which is *not* unique to humans?**
   a. Large, honing canine teeth specialized for shredding food
   b. Reliance on bipedalism for locomotion
   c. Dependence on material culture and tools to survive
   d. Spoken language for communication with other individuals

4. **In the scientific method, a theory is supported by**
   a. initial guesses and impressions.
   b. the collection of facts about a phenomenon.
   c. the creation of a hypothesis.
   d. rigorous testing of hypotheses.

KEY TERMS

anatomical
anthropology
arboreal
archaeology
artifacts
biocultural approach
biological anthropology
bipedalism
cultural anthropology
culture
data
empirical
evolvability
forensic anthropology
genome
hominins
hypotheses
language
linguistic anthropology
material culture
morphology
nonhoning canine
physical anthropology
primates
scientific law
scientific method
social learning
sociolinguistics
terrestrial
theory

STUDY QUIZ (CONTINUED)

5. Franz Boas helped establish that human societies

  a. are influenced both by biology and by culture.

  b. represent a biological evolution from simple to complex.

  c. are equivalent to nonhuman primate societies.

  d. cannot be studied using the scientific method.

EVOLUTION REVIEW

Biological Anthropology As Science

SYNOPSIS Anthropology is a holistic discipline in that it views humankind from the perspectives of all people and all eras. Anthropology is also an interdisciplinary science in that it both draws on and influences research in many related fields. Biological anthropology is one of the four subfields (along with cultural anthropology, archaeology, and linguistic anthropology) that make up anthropology as both a biological and a social science. The two main concepts that define biological anthropology are human biological evolution and human biocultural variation. By use of the scientific method, biological anthropologists study many different aspects of living humans, modern and extinct nonhuman primates, and fossil hominins, among other lines of research. Through all of these different ways of gathering knowledge about the human condition, biological anthropologists ultimately address research questions related to the two broad themes of evolution and variation.

Q1. Define the biocultural approach—a hallmark of biological anthropology.

Q2. Focusing on Figure 1.3, "The Six Big Events of Human Evolution," identify which two of these events were caused primarily by biological changes in humans and which four were caused by changes in both human biology and human culture.

Q3. Over time, has culture had a large or small effect on human evolution? Focusing on Figure 1.3, briefly explain your answer.

Q4. As a species, humans are unique in the degree to which culture influences our evolution. Consider Figure 1.3 again. How might aspects of human culture have affected the evolution of other species, such as livestock or wild animals?

Q5. Many nonscientists often critique evolution as "just a theory." What does it mean for evolution to be a theory in the context of the scientific method? How does the study of evolution illustrate the interdisciplinary nature of biological anthropology?

HINT What other scientific fields might contribute data that are used to test hypotheses related to biological evolution?

ADDITIONAL READINGS

Boyd, R., P. L. Richerson, and J. Henrich. 2011. The cultural niche: Why social learning is essential for human adaptation. *Proceedings of the National Academy of Sciences USA* 108(suppl. 2): 10918–10925.

Cartmill, M., P. T. Ellison, C. S. Larsen, C. B. Ruff, and E. J. E. Szathmáry, eds. 2018. Centennial anniversary issue of AJPA. *American Journal of Physical Anthropology*, special issue, 165(4): 611–954.

Larsen, C. S., ed. 2010. *A Companion to Biological Anthropology*. Chichester, UK: Wiley-Blackwell.

Trevathan, W., ed. 2018. *The International Encyclopedia of Biological Anthropology*. Hoboken, NJ: John Wiley & Sons.

Some Periodicals in Anthropology

Biological anthropology: *American Journal of Human Biology, American Journal of Physical Anthropology, American Journal of Primatology, Bioarchaeology International, Evolutionary Anthropology, Human Biology, International Journal of Paleopathology, Journal of Human Evolution, Yearbook of Physical Anthropology.*

Archaeology: *American Antiquity, Antiquity, Archaeology, Journal of Archaeological Science, Journal of Anthropological Archaeology, Latin American Antiquity, World Archaeology.*

Cultural anthropology: *American Anthropologist, Cultural Anthropology, Human Ecology.*

General anthropology: *American Anthropologist, Annual Review of Anthropology, Current Anthropology.*

PART I

THE PRESENT

Foundation for the Past

Some biological anthropologists learn about human evolution by studying living primates, including humans. Other biological anthropologists learn about human evolution by investigating the past, now represented mostly by fossilized bones and fossilized teeth. Together, the records of the living and the past enable us to understand evolution in the largest context. The fossil record provides us with the history of primates and our human and humanlike ancestors, whereas the living record provides the essential picture through which to view that history. Charles Darwin, the pioneering force behind our knowledge about evolution and natural selection, developed his ideas by studying living plants and animals. He had the extraordinary insight to realize that his theories and hypotheses based on the living applied to past organisms. For Darwin, living organisms were key to interpreting the past because they displayed evidence of evolution's elements and mechanics. In the same way, living organisms provide insights—into fundamental forces such as reproduction, DNA synthesis, protein synthesis, and behavior—that are not available, at least in the same way, within the record of the past. Part I of this book lays out observations and principles based on the study of living populations, the essential background for understanding evolution. Part II then digs into the past, into the study of ancestors whose descendants are present in today's world (all of us now living) and of those evolutionary lineages that did not survive. I start with the living because the living provides the evidence and mechanisms for how evolution and adaptation lead to biological change.

◄ The living primates—such as, here, orangutans and humans—have much in common, biologically and behaviorally. Studying them provides essential context for understanding variation and evolution, now and in the past.

Charles Darwin's observations provided the groundwork for his theory of natural selection, the basis of his 1859 book, *On the Origin of Species*.

2

Evolution

CONSTRUCTING A FUNDAMENTAL SCIENTIFIC THEORY

BIG QUESTIONS

1. How did the theory of evolution come to be?

2. What was Darwin's contribution to the theory of evolution?

3. What has happened since Darwin in the development of our understanding of evolution?

The nineteenth century was the century of scientific collecting. During the 1800s especially, the world discovered itself through collections. Collecting expeditions large and small—involving scientists, explorers, and adventurers—crossed the continents and investigated landmasses around the globe. These teams collected hundreds of thousands of samples: plants, animals, rocks, and preserved remains (or **fossils**—the subject of chapter 8). If it seemed worth picking off the ground or exposing in some other fashion, it was fair game. This kind of work, on one of these international expeditions, helped lay the foundation for the most important biological theory, arguably among the half dozen most important scientific theories—the theory of evolution.

In 1831, a 22-year-old Englishman and recent graduate of Cambridge University, Charles Darwin, was appointed the

(a)

(b)

(c)

FIGURE 2.1

Darwin's Voyage **(a)** Charles Darwin, ca. 1855, about 25 years after he set out on HMS *Beagle*. **(b)** In this illustration, the ship is passing through the Strait of Magellan, during the South American stretch of **(c)** its worldwide journey, whose ports of call are here mapped.

fossils Physical remains of part or all of once-living organisms, mostly bones and teeth, that have become mineralized by the replacement of organic with inorganic materials.

species A group of closely related organisms having the potential to interbreed and produce offspring.

habitat The specific area of the natural environment in which an organism lives.

naturalist for a 5-year voyage around the world on the ship HMS *Beagle* (**Figure 2.1**). Imagine that as your first job right out of college! Young Mr. Darwin, who was trained in medicine and theology, accepted a very difficult task. He was recruited to collect, document, and study the natural world—plants and animals, especially—everywhere the ship harbored. By the end of that voyage, Darwin had amassed a wonderfully comprehensive collection of plants, insects, birds, shells, fossils, and lots of other materials. The specimens he collected and the observations he made about the things he saw on that trip would form the basis of his lifetime of research. His discoveries would do no less than shape the future of the biological sciences, including biological anthropology. His ideas would provide the answers to big questions and the key to understanding the origin and evolution of life itself.

Soon after returning home from the voyage, Darwin began to formulate questions about the origins of plants and animals living in the many lands he and his shipmates had explored. His most prominent observations concerned the physical differences, or variation, between and among members of **species,** or like animals and like plants. He articulated the phenomenon best in his notes on finches that live in the Galápagos, a small cluster of islands 965 km (600 mi) off the coast of Ecuador (**Figure 2.2**). Not only did these birds differ from island to island, but even within a single island they seemed to vary according to **habitat,** or surroundings. For example, finches living on an island's coast had a different beak shape from finches living in an island's interior (**Figure 2.3**). These observations raised two questions for Darwin: (1) *Why* were the birds different from island to island and from habitat to habitat? (2) *How* did different species of finches arise? After years of study, Darwin answered these questions with an idea called "descent with modification," or the theory of evolution.

(a)

(b)

(c)

(d)

(e)

(f)

FIGURE 2.2

Galápagos Islands (a) An archipelago off the coast of Ecuador, South America, the Galápagos comprise 13 major volcanic islands and numerous smaller islands and islets. **(b–f)** These islands are well known for their many endemic, or native, species, such as the 13 species of Galápagos finches, also known as Darwin's finches, that are found only at this location.

Darwin also came to realize that the variations in physical characteristics of the different species of finches and other organisms were **adaptations**—physical characteristics that enhance an organism's ability to survive and reproduce. Darwin recognized many other adaptations in the natural world, and he concluded that adaptation was the crux of evolution. To connect these processes, he coined the term **natural selection**. According to the principle of natural selection, biological characteristics that enhance survival increase in frequency from generation to generation. Members of a population endowed with these characteristics produce more offspring that survive to reproductive age than do members that are not endowed with these characteristics. Natural selection is thus the primary driver of evolution. Recognizing that the different species of finches all derived from a single common

adaptations Changes in physical structure, function, or behavior that allow an organism or species to survive and reproduce in a given environment.

natural selection The process by which some organisms, with features that enable them to adapt to the environment, preferentially survive and reproduce, thereby increasing the frequency of those features in the population.

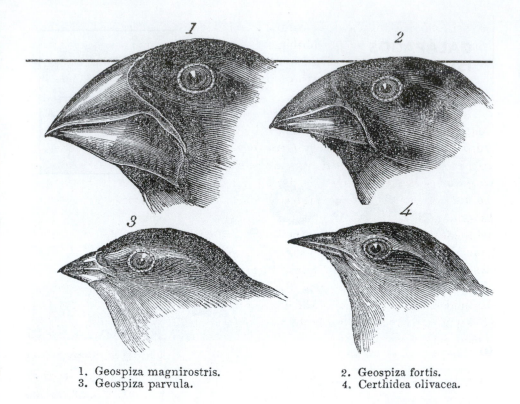

FIGURE 2.3

Darwin's Finches Darwin studied the physical variation in finches living on different islands of the Galápagos. Among other attributes, he studied beak shape, which varied from island to island. Eventually, Darwin related each beak shape to diet, especially to the texture of food and how the food was acquired. Finches with larger beaks typically consumed harder foods, such as seeds and nuts, while finches with smaller beaks ate softer foods, such as berries. Darwin concluded that each finch species had adapted to the particular environment and food resources of its island.

1. Geospiza magnirostris.
2. Geospiza fortis.
3. Geospiza parvula.
4. Certhidea olivacea.

adaptive radiation The diversification of an ancestral group of organisms into new forms that are adapted to specific environmental niches.

ancestor that had originated in South America, Darwin also postulated the process of **adaptive radiation:** out of one species branch multiple, closely related species.

Darwin regarded evolution as simply biological change from generation to generation. Many evolutionary biologists today limit their definition of evolution to genetic change only. However, nongenetic developmental change—biological change occurring within an individual's lifetime—can also give an adaptive advantage (or disadvantage) to an individual or individuals within a population. Moreover, genes control developmental processes, which likewise influence other genes.

In subsequent chapters, we will further explore these and other aspects of evolution. Although the core of this book is human evolution, or how human biology came to be, understanding human evolution requires understanding the term *evolution* as it applies to all living organisms. In this chapter, we will take a historical approach to defining the term and the theory behind it. After reading about its intellectual history before Darwin, Darwin's contribution, and developments since Darwin, you should have a clear idea of what biological anthropologists and other evolutionary biologists mean by *evolution*.

2.1 The Theory of Evolution: The Context for Darwin

Before Darwin's time, Western scientists' understanding of Earth and the organisms that inhabit it was strongly influenced by religious doctrine. In the Judeo-Christian view, the planet was relatively young, and both its surface and the life-forms on it had not changed since their miraculous creation. By the late 1700s, via their observations about the natural world, scientists had realized three key things about the world and its inhabitants: Earth is actually quite ancient; its surface is very different from what it was in the past; and plants and animals have changed over time. These realizations about the natural world provided the context for Darwin's theory of evolution.

To generate his theory, Darwin drew on information from five scientific disciplines: geology, paleontology, taxonomy and systematics, demography, and what is now called evolutionary biology. **Geology** is the study of Earth, especially with regard to its composition, activity, and history; this discipline has demonstrated the great age of our planet and the development of its landscape. **Paleontology** is the study of fossils; this discipline has detailed past life-forms, many now extinct. **Taxonomy** is the classification of past and living life-forms; this discipline laid the foundation for **systematics**, the study of biological relationships over time. **Demography** is the study of population, especially with regard to birth, survival, and death, and the major factors that influence these three key parts of life. **Evolutionary biology** is the study of organisms and their changes. By investigating the fundamental principles by which evolution operates, Darwin founded evolutionary biology as a discipline. In the following sections, we will look at these fields in more detail.

GEOLOGY: RECONSTRUCTING EARTH'S DYNAMIC HISTORY

We now know that our planet is 4.6 billion years old and that over time its surface has changed dramatically. If you had espoused these ideas in, say, the late 1600s, you would not have been believed, and you would have been condemned by the church because you had contradicted the Bible. According to a literal interpretation of the Bible, Earth is a few thousand years old and its surface is static. The Scottish scientist James Hutton (1726–1797) became dissatisfied with the biblical interpretation of the planet's history (**Figure 2.4**). He devoted his life to studying natural forces, such as wind and rain, and how they affected the landscape in Scotland. Hutton inferred from his observations that these forces changed Earth's surface in the past just as they do in the present. Wind and rain created erosion, which provided the raw materials—sand, rock, and soil—for the formation of new land surfaces. Over time, these surfaces became stacked one on top of the other, forming layers, or strata, of geologic deposits (**Figure 2.5**). From the (very long) time it took for these strata to build up, he calculated Earth's age in the millions of years. This was a revolutionary, indeed heretical, realization.

Hutton's idea—that the natural processes operating today are the same as the natural processes that operated in the past—is called **uniformitarianism**. Few paid much attention to Hutton's important contribution to our understanding of Earth's history until the rediscovery of the idea by the Scottish geologist Charles Lyell (1797–1875; **Figure 2.6**). Lyell devoted considerable energy to thinking and writing about uniformitarianism and its implications for explaining the history of our planet. His calculations of how long it would have taken for all known strata to build up created a mountain of evidence, an undeniable record, that Earth was at least millions of

FIGURE 2.4

James Hutton Hutton (here depicted ca. 1790) founded modern geology with his theory of Earth's formation. Hutton realized that the same natural processes he observed in Scotland had occurred in the past.

uniformitarianism The theory that processes that occurred in the geologic past are still at work today.

FIGURE 2.5

Geologic Strata The succession of strata from the oldest at the bottom to the youngest at the top (as seen here, in Utah's Bryce Canyon) marks the formation of new land surfaces over time.

FIGURE 2.6

Charles Lyell Lyell (here depicted ca. 1845) rediscovered Hutton's work and the idea of uniformitarianism. Lyell's research, based on examinations of geologic strata, confirmed Hutton's estimate of Earth's very old age.

years old. Hutton and Lyell, relying on empirical evidence and personal observation to develop their ideas and to test clear hypotheses about the natural world, had revised the timescale for the study of past life.

PALEONTOLOGY: RECONSTRUCTING THE HISTORY OF LIFE ON EARTH

For hundreds of years, people have been finding the preserved—that is, fossilized—remains of organisms all over the world (see also the full discussion of fossils in chapter 8). To test his hypothesis that fossils are the remains of past life, the English scientist Robert Hooke (1635–1703) studied the microscopic structure of fossil wood. After observing that the tissue structure of the fossil wood was identical to the tissue structure of living trees, Hooke concluded that the fossil wood derived from once-living trees (**Figure 2.7**).

The potential of fossils to illuminate the past was demonstrated by the French naturalist and zoologist Georges Cuvier (1769–1832). Cuvier dedicated himself to learning the anatomy, or structural makeup, of many kinds of animals (**Figure 2.8**). Pioneering what we now call paleontology and comparative anatomy, he applied his extensive knowledge of comparative anatomy to fossils. By doing so, he reconstructed the physical characteristics of past animals—their appearance, physiology, and behavior. Although not very accurate by today's standards, these efforts provided early tools for understanding past life-forms as once-living organisms. Through detailed reconstructions, Cuvier demonstrated that fossils found in geologic strata in France were the remains of animals that had gone extinct at some point in the remote past. Cuvier's work provided the first basic understanding of the history of life, from the earliest forms to recent ones.

Cuvier observed that each stratum seemed to contain a unique set of fossils. What happened to the animals represented by each set, each layer? Cuvier concluded that they must have gone extinct due to some powerful catastrophe, such as an earthquake or a volcanic eruption. He surmised that after each

FIGURE 2.7

Robert Hooke **(a)** Hooke did pioneering biological research using a very simple microscope. He was the first to identify cells; in fact, he coined the term *cell*. **(b)** This illustration of cork wood cells appeared in Hooke's *Micrographia* (1667), the first major book on microscopy. His examinations of cells like this enabled Hooke to determine that fossils represented past life-forms.

(a)

(b)

(a)

(b)

FIGURE 2.8

Georges Cuvier (a) One of Cuvier's most important contributions to science was the concept of extinction. Here, Cuvier is depicted examining a fish fossil. **(b)** In his 1796 paper on fossil and living elephants, Cuvier suggested that mammoth remains—such as those shown here, from one of his many publications—represented a species different from any living elephant species, and, therefore, mammoth remains were from a species that had gone extinct. This idea was revolutionary because it challenged the common perception that God had created all species, none of which had ever gone extinct.

catastrophe, the region was vacant of all life and was subsequently repopulated by a different group of animals moving into it from elsewhere. This perspective is called **catastrophism**.

We now know that Earth's history does not consist merely of sequential catastrophes and resulting extinctions. Past catastrophes, such as those leading to the extinction of the dinosaurs around 65 mya, *have* profoundly affected the direction of evolution, but they were not the leading factor in evolution.

Ultimately, such catastrophic events are rare and do not explain even the sequence of fossils Cuvier observed, mostly in the region called the Paris Basin in northern France. In addition to confirming that fossils were the remains of life in the distant past, Cuvier revealed that the most recent geologic strata contain mostly mammals and that earlier geologic strata contain mostly reptiles, including dinosaurs.

catastrophism The doctrine asserting that cataclysmic events (such as volcanoes, earthquakes, and floods), rather than evolutionary processes, are responsible for geologic changes throughout Earth's history.

TAXONOMY AND SYSTEMATICS: CLASSIFYING LIVING ORGANISMS AND IDENTIFYING THEIR BIOLOGICAL RELATIONSHIPS

Even before Darwin espoused his revolutionary ideas about evolution, most scientists who studied life-forms realized the importance of developing a taxonomy—a classification of life-forms—for identifying biological relationships. Early efforts at taxonomy took a commonsense approach. Animals were placed within major groups such as dogs, cats, horses, cattle, and people. Plants were placed within major groups such as trees, shrubs, vines, and weeds.

FIGURE 2.9

Carolus Linnaeus Linnaeus, a botanist, zoologist, and physician, is known for his contributions to the system of classification used today by all biological scientists, including biological anthropologists. He is also a founder of modern ecology.

genus A group of related species.

As late as the eighteenth century, scientists at the time generally believed that species were immutable. In their view, life had changed very little, or not at all, since the time of the single Creation. Thus, early taxonomists were not motivated by an interest in evolution. Rather, they were motivated by their desire to present the fullest and most accurate picture of the Creator's intentions for His newly created world. To construct the best possible taxonomy, the English naturalist John Ray (1627–1705) advocated personal observation, careful description, and consideration of plants' and animals' many attributes. Ray's attention to detail laid the groundwork for later taxonomy, especially for the binomial nomenclature (two-name) system developed by the Swedish naturalist Carl von Linné (1707–1778). Von Linné, better known by his Latinized name, Carolus Linnaeus, gave each plant and animal a higher-level **genus** (plural, *genera*) name and a lower-level species (plural is also *species*) name (**Figure 2.9**). A single genus could include one or more species. For example, when Linnaeus named human beings *Homo sapiens*—*Homo* being the genus, *sapiens* being the species—he thought there were species and subspecies of living humans (an idea discussed further in chapter 5). The presence of more than one level in his taxonomy acknowledged different degrees of physical similarity. Today, we recognize that *sapiens* is the only living species in the genus *Homo*.

Linnaeus presented the first version of his taxonomy in his book *Systema Naturae* (1735), or *System of Nature*. As he revised the taxonomy—his book would eventually go through 10 editions—he added more and more levels to the hierarchy. He classified groups of genera into orders, and groups of orders into classes. For example, he named one order "Primates"—the group of mammals that includes humans, apes, monkeys, and prosimians. Since the eighteenth century, this taxonomic system has evolved into multiple levels of classification, going from the subspecies at the bottom to the kingdom at the top (**Figure 2.10**).

Like Ray, Linnaeus was committed to the notion that life-forms were static, fixed at the time of the Creation. In later editions of his book, he hinted at the possibility that some species may be related to each other because they share an ancestor in common, but he never developed these ideas. His taxonomy is still used today, although viewed with a much stronger sense of present and past variation. The system's flexibility aided evolutionary biologists in their study of biological diversity, and the focus on taxonomic relationships over time is now called *systematics*.

DEMOGRAPHY: INFLUENCES ON POPULATION SIZE AND COMPETITION FOR LIMITED RESOURCES

After returning to England and while developing his ideas on natural selection, Darwin read the works of all the great scientists of the time. Probably the most important influence on his ideas was *An Essay on the Principle of Population*, by the English political economist Thomas Malthus (1766–1834). First published in 1798, Malthus's book made the case that an abundance of food—enough to feed everyone alive at any given time—would allow the human population to increase geometrically and indefinitely. In reality, the *Essay* argued that there simply is not enough food for everyone born, so population size is limited by food supply (**Figure 2.11**). Who survives to reproductive age? In Malthus's view, those who can successfully compete for food. Whose children thrive? Those of survivors who manage to feed their offspring. Applying Malthus's demographic ideas to human and nonhuman animals, Darwin concluded that some members of any species successfully compete

TAXONOMIC CATEGORY	TAXONOMIC LEVEL	COMMON CHARACTERISTICS
Kingdom	Animalia	Mobile multicellular organisms that consume other organisms for food and develop during an embryo stage.
Subkingdom	Eumetazoa	All major animals (except sponges) that contain true tissue layers, organized as germ layers, which develop into organs in humans.
Phylum	Chordata	Group of vertebrate and invertebrate animals that have a notochord, which becomes the vertebral column in humans and other primates.
Subphylum	Vertebrata	Animals with vertebral columns or backbones (including fish, amphibians, reptiles, birds, and mammals).
Superclass	Tetrapoda	Vertebrate animals with four feet or legs, including amphibians, birds, dinosaurs, and mammals.
Class	Mammalia	Group of warm-blooded vertebrate animals that produce milk for their young in mammary glands. They have hair or fur and specialized teeth.
Subclass	Theria	Group of mammals that produce live young without a shelled egg (including placental and marsupial mammals).
Order	Primates	Group of mammals specialized for life in the trees, with large brains, stereoscopic vision, opposable thumbs, and grasping hands and feet.
Suborder	Haplorhini	Group of primates, including monkeys, apes, humans, and tarsiers. They have in general long life cycles and are relatively large-bodied.
Infraorder	Anthropoidea	Group of haplorhines, including humans, apes, and monkeys.
Parvorder	Catarrhini	Group of anthropoids, including humans, apes, and Old World monkeys.
Superfamily	Hominoidea	Group of anthropoids, including humans, great apes, lesser apes, and humanlike ancestors. They have the largest bodies and brains of all primates.
Family	Hominidae	Great apes, humans, and humanlike ancestors.
Subfamily	Homininae	Chimpanzees, humans, and humanlike ancestors.
Tribe	Hominini	Commonly called "hominins," this level includes humans and humanlike ancestors, all of which are obligate bipeds.
Genus	*Homo*	Group of hominins including modern humans, their direct ancestors, and extinct relatives (e.g., Neandertals). They have the largest brains in the Hominini.
Species	*sapiens*	Modern and ancestral modern humans. They have culture, use language, and inhabit every continent except Antarctica.
Subspecies	*sapiens*	Modern humans alone.

FIGURE 2.10

The Place of Humans in Linnaeus's Taxonomy Linnaeus's system organized living things into various levels of hierarchical classification. Kingdom, at the top of the taxonomy, is the largest classification. The five kingdoms of the natural world—animals, plants, fungi, protists, and monera—include all living organisms. Through descending taxonomic levels, each group's size gets progressively smaller. For example, there are fewer organisms in a genus than there are in a phylum. Additionally, these classifications reflect the relationships of organisms to one another. For example, organisms within a genus are more closely related than are those from different genera.

(a)

(b)

FIGURE 2.11

Thomas Malthus **(a)** Malthus, the founder of demography, theorized that population size was limited by food supply. **(b)** London's crowded conditions influenced Malthus's view that an insufficient food supply causes some people to fall into poverty, while others are able to acquire the resources they need to thrive.

Lamarckism First proposed by Lamarck, the theory of evolution through the inheritance of acquired characteristics in which an organism can pass on features acquired during its lifetime.

for food because they have some special attribute or attributes. That an individual characteristic could facilitate survival was a revelation!

EVOLUTIONARY BIOLOGY: EXPLAINING THE TRANSFORMATION OF EARLIER LIFE-FORMS INTO LATER LIFE-FORMS

By the late 1700s, a handful of scientists had begun to argue that, contrary to religious doctrine, organisms' physical appearances are not fixed—they change over time, sometimes in dramatic ways. Simply, life evolved in the past and evolution is an ongoing, undirected process. Building on this concept, the French naturalist Jean-Baptiste de Monet (1744–1829), better known by his title, Chevalier de Lamarck, speculated that plants and animals not only change in form over time but do so for purposes of self-improvement. Lamarck believed that in response to new demands or needs, life-forms develop new anatomical modifications, such as new organs. His central idea—that when life-forms reproduce, they pass on to their offspring the modifications they have acquired to that point—is called *Lamarckian inheritance of acquired characteristics*, or **Lamarckism** (**Figure 2.12**). We now know Lamarck's mechanism for evolution to be wrong—offspring do not inherit traits acquired by their parents—but his work was the first major attempt to develop a theory built on the premise that living organisms arose from precursor species. Lamarck was also convinced that humans evolved from some ape-like animal.

Among the other scholars who believed that life had changed over time was the English physician, naturalist, and poet Erasmus Darwin (1731–1802), grandfather of Charles Darwin. Like Lamarck, he hypothesized that characteristics determined by wants and needs were acquired through inheritance; but he, too, was wrong about the mechanism underlying biological change over time.

CONCEPT CHECK

Darwin Borrows from Malthus

Five of Malthus's observations inspired Darwin's principle of natural selection.

OBSERVATION 1
For most organisms, every pair of parents produces multiple (sometimes many) offspring.

OBSERVATION 2
For most organisms, the population size remains the same. No increase occurs over time.

OBSERVATION 3
Population is limited by the food supply.

OBSERVATION 4
Members of populations compete for access to food.

OBSERVATION 5
No two members of a species are alike in their physical attributes—variation exists.

THEORY: EVOLUTION BY MEANS OF NATURAL SELECTION
Individuals having variation that is advantageous for survival to reproductive age produce more offspring (and more offspring that survive) than do individuals lacking this variation.

(a)

FIGURE 2.12

Jean-Baptiste Lamarck **(a)** Lamarck developed an early theory of evolution involving the inheritance of acquired characteristics. Although his mechanism of evolution was wrong, Lamarck's recognition of the dynamic nature of life in the past made an important contribution to the development of evolutionary theory.
(b) According to the classic (though incorrect) example of Lamarckism, giraffes stretched to reach food at the tops of trees, their necks grew as a result, and they passed on these long necks to their offspring.

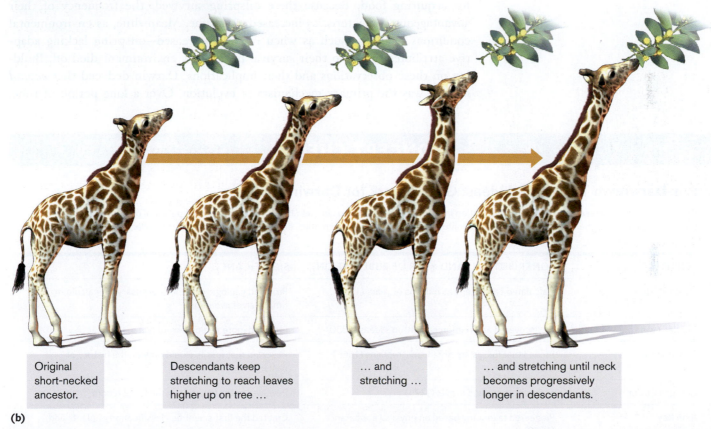

| Original short-necked ancestor. | Descendants keep stretching to reach leaves higher up on tree … | … and stretching … | … and stretching until neck becomes progressively longer in descendants. |

(b)

2.2 The Theory of Evolution: Darwin's Contribution

Darwin's remarkable attention to detail enabled him to connect his voluminous reading with his personal observations from the *Beagle* voyage. For example, while in Chile, Darwin had observed firsthand the power of earthquakes in shaping the landscape. Hutton's and Lyell's uniformitarianism led him to recognize that the accumulation of such catastrophes over a long period of time explains, at least in part, the appearance of the present-day landscape. This understanding of Earth's remarkably dynamic geologic history laid the groundwork for Darwin's view of evolution as a long, gradual process.

That process, he saw, could be reconstructed through the fossil record. He had read carefully Cuvier's studies of fossils, and in South America he saw fossils first-hand. Some of these fossils resembled living animals native to South America, such as the armadillo, ground sloth, and llama. This evidence strongly suggested that an earlier species had transformed into the modern species, most likely through a succession of species over time. Drawing on Malthus's ideas about reproduction, population, and variation, Darwin wrote, "It at once struck me that under these circumstances [that is, specific environmental conditions] favorable variations would tend to be preserved and unfavorable ones to be destroyed. The result of this would be the formation of new species." Another revelation!

Darwin hypothesized that surviving offspring had attributes advantageous for acquiring food. Because these offspring survived, the frequency of their advantageous characteristics increased over time. Meanwhile, as environmental conditions changed—such as when rainfall decreased—offspring lacking adaptive attributes suited to their survival in the new environment died off. Building on these observations and their implications, Darwin deduced that *natural selection* was the primary mechanism of evolution. Over a long period of time,

CONCEPT CHECK

Pre-Darwinian Theory and Ideas: Groundwork for Darwin's Theory

Charles Darwin first presented his theory of evolution in his book *On the Origin of Species* (1859). Based on years of personal observation and study, this unifying biological theory drew on geology, paleontology, taxonomy and systematics, demography, and what is now called evolutionary biology.

SCIENTIST	CONTRIBUTION (AND YEAR OF PUBLICATION)	SIGNIFICANCE
James Hutton	Calculated Earth's age as millions of years (1788)	Provided geologic evidence necessary for calculating time span of evolution
Charles Lyell	Rediscovered and reinforced Hutton's ideas (1830)	Provided more geologic evidence
Robert Hooke	Proved that fossils are organisms' remains (1665)	Revealed that fossils would provide the history of past life
Georges Cuvier	Extensively studied fossils (1796)	Revealed much variation in the fossil record
John Ray	Pioneered taxonomy based on physical appearance (1660)	Created the first scientific classification of plants and animals
Carolus Linnaeus	Wrote *Systema Naturae* (1735)	Presented the binomial nomenclature taxonomy of plants and animals
Thomas Malthus	Founded demography; theorized that only some will find enough food to survive (1798)	Provided the concept of characteristics advantageous for survival
Jean-Baptiste Lamarck	Posited that characteristics are acquired via inheritance (Lamarckism) (1809)	Provided the first serious model of physical traits passing from parents to offspring
Erasmus Darwin	Also posited that characteristics (determined by wants and needs) are acquired via inheritance (1794)	Advanced the notion that physical changes occurred in the past

(a)

(b)

(c)

FIGURE 2.13

Writing a Masterpiece **(a)** Darwin wrote most of *On the Origin of Species* at his beloved home, Down House, in Kent, England. **(b)** He generally worked in his study there. **(c)** The title page of the manuscript, written in Darwin's own hand, reads "An abstract of an Essay on the Origin of Species and Varieties Through Natural Selection, by Charles Darwin M.A., Fellow of the Royal, Geographical, and Linn[ean] Soc., London, 1859."

through generations' adaptation to different environments and different foods, a common ancestor gave rise to related species. Darwin's hypothesis was revolutionary, undermining the mid-nineteenth-century consensus that species were fixed types in a defined natural order of life. Now, species would have to be considered as populations with no predetermined limit on variation.

Darwin's background research had begun in the 1830s. It was not until 1856, however—fully two decades after his voyage around the world—that he had gathered enough evidence and had sufficiently developed his ideas to begin writing his great work about evolution by means of natural selection, *On the Origin of Species* (**Figure 2.13**). His colleagues had warned him that if he did not write his book soon, someone else might receive credit for the idea. Indeed, in 1858, Darwin received from the English naturalist and explorer Alfred Russel Wallace (1823–1913) a letter and a 20-page report outlining Wallace's theory of evolution by means of natural selection (**Figure 2.14**). Independently from Darwin, Wallace had arrived at most of the same conclusions that Darwin had. Both men had been aware of their shared interest in the subject, and both men formulated their theories independently. Concerned that Wallace would publish first, Darwin completed *Origin* over the next 15 months and published it in London in 1859. Who, then, "discovered" natural selection, the key mechanism that explains evolution? Some argue that Wallace should be given primary credit for the theory. However, because Wallace had not amassed the extensive body of evidence needed to support the theory, Darwin is recognized as the discoverer (**Figure 2.15**).

Darwin and Wallace made monumental discoveries, but neither man could come up with a compelling explanation of the physical mechanisms by which evolution takes place. That is, they could not explain what mechanisms result in evolutionary change. Half a continent away, a series of novel experiments led to the discovery of these biological mechanisms, paving the way for remarkable new insights into evolution.

FIGURE 2.14

Alfred Russel Wallace Although Darwin often gets sole credit for the development of the theory of evolution through natural selection, Wallace (here depicted ca. 1860) contributed substantially to evolutionary theory. Wallace was the leading authority on the geographic distribution of animals, for example, and was the first to recognize the concept of warning coloration in animals. In addition, he raised the issue of human impact on the environment a full century before it became a concern for the general public.

2.15

TIMELINE:
DARWIN'S THEORY OF EVOLUTION

Darwin's theory did not arise out of a vacuum. It arose from Darwin's experiences, the people he knew and respected, his interests in living plants and animals, and his dogged commitment to tracking down answers to questions about the natural world we live in.

3 · **DARWIN SEES THE WORLD, 1831–36**

As the *Beagle* made landfall at the rainforests, deserts, and mountains of South America, Darwin recorded detailed observations. He read the geology pioneer Charles Lyell's book *Principles of Geology* and became taken with Lyell's ideas about uniformitarianism, that the Earth is very old and that landmasses are constantly changing, rising, and falling.

SKELETON OF THE MEGATHERIUM. Page 106.

A prodigious collector, Darwin shipped back to England thousands of shells, bones, fossils, animal skins, and preserved plants. On the coast of Argentina, he excavated a fossil bed of megafauna, including the remains of an extinct giant sloth, noting the strong similarity between the fossils and living forms. On the Galápagos Islands, he saw tortoises, lizards, and mockingbirds (now known as Darwin's finches).

In organizing his notes, during the voyage home, he wrote that the variation in birds represented varieties of the same general kind of bird and concluded that species are not stable.

1 · **DARWIN GROWS UP, 1809–25**

Darwin belonged to a wealthy, cultured family and was raised to respect hard work and education. As a boy, he loved to walk through the countryside around his home in rural England, to think, and to speculate about the natural world around him. During these years, he began to study the variation of plants and animals.

2 · **DARWIN GOES TO COLLEGE, 1825–31**

While attending medical school at the University of Edinburgh, Darwin was drawn to natural history and became interested in marine invertebrates. He learned about Jean-Baptiste Lamarck's hypothesis that species change over time. A lecture by the American painter and ornithologist John James Audubon encouraged his interest in birds and wildlife. He left the University of Edinburgh for Cambridge University, where he continued to pursue natural history.

While collecting natural specimens on his own, Darwin studied with the English geology, archaeology, and botany pioneer John Stevens Henslow. Henslow introduced Darwin to the English geology pioneer Adam Sedgwick, who took him on a field trip to learn survey techniques. Henslow recommended that Darwin read the German pioneer naturalist Alexander von Humboldt's book on explorations in South America. In fact, Henslow was so impressed with Darwin's intellectual and personal abilities that he recommended him to serve as naturalist aboard HMS *Beagle*. Darwin enthusiastically accepted the position.

4 DARWIN RETURNS HOME AND DEVELOPS HIS IDEAS, 1837–55

In 1837, Darwin wrote that all forms of life had "transmuted" from a single life-form. He noted that fossils represent animals previous to living descendants, that some of the past forms went extinct, and that species evolve rather than being created. In 1838, Darwin read the work of the pioneer demographer and economist Thomas Malthus, who argued that the human population was too large to be supported by current resources. Darwin thought that, in the same way, weak plants and animals died off. Those with some kind of advantage—biological characteristics best suited for a particular setting—survived and produced offspring.

Realizing that his ideas would be challenged, Darwin decided not to publish them during his lifetime. To Lyell, the eminent geographical botanist Joseph Dalton Hooker, and the eminent biologist Thomas Henry Huxley, he showed a 230-page essay stating the ideas behind, and some of the evidence for, natural selection in particular and evolution in general. Darwin spent the next 15 years in his beloved rural home, Down House, preparing a major treatise on evolution. He studied barnacles and seed dispersions. He bred pigeons and studied the variations in their bones over generations.

5 DARWIN INTRODUCES HIS IDEAS TO THE WORLD, 1855–59

Alfred Russel Wallace had heard of Darwin and, having also read Malthus, drew the same conclusion about the driving force of natural selection and the mutability of species. Wallace's scientific paper "On the Law Which Has Regulated the Introduction of New Species" suggested that he might "scoop" Darwin, who was encouraged by colleagues to finish a big book that would present all his findings and theories. In 1858, Darwin and Wallace presented brief papers to the Linnean Society of London and published them later that year. Darwin abandoned his plan to finish the big book. Instead, he published a shorter version, *On the Origin of Species by Means of Natural Selection*. The book sold out immediately, beginning the modern era of biology and its affiliated sciences, including what would later become known as biological anthropology.

6 DARWIN'S LATER LIFE AND HIS IMPACT, 1859–82

For the next two decades, Darwin continued to gather data to support his theory. With a few exceptions, his ideas were accepted widely by the scientific community and viewed as fundamental to understanding the natural world. As a result, scientists came to see evolution as the source of life. The idea that all life, including humans and other primates, is related by descent provided the basis for some of the most important scientific discoveries and applications over the next century and a half. Later scientists' discoveries of the fossil record and, subsequently, the DNA revolution confirmed and expanded this remarkably powerful theory, which explains life and the world around us.

2.3 Since Darwin: Mechanisms of Inheritance, the Evolutionary Synthesis, and the Discovery of DNA

MECHANISMS OF INHERITANCE

Having articulated and supported his theory of evolution by means of natural selection, Darwin turned to the next fundamental question about natural selection: How do the traits that are being selected for (or against) pass from parent to offspring? Like other scientists of his day, Darwin believed that each body part contained invisible particles that he called **gemmules**. Darwin hypothesized that representative gemmules for all body parts resided in the reproductive organs. During fertilization, each parent contributed his or her gemmules to the potential offspring. The father's and the mother's gemmules then intermingled to form the characteristics observed in their progeny. Called **blending inheritance**, this process was a popular notion at the time.

Unknown to Darwin, research elsewhere in Europe was calling into question the idea of blending inheritance. In 1865, just 6 years after the publication of *On the Origin of Species*, Gregor Mendel (1822–1884), an Augustinian monk living in a monastery in Brno, Czech Republic, published in a local scientific journal the results of his revolutionary work on inheritance (**Figure 2.16**). Mendel had spent the previous 8 years crossbreeding different varieties of garden pea plants. Over the course of his experiments, he grew some 28,000 plants. These experiments enabled him to identify and carefully observe seven characteristics, or traits, that were especially informative about breeding and its outcome over the span of multiple generations (**Figure 2.17**). From his results, Mendel inferred that a *discrete* physical

FIGURE 2.16

Gregor Mendel Mendel, the father of modern genetics, was a Christian monk by profession but a scientist by nature. His observations provided the foundation for our understanding of genetics (the subject of chapters 3 and 4).

gemmules As proposed by Darwin, the units of inheritance, supposedly accumulated in the gametes so they could be passed on to offspring.

blending inheritance An outdated, refuted theory that the phenotype of an offspring was a uniform blend of the parents' phenotypes.

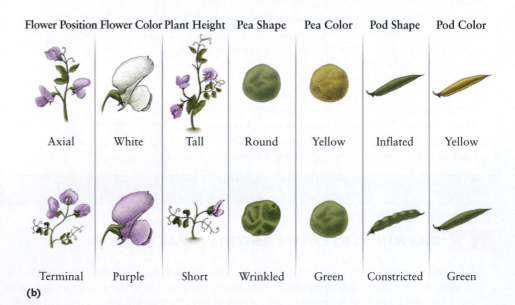

(a)

(b)

Flower Position	Flower Color	Plant Height	Pea Shape	Pea Color	Pod Shape	Pod Color
Axial	White	Tall	Round	Yellow	Inflated	Yellow
Terminal	Purple	Short	Wrinkled	Green	Constricted	Green

FIGURE 2.17

Mendel's Peas (a) This illustration—from the 1876 catalog of one of Mendel's seed suppliers—shows **(b)** the seven characteristics Mendel studied, each of which had two variants. Flower position, for example, could be axial or terminal, and flower color could be white or purple.

unit was responsible for each characteristic. This unit passed from parent to off-spring, and in this way the characteristic was inherited. In fact, the discrete unit could be traced over the course of multiple generations, and its passage (the inheritance) was determined by mathematical laws.

Mendel also discovered that the garden peas' traits did not blend. For example, plants and their offspring were either tall or short. Over time, the short plants diminished in frequency and eventually disappeared. Later scientists determined that the physical unit of inheritance—the **gene**—has two subunits, one subunit from the father and one subunit from the mother, each called an **allele**. Each allele is either **dominant** or **recessive**. In garden peas, the allele for tallness is dominant and the allele for shortness is recessive. If one parent provides a "tall" allele (*T*) and the other parent provides a "short" allele (*t*), then the offspring having one of each allele (*Tt*) would be tall because of the presence of the "tall" allele—the dominant allele is physically expressed, whereas the recessive allele is hidden. The pure strain for tall (*TT*) includes one tall maternal allele (*T*) and one tall paternal allele (*T*). The pure strain for short (*tt*) includes one short maternal allele (*t*) and one short paternal allele (*t*) (**Figure 2.18**).

While Darwin's theory generated immediate excitement in the scientific community and among the public and was supported by leading scientists of the time such as Thomas Henry Huxley (1825–1895; **Figure 2.19**), Mendel's crucial discovery (now known as **Mendelian inheritance**) went unnoticed. His writing was not widely distributed, as his work was simply ahead of its time; hence, the discovery was there but not the recognition. However, in 1900, three scientists working independently—the German botanist Carl Erich Correns (1864–1933), the Austrian botanist Erich Tschermak von Seysenegg (1871–1962), and the Dutch botanist Hugo de Vries (1848–1935)—discovered Mendel's research and replicated his findings. The Danish botanist Wilhelm Ludvig Johannsen (1857–1927) called the pair of alleles (for example, *TT, Tt, tt*) the **genotype** and the actual physical appearance (tall, short) the **phenotype**.

Mendel's theory of inheritance forms the basis of the modern discipline of **genetics**, the study of specific genes and their function and transmission (the subject of chapters 3 and 4). It makes clear that the physical units—the genes and the two component alleles of each gene—responsible for physical attributes are located in the reproductive cells: eggs and sperm. When microscope technology improved in the late nineteenth century, the cell structure and the units of inheritance were defined (see chapter 3).

Beginning in 1908, the American geneticist Thomas Hunt Morgan (1866–1945) and his associates bred the common fruit fly in experiments that built on Mendel's pea breeding. All genes, they discovered, are transmitted from parents to offspring in the ratios identified by Mendel. The genes are on **chromosomes**, and both the hereditary material and its carriers are duplicated during reproductive cell division (**Figure 2.20**).

THE EVOLUTIONARY SYNTHESIS, THE STUDY OF POPULATIONS, AND THE CAUSES OF EVOLUTION

The combination of Darwin's theory of evolution and Mendel's theory of heredity resulted in an **evolutionary synthesis**. Darwin's theory provided the mechanism for one cause of evolution (natural selection), and Mendel's theory showed how

gene The basic unit of inheritance; a sequence of DNA on a chromosome, coded to produce a specific protein.

allele One or more alternative forms of a gene.

dominant allele An allele that is expressed in an organism's phenotype and that simultaneously masks the effects of another allele, if another one is present.

recessive allele An allele that is expressed in an organism's phenotype if two copies are present but is masked if the dominant allele is present.

Mendelian inheritance The basic principles associated with the transmission of genetic material, forming the basis of genetics, including the law of segregation and the law of independent assortment.

genotype The genetic makeup of an organism; the combination of alleles for a given gene.

phenotype The physical expression of the genotype; it may be influenced by the environment.

chromosomes The strands of genetic material (DNA) found in the nucleus of multicelled organisms that contain hundreds or thousands of genes.

evolutionary synthesis A unified theory of evolution that combines genetics with natural selection.

Generation 1

Parent 1
(*TT*): Tall

	T	*T*
t	*Tt*	*Tt*
t	*Tt*	*Tt*

Parent 2
(*tt*): Short

100% *Tt* = Tall

If the tallness allele is expressed as *T* and the shortness allele is expressed as *t*, the pure strain for tall is *TT* (one *T* is the maternal allele, the other *T* is the paternal allele), and the pure strain for short is *tt* (one *t* is the maternal allele, and the other *t* is the paternal allele).

Generation 2

Parent 1
(*Tt*): Tall

When a *TT* plant is crossbred with a *tt* plant, one allele must come from the father (paternal) and one allele (maternal) must come from the mother, thereby producing a *Tt* offspring.

Because *T* is dominant, the offspring is tall.

	T	*t*
T	*TT*	*Tt*
t	*Tt*	*tt*

Parent 2
(*Tt*): Tall

25% *TT* = Tall
50% *Tt* = Tall   } 3:1 Tall:Short
25% *tt* = Short

When the offspring from two *Tt* parental plants are bred, the offspring's alleles independently redistribute, producing about equal numbers of the four possible combinations of *T* and *t* alleles: *TT*, *Tt*, *tT*, and *tt*.

Thus, three of the four plants (75%) will be tall owing to the dominance of the *T* allele, and one plant (25%) will be short owing to the recessiveness of the *t* allele. Note, however, that 25% of the offspring are tall with two dominant tall alleles (*TT*), while 50% are tall with one of each allele (*Tt*).

FIGURE 2.18
Mendel's Genetics

FIGURE 2.19

Thomas Henry Huxley Huxley, an English biologist, was known as "Darwin's bulldog" because he so forcefully promoted Darwin's theory of evolution by natural selection. Among Huxley's contributions to evolutionary theory was the concept that humans evolved from an apelike animal.

(a)

(b)

FIGURE 2.20

Thomas Hunt Morgan **(a)** In 1933, Morgan was awarded the Nobel Prize in Physiology or Medicine, largely for demonstrating that chromosomes carry genetic material in the form of genes. **(b)** A micrograph shows chromosomes of Morgan's research subject, the common fruit fly (*Drosophila melanogaster*).

traits are passed on systematically and predictably (Mendelian inheritance). The melding of natural selection and Mendelian inheritance led biologists to ask further questions about evolution, specifically about the origins of particular genes, genetic variation in general, and change in physical characteristics over time. *Why* do some genes increase in frequency, some decrease in frequency, and some show no change? *How* do completely new genes appear? These questions and a focus on population—viewed as the *gene pool*—provided the basis for a newly emerging field in evolutionary biology called **population genetics** (among the subjects of chapter 4).

Natural selection, the guiding force of evolution, could operate only on variation that already existed in a population. How did new variation—new characteristics—arise in a population? Through his experiments with fruit flies, Morgan showed that a new gene could appear as a result of spontaneous change in an existing gene. This kind of genetic change is called **mutation** (**Figure 2.21**). The only source of new genetic material, mutation is a second cause of evolution.

Gene flow, a third cause of evolution, is the diffusion, or spread, of new genetic material from one population to another. In other words, through sexual reproduction, genes from one gene pool are transferred to another gene pool. Take, for example, the gene that causes sickle-cell anemia (this disorder is discussed extensively in chapter 4). Among black West Africans, it has a frequency of about 10%. Among white Americans, it has a frequency of 0%. Because black West Africans and their descendants have long reproduced with white Americans, the frequency among people descended from both black West Africans and white Americans of the gene that causes sickle-cell anemia is approximately 5%, halfway between that of the two original populations. Over time, as the two populations have mixed, gene flow has decreased genetic difference. Traditionally, gene flow has been

population genetics A specialty within the field of genetics that focuses on the changes in gene frequencies and the effects of those changes on adaptation and evolution.

mutation A random change in a gene or chromosome, creating a new trait that may be advantageous, deleterious, or neutral in its effects on the organism.

gene flow Admixture, or the exchange of alleles between two populations.

(a)

(b)

(c)

FIGURE 2.21

Fruit Fly Mutations **(a)** Thomas Hunt Morgan's research on fruit flies focused on a variety of mutations, including eye color. This image shows the normal, or wild-type, eye color, as well as several possible mutations. Morgan first observed mutation when a white-eyed offspring appeared within a strain of red-eyed flies. **(b)** The normal fruit fly has two wings, while **(c)** the four-wing mutation has two wings on each side.

hybridization The process of interbreeding between members of different species.

genetic drift The random change in allele frequency from one generation to the next, with greater effect in small populations.

identified as interbreeding within members of a species only. However, many mammal groups show evidence of **hybridization** between members of different, but closely related, species.

Genetic drift, a fourth cause of evolution, is random change in the frequency of alleles of different gene forms. Such change affects a small population more powerfully than it affects a large population (**Figure 2.22**). Over time, it increases the genetic difference between two genetically related but not interbreeding populations.

By the mid-twentieth century, the four causes of evolution—natural selection, mutation, gene flow, and genetic drift—were well defined, thanks to a synthesis of ideas drawn from the full range of sciences that deal with biological variation. In effect, evolutionary synthesis unified the branches of biology and its affiliated sciences, including genetics, taxonomy, morphology, comparative anatomy, paleontology, and the subject of this book, biological anthropology. Similarly, evolution unites living and past worlds. *All organisms are related through common descent, and organisms more closely related than others share a more recent common ancestor.*

DNA: DISCOVERY OF THE MOLECULAR BASIS OF EVOLUTION

deoxyribonucleic acid (DNA) A double-stranded molecule that provides the genetic code for an organism, consisting of phosphate, deoxyribose sugar, and four types of nitrogen bases.

Once chromosomes were recognized as the carriers of genes, scientists sought to understand the structure of **deoxyribonucleic acid (DNA)**, the chemical that makes up chromosomes. In 1953, the American geneticist James Watson (b. 1928) and the British biophysicist Francis Crick (1916–2004) published their discovery that DNA molecules have a ladderlike, double-helical structure. Crucial to their discovery was the work of the British X-ray crystallographer Rosalind Franklin (1920–1958), who used a special technique, X-ray diffraction, to produce high-quality images of DNA. The combined efforts of Franklin, Watson, and Crick

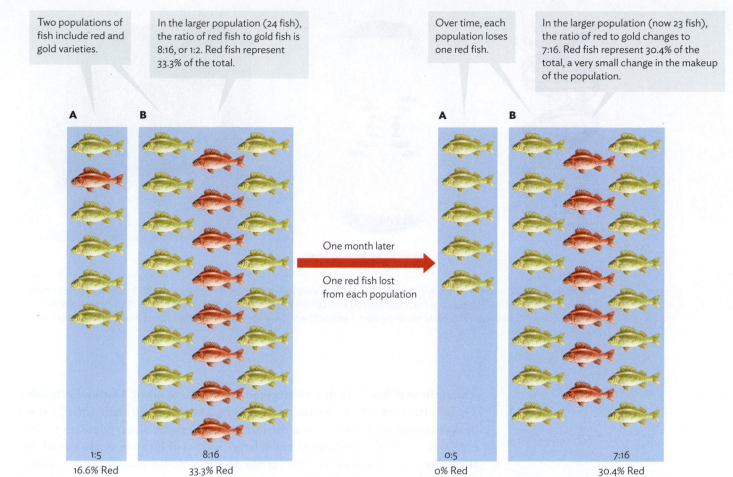

Two populations of fish include red and gold varieties.

In the larger population (24 fish), the ratio of red fish to gold fish is 8:16, or 1:2. Red fish represent 33.3% of the total.

Over time, each population loses one red fish.

In the larger population (now 23 fish), the ratio of red to gold changes to 7:16. Red fish represent 30.4% of the total, a very small change in the makeup of the population.

A   B

One month later

One red fish lost from each population

A   B

1:5   8:16   0:5   7:16
16.6% Red   33.3% Red   0% Red   30.4% Red

In the smaller population (6 fish), the ratio of red to gold is 1:5. Red fish represent 16.6% of the total.

In the smaller population (now 5 fish), the ratio of red to gold changes to 0:5. Red fish represent 0% of the total, a substantial change in the makeup of the population.

FIGURE 2.22
Genetic Drift's Effects on Small and Large Populations

opened up a whole new vista for biology by helping explain how chromosomes are replicated (**Figure 2.23**).

Analysis of the DNA from a wide variety of organisms, including primates, has provided both new perspectives on biological relationships and a molecular "clock" with which to time the branches of evolution (based on the similarity of species within those branches). In addition, as you will see in chapter 3, DNA provides a detailed road map of a wide range of diseases, such as viral and bacterial infections, cancer, heart disease, and stroke.

Little did Darwin realize just what a powerful foundation his evolutionary theory would build for science, ushering in the modern biological sciences. Long after his death, Darwin's search for the biological mechanisms involved in evolution would continue to inspire scientists, right up to the present day. Darwin would have been pleased to see the work of conservation biologist Christopher Cattau and his collaborators on the remarkably rapid morphological changes in the North

(a) (b)

(c)

FIGURE 2.23

Discovery of DNA In 1962, James Watson and Francis Crick were awarded a Nobel Prize for their 1953 discovery of **(a)** DNA's double-helical structure. Watson and Crick had worked with **(b)** X-ray diffraction photographs taken in 1953 by **(c)** Rosalind Franklin. Franklin's death in 1958 made her ineligible to receive the Nobel Prize with Watson and Crick because Nobels are not awarded posthumously.

American snail kite, a highly endangered raptor native to the Florida Everglades. These birds focus their diet on relatively small snails, using their small, curved beaks to consume the snails' meat directly out of the shells. Their population, however, was rapidly declining until a new, larger species of invasive snails spread into the region. Cattau and his research group documented the extraordinary increase in population size of the birds and the simultaneous increase in their beak length and body size. Cattau's study also revealed increased survival in birds with longer beaks and larger bodies—clear evidence for natural selection. Darwin provided the theory in the mid-nineteenth century, and modern evolutionary biologists continue to track the evidence in support of the theory. Notably, the documentation of the evolutionary process on North American snail kites in the Everglades shows that evolution can occur quickly. In that setting, it all happened within a few years, occurring only when the larger, invasive species of snails provided a new food source in a different package. Evolution does not have to occur over hundreds of thousands or millions of years.

The questions Darwin and his colleagues asked, especially about how physical attributes pass from parents to offspring, laid the foundation for the study of inheritance—the science of genetics—and eventually the DNA revolution and the field of **genomics**. Were Darwin alive today, he would have been fascinated by what DNA studies, genetics, and genomics can tell us about the evolution of animals and plants. He would also be thrilled to learn how our understanding of evolution has played such an essential role in developing our knowledge of viruses and other disease-causing agents and how they evolve and spread. For example, in 1976, the sudden outbreak of the Ebola virus came as a huge surprise, unfortunately with very high fatality rates for humans and other primates throughout West Africa; in the subsequent Ebola epidemic of 2014–16, thousands died, both humans and primates. It is likely that deadly viral **pandemics** will continue on a global scale, due to the capacity for viruses to

genomics The study of an organism's entire set of genes, or genome.

pandemic A global outbreak of a disease.

evolve in highly successful ways. Indeed, viruses' remarkably high level of evolvability makes them the most biologically successful occupants of Earth and increasingly problematic for many host species, including *H. sapiens*. We will discuss the devastation wrought by modern viruses and the COVID-19 virus, in particular, in Chapter 13. Today's knowledge of the mechanisms of genetic changes in viruses such as influenza, Ebola, and the novel coronavirus is built on the foundational work in evolution pioneered by Darwin in the nineteenth century. Our knowledge of evolution—especially the mechanisms of genetic change—has made possible the development of vaccines. Darwin's work created the revolution in biology that continues in the twenty-first century.

WATCH THE VIDEO

EBOLA

digital.wwwnorton.com/essanthro5

ANSWERING THE BIG QUESTIONS

1. **How did the theory of evolution come to be?**
   - In developing his theory of evolution by means of natural selection, Darwin drew on geology, paleontology, taxonomy and systematics, demography, and what is now called evolutionary biology.
   - Scientists working in these disciplines had shown that
     - Earth is quite old and has changed considerably over time
     - fossils represent the remains of once-living, often extinct organisms and thus provide a record of the history of life
     - life evolves over time
     - groups of related species help clarify evolutionary history
     - the number of adults in a population tends to remain the same over time

2. **What was Darwin's contribution to the theory of evolution?**
   - Darwin's key contribution was the principle of natural selection. Three principles allowed him to deduce that natural selection is the primary driver of evolution:
     - the number of adults in a population tends to remain the same over time even though, for most organisms, parents tend to produce multiple and sometimes many offspring
     - variation exists among members of populations
     - individuals having variation that boosts survival and reproduction increase in relative frequency over time

3. **What has happened since Darwin in the development of our understanding of evolution?**
   - Gregor Mendel discovered the principles of inheritance, the basis for our understanding of how physical attributes are passed from parents to offspring.

   - Mendel's revelation that attributes are passed as discrete units, which we now know as genes, laid the groundwork for our understanding of cell biology and chromosomes, and eventually for the field of population genetics.
   - We now know that evolution—genetic change in a population or species—occurs by one or more of four causes: natural selection, mutation, gene flow, and genetic drift.
   - We now know that each chromosome in an organism's cells consists of DNA molecules. DNA is the blueprint for all biological characteristics and functions.

STUDY QUIZ

1. **Which idea did *not* help Darwin form his theory of evolution?**
   a. Earth is very old, and its past organisms are preserved as fossils.
   b. Physically similar organisms tend to be closely related.
   c. Organisms compete for limited resources to survive to reproduce.
   d. Parents get new traits through their actions and pass them to offspring.

2. **Which observation supports the principle of natural selection?**
   a. Populations generally remain the same size over time.
   b. Individuals within a population tend to vary little in their physical traits.
   c. Trait variants that help organisms survive to reproduce become more common in a population over time.
   d. Whole populations are routinely wiped out by catastrophes.

KEY TERMS

adaptations
adaptive radiation
allele
blending inheritance
catastrophism
chromosomes
demography
deoxyribonucleic acid (DNA)

dominant allele
evolutionary biology
evolutionary synthesis
fossils
gemmules
gene flow
genes
genetic drift
genetics
genomics

genotype
genus
geology
habitat
hybridization
Lamarckism
Mendelian inheritance
mutation
natural selection
paleontology

pandemic
phenotype
population genetics
recessive allele
species
systematics
taxonomy
uniformitarianism

STUDY QUIZ (CONTINUED)

3. How would Lamarckism explain why the giraffe has a long neck?

a. A giraffe's neck grows as it stretches to reach food, and this trait is passed on to offspring.

b. Giraffes with long necks survive to reproduce at higher rates.

c. Giraffes have always had long necks because species do not change.

d. All short-necked giraffes went extinct because of a natural disaster.

4. Today we know that _____ pass on traits.

a. gemmules

b. genes

c. amino acids

d. phenotypes

5. The evolutionary synthesis combines natural selection with

a. genetics.

b. paleontology.

c. taxonomy.

d. geology.

EVOLUTION REVIEW

Past, Present, and Future of a Fundamental Scientific Theory

SYNOPSIS The theory of evolution forms the foundation of all the biological sciences, including biological anthropology. Although Charles Darwin is the most famous contributor to the formulation of this theory, his innovative idea of natural selection was partly influenced by the work of scientists across a number of disciplines, including geology, paleontology, taxonomy and systematics, demography, and what is now called evolutionary biology. The work of Gregor Mendel, rediscovered years after his death, provided a genetic basis for the evolutionary processes envisioned by Darwin and showed how evolution can occur in the natural world. Darwin's principle of natural selection and Mendel's principles of inheritance are intertwined in the modern evolutionary synthesis, the framework by which biological anthropologists address research questions related to human biological evolution and biocultural variation.

Q1. Darwin's principle of natural selection laid the foundations for all future biological thinking and discoveries. However, other scientists before Darwin argued in favor of biological evolution. Who is credited with one of the first major attempts to explain the process of evolutionary change through time? What is the erroneous mechanism hypothesized by this scientist to be a driving force of evolution?

Q2. Before the discoveries of Gregor Mendel, Darwin hypothesized that the characteristics of the father and mother intermingled in the offspring. What was this idea called at the time? What discovery, first made by Mendel and later by scientists such as Thomas Hunt Morgan, proved this hypothesis to be wrong?

Q3. Darwin was inspired by the idea of the demographer Thomas Malthus that population is limited by food supply. How is this idea a concern for human populations today? What steps might be taken to address this issue in the future?

Q4. Darwin originally did not publish his theory of evolution by means of natural selection, as he was well aware of the controversy it would generate. More than 150 years later, and backed by massive amounts of evidence spanning many scientific disciplines, evolution remains a subject of controversy among the general public. Why has evolution always been the subject of fierce debate?

Q5. Darwin gathered information from geology, paleontology, taxonomy and systemics, demography, and evolutionary biology to develop his theory of evolution, which includes the ideas of variation and natural selection. What are the five most important ideas from these other fields (described in this chapter) that contributed to Darwin's development of his theory?

ADDITIONAL READINGS

Alvarez, W. 1997. *T. rex and the Crater of Doom*. Princeton, NJ: Princeton University Press.

Berra, T. M. 2009. *Charles Darwin: The Concise Story of an Extraordinary Man*. Baltimore: Johns Hopkins University Press.

Bowler, P. J. 2003. *Evolution: The History of an Idea*. Berkeley: University of California Press.

Carroll, S. B. 2009. *Remarkable Creatures: Epic Adventures in the Search for the Origins of Species*. Boston: Houghton Mifflin Harcourt.

Gould, S. J. 1992. *Ever since Darwin: Reflections on Natural History*. New York: Norton.

Huxley, R. 2007. *The Great Naturalists*. New York: Thames & Hudson.

Repcheck, J. 2003. *The Man Who Found Time: James Hutton and the Discovery of the Earth's Antiquity*. Cambridge, MA: Perseus Publishing.

Wasik, B. R. and P. E. Turner. 2013. On the biological success of viruses. *Annual Review of Microbiology* 67: 519–541.

Wilson, E. O. 2006. *From So Simple a Beginning: Darwin's Four Great Books [Voyage of the H.M.S. Beagle, The Origin of Species, The Descent of Man, The Expression of Emotions in Man and Animals]*. New York: Norton.

On the surface, a human being and a chimpanzee might not seem to have much in common. However, they share 98% of their DNA. Chimpanzees are humans' closest living relatives, and both primates have many facial expressions, emotions, and body movements in common. In these and many other ways, these two primates share a considerable amount of biology.

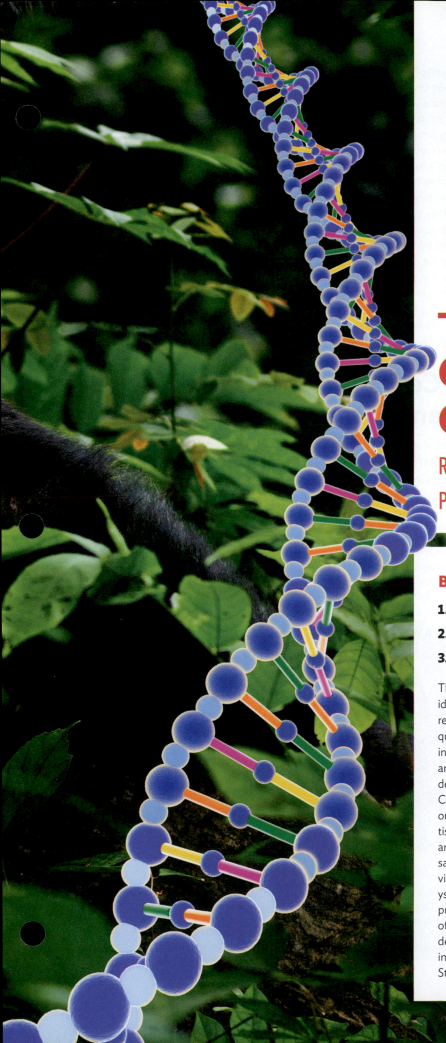

3

Genetics and Genomics
REPRODUCING LIFE AND
PRODUCING VARIATION

BIG QUESTIONS

1. **What is the genetic code?**
2. **What does the genetic code (DNA) do?**
3. **What is the genetic basis for human variation?**

There is a revolution going on in science: the discovery of DNA and the identification of its molecular structure have brought about a "DNA revolution." At no time in history have humans learned so much so quickly about the biology of plants and animals. In addition to bringing about developments in agriculture and food production, medicine, and other areas that affect billions of people every day, the information derived from DNA has transformed a number of scientific disciplines. Consider forensic science, where fingerprints and blood types were once the primary evidence. Thanks to DNA, far smaller samples—of tissue, bone, hair, and blood—can be used to identify victims' remains and to identify criminals with far greater accuracy. DNA in samples saved from old crime scenes has helped free scores of individuals convicted of crimes they had not committed. Beyond forensics, DNA analysis has helped determine family relationships. In medicine, DNA has proven critical for the identification of specific diseases and new ways of treating diseases having a genetic basis, and it has even been used to detect the presence of diseases, such as leprosy, plague, and syphilis, in ancient skeletons dating from hundreds and thousands of years ago. Study of DNA recovered from ancient hominin fossils is also helping anthropologists resolve long-standing issues pertaining to evolutionary relationships, population movements, and key adaptive shifts. Given the long and growing list of ways in which DNA can be used, it is little wonder that former US president Bill Clinton referred to the human DNA sequence, right after it was presented to the public in 2000, as "the most important, most wondrous map ever produced by humankind."

When I studied introductory biology in college in the early 1970s, knowledge of DNA was just a tiny fraction of what it is today. Evolution was understood in terms of entire organisms and their biological history. Now, DNA provides us with the information—a whole new window—whereby we can *see* how organisms are put together and *what* is actually evolving. Powerful stuff! In anthropology, it has meant new and fundamental insights into primate and human evolution. Before we can tie together the growing strands of DNA and evolution, though, we need to back up and examine the foundational work in genetics—the study of heredity.

Although the great nineteenth-century biologists discussed in chapter 2 knew a lot about phenotypic variation in species, they did not fully understand how this variation is produced or how it is transmitted from parents to offspring. For example, how do an organism's attributes grow from a fertilized egg? The answers to questions about variation—its origin and continuation—lie in the cell, its structures, and the myriad functions it performs from conception through full maturity. And governing each cell is the genetic code.

3.1 The Cell: Its Role in Reproducing Life and Producing Variation

prokaryotes Single-celled organisms with no nuclear membranes or organelles and with their genetic material as a single strand in the cytoplasm.

The cell is the basic unit of life for all organisms (**Figure 3.1**). Every organism has at least one cell (that is the baseline definition of an organism). Organisms having cells with no internal compartments are called **prokaryotes**. Prokaryotes were

The *nucleus* is the largest organelle in a cell. It houses one copy of nearly all the genetic material, or DNA, of that organism. It is covered by a nuclear membrane, or nuclear envelope, which keeps the contents of the nucleus separate from the rest of the cell.

The *cell membrane* is a semipermeable membrane surrounding the entire cell, separating one cell from the next.

The *mitochondrion* is considered the "powerhouse" of the cell, because it generates most of the energy. The number of mitochondria per cell varies by tissue type and by organism.

The *cytoplasm* is fluid that fills the cell and maintains the cell's shape. Organelles are suspended in the cytoplasm, which can also store chemical substances. The extranuclear DNA is in the mitochondria.

The *endoplasmic reticulum* is an organelle that usually surrounds the nucleus. It plays an especially important role in protein synthesis (a process discussed later in this chapter).

FIGURE 3.1

Cells and Their Organelles This illustration depicts the many components of cells found in plants and animals. Among the components are *organelles,* specialized parts analogous to organs.

likely the first life on Earth, appearing about 3.5 billion years ago (bya). Today, the prokaryotes are single-cell bacteria (**Figure 3.2**). Organisms with cells that have internal compartments separated by membranes are called **eukaryotes**. The membranes enclose the two main parts of individual cells, the **nucleus** and the **cytoplasm**, between which various communications and activities happen.

eukaryotes Multicelled organisms whose cells have a membrane-bound nucleus containing both the genetic material and specialized organelles.

nucleus A membrane-bound structure in eukaryotic cells that contains the genetic material.

cytoplasm The jellylike substance inside the cell membrane that surrounds the nucleus and in which the organelles are suspended.

The *nucleoid region* houses the genetic material of the prokaryotic cell, but unlike the nucleus of a eukaryotic cell it is not contained within a membrane. A prokaryotic cell has about one-thousandth the genetic material of a eukaryotic cell.

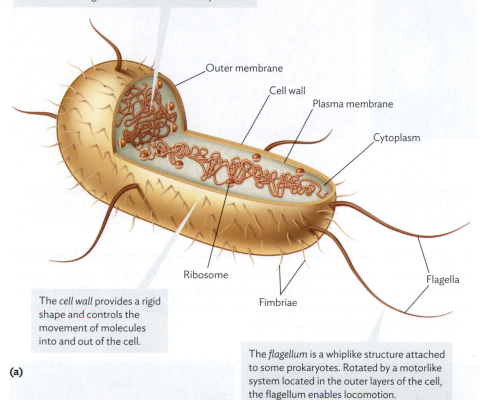

Outer membrane

Cell wall

Plasma membrane

Cytoplasm

Ribosome

Flagella

Fimbriae

The *cell wall* provides a rigid shape and controls the movement of molecules into and out of the cell.

(a)

The *flagellum* is a whiplike structure attached to some prokaryotes. Rotated by a motorlike system located in the outer layers of the cell, the flagellum enables locomotion.

Nucleus   Cytoplasm   Plasma membrane (also called *cell membrane*)

(c)

(b)

FIGURE 3.2

Prokaryotes and Eukaryotes **(a)** The many types of bacteria that we encounter in our daily lives are prokaryotic cells like this one. **(b)** For example, *Escherichia coli* (*E. coli*), two single cells of which are shown here, is a bacterium that aids digestion in the intestines of mammals, including humans. **(c)** This image shows the eukaryotic cells of a primate's kidney.

(a)

(b)

(c)

(d)

(e)

FIGURE 3.3

Somatic Cells Somatic cells in different tissues have different characteristics, but most somatic cells share a number of features. With the exception of red blood cells, somatic cells have a nucleus, which contains a complete copy of the organism's DNA. As a result, throughout the organism's body there are millions of copies of that DNA. Note the nuclei in these images of human anatomy: **(a)** heart muscle, **(b)** brain tissue, **(c)** motor neurons (nerve cells), **(d)** osteocyte (bone cell), and **(e)** skin cells.

Eukaryotes evolved much later than prokaryotes, appearing some 1.2 bya. Their quite complex structures require enormous amounts of energy to survive and reproduce. As they did in the past, eukaryotes come in many different forms, ranging from single-cell yeasts to large, complex, multicellular organisms, such as you, me, and all of our fellow human beings.

(a)

(b)

(c)

FIGURE 3.4

Gametes **(a)** Human male sex cells (sperm) have heads and tails; the tails are responsible for the sperm's motility. **(b)** A human female sex cell (ovum, in blue) is developing at the center of this ovarian follicle, or cavity. Once the egg reaches full maturity, it will be released at ovulation. If it is not fertilized by a sperm, the egg will be shed through menstruation. **(c)** Only one of the sperm surrounding this ovum will penetrate the external membrane and fertilize the ovum.

In all animals and plants, there are two types of eukaryotic cells. **Somatic cells**, also called *body cells*, compose most tissues, such as bone, muscle, skin, brain, lung, fat, and hair (**Figure 3.3**). **Gametes** are the sex cells, sperm in males and ova (or eggs) in females (**Figure 3.4**). The root of somatic cell and gamete production is in the chromosomes, located in the nucleus of each cell. In humans, somatic cells are **diploid**, having 46 chromosomes, whereas gametes are **haploid** with 23 chromosomes (**Figure 3.5**).

somatic cells Diploid cells that form the organs, tissues, and other parts of an organism's body.

gametes Sexual reproductive cells, ova and sperm, that have a haploid number of chromosomes and that can unite with a gamete of the opposite type to form a new organism.

diploid cell A cell that has a full complement of paired chromosomes.

haploid cell A cell that has a single set of unpaired chromosomes, half the number of chromosomes as a diploid cell.

 Camel: 70

 Potato: 48

 Guinea pig: 64

 Petunia: 14

 Salamander: 24

 Algae: 148

 Housefly: 12

 Ring-tailed lemur: 56

 Apple: 34

 Black-and-white colobus monkey: 44

 Orangutan: 48

(b)

(a)

FIGURE 3.5

Chromosomes **(a)** To get an idea of the incredibly minute size of chromosomes, consider that this pair has been magnified 35,000 times. If a penny (diameter approximately 2 cm, or 0.8 in) were magnified 35,000 times, it would be approximately 0.7 km, or 0.44 mi, in diameter. **(b)** An organism's complexity is not related to its number of chromosomes, as this comparison illustrates. While humans have 46 chromosomes, other primates have more (for example, ring-tailed lemurs) or fewer (for example, black-and-white colobus monkeys).

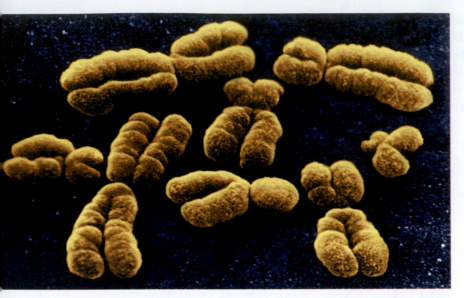

FIGURE 3.6

Nuclear DNA The cell's nucleus houses most of the body's DNA, in very long pieces called *chromosomes*. The different sizes of the human chromosomes reflect the relative amount of DNA in each.

3.2 The DNA Molecule: The Code for Life

The chemical that makes up each chromosome, DNA, is the body's genetic code. Because chromosomal DNA is contained in the nucleus of the cell, it is referred to as nuclear DNA, or nDNA (**Figure 3.6**). Within each chromosome, DNA molecules form sequences, or codes, that are templates for the production of proteins or parts of proteins in the body. Each protein has a specific function, and collectively the proteins determine all physical characteristics and govern the functions of all cells, tissues, and organs. Each DNA sequence, each protein-generating code, is a gene; and the complete set of all of your DNA, and the codes it carries, is your **genome**.

All plants and animals, past and present, have a genome. Although the number of chromosomes varies according to species (see Figure 3.5), all organisms share much the same genome. Chimpanzees have two more chromosomes than humans, but the DNA in chimpanzees and in humans is about 98% identical. Even the DNA in baker's yeast is 45% similar to human DNA. Within any organism, nDNA is **homoplasmic**, meaning that it is the same in each and every cell—the nDNA in a skin cell matches the nDNA in a bone cell. (An exception to the rule is mature red blood cells, which have no nuclei and, hence, no nuclear DNA.)

A small but significant amount of DNA is contained in tiny organelles, called **mitochondria**, within each cell's cytoplasm (**Figure 3.7**). These structures are the powerhouses of cell function; that is, they use oxygen to turn food molecules,

genome The complete set of genetic information—chromosomal and mitochondrial DNA—for an organism or species that represents all the inheritable traits.

homoplasmic Regarding nuclear DNA, the quality of being identical in each cell type (except red blood cells) within an organism.

mitochondria Energy-producing (ATP-producing) organelles in eukaryotic cells; mitochondria possess their own independent DNA.

adenosine triphosphate (ATP) An important cellular molecule created by the mitochondria and carrying the energy necessary for cellular functions.

matriline Lineage or inheritance that can be traced from mother to daughter or to son; mitochondrial DNA is matrilineal DNA.

heteroplasmic Regarding mitochondrial DNA or other organellar DNA, the quality of being different or varying among the parts of a single organism's body or even within cells of the same type, usually due to the mutation of the DNA in some organelles but not in others.

FIGURE 3.7

Mitochondrion Almost every cell includes mitochondria, sometimes thousands of them; they are known as the "powerhouses of the cell," and they are thought to have evolved from a free-living type of bacteria. The footprint-like shape pictured here is a single mitochondrion.

especially sugar and fat, into **adenosine triphosphate (ATP)**, a high-energy molecule that powers cells and, in turn, powers every tissue in the body. The number of mitochondria in a cell varies according to the cell's activity level. For example, the cells in highly active body tissues, such as muscles, contain far more mitochondria than do cells in relatively inactive tissues, such as hair.

The mitochondrial DNA (mtDNA), a kind of miniature chromosome containing 37 genes, is inherited from the mother. That is, the mtDNA comes from the ovum. Each of us, then, carries our mother's mtDNA, she carries or carried her mother's mtDNA, and so on for generation after generation. In theory, a maternal lineage, or **matriline**, can be traced back hundreds of thousands of years. (Ancient matrilines in fossil hominins are discussed in chapter 10.) Unlike nDNA, mtDNA is **heteroplasmic**, meaning it can differ among different parts of a person's body or even among the same kinds of cells.

DNA: THE BLUEPRINT OF LIFE

The DNA molecule is the blueprint of life. It serves as the chemical template for *every* aspect of biological organisms. As Watson and Crick discovered, the molecule has a right-twisted, double-helical structure (see "DNA: Discovery of the Molecular Basis of Evolution" in chapter 2). Understanding this structure is key to understanding the growth of any organism and all of its tissues, as well as the transmission of genes from parents to offspring. The starting point for looking at the DNA molecule in any detail is to unravel a chromosome and look at a tiny segment of it under supermagnification. Its helical, ladderlike structure consists of two uprights and many rungs. The uprights of the structure are made up of alternating sugar and phosphate molecules, and the rungs are composed of paired, complementary bases linked by a weak hydrogen bond (**Figure 3.8**).

On each side of the ladder, every unit of sugar, phosphate, and nitrogen base forms a single **nucleotide** (**Figure 3.9**). While the sugar and phosphate are the same throughout DNA, the base can be **adenine** (A), **thymine** (T), **guanine** (G), or **cytosine** (C). Owing to the bases' unvarying chemical configurations, adenine and thymine *always* pair with each other, and guanine and cytosine *always* pair up. In other words, apart from the rare errors in matching, adenine and thymine are **complementary bases,** and guanine and cytosine are complementary bases. This means that if on one side of the ladder the sequence is ATGCAG, on the other side the sequence will be complementary TACGTC. This predictability of base pairings ensures the high reliability of one key function of the DNA molecule, that of self-reproduction. Anthropologists and geneticists investigate the many thousands of single DNA base pairings that produce genetic differences between individuals. Known as **single nucleotide polymorphisms (SNPs,** pronounced "snips"), these pairings are spread uniformly throughout the genome. Groups of SNPs play a critical role in determining various attributes, such as hair color and blood type (see "Polymorphisms: Variations in Specific Genes" later in this chapter).

3.3 The DNA Molecule: Replicating the Code

One function of the DNA molecule is to replicate itself. **Replication** takes place in the nucleus and is part of cell division, leading to the production of new somatic cells (**mitosis**) or the production of new gametes (**meiosis**). Replication thus results

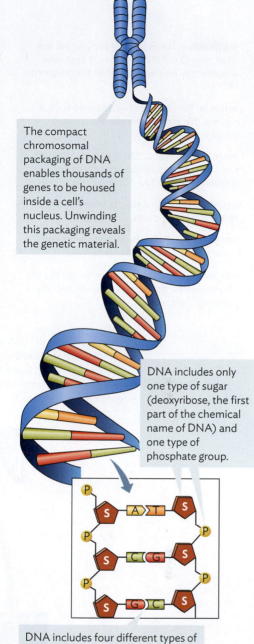

The compact chromosomal packaging of DNA enables thousands of genes to be housed inside a cell's nucleus. Unwinding this packaging reveals the genetic material.

DNA includes only one type of sugar (deoxyribose, the first part of the chemical name of DNA) and one type of phosphate group.

DNA includes four different types of nitrogen bases. A gene is a specific and unique sequence of these bases.

FIGURE 3.8
The Structure of DNA

FIGURE 3.9
Nucleotide A nucleotide is the building block of DNA and is made up of a phosphate group, a sugar, and a single nitrogen base.

replication The process of copying nuclear DNA prior to cell division, so that each new daughter cell receives a complete complement of DNA.

mitosis The process of cellular and nuclear division that creates two identical diploid daughter cells.

meiosis The production of gametes through one DNA replication and two cell (and nuclear) divisions, creating four haploid gametic cells.

zygote The cell that results from a sperm's fertilization of an ovum.

homologous Refers to chromosomes that occur in matching pairs in the genome.

autosomes All chromosomes, except the sex chromosomes, that occur in pairs in all somatic cells (not the gametes).

in continued cell production, from the single-celled **zygote** (the fertilized egg) to two cells, then four cells, and so on, to the fully mature body with all of its many different tissues and organs—within which cells are continually dying and being replaced by new cells.

In replication, DNA makes *identical* copies of itself, going from one double-stranded parent molecule of DNA to two double strands of daughter DNA. This means that where there was one chromosome, now there are two (**Figure 3.10**).

CHROMOSOME TYPES

Within somatic cells, chromosomes occur in **homologous**, or matching, pairs (**Figure 3.11**). Each pair includes the father's contribution (the paternal chromosome) and the mother's contribution (the maternal chromosome). These nonsex chromosomes are called **autosomes**.

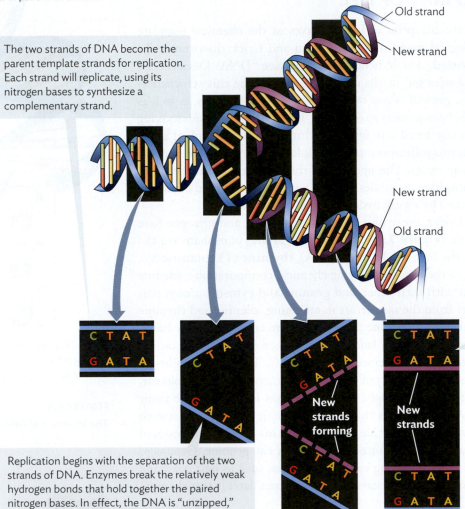

The two strands of DNA become the parent template strands for replication. Each strand will replicate, using its nitrogen bases to synthesize a complementary strand.

Old strand

New strand

New strand

Old strand

When all the nitrogen bases of the parent strands are paired with (formerly free-floating) nucleotides, replication is complete. There are now two complete DNA molecules, each consisting of one parent strand and one new strand.

New strands forming

New strands

Replication begins with the separation of the two strands of DNA. Enzymes break the relatively weak hydrogen bonds that hold together the paired nitrogen bases. In effect, the DNA is "unzipped," creating the two parent template strands.

Each parent strand serves as a template for the creation of a new complementary DNA strand. The exposed, unpaired nitrogen bases on the parent strands attract complementary free-floating nucleotides. The nitrogen bases of these nucleotides form hydrogen bonds with the existing nitrogen bases; for example, a free-floating nucleotide with a cytosine base will attach itself to a guanine base.

FIGURE 3.10
The Steps of DNA Replication

The **karyotype**, or complete set of chromosomes, includes all of the autosomes and one pair of **sex chromosomes**, so called because they determine an individual's biological sex (**Figure 3.12**). Females have two X chromosomes, and males have one X and one Y chromosome. The Y chromosome contains a small amount of genetic material, which determines only male characteristics. The interaction of gametes during fertilization determines the combination of chromosomes in the offspring. If an X-carrying sperm fertilizes an egg (which always carries an X),

FIGURE 3.11

Chromosome Pairs Homologous chromosomes are virtually identical in their physical and chemical structure. Each pair of chromosomes has the same genes, but the pair may have different alleles for specific genes.

(a)

karyotype The complete set of chromosomes for an individual organism or a species. The karyotype is typically presented as a photograph of an individual's chromosomes that have been arranged in homologous pairs and put in numerical order by size.

sex chromosomes The pair of chromosomes that determine an organism's biological sex.

(b)

FIGURE 3.12

Karyotype (a) Contained within each somatic cell, the human karyotype typically consists of 46 chromosomes of various sizes in 23 pairs. Of those 23, one pair determines the person's sex. Here, the label "X" means that these sex chromosomes are both Xs and thus belong to a human female. **(b)** In this karyotype, the pair labeled "XY" belongs to a human male.

the offspring will be female. If a Y-carrying sperm fertilizes an egg, the offspring will be male. Therefore, the male parent's gamete determines the sex of his offspring because the Y chromosome is present in males only; it is passed from father to son.

The Y chromosome can be highly informative about paternity over many generations. This **patriline**, or paternal lineage, is in part analogous to the matriline-based mtDNA, which is passed on only by females. However, mtDNA goes to all of a woman's children, whereas the Y chromosome is passed only to a man's sons.

patriline Lineage or inheritance that can be traced from father to son via the Y chromosome.

3.4 Mitosis: Production of Identical Somatic Cells

An organism starts life as a single cell, the zygote, which then produces identical copies of itself many, many times. A single human zygote, for example, eventually results in more than 10 trillion cells, each having the *exact* same DNA (**Figure 3.13**).

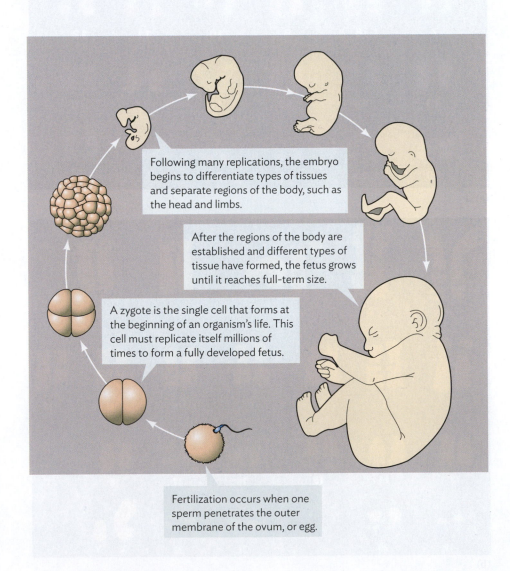

Following many replications, the embryo begins to differentiate types of tissues and separate regions of the body, such as the head and limbs.

After the regions of the body are established and different types of tissue have formed, the fetus grows until it reaches full-term size.

A zygote is the single cell that forms at the beginning of an organism's life. This cell must replicate itself millions of times to form a fully developed fetus.

Fertilization occurs when one sperm penetrates the outer membrane of the ovum, or egg.

FIGURE 3.13

Prenatal Development The stages of human development from fertilization of the ovum to a full-term infant.

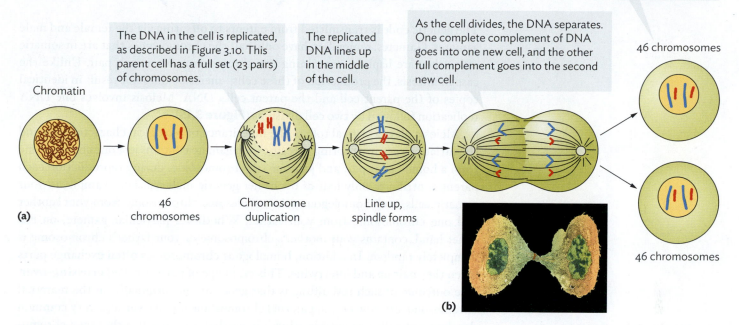

Each new cell has a full set of DNA, with 23 pairs of chromosomes.

The DNA in the cell is replicated, as described in Figure 3.10. This parent cell has a full set (23 pairs) of chromosomes.

The replicated DNA lines up in the middle of the cell.

As the cell divides, the DNA separates. One complete complement of DNA goes into one new cell, and the other full complement goes into the second new cell.

46 chromosomes

46 chromosomes

Chromatin

(a)

46 chromosomes

Chromosome duplication

Line up, spindle forms

46 chromosomes

(b)

FIGURE 3.14

Mitosis **(a)** The steps of mitosis in humans. **(b)** A human skin cell undergoing mitosis, dividing into two new daughter cells.

Here, the production of identical daughter cells from an original parental cell—mitosis—involves one DNA replication followed by *one* cell division (**Figure 3.14**). In this kind of cell division, a diploid cell—a cell having its organism's full set of chromosomes—divides to produce two cells, each of which also has the full set of chromosomes.

CONCEPT CHECK

The Two Steps of DNA Replication

The first function of DNA is to replicate itself. Templates from the original (parental) strand of DNA yield two exact (daughter) copies.

STEP		ACTIVITY
1.	Strand of DNA unzips to form templates.	Weak nucleotide bonds between bases break, exposing two parental strands of DNA.
2.	Templates plus nucleotides yield daughters.	Free-floating nucleotides match with the newly exposed template strands of DNA.

3.5 Meiosis: Production of Gametes (Sex Cells)

The genetic code is transmitted from parents to offspring via the female and male gametes. Gametes, remember, have only half the chromosomes that are in somatic cells—they are haploid, containing one chromosome from each pair. Unlike the case in mitosis, the production of these cells—meiosis—does not result in identical copies of the parent cell and the parent cell's DNA. Meiosis involves one DNA replication followed by two cell divisions (**Figure 3.15**).

Meiosis plays a critical role in the inheritance of biological characteristics and the variation seen in offspring. Because each gamete contains just one chromosome from a homologous pair and just one sex chromosome, during reproduction each parent contributes only half of his or her genetic material. For example, in your somatic cells, each homologous pair includes one chromosome from your mother and one chromosome from your father. Whether a particular gamete, on the other hand, contains your mother's chromosome or your father's chromosome is completely random. In addition, homologous chromosomes often exchange parts when they pair up and intertwine. This exchange of parts is called **crossing-over**. The outcome of such reshuffling is that gene variants originally on the maternal chromosome are now on the paternal chromosome (or vice versa), a very common development called **recombination**. Genes that are close together on a chromosome are much less likely to recombine. These units or blocks of genetic material are called **haplotypes**. Geneticists prefer to study haplotypes because they do not recombine and are passed on for many generations, potentially hundreds, over time.

Groups of related haplotypes, called **haplogroups**, are an important tool for studying both long-term evolution and populations' histories. For example, anthropologists have long speculated about the origins of Native Americans (where

recombination The exchange of genetic material between homologous chromosomes, resulting from a crossover event.

haplotypes A group of alleles that tend to be inherited as a unit because of their closely spaced loci on a single chromosome.

The parent cell is diploid, having 23 pairs of chromosomes.

Meiosis begins like mitosis. Initially, the cell's DNA is replicated.

Homologous pairs of chromosomes line up in the middle of the cell.

The pairs are separated and pulled to opposite sides as the cell divides.

46 chromosomes

Chromosome duplication

Homologous chromosome pairing

The cell divides, forming two daughter cells.

The chromosomes line up in the middle of the cell, but are not paired.

A second cell division follows, *without* DNA replication. The chromosomes are separated into single strands and are pulled to opposite sides as the cell divides.

Four haploid daughter cells result, each with 23 chromosomes, but *no pairs*.

FIGURE 3.15

Meiosis The steps of meiosis in humans. Compare this process to mitosis, shown in Figure 3.14.

F1
GgYy

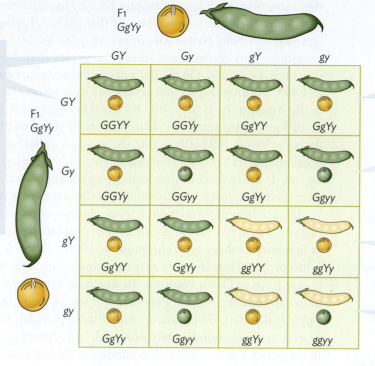

This Punnett square shows all possible combinations of two different genes, pod color and seed color:
G = green pod
g = yellow pod
Y = yellow seed
y = green seed

Because both parents have two different alleles for both traits, there are 16 possible combinations.

Of the 16 combinations, nine have green pods and yellow seeds. The genotypes vary and include: GGYY, GGYy, GgYY, GgYy.

Three of the resulting combinations have green pods and green seeds. They have one of two genotypes: GGyy or Ggyy.

Three of the resulting combinations have yellow pods and yellow seeds. There are two possible genotypes: ggYY or ggYy.

One of the resulting combinations has yellow pods and green seeds, with the genotype ggyy.

(a)

The small chromosomes have a gene that determines hair color: red represents brown hair, and blue represents blond hair.

The large chromosomes have a gene that determines eye color: red represents brown eyes, and blue represents blue eyes.

Alternatively, following the first cell division of meiosis, one cell has genes for brown eyes and blond hair, while the second has genes for blue eyes and brown hair.

Following the first cell division of meiosis, one cell has genes for brown eyes and brown hair, while the second cell has genes for blue eyes and blond hair.

The four daughter cells, or gametes, follow suit: two gametes have genes for brown eyes and brown hair, while the other two gametes have genes for blue eyes and blond hair.

Two equally probable chromosome arrangements in meiosis I:
— OR —

meiosis II:
— OR —

gametes:
— OR —

with genotypes:
— OR —

Again, the four daughter cells, or gametes, follow suit: two gametes have genes for brown eyes and blond hair, while the other two gametes have genes for blue eyes and brown hair.

(b)

FIGURE 3.16

Law of Independent Assortment Through his research with pea plants, Mendel formulated several laws pertaining to inheritance. **(a)** His second law, the law of independent assortment, asserts that traits linked to different chromosomes are inherited independently from one another. **(b)** Hair color, for example, is inherited independently from eye color.

they came from is a subject of chapter 12). Key to understanding their origins is their genetic diversity. Studies have revealed that the four haplogroups of mtDNA—A, B, C, and D—in living Native Americans are quite similar to the haplogroups of their ancestors. This resemblance strongly suggests that Native Americans' genetic structure is quite old. On the basis of current assumptions about mutation rates in mtDNA, anthropologists and geneticists have estimated that people first arrived in the Americas by 15,000 yBP (discussed in chapter 13). In addition, the presence of all four haplogroups and their variants in the skeletons of Native Americans dating to before 1492 tells us that the widespread decline of the Native American population after Columbus's arrival did not reduce their genetic, and therefore biological, diversity. Native Americans living today are likely as diverse genetically as were their ancestors living hundreds and thousands of years ago.

In rare instances, nonhomologous chromosomes exchange segments during meiosis. These rare exchanges are called **translocations**. The most common form in humans, involving both chromosome 13 and chromosome 14, affects about 1 in 1,300 people. Translocations may cause infertility, translocation Down syndrome (a rare form of Down syndrome in which an extra copy of chromosome 21 joins onto chromosome 14), and a number of diseases, including several forms of cancer (some leukemias). On occasion, chromosome pairs fail to separate during meiosis or mitosis. These **nondisjunctions** result in an incorrect number of chromosomes in the person's genome. A loss in number of chromosomes is a **monosomy**. A gain in number of chromosomes is a **trisomy**, the most common being trisomy 21, or Down syndrome (caused by an extra or part of an extra chromosome 21 associated with the homologous pair). As with many chromosomal abnormalities, the age of the mother determines the risk of the offspring's having Down syndrome. For 20- to 24-year-old mothers, the risk is 1 in 1,490. It rises to 1 in 106 by age 40, and 1 in 11 beyond age 49.

As Mendel recognized (see "Since Darwin: Mechanisms of Inheritance, the Evolutionary Synthesis, and the Discovery of DNA" in chapter 2), each physical unit (that is, each gene) passes from parent to offspring independently of other physical units. This independent inheritance—often called Mendel's **law of independent assortment** (**Figure 3.16**)—applies to genes from *different* chromosomes. However, what happens when genes are on the *same* chromosome? Because meiosis involves the separation of chromosome pairs (homologous chromosomes), genes on the same chromosome, especially ones near each other on that chromosome, have a greater chance of being inherited as a package. They are less subject to recombination. This gene linkage—the inheritance of a package of genes (such as haplotypes) from the same chromosome (**Figure 3.17**)—is an exception to Mendel's law of independent assortment.

3.6 Producing Proteins: The Other Function of DNA

In addition to replicating itself, DNA serves as the template for protein synthesis. Proteins are the complex chemicals that make up tissues and bring about the functions, repair, and growth of tissues (**Table 3.1**). Whereas some proteins work within cells—for example, the enzymes that unzip DNA during replication—others, such as hormones, work within the whole body. Proteins consist of **amino acids**, of which there are 20 (**Table 3.2**). Each kind of protein is defined by its

translocations Rearrangements of chromosomes due to the insertion of genetic material from one chromosome to another.

nondisjunctions Failures of chromosomes to properly segregate during meiosis, creating some gametes with abnormal numbers of chromosomes.

monosomy The condition in which only one of a specific pair of chromosomes is present in a cell's nucleus.

trisomy The condition in which an additional chromosome exists with the homologous pair.

law of independent assortment Mendel's second law, which asserts that the inheritance of one trait does not affect the inheritance of other traits.

amino acids Organic molecules combined in a specific sequence by ribosomes to form a protein.

FIGURE 3.17

Linkage Because alleles *A*, *B*, and *C* are on the same chromosome, they have a better chance of being inherited as a unit than of being combined and inherited with alleles *a*, *b*, and *c*, which are together on a separate chromosome and thus also have a good chance of being inherited as a unit. Meanwhile, because they are close together, alleles *A* and *B* (like alleles *a* and *b*) stand a better chance of being inherited together than do alleles *B* and *C* (like alleles *b* and *c*). If, for example, eye color and hair color were on the same chromosome, especially if they were close together on that chromosome, they would most likely *not* be inherited separately with all the combinations examined in Figure 3.16.

TABLE 3.1 The Seven Types of Proteins

NAME	FUNCTION	EXAMPLES
Enzymes	Catalyze chemical reactions	Lactase—breaks down lactose in milk products
Structural Proteins	Give structure or support to tissues	Keratin—found in hair; collagen—found in bone
Gas Transport Proteins	Carry vital gases to tissues	Hemoglobin—carries oxygen
Antibodies	Part of immune system	Anti-A and anti-B in ABO blood system
Hormones	Regulate metabolism	Insulin—regulates metabolism of carbohydrates and fats
Mechanical Proteins	Carry out specific functions or work	Actin and myosin—help muscles contract
Nutrients	Provide vital nutrients to tissues	Ovalbumin—main protein of egg whites

particular combination and number of linked amino acids. Most of the human body is composed of proteins, and the body produces 12 of the amino acids. The other eight, called **essential amino acids**, come from particular foods that we eat.

Two main categories of proteins are constantly being synthesized. **Structural proteins** are responsible for physical characteristics, such as hair form (for example, straight or wavy), eye color, tooth size, and basic bone shape (**Figure 3.18**). The other category, **regulatory proteins** (also called *functional proteins*), includes enzymes, hormones, and antibodies. Enzymes regulate activities within cells, hormones regulate activities between cells, and antibodies are key to fighting infections.

essential amino acids Those amino acids that cannot be synthesized in the body and, thus, must be supplied by the diet.

structural proteins Proteins that form an organism's physical attributes.

regulatory proteins Proteins involved in the expression of control genes.

(a)

(b)

FIGURE 3.18

Structural Proteins While culture and environment strongly influence the development of biological structures, those structures are initially determined by structural proteins. Two important structural proteins are keratin and collagen. **(a)** In humans, keratin is the primary component of hair (pictured here), skin, and fingernails. In other mammals and in amphibians, birds, and reptiles, it also contributes to structures such as hooves, antlers, claws, beaks, scales, and shells. **(b)** Collagen is the most abundant protein in humans and other mammals and is essential for connective tissues, such as bone (pictured here), cartilage, ligaments, and tendons. In addition, collagen strengthens the walls of blood vessels and, along with keratin, gives strength and elasticity to skin. In its crystalline form, collagen is found in the cornea and lens of the eye.

TABLE 3.2 The 20 Amino Acids and the DNA Triplet Codes Serving as Templates for Steps of Protein Synthesis

AMINO ACID	DNA TRIPLET CODE	FUNCTION	SOURCES
Alanine	CGA, CGG, CGT, CGC	Used in the production of glucose	Meat, poultry, dairy products
Arginine	GCA, GCG, GCT, GCC, TCT, TCC	Induces growth hormone release from pituitary gland	Chocolate, flour, dairy products
Asparagine	TTA, TTG	Used by central nervous system to maintain equilibrium	Plant proteins (e.g., asparagus), dairy products, poultry
Aspartic acid	CTA, CTG	Promotes mineral uptake in intestinal tract	Sugarcane, dairy products, beef
Cysteine	ACA, ACG	Promotes iron absorption	Meat, garlic, dairy products
Glutamic acid	CTT, CTC	Works as a neurotransmitter	Meat, poultry, fish, dairy products
Glutamine	GTT, GTG	Works as a carrier of urinary ammonia	Red meat, fish, beans
Glycine	CCA, CCG, CCT, CCC	Works as a neurotransmitter	Fish, meat, beans
Histidine	GTA, GTG	Detoxifies chemicals in the liver	Bananas, grapes, meat, dairy products
Isoleucine*	TAA, TAG, TAT	Helps to rebuild muscle tissue	Eggs, poultry, cereal grains, dairy products
Leucine*	AAT, AAC, GAA, GAG, GAT, GAC	Involved in energy release from muscles during work	Whole grains, dairy products
Lysine*	TTT, TTC	Stimulates secretion of gastric juices in digestion	Cereal grains, fish
Methionine*	TAC	Prevents fat deposits in liver	Fruits, vegetables, nuts
Phenylalanine*	AAA, AAG	Increases blood pressure in hypotension (low blood pressure)	Dairy products, legumes
Proline	GGA, GGG, GGT, GGC	Helps in repair of muscle and tendons	Meat
Serine	AGA, AGG, AGT, AGC, TCA, TCG	Takes part in metabolism	Meat, dairy products
Threonine*	TGA, TGG, TGT, TGC	Takes part in metabolism	Poultry, fish, beans
Tryptophan*	ACC	Aids in blood clotting	Oats, dairy products, red meat, poultry
Tyrosine	ATA, ATG	Aids in formation of thyroid hormones	Soy products, poultry
Valine*	CAA, CAG, CAT, CAC	Aids in building of muscles	Fish, poultry, beans

*Essential amino acid.

transcription The first step of protein synthesis, involving the creation of messenger RNA (mRNA) based on the DNA template.

translation The second step of protein synthesis, involving the transfer of amino acids by transfer RNA (tRNA) to the ribosomes, which are then added to the protein chain.

ribonucleic acid (RNA) A single-stranded molecule involved in protein synthesis, consisting of a phosphate, ribose sugar, and one of four nitrogen bases.

uracil One of four nitrogen bases that make up RNA; it pairs with adenine.

Protein synthesis is a two-step process (**Figure 3.19**). The first step, **transcription**, takes place mostly in the cell's nucleus. The second, **translation**, takes place in the cytoplasm. Transcription starts out just like the first step of DNA replication: a double strand of parental DNA unzips. Rather than producing daughter strands of DNA, the now-exposed bases in the DNA molecule serve as a single template for another kind of nucleic acid, **ribonucleic acid (RNA)**. RNA has the same nitrogen bases as DNA, except that **uracil** (U) replaces thymine (T). Uracil always matches with adenine (A), while guanine (G) continues to pair with cytosine (C).

Only one of the two DNA strands serves as the template for the production of RNA. This strand attracts free-floating RNA nucleotides. The strand of RNA—now called **messenger RNA (mRNA)**—then splits off from the DNA template, leaves the nucleus, and moves into the cytoplasm.

In the translation step, the mRNA attaches itself to structures called **ribosomes**. The mRNA is a "messenger" because (in the form of its own open bases) it carries the code for the protein being synthesized from the nucleus to the ribosomes. Ribosomes are made up of another kind of ribonucleic acid, **ribosomal RNA (rRNA)**. Once the mRNA is attached to the ribosome, the transcription step of protein synthesis is complete.

Floating in the cytoplasm is yet another kind of ribonucleic acid known as **transfer RNA (tRNA)**. tRNA occurs as triplets, or **anticodons**, that seek complementary triplet strands of mRNA, known as **triplets**, or **codons**. For example, a triplet of AUC mRNA would pair with the complementary UAG tRNA. The sets of three bases forming the DNA triplets that serve as templates for protein synthesis are shown in Table 3.2.

As the tRNA strand builds off the mRNA template, the amino acids are chemically linked together by a **peptide bond**, resulting in a chain of amino acids. A chain of these peptide bonds is called a **polypeptide**. Although a single polypeptide may function as a protein, in many cases multiple polypeptides must bind together and fold into a three-dimensional structure to form a functional protein. For example, hemoglobin, a molecule found on the surface of red blood cells, is composed of two pairs of polypeptide chains. Once the protein has formed, it breaks away from the tRNA and commences with its task, either structural or functional.

All of the DNA involved in protein synthesis is **coding DNA**, the molecular segments encoded for particular proteins. The total length of DNA in humans is about 3 billion nucleotides. Each of the 20,000 or so genes in humans has about 5,000 nucleotides, so (according to the math) only about 3% of the DNA contains protein-coding material. Thus, most human DNA is **noncoding DNA**. Often

messenger RNA (mRNA) The molecules that are responsible for making a chemical copy of a gene needed for a specific protein—that is, for the transcription phase of protein synthesis.

ribosomes The organelles attached to the surface of the endoplasmic reticulum, located in the cytoplasm of a cell; they are the site of protein synthesis.

ribosomal RNA (rRNA) A fundamental structural component of a ribosome.

transfer RNA (tRNA) The molecules that are responsible for transporting amino acids to the ribosomes during protein synthesis.

anticodons Sequences of three nitrogen bases carried by tRNA, they match up with the complementary mRNA codons, and each designates a specific amino acid during protein synthesis.

triplets Sequences of three nitrogen bases in DNA, known as codons in mRNA.

codons Sequences of three nitrogen bases carried by mRNA that are coded to produce specific amino acids in protein synthesis.

peptide bond A chemical bond that joins amino acids into a protein chain.

polypeptide Also known as a protein, a chain of amino acids held together by multiple peptide bonds.

coding DNA Sequences of a gene's DNA (also known as exons) that are coded to produce a specific protein and are transcribed and translated during protein synthesis.

noncoding DNA Sequences of a gene's DNA (also known as introns) that are not coded to produce specific proteins and are excised before protein synthesis.

CONCEPT CHECK

The Two Steps of Protein Synthesis

The second function of DNA is to synthesize proteins, which are responsible for all the structures and functions of the body.

STEP		ACTIVITY
1.	Transcription (nucleus)	The parental strand of DNA unzips, exposing two daughter strands of DNA.
		Free-floating RNA nucleotides match one exposed daughter strand of DNA.
		The strand of messenger RNA (mRNA) moves out of the nucleus and into the cytoplasm.
2.	Translation (cytoplasm)	The mRNA attaches to a ribosome in the cytoplasm.
		Triplets of transfer RNA (tRNA), with exposed bases and each carrying an amino acid specific to its set of three bases, recognize and bind with complementary base pairs of mRNA.
		The amino acids, linked by peptide bonds, form a chain called a polypeptide.
		The protein forms, either as a single polypeptide or as multiple polypeptides bound together.

As in DNA replication, transcription begins with enzymes "unzipping" the DNA. Unlike replication, however, transcription uses only one strand of DNA.

DNA template

mRNA strand

(b)

Once the DNA strands have opened, messenger RNA (mRNA) attaches free-floating RNA nitrogen bases to the exposed, unpaired DNA nitrogen bases.

Completed mRNA strand

Transcription, which occurs in the nucleus, involves the creation of mRNA from one strand of DNA.

After the mRNA strand is completed, it leaves the nucleus and goes to the ribosomes, in the cytoplasm.

Once completed, the DNA closes back up, and the mRNA strand leaves the nucleus and goes to one of the ribosomes in the cytoplasm.

(a)

DNA

Transcription

mRNA

Translation

Nucleus

Ribosome

Cytoplasm

Protein

Moves out of nucleus to ribosomes in cytoplasm

Translation takes place at the ribosomes. A protein is formed as the mRNA is "read" and the appropriate amino acids are linked together.

FIGURE 3.19

Protein Synthesis **(a)** As this overview of protein synthesis shows, transcription occurs mostly within the cell's nucleus, and translation follows at the ribosomes. **(b)** Here, the steps of protein synthesis are diagrammed for a hypothetical protein. **(c)** At the top is a computer model of a transfer RNA (tRNA) molecule, and below that is a diagram of the molecule.

Translation begins as the mRNA binds to a ribosome. In effect, the "message" carried by the mRNA is "translated" by a ribosome.

Ribosome

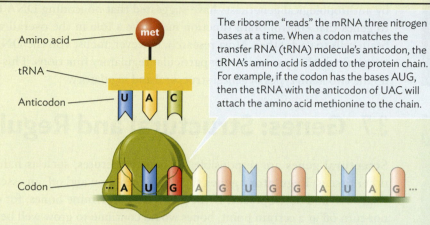

Amino acid

tRNA

Anticodon

The ribosome "reads" the mRNA three nitrogen bases at a time. When a codon matches the transfer RNA (tRNA) molecule's anticodon, the tRNA's amino acid is added to the protein chain. For example, if the codon has the bases AUG, then the tRNA with the anticodon of UAC will attach the amino acid methionine to the chain.

Codon

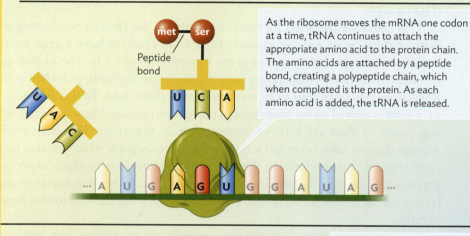

Peptide bond

As the ribosome moves the mRNA one codon at a time, tRNA continues to attach the appropriate amino acid to the protein chain. The amino acids are attached by a peptide bond, creating a polypeptide chain, which when completed is the protein. As each amino acid is added, the tRNA is released.

Protein: polypeptide chain

Eventually, a "stop" codon is reached, which indicates that the protein is completed. The mRNA leaves the ribosome, and the protein is released.

(c)

Amino acid

Anticodon

Amino acid — Serine

tRNA

Anticodon — UCG

mRNA — AGC

Codon

At a ribosome, a molecule of tRNA brings the anticodon for each codon on the mRNA. The tRNA carries its anticodon on one end and the associated amino acid on the other.

(a)

(b)

FIGURE 3.20

Marfan Syndrome **(a)** The hand on the right shows normal finger growth. The hand on the left has much longer and thinner fingers due to Marfan syndrome, a hereditary disorder of the regulatory genes that control connective tissue. As a result of Marfan syndrome, uncontrolled bone growth leads to long and thin fingers and toes, long and thin arms and legs, and increased stature. Organs such as the lungs and heart can also be negatively affected. **(b)** In the 1960s, a scientific paper asserted that US president Abraham Lincoln (1809–1865) was afflicted with Marfan syndrome. This still-controversial assessment was based entirely on Lincoln's unusual tallness and the length of his limbs.

interspersed with coding DNA from one end of the chromosome to the other, this noncoding DNA was long thought to have no function and was referred to as "junk DNA." However, non-protein-coding DNA is now known to perform a considerable number of regulatory functions throughout the genome; specifically, it plays a role in the regulation of gene activities by helping to turn these activities on or off. New work on the genome suggests that 80% of the noncoding DNA is functional in some manner, containing instructions for proteins controlling which genes a cell uses and determining whether and when a cell becomes a bone cell or a brain cell. In protein synthesis, the noncoding DNA is cut out before translation. Recent studies by anthropological geneticists have suggested that noncoding DNA located close to genes that control brain function may have a role in the overall wiring of the brain cells to each other. Most research, however, focuses on the DNA that codes for particular body structures or particular regulatory functions. This DNA makes up the two main types of genes: structural and regulatory.

3.7 Genes: Structural and Regulatory

Structural genes are responsible for body structures, such as hair, blood, and other tissues. **Regulatory genes** turn other genes on and off, an essential activity in growth and development. If the genes that determine bones, for example, did not turn off at a certain point, bones would continue to grow well beyond normal (**Figure 3.20**).

Chickens have the genes for tooth development, but they do not develop teeth because those genes are permanently turned off. Humans have a gene for total body hair coverage, but that gene is not turned on completely. The human genes for sexual maturity turn on during puberty, somewhat earlier in girls than in boys. Regulatory genes can lead to lactose intolerance in humans. In this instance, the *LCT* gene is turned off for most human populations around the world after weaning, usually by about age 4. However, most humans of northern European and East African descent have inherited a different regulatory gene, which creates lactase persistence. A person who lacks the *LCT* gene and eats dairy products experiences great gastrointestinal discomfort. A person who retains the gene is able to digest lactose owing to the persistence of lactase, thus enjoying the nutritional benefits of milk.

An organism's form and the arrangement of its tissues and organs are determined by regulatory genes called **homeotic (*Hox*) genes**. These master genes guide, for example, the embryological development of all the regions of an animal's body, such as the head, trunk, and limbs (**Figure 3.21**). This means that in the process of development, particular sets of *Hox* genes are turned on in a particular sequence, causing the correct structure or part of a structure to develop in each region. Until recently, scientists thought that the genes that control the development of the key structures and functions of the body differed from organism to organism. We now know, however, that the development of various body parts in complex organisms—such as the limbs, eyes, and vital organs—is governed by the *same* genes. *Hox* genes were first found in fruit flies, but research has shown that a common ancestral lineage has given organisms—ranging from flies to mice to humans—the same basic DNA structure in the key areas that control the development of form. Flies look like flies, mice look like mice, and humans look like humans because the *Hox* genes are turned on and off at different places and different times during the development process.

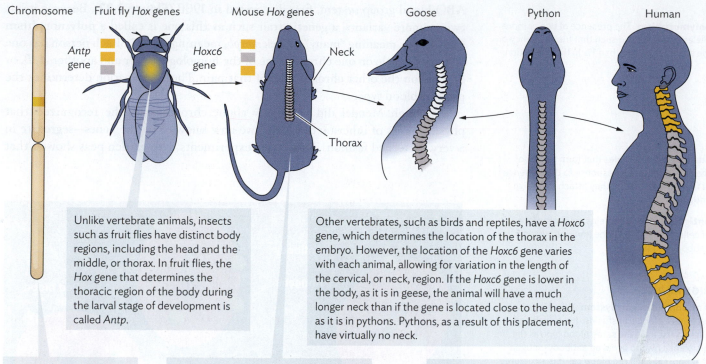

Chromosome   Fruit fly *Hox* genes   Mouse *Hox* genes   Goose   Python   Human

Antp gene

Hoxc6 gene

Neck

Thorax

Unlike vertebrate animals, insects such as fruit flies have distinct body regions, including the head and the middle, or thorax. In fruit flies, the *Hox* gene that determines the thoracic region of the body during the larval stage of development is called *Antp*.

Other vertebrates, such as birds and reptiles, have a *Hoxc6* gene, which determines the location of the thorax in the embryo. However, the location of the *Hoxc6* gene varies with each animal, allowing for variation in the length of the cervical, or neck, region. If the *Hoxc6* gene is lower in the body, as it is in geese, the animal will have a much longer neck than if the gene is located close to the head, as it is in pythons. Pythons, as a result of this placement, have virtually no neck.

Hox genes have been identified in all animals, plants, and fungi. They are found as a unique cluster known as the *Hox* cluster or *Hox* complex.

While the body regions of vertebrates, such as mice, are not as distinct as those of flies and other insects, *Hox* genes determine their body regions during embryological development. The *Hoxc6* gene in mice delimits the thoracic region, which is indicated by the thoracic vertebrae.

Humans, being vertebrates, also have a *Hoxc6* gene, which determines the location of the thoracic region. Humans have a neck of intermediate length when compared to geese and pythons; the *Hoxc6* gene is closer to the head in humans than in geese, but is lower than in pythons. The *Hoxc6* gene is responsible not just for determining the location of the thorax; in humans, this gene determines the development of the entire thoracic region, including mammary glands.

FIGURE 3.21

Homeotic (*Hox*) Genes Discovered in 1983 by Swiss and American researchers, these regulatory genes are coded to produce proteins that turn on many other genes, in particular those that determine the regions of the body during prenatal development. Without these genes, or if there are mutations in these genes, body development may be altered. For example, a mutation in the *Hox* genes of a fruit fly can cause a leg instead of an antenna to grow from the head. In the figure, the gray shading indicates the thorax location for the four vertebrates, which is controlled by the *Hoxc6* gene.

3.8 Polymorphisms: Variations in Specific Genes

Along each chromosome, a specific gene has a specific physical location, or **locus** (plural, *loci*). This locus is of intense interest to geneticists, especially in understanding the appearance and evolution of genetic variation (among the topics of chapter 4). Alleles, the genetic subunits (see "Mechanisms of Inheritance" in chapter 2), are slightly different chemical structures at the same loci on homologous chromosomes. That is, they are simply chemically alternative versions of the same gene. Some genes have only one allele, while others have 20 or more.

Human blood type is one genetic trait with different alleles. Each person has one of four blood types—A, B, AB, or O—and these four types compose the

locus The location on a chromosome of a specific gene.

polymorphism The presence of two or more alleles at a locus and such that the frequency of the alleles is greater than 1% in the population.

antibodies Molecules that form as part of the primary immune response to the presence of foreign substances; they attach to foreign antigens.

antigens Specific proteins, on the surfaces of cells, that stimulate the immune system's antibody production.

FIGURE 3.22

Antibody–Antigen System When a person receives a blood transfusion, the transfused blood must have the same blood type as the recipient's own to avoid an antibody–antigen reaction. **(a)** Each red blood cell has structures on its surface, known as **antigens,** that identify the cell as being type A, B, AB, or O. If the wrong type of blood is given to a person, the body's immune system recognizes the new antigens as foreign. Special proteins called **antibodies** are then produced in the blood in response to the "invaders." **(b)** The antibodies attach themselves to the foreign antigens, causing agglutination, or clumping, of the blood cells. Because the coagulated blood cannot pass through blood vessels properly, the recipient's tissues do not receive the blood they need. If not treated, the person might die.

For all the blood types in the ABO blood group system, **Table 3.3** shows the antigens, antibodies, and acceptable and unacceptable blood types in transfusions. For example, type A blood, which can result from *AO* alleles or *AA* alleles, has A antigens on its surface and anti-B antibodies, which will react with B or AB blood. (Genotypes and phenotypes are defined and discussed later in this section.)

ABO blood group system, first discovered in 1900 (**Figure 3.22**). Because it has two or more variants, a genetic trait such as this one is called a **polymorphism** (Greek *poly*, meaning "many"; Greek *morph*, meaning "form"). Each person has one *A*, *B*, or *O* allele on one chromosome of the homologous pair and another *A*, *B*, or *O* allele on the other chromosome of that pair. The combination determines the person's blood type.

Although Mendel did not know about chromosomes, he recognized that physical units of inheritance—which we now know to be the genes—segregate in a very patterned fashion. That is, his experiments with garden peas showed that

(a)

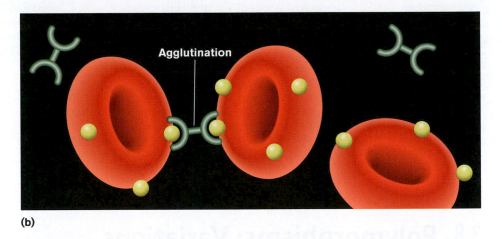

(b)

TABLE 3.3 The ABO Blood Group System

PHENOTYPES	GENOTYPES	ANTIGENS	ANTIBODIES	UNACCEPTABLE BLOOD TYPES	ACCEPTABLE BLOOD TYPES
A	*AO, AA*	A	Anti-B	B, AB	A, O
B	*BO, BB*	B	Anti-A	A, AB	B, O
AB	*AB*	A, B	None	None (universal recipient)	A, B, AB, O
O	*OO*	None (universal donor)	Anti-A, anti-B	A, B, AB	O

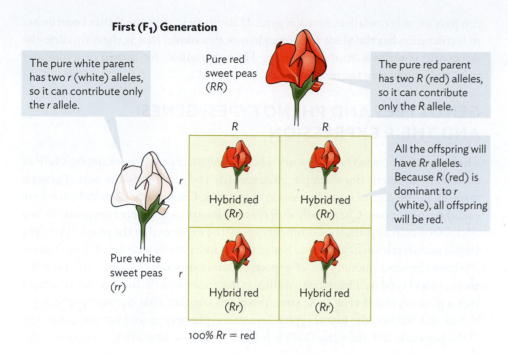

First (F₁) Generation

The pure white parent has two *r* (white) alleles, so it can contribute only the *r* allele.

Pure red sweet peas (*RR*)

The pure red parent has two *R* (red) alleles, so it can contribute only the *R* allele.

Pure white sweet peas (*rr*)

	R	*R*
r	Hybrid red (*Rr*)	Hybrid red (*Rr*)
r	Hybrid red (*Rr*)	Hybrid red (*Rr*)

All the offspring will have *Rr* alleles. Because *R* (red) is dominant to *r* (white), all offspring will be red.

100% *Rr* = red

Second (F₂) Generation

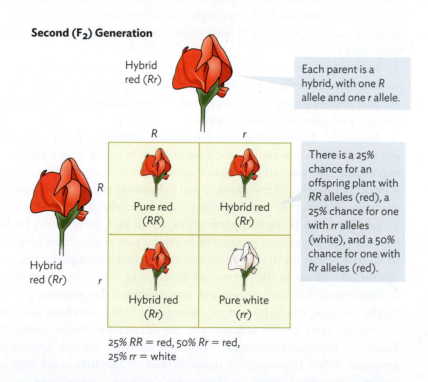

Hybrid red (*Rr*)

Each parent is a hybrid, with one *R* allele and one *r* allele.

Hybrid red (*Rr*)

	R	*r*
R	Pure red (*RR*)	Hybrid red (*Rr*)
r	Hybrid red (*Rr*)	Pure white (*rr*)

There is a 25% chance for an offspring plant with *RR* alleles (red), a 25% chance for one with *rr* alleles (white), and a 50% chance for one with *Rr* alleles (red).

25% *RR* = red, 50% *Rr* = red, 25% *rr* = white

FIGURE 3.23

Law of Segregation Mendel's first law, the law of segregation, declares that the mother and father contribute equally to an offspring's genetic makeup. For each gene, a person has two alleles (which can be the same or different). One allele is from the person's mother, and one is from the person's father.

the father contributes one physical unit and the mother contributes the other. This is Mendel's **law of segregation** (**Figure 3.23**). For example, a person with blood type AB will pass on either an *A* or a *B* allele to a child but not both. The other allele will come from the other parent. This discovery was revolutionary because it explained how new variation arises in reproduction.

Remember that meiosis (see Figure 3.15) creates four gametes, each of which has only one set of chromosomes and no pairs. Each gamete, having this one set,

law of segregation Mendel's first law, which asserts that the two alleles for any given gene (or trait) are inherited, one from each parent; during gamete production, only one of the two alleles will be present in each ovum or sperm.

can pass on only one allele for each gene. If the gamete that the father contributes to fertilization has the allele for brown hair, for example, that is the only allele the father will contribute to the offspring. The other allele, for brown or a different color, will come from the mother.

GENOTYPES AND PHENOTYPES: GENES AND THEIR EXPRESSION

The two alleles, whether they are chemically identical (for example, *AA*) or chemically different (for example, *AO*), identify the genotype—the actual genetic material in the pair of homologous chromosomes. Chemically identical alleles are called **homozygous**. Chemically different alleles are called **heterozygous**. When alleles are heterozygous, the dominant one will be expressed in the phenotype—the visible manifestation of the gene. For example, individuals who are *AA* or who are *AO* have the same phenotype—*A* expresses dominance over *O*, and both individuals are blood type A. The recessive allele is not expressed. When you know simply that a person's blood type is A, you cannot tell whether that person's genotype is *AA* or *AO*. Rather, the blood type refers to the phenotype and not the genotype. If the person is *AO*, then the *O* allele is hidden because that allele is recessive. For the recessive allele to be expressed, each of the homologous chromosomes must have the recessive allele. For example, the alleles for type O blood are *OO*. For a person to have type O blood, both alleles in the pair of homologous chromosomes have to be *O*.

Sometimes alleles exhibit **codominance**, where neither chemically different version dominates the other. In the ABO blood group system, the *A* and *B* alleles are codominant and both are expressed. If someone has type AB blood, you know that person's phenotype and genotype.

Biological anthropologists, geneticists, and the many other disciplines interested in understanding the relationship between genes and their physical expression have learned that gene expression is considerably more complex than previously thought. Many physical and behavioral traits are **polygenic**, meaning that they are affected by multiple loci. Moreover, new discoveries in gene mapping reveal that some polygenic phenotypes are in fact determined by hundreds or thousands of interacting genes. For example, new research on height shows that thousands of loci on the chromosome, representing multiple genes, account for a significant amount of the phenotype variation of this trait. Given the complexity of these many loci and association signals across the genome, phenotypes like height are best characterized as **omnigenic** traits, meaning they are affected by various parts of the genome and the interconnections among those parts. Similarly, neurodevelopmental disorders, such as autism spectrum disorder, attention deficit hyperactivity disorder, and schizophrenia are highly heritable, but in a complex fashion involving combinations, interactions, and sharing of dozens of genes.

On the other hand, **pleiotropy** may be operating in phenotype expression, whereby a single gene can have multiple effects. One classic example of a pleiotropic effect is Marfan syndrome (see Figure 3.20). This condition is a dominant collagen disorder caused by a single gene on chromosome 15. Collagen is a major protein, representing 25%–35% of all protein in the body. Because collagen is found in so many types of body tissues—for example, skeletal, visual, and cardiovascular—this single gene's effects are pervasive throughout the body. In fact, most complex traits are both polygenic and pleiotropic (**Figure 3.24**).

homozygous The condition in which the two alleles of a pair of alleles at a single locus on homologous chromosomes are the same.

heterozygous The condition in which the two alleles of a pair of alleles at a single locus on homologous chromosomes are different.

codominance The condition in which two different alleles are equally dominant; both alleles are fully expressed in a heterozygote's phenotype.

polygenic Refers to one phenotypic trait that is affected by two or more genes.

omnigenic Refers to complex traits that involve various parts of the genome and the interconnections among those parts.

pleiotropy The phenomenon of a single gene having multiple effects.

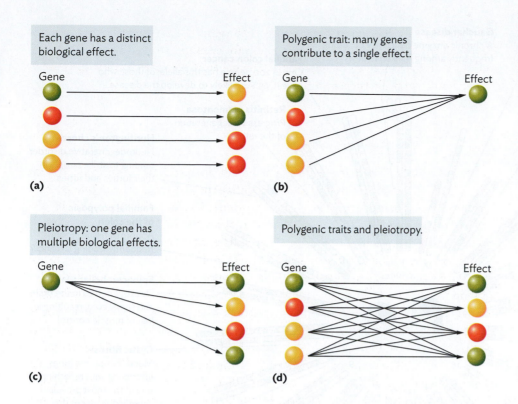

Each gene has a distinct biological effect.

Gene → Effect

(a)

Polygenic trait: many genes contribute to a single effect.

Gene → Effect

(b)

Pleiotropy: one gene has multiple biological effects.

Gene → Effect

(c)

Polygenic traits and pleiotropy.

Gene → Effect

(d)

FIGURE 3.24

Polygenic Traits and Pleiotropic Genes
(a) Mendel's simple rules of inheritance **(b)** do not apply when one trait is affected by many genes (a polygenic trait). Eye color, for example, is determined by at least three genes. Because this trait is polygenic, some children's eye colors are very different from those of their parents. **(c)** Pleiotropic genes affect more than one physical trait. The *PKU* allele, for example, affects mental abilities and the coloration of hair and skin. A person who inherits this allele will have the disease phenylketonuria, in which a missing enzyme leads to intellectual disability as well as reduced hair and skin pigmentation. **(d)** One trait can be affected by several genes, and each of those genes can affect several other traits as well.

3.9 The Human Genome: A Critical Window onto Human Variation

After the discovery of how the genetic code works (see chapter 2), the general impression about genes was that they simply represented specific locations of DNA coded to produce specific proteins. Much of the field of genetics, including anthropological genetics, was based on this "one gene–one protein" model. However, as we saw in the previous discussion, the story of our genes is not simple. In many ways, the mapping of the human genome, an ongoing process, provides new and deeper insights into the genetic structure and specific chromosomal locations of a large number of genes, and in turn provides insights into the phenotypes that those genes program. Even some of the most complex phenotypes of all—such as human height and cancers—are beginning to be mapped to specific multiple locations on multiple chromosomes. The maps of human genetic variation reveal, of course, that there is a common human genome, but each of us possesses singular details in our individual DNA structure that give us our unique personal genome.

When we look at the genome at the *individual* level—the basis of the science of **personal genomics**—we see how impossible it is to place individuals in biological categories, or so-called races (see chapter 5), and just how remarkably unique each of us is. There are clear geographic tendencies, but these tendencies reflect ancestral population distribution (for example, northeastern Europe, West Africa, East Asia, and so forth) and gene flow. Yes, we share considerable DNA with our parents, but in a wholly new fashion and with new twists and turns that make each of us different. Interest in personal genomics has grown in recent years, especially in part through commercial ancestry-tracing programs. With this burgeoning interest— and concerns about the way ancestry data are being calculated and interpreted—it

WATCH THE VIDEO
GENOMICS AND HUMAN EVOLUTION
digital.wwnorton.com/essanthro5

personal genomics The branch of genomics focused on sequencing individual genomes.

ALD (adrenoleukodystrophy)
Nerve disease portrayed in the movie *Lorenzo's Oil*

Gaucher disease
A chronic enzyme deficiency occurring frequently among Ashkenazi Jews

Familial colon cancer
One in 200 people has this allele; of those who have it, 65% are likely to develop the disease

Neurofibromatosis, type 2
Tumors of the auditory nerve and tissues surrounding the brain

Retinitis pigmentosa
Progressive degeneration of the retina

Huntington's chorea
Neurodegenerative disorder tending to strike people in their forties and fifties

Amyotrophic lateral sclerosis (Lou Gehrig's disease)
Fatal degenerative nerve ailment

ADA immune deficiency (ADA + adenosine deaminase)
Severe susceptibility to infections; first hereditary condition treated by gene therapy

Familial polyposis of the colon
Abnormal tissue growths frequently leading to cancer

Familial hypercholesterolemia
Extremely high cholesterol

Spinocerebellar ataxia
Destroys nerves in the brain and spinal cord, resulting in loss of muscle control

Amyloidosis
Accumulation in the tissues of an insoluble fibrillar protein

Cystic fibrosis
Mucus fills up the lungs, interfering with breathing; one of the most prevalent genetic diseases in the United States

Breast cancer
Roughly 5% of cases are caused by this allele

Multiple exostoses
A disorder of cartilage and bone

Polycystic kidney disease
Cysts resulting in enlarged kidneys and renal failure

Malignant melanoma
Tumors originating in the skin

Multiple endocrine neoplasia, type 2
Tumors in endocrine glands and other tissues

Tay–Sachs disease
Fatal hereditary disorder involving lipid metabolism; most common in Ashkenazi Jews and French Canadians

Alzheimer's disease
Degenerative nerve disease marked by premature senility

Sickle-cell anemia
Chronic inherited anemia, primarily affecting blacks, in which red blood cells sickle, or form crescents, plugging small blood vessels

Retinoblastoma
A relatively common eye tumor, accounting for 2% of childhood malignancies

PKU (phenylketonuria)
An inborn error of metabolism that results in intellectual disability if untreated

FIGURE 3.25

Disease and the Genome Researchers have identified the locations of hundreds of genes that control or influence a variety of diseases and disorders. For example, Cystic fibrosis is located on chromosome 7 of the human genome. The identification of gene location facilitates early detection and treatment for many illnesses.

is important to understand what genomics is, what it can and cannot say about our individual origins, and how anthropologists conduct research in this area.

Personal genomics has also become widely adopted in medicine, where it is referred to as *personalized medicine* because knowledge of one's genome, and the genetic markers it provides, may enable medical practitioners to identify potential risks for some diseases, such as sickle-cell anemia, cystic fibrosis, and some cancers (**Figure 3.25**). Comprehensive chromosomal screening helps physicians to identify potential life-threatening abnormalities *in utero*, even during early pregnancy.

However, this does not mean everyone should rush out to obtain their genome maps, expecting to discover all matters biological about themselves as individuals. Though the individualized genome map may reveal risks for specific genetic-based diseases, it will not, in many instances, predict that a person *will* have a specific disease. Moreover, especially with respect to identification of geographic ancestry and potential risk for disease, one's ancestry reflects many, many generations, and the remarkable degree of gene flow occurring over time across those many generations. An individual genome reflects both a person's immediate ancestry (that is, the contribution of the parents) and the tens, scores, hundreds, and thousands of ancestors who contributed to that person's genome. So, while this biological history is enriched by our growing understanding of our individual genomes at a number of levels, our individual genome maps cannot tell us with certainty if we have a certain percentage of ancestry from a particular geographical setting or if we will or will not develop a specific disease. Personal genomics can tell us some amazing things, but awareness of its limitations is important.

Some of the most exciting genomic research has revealed a whole new array of gene markers. Showing a tremendous amount of variation within and between human populations, SNPs (see "The DNA Molecule: The Code for Life" earlier) are known for well over 1 million marker sites on the human genome. Closer examination of the human genome has also revealed that DNA segments are often repeated, sometimes many times and for no apparent reason. These repeated sections, or **microsatellites**, are highly individualized, forming a unique DNA signature for each person. Microsatellites have quickly become the most important tool for individual identification, and they have proved especially valuable in forensic science, bioarchaeology, and other contexts. For example, they have been used to identify victims of the 9/11 attacks as well as genocides and mass murders in the Balkans, Iraq, Mexico, and Argentina; they are also valuable in studies of ancient human remains from archaeological contexts.

Individual genomes are now available for many thousands of persons around the globe, and some of the uniqueness of these genomes is due in part to their microsatellites. But in circumstances where small populations have been relatively isolated, individuals can recombine microsatellites through sexual reproduction. Over time, continued population isolation results in the presence of common microsatellite characteristics that may no longer be unique to an individual. Using microsatellite analysis, it is possible to identify patterns of genetic variation within and between traditional ethnic groups. For instance, in the United States, study of genomic variation of traditional ethnic groups (for example, African descent, European descent, East Asian descent) by geneticist Hua Tang and his research team revealed clear clusters of associated microsatellite markers corresponding to ethnicity. However, these clusters do not reveal biological categories but rather represent patterns of microsatellite variation resulting from social histories and migration patterns. That is, the same processes that produce geographic-associated variation also produce the observed microsatellite clusters. And while this kind of microsatellite study is important in understanding genomic variation, the medical community can also use microsatellite variation to identify specific genetic markers that indicate potential disease risk in individuals. Still in its preliminary stages, personal genomics may lead to a better understanding of individual genetic markers that are linked with specific diseases and their associated health risks, and not with so-called races (chapter 5 includes a discussion of race).

Adding to the complexity of the genome is the role of environment in influencing the **phenome**. That is, we are seeing the importance of environment as an influence

microsatellites Also called *short tandem repeats* (STRs); sequences of repeated base pairs of DNA, usually no more than two to six. If repeated excessively, they are often associated with neurologic disorders, such as Huntington's chorea.

phenome The total set of phenotypic traits in an organism.

in genomic programming. In humans, thousands of complex phenotypes—such as birth weight, height, skin color, head form, tooth size, and eye shape—have multiple genetic components and are influenced by environmental factors. Many other complex phenotypes—such as autism spectrum disorder and other behavioral and cognitive disorders—probably have environmental influences. Scientists have long understood that environment plays an important role in the physical manifestations of various aspects of one's genome. For example, environmental factors affecting the mother can also affect the developing fetus. If the fetus is female, then those offspring resulting from her developing ova may also be affected. In this way, environmental factors operating at a given point in time can affect the health and well-being of not just the immediate offspring but also subsequent generations. Such **epigenetic** effects represent potentially heritable changes in behavior or biology but without altering the DNA sequence. In other words, the sequence of base pairs remains fully intact, but the changes owing to environmental circumstances modify the way that DNA is regulated and expressed, without modifying the DNA itself.

A new and exciting area of research is showing that epigenetic mechanisms within cells may be activated by a variety of behavioral and environmental factors. In this regard, regulation of DNA in the offspring may be altered because of epigenetic phenomena, resulting in birth defects and other negative outcomes. These outcomes are due to **methylation**, a process in which a methyl group, a chemical, attaches to the DNA (**Figure 3.26**). In this process, methylation

epigenetic Refers to chemical changes in the genome affecting how the underlying DNA is used in the production of proteins, but without altering the DNA sequences.

methylation The attachment of a methyl group, a simple chemical, to DNA at certain sites throughout the genome.

CHROMOSOME

DNA methylation
Methyl group (an epigenetic factor found in some dietary sources) can tag DNA and activate or repress genes.

DNA

FIGURE 3.26
DNA Methylation

represses or fully stops gene expression, which may result in profoundly negative outcomes for offspring. Methylation can be activated by various factors such as exposure to temperature extremes or environmental chemicals, disease, poor nutrition, and a variety of behaviors such as smoking, excessive alcohol consumption, and inactivity.

The interaction between the environment and the genes of the mother and her offspring, from conception to birth, has considerable impact on the normal growth of the fetus as well as risk for disease after birth. Indeed, obesity and some birth defects, common diseases, and cancers appear to be influenced by epigenetic factors. For example, key nutrients—including vitamins A, B_3, C, and D—play roles in regulating DNA. An insufficiency of these nutrients is linked to diabetes, atherosclerosis, and cancer. By investigating the epigenetics of health and behavior, scientists have opened up a pathway toward understanding factors that influence parent and offspring health. In short, researchers have shown how environment interacts with the genome across generations. These discoveries have begun to revolutionize our understanding of the effects of environment on the genome, underscoring the role of environmental circumstances—both positive and negative—in health.

The emerging record of epigenetics is revealing that gene expression can be influenced in profound ways by social circumstances. For example, the American anthropological geneticist Connie Mulligan has found a probable link between stress and gene expression in mothers and their offspring in the Democratic Republic of the Congo, where communities have been subjected to warfare and violence for many years. In these settings, there is clear evidence of an association between war-related stress and genetic changes in infants, such as in the *NR3C1* gene, the gene located on chromosome 5 that codes for a protein associated with newborn birth weight. Similarly, exposure of the fetus to maternal stress associated with intimate partner violence and other violence-related stressors has been identified with changes in the *NR3C1* gene. These findings support the notion that various factors relating to exposure of the mother to violence may be an important methylation factor across generations.

The DNA revolution has made it possible to understand in much greater detail the underlying principles of inheritance and to explain variation over time—laid out so eloquently by Gregor Mendel more than a century and a half ago and built upon by thousands of scientists since then. In presenting the great breadth of knowledge about how genetic variation is transmitted from parents to offspring and the growing understanding of the human genome, this chapter has laid the groundwork for the topic of the next chapter, the study of genetic change in populations. Mendel could not have foreseen the amazing record of genetics and genomics that has been made possible by the greatly expanding genomic picture of life on Earth, past and present. But he would have quickly grasped the science being done and the commitment on the part of generations of scientists that have added to our growing understanding of life, past and present.

ANSWERING THE BIG QUESTIONS

1. What is the genetic code?

- The genetic code is DNA, packaged in chromosomes.
- Nuclear DNA provides most of the genetic code.

2. What does the genetic code (DNA) do?

- DNA serves as the chemical template for its own replication and for the creation of proteins.
- DNA replication is the first step in producing new cells.
  - Mitosis produces two identical somatic cells. In humans, each has 46 chromosomes in 23 homologous pairs.
  - Meiosis produces four gametes. In humans, each has 23 chromosomes.
- Proteins are combinations of amino acids. They compose the entire body and determine all of its functions, from conception through maturity.
  - The two categories of proteins are governed by two corresponding gene types: structural and regulatory.

3. What is the genetic basis for human variation?

- A gene is a linear sequence of nucleotides that codes for specific bodily structures and functions. Each gene has a particular locus on each chromosome.
- Each pair of homologous (like) chromosomes consists of a paternal chromosome and a maternal chromosome.

- An individual's genotype, or actual genetic composition, is based on two alleles, one from the father and one from the mother. Alleles can be chemically identical or chemically different. The genotype is expressed physically as a phenotype.
- Most phenotypes are determined by more than one gene (polygenic), sometimes involving networks and interactions of hundreds or thousands of genes (omnigenic).
- Some individual genes have multiple effects (pleiotropy).
- Genomics provides the complete set of genetic material, giving insight into health, ancestry, and evolution.
- Epigenetics, the study of environmental effects on gene function, is yielding revolutionary insights into how biological and cultural circumstances affect inheritance.

STUDY QUIZ

1. Which is *true* about gametes (sex cells)?

a. Gametes are diploid.
b. Gametes are produced through mitosis.
c. Gametes pass the genetic code from parent to offspring.
d. Gametes are found in every tissue of the body.

KEY TERMS

adenine
adenosine triphosphate (ATP)
amino acids
antibodies
anticodons
antigens
autosomes
coding DNA
codominance
codons
complementary bases
crossing-over
cytosine
cytoplasm
diploid cell
epigenetic
essential amino acids
eukaryotes
gametes
genome
guanine
haplogroups
haploid cell
haplotypes
heteroplasmic
heterozygous
homeotic (*Hox*) genes
homologous
homoplasmic
homozygous
karyotype
law of independent assortment
law of segregation
locus
matriline
meiosis
messenger RNA (mRNA)
methylation
microsatellites
mitochondria
mitosis
monosomy
noncoding DNA
nondisjunctions
nucleotide
nucleus
omnigenic
patriline
peptide bond
personal genomics
phenome
pleiotropy
polygenic
polymorphism
polypeptide
prokaryotes
recombination
regulatory genes
regulatory proteins
replication
ribonucleic acid (RNA)
ribosomal RNA (rRNA)
ribosomes
sex chromosomes
single nucleotide polymorphisms (SNPs)
somatic cells
structural genes
structural proteins
thymine
transcription
transfer RNA (tRNA)
translation
translocations
triplets
trisomy
uracil
zygote

STUDY QUIZ (CONTINUED)

2. What process is necessary for both mitosis and meiosis to occur?

a. DNA replication

b. Recombination

c. Crossing-over

d. Translocation

3. Which is *not* a role played by a type of RNA in protein synthesis?

a. mRNA (messenger RNA) transcribes the DNA template.

b. rRNA (ribosomal RNA) makes up ribosomes, which translate the genetic code into protein.

c. tRNA (transfer RNA) pairs RNA bases with amino acids.

d. pRNA (protein RNA) is the product of chemically linked amino acids.

4. For a Mendelian trait that is *not* codominant, an individual with a heterozygous genotype will express

a. the dominant phenotype.

b. the recessive phenotype.

c. a blend of the dominant phenotype and the recessive phenotype.

d. no phenotype for that trait.

5. Human height is affected by many genes, so it is a _____ trait.

a. pleiotropic

b. codominant

c. epigenetic

d. omnigenic

EVOLUTION REVIEW

Insights from Genetics and Genomics

SYNOPSIS DNA is often described as a genetic blueprint because it encodes the plan for an organism's traits and ensures that these traits are passed on to future generations. One of the major functions of the DNA molecule is replication: creating identical copies of itself. The reliability of this process influences evolution by making variation heritable; that is, traits will be passed on to offspring, who will be similar to their parents. A second major function of DNA is directing protein synthesis, which is how genotype (genetic code) is translated to phenotype (physical expression of this code). Protein synthesis is the basis for the traits that allow organisms to interact with their environment and undergo natural selection. Molecular genetics can be complex. Many traits are polygenic (influenced by more than one gene), and many genes are pleiotropic (operating on more than one trait). The record also shows that some phenotypes—for example, body height—involve the interaction of networks of thousands of genes. Furthermore, epigenetic (environmental, nongenetic) phenomena can alter DNA regulation and phenotype without altering the DNA sequence itself. Thus, genetics both complicates and illuminates our understanding of human variation and evolution.

Q1. What are the two types of cell division? How does each type affect individual genetic variation?

Q2. What is recombination? How does the effect of recombination differ from that of mutation?

Q3. Given our growing knowledge of humans from a genetic perspective, why is it still important for biological anthropologists to study physical remains (for example, bones and teeth) when testing hypotheses about evolution and variation among ourselves and our closest living and fossil relatives?

   HINT Think about the types of remains available for living and fossil organisms and about how genetics is related to physical characteristics.

Q4. Consider various human characteristics, such as height, weight, skin color, head form, and eye shape. Are the phenotypic expressions of these characteristics discontinuous (able to be assigned to discrete categories) or continuous (on a continuum rather than separable into discrete categories)? What might they tell us about the mechanisms behind human variation?

Q5. Why is the knowledge of the human genome so important to our understanding of human biological variation, past and present?

ADDITIONAL READINGS

Carey, N. 2012. *The Epigenetics Revolution: How Modern Biology Is Rewriting Our Understanding of Genetics, Disease, and Inheritance.* New York: Columbia University Press.

Harris, E. E. 2014. *Ancestors in Our Genome: The New Science of Human Evolution.* Oxford, UK: Oxford University Press.

Mukherjee, S. 2017. *The Gene: An Intimate History.* New York: Scribner.

Relethford, J. H. and D. A. Bolnick. 2018. *Reflections of Our Past: How Human History Is Revealed in Our Genes,* 2nd ed. New York, NY: Routledge.

Skoglund, P. and I. Mathieson. 2018. Ancient genomics of modern humans: The first decade. *Annual Review of Genomics and Human Genetics* 19: 381–404.

The key driver of evolution is natural selection. Members of species having genetic variation that enhances survival to reproductive age will tend to live to reproductive age. In the leafy sea dragon, for example, there is selection for genes controlling for pigmentation and other attributes of body phenotype. These phenotypes make it difficult for predators to see this animal. This "visual" selection is commonplace worldwide now, as it must have been in the past.

4

Genes and Their Evolution

POPULATION GENETICS

BIG QUESTIONS

1. What causes evolutionary (genetic) change?
2. How is evolutionary (genetic) change measured, and how is the cause determined?

One of the great stories about genetics comes not from a research program of a famous scientist in charge of a large laboratory filled with technicians, graduate students, and post-doctoral fellows and funded by a multimillion-dollar grant, but rather from a student with a simple hypothesis and a passionate interest in testing a hypothesis. At Oxford University in the late 1940s, a 20-something Anthony Allison (1925–2014) was finishing his coursework in basic sciences and was about to start his clinical medical training. Allison had grown up in Kenya; his interest in anthropology reflected his intellectual curiosity, but his desire to become a doctor was motivated by an ambition to help improve native Kenyans' quality of life. While at Oxford, he was exposed to the ideas of the English scientists R. A. Fisher and J. B. S. Haldane and the American scientist Sewall Wright, pioneers of the new field of population genetics and advocates of the novel idea that gene frequencies were tied to natural selection.

After a bout of malaria, Allison decided to help Kenyans (and other peoples) by seeking a cure for this disease. In 1949, he joined an expedition to document blood groups and genetic traits in native Kenyans. On this expedition, Allison discovered that in areas affected by malaria, especially along Kenya's coast (southeast) and near Lake Victoria (southwest), a remarkably high 20%–30% of the population carried the gene for sickle-cell anemia. But in the highlands (west), where there was no malaria, less than 1% of the people carried the gene. In what he described as a "flash of inspiration," he hypothesized that individuals with the sickle-cell allele were resistant to malaria and that natural selection was operating on the gene. *But how?* he wondered.

Before pursuing these ideas, Allison completed his medical education. In 1953, with just enough money to buy passage back to Kenya and for food and simple lodging, he spent a year researching the relationship between malaria and sickle-cell anemia. He generated lab and field data, looking at malaria infection rates in people with and without the sickle-cell allele. His results showed that carriers of the gene are much more likely to survive malaria than are noncarriers. Natural selection was favoring the carriers.

The next year, Allison published three landmark scientific articles in rapid succession, laying out the proof for his hypothesis. Gene frequencies *are* tied to natural selection: carriers of the sickle-cell allele survive longer and produce more offspring than do noncarriers. In Allison's words, "disease is an agent of natural selection." Although his ideas met with strong skepticism, eventually Allison's hypothesis was accepted by most scientists. His research enabled generations of geneticists and anthropologists to further investigate genes and their evolution, all of these researchers asking why some gene frequencies remain the same while others change over time.

Human populations exhibit some remarkable biological differences, and the science of genetics helps biologists answer questions about those differences. The questions and the answers are founded on Darwin's discovery that phenotypes—the physical manifestations of genes—change over time. In addition, Mendel's research on garden peas revealed how the inheritance of genes produces variation in phenotypes. These two revolutionary scientific discoveries inform our understanding of biological variation and its evolution.

Before considering this chapter's big questions, we need to look at populations and species, the units that evolutionary biologists work with.

4.1 Demes, Reproductive Isolation, and Species

To show how genetic variation is produced, the previous chapter focused on the individual and the transmission of genes from parents to offspring. When biological anthropologists and geneticists study the genetics of individuals, they focus on the reproductive population, or **deme**: members of a species that produce offspring. That is, evolution is about groups of organisms that have the potential to reproduce. When biological anthropologists talk about populations, they often refer to the **gene pool**, which is all the genetic material within a population. When geneticists talk about the gene pool, they are even more specific, referring to all the variation within a specific genetic locus. For example, some people carry the sickle-cell allele and some do not.

deme A local population of organisms that have similar genes, interbreed, and produce offspring.

gene pool All the genetic information in a breeding population.

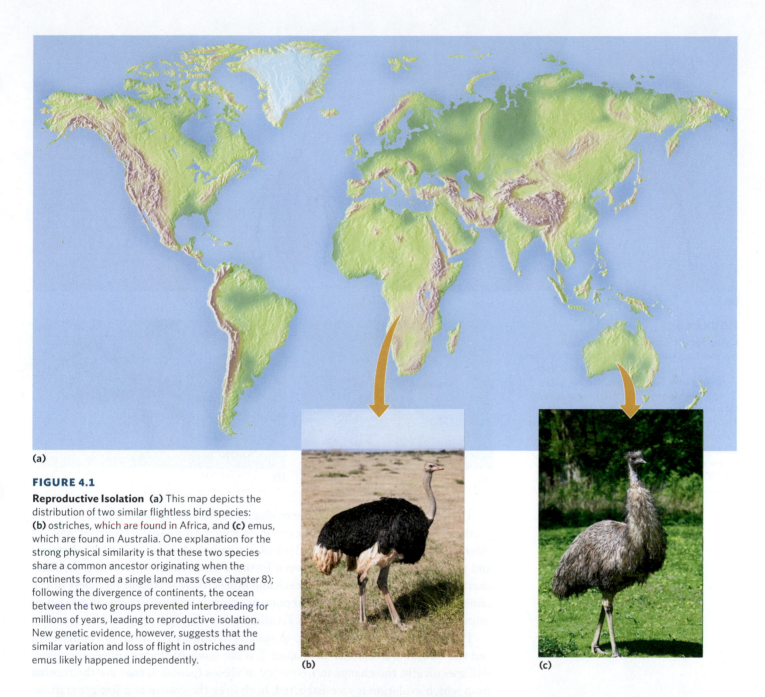

(a)

FIGURE 4.1

Reproductive Isolation **(a)** This map depicts the distribution of two similar flightless bird species: **(b)** ostriches, which are found in Africa, and **(c)** emus, which are found in Australia. One explanation for the strong physical similarity is that these two species share a common ancestor originating when the continents formed a single land mass (see chapter 8); following the divergence of continents, the ocean between the two groups prevented interbreeding for millions of years, leading to reproductive isolation. New genetic evidence, however, suggests that the similar variation and loss of flight in ostriches and emus likely happened independently.

(b)

(c)

The concept of the breeding population is also central to the definition of *species*. A species is composed of all the populations (and their individual members) that are capable of breeding with each other and producing viable (fertile) offspring. Species, therefore, are defined on the basis of **reproductive isolation** (**Figure 4.1**). In biological terms, if two populations are reproductively isolated, members of one population cannot interbreed with members of the other. Reproductive isolation is largely related to geographic isolation. If two populations of the same species become isolated, such as by a mountain range or a large body of water, then enough genetic differences could accumulate for two entirely different species to emerge. On the other hand, the similarity of two species, such as the ostriches in Africa and the emus in Australia, may not be due to sharing a common ancestor. The genetic evidence suggests that their similarity is due to convergent evolution, whereby the two birds evolved similar body forms and flightlessness independently.

reproductive isolation Any circumstance that prevents two populations from interbreeding and exchanging genetic material, such as when two populations are separated by a large body of water or a major mountain range.

(a)

(b)

(c)

(d)

FIGURE 4.2

Living Fossils Fossilized remains might represent animals and plants that lived thousands or millions of years ago, but a number of such organisms have counterparts that live today. Compare the forms of the following organisms: **(a)** a living horseshoe crab and **(b)** a fossil *Mesolimulus walchii*, the ancestor to the modern horseshoe crab; **(c)** a living cockroach and **(d)** a fossil cockroach; and **(e)** a living assassin bug (of the family Reduviidae) and **(f)** a 50-million-year-old fossil assassin bug (Reduviidae).

(e)

(f)

microevolution Small-scale evolution, such as changes in allele frequency, that occurs from one generation to the next.

macroevolution Large-scale evolution, such as a speciation event, that occurs after hundreds or thousands of generations.

equilibrium A condition in which a system is stable, balanced, and unchanging.

In the living world, we can observe members of a species to verify that they can produce offspring. Obviously, we cannot do this with fossils. Rather, we have to infer reproductive isolation in fossil populations on the basis of geographic distance and the physical resemblance between fossils. Fossil remains that share the same characteristics in morphology of teeth and bones likely represent members of the same species (**Figure 4.2**). (This important concept will inform the discussion of primate evolution in chapters 9–13. Fossils are the subject of chapter 8.)

Population genetics (see "The Evolutionary Synthesis, the Study of Populations, and the Causes of Evolution" in chapter 2) is the study of changes in genetic material; specifically, the change in frequency of alleles (genes). Genes are the records from which evolution is reconstructed, both over the course of a few generations (**microevolution**) and over many generations (**macroevolution**; **Figure 4.3**). Geneticists strive to *document* genetic change and to explain *why* it occurred. Such documentation and explanation are the central issues of evolutionary biology. Population geneticists, biological anthropologists, and other evolutionary biologists tend to focus on genetic change over time. For example, if a trait in a population has two alleles, *A* and *a,* and the parent generation is 60% *A* and 40% *a* and the next generation is 65% *A* and 35% *a,* scientists would want to know why the evolution occurred—why the frequency of the *A* allele increased in the population.

Just as interesting, however, are instances in which frequency does not change over time; that is, when the frequencies of a population's alleles for a particular trait are in a state of **equilibrium**. For example, in areas of West Africa where malaria is common, the frequency of the sickle-cell allele remains relatively constant. What factors—forces of evolution—account for deviations from equilibrium?

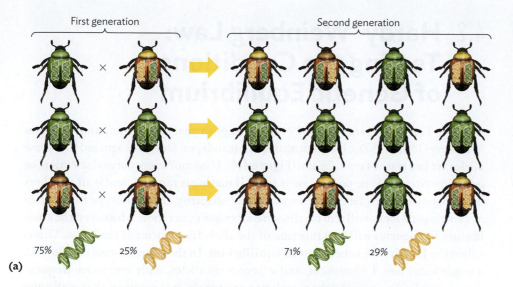

First generation   Second generation

75%   25%   71%   29%

(a)

FIGURE 4.3

Microevolution and Macroevolution
(a) Microevolution is change in gene frequency over a few generations. For example, the beetles in this diagram have either of two colors, represented by two alleles. In the first generation, 75% of the color alleles are green and 25% are brown. In the second generation, 71% of the color alleles are green and 29% are brown. Thus, the frequencies of the green and brown alleles have undergone a microevolutionary change. **(b)** Macroevolution is substantial change over many generations—the creation of new species. For example, over 60 million years, the eohippus—a small, dog-sized animal with multitoed feet that inhabited rainforests—evolved into the modern horse. Among the species' large-scale changes were increases in overall body size and height, as well as the loss of toes. Horses' single-toed hooves enable them to run more efficiently in the open grasslands they naturally inhabit.

Equus
3 mya
height
1.6 m
(5.25 ft)

Pliohippus
10 mya
height
1.0 m
(3.28 ft)

Merychippus
20 mya
height
1.0 m
(3.28 ft)

Mesohippus
40 mya
height
0.6 m
(1.97 ft)

Eohippus
50 mya
height
0.4 m
(1.31 ft)

(b)

FIGURE 4.4

Godfrey Hardy Hardy and Wilhelm Weinberg independently discovered the equilibrium that bears their names and is still used in population genetics. This equilibrium, worked out in a simple Punnett square, is used to assess whether gene frequencies have changed from one generation to the next. It can also be used to estimate the genotype frequencies of the subsequent generation.

Hardy–Weinberg law of equilibrium
A mathematical model in population genetics that reflects the relationship between frequencies of alleles and of genotypes; it can be used to determine whether a population is undergoing evolutionary changes.

4.2 Hardy–Weinberg Law: Testing the Conditions of Genetic Equilibrium

In 1908, Godfrey Hardy (1877–1947), an English mathematician, and Wilhelm Weinberg (1862–1937), a German obstetrician, independently recognized that some alleles are in a state of equilibrium (**Figure 4.4**). If no mutation, natural selection, or gene flow occurs; if the population is large; if mating is random; and if all members of the population produce the same number of offspring, then genotype frequencies at a single gene locus will remain the same after one generation. Moreover, the equilibrium frequencies will be a function of the allele frequencies at the locus. This is called the **Hardy–Weinberg law of equilibrium**. In the simplest case (**Table 4.1**), a single locus has A (dominant) and a (recessive) alleles, with respective frequencies of p and q. In assessing the population as a whole, it is assumed that males and females have both alleles. The Hardy–Weinberg law predicts the genotype frequencies for the next generation after one mating, where p^2 is the genotype frequency for the AA homozygous alleles, $2pq$ is the genotype frequency for the Aa (heterozygous) alleles, and q^2 is the genotype frequency for the aa homozygous alleles. In other words, the total population (100%) should be the sum of the frequencies of three genotypes, expressed by the simple mathematical equation $p^2 + 2pq + q^2 = 1$. If a hypothetical population were 60% A ($p = .6$) and 40% a ($q = .4$), then the genotype frequencies in the next generation would work out to $AA = .36$, $Aa = .48$, and $aa = .16$. The frequencies can be expressed as decimals or percentages, but they are expressed most often as decimals. Because the three genotypes are the only genotypes for the gene in question in the population, the frequencies must add up to 1, or 100%. So, if the frequency of AA is .36 (or 36%), the frequency of Aa is .48 (or 48%), and the frequency of aa is .16 (or 16%), together they add up to 1 (or 100%).

In the absence of evolution, the frequencies of the genotypes will in theory remain the same forever. In this way, the Hardy–Weinberg law of equilibrium hypothesizes that when gene frequencies remain the same, it is because no evolutionary change takes place (**Figure 4.5**).

By determining the genotype frequencies for a population at different points in time, however, the Hardy–Weinberg equation establishes expectations as to whether evolution is operating on a particular gene. If the genotype frequencies change from one generation to the next, the population is not in equilibrium—it is evolving. If the frequencies remain the same, the population is in equilibrium—the population is not evolving, at least with respect to the locus being studied.

What might cause a population to change its allele frequencies and go out of equilibrium? As discussed in chapters 2 and 3, genes are passed from generation to generation by interbreeding within populations in particular and among members of the same species in general, and genetic changes result from one or a combination

TABLE 4.1 **Punnett Square for Hardy–Weinberg Equilibrium**

		FEMALES	
		A (p)	a (q)
MALES	A (p)	AA (p^2)	Aa (pq)
	a (q)	Aa (pq)	aa (q^2)

FIGURE 4.5

Gene Frequencies in Equilibrium As this Punnett square illustrates, the Hardy–Weinberg equilibrium captures gene frequencies in a static moment, when no evolutionary change is taking place. Crossing the males (sperm pool) and females (egg pool) of the population produces theoretical genotype frequencies of the next generation.

Once evolutionary change takes place, the actual genotype frequencies will differ significantly from the theoretical genotype frequencies expressed in this Punnett square. For example, if the population later turns out to be 5% *AA*, 65% *aa*, and 30% *Aa*, an evolutionary force has most likely altered its genotype frequencies.

Approximately 36% of the offspring will have the genotype *AA*. The estimate is made by multiplying the male *p* (frequency of *A* allele = .6) with the female *p* (.6). Thus, $p \times p = p^2$, and $.6 \times .6 = .36$. The frequency of the *AA* genotype is represented by p^2.

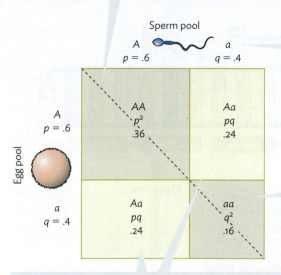

Sperm pool

The allele frequencies for males and females in this population are the same: *p* (frequency of *A* allele) is .6 and *q* (frequency of *a* allele) is .4.

Approximately 16% of the offspring will have the genotype *aa*. This estimate is made by multiplying the male *q* (frequency of *a* allele = .4) with the female *q* (.4). Thus, $q \times q = q^2$, and $.4 \times .4 = .16$. The frequency of the *aa* genotype is represented by q^2.

Approximately 48% of the offspring will have the genotype *Aa*. This estimate is made by multiplying the male *p* (.6) with the female *q* (.4) and the male *q* (.4) with the female *p* (.6). Thus, $p \times q = pq$ and $q \times p = qp$; $.6 \times .4 = .24$ and $.4 \times .6 = .24$. Because both $p \times q$ and $q \times p$ must be included, the two results are added together. $2pq = 2 \times .24$ (or $.24 + .24$) $= .48$. The frequency of the *Aa* genotype is represented by *2pq*.

of the four forces of evolution: natural selection, mutation, gene flow, and genetic drift (see "The Evolutionary Synthesis, the Study of Populations, and the Causes of Evolution" in chapter 2).

4.3 Mutation: The Only Source of New Alleles

During cell reproduction, DNA almost always replicates itself exactly. Sometimes, however, the replication process produces an error or a collection of errors in the DNA code. If the problem is not at once detected and corrected by a set of enzymes that monitor DNA, a mutation results. The mutation can be any heritable change in the structure or amount of genetic material.

Some of any person's DNA is noncoding (see "Producing Proteins: The Other Function of DNA" in chapter 3) and nonfunctional in many respects. Although the effects of mutations in noncoding DNA are not as obvious as those in coding DNA, mutations associated with noncoding DNA can still affect an individual's health. For example, some cancers can be caused by mutations in noncoding DNA.

A new sequence in *coding* DNA that results from mutation may have profound consequences, positive or negative. For instance, the mutation might code the DNA for a protein with an altered or different function from that performed by the protein coded for in the original parent strand of DNA, or the mutation might create a sequence that results in either no protein or an abnormal protein (**Figure 4.6**).

FIGURE 4.6

DNA Mutations During the transcription phase of protein synthesis, errors in the DNA template can affect the resulting protein. Two types of DNA mutation are illustrated in these diagrams: **(a)** base substitution and **(b)** base insertion.

(a) Base substitution

A *base substitution*, the simplest kind of mutation, occurs when a single nitrogen base is substituted by another base. Here, thymine is being replaced by cytosine.

As a result of the base substitution, the mRNA strand receives complementary guanine rather than the adenine that pairs with thymine. This further substitution changes the amino acid that is added to the polypeptide chain at the ribosomes. Instead of isoleucine, valine is inserted (see Table 3.2 in chapter 3). This amino acid change may or may not affect the resulting protein.

(b) Base insertion

A *base insertion* occurs when a nitrogen base is added to the DNA template. Here, adenine is inserted.

The mRNA receives the appropriate complementary nitrogen base, uracil. When the mRNA reaches the ribosomes, the series of codons is changed because of the insertion. Instead of reading the correct AUU, the ribosomes read UAU, which codes for the amino acid tyrosine instead of isoleucine. Again, this amino acid change may or may not affect the resulting protein.

Mutations occur at random and can occur in any cell, but the ones with consequences for future generations take place in gametes. Gametes may transfer mutations to offspring, depending on what happens during meiosis in the parents. Regardless of their causes or outcomes, in the absence of gene flow (see "Gene Flow: Spread of Genes across Population Boundaries" later in this chapter) *mutations are the only source of new genetic variation in a population*.

Mutations involving incorrect base pairing are called **point mutations**. A **synonymous point mutation** creates an altered triplet in the DNA, but the alteration carries with it the original amino acid. Because the amino acid is the same, the protein formed is the same. A **nonsynonymous point mutation** results in a matchup that brings along a different amino acid. Such a mutation can have dramatic results for the individual carrying it. For example, a mutation on human chromosome 11 results in a GUG codon instead of a GAG codon. The GUG codon is encoded to produce the amino acid valine, whereas the GAG codon would have normally led to the production of glutamic acid. This substitution leads to the abnormal hemoglobin that results in sickle-cell anemia (discussed later in this chapter).

As a result of the shifting base pairs caused by base insertion, the reading frame of a gene is altered or stopped entirely. This **frameshift mutation** produces a protein having no function. Such a mutation usually involves a small part of the DNA sequence, often just a base pair or a relatively limited number of base pairs.

Other kinds of mutations can affect far more of the genome. **Transposable elements** are genes that can copy themselves to entirely different places along the DNA sequence. If such a gene inserts itself into another gene, it can fundamentally alter the other gene, doing real damage. If, as is likely, the gene transposes itself to a noncoding area of the DNA sequence, little or no significant alteration will occur.

Large parts of DNA sequences or entire chromosomes can be affected by mutations. An entire piece of chromosome can be moved to another chromosome, can be placed differently on the same chromosome, or can be positioned backward in a chromosome. The effects of these mutations are highly variable and depend on the loci of the mutations.

In the most extreme mutations, entire chromosomes can be duplicated (a trisomy) or lost altogether (a monosomy). Examples of trisomies are Down syndrome, with its extra chromosome 21 (see "Meiosis: Production of Gametes [Sex Cells]" in chapter 3) and **Klinefelter's syndrome**, a common sex chromosome variant that appears in about 1 of 500–1,000 births (**Figure 4.7**).

point mutations Replacements of a single nitrogen base with another base, which may or may not affect the amino acid for which the triplet codes.

synonymous point mutation A neutral point mutation in which the substituted nitrogen base creates a triplet coded to produce the same amino acid as that of the original triplet.

nonsynonymous point mutation A point mutation that creates a triplet coded to produce a different amino acid from that of the original triplet.

frameshift mutation A change in a gene due to the insertion or deletion of one or more nitrogen bases, which causes the subsequent triplets to be rearranged and the codons to be read incorrectly during translation.

transposable elements Mobile pieces of DNA that can copy themselves into entirely new areas of chromosomes.

Klinefelter's syndrome A chromosomal trisomy in which males have an extra X chromosome, resulting in an XXY condition; affected individuals typically have reduced fertility.

FIGURE 4.7

Klinefelter's Syndrome This karyotype belongs to a male human with Klinefelter's syndrome, a disorder that results from chromosome duplication. Only men receive the additional X chromosome that makes for a total of 47 chromosomes rather than the normal 46. This extra chromosome usually leads to sterility and can produce a range of physical effects, from a youthful, lanky appearance to a rounded, generally feminized body with gynecomastia (additional breast tissue).

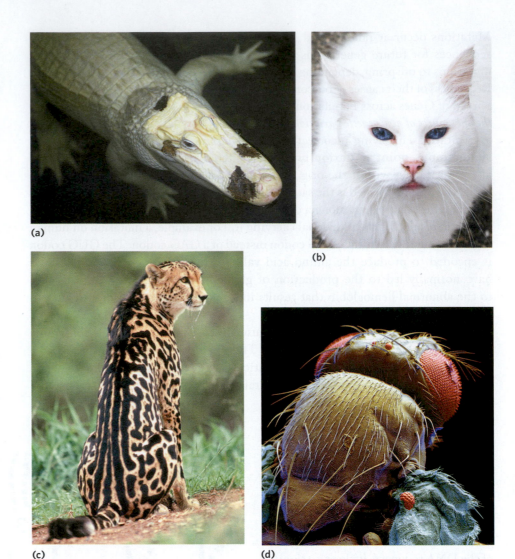

(a)

(b)

(c)

(d)

FIGURE 4.8

Spontaneous Mutations Spontaneous mutations can affect only physical appearance or can have health consequences, sometimes extreme ones. **(a)** A mutation called *leucism* has made this American alligator white. On its head are some spots of the normal, dark color of alligators. **(b)** The mutation that gives some cats white fur and blue eyes can also produce deafness and timidity. **(c)** Cheetahs normally have spotted coats, but a genetic mutation has produced stripes on this cheetah's back. **(d)** Mutations can affect the wing count, eye color, and eye placement in fruit flies. A mutation has given this fruit fly abnormally placed, or ectopic, eyes, one of which is visible here as the red area on the wing.

spontaneous mutations Random changes in DNA that occur during cell division.

induced mutations Mutations in DNA resulting from exposure to toxic chemicals or to radiation.

mutagens Substances, such as toxins, chemicals, or radiation, that may induce genetic mutations.

All mutations fall into one of two types: **spontaneous mutations**, which have no known cause (**Figure 4.8**); and **induced mutations**, which are caused by specific environmental agents, usually associated with human activity. These agents, or **mutagens**, are increasingly becoming known. For example, ionizing radiation (X-rays) and various toxic chemicals have been linked to mutations in animals and humans. Most mutations are spontaneous, however, and are simply DNA copying errors. The human mutation rate is higher in male sex cells (sperm) than in female sex cells (eggs) but is generally on the order of one per million per nucleotide per generation. The human genome includes about 3 billion base pairs, about 1.5% of which code for proteins, so the average mutation rate in humans is 0.45 mutations in protein-coding genes per generation, or about one new, potentially significant mutation in every other person born.

For individuals, most mutations are relatively harmless, while a few may have profound consequences. For populations, mutations are inconsequential unless they offer selective adaptive advantages.

4.4 Natural Selection: Advantageous Characteristics, Survival, and Reproduction

Darwin's theory of evolution by means of natural selection provided the conceptual framework for understanding adaptation. That framework has become even more powerful over the past 150 years because it has allowed for many refinements. The principle of natural selection is based on Darwin's conclusion that individuals with advantageous characteristics will survive in higher numbers and produce more off-spring than will members of a population lacking advantageous characteristics. Natural selection, therefore, focuses on reproductive success, or **fitness**. In particular, fitness is defined as some measure of the propensity to contribute offspring to future generations, usually by the next generation. Fitness can be defined in reference to individuals in a population or to specific genotypes. For our purposes, fitness is defined on the basis of genotypes. This means some genotypes have more (or less) fitness than other genotypes. The implication is that fitness differences can result in changes to allele frequencies. For example, if the genotype for darker coloring confers an adaptive advantage over the genotype for lighter coloring, the dark-color genotype will likely increase in frequency over time.

fitness Average number of offspring produced by parents with a particular genotype compared to the number of offspring produced by parents with another genotype.

PATTERNS OF NATURAL SELECTION

Evolutionary biologists have identified three alternative patterns by which natural selection can act on a specific trait. **Directional selection** favors one extreme form of a trait—more children are produced by individuals who have that extreme trait, so selection moves in that direction. Human evolution, for example, has clearly favored larger brains (for more on these topics, see chapters 10 and 11). **Stabilizing selection** favors the average version of a trait. For example, living humans whose birth weights are in the middle of the range have a better chance of surviving and reproducing than do those born with the lowest and highest weights. In **disruptive selection**, the pattern of variation is discontinuous. Individuals at both extreme ends of the range produce more offspring than does the remainder of the population. Given enough time, this pattern can result in a speciation event, as those in the middle fail to survive and reproduce and two new species arise at the extremes (**Figure 4.9**).

directional selection Selection for one allele over other alleles, causing allele frequencies to shift in one direction.

stabilizing selection Selection against the extremes of a phenotypic distribution, decreasing the genetic diversity for a trait in the population.

disruptive selection Selection for both extremes of a phenotypic distribution; may eventually lead to a speciation event.

NATURAL SELECTION IN ANIMALS: THE CASE OF THE PEPPERED MOTH AND INDUSTRIAL MELANISM

Examples of natural selection in animals are wide-ranging. Among them are animals that "blend in" with their surrounding habitat (**Figure 4.10**). Perhaps the best evidence ever documented of natural selection operating on a heritable trait concerns the peppered moth, *Biston betularia*, a species common throughout Great Britain (**Figure 4.11**). This moth is nocturnal, eating and breeding by night and attaching itself to trees, especially in the upper branches, during the day. Prior to the mid-1800s, all members of the species had a peppered appearance, their white coloring sprinkled with black. Trees throughout Great Britain were covered with lichen, and the moths' coloration provided excellent camouflage against the trees'

FIGURE 4.9

Types of Selection **(a) Top:** In the population represented here, smaller body size is more favorable than larger body size, so the frequency of smaller body size will increase thanks to directional selection. **Middle:** The fitness of individuals with smaller body sizes will be greater than that of individuals with larger body sizes. **Bottom:** Over time, the population's average body size will decrease.

(b) Top: In this population, medium body size is favored, so the frequency of medium body size will increase thanks to stabilizing selection. **Middle:** The fitness of individuals with medium body sizes will be much greater. **Bottom:** However, the population's average body size will remain relatively stable over time.

(c) Top: Here, owing to disruptive selection, the frequencies of small and large body sizes will increase, while the frequency of medium body size will decrease. **Middle:** The fitness levels are highest at the extremes and lowest in the middle. **Bottom:** Over time, the population will split between those with large bodies and those with small bodies.

(d) Top: In the absence of selection, the population will have a range of sizes. **Middle:** Fitness levels will vary independently of size. **Bottom:** The population's average body size will not change over time.

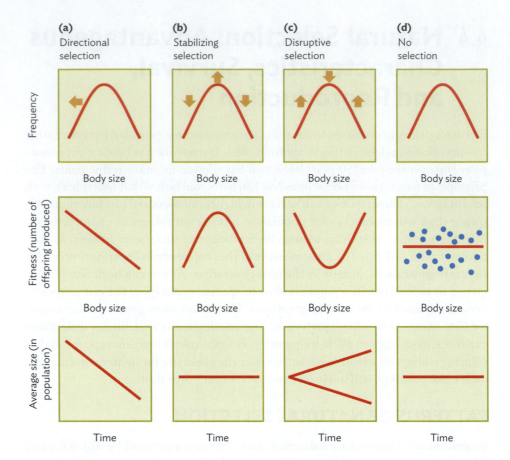

variable-colored surface and thus protected the moths from their major predator, birds. In 1848, a naturalist exploring the countryside near Manchester, England, spotted a melanic (dark) variety of the moth. The frequency of the melanic form relative to the nonmelanic (light) form remained low for a couple of decades but then climbed rapidly in the late nineteenth century. By the 1950s, 90% or more of peppered moths were melanic (**Figure 4.12**).

FIGURE 4.10

Leafy Sea Dragon As a result of natural selection, the leafy sea dragon looks just like the sea plants around it in its ocean setting.

This rapid increase in melanic frequency was a case of evolution profoundly changing phenotype. Directional selection had favored the melanic form over the nonmelanic form of *B. betularia*, and the melanic form exhibited a greater fitness. But what was this form's adaptive advantage?

The selecting factor was the Industrial Revolution. With the rise of industry throughout England and elsewhere in the middle to late nineteenth century, mills, fueled entirely by coal, spewed coal particles from smokestacks—50 tons per square mile per month, in some places—blackening the sky and covering the landscape. The trees survived this pollution onslaught, but the lichen covering the trees did not. The surfaces of the trees changed from light-colored to black, greatly altering the peppered moth's habitat. This pollution crisis provided a huge selective advantage for the melanic moths, which were now perfectly camouflaged against blackened trees. Nonmelanic moths became easy prey.

How did the genetics of this evolutionary change work? Breeding experiments revealed that, in a classic case of Mendelian genetics, the color difference between the two *B. betularia* forms was determined by one locus. The nonmelanic variety had a genotype of *cc* (homozygous recessive), while the melanic variety was either heterozygous, *Cc*, or homozygous, *CC*. The dominant allele, *C*, likely first appeared as a mutation, perhaps in the first half of the nineteenth century or earlier, long before the first melanic moth was observed in 1848. The *C* allele may have been in the population, maintained by the mutation's reoccurrence. Recent estimates suggest that the frequency of the nonmelanic variety was only 1%–10% in polluted regions of England and no more than 5% around Manchester (**Figure 4.13**). Plugged into the Hardy–Weinberg equilibrium equation, this information in turn suggests that 46% of the population had the *CC* genotype, 44% had the *Cc* genotype, and 10% had the *cc* genotype (**Table 4.2**). Beginning in the late 1960s and early 1970s, the stricter pollution laws, changes in coal burning, and decline of mill-based industry in Great Britain profoundly affected the moth population, once again illustrating natural selection. That is, in areas that were no longer polluted, the frequency of melanic *B. betularia* dropped. In Manchester, for example, the frequency of the melanic moth decreased from 90% in 1983 to well under 10% in the late 1990s. Plugged into the Hardy–Weinberg equation, these numbers reveal that the *CC* genotype decreased to 0.25%, the *Cc* genotype decreased to 9.5%, and the *cc* genotype increased to 90% (**Table 4.3**). This rapid evolutionary change reflected the return of the original coloration of the trees, which conferred

FIGURE 4.11

Peppered Moths The species *Biston betularia* includes two forms: light (nonmelanic) and dark (melanic).

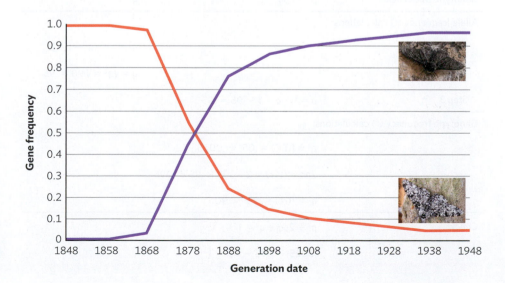

Generation date

FIGURE 4.12

Changes in the Peppered Moth Gene Frequency The frequency of the melanic gene in peppered moths increased from 1848 through 1948. The frequency of the nonmelanic gene decreased during that same period.

FIGURE 4.13

Melanic Moths This map of Great Britain illustrates the prevalence of melanic (dark) moths there during the Industrial Revolution. Highly industrialized areas, such as Manchester, had almost no light moths, while rural, nonindustrial areas, such as Scotland (north) and southwestern England, had substantially more light moths, almost to the exclusion of dark moths. What would this map look like for the preindustrialization period?

TABLE 4.2 Moth (*Biston betularia*) Genotype Frequencies—Industrialization Period

PHENOTYPE	MELANIC	NONMELANIC
Phenotype frequencies	.90	.10
Genotype	$CC + Cc$	cc
Genotype frequencies	$p^2 + 2pq$	q^2

Allele frequency (f) calculations:

Step 1		$q^2 = .10$ $(q^2 = f[cc])$
Step 2		$q = \sqrt{q^2} = \sqrt{.10} = .32$
Step 3	$p = 1 - q = 1 - .32 = .68$	

Genotype frequency (f) calculations:

$$p^2 = f(CC) = .68^2 = .46$$

$$2pq = f(Cc) = 2 \times .68 \times .32 = .44$$

$$q^2 = f(cc) = .32^2 = .10$$

Check:	$p^2 + 2pq + q^2 = 1$
	$.46 + .44 + .10 = 1$

TABLE 4.3 Moth (*Biston betularia*) Genotype Frequencies—Postindustrialization Period

PHENOTYPE	MELANIC	NONMELANIC
Phenotype frequencies	.10	.90
Genotype	$CC + Cc$	cc
Genotype frequencies	$p^2 + 2pq$	q^2

Allele frequency (f) calculations:

Step 1		$q^2 = .90$ $(q^2 = f[cc])$
Step 2		$q = \sqrt{q^2} = \sqrt{.90} = .95$
Step 3	$p = 1 - q = 1 - .95 = .05$	

Genotype frequency (f) calculations:

$$p^2 = f(CC) = .05^2 = .0025$$

$$2pq = f(Cc) = 2 \times .05 \times .95 = .095$$

$$q^2 = f(cc) = .95^2 = .90$$

Check:	$p^2 + 2pq + q^2 = 1$
	$.0025 + .095 + .90 = 1$

a selective disadvantage—predation visibility—on the melanic variety. This postscript adds even more power to the story of how natural selection brought about biological changes in *B. betularia*.

NATURAL SELECTION IN HUMANS: ABNORMAL HEMOGLOBINS AND RESISTANCE TO MALARIA

The preceding case of industrial melanism is an example of **positive selection**, whereby an organism's biology is shaped by selection for beneficial traits. Natural selection for beneficial traits in humans is best understood by studying genes that control specific traits. Of the 90 or so different loci that are targets of natural selection (**Figure 4.14**), among the most compelling examples is the sickle-cell allele—the hemoglobin *S* (or simply *S*) allele—which causes **sickle-cell anemia** (**Figure 4.15**). Millions of people suffer from such **hemolytic anemias**, which involve the destruction of red blood cells. A low number of red blood cells can produce health problems because of the resultant lack of hemoglobin, the chemical in red blood cells that carries oxygen to all the body tissues. The *S* gene yields a specific kind of **abnormal hemoglobin**.

Sickle-cell anemia has been known to the medical community since the early 1900s, and the genetics behind it was documented in the 1950s. The *S* gene is a

positive selection The process by which advantageous genetic variants quickly increase in frequency in a population.

sickle-cell anemia A genetic blood disease in which the red blood cells become deformed and sickle-shaped, decreasing their ability to carry oxygen to tissues.

hemolytic anemias Conditions of insufficient iron in the blood due to the destruction of red blood cells resulting from genetic blood diseases, toxins, or infectious pathogens.

abnormal hemoglobin Hemoglobin altered so that it is less efficient in binding to and carrying oxygen.

X chromosome

G6PD

FIGURE 4.14

***G6pd* Gene** One target of natural selection in humans is the *G6pd* gene, located on the X chromosome.

Chromosome 11

Hemoglobin *S*

FIGURE 4.15

Sickle-Cell Gene Hemoglobin *S* appears on human chromosome 11.

FIGURE 4.16

Sickle-Cell Mutation Sickle-cell anemia begins with a single nitrogen base mutation—a base substitution. The abnormal hemoglobin that results is less efficient at binding to oxygen and causes red blood cells to become sickle-shaped.

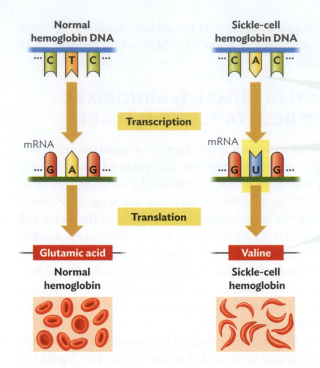

The *S* allele arises from a nitrogen base substitution: adenine replaces thymine in the hemoglobin DNA.

The codon changes from GAG in normal hemoglobin mRNA to GUG in the sickle-cell hemoglobin mRNA (the adenine in the normal mRNA is replaced with uracil).

The changed codon in the mRNA is coded to produce a different amino acid. Instead of glutamic acid, valine is inserted in the polypeptide chain. This amino acid change causes a change in the functioning of the hemoglobin so that it cannot bind to oxygen.

capillaries Small blood vessels between the terminal ends of arteries and the veins.

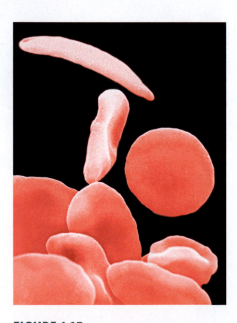

FIGURE 4.17

Sickle-Shaped Red Blood Cells This image shows normal red blood cells, which are round; a long, slender, sickle-shaped cell (at top); and other irregularly shaped cells. The abnormal cells are very fragile and easily damaged or destroyed.

simple base-pair mutation (**Figure 4.16**). Genetically, people with normal hemoglobin have the alleles *AA,* the homozygous condition. People who carry the sickle-cell allele on one of the two homologous chromosomes only are *AS,* and people who have the homozygous form of the disease are *SS*. *AS* individuals are for all practical purposes normal in their survival and reproduction rates. There is no cure for sickle-cell anemia, and in the absence of modern medical treatment, some 80% of people who are *SS* die before their reproductive years, usually considerably earlier. The *SS* genotype results in many red blood cells having a sickle shape caused by the abnormal hemoglobin, in sharp contrast to the round appearance of red blood cells in people with normal hemoglobin (**Figure 4.17**). The abnormal shape of the cells prevents them from passing through the **capillaries**, the narrow blood vessels that form networks throughout tissues. When the clogging of capillaries cuts off the oxygen supply in vital tissues, severe anemia and death can result.

The Geography of Sickle-Cell Anemia and the Association with Malaria Beginning in the mid-twentieth century, the medical community observed that many people living in equatorial Africa—as many as 20%–30%—had the *S* gene. This finding represented a huge puzzle: as the gene was so bad for survival, why was its frequency so high? In other words, one would expect strong selection against this nonbeneficial gene. The solution to the puzzle began to emerge with the discovery that high heterozygous (*AS*) frequencies appear in regions of Africa where malaria is endemic. In other words, where malaria—a potentially lethal parasitic infection in which the parasite is introduced to a human host by a mosquito—is always present, there is a high frequency of carriers of the gene (**Figure 4.18**). Moreover, *AS* people (sickle-gene carriers) die of malaria in far fewer numbers than do *AA* people.

As described at the beginning of this chapter, Anthony Allison discovered that in low-lying, wet areas of Kenya (where the number of mosquitoes was great and the rate of malaria was high), the frequency of the sickle-cell allele was considerably higher than in highland or arid areas. He developed the simple but elegant hypothesis that the infection and the genetic mutation were related. Individuals homozygous

(a)

(b)

FIGURE 4.18

Frequency Distributions of the Sickle-Cell Allele and Malaria In equatorial Africa, **(a)** the frequency distribution of the sickle-cell allele coincides with **(b)** areas of high malarial parasite concentration.

for normal hemoglobin (*AA*) were highly susceptible to dying from malaria; individuals homozygous for sickle-cell anemia (*SS*) did not survive to reproduce; however, individuals heterozygous for normal hemoglobin and the sickle-cell mutation (*AS*) either did not contract malaria or suffered a less severe malarial infection. That these frequencies were being maintained indicated that the *AS* heterozygote was a **balanced polymorphism**. It was also a fitness trade-off: carriers could pass on the sickle-cell allele, but they received immunity from malaria.

balanced polymorphism A situation in which selection maintains two or more phenotypes for a specific gene in a population.

The Biology of Sickle-Cell Anemia and Malarial Infection Why do people who are heterozygous for the sickle-cell allele survive malaria or not contract it at all? Unlike *SS* red blood cells, *AS* red blood cells do not sickle under most conditions (that is, except when severely deprived of oxygen). They are, however, somewhat smaller than normal cells, and their oxygen levels are somewhat lower. For reasons not yet understood, the *AS* red blood cells are simply a poor host—a nonconducive living and reproduction environment—for the parasite that causes malaria (**Figure 4.19**).

The Historical Link between Sickle-Cell Anemia and Malaria In the late 1950s, the American biological anthropologist Frank B. Livingstone (1928–2005) sought to strengthen the case for natural selection by historically linking sickle-cell anemia and malaria. Livingstone asked two important questions: *Where and when did the sickle-cell allele first appear in equatorial Africa?* and *What conditions led to the allele being naturally selected?* He hypothesized that the Bantu, a group of peoples who speak Bantu languages, carried the mutation with them when they migrated southward from the region of Cameroon and Nigeria (**Figure 4.20**). Prior to the Bantu's arrival, the region was a largely unbroken forest. Bantu populations introduced agriculture there, clearing large swaths of the forest for cultivation. The peoples' iron-working technology made possible the creation of tools for cutting down large trees, clearing and plowing fields, and planting crops—mostly yams and cassava.

Even under the best conditions, tropical forests are fragile ecosystems. Once their trees have been cleared and their fields have been planted, their relatively poor soil, which normally soaks up rainwater, becomes thin or disappears. Geologic evidence shows a dramatic increase in soil erosion in the region after the arrival of Bantu populations, due in large part to **anthropogenic** deforestation and the overall environmental impact of humans on the landscape. As a result of these erosive processes, pools of water collected and became stagnant, providing ideal conditions

anthropogenic Relating to any effect caused by humans.

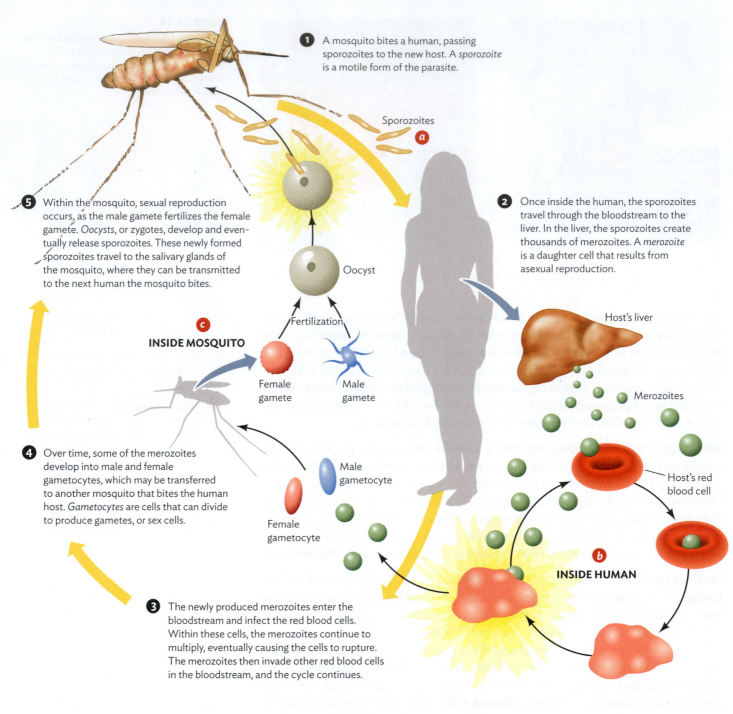

1 A mosquito bites a human, passing sporozoites to the new host. A *sporozoite* is a motile form of the parasite.

Sporozoites
a

5 Within the mosquito, sexual reproduction occurs, as the male gamete fertilizes the female gamete. *Oocysts*, or zygotes, develop and eventually release sporozoites. These newly formed sporozoites travel to the salivary glands of the mosquito, where they can be transmitted to the next human the mosquito bites.

Oocyst

Fertilization

c

INSIDE MOSQUITO

Female gamete

Male gamete

2 Once inside the human, the sporozoites travel through the bloodstream to the liver. In the liver, the sporozoites create thousands of merozoites. A *merozoite* is a daughter cell that results from asexual reproduction.

Host's liver

Merozoites

Host's red blood cell

b

INSIDE HUMAN

4 Over time, some of the merozoites develop into male and female gametocytes, which may be transferred to another mosquito that bites the human host. *Gametocytes* are cells that can divide to produce gametes, or sex cells.

Male gametocyte

Female gametocyte

3 The newly produced merozoites enter the bloodstream and infect the red blood cells. Within these cells, the merozoites continue to multiply, eventually causing the cells to rupture. The merozoites then invade other red blood cells in the bloodstream, and the cycle continues.

VACCINE TARGETS

a Sporozoite: The goal of sporozoite vaccines is to block parasites from entering or growing within human liver cells.

b Merozoite: Vaccines based on merozoite antigens lessen malaria's severity by hobbling the invasion of new generations of red blood cells or by reducing complications.

c Gametocyte: So-called altruistic gametocyte-based vaccines do not affect human disease but are designed to evoke human antibodies that derail parasite development within the mosquito.

FIGURE 4.19

Life Cycle of *Plasmodium falciparum* The life cycle of the malarial parasite, *Plasmodium falciparum*, takes place in two hosts: mosquito and human. Both hosts are needed if the parasite is to survive.

(a)   (b)

FIGURE 4.21

The Spread of Malaria As the Bantu cleared forests for agricultural fields, **(a)** pools of stagnant water became an ideal breeding ground for **(b)** mosquito larvae, which carried the malarial parasites.

FIGURE 4.20

The Ecology of Malarial Parasites Beginning about 4,000 to 5,000 yBP, Bantu people began a series of migrations, originating from west-central Africa and pushing southward eventually into southern Africa. In addition to agriculture, they carried the mutation for the sickle-cell allele. The Khoisan were the inhabitants of southern Africa encountered by the Bantu as they spread southward.

for the breeding of parasite-carrying mosquitoes (**Figure 4.21**). This picture became clear to Livingstone as he developed his research: the newly created ecological circumstances fostered mosquito reproduction and the spread of malaria, and the growing host of humans made possible by agriculture-fueled population growth provided the food resources needed by the mosquitoes. The infectious disease gave those individuals with a very rare mutation—the sickle-cell allele—an adaptive advantage and the ability to survive and reproduce in these new environmental circumstances. Because of the advantage the heterozygous condition provides, the *S* allele was maintained and passed from generation to generation. For this reason, sickle-cell anemia predominantly affects those whose descendants came from the malarial environments in large parts of equatorial Africa. Outside of such malarial environments, the *S* allele never became advantageous.

Other Hemoglobin and Enzyme Abnormalities Sickle-cell anemia turns out to be just one of a number of **hemoglobinopathies** and other genetic abnormalities in Africa, Asia, and Europe that provide a strong selective advantage in regions of endemic malaria (**Figure 4.22**). Heterozygous carriers of abnormal hemoglobins apparently make poor hosts for malarial parasites.

Thalassemia, a genetic anemia found in Europe (especially in Italy and Greece), Asia, and the Pacific, reduces or eliminates hemoglobin synthesis. In some

hemoglobinopathies A group of related genetic blood diseases characterized by abnormal hemoglobin.

thalassemia A genetic blood disease in which hemoglobin is improperly synthesized, causing red blood cells to have a much shorter life span.

Hemoglobin C
Hemoglobin E
Hemoglobin S

FIGURE 4.22

Distribution of Hemoglobinopathies This map shows the distribution of hemoglobin *C*, hemoglobin *E*, and hemoglobin *S* in Southeast Asia and Africa. People with hemoglobin *E* may have mild hemolytic anemia or other mild effects. Like hemoglobin *S*, hemoglobin *C* appears primarily in equatorial Africa. Like hemoglobin *E*, hemoglobin *C* has generally minor effects, most often mild hemolytic anemia.

FIGURE 4.23

***G6pd* Gene Distribution** This map shows the distribution of the *G6pd* gene, with the highest levels in Africa and Southeast Asia.

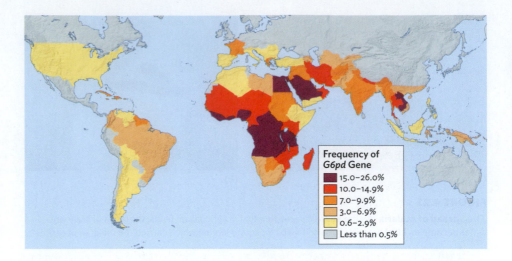

Frequency of *G6pd* Gene
- 15.0–26.0%
- 10.0–14.9%
- 7.0–9.9%
- 3.0–6.9%
- 0.6–2.9%
- Less than 0.5%

glucose-6-phosphate dehydrogenase (G6PD) An enzyme that aids in the proper functioning of red blood cells; G6PD deficiency, a genetic condition, leads to hemolytic anemia.

homozygous forms of the mutation, hemoglobin becomes clumped inside the red blood cells. The spleen then destroys the red blood cells, resulting in severe anemia. In the areas around the Mediterranean where the genetic frequency is highest—as high as 80%—the presence of malaria makes a strong case for a selective advantage for heterozygous individuals, for whom the condition and malaria are not lethal.

An association has long been recognized between deficiency of the enzyme **glucose-6-phosphate dehydrogenase (G6PD)** and malaria. A recessive hereditary mutation leads more males than females to lack the gene that is coded to produce this enzyme (see Figure 4.14). Without the G6PD enzyme, a person who takes sulfa-based antibiotics or eats fava beans risks the destruction of red blood cells, severe anemia, and occasionally death. Because of the connection with fava beans, this severe hemolytic disease is called *favism*. Its 130 genetic variants occur in high frequencies in some populations, the highest being 70% among Kurdish Jews (**Figure 4.23**). Heterozygous carriers have a strong selective advantage because they produce some of the enzyme but are protected from malaria (here again, the parasite cannot live in the abnormal red blood cells).

Analysis of genetic data by the biological anthropologist Sarah Tishkoff indicates that the mutation for the disease arose between about 4,000 and 12,000 yBP, at the same time as the abnormal hemoglobins. Populations whose descendants did not encounter malaria do not have the *G6pd* gene mutation or abnormal hemoglobins. Today, for example, malaria appears throughout the tropical regions of the Americas, but Native Americans are 100% homozygous for normal alleles at the *G6pd* and hemoglobin loci. That these particular genes do not appear to have mutated in the New World strongly suggests that malaria was introduced to North and South America only after the Europeans' arrival. Indeed, the introduction of malaria and other Old World diseases—by either Spaniards or their African slaves—likely played an instrumental role in the precipitous decline in the native populations.

If malaria had been introduced in the Americas much earlier than the past few centuries—say thousands of years ago—and the mutations occurred, there might have been time for a natural selection to develop for the mutations. If the mutations did appear before the Europeans' arrival, however, they would have exhibited a clear selective disadvantage in the absence of malaria and been weeded out of the gene pool. Thus, red blood cell polymorphisms in the abnormal hemoglobin and *G6pd* loci reflect the fundamental interactions among environment, genes, and culture that have resulted in the modern human genome. The genes provide an important record about human evolution and the role of natural selection in shaping genetic variation.

4.5 Genetic Drift: Genetic Change Due to Chance

Genetic drift, one of the four forces in evolution, is random change in allele frequency over time. Provided that no allele confers a selective advantage over another, a random change can lead to a change in gene frequency, such as one allele being lost and the other becoming fixated—or fixed, the only allele of its kind in the population. This force makes possible the measuring of evolution as a statistical probability.

Coin tosses can demonstrate the effects of genetic drift (**Table 4.4**). Imagine that heads and tails are two alleles in a population. If there are only two members of the population (two coin tosses), then there is a chance that both will be heads. In effect, the "heads" allele will become fixed in the small population, while the "tails" allele will be lost. As the population size (number of coin tosses) increases, it becomes less likely that one allele will become fixed and the other lost. In very large populations (1 million coin tosses), both alleles may be present in equal proportions.

How does such statistical probability translate to populations? Now imagine that before the election of your student government you have been asked to predict the winners. The best way for you to predict would be to ask each voting-eligible student how he or she planned to vote. It is *highly* likely that the outcome of such a comprehensive poll would be close to the actual election results. The shortcomings of this approach might include the very large size of the target population. No one would interview, for example, 50,000 students! The second-best approach would

TABLE 4.4 Heads versus Tails: Genetic Drift and Probability

COIN TOSSES	HEADS	TAILS	HEADS:TAILS RATIO
2	2	0	2:0
10	4	6	4:6
50	22	28	11:14
100	55	45	11:9
200	199	201	199:201
500	253	247	253:247
1,000	501	499	501:499
5,000	2,500	2,500	1:1
10,000	5,000	5,000	1:1
100,000	50,000	50,000	1:1
500,000	250,000	250,000	1:1
1,000,000	500,000	500,000	1:1

FIGURE 4.24

Genetic Drift over Time The effects of genetic drift appear in this graph, which plots the frequencies over time (measured in number of generations) of one gene in three differently sized populations. Assume that population A is the smallest of the three and population C is the largest. At the start, each population has the gene at 50% frequency. At around 38 generations, population A has drifted significantly; the gene is now fixed at 100% frequency. At 50 generations, population B has also drifted. Its gene frequency has declined to 10%. Although the frequency in population C has changed over time, it is still approximately 50% after 50 generations, owing to the largeness of the population.

endogamous Characterized by endogamy, which is the practice (by a population or group) of breeding only within the population.

exogamous Characterized by exogamy, which is the practice (by a population or group) of breeding outside the population.

founder effect The accumulation of random genetic changes in a small population that has become isolated from the parent population due to the genetic input of only a few colonizers.

be to select a sample, preferably a random sample that represented the entire student body. If you selected five students out of the 50,000, chances are very slim that those five would represent all the ethnic, national, regional, and economic backgrounds of the student body. In fact, chances are very high that this sample (0.01% of the total population) would provide a voting outcome very different from the actual one. If you interviewed 500 students (1% of the population), the chances of representation would be much greater; and if you chose 5,000 students (10% of the population), they would be greater still. The larger the sample size, the greater the probability of an accurate prediction.

Variations in human populations work the exact same way, except that genetic drift operates over a period of time rather than at a single point. The probability of an allele's frequency changing in a relatively short period of time increases with decreasing population size. The larger the population, the less divergence from the original gene frequency over time (**Figure 4.24**).

How does this effect play out in real life? Among humans, for example, genetic drift might occur in a small group that is **endogamous**, discouraging reproduction outside the group. (An **exogamous** society extends reproduction outside its community.) Within such a group, the chances are great that the frequencies of genetic markers will differ from those of a larger population. When the Dunkers, a small religious sect that discourages outside marriage (and thus reproduction), first emigrated from Germany to Pennsylvania in 1719, the group included just 28 members. Over the next few decades, several hundred more arrived in Pennsylvania; but the breeding population remained quite small. Comparisons of contemporary blood type percentages among Dunkers, Germans, and Americans reflect significant changes in the Dunkers and a likely lack of change in the larger populations (**Figure 4.25**). That is, frequencies for ABO and MN blood types among Germans and Americans remain basically the same as they were in the 1700s. The Dunkers' original frequencies were probably much like those of the Germans, but the small Dunker population meant a much greater chance for genetic drift. The frequencies diverged dramatically over time simply due to chance.

FOUNDER EFFECT: A SPECIAL KIND OF GENETIC DRIFT

The **founder effect**, one form of genetic drift, occurs when a small group (fewer than several hundred members) of a large parent population migrates to a new region and is reproductively isolated. The new region is either unoccupied or

(a) ABO blood type frequencies

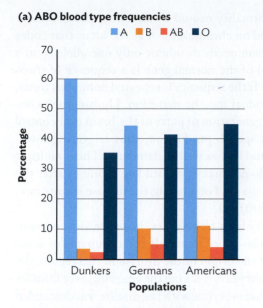

(b) MN blood type frequencies

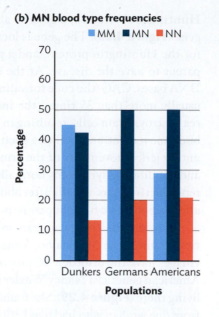

FIGURE 4.25

Genetic Drift in the Dunker Population
Comparisons of ABO and MN blood type frequencies among Dunkers, Germans, and Americans reveal genetic drift. **(a)** Dunkers have a higher percentage of blood type A and lower percentages of blood types O, B, and AB than do Germans and Americans. **(b)** Dunkers have a higher percentage of blood type MM and lower percentages of MN and NN.

occupied by species with which the small group cannot breed. Because the founding population is so small, there is a very good chance that its genetic composition is not representative of the parent population's. Because of the founder effect, as the founding population grows, its gene pool diverges even further from the source (**Figure 4.26**). For example, about 15,000 yBP, a very small number of individuals—perhaps just a few hundred—migrated from eastern Asia to North America (this movement is among the topics of chapter 12). Today, Native Americans have very high frequencies of type O blood—in many places the frequency is 100%—while eastern Asian populations have among the world's lowest frequencies of type O blood (**Figure 4.27**). This discrepancy strongly suggests that the original East Asian immigrants, the founding "Native Americans," had a higher frequency of type O blood than their parent population had.

The founder effect has also been documented in several genetic diseases that affect humans. Among the best known is a type of microsatellite called

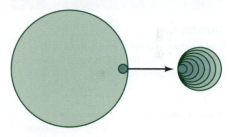

FIGURE 4.26

Founder Effect The large circle on the left represents a parent population, from which a very small proportion is removed to begin a new population. Over time, the founding population grows, and its gene pool looks less and less like that of the parent population.

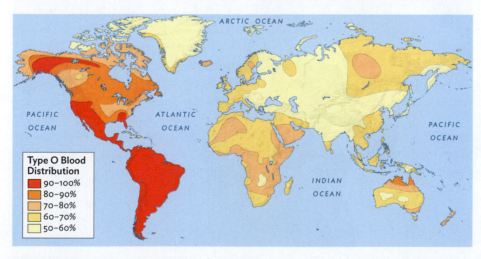

FIGURE 4.27

Type O Blood Frequency Distribution Native Americans in North and South America have much higher percentages of type O blood than do East Asians, with whom they share ancestors.

FIGURE 4.28

Huntington's Chorea The woman in the wheelchair suffers from Huntington's chorea, a degenerative genetic disorder.

Huntington's chorea A rare genetic disease in which the central nervous system degenerates and the individual loses control over voluntary movements, with the symptoms often appearing between ages 30 and 50.

Huntington's chorea, a genetic abnormality caused by an autosomal dominant gene (**Figure 4.28**). The gene is located on chromosome 4 at the locus that codes for the Huntingtin protein, and a person needs to inherit only one allele from a parent to have the disease. At the end of the normal gene is a sequence of three DNA bases, CAG (the code for valine). If the sequence is repeated numerous times, usually more than 35 times, the individual has the mutation. Huntington's chorea destroys brain cells, resulting in degeneration of parts of the brain that control body movement and abilities such as speech production, thus triggering involuntary jerky movements of the arms and legs as well as dementia. These multiple and debilitating symptoms normally do not manifest until late in life or after the reproductive years, usually after about age 40. Fortunately, the disease is quite rare, affecting only five to eight people per 100,000.

Huntington's chorea appears in very high frequencies, however, in communities around Lake Maracaibo, Venezuela—more than half the occupants of some villages have the disorder. To pinpoint the origin of the disease in this region, the American geneticist Nancy Wexler spent years tracking the genealogies of families living there (**Figure 4.29**). She found that everyone with the disease was descended from one woman who had lived 200 years earlier and carried the allele. This original carrier was not representative of her parent population, which would have had a much lower frequency of the allele. In accordance with the statistical probability, the genetic frequency had increased within the small population.

Why had such a debilitating disease not been removed from the gene pool via natural selection? Because the effects of the gene are not expressed until later in life, people might not have known they had the disease until after they had passed on the detrimental allele to their offspring.

Today, most human populations are not small and isolated, and they interbreed relatively freely with surrounding groups. Whenever interbreeding occurs across population boundaries, gene flow occurs.

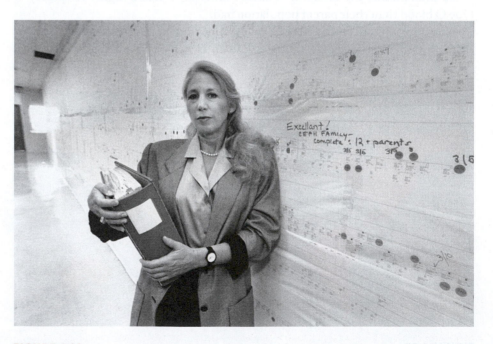

FIGURE 4.29

Nancy Wexler Wexler, whose mother died of Huntington's chorea, here stands in front of a chart showing genetic histories she tracked in studying the disease.

4.6 Gene Flow: Spread of Genes across Population Boundaries

Another force of evolution, gene flow (or **admixture**) is the transfer of genes across population boundaries. Simply, members of two populations produce offspring (**Figure 4.30**). The key determinant for the amount of gene flow is accessibility to mates—the smaller the physical distance between populations, the greater the chance of gene flow. While mutation increases genetic variation between two populations over time, gene flow decreases such variation. Anthropologists and geneticists have found that for many kinds of biological traits, ranging from cranial shapes to blood types to microsatellite DNA markers (see "Polymorphisms: Variations in Specific Genes" in chapter 3), similarity increases the closer geographically one population is to another population.

Migration does not necessarily bring about gene flow. For example, when East Asians first migrated to North America some 15,000 yBP, they reached a continental landmass where no humans had ever lived. Written records suggest that Vikings first traveled from Greenland to Newfoundland around AD 1000, but there is no evidence that they interbred with the native people. The first significant gene flow involving Native Americans and Europeans seems to have occurred soon after Christopher Columbus and his crew arrived in the New World in 1492. From that point on, gene flow in North America and South America has been extensive.

Gene flow and genetic variation are also highly influenced by social structure. Endogamous societies—for example, Australian Aborigines—have relatively little genetic diversity because few individuals migrate into the community and thus little new genetic material is introduced. Exogamous societies have relatively high genetic diversity because proportionately more genetic material is brought into the gene pool.

admixture The exchange of genetic material between two or more populations.

Generation 1   Generation 2

FIGURE 4.30

Gene Flow New genetic material can be introduced into a population through gene flow from another population. Say, for example, a population in one place has genes for only brown hair. Members of that population interbreed with an adjacent population, which has genes for only blond hair. After interbreeding for a generation, both populations have genes for blond and brown hair. As a result, when people from either population interbreed with yet another population, they may contribute alleles for brown, blond, or both.

Gene flow has always been an important force in human evolution. New studies of genomes recovered from fossil hominins, along with the remarkable expansion of the investigations of genomes of living people, are giving anthropologists answers to fundamental questions about the origins of genetic variation that we see in humans today. These studies reveal patterns of **introgression**, whereby some early hominins ancestral to later branches of hominin populations had at one time in their past disconnected, evolved, and later reconnected and exchanged genetic material (see Chapter 12). The study of these introgressed genomes provides a record of gene flow involving hominins who were likely reproductively isolated for many generations. The effects of gene flow have greatly increased in recent human evolution. Originally, human populations tended to be small and isolated. Only during the past 10,000 years, with the development of agriculture and with major population increases, have humans had widespread interaction.

Specific genetic markers in living populations, such as the ABO blood group system, provide evidence of gene flow across large regions. For example, the frequencies of type B blood change gradually from eastern Asia to far-western Europe (**Figure 4.31**). This clinal—that is, sloping—trend was first noted in the early 1940s by the American geneticist Pompeo Candela, who made the case that the gradient from east to west reflects significant gene flow that occurred as Mongol populations migrated westward from AD 500 to 1500. That is, if Mongols had higher frequencies of the *B* allele, they might have passed on that allele as they interbred with local populations.

Subsequent data on blood groups, however, have revealed sharp distinctions in frequencies between adjacent populations. These distinctions suggest that, in

FIGURE 4.31

Type B Blood Frequency Distribution The frequency of blood type B ranges from 30% in eastern Asia to almost 0% in far-western Europe. The main factor contributing to this change was probably gene flow between populations in an east-to-west direction (shown by arrow).

What Causes Evolution?

Evolution is caused by one of (or a combination of) four forces: mutation, natural selection, genetic drift, and gene flow. Although all four forces are important, natural selection accounts for most evolution.

CAUSE	DEFINITION	EXAMPLES
Mutation	A random change in a gene or chromosome, creating a new trait that may be advantageous, deleterious, or neutral in its effects on the organism	Sickle-cell anemia Huntington's chorea Klinefelter's syndrome Down syndrome
Natural selection	The process by which some organisms, with features that enable them to adapt to the environment, preferentially survive and reproduce, thereby increasing the frequency of those features in the population	Sickle-cell anemia Industrial melanism Thalassemia G6PD deficiency Lactase deficiency
Genetic drift	The random change in allele frequency from one generation to the next, with greater effect in small populations	Klinefelter's syndrome Blood types
Gene flow	Admixture, or the exchange of alleles between two populations	Blood types

addition to gene flow, genetic drift within small, isolated groups contributed to the frequency variations.

This chapter and the previous one discussed inheritance, the genetic code, and genetic change in terms of evolution. Prior to the emergence of evolutionary approaches to the study of human variation, many scientists believed that human variation could be understood through discrete categories called *races*. The next chapter will address the study of biological diversity, the uses and misuses of biological classification, and the ways that variation in living people reflects adaptations to diverse and sometimes extreme environments across the planet.

ANSWERING THE BIG QUESTIONS

1. **What causes evolutionary (genetic) change?**
   - There are four forces of evolution: mutation, natural selection, genetic drift, and gene flow. These forces result in genetic change over time.
   - Mutations are DNA coding errors involving permanent changes in the structure or amount of genetic material in cells. They are the only source of new genetic material.
   - Only mutations in gametes can affect offspring, so they have greater importance for evolution than do mutations in somatic cells.
   - During natural selection, population members with advantageous characteristics survive and reproduce in greater numbers than do members lacking the same characteristics. Allele frequencies can increase, decrease, or remain the same owing to natural selection.
   - Advantageous characteristics can be visible physical attributes and/or invisible, biochemical attributes.
   - Genetic drift is change in gene frequency due to chance. It is likelier within smaller populations.
   - Gene flow is the transfer of genes across population boundaries.

2. **How is evolutionary (genetic) change measured, and how is the cause determined?**
   - Deviation from the proportions of gene frequencies and genotype frequencies as defined by the Hardy–Weinberg law of equilibrium is used to measure evolutionary change.
   - There is no apparent evolution of a gene in a population if there is no change in frequency over time.
   - If gene frequency is changing, then evolution is likely occurring owing to one or more forces of evolution, but the Hardy–Weinberg law does not indicate which particular force (or forces) is the cause. The scientist examines the context for change, such as change in climate, migration of populations across territorial or geographic boundaries, introduction of new diseases, and change in diet.

STUDY QUIZ

1. **Mutation, natural selection, genetic drift, and gene flow can all**
   a. create new alleles that have never existed before.
   b. increase reproductive success of individuals in a population.
   c. change allele frequency in a population.
   d. drive alleles to become lost or fixed in small populations.

2. **A population at equilibrium according to the Hardy–Weinberg law**
   a. is rapidly evolving with respect to a given gene.
   b. is not evolving with respect to a given gene.
   c. is experiencing random changes in gene frequency.
   d. must be either a small or a migrating population.

3. **Evolutionary fitness measures**
   a. physical strength.
   b. life span.
   c. intelligence.
   d. reproductive success.

4. **Why is the heterozygous sickle-cell genotype common only in malarial regions?**
   a. The sickle-cell allele is a new mutation and will eventually spread worldwide.
   b. Immunity to malaria outweighs the fitness risk of the sickle-cell allele.
   c. The association of the sickle-cell allele and malaria is a random coincidence due to genetic drift.
   d. Gene flow spread the sickle-cell allele only in malarial regions.

KEY TERMS

abnormal hemoglobin
admixture
anthropogenic
balanced polymorphism
capillaries
deme
directional selection
disruptive selection
endogamous
equilibrium
exogamous
fitness
founder effect
frameshift mutation
gene pool
glucose-6-phosphate dehydrogenase (G6PD)
Hardy–Weinberg law of equilibrium
hemoglobinopathies
hemolytic anemias
Huntington's chorea
induced mutations
introgression
Klinefelter's syndrome
macroevolution
microevolution
mutagens
nonsynonymous point mutation
point mutations
positive selection
reproductive isolation
sickle-cell anemia
spontaneous mutations
stabilizing selection
synonymous point mutation
thalassemia
transposable elements

STUDY QUIZ (CONTINUED)

5. Gene flow involves

a. humans only.

b. members of one species only.

c. members within a species or members of different species.

d. immunity to genetic drift.

EVOLUTION REVIEW

The Four Forces of Evolution

SYNOPSIS Biological anthropologists carry out population genetics studies to measure the changes in genetic makeup (allele frequencies) from one generation to the next and to explain the evolutionary processes behind these changes. Researchers use the Hardy–Weinberg law to mathematically demonstrate whether or not a population is undergoing evolutionary change with respect to a particular trait. When there is no change in allele frequencies for a trait (and therefore no evolutionary change), the population is said to be in genetic equilibrium for that trait. Deviations from genetic equilibrium are brought about by the four forces of evolution: mutation, natural selection, genetic drift, and gene flow. Each of these four forces affects the level of genetic variation within a population and between populations in different ways, and any one or a combination of these forces may be acting on a population at any given time. Throughout our evolutionary history, humans have been and continue to be subject to the operation of these four forces. Biological anthropologists explain much of the variation observed among modern humans today within the specific context of one or more of these forces.

Q1. In the chapter, microevolution is defined as small-scale evolution that occurs over a few generations, while macroevolution is defined as large-scale evolution that occurs over many (hundreds or thousands of) generations. Microevolution can also be defined as changes occurring below the level of species (such as within or between populations), while macroevolution can also be defined as changes at the species level or above (family, class, order, etc.). Provide an example for each type (each definition) of microevolution and each type of macroevolution. Considering these definitions and your examples, which one of the four forces of evolution will *not* be operating on groups undergoing macroevolution?

HINT Think about what defines a species.

Q2. Describe the three patterns of natural selection discussed in this chapter. Of these three, which pattern of selection would be most likely to eventually result in a speciation event?

Q3. Mutations can be either spontaneous (no known cause) or induced (caused by specific environmental agents). What are some environmental agents that could increase the rates of genetic mutations among humans today? What types of mutation have the potential to be the most significant from an evolutionary perspective?

HINT Think about how mutations are passed from one generation to the next.

Q4. Discuss the example of lactase persistence as it relates to human biocultural variation and evolution. Under what environmental conditions would those individuals carrying alleles for lactase persistence be favored, while their counterparts unable to produce this enzyme would be strongly selected against?

HINT Think about the ways this trait would contribute to greater fitness or reproductive success.

Q5. Provide at least one example each of a modern human population and nonhuman population in which genetic drift may be an especially important factor affecting variation and evolution.

HINT Think about whether genetic drift is more influential in smaller populations or larger populations.

ADDITIONAL READINGS

Kettlewell, H. B. D. 1973. *The Evolution of Melanism*. Oxford, UK: Oxford University Press.

Livingstone, F. B. 1958. Anthropological implications of sickle cell gene distribution in West Africa. *American Anthropologist* 60: 533–562.

Mielke, J. H., L. W. Konigsberg, and J. H. Relethford. 2011. *Human Biological Variation*, 2nd ed. New York: Oxford University Press.

Relethford, J. H. 2012. *Human Population Genetics*. Hoboken, NJ: Wiley-Blackwell.

Ridley, M. 2004. *Evolution*, 3rd ed. Malden, MA: Blackwell Science.

Modern human skin colors range from very light to very dark. If all the variants were lined up from lightest to darkest, it would be hard to determine the dividing lines between so-called racial categories. In fact, the number of racial categories differs by whom you ask, from three to 10 or more. Although skin color is an easily observable form of biological variation among humans, it is not the main form. Most of our variation as a species is invisible to the naked eye and does not divide up into discrete categories.

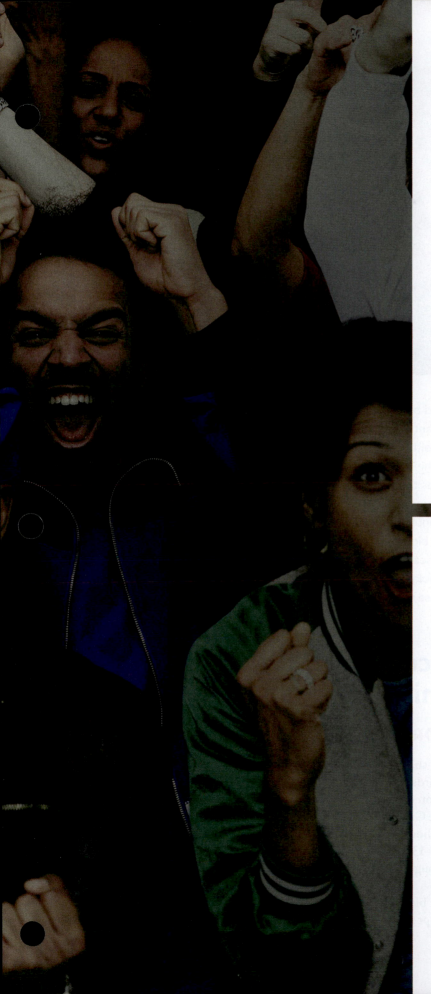

5

Biology in the Present

LIVING PEOPLE

BIG QUESTIONS

1. Is race a valid, biologically meaningful concept?

2. What do growth and development tell us about human variation? What are the benefits of our life history pattern?

3. How do people adapt to environmental extremes and other circumstances?

I was first introduced to the biology of and variation in living people in high school, when my biology teacher assigned the section on race in our textbook. From that reading and class discussion about it, I learned that race is complex and important, especially with regard to poverty and inequality. I also learned that, from a biological perspective, race is a useful way to classify human beings. The teacher informed the class that each human being belongs to one of three so-called races: "Caucasoid," "Negroid," and "Mongoloid," referring respectively to Europeans and western Asians, Africans south of the Sahara Desert, and all other Asians and Native Americans. Simple.

But is racial categorization in fact all that simple? Can human biological variation be classified? Is race a means of understanding why humans differ in appearance and biology

FIGURE 5.1

Christopher Columbus's Ships In 1492, on his voyage from Spain to what he thought was India but turned out to be the Americas, Columbus commanded a group of ships that included, as depicted at right, the now famous *Niña, Pinta,* and *Santa Maria.* Once ships and boats enabled explorers and other travelers to reach places that had previously been too far away to visit, people of different lands—who had different physical features—began to meet. Observations of physical and cultural differences led to notions of "us" versus "them," creating the foundation for the race concept.

around the world? If the answer to these questions is no, then is there a better way to comprehend the enormous variation among humans today? In addressing these questions in this chapter, I will show that race, as it was presented in my high school biology class, has deep historical roots going back centuries. These historical roots have led to a largely incorrect understanding of human biological variation, an incorrect understanding that persists to the present day.

In fact, race symbolizes the misperceptions that many Americans and others around the world have about human variation. Traits that are often seen as racial in origin are actually biological adaptations that have been strongly influenced by natural selection operating in regional and other contexts. As interpreted by anthropologists, human biological variation consists not of categories but of an evolutionary continuum. A key underlying concept here is humans' flexibility toward their environmental circumstances, a process that begins before birth and continues through adulthood. The study of living human biology, then, emphasizes the enormous developmental flexibility that characterizes *Homo sapiens.* Simply, the popular perception is that race is biology. As you will explore in this chapter, race is *not* biology. Rather, human biological variation is driven by evolution. In some very significant ways, this may be one of the most important chapters that you read in this book, mainly because it addresses general misperceptions of what race is and how these misperceptions serve to incorrectly frame our understanding of human biology.

5.1 Is Race a Valid, Biologically Meaningful Concept?

BRIEF HISTORY OF THE RACE CONCEPT

The idea of race—that human variation can be classified—is a recent invention. Early written records do not use the concept. For example, even though ancient Egyptians represented sub-Saharan Africans in their art, they never referred to the Africans' race. The Greek historian Herodotus (ca. 484–ca. 420 bc) traveled widely but never wrote about race. Similarly, the great Venetian historian and traveler Marco Polo (1254–1324), who saw more of the known world than anyone else of his day, recorded huge amounts of information about his sojourns in Asia without mentioning race.

The American biological anthropologist C. Loring Brace (1930–2019) argued that the race concept got its start in the fourteenth century, during the Renaissance.

Before that time, people traveled gradually, either by walking or on horseback. A day's journey averaged 40 km (25 mi), over which travelers could observe subtle changes in human variation, such as in skin color, from place to place. When Renaissance-era travelers began covering long distances via oceangoing vessels, they also began categorizing people into discrete groups (**Figure 5.1**). In simply departing from seaports, covering vast bodies of water, and landing at their destinations, these travelers noted obvious and sometimes profound physical differences in people—say between western Europeans and equatorial Africans—without all the gradations that came between.

The early scientific articulation of the race concept—namely, that living humans could be lumped into different taxonomic groups—first emerged in the eighteenth century. By the 1700s, Europeans had encountered most of the biological diversity of the world's populations. Building on Linnaeus's taxonomy of organisms (see "Taxonomy and Systematics: Classifying Living Organisms and Identifying Their Biological Relationships" in chapter 2), the eminent German anatomist Johann Friedrich Blumenbach (1752–1840) developed a biological taxonomy of human races, which he published as his MD thesis at the University of Göttingen in 1775. Blumenbach based his taxonomy on human skin color and other physical traits, but mainly on features of the skull, such as the facial projection (**Figure 5.2**). After studying several hundred skulls he had collected from around the world, Blumenbach concluded that there were five races of people: Mongoloids, Malays, Ethiopians (Africans), American Indians, and Caucasoids. These types were static—they did not change over time. And while Blumenbach had focused on skulls, his racial taxonomy was subsequently applied to the living populations represented by those skulls. More than any other work, Blumenbach's study set the tone for the popular perception of human variation: that human beings come in categorical types called *races*.

DEBUNKING THE RACE CONCEPT

Franz Boas, the founder of American anthropology, was among the first scientists to challenge the taxonomic approach to human biological variation. Specifically, he wanted to test the widely held notion that head shape and other so-called racial markers were static entities, essentially unchanging through time. In the early 1900s, he and his researchers studied some 18,000 immigrant families, calculating the cephalic index—the ratio of head length to head breadth—of parents born in Europe and of their children born in the United States (**Figure 5.3**). The results of this study revealed that the adults' and children's head shapes differed, not by a lot but by a degree that could be expressed mathematically. This finding undermined the idea, prevalent at the time, that racial types were innately stable. Because the differences that had been cited among various races were not immutable, Boas concluded that the race concept was invalid. Boas's work laid the foundation for a scientific focus on biological process and variation rather than on typological classification.

Other social scientists in the early twentieth century were drawing similar conclusions regarding the lack of validity of racial categories. Contrary to the view held by most of the public, American sociologist and civil rights leader W. E. B. Du Bois (1868–1963) argued that health differences between people of European descent and people of African descent in the United States were due to social inequality and not biology. The emerging understanding, simply put, was that race is a social construction.

FIGURE 5.2

Blumenbach's Skulls Johann Blumenbach created a classification system for humans based on the shapes of crania he collected. Here, he has sketched the four skulls representing four of his five main groups: (from top to bottom) African (*Aethiopis*), Asian or Mongoloid (*Tungusae*), Caucasoid (*Georgianae*), and American Indian (*Americani illinoici*). This scheme as applied to living humans is still prevalent in the popular perception of human variation. Biological anthropologists have long discredited this classification scheme and other classification approaches to human variation.

FIGURE 5.3

Immigrant Family To test the hypothesis that head shapes change from one generation to the next, Franz Boas studied immigrant families in America like this one, photographed ca. 1888–1912. His conclusion—that cranial proportions were both inherited and influenced by environment—showed the biological malleability of human beings, a foundational principle in modern biological anthropology.

WATCH THE VIDEO

IS RACE REAL?

digital.wwnorton.com/essanthro5

SO-CALLED RACIAL TRAITS ARE NOT CONCORDANT: RACE IS A SOCIAL CONSTRUCT AND NOT A BIOLOGICALLY MEANINGFUL CONCEPT

Single biological traits, such as cranial shape, had seemed to be a firm basis for racial categories partly because categorization is very easy when focusing on just one characteristic. What happens when human populations are grouped according to multiple characteristics? In the early 1970s, the American geneticist R. C. Lewontin tested the race concept by studying global genetic variation. If human races existed, most genetic diversity would be accounted for by them. Focusing on blood groups, serum proteins, and red blood cell enzyme variants, Lewontin found that the so-called races accounted for only about 5%–10% of the overall genetic diversity. In other words, most variation occurred *across* human populations regardless of "racial" makeup—human "races" have no taxonomic significance. Since Lewontin's study, many other genetic studies have reached the same conclusion.

Subsequent research by other scientists, including studies of wide-ranging characteristics such as genetic traits and cranial morphology, have all shown the same thing: so-called races account for a very small amount of biological variation. Multiple biological traits do not lead to clear-cut racial classifications because traits simply do not agree in their frequency or distribution. One trait might cut across human populations in one way, but another trait cuts across them in another way.

Yet, most Americans view differences in skin pigmentation and other phenotypes as representing fundamental, categorical differences between peoples in the United States and elsewhere around the world. American biological anthropologist Rachel Caspari argues that this typological thinking, while it does not characterize human variation, persists both in modern society and across a range of sciences. She suggests that racial or typological ways of thinking may be a natural (although flawed), "built-in" mental construct for organizing the variation that we see around us. Thus, categorical thinking about variation that is not, in fact, categorical may be hardwired into all of our brains. Simply, though, categories of discrete races are not accurate representations of human biological variation.

HUMAN VARIATION: GEOGRAPHIC CLINES, NOT RACIAL CATEGORIES

If race is not a valid way to account for human diversity, then how do we speak meaningfully about the enormous range of variation in all kinds of human characteristics around the globe? One important finding from biological anthropologists' studies of human variation is that specific biological traits generally follow a geographic continuum, also called a **cline**. Think, for example, of two patterns discussed in chapter 4: first, the frequencies of type B blood changing gradually from eastern Asia to far-western Europe (see Figure 4.31 in chapter 4); second, the frequency of the human gene that causes the disorder sickle-cell anemia, hemoglobin *S*, increasing in areas where the parasitic disease malaria is endemic and decreasing (to nearly zero) in areas where malaria is not endemic (see Figure 4.22 in chapter 4). Because living humans are a single, geographically diverse species, their variation is continuously distributed in ways like these—along various geographic continuums—rather than grouped in discrete categories.

Among the best examples of clinal variation are highly visible phenotypes such as skin pigmentations of living people. From equatorial to higher latitudes, skin color changes in a gradient from dark to light. Exceptions to this pattern exist, such as the relatively dark skin of Native Americans in the Canadian Arctic, but the single strongest factor in determining skin pigmentation is exposure to ultraviolet radiation (see "Solar Radiation and Skin Color" later in this chapter).

One of the most important outcomes of research on human variation at all levels shows that human variation cannot be subdivided into racial categories. As said best by the biological anthropologist Frank B. Livingstone, "There are no races, there are only clines." Human variation can be understood far more meaningfully in terms of **life history**, the biology of growth and development in an evolutionary context.

5.2 Life History: Growth and Development

Various factors, genetic and external, influence the human body's growth (increase in size) and development (progression from immaturity to maturity). DNA provides a blueprint that schedules growth, but environment and external events very much influence the actual development from conception through death.

THE GROWTH CYCLE: CONCEPTION THROUGH ADULTHOOD

The bodies of large mammals such as adult humans are made of more than 10 trillion cells, which are produced over the course of about 2^{38} mitoses (or cell divisions; see "Mitosis: Production of Identical Somatic Cells" in chapter 3). Mitoses result in all the various types of tissues (bone, blood, and muscle, for example) and organs (brain, stomach, heart, and so on), and they begin from the moment of fertilization (**Figure 5.4**). The human growth cycle, from embryo to fetus to child to adult, consists of three stages:

1. The **prenatal stage**, which includes the three periods, or trimesters, of pregnancy and ends with birth (40 weeks after conception)

cline A gradual change in a phenotypic characteristic from one geographic population to the next.

prenatal stage The first stage of life, beginning with the zygote in utero, terminating with birth, and involving multiple mitotic events and the differentiation of the body into the appropriate segments and regions.

FIGURE 5.4

Fertilization Growth, in the form of mitoses that result in tissues, begins with the fertilization of an egg by a sperm. Of the many human sperm pictured here, only one will penetrate the ovum's outer layers.

postnatal stage The second stage of life, beginning with birth, terminating with the shift to the adult stage, and involving substantial increases in height, weight, and brain growth and development.

lactation The production and secretion of milk from a female mammal's mammary glands, providing a food source to the female's young.

adult stage The third stage of life, involving the reproductive years and senescence.

stressors Factors that can cause stress in an organism, potentially affecting the body's proper functioning and its homeostasis.

intrauterine Within the uterus.

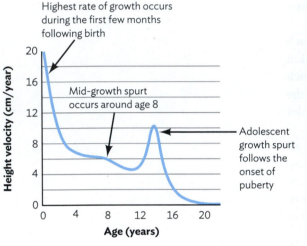

Highest rate of growth occurs during the first few months following birth

Mid-growth spurt occurs around age 8

Adolescent growth spurt follows the onset of puberty

FIGURE 5.5

Human Growth Curve During postnatal life, a human grows at different rates. The highest rate of growth (on this graph, 20 cm, or 7.9 in, per year) occurs during the first few months following birth. Growth velocity decreases throughout the rest of life, apart from a mid-growth spurt (here, approximately 6 cm, or 2.4 in, per year) around age 8 and an adolescent growth spurt (10 cm, or 3.9 in, per year) following the onset of puberty.

FIGURE 5.6

Deciduous Teeth Deciduous teeth, or baby teeth, begin to form in the fetus and erupt shortly after birth.

2. The **postnatal stage**, which includes the *neonatal* period (about the first month), *infancy* (the second month to the end of **lactation**, usually by the end of the third year), *childhood* (ages 3–7, generally postweaning), the *juvenile* period (ages 7–10 for girls and 7–12 for boys), *puberty* (days to weeks at the end of the juvenile years), and *adolescence* (5–10 years after puberty)
3. The **adult stage**, which includes the reproductive period (from about age 20 to the end of the childbearing years, usually by age 50 for women and later for men) and *senescence* (the period of time after the childbearing years)

PRENATAL STAGE: SENSITIVE TO ENVIRONMENTAL STRESS, PREDICTIVE OF ADULT HEALTH

In humans, the prenatal stage, or pregnancy, lasts 40 weeks. In the first trimester, or 3-month period, the fertilized ovum multiplies into millions of cells. Distinctive cell groupings first represent different kinds of tissues, then give rise to the tissues, the organs, the brain, and the various physiological systems. By the end of the second month, the embryo is about 2.5 cm (1 in) long but is recognizably human. Because growth and development are at their most dynamic during this trimester, the embryo is highly susceptible to disruption and disease caused by mutation or environmental factors. Specific **stressors**, or potentially harmful agents, include the mother's smoking, consuming alcohol, taking drugs, and providing inadequate nutrition.

In the second trimester, the fetus mainly grows longer, from about 20.3 cm (8 in) at the end of the first month of this trimester to about 35.6 cm (14 in), or three-quarters the length of an average newborn.

The third trimester involves rapid weight growth and organ development. Humans are unique among primates in having a very high percentage of body fat. This general pattern of humans producing fat babies may be related to the large brain of *Homo sapiens*, suggesting that the fat serves as a kind of energy "bank" or reserve supporting the high energy needs of the developing brain. During the final month, the lungs develop and most reflexes become fully coordinated. The fetus's wide range of movement includes the ability to grasp and to respond to light, sound, and touch.

This trimester culminates in birth, the profoundly stressful transition from the **intrauterine** environment to the external environment. Half of all neonatal deaths occur during the first 24 hours after birth. Most of these deaths are caused by low birth weight (less than 2.5 kg, or 5.5 lb), which is generally linked to one or a combination of multiple stressors, such as maternal malnutrition, smoking, and alcohol consumption. Because individuals of low socioeconomic status tend to be exposed to environmental stresses, their children are prone to low birth weights and early deaths. A poor intrauterine environment predisposes a person to develop specific diseases later in life.

POSTNATAL STAGE: THE MATURING BRAIN, PREPARING FOR ADULTHOOD

Each of the six postnatal periods has a different **growth velocity**, or rate of growth per year (**Figure 5.5**). During infancy, the period of most rapid growth, the **deciduous** (or primary) **dentition** erupts through the gums (**Figure 5.6**). By the time an infant has completed weaning—when the infant shifts from consuming only milk provided

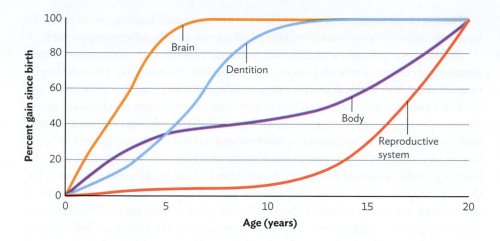

FIGURE 5.7

Growth Curves of Body Tissues This chart shows the varying growth curves of the brain, body, dentition, and reproductive system in humans. The brain grows the fastest, reaching full cognitive development around age 6 years. In fact, humans have such a large brain that much of it needs to be attained after birth; if the brain reached full size before birth, women would not be able to pass newborns' heads through their pelvic regions. Dentition has the next highest growth velocity (see Figures 5.6 and 5.8). The body grows more slowly and continues to grow until as late as 24 or 25 years of age. The reproductive system does not begin substantial growth and development until the onset of puberty, but it reaches completion around age 15–16 for girls.

by the mother to consuming external foods—all 20 deciduous teeth have erupted. The time of weaning varies, but the process is often finished by the end of the second or third year. **Motor skills** such as walking and running develop during the first 2 years. **Cognitive abilities** also progress rapidly during this time, reflecting the very rapid growth and development of the brain during infancy (**Figure 5.7**).

During childhood (ages 3–7), general growth levels off, but the still rapidly growing brain requires the child to have a diet rich in fats, protein, and energy. The child learns behaviors important to later survival but still depends on adults for food and other resources. Because the child's dentition and digestive system are immature, adults sometimes prepare food that is soft and easy to chew. By age 2, however, children normally can consume most adult foods.

By about age 6, permanent teeth begin to replace primary teeth, and brain growth is completed (**Figure 5.8**). These hallmark developmental events occur nearly simultaneously, as they do in many other primate species. The eruption of the first permanent molar signals the ability to eat adult food, and very high nutritional requirements cease once the brain reaches its final weight.

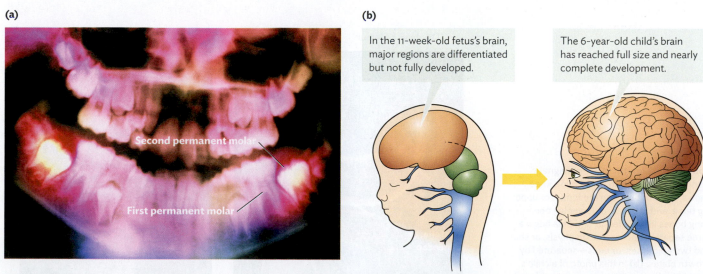

(a)

(b)

In the 11-week-old fetus's brain, major regions are differentiated but not fully developed.

The 6-year-old child's brain has reached full size and nearly complete development.

FIGURE 5.8

Molar Eruption and Brain Development (a) Permanent teeth form during the early years of life and begin to erupt around age 6. In this X-ray image, the first permanent molars, called the 6-year molars, have erupted. The second permanent molars, the 12-year molars, are still forming and will not erupt for another 6 years. The crowded anterior dentition, or front teeth, includes the deciduous teeth and new permanent teeth waiting to erupt and take their places. **(b)** Brain growth and development finish at around the same time as the full eruption of the first permanent molar.

During the juvenile years, growth slows. Although much learning occurs in childhood, the full-size brain makes formalized education and social learning possible.

Adolescence presents a number of profound biological developments. Sexual maturation commences with puberty, and its visible characteristics are the beginning of breast development and menstruation (**menarche**) in girls, the deepening of the voice and emergence of facial hair in boys, the development of secondary sexual characteristics (changes to genitals), and **sexual dimorphism** of girls' and boys' body sizes. Unlike other primates, humans experience increased growth velocity during this time. When nutrition is adequate and stressors are minimal, the adolescent growth spurt can add as much as 8.9 cm (3.5 in) to boys and somewhat less than 7.6 cm (3 in) to girls. Boys complete their growth later than girls, whose growth spurts peak earlier than those of boys. Growth spurts either do not happen or are minimized in very highly stressed populations, such as the Quechua Indians, who live at high altitudes in Peru and suffer from cold, overwork, malnutrition, and hypoxia (a condition discussed later in this chapter; see "High Altitude and Access to Oxygen").

Prior to the completion of growth, the ends of the long bones—the humerus, radius, and ulna in the arm and the femur, tibia, and fibula in the leg—are separate growth centers called **epiphyses**. The epiphyses are separated from the main bone shafts, or **diaphyses**, by growth plates containing cells that produce **nonmineralized** bone substance. As long as bone cells are producing bone substance and the epiphyses remain unfused, the long bones will continue to grow. The bones continually grow in width throughout life, but once the epiphyses have fused to the diaphyses, the growth in length stops and the individual's height is set (**Figure 5.9**).

Biologically, adulthood is signaled by the completion of sexual maturity, the reaching of full height, and the fusion of the epiphyses. The social maturity and behavioral maturity associated with adulthood, however, are difficult to define. In fact, sociologists and social psychologists argue that social maturity is a lifelong process, developing earlier in some biologically mature individuals than in others.

While bone growth and epiphyseal fusion are influenced by genes and sex hormones (androgens and estrogens), the amount of growth and the terminal length

epiphyses The end portions of long bones; once they fuse to the diaphyses, the bones stop growing longer.

diaphyses The main midsection, or shaft, portions of long bones; each diaphysis contains a medullary cavity.

nonmineralized (bone) Bone reduced to its organic component.

FIGURE 5.9

Long-Bone Growth **(a)** This magnetic resonance image (MRI) of a child's knee shows the joint between the femur, or upper leg bone, and the tibia, or lower leg bone. Long bones like the femur and tibia begin as three separate bones—the diaphysis, or shaft, and two epiphyses, or ends—separated by growth plates. **(b)** In this photo of a child's knee joint, the epiphyses have not yet fused to the diaphyses. The line of union may be visible for several years after the attachment occurs; when it eventually disappears, the bone appears as a single element.

Diaphysis of femur   Epiphysis of femur

Growth plate

Patella, or kneecap

Epiphysis of tibia   Diaphysis of tibia

(a)   (b)

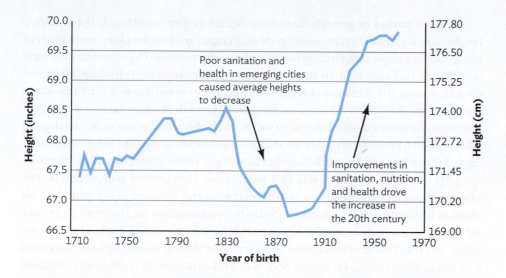

FIGURE 5.10

Changes in Height Beginning in the 1700s, the heights of soldiers, students, and slaves were routinely collected for identification or registration purposes. By combining these data with subsequent figures, Costa and Steckel discovered patterns of increase and decline in the heights of American-born males of European descent. From about 171.45 cm (67.5 in) in the early 1700s, heights rose to about 174 cm (68.5 in) around 1830, then sharply declined by 5.1 cm (2 in) over the next 50 years. After the late 1800s, heights increased by roughly 7.5 cm, or 3 in, during the twentieth century. Simply put, the extraordinarily poor sanitation and health conditions in nineteenth-century cities resulted in increased disease, stress, and attenuated growth. The subsequent increase in Americans' heights reflected improvements in sanitation, nutrition, and health.

of bones are strongly affected by environmental factors, especially by nutrition and general health. Negative environmental effects in the present and in the historical past, such as downturns in nutrition, have been documented worldwide. The American economic historians Dora Costa and Richard Steckel have shown, for example, that between 1710 and 1970, substantial changes occurred in the heights of American males of European descent (**Figure 5.10**). Initially, a gradual increase in heights likely reflected improved living conditions and food availability. The sharp decline in heights around 1830 coincided with the urbanization trend. As people moved from rural, agricultural settings to overly crowded cities, they were exposed to more diseases that were easily passed from person to person. In addition, high population densities caused great accumulations of garbage and waste, which may have polluted water supplies and thus exposed people to more bacteria, viruses, and parasites that caused infection and disease. As living conditions improved at the beginning of the twentieth century, as trash removal became mandatory and sewers were constructed, height increased. Today, Americans' heights are among the greatest in the country's history, thanks to reliable food supplies, unpolluted water, and access to medical care.

This twentieth-century trend of increasing tallness, sometimes called a **secular trend**, has been noted in many other countries as well. Multiple factors have contributed to particular causes from place to place, but the collective increase in height within many societies across the world has resulted from improvements in disease control and nutrition over the last several decades. In wealthy nations, the increase in height has now come to a stop or slowed considerably, most likely because growth has reached its genetic limit. Conversely, in many less wealthy (and thus less healthy) nations, growth potential has not been reached, and growth periods remain comparatively slow. As a result, members of many populations around the world are relatively short-statured during the years of growth and development and remain so upon reaching adulthood. The growth and development of males, prenatally and postnatally, are more sensitive to environmental stressors than are the growth and development of females. Scientists who study human biology have found much evidence of these differences in developing countries, but they have not been able to explain the mechanisms at work. In terms of evolution, it would make sense for females to have developed buffers from stress because females' roles in reproduction, including pregnancy and lactation, are much more demanding than the roles of males.

secular trend A phenotypic change over time, due to multiple factors; such trends can be positive (e.g., increased height) or negative (e.g., decreased height).

When a period of growth disruption occurs before adulthood, the resulting height deficit can later on be made up through rapid growth. In a long-term study of the Turkana people in Kenya, growth has been documented to continue into early adulthood. Turkana children tend to be shorter than American children. However, growth among the Turkana extends well into their twenties, and Turkana adults are as tall as American adults. Few long-term growth studies have been done of nutritionally stressed populations, so we do not know about many other settings in which growth extends into adulthood. But by and large, in areas of the world experiencing nutritional stress, adults are short, owing to lifelong nutritional deprivation.

This is not to say, however, that heights are determined completely by the environment. In fact, height is highly heritable, and in some geographic regions there is likely a selective advantage to body size variation. In the central African rainforests, for example, small body size has long been observed. Earlier hypotheses suggested that this trait was due to populations in the region having been subjected to a range of stressors, including poor diet and exposure to a range of infectious diseases, such as hepatitis B and hepatitis C. Recent genomic analysis, however, has revealed evidence of natural selection operating on a region of chromosome 8 associated with body height. This suggests that there is a selective advantage for short stature in this geographic region. The finding makes clear that the forces of evolution, including natural selection, can be regionally specific.

ADULT STAGE: AGING AND SENESCENCE

Throughout life, the body continually grows and develops—it is dynamic. By adulthood, its basic structure has been formed, so during this period most growth and development involves the replacement of cells and of tissues. In fact, over a person's lifetime nearly every cell and tissue in the body is replaced at least once every 7 years. Indeed, your body is a very different one now from the body you had 10 years ago.

Aging basically means "becoming older," but it refers collectively to various social, cultural, biological, and behavioral events that occur over a lifetime yet do not by themselves increase the probability of death. **Senescence**, which accompanies aging, is a biological process characterized by a reduction in **homeostasis**, the body's ability to keep its organs and its physiological systems stable in the face of environmental stress. Senescing persons are increasingly susceptible to stress and death and have a decreased capacity to reproduce. For example, older adults produce less body heat than do younger adults and hence are more uncomfortable in cold temperatures.

Whereas the previous life stages are generally predictable in their timing (mostly due to genetic programming), the chronology of senescence is highly variable but occurs in midlife. **Menopause**, the loss of ovarian function, is a key element of female senescence, marking the end of the reproductive phase and the end of childbearing. As a human biological universal, menopause usually occurs by age 50, but it varies by several years in different populations. Male senescence is different in that men normally produce sperm well into their seventies and eighties. However, the number of well-formed sperm and their motility decline by half after age 70. Male and female individuals older than 70 years, having lived through senescence, are considered elderly. These patterns of aging and senescence are unique to humans. That is, reproductive senescence is extremely rare in nonhuman primates. For all but a few species of nonhuman primates, fertility occurs throughout the adult life span. Where reproductive senescence has been found in nonhuman primates, it is present in very few individuals. American primatologist Susan Alberts and her

aging The process of maturation.

senescence An organism's biological changes in later adulthood.

homeostasis The maintenance of the internal environment of an organism within an acceptable range.

menopause The cessation of the menstrual cycle, signifying the end of a female's ability to bear children.

(a)

(b)

Grayish areas indicate porous bone mass

FIGURE 5.11

Osteoporosis **(a)** As this graph shows, men and women reach their maximum bone mass around age 30. **(b)** The loss of bone mass becomes evident in the grayish areas of X-rays (arrows). The normal bone mass would be solid white.

research team found that just a few elderly individuals in three primate taxanomic groups were not fertile at the time of death: baboons, blue monkeys, and sifakas.

As discussed in chapter 3, bone loss is an effect of senescence that is universal in humans: after age 40, humans suffer increased bone porosity and reduction in bone mass. The increased susceptibility to bone fracture that comes with this loss is called **osteoporosis (Figure 5.11)**. In extreme cases, osteoporosis can weaken bone to the point that it easily fractures under small amounts of stress. This fragile nature commonly leads to fractures, such as broken hips, or to "compression" fractures of vertebrae, in which the bone simply cannot support the normal body weight and collapses. The collapse of several vertebrae can give the person a hunchback. Far more common in women than in men—because a loss of the hormone estrogen is linked to bone loss—osteoporosis shows less age variation than menopause does. Other factors that can predispose people to this condition are smoking, chronic diseases, and certain medications.

For every stage—from conception through senescence—humans (and other primates) have evolved strategies for enhancing their survival and reproductive potential, the prime movers of natural selection. In the next subsection, we will examine behaviors that are central to this adaptive success.

osteoporosis The loss of bone mass, often due to age, causing the bones to become porous, brittle, and easily fractured.

EVOLUTION OF HUMAN LIFE HISTORY: FOOD, SEX, AND STRATEGIES FOR SURVIVAL AND REPRODUCTION

Two behaviors make possible the survival and adaptive success of humans and other primates: acquisition of food and reproduction. Unlike the other primates, humans acquire food and reproduce within the contexts of culture and society. For example, humans have created social institutions—especially kinship and marriage—and beliefs and rules supporting these institutions. Anthropologists are keenly interested in the relations between humans' sociocultural behaviors and the evolution of our unique life history, especially in comparison with other primates' life histories.

Prolonged Childhood: Fat-Bodied Moms and Their Big-Brained Babies Humans have a relatively prolonged childhood. However, within this life period, the spans of infancy and lactation are quite short. The mother's brief, intensive child care allows her, theoretically, to have more births and to invest her resources among all her children.

The cost of this fertility advantage is the large amount of food the mother must provide for her children. The energy demands of the children's maturing brains require that this food be highly nutritious: rich in fats, protein, and energy. For only the first several years of a child's postnatal life can the mother provide these resources, via lactation, from her own stored body fats and other nutrients. Even during this period, a mother will begin to supplement the child's diet with other solids (at around age 4–6 months).

Grandmothering: Part of Human Adaptive Success Humans are also the only primates that experience prolonged postmenopausal survival at the other end of the life history. Some apes have a postmenopausal period, but it is briefer than that of humans. Ethnographic evidence from cultures around the world shows that postmenopausal

CONCEPT CHECK

Life History Stages in Humans: Prenatal, Postnatal, and Adult

A life history is the biological story—from conception to death—of an individual, a population, or a species. A life history provides insight into how energy is allocated to key events, such as reproduction, brain growth, and the care of offspring. It also sheds light on the interactions between genes and environment at crucial stages.

STAGE	PERIOD	TIMING AND CHARACTERISTICS
Prenatal	First trimester	Fertilization to 12th week; embryo development; organ development
	Second trimester	Fourth through sixth lunar months; rapid growth in length
	Third trimester	Seventh month to birth; rapid growth in weight and organ development
Postnatal	Neonatal	Birth to 28 days; first exposure to extrauterine environment; most rapid postnatal growth and development
	Infancy	Second month to 36 months; rapid growth; breastfeeding; deciduous tooth development; other milestones (e.g., walking); weaning at end of period
	Childhood	3–7 years; moderate growth; eruption of first permanent molar; completion of brain growth
	Juvenile	7–10 years (girls), 7–12 years (boys); slower growth; self-feeding; cognitive transition in learning and increased ability to learn
	Puberty	Days to a few weeks at end of juvenile years; activation of sexual development; marked increase in secretion of sex hormones
	Adolescence	5- to 10-year period after puberty; growth spurt (earlier in girls than in boys); completion of permanent dental development and eruption; development of secondary sex characteristics; interest in adult social, sexual, and economic behaviors
Adult	Reproductive period	20 years to end of reproductive years; stability in physiology, behavior, and cognition; menopause in women, commencing at about age 50
	Senescence	End of reproductive years to death; decline in function of many tissues and organs; homeostasis more easily disrupted than in earlier years; grandmother social behaviors

Source: Adapted from Table 11.1 in B. Bogin and B. H. Smith. 2012. Evolution of the human life cycle. Pp. 515–586 in S. Stinson, B. Bogin, and D. O'Rourke, eds. *Human Biology: An Evolutionary and Biocultural Perspective*, 2nd ed. Hoboken, NJ: Wiley-Blackwell.

FIGURE 5.12

Grandmothering Postmenopausal women are often caregivers to children, frequently to their grandchildren. As more and more families have both parents working, child care by grandparents, and by grandmothers in particular, has become especially important.

women, most often grandmothers, play important roles in caring for children, provisioning food to children, and providing essential information about the world to various members of their social groups (**Figure 5.12**). Because older people can become key repositories of knowledge about culture and society, longevity may have a selective advantage in humans but not in other primates.

5.3 Adaptation: Meeting the Challenges of Living

Humans adjust remarkably well to new conditions and to challenges. As in other organisms, such adaptations—functional responses within particular environmental contexts—occur at four different levels. *Genetic* adaptation, as discussed in previous chapters, occurs at the population level via natural selection. Here, the biological change is inherited and is not reversible in a person (for example, someone with sickle-cell anemia). *Developmental* (or *ontogenetic*) adaptation occurs at the level of the individual during a critical period of growth and development, childhood especially. The capacity to make the change is inherited, but the change is not inherited and is not reversible. For example, children living at high altitudes develop greater chest size prior to reaching adulthood than do children living at low altitudes. The expanded chest reflects the need for increased lung capacity in settings where less oxygen is available (discussed further later; see "High Altitude and Access to Oxygen"). *Acclimatization* (or *physiological* adaptation) also occurs at the individual level, but unlike developmental adaptation it can occur anytime during a person's life. In this kind of adaptation, the change is not inherited and can be reversed. For example, exposure to sunlight for extended periods of time results in tanning (also discussed further later; see "Solar Radiation and Skin Color"). Lastly, *cultural* (or *behavioral*) adaptation involves the use of material culture to make living possible in certain settings. For example, wearing insulated clothing or living in warmed interiors of built structures (e.g., our homes) keeps people from freezing in extreme cold in these artificial, culturally determined circumstances.

The American biological anthropologist Roberto Frisancho applies the general term **functional adaptations** to the biological adjustments that occur within the individual's lifetime (that is, developmental adaptations and acclimatizations). Most functional adaptations are associated with extreme environmental conditions, such as heat, cold, high altitude, and heavy workload. Some of these conditions appear to have brought about genetic changes in humans. That is, over hundreds of generations humans have adapted to settings in which specific attributes enhance the potential for survival and reproduction. Skin pigmentation, for example, is related genetically to solar radiation exposure.

All adaptations have one purpose: *maintenance of internal homeostasis,* or maintenance of the normal functioning of all organs and physiological systems. Not to maintain homeostasis in body temperature, for example, or in oxygen accessibility or in strength of the bones of the skeleton has severe consequences for the individual, including work impairment and loss of productivity, decline in quality of life, and even death. The maintenance of homeostasis involves all levels of any organism's biology, from biochemical pathways to cells, tissues, organs, and ultimately the entire organism.

To determine how humans maintain internal homeostasis, anthropologists use indirect approaches and direct ones. *Indirect* approaches involve the study of populations in their natural environments, such as the Quechua Indians living in highland Peru or the Inuit living in Greenland. The observation of living populations as they engage in various activities in various settings provides great insight into functional adaptations, helping establish associations between specific biological attributes and environmental settings or circumstances. *Direct* approaches, by contrast, involve the replication of environmental conditions and of human responses to these conditions. In the course of such experiments, anthropologists determine cause-and-effect relationships, such as body response to temperature extremes.

THE ROLE OF CLIMATE IN HUMAN ADAPTATION: LIVING ON THE MARGINS

Heat Stress and Thermoregulation Like all other mammals, humans are **homeothermic**, meaning that they maintain a constant body temperature. A constant core temperature is essential for normal physiology, including brain function, limb function, and general body mobility. Humans can tolerate a body temperature higher than their normal 98.6 °F, but a body temperature above 104–107 °F for an extended period leads to organ failure and eventually death. Extremely hot weather can thus result in many deaths, such as in the summer of 2003, when at least 35,000 and perhaps as many as 50,000 people died in Europe during one of the hottest seasons ever recorded. Severe heat stress is experienced mostly in tropical settings, where it is hot much of the year, and during hot spells in temperate regions.

A body experiencing heat stress attempts to rid itself of internally and externally derived heat sources. Internal heat is produced by the body's metabolism, especially during activities involving movement, such as physical labor, walking, and running. External heat is derived from the air temperature. The initial physiological response to an elevated temperature is **vasodilation**, the dilation (expansion) of the blood vessels near the body's surface. By increasing the diameter of blood vessels, the body is able to move more blood (and associated heat) away from the body's core to the body's surface. The red face of a person who is in a hot environment is the visible expression of vasodilation.

Sweating is another response to heat. Sweat is mostly water produced by the eccrine glands, which are located over the entire body's surface. Evaporation of the thin layer of water on the skin results in cooling of the surface. Humans can sweat a remarkably high volume of water, and this physiological process is central to humans' long-term functional adaptation to heat.

Sweating is less effective in areas of the body having a dense hair cover than in areas of the body having little or no hair. This relationship suggests that sweating evolved as a thermoregulatory adaptation in association with the general loss of body hair. Humans' loss of body hair is unique among the primates, indicating that the thermoregulatory adaptation of hair loss and sweating occurred in human evolution only.

Humans have a strong capacity to adapt to excessive heat. Individuals who have not often experienced such heat are less able to conduct heat away from their cores and less able to sweat than are individuals living in hot climates. Individuals exposed for the first time to a hot climate, however, rapidly adjust over a period of 10–14 days. This adjustment involves a lowering of the body's core temperature, a lowering of the threshold for when vasodilation and sweating begin, and a reduction of the heart rate and metabolic rate. Overall, women are less able to tolerate heat than are men, in part due to a relatively reduced ability to move blood to the skin through vasodilation and the presence of more body fat.

Human populations who have lived in hot climates for most of their history—such as native equatorial Africans and South Americans—have the same number of sweat glands as that of other populations. However, heat-adapted populations sweat less and perform their jobs and other physical functions better in conditions involving excessive heat than do non-heat-adapted populations.

Body Shape and Adaptation to Heat Stress The relationship between body shape and temperature adaptation was first described in the 1800s by a combination of two biogeographic rules, one developed by the German biologist Carl Bergmann (1814–1865) and the other developed by the American zoologist Joel Allen (1838–1921). **Bergmann's rule** states that heat-adapted mammal populations will have smaller bodies than those of cold-adapted mammal populations. Relative to body volume, small bodies have more surface area, facilitating more rapid heat dissipation. Conversely, large bodies have less surface area relative to body volume, thus conserving heat in cold climates (**Figure 5.13**). Consequently, human populations adapted to hot climates tend to have small and narrow bodies (discussed further in chapter 12). **Allen's rule** states that heat-adapted mammal populations will have long limbs, which maximize the body's surface area and thus promote heat dissipation, whereas cold-adapted mammal populations will have short limbs, which minimize the body's surface area and thus promote heat conservation.

Exceptions exist to Bergmann's and Allen's rules, but by and large these rules explain variation in human shapes that goes back at least 1.5 million years. Populations living in hot climates tend to have narrow bodies and long limbs. Populations living in cold climates tend to have wide bodies and short limbs. This long-term association between body shape and climate means that body shape is mostly a genetic adaptation. However, body shape also involves childhood developmental processes that respond to climatic and other stressors, such as poor nutrition. For example, poor nutrition during early childhood can retard limb growth, especially of the forearm and lower leg, resulting in shorter arms and legs. Ultimately, then, body shape and morphology reflect both evolutionary and developmental processes.

Bergmann's rule The principle that an animal's size is heat-related; smaller bodies are adapted to hot environments, and larger bodies are adapted to cold environments.

Allen's rule The principle that an animal's limb lengths are heat-related; limbs are longer in hot environments and shorter in cold environments.

FIGURE 5.13

Bergmann's Rule This graph illustrates Carl Bergmann's biogeographic rule: as latitude increases (and temperature decreases), body breadth (as measured by bi-iliac breadth, or the maximum breadth between the pelvic bones) also increases. Bergmann's rule applies to all warm-blooded animals (including humans), which need to maintain a constant body temperature. Physically and physiologically, humans can adapt to a wide range of climates; but because humans are able to move about the Earth, human body size may not strictly adhere to the latitude at which a person is living.

hypothermia A condition in which an organism's body temperature falls below the normal range, which may lead to the loss of proper body functions and, eventually, death.

vasoconstriction The decrease in blood vessels' diameter due to the action of a nerve or of a drug; it can also occur in response to cold temperatures.

basal metabolic rate (BMR) The rate at which an organism's body, while at rest, expends energy to maintain basic bodily functions; measured by the amount of heat given off per kilogram of body weight.

Cold Stress and Thermoregulation Severe cold stress is experienced mostly in places close to Earth's magnetic poles, such as the Arctic; at altitudes higher than 3 km (roughly 10,000 ft); and during cold spells in temperate settings. **Hypothermia**, or low body temperature, occurs in excessively cold air or immersion in cold water. During the great *Titanic* disaster in 1912, many hundreds of passengers and ship's crew members escaped the sinking vessel but died from hypothermia after floating in the northern Atlantic Ocean (28 °F) for 2 hours before rescue ships arrived.

Maintaining homeostasis against cold stress involves heat conservation and heat production. The human body's first response to cold stress is **vasoconstriction**, the constriction of the blood vessels beneath the skin. Decreasing the diameter of the blood vessels reduces blood flow and heat loss from the body's core to the skin. The chief mechanism for producing heat is shivering.

Humans adapt to cold, but the adaptation includes cultural and behavioral factors, practices that societies living in extremely cold settings pass from one generation to the next. That is, people teach their children how to avoid situations involving heat loss. They teach them what clothing to wear, what kinds of shelters to build, and how to keep the interiors of shelters warm. Cold-adapted cultures also know that alcohol consumption contributes to the loss of body heat, increasing the chances of hypothermia and death.

After being exposed to survivable cold for more than a few days, humans shiver less, produce more heat, and have higher skin temperatures. Overall, adjusting to cold means becoming able to tolerate lower temperatures—simply, feeling better in the cold.

To measure heat production, anthropologists take a specific kind of measurement called the **basal metabolic rate (BMR)**. Indigenous people living in cold settings, such as the Indians at high altitudes in the Peruvian Andes, have a significantly higher BMR than that of other human populations. The Inuit are among the most studied populations on Earth, owing to their adaptation to the very cold, dry conditions in the Arctic Circle, where average winter temperatures range from –50 °F to –35 °F and even summer temperatures usually do not climb above 46 °F. In part, their high BMR is produced by their diet, which is high in animal protein and fat (about 9 calories per gram) and low in carbohydrates (about 3 calories per gram). Like most cold-adapted populations, however, the Inuit have adapted physiologically by developing a capacity for tolerating excessive cold. For example, their peripheral body temperatures, in the hands and feet, are higher than those of other peoples because of a higher rate of blood flow from the body's core to the skin.

The Inuit conform to Bergmann's and Allen's rules, having large, wide bodies and short limbs. Moreover, they have developed a technology that conserves heat: their traditional housing focuses on insulation. For example, the walls of ice-constructed "igloos" include whale-rib rafters that are covered with alternating layers of seal skin and moss. Heat conductivity from a fire built beneath the main floor of the house serves to warm cold air as it rises, which is a simple but highly efficient way to heat a small interior environment.

Solar Radiation and Skin Color One of the most profound environmental factors that humans deal with daily is solar radiation, or the sun's energy output, which plays a central role in the evolution and development of skin color (**Figure 5.14**). In daylight, skin—the largest organ and the most conspicuous feature of the human body, accounting for 15% of total body weight—is exposed to ultraviolet (UV)

(a)

Epidermis

Dermis

Sweat gland   Oil gland   Hair follicle

(b)

Epidermis

Dermis

Melanocyte

Melanosome

Keratinocytes with aggregations of small melanosomes

Lightly pigmented or untanned skin

Keratinocytes with larger, nonaggregated melanosomes

Darkly pigmented or heavily tanned skin

Keratinocytes

Lightly pigmented or untanned skin

Keratinocytes with melanin granules

Darkly pigmented or heavily tanned skin

FIGURE 5.14

Structure of Skin (a) Skin's two main layers are the *epidermis,* which is external, and the *dermis,* which is internal. The epidermis makes the skin waterproof and contains *keratinocytes,* building blocks that manufacture the protein keratin, and *melanocytes,* specialized cells that produce the skin pigment *melanin.* The dermis, a thicker layer of tissue, contains hair follicles, sweat glands, blood vessels, and oil glands. **(b)** Within melanocytes, specialized organelles called *melanosomes* synthesize melanin; skin color varies based on the amount and type of melanin in the skin. People with darker skin have greater melanin production, rather than a greater number of melanocytes or melanosomes. Melanin comes in two varieties, one that is a brown to black pigment and one that is a yellow to red pigment. Varying production of these two melanin pigments accounts for the wide range of skin color.

skin reflectance The amount of light reflected from the skin that can be measured and used to assess skin color.

radiation, a component of solar radiation. The American anthropologists Nina Jablonski and George Chaplin have shown that the best predictor of skin color, as measured by **skin reflectance**, is UV radiation exposure. That is, the darkest skin (low skin reflectance) is associated with the highest levels of UV radiation, and the lightest skin (high skin reflectance) is associated with the lowest levels of UV radiation. UV radiation is highest at noon, during the summer, at the equator, and in higher altitudes, and skin becomes darker (more pigmented) at these times and in these settings. As a result, individuals living in low latitudes or equatorial regions of the globe have some of the darkest skin pigmentation because of the more direct and prolonged UV radiation throughout the year. As latitude increases, the amount of UV radiation decreases and so, too, does the amount of **melanin** in the skin; therefore, the lightest-skinned individuals are usually in the highest latitudes. In general, populations between latitude 20° N and latitude 20° S have the darkest skin (**Figure 5.15**). On the other hand, dark-skin pigmentation is not just associated with Africa. In fact, very dark-pigmented populations extend as far east as South Asia and beyond. Moreover, populations in the African continent possess some of the most diverse phenotypic variation in skin pigmentation globally, ranging from very light to very dark. This variation is due to natural selection, but also gene flow, representing an enormous amount of population migration, a hallmark feature of human evolution generally.

melanin A brown pigment that determines the darkness or lightness of a human's skin color due to its concentration in the skin.

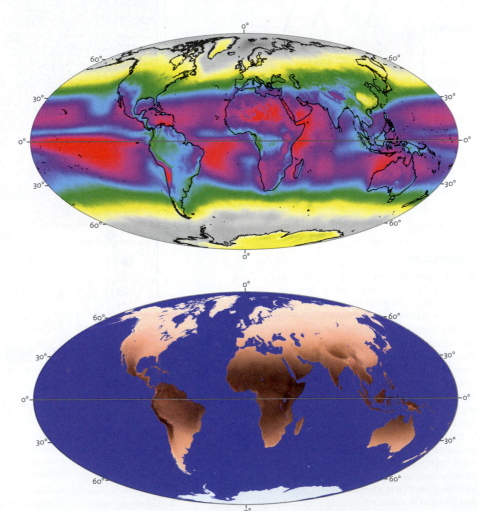

FIGURE 5.15

Skin Color Variation Humans inherit a certain amount of pigmentation, but exposure to solar radiation can alter skin color dramatically. Because melanin provides a protective barrier against UV radiation, the production of more melanin is an adaptation to areas with greater amounts of UV radiation. These maps show (top) how solar radiation shifts from the highest levels near the equator to the lowest levels at the poles and (bottom) how skin color varies from the darkest pigmentation at the equator to the lightest pigmentation at the poles.

When first exposed to UV radiation, light skin reddens—the condition commonly called *sunburn*. With ongoing exposure, the **melanocytes** increase the number and size of melanin granules. In addition, the outer layer of the epidermis thickens. This darkening—that is, tanning—and thickening serves to retard penetration of the epidermis and dermis by UV radiation, protecting the individual from sunburn and possibly cancer. Because melanin is a natural sunscreen, individuals with high melanin content receive the most protection. Thus, people with dark skin, such as in equatorial Africa, are able to tolerate more exposure to the sun than are those with light skin. Dark-skinned people have a **sun protection factor (SPF)** of 10–15; light-skinned people have an SPF of between 2 and 3. Around the world, populations with the most melanin have the fewest skin cancers and malignant melanomas. However, these effects occur largely during or after the late reproductive years, suggesting that skin cancer is not an element of natural selection.

Solar Radiation and Vitamin D Synthesis The body needs UV radiation for the synthesis of vitamin D, a steroid hormone that regulates calcium absorption and mineralization of the skeleton. Today, people obtain some vitamin D through fortified foods and by eating fatty fish such as salmon, but most vitamin D is produced in the skin. UV radiation in the form of UV photons penetrates the skin and is absorbed by a cholesterol-like substance, 7-dehydrocholesterol, in the epidermis (keratinocytes) and dermis (fibroblasts) layers (see Figure 5.14). This process produces a previtamin D that eventually converts to vitamin D, which is released from the skin and transported via the circulatory system to the liver and kidneys. There, more chemical reactions produce the active form of vitamin D. Without this form, the bones do not mineralize properly, resulting in a condition called *rickets* in children and *osteomalacia* in adults (**Figure 5.16**).

In addition to lower-limb deformation, a telltale sign of rickets in children is malformed pelvic bones. Both conditions result when poorly developed bone is unable to withstand the forces of body weight. Women who, as children, had severe enough rickets to affect the pelvic bones have trouble giving birth because the space for the fetus's passage during birth is restricted. Because a key element of natural selection is a greater number of births, this decreased reproductive capacity means that the trait—malformed pelvic bones caused by rickets—is disadvantageous.

Melanin, the primary influence on vitamin D synthesis, can be advantageous or disadvantageous. That is, because melanin provides protection from solar radiation, substantial amounts of this pigment can inhibit vitamin D production. As a result, at high latitudes where there is less UV radiation, lighter skin, with less melanin, is favorable because it allows more solar radiation to be absorbed, enabling vitamin D production. In fact, as world populations today reveal, there is a strong correlation between the distance of a population from the equator and the degree of skin pigmentation: the closer a population is to the equator, the darker the skin pigmentation. Simply, skin needs to be dark enough to protect from UV radiation but light enough to allow solar radiation sufficient for vitamin D production.

The American physiologist William Loomis has hypothesized that as human ancestors moved out of Africa into the more northerly latitudes of Europe and elsewhere, their dark skin would not have produced enough vitamin D to bring about calcium absorption and skeletal development. Therefore, in those latitudes, natural selection strongly favored alleles for light skin. This scenario suggests that prior to 1 mya, all of our ancestors lived in what is now Africa and that their skin was pigmented highly so that it would block dangerous UV radiation.

melanocytes Melanin-producing cells located in the skin's epidermis.

sun protection factor (SPF) The rating calculated by comparing the length of time needed for protected skin to burn to the length of time needed for unprotected skin to burn.

FIGURE 5.16

Rickets Photographed in Hungary in 1895, these children are suffering from rickets, a disorder in which poorly mineralized bones, especially the weight-bearing leg bones, become soft, are prone to fracture, and can warp or bow. Rickets was especially prevalent in the 1800s in Europe and America. In urban settings in particular, indoor work and air pollution decreased access to sunlight and exposure to UV radiation.

Solar Radiation and Folate Protection Support for the evolution of skin pigmentation in humans is provided by the fundamental role of melanin in the protection of stored folate (folic acid) in our bodies. New research shows that folate is essential for the synthesis and repair of DNA and therefore directly affects cell division and homeostasis. Even very tiny deficiencies of folate have been linked to a range of health issues, including neural tube defects whereby the brain or spinal cord does not form properly, cleft palate, pregnancy loss, and reduced sperm production. Folate levels decline dramatically with exposure to high and prolonged levels of UV radiation. However, skin color and melanin production are key elements in protecting the body from folate depletion. Thus, natural selection would have played a key role in maintaining relatively dark skin in regions of the world with high UV-radiation exposure.

High Altitude and Access to Oxygen At high altitudes, generally defined as greater than 3,000 m (roughly 10,000 ft) above sea level, a fall in barometric pressure reduces the number of oxygen molecules. The primary environmental stress in such places is **hypoxia**, the condition in which body tissues receive insufficient amounts of oxygen (**Figure 5.17**). Secondary stresses include high UV radiation, cold, wind, nutritional deprivation, and the rigors of living in highly variable, generally rugged terrain.

The severity of hypoxia increases as a person moves higher, and the associated risk increases because all body tissues and physiological processes require an uninterrupted oxygen supply. Hypoxia results in mountain sickness, with headache, nausea, loss of appetite, fatigue, and breathlessness occurring at about 2,400 m (roughly 8,000 ft) during rest and about 1,900 m (roughly 6,500 ft) during physical activity. For some individuals living at sea level or in prehypoxic conditions who travel to high altitudes or otherwise experience hypoxia, mountain sickness becomes a life-threatening condition. For most people, the symptoms disappear within the first few days of exposure as the body begins to more efficiently use the

hypoxia A condition characterized by less than the usual sea-level amount of oxygen in the air or in the body.

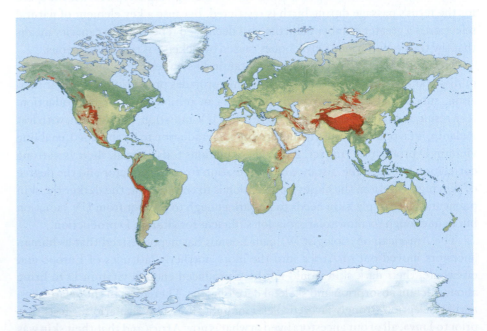

FIGURE 5.17

High Altitudes As this map shows, each continent, except for Australia and Antarctica, has at least one high-altitude area (shaded in red). A lack of oxygen is among the conditions to which humans must adapt at high altitudes.

FIGURE 5.18

Tibetan Farmers Tibetan farmers live in high-altitude areas and are shorter than Tibetans living in lowlands. Among the farmers' physiological adaptations to their environment are large lungs, better lung function, and higher oxygen saturation in arteries.

reduced amounts of oxygen in the air and homeostasis is restored. Extra red blood cells and oxygen-saturated hemoglobin are produced. The hemoglobin transports oxygen to body tissues, while an expansion in the diameter of arteries and of veins allows increased blood flow and increased access to oxygen.

Additional physiological changes represent a long-term response to hypoxia. A person who moves to the high-altitude settings of the Himalayas, for example, will function better there over time. A young child who moves there will, through the process of growth, develop greater lung volume and the ability to use oxygen more efficiently. Human populations who have lived at high altitudes for many generations—such as those in the Peruvian Andes—have larger chest cavities than those of populations at low altitudes, reflecting the high-altitude populations' inherited increases in lung volume. However, these populations are generally shorter than their low-altitude counterparts. Widespread growth retardation results from the increased energy required to live in cold environments with little oxygen and poor nutrition. But some biological attributes associated with living at high altitudes may offer selective advantages. For example, the American biological anthropologist Cynthia Beall and colleagues have found that Tibetan women with alleles for high oxygen saturation in their hemoglobin, a factor that enhances the body's access to oxygen, have more surviving children. Thus, hypoxia at high altitudes can be an agent of natural selection (**Figure 5.18**). Similarly, Peruvian Quechua show an elevated exercise capacity at high altitudes. The high level of exercise capacity in this setting is associated with five genetic markers in close proximity to the *Egln1* gene, the gene linked to increased aerobic capacity.

THE ROLE OF NUTRITION IN ADAPTATION: NUTRIENTS, ENERGY, AND FUNCTION

Macronutrients and Micronutrients Climate is only one key context in which humans adapt. As with any other living organism, our success in adaptation is also closely tied to diet, or the kinds of foods we eat, and nutrition, or the deriving of nutrients from those foods. Nutrition is crucial in the acquisition of the necessary energy and nutrients for reproduction, growth, and development.

CONCEPT CHECK

Adaptation: Heat, Cold, Solar Radiation, and High Altitude

Humans display both short-term adjustments and long-term adaptations to environmental extremes. These responses are crucial for maintaining homeostasis.

SETTING	EXPOSURE AND ADAPTATION	CHARACTERISTICS
Heat	First exposure	Vasodilation and profuse sweating; effects reduce with continual exposure
	Functional adaptation	Less sweating; normal work performance
	Genetic adaptation	Narrow body; long limbs
Cold	First exposure	Vasoconstriction and shivering; effects reduce after continual exposure brings warmer skin temperature
	Functional adaptation	Tolerance to cold and to lowering of skin temperature; metabolic rate higher than that of nonadapted populations; peripheral body temperature higher than that of nonadapted populations
	Genetic adaptation	Large, wide body; short limbs
Solar/UV radiation	First exposure	Reddening of skin (sunburn), followed by increased melanin production by melanocytes
	Functional adaptation	Tanning; thickening of skin
	Genetic adaptation	High melanin production (dark skin)
High altitude	First exposure	Hypoxia resulting in headache, nausea, loss of appetite, fatigue, and breathlessness; symptoms disappear after a few days
	Functional adaptation	Greater diameter of arteries and veins; greater relative blood flow to body tissues; greater lung volume; more efficient use of oxygen; larger chest size in some populations (reflecting greater lung volume)
	Genetic adaptation	High oxygen saturation in hemoglobin

basal metabolic requirement The minimum amount of energy needed to keep an organism alive.

total daily energy expenditure (TDEE) The number of calories used by an organism's body during a 24-hour period.

macronutrients Essential chemical nutrients, including fats, carbohydrates, and proteins, that a body needs to live and to function normally.

micronutrients Essential substances, such as minerals or vitamins, needed in very small amounts to maintain normal body functioning.

Each body function requires a certain amount of energy and particular nutrients, and a lack of energy or of nutrients can hamper body functions. Like many other primates (the other primates are discussed in chapter 6), humans are omnivorous, eating a wide range of both plants and animals. This dietary plasticity enhances our access to the nutrients we need for function and survival; and in terms of adaptability and evolution, it reflects humans' unique combination of biology and culture.

Nutritionists have developed two sets of dietary recommendations: those based on energy requirements and those based on nutrient requirements. Measured in calories, the minimum energy needed to keep a person alive is called the **basal metabolic requirement**. A person needs additional energy for other functions, such as work and exercise, thermoregulation, growth, and reproduction (pregnancy and lactation). The **total daily energy expenditure (TDEE)** consists of the basal metabolic requirement plus all the other energy requirements, and we fulfill all these energy requirements by consuming specific **macronutrients** (carbohydrates, fats, and proteins) in food and **micronutrients** (vitamins and minerals) in food as well as in multivitamins. **Table 5.1** shows the daily minimum amounts (called dietary reference intakes) of nutrients recommended in the United States. A lack of

TABLE 5.1 Dietary Reference Intakes for Selected Nutrients

NUTRIENT (UNITS)	CHILD 1–3 YEARS	FEMALE 19–30 YEARS	MALE 19–30 YEARS
Macronutrients			
Protein (g)	13	46	56
(% of calories)	5–20	10–35	10–35
Carbohydrate (g)	130	130	130
(% of calories)	45–65	45–65	45–65
Total fiber (g)	14	28	34
Total fat (% kcal)	30–40	20–35	20–35
Saturated fat (% kcal)	<10	<10	<10
Linoleic acid (g)	7	12	17
(% kcal)	5–10	5–10	5–10
α-Linoleic acid (g)	0.7	1.1	1.6
(% kcal)	0.6–1.2	0.6–1.2	0.6–1.2
Cholesterol (mg)	<300	<300	<300
Minerals			
Calcium (mg)	500	1,000	1,000
Iron (mg)	7	18	8
Magnesium (mg)	80	310	400
Phosphorus (mg)	460	700	700
Potassium (mg)	3,000	4,700	4,700
Sodium (mg)	<1,500	<2,300	<2,300
Zinc (mg)	3	8	11
Copper (g)	340	900	900
Selenium (g)	20	55	55
Vitamins			
Vitamin A (g RAE)	300	700	900
Vitamin D (g)	5	5	5
Vitamin E (mg AT)	6	15	15
Vitamin C (mg)	15	75	90
Thiamin (mg)	0.5	1.1	1.2
Riboflavin (mg)	0.5	1.1	1.3
Niacin (mg)	6	14	16
Vitamin B_6 (mg)	0.5	1.3	1.3
Vitamin B_{12} (g)	0.9	2.4	2.4
Choline (mg)	200	425	550
Vitamin K (g)	30	90	120
Folate (g DFE)	150	400	400
USDA food pattern using goals as targets	1,000	2,000	2,400

AT = alpha-tocopherol; DFE = dietary folate equivalent; RAE = retinol activity equivalent; USDA = United States Department of Agriculture.

Source: United States Department of Agriculture, https://www.nal.usda.gov/fnic.

these essential vitamins and minerals, even those recommended in small amounts, can have devastating effects. For example, a lack of folate in a pregnant woman can lead to neural tube defects, such as spina bifida, in the fetus. Many foods we commonly eat in the United States, such as cereal, bread, and milk, are fortified with some of these essential nutrients.

Human Nutrition Today The majority of human populations across the world are undernourished (consuming fewer than 2,000 calories per day), especially in developing nations in Africa, in South and Central America, and across large regions of Asia (**Figure 5.19**).

Called the **nutrition transition**, in many settings of the world local populations have shifted from eating minimally refined, locally grown foods that generally provide sufficient calories and nutrients to eating highly processed foods that are high in saturated fats and sugar and low in fiber. The American anthropologist Barry Bogin has documented the increasingly globalized diets of the Maya people of Mexico. In this setting, health has shown a precipitous decline owing to the shift to poor diets.

In the late twentieth century and the early twenty-first century, governments across the world have collaborated on increasing agricultural production to relieve famine and starvation. Currently, resources are directed at enhancing the nutritional attributes of key grains, particularly rice and corn. As a result of these international efforts, grains are more readily available and of better nutritional quality. This focus on grains has contributed, however, to a growing decline in the diversity of foods consumed by human populations, especially in nutritionally stressed settings. Increased agricultural production might help meet populations' caloric needs, but attention is shifting to increasing the availability of additional micronutrients—such as vitamin A, vitamins B_6 and B_{12}, vitamin D, iodine, iron, and zinc—through meat and other animal products.

Despite these efforts, the increasing trend of declining nutrition is having significant consequences for human populations around the world. Among the consequences of poor nutrition is the suppression of the immune system. Owing to poor living circumstances and poor sanitation conditions, meanwhile, undernourished populations are especially susceptible to the spread and maintenance of infectious disease. Thus, undernutrition and infection work hand in hand—each exacerbates the other, and the combination is much worse for the health and well-being of the individual than is either one alone.

Universally, undernourished populations experience stunted growth, resulting in shortness for age. The American economist David Seckler has hypothesized that shortness in height is an adaptation to reduced food supplies, one with no costs to individual health. The record shows quite the opposite, however: individuals who are undernourished typically have poor general functioning, reduced work capacity, ill health, and shortened life expectancy. Short individuals might require fewer calories and nutrients, but the associated health cost for them can be profound. Moreover, it is highly unlikely that undernourished populations' shortness is a genetic adaptation. Where energy and nutrition became adequate or abundant after periods of disruption and deprivation, body size rebounded. For example, in many countries, especially nations in Europe and Asia, World War II had a profoundly negative impact on growth. In the Netherlands, 1944 and 1945 were known as the "starving years." After the war, children and adults began growing again thanks to the return of adequate nutrition (**Figure 5.20**).

nutrition transition Change in diet involving a shift from a traditional diet of low-fat foods, cereals, and fiber to a Western diet of high-fat, high-carbohydrate, animal-sourced foods.

FIGURE 5.19

Malnutrition Malnutrition is a substantial problem in many parts of the world. Both of its forms—undernutrition, or insufficient consumption of calories and/or micronutrients, and overnutrition, or excessive consumption of calories and/or micronutrients—can have detrimental health consequences. Chronic undernutrition is a persistent problem for populations of many developing nations. This emaciated Somali man, for example, has not been able to consume enough food to sustain normal body weight.

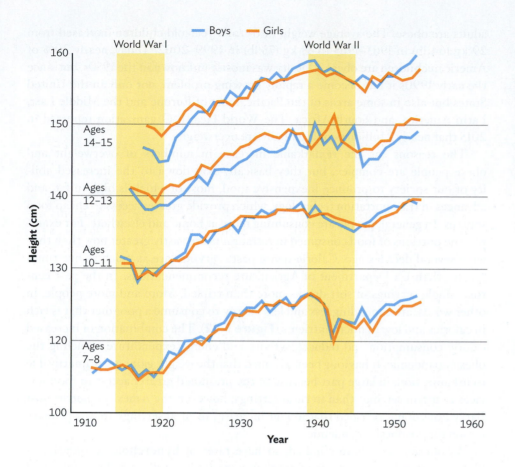

FIGURE 5.20

Malnutrition and Height Height is a sensitive indicator of diet and health. During periods of insufficient nutrition, growth can be slowed or arrested, leading to reduced adult stature. If, however, proper nutrition is restored before adulthood, a recovery period can follow, during which growth "catches up" to where it should be. This graph shows the heights of boys and girls of various ages in Germany during and after World Wars I and II. During the wars, food shortages negatively affected growth in height. After the wars, food was more abundant and growth was not inhibited. What might account for the general increase in growth from 1910 through 1950?

Overnutrition and the Consequences of Dietary Excess Much of the preceding discussion about nutrition focused on shortfalls and the consequences of not getting enough of some nutrient or food or energy. Increasingly around the world, the problem is becoming just the opposite: too much food and too many of the wrong kinds of food. These dietary choices have their own negative consequences for health and well-being (**Figure 5.21**). In the United States, adults have increased their body weight by an average of 11 kg (24 lb) over the past four decades, and nearly 50% of

FIGURE 5.21

Overnutrition Like undernutrition, overnutrition has many negative consequences for health and well-being. As this graph shows, the risks of diabetes, high blood pressure, and high cholesterol increase substantially as BMI increases. BMI, or body mass index, is a statistical measure of weight according to height. A BMI between 18.5 and 24.9 indicates that a person has normal weight for his or her height. A BMI between 25 and 29.9 means "overweight," while 30 or above means "obese," where excess weight is so extreme that health and function are compromised.

adults are obese. The average weight of 6- to 11-year-old children increased from 29 kg (64 lb) in 1963–1965 to 33 kg (73 lb) in 1999–2002. Today, nearly 20% of American children are obese. Obesity was mostly unknown in the 1950s, but since the early 1990s it has become a rapidly growing problem, not only in the United States but also in some areas of the Pacific, most of Europe and the Middle East, Latin America, and South Africa. The World Health Organization reported in 2015 that nearly 2 billion people globally are overweight.

The reasons for the remarkable increase in numbers of overweight and obese people are complex, but they basically boil down to the increased ability of our society to produce inexpensive food, most of which is high in fat, and advances in transportation technology, which provide greater access to cheap food sources. In general, people are consuming more at home and elsewhere. For example, the portions of food consumed in restaurants are vastly greater now than they were several decades ago. Calorie-dense pasta servings are as much as five times greater than US Department of Agriculture recommendations. In the past century, single servings of soft drinks more than tripled. More and more people, in other words, are expending less and less energy to consume a poor diet that is rich in calories and low in micronutrients (**Figure 5.22**). The combination of increased calorie consumption and reduced activity and energy expenditure is fueling the obesity pandemic. It has long been assumed that the weight gains are primarily due to urbanization, in large part because of the presumed greater access to food services in urban settings than in rural settings; however, the American nutritionist Barry Popkin has revealed that weight increases in rural settings are the primary reason for the obesity pandemic.

As obesity rates have climbed, so have rates of **hypercholesterolemia**, or high cholesterol, a predisposing factor for coronary heart disease. The cholesterol levels of traditional hunter-gatherers (and of our ancestors) averaged 125 mg/dl (milligrams per deciliter of blood), but the average cholesterol level of Americans

hypercholesterolemia The presence of high levels of cholesterol in an organism's blood; this condition may result from the dietary consumption of foods that promote high cholesterol or through the inheritance of a genetic disorder.

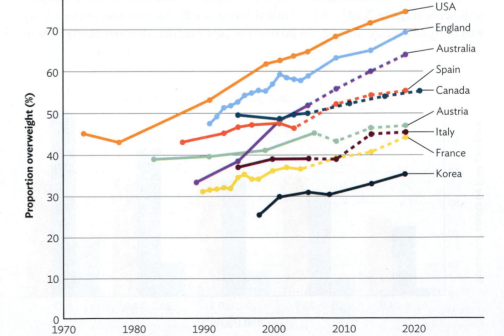

FIGURE 5.22

People around the World Are Becoming Overweight While excessive body weight is reaching epidemic levels in the United States, it is also becoming a problem in other countries. As Western culture in general, and American fast-food chains in particular, move into developing countries, excessive body weight increases follow. This graph shows the percentage of overweight individuals in select countries over the past several decades.

TSEGA GEBREYESUS, PHD, MPH

Centers for Disease Control and Prevention

What do I do? I am a researcher who explores the root contributors to public health challenges and works to identify practical and sustainable solutions to them. Recently, I worked and trained at the Centers for Disease Control and Prevention (CDC). While working in risk mitigation at the CDC's Division for Emergency Operations during the hurricane season, I learned about the direct and indirect effects of natural disasters on health, the importance of tailoring interventions to the needs of the diverse populations within the continental United States and its territories, and the barriers to efficiency that result, in part, from the complexity of the ever changing US public health system. Later, as an Oak Ridge Institute for Science and Education (ORISE) postdoctoral fellow with the policy branch of the CDC's Office on Smoking and Health, I assessed state and local efforts to surmount the barriers to decreasing tobacco prevalence among marginalized communities, in order to support the development of locally relevant initiatives at the federal level.

What excites me most about my work? Throughout my career in public health, I have worked in the United States and internationally to identify barriers to accessing health care for marginalized populations. Every geographic location has different cultural mores, health systems, and burdens of diseases, and each has varying levels of the political will necessary to address the root causes of health disparities. Despite these dissimilarities, the role of social determinants in health outcomes has been a common thread: the wider political, economic, and sociocultural environment often determines what diseases people develop and their ability to manage them. Despite the seemingly insurmountable challenges they face, I am continually impressed by the innovative and collaborative nature of local communities' strategies to improve their health outcomes. I really value my work in the translation of scientific evidence into public health practice and am grateful to have developed the skill sets necessary to facilitate community-informed and community-supported mechanisms for combating the diseases that plague marginalized communities in the world today.

Why did I study anthropology? I was raised in an immigrant community in the United States, where I learned early on that context and biology play an influential role in the development of social norms and subsequent life outcomes. In college, I explored my interest in understanding the roots of social behavior by majoring in anthropology. I have a proclivity for languages and, in addition to English, Tigrinya, and Amharic, I learned Spanish and Arabic because linguistic competency provides a more nuanced lens into the life patterns and social decisions of communities. I lived, worked, and studied in different parts of Latin America, Africa, and the Middle East and chose to embed myself within local communities in order to contextualize behavior within the wider political, historical, environmental, genetic, economic, and social contexts in which they lived.

My anthropological background has been invaluable throughout my public health education and career. Both biological and cultural anthropological insights enhance the research I conduct because they allow me to explore the underlying and determinative roles of family structure, religion, economics, genetics, topography, and politics on individual health decision-making. My anthropological training has reinforced how I value the importance of being in the field and actively participating in data collection, in order to contextualize health behaviors and develop effective, locally valued, and sustainable interventions.

today well exceeds 200 mg/dl. The hunter-gatherers ate a lot of meat, just as we do, but the nondomesticated animals of 15,000 yBP contained very low levels of cholesterol-elevating saturated fatty acids, especially compared with the very high fat content of today's domesticated animals. In addition, hydrogenated vegetable fats and oils and very high levels of trans fatty acids contribute some 15% of the energy in the average American diet. Clearly, these changes in consumption are culturally influenced; that is, people *learn* to eat what they eat. This is an important characteristic of our evolution and a key element of social learning (see chapter 1).

Simultaneous to the global pandemic of obesity is an epidemic of non-insulin-dependent diabetes mellitus, or **type 2 diabetes**. More than 100 million people suffer from the disease worldwide. Historically, type 2 diabetes was associated with overweight individuals older than 40. Since about 1990, however, more and more young adults and adolescents have been affected. The key elements of this complex disease are abnormally high blood glucose levels and excessive body weight, both of which result from excessive caloric consumption. Glucose, weight, and other biological signals prompt the pancreas to produce and secrete insufficient amounts of the hormone insulin. Eventually, insulin resistance develops at specific target tissues: muscle, fat, and the liver. The lack of insulin and presence of insulin resistance denies these target tissues key nutrients used for fuel and storage. This denial of nutrients is not the major health problem, however, because glucose—a necessary source of energy—is still stored as fatty acids in fat tissue. From the fat tissue, glucose is pushed into liver and muscle cells, so a person with type 2 diabetes typically becomes fatter and fatter.

The major health problem is that the extra glucose increases the blood's viscosity, and the thickened blood damages blood vessels in the kidneys, eyes, and extremities. In advanced stages of the disease, the kidneys function poorly, vision is reduced, and blood does not flow adequately to the hands, arms, feet, and legs. There is also a greater chance of cardiac disease and stroke.

Is there an adaptive component to the disease? In the early 1960s, the American geneticist James V. Neel noted the high incidence of type 2 diabetes among Native Americans. In the early twentieth century, the disease had been virtually nonexistent in Native Americans, but after World War II it increased to the point of affecting more than half the members of some Native American tribes. Neel hypothesized a "thrifty genotype," one that during times of plenty stored energy efficiently in the form of glucose in fat tissue. For Native Americans, who lived a feast-or-famine life, such a thrifty genotype for a rapid insulin trigger would have been a benefit. For populations that lived an abundant life, the consequences of type 2 diabetes would have triggered a selection against the thrifty genotype.

Given the data in the 1960s, when only some populations around the world had type 2 diabetes, Neel's hypothesis made a lot of sense. Since that time, however, populations around the world have been experiencing an alarming increase in the disease, all in regions where people are becoming obese. Current projections indicate that by 2020, one-quarter of the US population will develop the disease. Little evidence supports the idea that some populations, such as Native Americans, have a thrifty genotype.

If genetic causes or susceptibilities do not explain the remarkable increase in type 2 diabetes, then why is there such a high frequency in some Native Americans, such as in the Pima of the American Southwest, where 50% of adults are afflicted? To understand the cause of the disease among Native American and other highly susceptible groups, we need to view the disease in terms of nutritional history. Studies of populations show a strong association between poor maternal nutrition during pregnancy (usually leading to low-birth-weight babies) and development of type 2 diabetes among these offspring in later life. The American anthropologist Daniel Benyshek and his colleagues have made a strong case that Native Americans and other populations with a high incidence of type 2 diabetes share a common

type 2 diabetes A disease in which the body does not produce enough insulin or the cells do not use the available insulin, causing a buildup of glucose in the cells.

history of severe nutritional deprivation. Moreover, the effects of malnutrition are perpetuated for generations, even in subsequent generations no longer experiencing malnutrition. That is, the metabolism of children gestated under such conditions becomes permanently "programmed," in turn leading to comparable developmental programming effects in their children. Thus, the cycle can continue for generations.

In other Native American populations, such as those inhabiting the Aleutian Islands of Alaska, the incidence of type 2 diabetes is relatively low. Unlike native populations in the American Southwest, Aleutian Islanders do not have a history of severe malnutrition. During adulthood, too little activity and too many calories are risk factors for any population. But the impact of poor diet on the growing fetus is crucial for understanding the high prevalence of type 2 diabetes in humans today.

THE ROLE OF WORKLOAD AND ACTIVITY IN ADAPTATION: SKELETAL HOMEOSTASIS AND FUNCTION

Homeostasis depends on the health of all the body's tissues, including the bone tissues. The skeleton must be maintained so that it can support the body and enable the body to move. Without this essential framework, where would tendons, ligaments, and muscles be attached and how would they get the leverage needed for their use?

The growth and development of bones are subject to a range of factors. Strongly controlled by genes, they are also affected by various physiological processes, disease, and nutrition. As discussed earlier, poor nutrition in childhood may result in short stature, both in children and in the adults they become. Various mechanical forces associated with workload and activity also affect the growth and development of bones. The bones of the arms and legs, for example, are subject to bending and torsion, or twisting, whenever they are used. Bones' **rigidity**, or strength, is a functional adaptation to these forces, preventing fracture in the course of normal use (**Figure 5.23**). During growth and development, physical

FIGURE 5.23

Framework of the Human Body Just as a building needs its framework, the human body needs the skeleton for support and rigidity. In addition to maintaining the body's shape and enabling its movement, the skeleton protects the many vital organs (the brain, for example, is safely encased in the cranium). It makes possible the production of red blood cells (within the marrow cavities of bones). And it serves as a storage facility for minerals, which can be retrieved at any time. Which minerals would you expect to be stored in bone?

rigidity (bone) The strength of bone to resist bending and torsion.

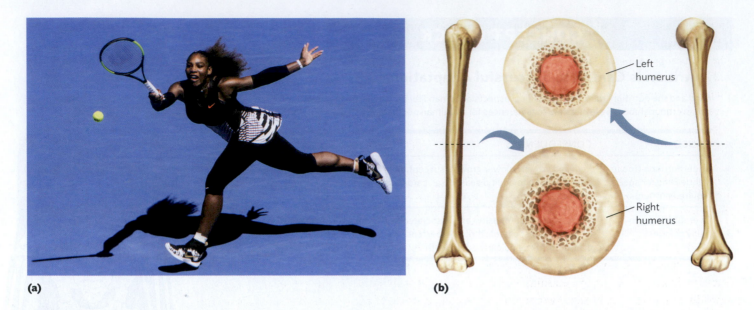

(a)   (b)

FIGURE 5.24

Skeletal Remodeling and Athletics The "playing" arms of athletes in certain sports undergo remodeling as a result of stress. **(a)** A baseball pitcher or a tennis player (such as, here, the professional player Serena Williams) typically has a dominant arm, which is used to a much greater degree than the nondominant arm. **(b)** The upper arm bone, or humerus, of the dominant arm is much stronger than that of the nondominant arm. In these cross sections, note the greater diameter of the right humerus.

osteoblasts Cells responsible for bone formation.

bone mass The density of bone per unit of measure.

osteoclasts Cells responsible for bone resorption.

Wolff's law The principle that bone is placed in the direction of functional demand; that is, bone develops where needed and recedes where it is not needed.

activity stimulates bone-forming cells, called **osteoblasts**, which produce **bone mass** where it is needed to maintain the rigidity of specific bones and bone regions. In the absence of physical activity, other cells, called **osteoclasts**, remove bone mass. A principle called **Wolff's law** lays out the homeostatic balance of osteoblastic and osteoclastic activity, in which bone mass is produced where it is needed and taken away where it is not needed.

Wolff's law also accounts for the remodeling of bone that occurs during life—the changing of certain bones' shapes as the result of particular activities. Because the movements of tendons, ligaments, and muscles put stress on individual bones, repetitive actions eventually can cause those bones to reinforce themselves by adding more material. Just as you need to reinforce a shelf if it starts to buckle under the weight it holds, so the body is likely to try to prevent a bone from breaking under added weight or stress (**Figure 5.24**).

At the other end of the spectrum, people who are physically inactive—such as from partial or full immobilization—have less dense bones because osteoblasts are not stimulated to produce bone mass (**Figure 5.25**). The resulting decline in bone density may weaken the skeleton. For example, the skeletons of astronauts who have been in outer space for extended periods of time have remarkable loss in bone density. Around the world, children who are less physically active tend to have smaller and less developed bones than those of children who are more physically active. Children with less bone mass due to habitual physical inactivity become predisposed, as adults, to osteoporosis and fracture. Similarly, in one study of military recruits' leg bones, young men and women who had better developed muscles and greater bone mass were less susceptible to fractures than were young men and women who had less developed muscles and less bone mass.

Studying the larger picture of human variation, anthropologists have learned that highly physically active human populations—those that do lots of walking, lifting, carrying, or anything else that "stresses" the skeleton—have bones with optimum density. In addition, the diameters of long bones in populations with active lifestyles are greater than those in populations that are physically inactive. These greater diameters provide the bones with higher rigidity, increasing their ability to resist bending and torsion (this phenomenon is discussed further in chapter 12). In addition, greater amounts of bone gained during growth and development are kept in later adulthood.

EXCESSIVE ACTIVITY AND REPRODUCTIVE ECOLOGY

The biological benefits of physical activity are clear. Exercise improves physical fitness by contributing to bone strength, helping to lower blood pressure and cholesterol, increasing heart function and lung function, and so on. Exercise that becomes an excessive workload, however, can hinder female reproductive function, a crucial factor in evolution. Many studies have shown that an excessive workload, such as regular intense aerobic exercise, can interrupt menstrual function, resulting in lower fertility. Even milder levels of physical activity have reduced the reproductive potential of some women. For example, a study of a large number of women from Washington State revealed that women who engage in more than an hour of exercise per day and whose body weights are 85% that of the average American woman are five to six times more likely to not be able to conceive within 1 year than women who do not exercise and have normal weight. Two important implications stand out from this and other studies on workload and ovarian function: First, human populations requiring heavy work by reproductive-age women will have reduced birthrates. Second, and in the larger picture of human adaptation and evolution, amount of work is an important selective factor—a population with relatively high fitness will likely not require excessive energy expenditure, at least for reproductive-age women.

Anthropologists have shown that the classification of humans into different types, or races, simply does not provide meaningful information about variation. While race may be an enduring social concept, it is not valid biologically. Understanding human variation in an evolutionary context—that is, understanding people's remarkable adaptability to a wide range of environmental circumstances throughout the stages of growth, from conception through old age and senescence—is far more productive than attempting to classify different types of the human organism. Just as humans represent a continuum, so are they part of a larger continuum that includes their fellow primates, with whom they share a range of characteristics, many common adaptations, and much evolutionary history. As we will explore in the next chapter, the nonhuman primates provide an important record of adaptability and flexibility, one of the great success stories of mammalian evolution.

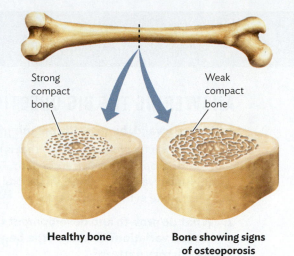

Strong compact bone

Weak compact bone

Healthy bone

Bone showing signs of osteoporosis

FIGURE 5.25

Bone Disuse When bones are not used routinely or for extended periods of time, bone density can decrease. Typically, the loss occurs on the inner surface of the bone, making the bone more fragile. The outer, compact bone becomes thinner as the bone marrow, or medullary cavity, in the middle increases in diameter. In this drawing, the osteoporotic bone, on the right, has a much thinner outer compact bone and a larger bone marrow cavity than those of the healthy bone.

ANSWERING THE BIG QUESTIONS

1. **Is race a valid, biologically meaningful concept?**
   - Race is a typological leftover that is neither a useful nor an appropriate biological concept.
   - Human variation is clinal. In general, traits do not correlate in their distribution.

2. **What do growth and development tell us about human variation? What are the benefits of our life-history pattern?**
   - Differentiation and development of all the body's organs occur during the prenatal stage of life.
   - The postnatal stage involves growth acceleration and deceleration. Childhood and adolescence are long events, in which individuals become physically and emotionally mature.
   - Reproductive senescence is unique to humans. Individuals older than 50 play important roles in the care of young and as sources of information.

3. **How do people adapt to environmental extremes and other circumstances?**
   - Some adaptations to the environment are genetic, whereas others occur within the individual's lifetime and either are inherited and are irreversible or are *not* inherited and are reversible. Biological change associated with all forms of adaptation occurs to maintain homeostasis.
   - Most functional adaptations—adaptations that occur during the individual's lifetime—have important implications for evolution.

   - Adaptations to UV radiation, high altitudes, and workloads are all seen in humans and can be subject to the forces of evolution. While many adaptations are beneficial, some can be disruptive, such as the negative effect of high levels of physical activity on female reproductive potential.
   - Undernutrition and obesity are not the result of adaptation—the body either receives adequate (or too much) nutrition or it does not. Nutritional deficiencies and overabundance both negatively affect health.

STUDY QUIZ

1. **Which is true about race?**
   a. Racial traits change very suddenly across geographic regions.
   b. Racial categories explain a very high percentage of genetic variation.
   c. Race is socially constructed and is not a biological concept.
   d. Personal genomic research supports racial categories.

2. **Which is an example of a physiological adaptation (acclimatization) to climate?**
   a. The loss of body hair in humans
   b. Variation in the breadth and length of the body and limbs
   c. Vasodilation of blood vessels in response to temperature
   d. The development of human technologies to conserve heat

KEY TERMS

adult stage
aging
Allen's rule
basal metabolic rate (BMR)
basal metabolic requirement
Bergmann's rule
bone mass
cline
cognitive abilities
deciduous dentition
diaphysis
epiphyses
functional adaptations
growth velocity
homeostasis
homeothermic
hypercholesterolemia
hypothermia
hypoxia
intrauterine
lactation
life history
macronutrients
melanin
melanocytes
menarche
menopause
micronutrients
motor skills
nonmineralized
nutrition transition
osteoblasts
osteoclasts
osteoporosis
postnatal stage
prenatal stage
rigidity (bone)
secular trend
senescence
sexual dimorphism
skin reflectance
stressors
sun protection factor (SPF)
total daily energy expenditure (TDEE)
type 2 diabetes
vasoconstriction
vasodilation
Wolff's law

STUDY QUIZ (CONTINUED)

3. **What *reproductive benefit* from reduced absorption of UV radiation could be driving natural selection for dark skin?**
   a. Lower risk of sunburn
   b. Lower risk of skin cancer
   c. Increased vitamin D synthesis
   d. Protection of stored folate

4. **Which is a developmental adaptation to high-altitude hypoxia?**
   a. Alleles for hemoglobin with higher oxygen saturation
   b. Growth of an expanded chest during childhood
   c. Production of more red blood cells
   d. Mountain sickness

5. **The *nutrition transition* refers to the**
   a. transition from hunting and gathering to agriculture.
   b. domestication of wild plants and animals.
   c. resumed growth of a formerly malnourished population.
   d. shift from eating local foods to eating highly processed foods.

EVOLUTION REVIEW

Human Variation Today

SYNOPSIS The biocultural approach of biological anthropology emphasizes that human evolution and variation are shaped by both biology and culture—that is, by both genetic factors and environmental factors. Biological anthropologists apply this concept in various ways. For instance, the relationship between the unique life history stages of humans and our sociocultural behaviors is an area of interest. Additionally, human populations across the globe vary in the ways that homeostasis (physiological equilibrium) is maintained, and such adaptations are a product of evolutionary processes operating over a wide range of environmental settings. The broad range of human adaptability—to life in hot and cold climates, among extremes of latitude and altitude, and with variable access to key nutrients—is a major contributor to the success of our species: humans survive and reproduce across a diverse array of environments worldwide.

Q1. Define Bergmann's rule and Allen's rule in relation to adaptation. What is one example of an environmental factor that can lead to the development of body-shape characteristics that deviate from those predicted by these two rules?

Q2. What is clinal variation? Identify two physiological effects of solar radiation that likely acted as selective pressures in shaping the pattern of clinal variation observed for human skin color.

Q3. In early life, human females are more highly buffered against environmental stresses than are human males. In addition, human females enter puberty, adolescence, and reproductive senescence earlier than human males do. Why are such features advantageous from an evolutionary standpoint?

HINT Focus on implications for fitness, or reproductive success.

Q4. In what ways have each of the four types (or levels) of adaptation discussed in this chapter contributed to the ability of human populations to inhabit areas spanning the entire surface of the globe? Consider various factors, including climate and nutrition.

HINT Think about an extreme geographic setting. How might the ways that a resident maintains homeostasis differ from the ways a visitor maintains homeostasis?

Q5. Many scientists characterize the conditions of modern populations worldwide (but especially Western societies) as conducive to an obesity pandemic. Discuss the ways in which adaptive features from our evolutionary past may have become modern maladaptations.

HINT Think about the differences in nutritional resources and activity patterns between ourselves and our hominin ancestors.

ADDITIONAL READINGS

Barker, D. J. P. 1996. The origins of coronary heart disease in early life. Pp. 155–162 in C. J. K. Henry and S. J. Ulijaszek, eds. *Long-Term Consequences of Early Environment: Growth, Development and the Lifespan Developmental Perspective.* Cambridge, UK: Cambridge University Press.

Bogin, B. 2020. *Patterns of Human Growth*, 3rd ed. Cambridge, UK: Cambridge University Press.

Frisancho, A. R. 1993. *Human Adaptation and Accommodation.* Ann Arbor: University of Michigan Press.

Jablonski, N. G. 2006. *Skin: A Natural History.* Berkeley: University of California Press.

Stinson, S., B. Bogin, and D. O'Rourke, eds. 2012. *Human Biology: An Evolutionary and Biocultural Perspective*, 2nd ed. Hoboken, NJ: Wiley-Blackwell.

Sussman, R. W. 2014. *The Myth of Race: The Troubling Persistence of an Unscientific Idea.* Cambridge, MA: Harvard University Press.

Van Arsdale, A. P. 2019. Population demography, ancestry, and the biological concept of race. *Annual Review of Anthropology* 48: 227–241.

Olive baboons (*Papio anubis*) from the Mole National Park, Ghana, are one of multiple species of baboons. These primates represent one of the most successful and widespread adaptations in African monkeys. Some olive baboons are adapted to open grasslands, whereas others are adapted to deserts and forest.

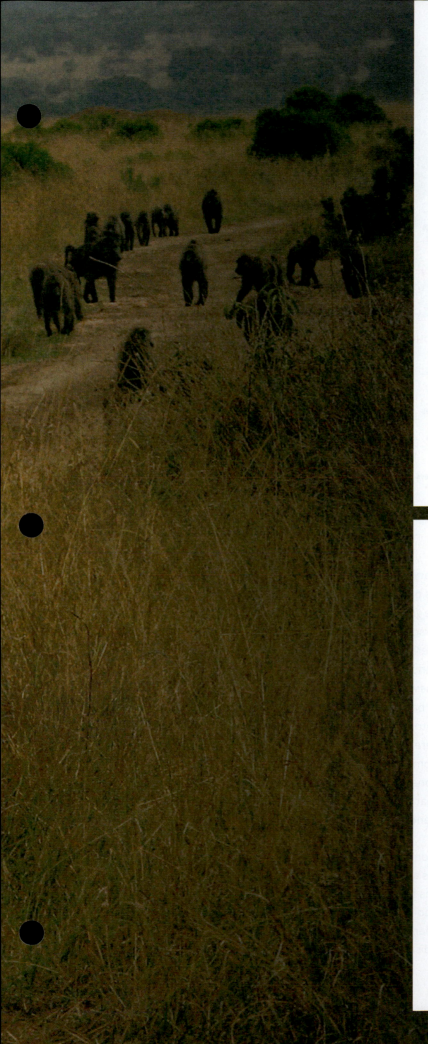

6

Biology in the Present

THE OTHER LIVING PRIMATES

BIG QUESTIONS

1. **Why study primates?**
2. **What is a primate?**
3. **What are the kinds of primates?**

Do you remember the first time you saw a primate (besides a human one, that is)?[1] I first saw a primate on a school trip to the Kansas City Zoo. My third-grade class and our teacher walked up to an enclosure containing several monkeys. I could not take my eyes off the faces of those animals. In so many ways, they looked just like us! Their eyes were on the fronts of their faces, they had different facial expressions, and they had grasping hands. For fear of retaliation from my fellow classmates, I did not point out the resemblances I saw between monkeys and people, including them. But I came away from that experience wondering why monkeys shared so many physical attributes with humans.

I did not think much about that trip to the zoo until I took my first biological anthropology class in college, 10 years later. My professor explained that monkeys, like humans, are members of

---

[1] Throughout this chapter and the remainder of the book, *primate* or *primates* refers to nonhuman primates except where otherwise specified.

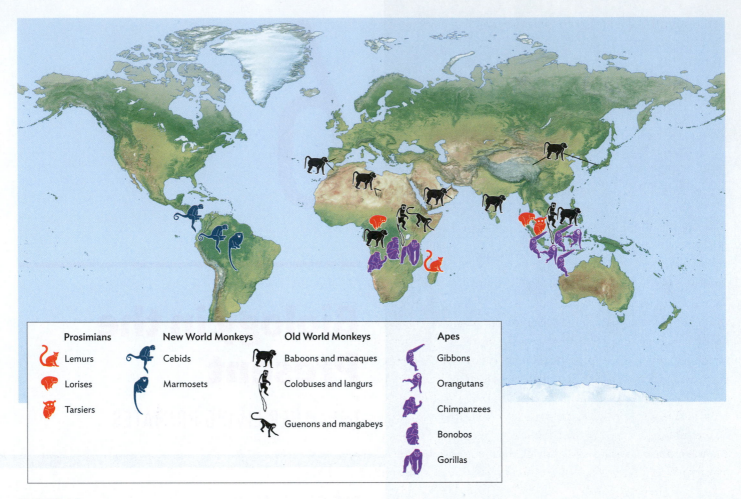

Prosimians

Lemurs

Lorises

Tarsiers

New World Monkeys

Cebids

Marmosets

Old World Monkeys

Baboons and macaques

Colobuses and langurs

Guenons and mangabeys

Apes

Gibbons

Orangutans

Chimpanzees

Bonobos

Gorillas

FIGURE 6.1

Primate Distribution As shown on this map, primates inhabit every continent except Antarctica and Australia. New World primates live in North and South America, while Old World primates live in Europe, Africa, and Asia. Although they are often considered tropical animals that live in forested settings, primate species exist in a wide range of environments.

the order Primates and that one key unifying feature of all primates is forward-facing eyes. This feature is part of the generalized and arboreal adaptation that unites this amazing and diverse group of animals and indicates their common ancestry. Research by primatologists—scientists who study primates—had revealed one of the most impressive characteristics of primates: their marvelous ability to adapt to new or changing circumstances. My question was answered! Monkeys and humans share features because they share ancestry. They are not identical today because at some point in the remote past, the evolutionary paths of their ancestors diverged.

One key indicator of primates' adaptability is the fact that they are able to live almost anywhere—they inhabit many kinds of landscapes and widely diverse climates, ranging from the bitter cold of northern Japan to the humid tropics of Brazil (**Figure 6.1**). Anyone who has ever studied nonhuman primates for any length of time will tell you that they have other characteristics as impressive as their adaptability: their intelligence, their long lives, their variable diets, and their complex social behavior.

Primatologists come from a range of disciplines. Many are in anthropology departments in universities and colleges around the world, but primate studies are also part of disciplines such as biology, ecology, psychology, paleontology, anatomy, zoology, and genetics. In addition, animal and plant conservationists study primates as a barometer of broader species losses and extinctions. Many primates live in tropical forests, which are disappearing by the hundreds of thousands of acres around the world annually, mostly due to forest clearing and encroachment by people; if primates are disappearing, then so are many other animals (a subject discussed further in chapter 14).

Among the practical applications for the study of primates are advances in medicine. Many types of primates have some of the same (or closely related) diseases as humans. In the past 50 years, millions of human lives have been saved around the world because of the study of diseases found in both primates and humans. For example, chimpanzees are susceptible to polio. The vaccine for polio, a once-dreaded disease that killed and debilitated millions of people and many chimpanzees around the world, was developed via primate research in the 1950s.

The physical and behavioral similarities between apes and humans provide important clues about the origins of humans (discussed further in chapter 9). The similarities between the muscles and bones of apes and of humans, for example, enable us to conjecture about what the common ancestor and the earliest hominin may have looked like. The study of primate behavior provides insights into our own behavior and perhaps into the origins of specific behaviors, such as cognition, parenting, social interactions, and (some argue) even conflict and warfare.

These diverse issues make the study of primates so interesting and important, far more than I imagined that day at the zoo. In this chapter, we will define the order Primates and discuss how primates are classified (taxonomy), where they live (ecology and geography), and their physical characteristics (anatomy). In the next chapter, we will look at key aspects of primates' social behavior, especially in the important linkage between social organization, ecology, and diet (socioecology). What you learn in this and the following chapter will provide the essential context for your understanding part II of this book, which is about the evolution of primates and of humans.

6.1 What Is a Primate?

When Linnaeus first defined the order Primates in the eighteenth century (see "Taxonomy and Systematics: Classifying Living Organisms and Identifying Their Biological Relationships" in chapter 2), he did so purely for classification purposes and focused on descriptive traits. Biological anthropologists, however, define primates on the basis of behavioral, adaptive, or evolutionary tendencies. The eminent British anatomist Sir Wilfrid E. Le Gros Clark (1895–1971) identified three prominent tendencies:

1. Primates are adapted to life in the trees—they express **arboreal adaptation** in a set of behaviors and anatomical characteristics that is unique among mammals.
2. Primates eat a wide variety of foods—they express **dietary plasticity**.
3. Primates invest a lot of time and care in few offspring—they express **parental investment**.

In addition to these tendencies, the physical and behavioral characteristics discussed in the subsections that follow identify primates as a separate order of mammals.

One thing that all anthropologists agree on when they talk about primates is the order's remarkable diversity. The panoramic view displayed in **Figure 6.2** provides a sense of that diversity. Depicted in the Taï National Park, in Ivory Coast, West

arboreal adaptation Adaptation to life in the trees.

dietary plasticity The ability of an organism to utilize a wide range of foods in meeting its nutritional requirements.

parental investment The time and energy parents expend for their offspring's benefit.

PRIMATE ADAPTATION IN MICROCOSM:

THE TAÏ NATIONAL PARK, IVORY COAST, WEST AFRICA

1   GENERALIZED SKELETAL STRUCTURE

Primates have a generalized skeletal structure. The highly mobile articulations in the shoulders, upper and lower limbs, and hands and feet give primates a great deal of flexibility when moving in trees. In this monkey skeleton, note the grasping hands and feet, the long tail, and the equal length of the front and hind limbs relative to each other.

Human   Potto

2   ENHANCED TOUCH

Primates have an enhanced sense of touch. This sensitivity is due in part to the presence of dermal ridges (fingerprints and toe prints) on the inside surfaces of the hands and feet. The potto, a prosimian, has primitive dermal ridges, whereas the human, a higher primate, has more derived ridges, which provide better gripping ability.

Emerging canopy

Main canopy

Understory

■ Black-and-white colobus	■ Human	■ Red colobus
■ Campbell's	■ Lesser spot-nosed	■ Sooty mangabey
■ Chimpanzee	■ Olive colobus	■ Thomas's galago
■ Demidoff's galago	■ Potto	■ Eagle
■ Diana monkey	■ Putty-nosed	

Taï National
Park

Overlapping
visual fields

3 | ENHANCED VISION

Primates have an enhanced sense of vision. Evolution
has given primates better vision, including increased
depth perception and seeing in color. The eyes'
convergence provides significant overlap in the visual
fields and thus greater sense of depth.

Reduced
snout length

Dog   **Monkey**

4 | REDUCED SMELL

Primates have a reduced sense of smell. The smaller
and less projecting snouts of most primates indicate
their decreased reliance on smell.

5 | DIETARY VERSATILITY

Primates have dietary versatility. Part of the record of
primate dietary adaptation is found in the teeth. The
red colobus monkey dentition shown here is typical of
a catarrhine dentition with a 2/1/2/3 dental formula.
Note the differences in morphology of the four
different tooth types: incisors (I1, I2), canines (C),
premolars (P3, P4), and molars (M1, M2, M3).

Africa, are one kind of ape (chimpanzee), eight kinds of monkeys (black-and-white colobus, Campbell's, Diana, lesser spot-nosed, putty-nosed, red colobus, olive colobus, sooty mangabey), and three kinds of strepsirrhines (potto, Demidoff's galago, Thomas's galago). All but the strepsirrhines are active during the day. (The humans are, of course, primates as well. The eagle is an important predator of monkeys, especially the red colobus.)

ARBOREAL ADAPTATION—PRIMATES LIVE IN TREES AND ARE GOOD AT IT

Many animals—such as squirrels, nondomesticated cats, some snakes, and birds—have successfully adapted to living in trees. Primates, however, display a unique combination of specific arboreal adaptations. Even the few primates that spend all or most of their time on the ground have retained, over the course of their evolution, a number of features shared with an arboreal common ancestor.

Primates Have a Versatile Skeletal Structure Primates get around in trees using an unusually wide range of motions involving the limbs and body trunk. One has only to watch many of the primates perform their acrobatics in the forest canopy to appreciate this versatility, a function of the primate body's anatomy. That is, the bones making up the shoulders, limbs, hands, and feet tend to be separate, and these separate bones are articulated at highly mobile joints.

Atop the list of separate bones is the collarbone (the clavicle), which acts as a strut, keeping the upper limbs to the sides of the body. The lower forelimb (the ulna and radius) and the fingers and toes (the phalanges) also have separate bones. The forearm rotates from side to side with relative ease, and the dexterity of the hands and feet is unparalleled among mammals.

One of the most important attributes of the primate hand is the **opposable thumb**—on either hand, the tip of the thumb can touch the tips of the other four fingers. Thus, the primate can grasp an object or manipulate a small one. Humans have the longest thumb, or pollex, among primates and therefore the greatest opposability (**Figure 6.3**). This elongated thumb is part of the unique adaptation of the human hand for what the English anatomist and evolutionary biologist John Napier (1917–1987) calls the **power grip** and the **precision grip**. In the power grip, the palm grips an object, such as a hammer's handle, while the thumb and fingers wrap around it in opposite directions. In the precision grip, the thumb and one

opposable thumb As found in primates, a thumb that can touch each of the four fingertips, enabling a grasping ability.

power grip A fistlike grip in which the fingers and thumb wrap around an object in opposite directions.

precision grip A grip in which the tips of the fingers and thumb come together, enabling fine manipulation.

FIGURE 6.3
Grips and Opposable Thumbs Apes and humans have two kinds of grips: power and precision. **(a)** The power grip shown here, as a human holds a hammer, preceded the evolution of the precision grip. **(b)** The precision grip of apes is not nearly as developed as that of humans. **(c)** The finer precision grip of humans—in part due to the greater opposability of their thumbs—lets them finely manipulate objects.

(a) Power grip (human)

(b) Precision grip (ape)

(c) Precision grip (human)

or more of the other fingers' ends provide fine dexterity, as when holding a screwdriver, picking up a small object (such as a coin), or writing with a pen or pencil. The American paleoanthropologist Randall Susman has identified in early hominins the anatomy that would have supported a power grip and a precision grip (discussed further in chapter 9).

Many primates also have opposable big toes (the halluces). Humans are not among these primates, mainly because of changes in the foot that took place when our prehuman ancestors shifted from quadrupedal locomotion to bipedalism (**Figure 6.4**). (See also "What Makes Humans So Different from Other Animals?

(a) **Chimpanzee**   **Human**

(b)

(c)

FIGURE 6.4

Opposable Big Toes Nonhuman primates' opposable big toes, like their opposable thumbs, enable their feet to grasp things such as tree branches. Humans lack this feature due to their adaptation to life on the ground. **(a)** Its curved hallux and large gap between the hallux and second toe make **(b)** the chimpanzee foot look more like a human hand (not shown) than like **(c)** a human foot.

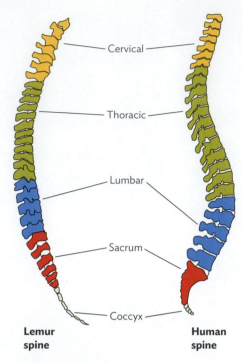

FIGURE 6.5

Primate Vertebrae The five types of vertebrae in primates, including lemurs and humans, create a flexible column allowing a wide range of movement. The cervical, thoracic, and lumbar vertebrae are the true, or movable, vertebrae, responsible for bending, twisting, and stretching. The sacral vertebrae are much less movable because they form part of the pelvis. In most nonhuman primates, the vertebrae of the coccyx form the tail; in humans, these vertebrae are reduced to three to five very short, fused segments. Notice, too, the S-shaped spine in humans versus the C-shaped spine in other primates, such as the lemur.

preadaptation An organism's use of an anatomical feature in a way unrelated to the feature's original function.

nocturnal Normally awake and active during the night.

diurnal Normally awake and active during daylight hours.

FIGURE 6.6

Flat Fingernails Finger pads with nail support help primates, such as this orangutan, securely hold tree branches that are smaller than their hands. By contrast, claws enable nonprimate mammals to dig into tree bark, an especially helpful ability when limbs or tree trunks are larger than the animals' paws.

The Six Steps to Humanness" in chapter 1.) To walk or run, humans need all five toes firmly planted on the ground. The mobility of recent humans' toes has been even further reduced by the wearing of shoes.

The body trunk of primates is also distinctive. The backbone has five functionally distinct types of vertebrae—from top to bottom, the cervical, thoracic, lumbar, sacral (forming the sacrum of the pelvis), and coccygeal vertebrae—which give primates a greater range of movement than other animals have (**Figure 6.5**). The body trunk also tends to be vertically oriented, such as when the primate climbs, swings from tree limb to tree limb, or sits. The vertical tendency in a prehuman ancestor was an essential **preadaptation** to humans' bipedalism.

Primates Have an Enhanced Sense of Touch The ends of the fingers and toes are highly sensitive in primates. This enhancement helps inform primates about texture and other physical properties of objects, such as potential food items. On the inside surfaces of the fingers, toes, palms of the hands, and soles of the feet, the skin surface is covered with series of fine ridges called dermal ridges (fingerprints and toe prints). These ridges further enhance the tactile sense, and they increase the amount of friction, or resistance to slipping, when grasping an object, such as a tree branch. On the backs of the ends of the fingers and toes, most primates have flat nails instead of claws (**Figure 6.6**). (A few primates have specializations, such as a grooming claw on the second toe in lemurs and lorises.) Made of keratin, the strong protein also found in hair, flat nails may protect the ends of the fingers and toes. They may aid in picking up small objects. Most important, however, they provide broad support to the ends of the fingers and toes by spreading out the forces generated in the digits by gripping.

Primates Have an Enhanced Sense of Vision The enhanced vision of primates stems from two developments in the order's evolutionary history. First, very early in primate evolution, the eyes rotated forward from the sides of the head to the front of the head (**Figure 6.7**). As a result, the two fields of vision overlapped, providing the primate with depth perception. (Along with convergence of the eyes, fully enclosed or partially enclosed eye orbits evolved.) Second, color vision evolved. Crucial for spotting insects and other prey within the surrounding vegetation, color vision likely evolved as early primates shifted from a **nocturnal** adaptation to a **diurnal** adaptation.

(a)

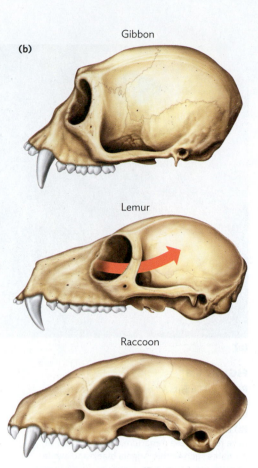
Gibbon

Lemur

Raccoon

FIGURE 6.7

Primate Vision **(a)** Primates' forward-facing eyes enable depth perception, a vital adaptation to life in the trees that has a selective advantage beyond arboreal life. Consider what would happen if a primate attempted to leap from one branch to another without being able to determine the distance between the two branches. Now imagine a human leaping over a (relatively) narrow chasm without knowing how far to leap. **(b)** In most primates, such as the gibbon, the eye orbit is fully enclosed. In animals such as the lemur, a postorbital bar lines the back of the eye orbit but does not fully enclose it. In other animals, such as the raccoon, the eye orbit is open, with no bone enclosing it at the rear.

CONCEPT CHECK

What Makes Primates Good at Living in Trees?

Primates show a series of behavioral and anatomical tendencies that make them especially good at living in trees.

CHARACTERISTIC	FEATURES
Versatile skeletal structure emphasizing mobility and flexibility	Separation of bones in articular joints associated with mobility: clavicle, radius and ulna, wrist, opposable thumb, opposable big toe in many primates
	Five functionally distinct vertebral types: cervical, thoracic, lumbar, sacral, coccygeal
Enhanced sense of touch	Dermal ridges at ends of fingers and toes; nails instead of claws
Enhanced sense of vision	Convergence of eyes; color vision

Primates Have a Reduced Reliance on Senses of Smell and Hearing For most primates, enhanced vision led to greatly reduced senses of smell and hearing. Most primates have lost the **rhinarium** (the external wet nose, which most mammals have) and the long snout. Some of the strepsirrhines—the more primitive primates, such as lemurs and lorises—have retained the rhinarium, and they continue to rely on a well-developed sense of smell (**Figure 6.8**). The reduction in snout length

rhinarium The naked surface around the nostrils, typically wet in mammals.

(a)

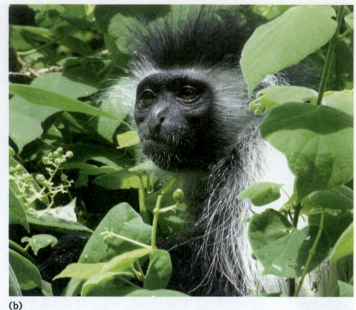

(b)

FIGURE 6.8

Reduced Snout As primates have increased their reliance on vision, they have reduced their reliance on olfaction, the sense of smell. **(a)** Lemurs are among the few primates that have retained the rhinarium. **(b)** The snout of primates such as this Angola black-and-white colobus monkey has no rhinarium.

dental formula The numerical description of a species' teeth, listing the number, in one quadrant of the jaws, of incisors, canines, premolars, and molars (in that order).

loph An enamel ridge connecting cusps on a tooth's surface.

bilophodont (molar) Having two ridges, as the lower molars in Old World monkeys.

FIGURE 6.9

Baboon Snout Baboons do not rely on olfaction. Their snout remains large because of oversized canines. (See also Figure 6.14.)

resulted from a loss of internal surface area of the nasal passage, the location of the chemistry involved in smell. But some primates, such as baboons, later evolved a large and projecting snout to accommodate massive canine roots, especially in adult males (**Figure 6.9**).

DIETARY PLASTICITY—PRIMATES EAT A HIGHLY VARIED DIET, AND THEIR TEETH REFLECT THIS ADAPTIVE VERSATILITY

Primates Have Retained Primitive Characteristics in Their Teeth One fundamental anatomical feature in primates that reflects their high degree of dietary diversity is the retention of primitive dental characteristics, especially of four functionally distinctive tooth types: incisors, canines, premolars, and molars (**Figure 6.10**). The mammalian ancestors of primates had these same tooth types and so must have eaten a range of foods.

Primates Have a Reduced Number of Teeth Because the numbers of the different types of teeth are the same in the upper and lower jaws and the left and right sides of the jaws, anthropologists record each primate species' **dental formula** with respect to one quadrant of the dentition. Primates' early mammalian ancestor, for example, had a dental formula of 3/1/4/3—three incisors, one canine, four premolars, and three molars—in one quadrant of its dentition. As indicated in **Table 6.1**, the Old World anthropoids have a dental formula of 2/1/2/3. Most New World primates have retained one more premolar and have a dental formula of 2/1/3/3. Some primates, such as tarsiers, have different numbers of teeth in the upper and lower jaws. Over the course of the order's evolution, primates' teeth have tended to reduce in number. Thus, the dental formula can be very useful in studies of ancestral primate species. For example, the ancestors of modern Old World monkeys had a dental formula of 2/1/2/3, the same as today's Old World monkeys, and if fossilized remains of a primate ancestor have a dental formula of 2/1/3/3, the ancestor was likely related to New World monkeys, strepsirrhines (lemurs, lorises, galagos), or perhaps tarsiers, because these primates have retained the extra premolar.

TABLE 6.1 Primate Dental Formulae

The major primate groups are distinguished dentally by the number of incisors, canines, premolars, and molars.

PRIMATE GROUP	UPPER	LOWER
Tarsiers	2/1/3/3	1/1/3/3
Lemurs	2/1/3/3	2/1/3/3 (although there is much variation with lemurs)
Lorises	2/1/3/3	2/1/3/3
New World monkeys	2/1/3/2 or 2/1/3/3	2/1/3/2 or 2/1/3/3
Old World monkeys	2/1/2/3	2/1/2/3
Apes and humans	2/1/2/3	2/1/2/3

FIGURE 6.10

Primate Dentitions These five sets of dentitions represent, from top to bottom, human, chimpanzee, gorilla, orangutan, and baboon. Notice that humans do not have the large projecting canines evident in the other four primate dentitions. In the side view, the large upper canines fit into a diastema, or space, between the lower canines and the third premolars. Each time the jaws are closed, the upper canines are sharpened against the lower third premolars.

Primates Have Evolved Different Dental Specializations and Functional Emphases The premolars and molars of primates have undergone little evolutionary change compared with those of other mammals. This evolutionary conservatism reflects the continued function of these teeth, especially of the molars: grinding and crushing food. Specialized attributes of some primates' teeth reflect particular food preferences. For example, some primates have high, pointed cusps on the occlusal, or chewing, surfaces of their molars, for puncturing and crushing insects. Others have crests on their molars, for shearing leaves. The many primates that eat fruit and seeds tend to have low, round cusps on their molars, for crushing and pulping.

The molars of monkeys, apes, and humans have distinctive occlusal surfaces (**Figure 6.11**). Old World monkeys have four cusps on their upper and lower molars, with two of the cusps on the front and two of the cusps on the back of the tooth's occlusal surface. Each pair of cusps, front and back, is connected by an enamel ridge, or **loph**. This is called a **bilophodont** (meaning "two-ridge tooth") molar. Apes and humans have a lower molar with five separate cusps that are separated by

Bilophodont

(a)

(b)

Y-5

(c)

(d)

FIGURE 6.11

Primate Molars The morphology of lower molars in primates has two main variants: the Old World monkeys' bilophodont pattern, such as in **(a)** the colobus monkey; and the apes' Y-5 pattern, such as in **(b)** the gibbon, **(c)** the chimpanzee, and **(d)** the orangutan. Like the dental formula, molar morphology can be used to determine whether fossilized remains of a primate represent an ancestor of Old World monkeys or of apes and humans.

FIGURE 6.12

Tooth Comb Lemurs and lorises possess this unique morphology of lower incisors and canines—seen here from **(a)** above and **(b)** the side—that is useful for scraping and for grooming fur.

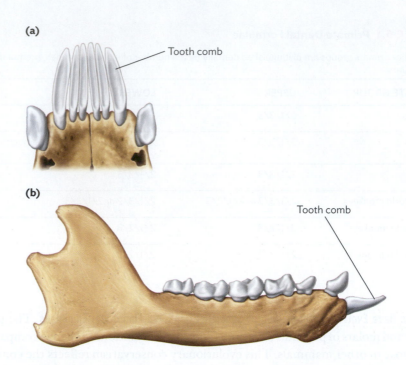

(a)

Tooth comb

(b)

Tooth comb

Y-5 Hominoids' pattern of lower molar cusps.

tooth comb Anterior teeth (incisors and canines) that have been tilted forward, creating a scraper.

canine–premolar honing complex The dental form in which the upper canines are sharpened against the lower third premolars when the jaws are opened and closed.

diastema A space between two teeth.

sectorial (premolar) Adapted for cutting.

grooves. A Υ-shaped groove is dominant, with the fork of the Υ directed toward the outside of the tooth. This is called a **Y-5** molar. The upper molars of apes and humans generally have four cusps, separated by grooves.

While most primates have flat, vertically oriented incisors that are used to prepare food before it is chewed by the premolars and molars, strepsirrhines have elongated lower incisors and canines that are crowded together and project forward. This specialized feature, a **tooth comb**, is especially useful for grooming (**Figure 6.12**).

The horizontally oriented canine is one of three different kinds of canines in primates. The small, vertical, incisor-shaped canine appears only in humans, and only in humans (and all their hominin ancestors) are the canines subject to wear at the tip of the tooth. The projecting, pointed canine is present in all monkeys and all apes. In Old World monkeys and apes, the canines are part of a **canine–premolar honing complex**, in which the upper canine fits in a space, or **diastema**, between the lower canine and lower third premolar. This configuration slices food, especially leaves and other plants. When the primate chews, the movement of the back of the upper canine against the front of the lower first premolar creates and maintains a sharp edge on each of the two teeth (**Figure 6.13**).

The lower third premolar is **sectorial**, meaning that it has a single dominant cusp and a sharp cutting edge. The upper canine tends to be large, especially in males. In addition to its masticatory function, the large upper canine provides a strong social signal for establishing and maintaining dominance among male members of the primate society, such as in baboons (**Figure 6.14**). (In chapter 7, I talk more about dominance in primates, an important concept in social behavior.) The large upper canine is also displayed by adult males as a warning signal to potential predators.

Thickness of tooth enamel varies across primate species. Orangutans and humans have thick enamel, whereas chimpanzees and gorillas have thin enamel. Thick enamel reflects an adaptation to eating tough, hard foods. Although humans today rarely eat hard foods, they have retained this primitive characteristic.

(a) (b)

Diastema

No diastema

FIGURE 6.13

Honing Complex **(a)** In Old World monkeys and apes, the lower jaw has a diastema to accommodate the very large upper canines. **(b)** Humans lack such a space because they do not have large, projecting upper canines. Notice the different size and orientation of the canines in **(a)** and **(b)** and in Figure 6.12.

PARENTAL INVESTMENT—PRIMATE PARENTS PROVIDE PROLONGED CARE FOR FEWER BUT SMARTER, MORE SOCIALLY COMPLEX, AND LONGER-LIVED OFFSPRING

Female primates give birth to fewer offspring than do other female mammals. A single female primate's births are spaced out over time—sometimes by several years in the cases of some apes. Primate mothers invest a lot of time and energy in caring for each of their offspring (**Figure 6.15**). By caring for their offspring, providing them with food, and teaching them about social roles and social behavior generally, primates increase the chances of their species' survival.

Primates have long growth and development periods, in part because of their high level of intelligence, cognitive abilities, social learning, and cultural capabilities relative to other animals (**Figure 6.16**). The timeline of growth stages of the primates also reveals that humans have an extraordinarily long life span. It is likely

FIGURE 6.14

Canine Size In some primate species, such as baboons, the canines differ in size between males and females. Because the canines can be used as weapons, the fierce appearance of these large teeth serves to warn competitors and predators.

CONCEPT CHECK

What Gives Primates Their Dietary Flexibility?

Primates display a broad range of dietary adaptations. Although the teeth of strepsirrhines and haplorrhines have evolved specializations, such as the tooth comb in lemurs, the overall retention of a nonspecialized, primitive dentition reflects the order's diverse diet.

CHARACTERISTIC	FEATURES
Multiple tooth types	Incisors, canines, premolars, molars
Reduced number of teeth	Fewer incisors, premolars, and molars

FIGURE 6.15

Parental Investment Because a female primate generally expends so much energy in rearing each of her offspring, she generally will have few offspring. Here, a chimpanzee mother holds her infant.

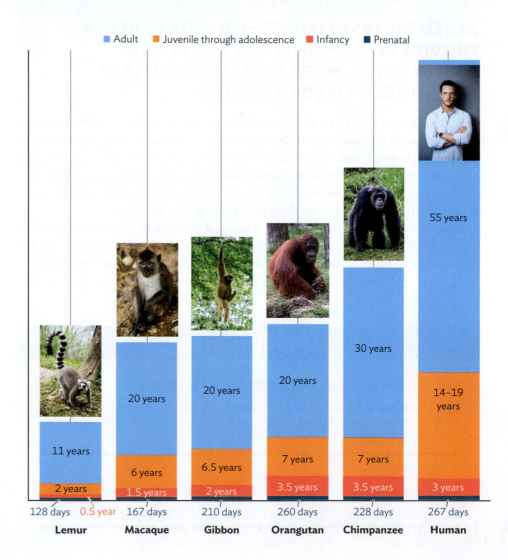

Adult ■ Juvenile through adolescence ■ Infancy ■ Prenatal

Lemur	Macaque	Gibbon	Orangutan	Chimpanzee	Human
11 years	20 years	20 years	20 years	30 years	55 years
	6 years	6.5 years	7 years	7 years	14–19 years
2 years	1.5 years	2 years	3.5 years	3.5 years	3 years
128 days 0.5 year	167 days	210 days	260 days	228 days	267 days

FIGURE 6.16

Growth Stages of Six Primates Lemurs and macaques have the shortest growth period; apes and humans have the longest. The longer growth period reflects the greater behavioral complexity in apes and humans than in lemurs and macaques.

that the high level of sociality in general and social learning in particular has contributed to prolonged lifetimes, especially in the modern era.

That primates' brains are so large and complex reflects the crucial importance of intelligence—brainpower—in primate evolution (**Figure 6.17**). The back portion of the brain where visual signals are processed is expanded in primates, whereas the areas of the brain associated with smell (**olfactory bulb**) and hearing are considerably smaller than in other mammals. Among all primates, humans have the largest brain relative to body size and the most elaborate neural connections between different regions of the brain. This combination of greater mass and complexity provides humans with greater intelligence compared with other primates and has led humans to develop language and highly complex material and behavioral culture.

olfactory bulb The portion of the anterior brain that processes odor-detection signals.

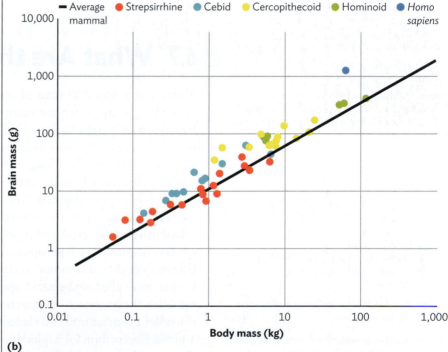

(b)

FIGURE 6.17

Primate Brain Morphology **(a)** The main regions of the brain are delineated in these drawings of primates' brains. The drawings are out of scale to show differences in anatomy. **(b)** As this graph shows, primates with the greatest body mass also have the greatest brain mass and thus the greatest intelligence. Most primates also have a larger brain relative to body size than the average mammal, a reflection of primates' higher intelligence. The *Homo sapiens* dot is way off the line because humans have a much bigger brain relative to body mass. The human brain is not just a large version of an ape's, monkey's, or strepsirrhine's brain. Rather, during evolution, in addition to a size increase, the human brain has undergone important qualitative and quantitative changes in some key regions. What are these changes, and how are they associated with behavior?

6.2 What Are the Kinds of Primates?

taxa Plural of *taxon*, which is any unit in biological classification (taxonomy), such as genus, species, class, order, family, and the like.

grade A group of organisms sharing the same complexity and level of evolution.

clade A group of organisms that evolved from a common ancestor.

primitive characteristics Characteristics present in multiple species of a group.

derived characteristics Characteristics present in only one or a few species of a group.

Today, more than 200 **taxa** of primates live in various parts of the world. If we count subspecies, there are more than 600 kinds of primates, from the mouse lemur, which weighs less than 0.5 kg (1 lb), to the gorilla, which weighs several hundred pounds. Primate biological diversity is reflected in two different classification systems. The long-standing approach, called *traditional* or *gradistic*, separates the order Primates into two suborders, the Prosimii (prosimians) and the Anthropoidea (anthropoids). This approach is based on **grades**, or levels of anatomical complexity, without consideration of identifying ancestral–descendant relationships. Biological anthropologists are increasingly using an alternative form of classification, which groups primates on the basis of lines of descent and identification of shared common ancestry (**Figure 6.18**). This *cladistic*, or *evolutionary* (sometimes called *phylogenetic*), approach uses anatomical and genetic evidence to establish the ancestral–descendant lines that link **clades**. This approach divides the order Primates into two clades (suborders): the Strepsirrhini (or strepsirrhines) and the Haplorrhini (or haplorrhines). The strepsirrhines have retained **primitive characteristics**, such as the rhinarium and heightened sense of smell, and tend to have relatively specialized diets and behaviors. The haplorrhines have the range of features that define primates as described earlier, but they have lost over the course of their evolution a number of primitive primate characteristics that strepsirrhines have retained, such as the rhinarium.

The classification approaches—traditional (gradistic) and evolutionary (cladistic)—result in similar outcomes in the way primates are categorized. The major difference is that the traditional approach groups tarsiers, a relatively specialized primate, with the prosimians. However, tarsiers share a number of **derived characteristics** with anthropoids, such as both lacking a rhinarium. Tarsiers' teeth are like anthropoids'—their canines are large and projecting, the lower incisors are relatively small, and the upper central incisors are large. Many authorities argue that tarsiers share a common ancestor with anthropoids and not with the other prosimians (lorises, galagos, and lemurs) and should be considered part of a single (haplorrhine) clade. Given the priority of and focus on evolution,

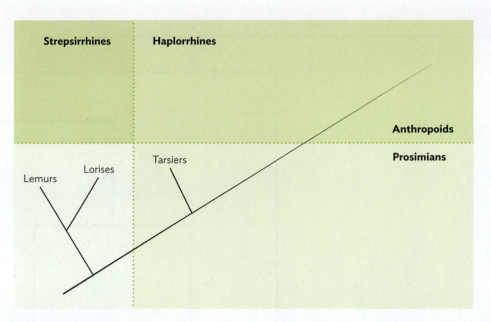

FIGURE 6.18

Cladistic (Evolutionary or Phylogenetic) versus Gradistic (Traditional) Classification
According to the cladistic categorization (upper left), lemurs and lorises belong to the category strepsirrhines, and anthropoids and tarsiers belong to the category haplorrhines. By contrast, according to the gradistic categorization (right), lorises, lemurs, and tarsiers belong to the category prosimians, which is distinct from anthropoids.

and not description, in this book, I use the cladistic approach, placing the tarsiers with the anthropoids (monkeys, apes, and humans) in a haplorrhine clade and the lorises, galagos, and lemurs in the strepsirrhine clade (**Figure 6.19**).

There are two clades of haplorrhines: the anthropoids and tarsiers. Anthropoids include catarrhines (Old World monkeys, apes, and humans) and platyrrhines (New World monkeys). These clades encompass monkeys (cercopithecoids, or Old World monkeys, and ceboids, or New World monkeys), apes (hylobatids, or lesser apes, and nonhuman hominids, or great apes), and humans (hominins). Tarsiers have a number of primitive features, especially with respect to having large, bulbous eyes for nocturnal vision. Rather than having four lower incisors, two on the left and two on the right, tarsiers have only two. Like some of the strepsirrhines, they have retained three premolars on each side of the upper and lower jaws, giving them 34 teeth. Their name refers to the presence of two highly elongated tarsal bones in their feet. These long bones give extra leverage for leaping in search of prey, such as small birds. Tarsiers' eyes and eye sockets are enormous, reflecting their nocturnal adaptation (**Figure 6.20**).

Anthropoids are found in many places around the world, whereas tarsiers are restricted to a series of islands, especially Sulawesi, Borneo, and the Philippines. Both major clades of primates—strepsirrhines and haplorrhines—are hierarchically arranged, culminating at the bottom with genus and species (see Figure 6.19). Some genera are very diverse and are represented by multiple species, whereas others are not as diverse and have today just one species (for example, living humans). Among the hominoids, humans and African great apes (gorillas, chimpanzees, and bonobos) are more closely related to each other than they are to the Asian great apes (orangutans). In addition, DNA comparisons reveal that chimpanzees and humans are more closely related than either is to gorillas (**Figure 6.21**).

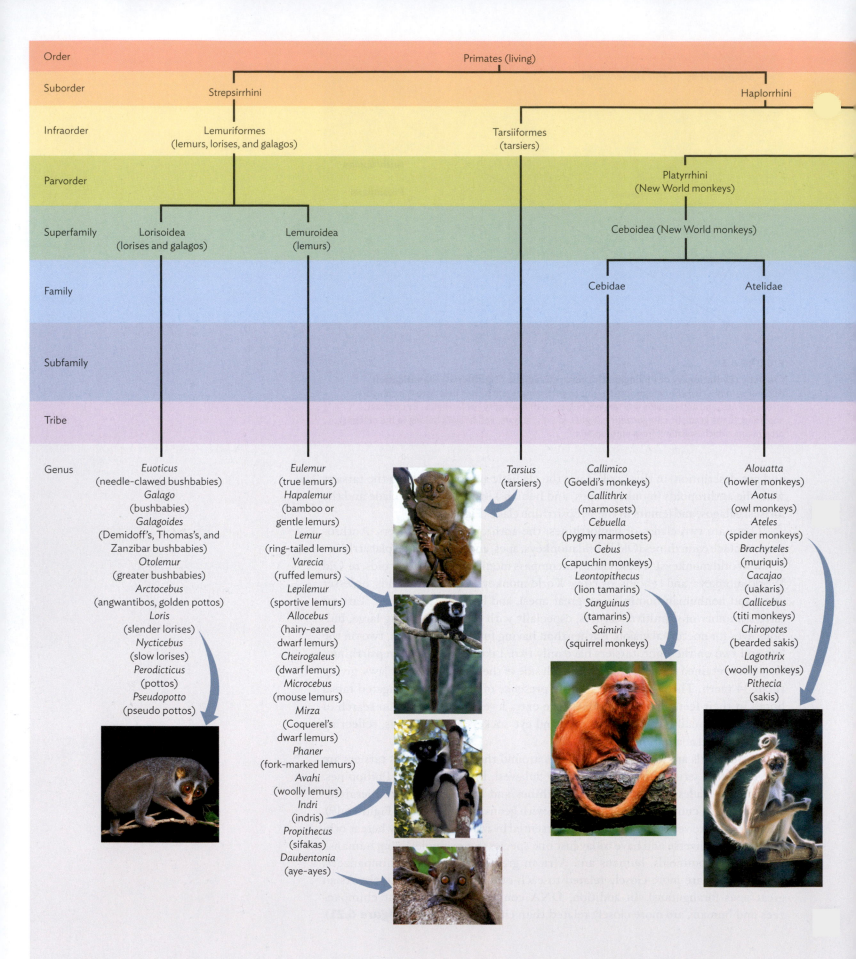

Order	Primates (living)			
Suborder	Strepsirrhini			Haplorrhini
Infraorder	Lemuriformes (lemurs, lorises, and galagos)		Tarsiiformes (tarsiers)	
Parvorder			Platyrrhini (New World monkeys)	
Superfamily	Lorisoidea (lorises and galagos)	Lemuroidea (lemurs)	Ceboidea (New World monkeys)	
Family			Cebidae	Atelidae
Subfamily				
Tribe				

Genus

Euoticus
(needle-clawed bushbabies)
Galago
(bushbabies)
Galagoides
(Demidoff's, Thomas's, and
Zanzibar bushbabies)
Otolemur
(greater bushbabies)
Arctocebus
(angwantibos, golden pottos)
Loris
(slender lorises)
Nycticebus
(slow lorises)
Perodicticus
(pottos)
Pseudopotto
(pseudo pottos)

Eulemur
(true lemurs)
Hapalemur
(bamboo or
gentle lemurs)
Lemur
(ring-tailed lemurs)
Varecia
(ruffed lemurs)
Lepilemur
(sportive lemurs)
Allocebus
(hairy-eared
dwarf lemurs)
Cheirogaleus
(dwarf lemurs)
Microcebus
(mouse lemurs)
Mirza
(Coquerel's
dwarf lemurs)
Phaner
(fork-marked lemurs)
Avahi
(woolly lemurs)
Indri
(indris)
Propithecus
(sifakas)
Daubentonia
(aye-ayes)

Tarsius
(tarsiers)

Callimico
(Goeldi's monkeys)
Callithrix
(marmosets)
Cebuella
(pygmy marmosets)
Cebus
(capuchin monkeys)
Leontopithecus
(lion tamarins)
Sanguinus
(tamarins)
Saimiri
(squirrel monkeys)

Alouatta
(howler monkeys)
Aotus
(owl monkeys)
Ateles
(spider monkeys)
Brachyteles
(muriquis)
Cacajao
(uakaris)
Callicebus
(titi monkeys)
Chiropotes
(bearded sakis)
Lagothrix
(woolly monkeys)
Pithecia
(sakis)

Anthropoidea (monkeys, apes, and humans)

Catarrhini
(Old World monkeys, apes, and humans)

Cercopithecoidea
(Old World monkeys)

Hominoidea
(apes and humans)

Hylobatidae
(lesser apes)

Hominidae
(great apes and humans)

Colobinae

Cercopithecinae

Ponginae
(orangutans)

Gorillinae
(gorillas)

Homininae
(chimpanzees, bonobos,
and humans)

Panini

Hominini

Colobus
(black-and-white
colobus monkeys)
Nasalis
(proboscis monkeys)
Presbytis
(leaf monkeys)
Procolobus
(red and olive
colobus monkeys)
Pygathrix
(snub-nosed monkeys)
Semnopithecus
(Hanuman langurs)
Simias
(pig-tailed monkeys)
Trachypithecus
(langurs)

Allenopithecus
(swamp monkeys)
Cercocebus
(mangabeys)
Cercopithecus
(guenons)
Erythrocebus
(patas monkeys)
Macaca
(macaques)
Mandrillus
(drills, mandrills)
Miopithecus
(talapoin monkeys)
Papio
(baboons)
Theropithecus
(geladas)

Hylobates
(gibbons and
siamangs)

Pongo
(orangutans)

Gorilla
(gorillas)

Pan
(chimpanzees,
including
bonobos)

Homo
(humans)

FIGURE 6.19

Order Primates This classification of primate species uses the Linnaean taxonomy and places primates into two major groups: strepsirrhines and haplorrhines. Shared adaptive physical features help determine the degree of relatedness among primate species. (Not all species of primates are listed.)

(b)

Talus

Calcaneus

Tarsier foot

Talus

Calcaneus

Human foot

FIGURE 6.20

Tarsier Eyes and Feet **(a)** Tarsiers are unique among haplorrhines in that their eyes have a fovea, a region of the retina that enables the sharp central vision needed for seeing details. This trait is unusual in nocturnal animals because dim light typically prevents them from seeing things that clearly. **(b)** Thanks to their elongated tarsals (shown in color), especially the talus and calcaneus bones, tarsiers are superb leapers.

I KNOW IT'S HARD TO BELIEVE, BUT BIOLOGICALLY SPEAKING, THEY'RE OUR CLOSEST RELATIVES.

FIGURE 6.21

Chimpanzee–Human Relationship As noted in chapter 3, humans and chimpanzees have approximately 98% of their genetic material in common. Perhaps we often seem as chimplike to them as chimps often seem humanlike to us. (*Brevity* © 2006. Dist. by Andrews McMeel Syndication. Reprinted with permission. All rights reserved.)

Therefore, traditional and cladistic taxonomies produce somewhat different results for these primates (**Table 6.2**). The traditional classification includes three families: hylobatids (gibbons), pongids (great apes), and hominids (humans). By contrast, the cladistic classification includes two families: hylobatids (gibbons) and hominids (great apes, including humans); and three subfamilies: pongines (orangutans), gorillines (gorillas), and hominines (chimpanzees, bonobos, and humans). The hominines are further subdivided into two tribes: panins (chimpanzees, bonobos) and hominins (humans).

The differences between the major primate groups—for example, the differences between an ape and a monkey—matter, first, because they are a means of understanding the variation among primates. Second, the key characteristics of the different primate taxa appear at specific points in the evolutionary record. Paleontologists look for these characteristics in their study of the origins and evolution of the different primate groups. For example, when did the Y-5 molar, a defining characteristic of apes, first appear? When did bipedalism first occur? When did monkeys living in the New World first differ noticeably from those living in the Old World? Such questions are central to the study of both primates and their evolution. They can be answered only by knowing the characteristics unique to different primate taxa. These characteristics, then, help paleontologists and anthropologists reconstruct the evolutionary relationships and history of living species and their fossil ancestors. These evolutionary relationships, or **phylogeny**, are based on shared characteristics, including physical traits, genetics, and behavior. Organisms that share characteristics are more closely related than are organisms

TABLE 6.2 Hominoid Classifications

	GRADISTIC (TRADITIONAL) CLASSIFICATION					CLADISTIC (PHYLOGENETIC) CLASSIFICATION				
Superfamily		Hominoid					Hominoid			
Family	Hylobatid	Pongid			Hominid	Hylobatid	Hominid			
Subfamily							Pongine	Gorilline	Hominine	
Tribe									Panini	Hominini
Genus	*Hylobates*	*Pongo*	*Pan*	*Gorilla*	*Homo*	*Hylobates*	*Pongo*	*Gorilla*	*Pan*	*Homo*
Common name	Gibbon	Orangutan	Chimpanzee Bonobo	Gorilla	Human	Gibbon	Orangutan	Gorilla	Chimpanzee Bonobo	Human

that do not share characteristics. For example, all mammals are homeothermic—all mammal species share this primitive trait. All apes have a sectorial complex—but humans lack this derived trait.

In addition, it is important to know about the physical differences between primate taxa because the variation in the living primates provides models for understanding the morphology, the behavior, and the adaptation in the evolutionary past. For example, the Y-5 lower molar pattern seen today in apes and humans first appeared in anthropoids 20–30 mya. This morphology indicates that apes originated at that time. (Humans have the pattern but evolved after apes.) Similarly, characteristics that define bipedalism in humans—long lower limbs and short upper limbs—first appeared 5 mya or so. When anthropologists find these anatomical characteristics in fossilized remains (fossils are the subject of chapter 8), they are able to identify the origins of humanlike ancestors. And knowing how those ancestors walked helps complete a timeline of adaptation.

phylogeny The evolutionary relationships of a group of organisms.

THE STREPSIRRHINES

In acquiring food, strepsirrhines rely heavily on their highly developed sense of smell. Reflecting this focus on smell, they have a rhinarium, enlarged nasal passages, scent glands, and a large olfactory bulb in the area in the front of the brain that controls the sense of smell. They also have the aforementioned tooth comb. Strepsirrhines have nails at the ends of their fingers and toes, but the second toe has a toilet claw, which is a claw used primarily for grooming. Virtually all strepsirrhines communicate with distinctive calls and mark their travel routes and territory with urine.

In evolutionary terms, the three strepsirrhines—lemurs, lorises, and galagos—are among the most primitive primates (primate evolution is the subject of chapter 9). Many of the primitive characteristics seen in these primates have been

FIGURE 6.22

around for many millions of years. There are a number of behaviors that almost all strepsirrhines share, such as a focus on grooming and relatively simple social groupings. On the other hand, there is considerable variation in the biology and ecology of these highly diverse primates, associated with habitats and available foods, terrain, and climate.

Lemurs express the highest degree of diversity among primates today, so much so that they represent some 21% of primate genera worldwide (**Figure 6.22**). However, all of this remarkable diversity is highly constricted geographically. That is, lemurs are restricted to the large island of Madagascar off the southeast coast of Africa. Until humans first arrived on Madagascar, beginning around 2,000 years ago, many species of lemurs were present on the island, including the large *Megaladapis*, which reached 50 kg (110 lb) in adulthood (**Figure 6.23**). These and many other so-called subfossil lemurs are now extinct, owing mostly to human encroachment and exploitations of these primate species.

Today, there are about 100 taxa of lemurs, ranging from the tiny mouse lemur (*Microcebus berthae*), weighing only about 30 g (1 oz), to the indri (*Indri indri*), weighing around 9 kg (20 lb). They are extraordinarily primitive, having very small brains relative to body size and an enhanced sense of smell. Their high degree of anatomical diversity is also reflected in some species having relatively long hind limbs, an anatomical specialization used for leaping from tree branch to tree branch.

Lemurs are highly social, traveling in groups dominated by adult females. Reflecting their biological variation, lemurs have considerable dietary variation, with most depending on leaves and fruits, but with some having a relatively narrow

(a)

Gorilla

Megaladapis

(b)

Megaladapis edwardsi

Megaladapis madagascariensis

Palaeopropithecus   Hadropithecus   Archaeolemur   Babakotia

mouse lemur   indri

10 cm

FIGURE 6.23

Megaladapis **(a)** The skull at the bottom of the photo belonged to a species of very large lemurs, the now extinct *Megaladapis*, on Madagascar. Skulls of *Megaladapis* were larger than a modern gorilla's, though *Megaladapis*'s body was smaller than a gorilla's. **(b)** In the right foreground, the skulls of a modern mouse lemur (middle) and an indri (right) represent the range of sizes in living lemurs. The crania in the back row and the skull to the left of the mouse lemur's show the range of sizes in extinct lemurs. The sizes of living and extinct lemurs overlap somewhat, but *Megaladapis*, the largest extinct lemur (far left), was substantially larger than any living lemur.

diet. Lemurs reflect the diversity of primates generally, with Madagascar serving as a kind of microcosm of environments globally, ranging from dense, tropical forest to open grasslands. Lemurs have successfully adapted to these diverse ecological contexts.

Owing to the continued expansion of the human population on Madagascar, virtually all lemur taxa are threatened in some manner. Although a number of research centers are successful in breeding and maintaining populations, such as the Duke Lemur Center at Duke University, North Carolina, and a group working on St. Catherines Island, Georgia, the degree of loss in their natural settings is alarming.

Lorises today are found in Southeast Asia, Sri Lanka, and Africa. Unlike the enormous variation seen in lemurs, lorises are less diverse and are represented by far fewer species (**Figure 6.24**). They are generally nocturnal and arboreal, making it more difficult for primatologists to study their biology, behavior, and ecology. Unlike many other strepsirrhines, lorises lack an external tail. The Sunda slow loris (*Nycticebus coucang*) is unique in having a toxic bite, whereby the primate licks its arm gland and the associated toxin is activated via mixing with its saliva. The toxin protects the adult and its infant from predators.

The very large, forward-facing eyes of lorises are an adaptation to their limitation to nocturnal activity. Their limbs are relatively long, but with some having specializations, such as opposability of the big toe with the other four toes, providing stability on branches and for acquisition of food. The Sunda slow loris has a long trunk, an anatomical adaptation for twisting around branches. Generally, multiple males compete for access to a single female. At dusk, lorises emerge from their nests. Over the course of the night, lorises interact regularly and sleep in groups. During the day, females and young sleep in groups. Food sources are limited primarily to insects.

Galagos (or bushbabies) live in Africa. Like lorises, galagos feed and reproduce at night. Their most distinctive physical characteristics—very large, forward-facing eyes and very large eye orbits—reflect an adaptation that is exclusively nocturnal (**Figure 6.25**). They also have the specialized tooth comb. Galagos are primarily

(a)

(c)

(b)

FIGURE 6.24

Lorises Lorises are widespread, today found in Southeast Asia, Sri Lanka, and Africa. Unlike most primate taxa, these primates have a very small tail and do not leap. Shown here are **(a)** Sunda slow loris (*Nycticebus coucang*), **(b)** gray slender loris (*Loris lydekkerianus*), and **(c)** pygmy slow loris (*Nycticebus pygmaeus*).

(a)

(b)

(c)

FIGURE 6.25

Galagos The galagos, or bushbabies, live in Africa and are exclusively nocturnal primates. There are multiple genera and species, including **(a)** Senegal bushbaby (*Galago senegalensis*), **(b)** southern lesser galago (*Galago moholi*), and **(c)** thick-tailed bushbaby (*Otolemur crassicaudatus*).

Monkey or Ape? Differences Matter

Differences between monkeys and apes track different evolutionary histories.

CHARACTERISTIC	MONKEY	APE
Body size	Generally smaller	Generally larger
Posture/locomotion	Generally horizontal body trunk	Relatively vertical body trunk
Body trunk	Narrow	Broad
Tail	Has a tail	Lacks a tail
Lower molars	Bilophodont lower molar (cercopithecoids only)	Y-5 molar pattern
Brain	Relatively small	Relatively large
Growth	Relatively fast	Relatively slow
Interspecies variability	High	Low

insectivorous but will occasionally consume small animals and fruit. Like many other strepsirrhines, the common social grouping includes an adult female and her young.

Perhaps what is most distinctive about galagos is their predilection to jumping upward, often to heights exceeding 2 m (6.5 ft). Therefore, a considerable 25% of their overall body mass is muscle in the hind limbs. Their remarkably powerful hind limbs facilitate movement over great distances in a short amount of time. The rapid travel is associated with both acquisition of food—such as fast-moving insects—and fleeing from predators.

THE HAPLORRHINES

Haplorrhines differ from strepsirrhines in a number of important ways. In general, haplorrhines have larger brains, are more dimorphic sexually in body size and other anatomical characteristics, and have fewer teeth (premolars, in particular) than strepsirrhines. Moreover, unlike strepsirrhines' eyes, haplorrhines' eyes are convergent and enclosed by a continuous ring of bone. Haplorrhines also see in color, whereas strepsirrhines see mostly in black and white.

The two parvorders of anthropoids—platyrrhines, or New World monkeys, and catarrhines, including Old World monkeys, apes, and hominins (see Figure 6.19)—are named for the morphologies of their noses (**Figure 6.26**). Platyrrhine (from the Greek, meaning "broad-nosed") nostrils are round and separated by a wide nasal septum, the area of soft tissue between the nostrils. Catarrhine ("hook-nosed") nostrils are close together and point downward. (To understand nostril orientation, look at your own nostrils in a mirror. They should be directed downward, as you are a catarrhine.)

The one superfamily of platyrrhines is the ceboids (see Figure 6.19). The two ceboid families, cebids and atelids, are widespread in Latin America, from southern

Platyrrhines
New World

Catarrhines
Old World

FIGURE 6.26

Platyrrhines versus Catarrhines In addition to their differently shaped noses, these two groups differ in their numbers of premolars: platyrrhines have six upper and six lower premolars, whereas catarrhines have four upper and four lower premolars.

prehensile tail A tail that acts as a kind of a hand for support in trees; common in New World monkeys.

FIGURE 6.27

Prehensile Tails Atelines, such as the muriquis (or woolly spider monkeys) shown here, are the only primates with a fully prehensile tail. (Opossums and kinkajous are among the other mammals with a fully prehensile tail.) The prehensile tail is very muscular, and its undersurface has dermal ridges, like fingerprints and toe prints, that improve the tail's grip.

Argentina to Mexico. Ceboids are arboreal, spending nearly all their time in trees. They use suspensory locomotion, in which all four limbs grasp on to branches and help move the body from one tree or branch to another. Within the atelids are two subfamilies, one of which, the atelines, is distinctive in that each of its four types (howler monkeys, spider monkeys, woolly monkeys, and woolly spider monkeys) has a **prehensile tail** (**Figure 6.27**). In addition to locomotion functions in the trees, the prehensile tail can be used to suspend the body from a branch so that the hands and feet can be used to feed. Ceboids have a diverse diet, ranging from insects (that is, they practice insectivory) to fruits (frugivory) and leaves (folivory). Smaller ceboids obtain protein from insects, whereas larger ones obtain it from leaves.

The Old World monkeys, cercopithecoids, are the most diverse and successful nonhuman primates. They inhabit a wide range of habitats throughout Africa and Asia but mostly live in the tropics or subtropics. Some are arboreal and some are terrestrial. Cercopithecoids have bilophodont upper and lower molars, a narrow face, a sitting pad on the rear, and a long body trunk that terminates with a nonprehensile tail. Their canines are highly dimorphic sexually—males' canines are larger than females' canines, sometimes considerably so.

Cercopithecoids are divided into two subfamilies: colobines and cercopithecines (**Figure 6.28**). Colobines are closely related, medium-sized primates with a long tail and a wide array of coloration. They are mostly arboreal and live in a variety of climates, though not in dry areas. Colobines are folivores, and their anatomical features have adapted to accommodate a diet rich in leaves. The high, pointed cusps of their molars shear leaves and thus maximize the amount of nutrition obtained from them. Conversely, cercopithecines have rounded, lower cusps on their molars as their diet is rich in fruit, which does not need as much processing to extract its nutrients. Colobines' large three- or four-chambered stomach, resembling a cow's stomach, contains microorganisms that break down cellulose, again to maximize the amount of nutrition extracted from the leaves. By contrast, cercopithecines are often called "cheek-pouch monkeys" because inside each cheek they have a pouch

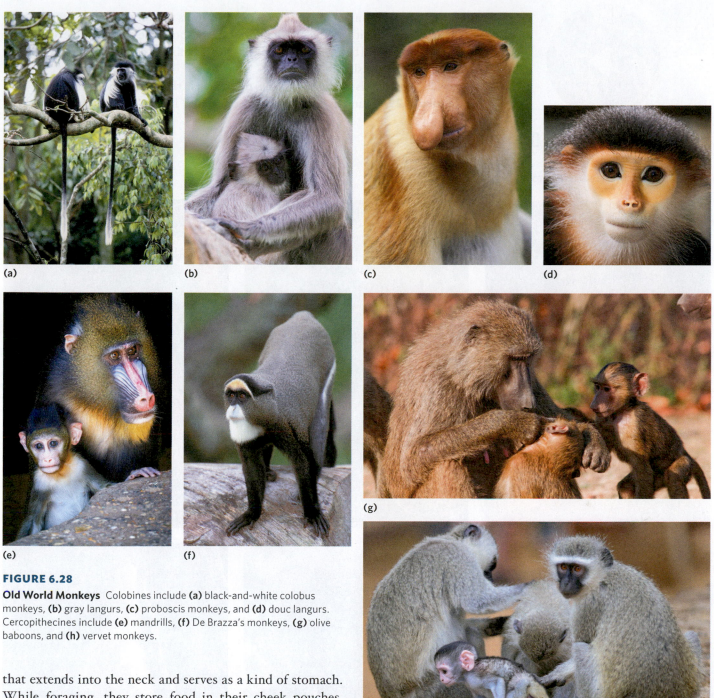

FIGURE 6.28

Old World Monkeys Colobines include **(a)** black-and-white colobus monkeys, **(b)** gray langurs, **(c)** proboscis monkeys, and **(d)** douc langurs. Cercopithecines include **(e)** mandrills, **(f)** De Brazza's monkeys, **(g)** olive baboons, and **(h)** vervet monkeys.

that extends into the neck and serves as a kind of stomach. While foraging, they store food in their cheek pouches, which are especially useful when they need to gather food quickly in a dangerous area. Arboreal cercopithecines tend to have a longer tail, while terrestrial species have a short or no tail.

Colobines are receiving a lot of attention because some taxa are highly threatened. One colobine species, Miss Waldron's red colobus monkey, is the first primate to have gone extinct in the past five centuries.

The most studied cercopithecoids are the cercopithecines, which include baboons and baboonlike monkeys (geladas, mandrills, macaques). Many cercopithecines live in the savannas of East Africa. Some of them have highly dexterous fingers, adapted for picking up small seeds from the ground. Because these primates live in habitats similar to those of early hominins (see chapter 10), they provide anthropologists with the means of understanding both the origins and evolution of early human social behavior and some physical attributes characteristic of primates living in open grasslands.

The hominoids are, in addition to humans, the great apes and lesser apes (**Figure 6.29**). Humans live on every continent. Today, the only great ape that

FIGURE 6.29

Great Apes and Lesser Apes The great apes—**(a)** chimpanzees, **(b)** bonobos, **(c)** orangutans, and **(d)** gorillas—tend to be larger than other primates. All but gorillas are smaller than humans, with whom they are highly genetically similar. While great apes have a variety of social groupings, lesser apes— **(e)** gibbons and (not pictured) siamangs—are unique in that they form pair bonds, in which one male, one female, and their offspring are the basic social unit.

lives in Asia is the orangutan. The lesser apes live in Southeast Asia. The great apes of Africa—the chimpanzee, the closely related bonobo (or pygmy chimpanzee), and the gorilla—are restricted to small equatorial areas. All of these hominoids have large brains, broad faces, and premolars and molars with little occlusal surface relief. They all have a Y-5 lower molar pattern. All apes have the canine–premolar honing complex. None of the hominoids have an external tail.

All hominoids except humans—gibbons, siamangs, gorillas, chimpanzees, bonobos, and orangutans—have very long forelimbs (arms) compared with the hind limbs. The fingers and toes are also quite long, for grasping trees and branches of various shapes and sizes. These characteristics are important adaptations used in the forest in a range of suspensory postures and movements (**Figure 6.30**). Gibbons and siamangs are skilled **brachiators**, using their upper limbs to move from tree limb to tree limb. Chimpanzees, bonobos, and gorillas are efficient at various suspensory postures, but their large sizes—especially in adult males—lead them to spend significant amounts of time on the ground in feeding and in locomotion. They use a specialized form of quadrupedalism called knuckle-walking, in which the very strong arms are used to support the upper body weight while positioned on the backs of the fingers' middle phalanges. The knuckles bear the weight, while the fingers are flexed toward the palms (**Figure 6.31**).

In orangutans and gorillas, males have enormous masticatory muscles, which are accommodated by a large, well-developed sagittal crest, the ridge of bone running along the midline (mid-sagittal) plane of the skull. The sagittal crest is the terminal attachment site for the temporalis muscle

Long, curved fingers

Long arms

FIGURE 6.30

Suspensory Apes That the great apes and lesser apes regularly use suspensory locomotion can be seen in various features of their skeletal anatomy. For example, this gibbon's arms are long compared with its legs; its fingers and toes are long; and its fingers are curved and thus have enhanced grasping ability. If an ancestral primate's forelimbs were considerably longer than its hind limbs, the animal was likely suspensory.

FIGURE 6.31

Knuckle-Walking This unique type of quadrupedalism enables chimpanzees and gorillas, like the gorilla pictured here, to move very quickly. In contrast, orangutans typically use fist-walking, supporting their upper body weight on the palms, which are closed in fists.

(a)

(b)

Sagittal crest

Temporalis
muscle

Nuchal
crest

Masseter
muscle

FIGURE 6.32

Sagittal Crest **(a)** This ridge of bone is located at the
sagittal suture along the midline of the cranium.
(b) The more highly developed the sagittal crest is, the
more highly developed the masticatory muscles are. This
feature appears in gorillas and orangutans, as well as
a variety of other animals, especially carnivores. It has
been found in some human and primate ancestors.

(**Figure 6.32**). Gorillas devote considerable time to eating leaves and plant stems.
In contrast, chimpanzees are omnivorous—they eat fruit, leaves, bark, insects,
and meat, depending on the season, their habitat (ranging from dense rainforests
to savanna–woodlands), and local tradition. When meat is not available, chimpanzees' body weight goes down, suggesting that they rely on animal sources
for protein.

The general body plan of humans resembles that of the large-bodied apes of
Africa, a fact that has been recognized since at least the middle of the nineteenth
century, when Thomas Huxley wrote his famous treatise on primate anatomy and
human evolution, *Man's Place in Nature* (Huxley's research is discussed further in
chapter 10). Humans have several unique anatomical attributes, however, many
of which are related to the fact that humans are the only obligate, or restrictedly,
bipedal primate (see "What Makes Humans So Different from Other Animals?
The Six Steps to Humanness" in chapter 1).

The skeletal indicators of bipedalism are found in the skull and the postcranial
skeleton. In bipeds, the foramen magnum—the large opening for the passage of the
spinal cord to the brain—is located at the bottom of the skull. The skull sits atop
the body, whereas in quadrupeds the foramen magnum is located on the back of
the skull and the skull is positioned on the front of the body. Many of the postcranial characteristics associated with bipedalism are in the pelvis. The pelvis of the
human (the biped) is short and directed to the side of the body, whereas the pelvis
of the ape (the quadruped) is long and directed to the back of the body. These differently shaped pelvises reflect the different positions and functions of two gluteal
muscles—gluteus medius and gluteus minimus—which attach across the hip joints
of both humans and apes. In apes, these two muscles act as thigh straighteners, or

extensors; but in humans, they abduct the thigh on the side of the hip that supports the body weight when a person walks. The muscles' contraction on the abducted side keeps the hip stable while the other leg swings forward (**Figure 6.33**). (Next time you walk, notice how only one foot is on the ground at any one time, and feel how on that side of your hip the gluteal muscles have contracted.)

The position of the foramen magnum in apes, monkeys, and other quadrupedal animals is toward the back of the skull.

In apes, the medius and minimus gluteal muscles pull the leg backward, extending the leg at the hip.

In humans, the foramen magnum is on the bottom of the skull.

In humans, the medius and minimus gluteal muscles abduct the leg; that is, they pull the thigh away from the midline of the body when the leg is extended. As the thigh is abducted, it is also rotated inward, providing a more stable support for the hip during walking.

FIGURE 6.33

Quadrupedalism versus Bipedalism Various morphological features differentiate these two forms of locomotion.

Strepsirrhines and Haplorrhines Differ in Their Anatomy and Senses

Strepsirrhines tend to be more primitive than haplorrhines.

CHARACTERISTIC/ ADAPTATION	STREPSIRRHINE TENDENCIES	HAPLORRHINE TENDENCIES
Smell	More developed	Less developed
Vision	Nocturnal for many	Diurnal
Touch	Claws in some Less developed	Nails More developed
Diet	More specialized More teeth in some	More generalized Reduced number of teeth
Intelligence	Less developed Small brain	More developed Large brain

Among the other anatomical differences between humans and apes are the relative lengths of the limbs, the curvature of the spine, and the angle of the femur in standing, walking, and running bipeds (**Figure 6.34**). In addition, unlike apes and monkeys, humans do not hone their canines and premolars. These differences are discussed more fully in chapter 10. Moreover, humans also have a greatly reduced digestive system compared to the other hominoids. In this regard, humans

FIGURE 6.34

Limb Proportions In suspensory apes (left), the arms are long compared with the legs. In humans (right), the arms are relatively short because they are no longer used in locomotion. In addition, humans' fingers and toes are relatively shorter and straighter than those of apes, again as a result of bipedalism.

have smaller teeth, smaller masticatory muscles and bony architecture supporting these muscles, and a diminutive stomach and intestinal tract. The reduction of the digestive system—from ingestion through digestion and elimination of waste products—reflects the long evolutionary history of hominins and especially their increasing dependence on tools to process foods and the use of fire to cook foods, thus reducing the consistency and increasing the digestibility of plants and animals eaten.

So far, we have concentrated on the anatomical differences among the different taxa of living primates. Of course, primates are not just about bones and teeth and other physical components. Like their anatomical variation, primates' behavioral variation reflects millions of years of evolution, during which adaptive strategies have enhanced the survival and reproduction of individuals and societies.

ANSWERING THE BIG QUESTIONS

1. Why study primates?

- Nonhuman primates (referred to simply as *primates* except where noted) are physically and behaviorally similar to humans in numerous ways. For example, forward-facing eyes and grasping hands in both groups indicate a common ancestry.
- Primates, including humans, are remarkably diverse, yet they all show ability to adapt to a wide range of circumstances.
- Owing to biological similarities between primates and humans, the study of diseases in primates helps us understand and cure diseases in humans.
- Primate diversity reflects the diversity of animal species. Reduction in primate diversity is a barometer of the "health" of the animal kingdom.

2. What is a primate?

- Primates, an order of mammals, are best defined on the basis of their evolutionary trends: they are arboreal, have highly flexible diets, and invest a great deal of time in their young. Overall, they are generalized—primates have specialized in not specializing.
- The physical characteristics of primates reflect their adaptation to life in the trees. A highly versatile body structure facilitates great mobility and manual dexterity. Vision is highly developed, but the senses of hearing and smell are greatly de-emphasized in most primate taxa.
- Primates' highly varied diet is reflected in a generally nonspecialized dentition including functionally distinctive tooth types.
- Primates' prolonged care for their young reflects the fact that primates have a lot to teach, especially in the area of complex social behaviors.

3. What are the kinds of primates?

- The more than 200 primate species living today are subdivided into two suborders: strepsirrhines and haplorrhines. Strepsirrhines include lemurs, lorises, and galagos. Haplorrhines are the tarsiers, monkeys, apes, and humans. Tarsiers are included in the haplorrhines but retain a significant suite of primitive characteristics.

STUDY QUIZ

1. Which is *not* an arboreal adaptation shared by most primates?

- a. Mobile joints connecting bones of the shoulders, limbs, hands, and feet
- b. An opposable thumb and often an opposable big toe
- c. Dermal ridges and flat nails on fingertips
- d. Rigidly connected, identical vertebrae in the backbone

2. Which evolutionary adaptation provides primates with depth perception?

- a. Forward-facing eyes
- b. Color vision
- c. Loss of the rhinarium
- d. Smaller olfactory bulb

3. _____ retain more primitive characteristics than other primates, such as a partially enclosed eye orbit.

- a. Strepsirrhines
- b. Haplorrhines
- c. Platyrrhines
- d. Catarrhines

KEY TERMS

arboreal adaptation
bilophodont (thumb)
brachiators
canine–premolar
   honing complex
clade

dental formula
derived characteristics
diastema
dietary plasticity
diurnal
grade
loph
nocturnal

olfactory bulb
opposable thumb
parental investment
phylogeny
power grip
preadaptation
precision grip
prehensile tail

primitive characteristics
rhinarium
sectorial (premolar)
taxa
tooth comb
Y-5

STUDY QUIZ (CONTINUED)

4. _____ have a dental formula of 2/1/2/3 and hook-shaped nostrils.

   a. Atelids

   b. Catarrhines

   c. Cebids

   d. Platyrrhines

5. Which feature is shared by both apes and Old World monkeys?

   a. Long tail

   b. Lower molar morphology

   c. Canine–premolar honing complex

   d. Large bodies and brains

EVOLUTION REVIEW

Our Closest Living Relatives

SYNOPSIS As a group, the members of the order Primates differ from other mammals in three key respects related to the evolutionary history that shaped their morphology and behavior. Primates are characterized by (1) arboreal adaptations (associated with life in the trees), (2) dietary flexibility (associated with the wide variety of foods that they eat), and (3) parental investment (associated with offspring that require a large amount of care). Despite these key similarities among its members, perhaps the most remarkable feature of the order Primates is its immense diversity. Some primates are nocturnal, whereas others are diurnal. Some primates spend most of their time in the trees, whereas others spend a great deal of time on the ground. Some primates have specialized diets, whereas others might eat just about anything. The immense diversity among living primates was shaped by evolutionary forces over tens of millions of years, and this diversity reflects the interactions between species and their environmental settings.

Q1. Primates are characterized by adaptations for life in trees and for eating a broad diet. Provide two examples of primate adaptations for life in the trees and two examples of primate adaptations for eating a wide variety of foods.

Q2. Primates are also characterized by unique patterns of parental investment compared to other mammalian species. Describe three major features of primate parenting. What are the implications of these parenting features for intelligence, socialization, and fitness?

Q3. Compare and contrast the traditional (gradistic) and evolutionary (cladistic) approaches to primate classification. How do morphological and genetic features contribute to defining evolutionary (ancestral–descendant) relationships more accurately in the cladistic approach? Which scheme, traditional or evolutionary, more accurately represents the similarities and differences between all members of the order Primates?

HINT See Table 6.2.

Q4. Discuss the ways in which evolutionary forces might operate to produce the huge amount of anatomical and behavioral diversity seen in the order Primates today. How does such diversity reflect the adaptability and evolutionary "success" of the order?

HINT Consider the ways in which different primates occupy distinct ecological niches.

Q5. As humans, we are obviously accustomed to thinking about most issues from a "people-centric" perspective. Pretend for a moment that you are a chimpanzee, gorilla, howler monkey, tarsier, ring-tailed lemur, or one of the many other nonhuman primate species discussed in this chapter. Which ecological and environmental factors have the greatest potential to affect the evolutionary future of your species? What types of adaptations might be most beneficial in response to these selective pressures?

ADDITIONAL READINGS

Caldecott, J. and L. Miles, eds. 2005. *World Atlas of Great Apes and Their Conservation*. Berkeley: University of California Press.

Campbell, C. J., A. Fuentes, K. C. MacKinnon, M. Panger, and S. K. Bearder, eds. 2006. *Primates in Perspective*. New York: Oxford University Press.

Estrada, A., P. A. Garber, A. B. Rylands, C. Roos, E. Fernandez-Duque, et al. 2017. Impending extinction crisis of the world's primates: Why primates matter. *Science Advances* 3(1): e1600946. DOI: 10.1126/sciadv.1600946.

McGraw, W. S. 2010. Primates defined. Pp. 222–242 in C. S. Larsen, ed. *A Companion to Biological Anthropology*. Chichester, UK: Wiley-Blackwell.

Nowak, R. M. 1999. *Walker's Primates of the World*. Baltimore: Johns Hopkins University Press.

Swindler, D. R. 1998. *Introduction to the Primates*. Seattle: University of Washington Press.

At Gombe National Park, Tanzania, in 1965, a chimpanzee plays with Jane Goodall, who sometimes hid bananas for her research subjects beneath her shirt. A world-renowned primatologist, Goodall established the Jane Goodall Institute, dedicated to preserving wildlife worldwide. Projects spearheaded by the institute, such as sanctuaries in Africa for orphaned chimpanzees, provide opportunities for continued research and educational outreach, as well as employment for members of local communities.

Gombe
National Park,
Tanzania

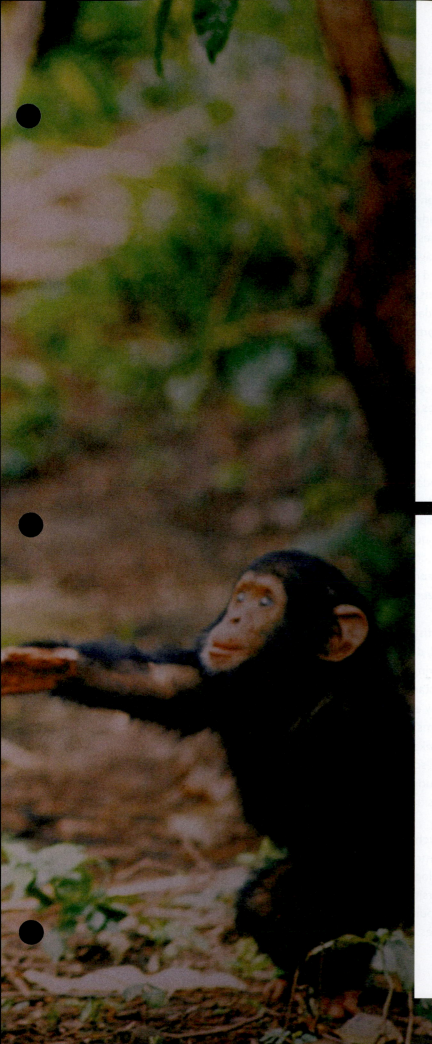

7

Primate Sociality, Social Behavior, and Culture

BIG QUESTIONS

1. **Why are primates social?**
2. **What is special about primate societies and social behavior?**
3. **How do primates acquire food?**
4. **How do primates communicate?**

Of all the scientists mentioned in this book so far, the British primatologist Jane Goodall may be the most famous. But when Goodall began doing what she loves most—observing and talking about primates—probably the only people who had heard of her were her family and friends in England. From childhood, Goodall had dreamed of living in Africa, and in 1957—after graduating from secretarial school, holding a series of odd jobs, and saving her money for 2 years—she traveled with a friend to Kenya. Within 2 months of her arrival, she had met the famous fossil hunter Louis Leakey (fossils are the subject of chapter 8; you will hear more about Leakey in chapter 10), who eventually employed her at the national museum in Nairobi.

Leakey was interested in human origins and had long thought that studying chimpanzees in the wild would open a window onto the behavior and social organization of early apes and humans. Other scientists, such as the American biological anthropologists Sherwood Washburn (1911–2000) and Irven DeVore (1934–2014), were doing pioneering field studies of baboon behavior in Kenya, but Leakey thought that chimpanzees would provide an even better understanding of the origins of ape and human social behavior. After getting to know the energetic and highly competent Goodall, and including her as his assistant at Olduvai Gorge, Tanzania, he decided she was the right person to pursue this line of inquiry. She enthusiastically agreed to live among and study chimpanzees in Gombe National Park, located in a remote area along the shores of Lake Tanganyika in western Tanzania. This venture would have been discouraging to most. No one had ever observed chimpanzees in the wild for an extended period or at the level of detail needed to record their behavior and draw conclusions. Moreover, living in the jungle was no easy undertaking—it was full of uncertainty, danger, and isolation.

habituate Undertake the process of accustoming animals to human observers.

The outcome proved even more amazing than Leakey might have imagined. A few months after reaching her field site in 1960, Goodall was able to **habituate** the chimpanzees to her presence, observe them for hours on end, and record their behaviors in unprecedented detail. Her findings bowled over the anthropological world. Chimpanzees proved highly intelligent, for example, and close social bonds existed between chimpanzee mothers and their offspring and between chimpanzee siblings. Goodall also discovered behaviors that other scientists found quite hard to believe, mainly because the behaviors did not fit expectations about the species. First, Goodall documented in words and on film how chimps made stick probes to harvest termites from termite nests and how they crumpled up leaves to make a kind of sponge, with which they soaked up rainwater from the crooks of trees and then squeezed the water into their mouths. That chimps used tools was an exciting discovery because it narrowed the perceived behavioral chasm between humans and apes, our closest living relatives. Second, Goodall discovered that chimpanzees regularly hunted other primates and animals. Chimps were not vegetarians!

A skilled scientist—formulating hypotheses, testing them with careful field observations, and drawing conclusions based on her observations—Goodall performed pioneering research that underscored the importance of the study of primates to understanding ourselves. Among her many accomplishments, Goodall documented key elements of primate societies and of primate social behavior in its broadest terms. This chapter considers primate social behavior, especially in the important linkage between learning, behavior, and socioecology (the connections between social organization, ecology, and diet). Exciting new developments in the study of primates challenge long-held notions in the social and behavioral sciences that only humans have distinctive, socially transmitted cultural traditions.

Underlying much of what motivates primatologists to study primate social behavior is one central question: *Why are primates social?* To seek answers to this question, primatologists study primate societies all over the world with an eye toward social diversity and ways that primate societies are organized. To understand sociality in our nearest living relatives is to gain insight into the origins of sociality in ourselves.

7.1 Primate Societies: Diverse, Complex, Long-Lasting

Primate societies are characterized by diverse social behaviors, complex social structures, and the forming of long-lasting relationships. The sections that follow will examine various aspects of these social characteristics.

Primates express themselves socially through a range of behaviors. Some of the more obvious behaviors include touching, hugging, mouthing, mounting, lip smacking, vocalizing, greeting, and grooming. Far more so than any other animal, primates use these diverse social signals to express different kinds of relationships, many of them complex and reciprocal. These signals can serve as a kind of "currency" for items or activities they are interested in, such as grooming another individual to establish an alliance at the moment or in some future event.

Many primate societies are complexly organized. Within any primate group, individuals representing different kinships, ranks, ages, and sexes often form alliances.

Primates form various social relationships for the long term. Primates form relationships for immediate payoff (for example, access to food or to mates), but they also establish and maintain long-lasting alliances that, at first glance, do not appear to be beneficial, especially with regard to reproductive success and gaining access to food and other resources. For example, we might be surprised to learn that male chimpanzees groom each other or travel together, especially since these activities entail forming social relationships with potential rivals for food or mates. But males who frequently engage in these and other cooperative activities might later work together to compete, for food or mates, against other groups.

PRIMATE SOCIAL BEHAVIOR: ENHANCING SURVIVAL AND REPRODUCTION

As was recognized by the American evolutionary biologist Edward O. Wilson in his study of social behavior in animals generally, primate social behavior is influenced by evolution. Basically, natural selection favors primate behaviors that enhance survival and reproduction. In this way, the genes of individuals who engage in such behaviors pass from generation to generation. Primatologists explore the relationships between specific social behaviors and reproductive fitness. Such behaviors may be purely natural or they may be learned. In other words, sometimes primates are not conscious of their actions, and other times they strategize, learning by observation and imitation. These extremely important processes are highly elaborated in primates. Social contexts play an especially important role in survival and length of life. For example, in wild female baboons at Amboseli National Park, Kenya, both same-sex and opposite-sex social relationships and connectedness are clear predictors of longer life. In that setting, female baboons who are socially tied to either adult female or adult male baboons live significantly longer lives than do socially isolated female baboons. Social connectedness is a key element of survival and reproduction in these primates.

As for most animals, primate males and females have very different reproductive roles and life histories in adulthood. Males provide the sperm to produce offspring. Females provide the ova to conceive the young, grow the young within them, give birth, and nurse the young. Overall, females expend far more energy in the creation of and caring for offspring than males do. As a general rule for many

FIGURE 7.1

Competition and Sexual Dimorphism
Among primates, as shown in this chart, sexual dimorphism in body size is directly related to group composition. Here, a value of 1.0 indicates no sexual dimorphism. In primate species with monogamous pairs (such as gibbons), there is less competition for females and thus little sexual dimorphism. In primate species where a single dominant male competes for multiple females (such as with gorillas), there is substantial competition among males to hold the dominant position and thus great sexual dimorphism. In primate species where multiple males compete for multiple females (such as with chimpanzees), the sexual dimorphism is not as extreme as in single-male groups.

polygynous Pertaining to a social group that includes one adult male, several adult females, and their offspring.

polyandrous Pertaining to a social group that includes one reproductively active female, several adult males, and their offspring.

animals, including primates, those members of the sex that expends less energy in this way (the males) compete more aggressively among themselves for sexual access to members of the sex that expends more energy (the females).

When male primates compete for females, whether they are competing singly or in groups, the males' bodies adapt. Sexual dimorphism in body size and canine size is considerably higher in such societies than in societies where males do not compete. This difference reflects the fact that to compete for females successfully, males must be big and aggressive (**Figure 7.1**). In these societies, males are generally unrelated. In societies where males are related, live in the group in which they were born (the natal group), and compete with related males, sexual dimorphism tends to be lower than in groups where males disperse and compete with nonrelated males.

Finally, although all the life periods of primates are generally longer than those of other animals, humans have the longest life span of the primates (see Figure 6.16). The average human life lasts nearly 70 years, longer than that of the chimpanzee (44 years), the gibbon (30 years), the macaque (29 years), and the lemur (13 years). The American anthropologist and demographer Timothy Gage suggests that humans are the only primates to have "baby booms"; that is, variation in numbers of offspring in a population, fluctuating from small numbers to large numbers over time.

PRIMATE RESIDENCE PATTERNS

Animals such as birds and nonprimate mammals tend to be regimented in their social structures and residence patterns. By contrast, individual primate species combine different patterns, and their social groups are strongly influenced by factors such as food availability, environment, and competition. Although it is, thus, exceedingly difficult to fully understand primate social behavior, primatologists have identified six main types of primate residence patterns (**Figure 7.2**):

1. *One male, multifemale.* This haremlike organization consists of one reproductive-age male, several mature females, and the immature offspring. The society is **polygynous**, meaning that the one male has more than one partner. Gorillas, orangutans, some howler monkeys, some langurs, and some Old World monkeys, such as gelada baboons, practice this social system. Although male orangutans are solitary (see pattern number 6), their reproductive strategy of establishing territories inhabited by two or more females means orangutans can be deemed polygynous as well.

2. *One female, multimale.* This residence pattern consists of one reproductive-age female, several mature males, and the immature offspring. The society is **polyandrous**, meaning that the one female mates with nonpolygynous males. The males often cooperate with the females in parenting activities. Only some New World monkeys practice this social system, and only rarely.

3. *Multimale, multifemale.* This social grouping consists of many adults, male and female, and the offspring. Both sexes mate promiscuously. Competition for mates tends to be relatively low, especially among males. Many Old World monkeys, a few New World monkeys, and chimpanzees fit in this category (**Figure 7.3**).

4. *All male.* In some species, such as baboons, males form at least temporary groups, typically before joining or forming groups that include males and females. All-male groups commonly exist together with multimale, multifemale groups.

1 One male, multifemale

2 One female, multimale

3 Multimale, multifemale

4 All male

5 One male, one female

6 Solitary

FIGURE 7.2

Primate Residence Patterns Primates exhibit these six social groupings, which in many cases can change. In some species, for example, groups break apart if food is scarce and reunite when food becomes more ample.

5. *One male, one female*. This pattern consists of an adult male, an adult female, and their immature offspring. Mating is typically **monogamous**, so each partner's reproductive success is tied to that of the other, and the male invests a relatively large amount of time and energy in the young (for example, through protection and food acquisition). Gibbons, siamangs, two ceboids (owl monkeys and titi monkeys), and several species of strepsirrhines practice this form of society.

6. *Solitary*. Solitary primates go it alone—rarely are these individuals seen with others. Interaction between adult males and adult females occurs only for sexual activity. Only orangutans and a few strepsirrhines are solitary. An orangutan male has greater reproductive success if he maintains a territory with areas traversed by two or more females. Orangutan sexual dimorphism is predictably quite high—adult males are twice the size of adult females and have large canines, large cheek pads, and very loud calls over long distances. Males that have been relatively unsuccessful at competing for access to females tend to be more solitary than successful males.

These categories of primate residence patterns capture only some of the variation primatologists have identified in social interactions. Considerably more is understood now about social behaviors that develop within individual primate taxa, reflecting the remarkable complexity of primate social interactions, even

monogamous Pertaining to a social group that includes an adult male, an adult female, and their offspring.

FIGURE 7.3

Observing Primate Residence Patterns Snub-nosed monkeys are an example of Old World monkeys that live in multimale, multifemale groups. Here, researcher Guo Songtao studies a group that has become habituated to his presence.

when comparing closely related taxa. For example, primatologists Amy Parish and Frans de Waal have documented key differences in social interactions among chimpanzees (*Pan troglodytes*) and bonobos (*Pan paniscus*). Whereas chimpanzee societies are male dominated, bonobo societies are largely female dominated. In the former, males regularly form bonds, whereas in the latter, female–female social bonds are far more commonplace. In addition, female–female sexual interactions occur regularly in bonobos, far more so than in chimpanzees.

PRIMATE REPRODUCTIVE STRATEGIES: MALES' DIFFER FROM FEMALES'

Because reproduction makes very different demands on males and females in terms of energy expenditure and time investment, each sex has a different set of reproductive strategies and interests. As discussed earlier, the primary strategy of males, with few exceptions, is to physically compete for access to reproductively mature females, resulting in a strong degree of natural selection in males for both large bodies and large canines. This form of natural selection is called **sexual selection**. Another male strategy is **infanticide**—the killing of a nursing infant, primarily by a foreign male that has driven the single male out of a one-male, multifemale group. The American primatologist Sarah Blaffer Hrdy has hypothesized that the new male kills the nursing infant so that its mother stops lactating, resumes ovulation, and becomes sexually receptive to him. As a result, the new male enhances his reproductive fitness, largely at the expense of the previous male.

Whereas males compete with each other for mates, females compete with each other for resources that enable them to care for young. In various New World and Old World monkeys, including macaques and some baboons, the competition for resources happens within the context of stable *dominance hierarchies*. **Dominance** is key to how a primate acquires resources and access to mates. Specifically, a dominance hierarchy represents how individuals in a primate

sexual selection The frequency of traits that change due to the attractiveness of those traits to members of the opposite sex.

infanticide The killing of a juvenile.

dominance The ability to intimidate or defeat another individual in a pairwise, or dyadic, encounter.

Male and Female Reproductive Strategies

Reproductive strategies differ in male and female primates. Males compete for mates, whereas females compete for resources and invest time and energy in the care of offspring.

SEX	REPRODUCTIVE STRATEGY AND OUTCOME
Males	*Strategy:* Physical competition for access to females
	Outcome: Selection for large body size and for large canines; selection for loud vocalization ability in some territorial primates
	Strategy: Sometime killing of nursing young (infanticide)
	Outcome: Suppressed lactation and resumption of ovulation in female; receptiveness of female to new male partner
Females	*Strategy:* Acquisition of resources for raising young, usually in competition with other females
	Outcome: Higher-ranked females provide more resources to offspring than low-ranked females do

society are ranked relative to one another. For males, the alpha, or most dominant, male has successfully defeated all other males in a series of aggressive encounters. The second-rank male is in second rank because he has defeated all but the dominant male, and so on down the line to the least-dominant male, who has defeated no other male in an aggressive encounter. For females, hierarchical ranks usually pass from mother to daughter, and younger sisters usually rank higher than older sisters. The younger sister is protected more by the mother than is the older sister, thereby giving the younger sister a higher rank. The mother maintains her rank above all of them, except when the juvenile offspring become adults. In general, though, the higher the rank in primate societies, the greater the ability to acquire important resources, such as food. Higher-ranked females also tend to have more offspring, such as in gelada baboons in East Africa (**Figure 7.4**). In some primates, higher-ranked females have a greater number of offspring because they begin mating and producing offspring months before lower-ranked females do. For example, dominant yellow baboons in Kenya start reproducing some 200 days before lower-ranked ones.

Primatologists have observed that some female primates are relatively more selective in choosing mates than are others, making their selections on the basis of characteristics such as disposition, physical appearance, and position in social hierarchy. Some adult females' social behaviors encourage support for and investment in their offspring by other members of the group. And some adult females protect their infants from aggression, as when they attempt to prevent infanticide.

THE OTHER SIDE OF COMPETITION: COOPERATION IN PRIMATES

Although competition and dominance are central to primate social behavior, primates are also highly cooperative social animals. Chimpanzees, which are about half the size of gorillas and not very dimorphic sexually, hunt in groups of

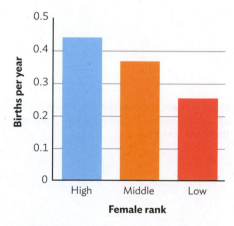

FIGURE 7.4

Female Dominance Hierarchy This graph compares the birthrates among high-, middle-, and low-ranked adult female gelada baboons. The higher the rank, the greater a female's access to resources and the more offspring she will bear.

(a)

(b)

FIGURE 7.5

Grooming Among many primates, including **(a)** chimpanzees and **(b)** humans, grooming is one of the most important social bonding behaviors. While helping ensure proper hygiene and good health, it can also cement social bonds between individuals, resolve conflicts, and reinforce social structures or family links.

altruistic Relating to behavior that benefits others while being disadvantageous to the individual.

kin selection Natural selection in favor of altruistic behaviors that increase the fitness of the donor's relatives.

cooperating males, often preying on juvenile monkeys such as the red colobus. Chimpanzees also share food after a hunt. By contrast, in the bonobo community, it is the females that are highly cooperative with each other; males are far less so. Some primates issue warning calls to their social group when predators approach. Many primates also groom one another (**Figure 7.5**). In nonhuman primates, grooming involves one individual picking through the skin and hair of another individual, removing insects or other foreign objects, and sometimes eating these materials. Among this practice's functions are bonding two members of a social group, calming the primate being groomed, or appeasing that primate if he or she has a higher position in a dominance hierarchy.

Some cooperative behaviors are **altruistic**, in that they appear to reduce the reproductive fitness of the individuals performing the behavior but enhance the reproductive fitness of the recipients. For example, adult baboons might give warning calls to their social group or even attack predators and, in doing so, place themselves in jeopardy. Grooming, food sharing, and caregiving are also altruistic, because one primate invests time and effort in another.

Why should a primate engage in altruistic behavior? Altruism seems not to be directed haphazardly; rather, it seems to be aimed primarily at relatives. According to the hypothesis of **kin selection**, as put forth by the British evolutionary theorist William Hamilton, the evolutionary benefits of an altruistic behavior to the kin group outweigh the costs to the individual acting altruistically. A primate will most strongly and consistently act altruistically when living with relatives. This is particularly true among cercopithecoids, such as baboons and macaques, where females live mostly in the natal group, or in chimpanzees, where males live in the natal group. Primatologist Richard Wrangham has observed groups of cooperating related male chimpanzees attacking groups of male chimps unrelated to them. He has also observed groups of cooperating male chimps patrolling territorial boundaries. Such behaviors in living chimpanzees may be the best model for early hominin behavior and for the origins of human aggression.

Cooperation has many advantages, but it ultimately provides most primate taxa with their distinctive behavioral characteristic: **sociality**, or the tendency to live in social groups. And the most likely reason for sociality is that while many primates are proficient predators, they are also preyed upon by a range of predators. The American primatologist Susanne Shultz and her associates suggest that the earliest primates were largely nocturnal and led a solitary existence. This understanding is suggested by the fossil record (see chapter 8) and by the fact that the nocturnal primates today are also the most primitive (many of the strepsirrhines). As soon as primates began a diurnal lifestyle, they became subject to increased predation, which in turn placed an adaptive advantage on cooperative behavior and group living. Under circumstances of increased predation, primates' joining together to defend themselves from predators would seem to be an important form of cooperative behavior. While primatologists have observed the kinds of warning calls and direct physical defenses described earlier, the evidence of primates' protecting each other from predators is slim. It is difficult to directly observe predation, for example, because predators tend to be afraid of humans and avoid primate groups being studied.

Many primates are preyed upon by large birds, such as eagles. Shultz and her fellow American primatologist Scott McGraw have studied eagles' nests because the remains left in them—representative samples of "meals"—provide proxy information about what the eagles hunt and how often (**Figure 7.6**, pp. 190–191). The results show that predation rates are lower among larger primate groups than among smaller primate groups. Predation is a very strong selective pressure, and mutual cooperation—sociality—has been favored among primates because of the protection it provides. Sociality also provides access to mates, but the predation-related advantage of cooperation within a society is the underlying explanation for primates' living in social groups.

7.2 Getting Food

Primates acquire their food through a wide variety of foraging practices, which entail looking for food, then handling and processing the food for consumption. The American biological anthropologist Karen Strier estimates that, on average, foraging can take up more than 50% of a primate's waking time. This burden is especially great on mothers. Not only do mothers need to eat food that will provide the energy for gestation and lactation, but they also need to look for food and then handle and process it for their young to consume. In a few primate species, the father is involved in caring for and providing food for the young, but generally the mother is the sole provider of her offspring's food. The American primatologist P. C. Lee estimates that in adult female primates, a mother's energy requirements are between two and five times higher than a nonmother's. For the female primate, success in caring for young, both before and after their birth, is very much tied to adequate nutrition. Females with good nutrition give birth at an earlier age, have healthier young, experience shorter intervals between births, and live longer than those with suboptimal nutrition.

Three key factors contribute to a primate's success at feeding: quality of food, distribution of food, and availability of food. *Quality* foods are those that provide readily digestible energy and protein. Mature leaves and mature grasses, for example, are of relatively little value to many primates because the cellulose

sociality The tendency within certain animal populations for individuals to form social groups and cooperative communities.

Crowned Eagle Found throughout Africa south of the Sahara Desert, the crowned eagle (*Stephanoaetus coronatus*) is among the most successful raptors in the world. This carnivore preys on a range of animals, including primates.

1 ▸ RAPTORS

Eagles, hawks, buzzards, falcons, and owls are predators known collectively as raptors, or birds of prey. Anthropologists, field ecologists, and other scientists have long been skeptical that primates could be preyed upon by these predators, owing to doubts about the birds' being able to lift something as heavy as some primates off the ground. Extensive field studies have revealed, however, that small primates worldwide—indeed, most primates—are routinely and efficiently killed by raptors.

Some of our best understanding of primates as prey is derived from the study of primate skeletal remains recovered from eagle nests, most of which are enormous. Study of the contents of these nests in the Taï National Park, Ivory Coast (see Figure 6.2, pp. 148–149), provides important insight into not only what African crowned eagles hunt but also the manner in which the primates are killed and processed for food. In this setting, scientists have studied more than 1,200 bones from nests, representing about 35 species routinely preyed upon in this corner of West Africa. Some of these prey species weigh upwards of three to four times the weight of the eagle predators. Anthropologists' study of the primate remains—sometimes numbering in the hundreds of bones—provides a remarkably complete story of predator–prey interactions.

2 ▸ PRIMATES

Which primates are the crowned eagles preying upon? Despite the fast movement and well-developed vocalized warnings of the Diana monkey and the inconspicuous nature of the Campbell's guenon, both species commonly fall victim to crowned eagle predation. Sooty mangabeys (*Cercocebus atys*), the largest cercopithecoid monkeys in the Taï National Park, are also among the most common victims. Prior to her study, Susanne Shultz predicted that the sooty mangabeys' large body size and group-oriented social structure limited predation by even these highly aggressive birds. Her study revealed instead that raptors are fully able to prey upon primates weighing more than 11 kg (24.25 lb) and living in large groups. (The upper limit appears to be about 13 kg [28.66 lb]).

Campbell's Guenon The Campbell's guenon (*Cercopithecus campbelli*) has a distinctive yellow band across the brow and blue shading around the eyes. It is among the most common monkeys in West Africa. Although adapted to the shelter of the dark understory of the Taï National Park, the Campbell's guenon is choice prey for crowned eagles.

Diana Monkey The Diana monkey (*Cercopithecus diana*) is one of the most active monkeys in the Taï National Park. Diana monkeys have a highly visible black face framed by a striking white beard. They are noisy, fast moving, and on high alert for predators. Through their vocalized early detection of predators, they provide an important warning system to other primates in the vicinity.

The study of these primate bones also shows that the eagles have a clear pattern of processing their prey. They first disable the primates by powerfully thrusting their sharp talons and beaks into the primate prey. The eagles then dismember their victims on the ground. They place portions of the flesh in nearby trees. Via trips to and from these cache sites, the eagles carry food to the nest for consumption by young eagles. The dismemberment of the prey's carcass explains why there are no complete skeletons of prey found in the nests or on the ground below the nests. It also means that transport of parts does not require the thrust to lift even the largest of the primates. These findings have important implications for predation on primates generally, including ancient hominins. We now know that raptors prey on primates. This finding means that primate social behavior and social organization are almost certainly influenced by the behavior of birds of prey—and were likewise influenced in the distant past.

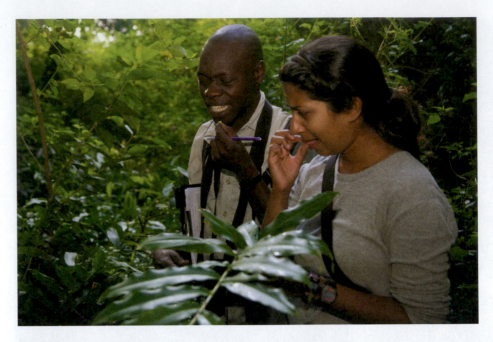

FIGURE 7.7

Researching Primate Diets Primatologists can learn about primates' diets and ecologies by examining the foods they eat. Here, two researchers (PhD student Zarin Machanda and senior field assistant Geresomu Muhumuza) taste bitter food items of chimpanzees.

and dietary fiber are much harder to digest for nutrients than are the cellulose and dietary fiber of young leaves and young grasses (**Figure 7.7**). As discussed in chapter 6, sharp-crested teeth and compartmentalized stomachs have evolved in some primates, especially in leaf-eating monkeys. For example, folivorous Old World monkeys have sharp crests connecting the cusps on the fronts and backs of the occlusal surfaces of their bilophodont molars.

Distribution refers to the location of food across the landscape. Ideally, primates would have to expend relatively little energy to acquire food; therefore, in terms of evolution, behaviors that minimize the energy costs of acquiring food are selected for. Many primates focus on patches of food, such as a fruit-bearing tree or a group of such trees, whose fruit provides a ready and concentrated source of nutrients. However, a small patch will support only a relatively small group. All primates are able to adjust the size of the feeding group in relation to the amount of food available in a patch. Food *availability* can be highly fluid, depending on season and rainfall. The farther a region is from the equator, the more defined are its seasons and the less available are fruit and leaves, primates' main food sources. Thus, primates are generally restricted to equatorial regions.

Chimpanzees are enormously flexible in their ability to access preferred foods. Primatologist Karline Janmaat and colleagues have documented acquisition patterns of these ripe-fruit specialists in the Taï National Park, Ivory Coast (see Figure 7.6). In this setting, chimpanzees strategically locate their nesting sites, increasing the likelihood that they will encounter trees bearing the best and most ripe fruit. Janmaat's study reveals that chimpanzees possess a mental map of food landscapes and display a strong sense of *where* the fruit-bearing trees are located and *when* the fruit will be ripe. In the group of chimpanzees they studied, a number of individuals built their evening nests directly on the route to a fruit-bearing tree. Moreover, these chimpanzees tended to rise earlier in the morning and increase their travel speed. Importantly, knowledge of the food landscape and planning gave these chimpanzees a competitive edge for acquiring the fruit, well ahead of other animals interested in the same foods. These findings make clear that chimpanzees in this setting apply their intelligence to acquiring food in the highly competitive landscape of the rainforest of West Africa. Moreover, increasing evidence indicates that the memory of locations of fruit-bearing trees spans a period of years. The success of acquiring food is not limited to hearing, vision, or smell. Rather, it is a behavior that emphasizes memory over the long term.

In Africa, and in an increasing number of settings elsewhere, the food resources of primates overlap to a large degree with those of humans. Primatologists are learning that the coexistence of humans and primates in one place at one time is changing how the latter are acquiring food. For example, on the Indonesian islands of Bali and Sulawesi—places of enormous human population increase—there are very close and competitive interactions between people and primates. For a region having one of the highest human populations in the world (Indonesia now ranks fourth) coupled with the highest diversity of primates (at least 45 species representing five families—Lorisidae, Tarsiidae, Cercopithecidae, Hylobatidae, and Pongidae), anthropologists are asking: How can we humans sustain the remarkable diversity and success of primates in such crowded spaces? Erin Riley, Agustín Fuentes, and other primatologists have pioneered a new field called **ethnoprimatology** to study the ecological and cultural interactions between humans and primates to develop better practices for the long-term success of primates. The failure to develop better interactions between people and primates puts now-threatened species in jeopardy. Ethnoprimatologists make the strong case that the study of the interlinkages of social and cultural behaviors of humans and primates will lead to more informed efforts for ensuring the long-term success of both.

7.3 Acquiring Resources and Transmitting Knowledge: Got Culture?

Primates and humans acquire food in vastly different ways. While primates can acquire food using primarily their bodies, humans depend on technology—material culture—to acquire food. But this distinction does not mean that primates have no material culture.

In the 1960s, Jane Goodall became the first to question the assumption that primates lack material culture when she observed adult chimps poking twigs into a termite hill, withdrawing them, and eating the termites that clung to the twigs (**Figure 7.8**). Goodall realized that one fundamental assumption about what it means to be human—namely, that material culture (and culture in general) is exclusive to human beings—seemed incorrect. Other scientists then realized that tool use by living chimpanzees may be the best model for understanding our prehuman ancestors' earliest cultures and the origins of tool use in hominins (among the topics of chapter 10).

Based on Goodall's research and a great deal of work since, anthropologists have identified three central features about chimpanzees' tool use. First, chimpanzees are extraordinarily intelligent and have

WATCH THE VIDEO
ETHNOPRIMATOLOGY
digital.wwwnorton.com/essanthro5

ethnoprimatology The study of ecological and cultural interactions between humans and primates.

FIGURE 7.8

Chimpanzee Tool Use When "fishing" for termites (which are highly nutritious), a chimpanzee selects a branch or twig thin enough to pass through the holes of a termite nest, then removes all extra branches and leaves and inserts the twig into the nest. Simple and disposable, even primitive, tools like this might have been used by our ancestors long before the appearance of stone tools some 3.3 mya.

FIGURE 7.9

Chimpanzee Social Learning A juvenile chimpanzee watches its mother crack open palm nuts with a stone hammer and anvil in Guinea, West Africa.

the complex cognitive skills necessary for at least some kinds of behaviors that require learning and the ability to understand complex symbolization. The evidence for this ability is impressive, and it is growing. For example, chimpanzees are able to accomplish a number of complex behaviors for which visual acumen and ability to think abstractly are essential elements. In laboratory or otherwise controlled settings, humans have taught young chimpanzees to crack open nuts with stones. In turn, these chimpanzees have taught other young chimpanzees to crack open nuts. Chimpanzees have also been shown how to use a sharp stone tool to cut a cord in order to gain access to food in a box. Similarly, they have been shown how to make simple stone tools, and they subsequently have passed on that behavior to relatives.

Second, in natural settings where chimpanzees have not been taught by humans, mothers have also shown their young how to use tools (**Figure 7.9**). Most of the tools chimpanzees produce are for acquiring and consuming food. Among the rare examples of primate tool use unrelated to food is that of chimpanzees in Gombe throwing stones as part of a dominance conflict between adult males. One of chimps' most fascinating food-based innovations, observed by the American primatologist Jill Pruetz at Fongoli, Senegal, is the creation and use of a spearlike object—a trimmed, pointed twig—to skewer strepsirrhines, especially galagos, for food (**Figure 7.10**). This is the only known setting where a nonhuman animal has been observed to hunt vertebrate prey using a tool purposefully prepared for this task.

Third, tool production and tool use are sometimes highly localized. For example, although some adjacent chimpanzee groups use stones to crack open hard-shelled nuts, only one group has been observed to produce and use simple spears, and these tools have not been seen anywhere else in Africa.

(a)

(b)

FIGURE 7.10

Chimpanzee Spears **(a)** A chimpanzee made this spear from a tree branch, sharpening one end with its teeth. **(b)** Chimpanzees who make such spears use them to thrust into the hollows of trees and kill bushbabies. Here, an adolescent female holds a dead bushbaby that had been killed with the use of a spear. This method is the first (and only) observation of primates' use of tools to hunt other vertebrates, including other primates.

While chimpanzees do not depend on material culture for survival—certainly not to the extent of living humans—they nonetheless use material culture. Laboratory experiments and natural-setting research from a range of places in Africa show that chimpanzees use several forms of tools and that not all forms occur in all chimpanzee groups. Perhaps local traditions are passed from generation to generation via social learning—parents pass the information to offspring, and the young share it with other young. In at least one setting in the Budongo Forest, Uganda, researchers found a clear kin-based association with mothers passing knowledge on to their young. In a very real sense, then, tool use in primates is an important form of social and cultural transmission. Moreover, the widespread nature of chimpanzee tool use suggests that it dates back to antiquity. Sites in Ivory Coast contain chimpanzee tools from 4,000 to 5,000 yBP, but tool use likely started earlier.

What about other primates? Field observations by the Swiss anthropologist Carel van Schaik and his associates show that, like chimpanzees, orangutans in Borneo and Sumatra habitually use probes to obtain insects for food. Across the Atlantic in South America, the psychologist Dorothy Fragaszy and her research team have documented how some capuchin (*Cebus*) monkeys use stones to dig for food and to crack open nuts. The complexity here is far less than that of human technology, but these simple behaviors show that chimpanzees are not the only primates that interact with the environment through tools they make.

7.4 Vocal and Nonvocal Communication Is Fundamental Behavior in Primate Societies

All primates communicate vocally and nonvocally, and these two types of communication serve various functions. Nonvocal communication, such as gesturing and signing, will be discussed later in this section, but first let's look at vocal communication. Among primates, some quiet vocal calls can be heard only by nearby group members, while some loud calls convey information over great distances and through dense vegetation in tropical forests. Scientists once believed that primate vocalizations were merely innate, emotional utterances produced involuntarily in response to stimuli and, therefore, could tell us nothing about the evolution of human language. Research has shown, however, that these vocal systems are actually rich and complex and largely under the callers' control. There is also some evidence for language-like behaviors in primates. No single taxon of primate has the full suite of human language characteristics—such as dialect, humanlike vocal sounds, vocal-tract anatomy, or turn taking. However, the range of information collected by primatologists and other scientists points to some compelling similarities between human and nonhuman primates in the communication patterns. The study of primate vocal communication can give us important insights into the selective pressures that may have shaped the evolution of language unique to humans and their ancestors.

TRANSLATING PRIMATE COMMUNICATION: IT'S ABOUT THE CONTEXT

To "translate" the calls of primates, scientists first catalog a population's vocal repertoire. They then determine the contexts in which the members of that population produce the different vocalizations. Primate voices vary just as human voices do, but individuals in groups produce similar calls in categories.

Determining the context of a given call does not unequivocally prove that call's function. The use of playback experiments has revolutionized what scientists can say about a call's meaning, albeit only from the listener's perspective. In conducting such an experiment, the researchers record naturally occurring calls (**Figure 7.11**). They then use hidden speakers to broadcast call sequences to the primate group. In a classic example, the American primatologists Dorothy Cheney and Robert Seyfarth played the sound of an infant vervet monkey screaming

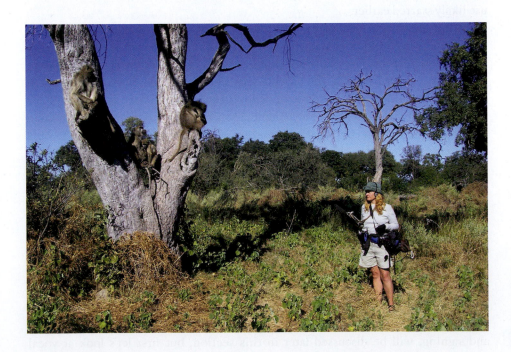

FIGURE 7.11

Recording Alarm Calls Dawn Kitchen records chacma baboon alarm calls in Botswana. The lion prompting these calls is lying in the grass, about 75 m (250 ft) behind Kitchen.

to a group of mothers whose infants had all wandered off. Only the mother of that particular infant looked toward the hidden speaker, a finding that suggests females recognize the voices of their own infants. To Cheney's and Seyfarth's surprise, however, the other females looked at the mother of the screaming infant. This finding gave the researchers insight into what primates "know" about each other. Their study laid the groundwork for a field of research in which scientists use carefully designed playback experiments to "interview" free-ranging primates about their social cognitive abilities.

In this way, researchers have determined that some quiet calls produced by primates mediate social encounters within a group. For example, Cheney, Seyfarth, and their colleagues, in studying chacma baboons in Botswana, found that a subordinate baboon was less likely to move away from a dominant animal if the dominant quietly "grunted" as it approached the subordinate. Conversely, if the dominant animal did not grunt, the subordinate would almost always move off. If the approaching dominant produced a "threat-grunt," a version of the call that indicates aggressive intent, the listener would likely flee rapidly.

PREDATOR ALARMS: IN DEFENSE OF THE PRIMATE SOCIETY

Unlike quiet calls exchanged among nearby animals, the loudest calls in a primate species' repertoire transmit information over long distances and are typically produced during events such as an encounter with predators, an aggressive contest with another group, and one animal's separation from its group. In howler monkey societies, for example, adult males in different groups compete through their long, loud calls, warning potential competitors to stay off their turf. (Once you hear one of these bizarre calls, you understand why they are called "howlers.") The American primatologist Dawn Kitchen documented extremely loud choruses by male black howler monkeys in Belize. She found that the voices of individual callers within a group do not completely overlap during a chorus; thus, it is possible for listeners in another group to "count" the number of rivals they will face based on vocal cues alone. Howlers can assess the strength of opposing groups according to these criteria. Using playback experiments, Kitchen found that howler groups that thought they were outnumbered by invaders retreated, whereas groups that thought they outnumbered intruders not only vocalized in return but also advanced on the simulated rivals (**Figure 7.12**). Likewise, Kitchen found that during aggressive male–male competition in chacma baboons, the loud, repetitive call displays ("wahoos") produced by adult males reliably indicated the caller's physical condition. By judging each other's calls, rival baboons can assess an opponent's fighting ability and avoid a contest with a superior opponent.

Although primate vocalizations (such as the screams of an attack victim) can indicate a caller's emotional state, many also seem to convey information about the world around the caller. In the Taï National Park (see Figure 6.2), Diana monkeys produce two different loud alarm calls in response to predators, depending on whether the predator is terrestrial (such as a leopard) or aerial (such as an eagle). Importantly, each type of predator requires a very different escape response from the Diana monkey. Using playback experiments, the Swiss primatologist Klaus Zuberbühler and his team found that listeners treat all sounds in the forest associated with one type of predator the same. For example, a leopard's

FIGURE 7.12

Primate Vocalizations (a) Male howler monkeys, such as the one in action here, are among the male primates that vocalize to protect their territories, their resources, and/or their females. Their notorious calls can be heard over great distances. Howler monkeys are the loudest land animal and the second loudest of all animals, outdone only by the blue whale. **(b)** This chimpanzee is presenting a series of whoops, perhaps characterizing a food source. Chimpanzee vocalizations are diverse and difficult to interpret.

growl produces the same response as the leopard alarm call of a male Diana monkey, despite the acoustic differences between these sounds. These and other experimental results suggest that primate calls can be functionally referential. That is, these calls convey semantic-like meaning, which makes them similar to human words, at least from the listener's perspective.

The variation in predator-specific vocalizations indicates that Diana monkeys have evolved an ability to modify their vocalizations and behavior based on the type of predator and the predator's attack strategy. For example, Diana monkeys issue loud alarm calls when they are confronted by "ambush" predators such as leopards or eagles, both of which are especially efficient hunters when they are able to surprise their prey. When "pursuit" predators such as chimpanzees or humans are also nearby, however, the Diana monkeys' loud alarm calls enable the predators to locate the monkeys. Zuberbühler found that Diana monkeys with a lot of exposure to chimpanzees respond more appropriately to playbacks of chimpanzee vocalizations—remaining silent and quietly moving away—than did monkeys with little chimpanzee experience. This finding strongly suggests that the perception of and response to certain vocalizations are learned.

CHIMPANZEE VOCALIZATION: LABELING THE WORLD AROUND THEM

Like monkeys, chimpanzees can label events and objects. They and many other primates have displayed food-associated vocalizations. In controlled laboratory studies of chimpanzees, Zuberbühler and his colleague Katie Slocombe found that chimpanzees express a specific kind of "rough grunt" when they see food. This grunt can vary in specific ways, depending on the type of food and how much the chimpanzee wants that food. Interpretations of distinctive sounds made by chimpanzees in field settings are beginning to provide new insights into how these apes communicate, insights going far beyond what can be learned in

FIGURE 7.13

Chimpanzee Communication Research on animal communication is conducted with a habituated group of chimpanzees in the Budongo Forest Reserve in Uganda.

laboratory settings alone. The English primatologist Catherine Crockford and her associates have been studying chimpanzee communication in the Budongo Forest, Uganda. Their work shows that chimpanzee communication involves different combinations of sounds—grunts, pants, hoots, screams, barks, and other vocalizations—most of which have meaning for the individual that is vocalizing and for the intended audience. The work of Crockford and her colleagues shows that, as with most communication in other primates, understanding chimpanzee communication requires knowledge of both the vocalizations and their contexts. The vocalizations can be studied through recordings, but the contexts must be observed in the primates' natural setting (**Figure 7.13**). The natural environment provides critical clues to the meanings of vocalizations.

Because some calls within a species' repertoire vary so subtly that the human ear cannot easily differentiate them, the analysis of acoustic properties of vocal recordings (such as duration, amplitude, and frequency of a call) is a critical step in translating primate vocalizations. For example, the German scientist Julia Fischer and her colleagues found that female baboons produce two loud calls that are very similar: one when they encounter a predator and another when they are separated from their group. Using specially designed computer software, Fischer found that these two call types grade into each other along an acoustic continuum (in the same way that the words *fire* and *far* seem to overlap when spoken with a southern US accent). Furthermore, these subtle differences were detectable to baboons—adult females hearing the two call types during playback experiments responded strongly only to the alarm calls. These and other experiments suggest that, like humans, primates can perceive acoustically graded calls in discrete ways.

Primatologists are also learning that vocalizations have clear patterns, some of which bear a striking resemblance to the structural elements of human language. Humans change word structure to change meaning. One of the most important examples is what linguists call *affixation*, whereby a small unit is added at either the beginning (prefix) or the end (suffix) of the word stem (the part of the word that is never altered). Exciting new work by Zuberbühler and his group on Campbell's monkeys (**Figure 7.14**), also inhabitants of the Taï National Park, reveals

FIGURE 7.14

Monkey Alarm Calls Campbell's monkeys use specific alarm calls containing prefixes and suffixes.

that these primates use a kind of affixation by adding suffixes (similar in some respects to English speakers' changing the present tense of a verb to past tense by adding -ed). These researchers recorded a loud "krak" sound produced by adult male Campbell's monkeys that had seen a leopard in the area. Sharing the same forest, Diana monkeys and Campbell's monkeys have learned to respond to one another's alarm calls with their own alarm calls. However, when Campbell's monkeys issue a leopard alarm call in response to the leopard alarm call of Diana monkeys, they affix an "oo" sound to the warning call. This "krak-oo" alarm call indicates that they have heard the initial alarm call from a different primate taxon. These primates' altering of a stem term through the addition of a suffix is a very important discovery because it provides a strong parallel with human word construction. While human language is extremely complex and most of its characteristics are completely different from those of other animals' (including nonhuman primates') communication, this parallel suggests what the first form of speech of early hominins may have been like.

· Humans routinely invent new vocalizations throughout their lives. In contrast, nonhuman primates appear to be basically preprogrammed, producing most of the calls typical of their species shortly after birth. However, as the earlier Diana monkey example illustrates, primates must still learn to use and to respond to these vocalizations appropriately. For example, vervet monkeys are susceptible to predation by raptors (birds of prey) and are born able to produce predator-specific alarm calls. Cheney and Seyfarth, in systematically recording the developmental changes in vocal usage among vervets living in Kenya, discovered that very young monkeys will produce these alarm calls in response to anything startling that appears in the sky—an actual raptor, a harmless songbird, even a falling leaf. As vervets age, they refine their call production, limiting it first to all raptors and finally, by the time they are adults, to only that subset of raptors large enough to prey on vervets. Likewise, until a vervet is about 7 months old, before it reacts to alarm calls with an appropriate predator-escape response, it will look toward an adult or run toward its mother.

GESTURING IS NOT LIMITED TO HUMANS

Not all communication is vocal. Like humans, apes gesture with their hands, limbs, and bodies, and many of these behaviors are learned. Some 20 different gestures have been cataloged in siamangs, for example. Chimpanzees have been found to extensively and flexibly use gestural communication, even developing novel gestures in new situations. The primatologist William McGrew and his colleagues, while observing chimpanzees in Mahale National Park, Tanzania, were the first to note an unusual grooming technique, the *hand clasp*: The two participants face one another. Each one holds a hand up over its head and clasps the other's hand, forming an *A*-frame, and each uses his or her free hand to pick parasites and other detritus off the other participant (**Figure 7.15**). Although this is the customary way to groom at Mahale, the nearby chimpanzees of Gombe National Park, Tanzania, do not groom in this manner, and these differences are not likely explained by ecological or genetic differences in the two populations. In addition to differences in grooming, chimpanzees show different kinds of vocalizations unique to specific groups and regions. These differences suggest that some vocal features may be transmitted through social learning. Group-specific patterns of grooming, gesturing, and vocalizing are just a sample of the many behaviors identified by primatologists that represent nonmaterial aspects of

FIGURE 7.15

Hand Clasp Grooming The distinctive type of grooming depicted here has been observed only in groups of chimpanzees in Tanzania. Here, the paired chimpanzees grasp each other's wrist, while in other groups they grasp each other's hand. Such specific social customs are unique to individual groups of chimpanzees and thus must be learned within each group—a fundamental aspect of culture.

MARCELA BENÍTEZ, PHD

Georgia State University

What do I do? I'm a primatologist studying how primates make informed social decisions. From 2009 to 2016, I studied how male gelada baboons in the Simien Mountains National Park, Ethiopia, sized up their rivals. My research focused on a loud call used in male displays. I recorded 272 call bouts from 79 males of different condition (age, status, and stamina) and found that the strongest males in gelada society produced more calls and calls that were lower in pitch. I then played these calls back (a playback experiment) to males to see how they responded. I found that bachelors—males that must fight a leader male to gain access to females—exhibited a stronger response to calls from weak males (an easy target), while harem-holding leader males exhibited a stronger response to calls from strong males (a potential threat). This suggests that gelada males attend to differences in loud calls and make important decisions on which males to challenge and which to avoid based on these calls.

What excites me most about my work? I'm very interested in what monkeys know about others and how they use this information when making decisions. Knowing this can tell us a lot about the evolution of our own intelligence as humans. But the challenge in studying monkey minds, of course, is that we can't ask them what they know or what they are thinking. That's what excites me so much about my work setting

WATCH THE VIDEO

digital.wwwnorton
.com/essanthro5

up playback studies and controlled experimental tasks—this type of fieldwork can give us valuable insight into the minds of our closest living relatives. For example, in the study just described, we knew that gelada males were attending to two important pieces of information: information about the strength of a rival and information about their own status (leader or bachelor). In observational studies, we found that males were more likely to loud-call after they heard males of similar quality calling. In other words, strong males would call in response to other strong males. This suggests that males know their own strength as well as that of their rival, and compare the two. This type of mutual assessment is rare in species, perhaps because it is thought to be quite cognitively complex.

Why did I study biological anthropology? Our cognitive abilities as humans are certainly remarkable, but are they exceptional? I study biological anthropology because I'm fascinated by this question and interested in figuring out how to unpack it. By studying the cognitive abilities of other primates, we can begin to understand the origin of human cognitive abilities, the driving factors that were important in the evolution of the human mind, and exactly how special we really are. My current research on social cognition in capuchin monkeys takes me from the lab at Georgia State University to the field in Argentina and Costa Rica to try and get at these important questions. It is essential to remember that our knowledge of what nonhuman primates are cognitively capable of is not limited by *their* mental abilities, but rather by *our* ability to understand what they are thinking. What I love about my work as a biological anthropologist is how it helps contribute to the advancement of that ability.

primate culture. In the larger picture, the great apes—especially chimpanzees—are the nonhuman primates with the highest degree of flexibility, and most extensive use, of material and nonmaterial culture.

NONVOCAL COMMUNICATION: LEARNING SIGNING

Although great apes lack the physical ability to produce human speech, the findings of several "ape language" research projects indicate that they have some of the rudimentary cognitive abilities necessary to understand human speech. Different

FIGURE 7.16

Chimpanzee Signing Student teacher Joyce Butler shows the famous chimpanzee Nim Chimpsky the American Sign Language sign configuration for "drank," and Nim imitates her.

groups of scientists have taught orangutan, gorilla, chimpanzee, and bonobo subjects to communicate with humans using either American Sign Language (**Figure 7.16**) or graphical symbols on computerized keyboards (lexigrams). While watching his mother being taught by Sue Savage-Rumbaugh and her colleagues, a captive bonobo named Kanzi spontaneously learned to use lexigrams (this process is in fact similar to the way human children learn to speak). Kanzi remains one of the most successful nonhuman users of such a symbolic communication system. He can understand English at the level of a 2-year-old human, and he combines lexigrams in new ways according to a set of rules. The researchers argue that Kanzi's competence reflects an ancient history for a form of proto-grammar. Although such research has its share of critics, the ape language projects will continue to enrich what we know about the cognitive abilities of our closest living relatives, and they may shed light on the behaviors and linguistic abilities of our common ancestor.

This chapter has discussed primates' social behaviors, the methods that primates use for acquiring food, and the growing understanding of the essential role of material culture and nonmaterial culture and communication. All the information presented in this and the previous chapter lays the foundation for understanding the next part of this book, on roughly the past 50 million years of primate and human evolution.

ANSWERING THE BIG QUESTIONS

1. Why are primates social?

- Generally, primates that cooperate in social groups are better able to protect themselves from predators. The larger the group, the better the protection.
- Living in social groups provides access to mates and enhances reproductive success.

2. What is special about primate societies and social behavior?

- Primate societies range from solitary animals to complex multimale, multifemale groups. Most primates live in some kind of social group and do so on a long-term basis.
- Male reproductive strategies emphasize competition between males for access to reproductive-age females. Female reproductive strategies emphasize care of young and access to food for mothers and their offspring.

3. How do primates acquire food?

- Primates' wide variety of habitats requires them to use a wide variety of food-foraging strategies.
- Primates rely entirely on their bodies for acquiring and processing food for consumption. Humans rely on material culture to acquire and process food.
- Some primates have material culture. They have displayed some learned behavior and cultural tradition, such as forms of social grooming, tool use, and vocalization that are unique to specific groups and regions.

4. How do primates communicate?

- Primates communicate information through a wide variety of means, especially through vocalization.
- Vocalizations serve a range of functions and vary in different contexts; they include the transmissions from one individual to another or one group to another.
- Humans are the only primate to have speech, but use of symbols by apes in experimental contexts provides important insight into their cognitive abilities.

STUDY QUIZ

1. In primates, males and females primarily differ in
  a. body and canine size.
  b. mode of locomotion.
  c. tool use.
  d. color.

2. How do male and female primates differ in reproductive strategies?
  a. Males and females of the same species usually have different residence patterns.
  b. Males compete for mates, while females compete for resources.
  c. Some males are part of dominance hierarchies, but females never are.
  d. Females typically commit infanticide when a new male enters the group.

3. A primate's feeding success would be increased by
  a. consuming large quantities of low-quality foods.
  b. living in a geographic region with widely distributed food sources.
  c. consuming a single type of food.
  d. memorizing locations and seasonal availability of food patches.

4. Which statement is _false_ regarding chimpanzee material culture?
  a. Chimpanzees use tools in the wild.
  b. Chimpanzee tool use in the wild can be highly specific to a group.
  c. Chimpanzees can learn tool use from humans.
  d. Chimpanzees depend on tools to survive.

5. Which feature of communication is found only in humans?
  a. Different vocalizations that refer to specific events or objects
  b. Modifying vocalizations based on life experience
  c. Using gestures or symbols
  d. Physical ability to produce speech

KEY TERMS

altruistic
dominance
ethnoprimatology

habituate
infanticide
kin selection
monogamous
polyandrous

polygynous
sexual selection
sociality

EVOLUTION REVIEW

Primate Social Organization and Behavior

SYNOPSIS In addition to the wide variation of morphological characteristics present within the order Primates (see chapter 6), nonhuman primate species exhibit considerable diversity in social organization and behavior. Different primate species engage in various patterns of residence (social groupings), which influence the number of males, females, and juveniles present within the group at any one time. Within a species, males and females might have vastly different reproductive strategies, which can be associated with morphological and behavioral disparities between the two sexes. Primates also engage in cooperation, communication, and cultural behaviors, all of which vary drastically across this taxonomic order. As with their morphological characteristics, the immense diversity of behaviors among living primates has been shaped by the evolutionary histories of different species and continues to be shaped by environmental and social pressures.

Q1. List three ways in which reproductive strategies might differ among male and female primates of the same species. Describe the outcomes, in relation to morphology, behavior, and fitness, of these different reproductive strategies for both males and females.

Q2. Refer to Figure 7.1 and consider the following three primate species: bonobos, owl monkeys, and howler monkeys. Bonobos live in multimale, multifemale groups; owl monkeys in monogamous groups; and howler monkeys in one-male, multifemale (polygynous) groups. Based on their residence patterns, which of these species do you expect is the most sexually dimorphic in terms of body size, the least sexually dimorphic, and somewhere in between?

Q3. What kinds of advantages, in terms of evolutionary fitness, do cooperative behaviors provide among different species of nonhuman primates? Under what selective pressures would altruism (toward kin and nonkin) be likely to evolve?

Q4. Provide at least three examples (material or nonmaterial) from studies of chimpanzees or other nonhuman primates that fit the definition of *culture* (that is, learned behavior transmitted from individual to individual). Identify those that are likely adaptations that help the primate species survive and any that are more likely differences in behavior occurring between two populations for no apparent (or at least adaptive) reason.

Q5. In the strictest sense, *anthropology* is defined as "the study of humankind." Explain why studies of nonhuman primates are within the scope of biological anthropology. How can studies of nonhuman primate sociality and behavior enhance our understanding of our evolutionary past, and why are they important (and anthropological) in their own right?

ADDITIONAL READINGS

Arcadi, A. C. 2018. *Wild Chimpanzees: Social Behavior of an Endangered Species*. Cambridge, UK: Cambridge University Press.

Cheney, D. L. and R. M. Seyfarth. 2007. *Baboon Metaphysics: The Evolution of a Social Mind*. Chicago: University of Chicago Press.

Dore, K. M., E. P. Riley, and A. Fuentes, eds. 2017. *Ethnoprimatology: A Practical Guide to Research at the Human-Nonhuman Primate Interface*. Cambridge, UK: Cambridge University Press.

Goodall, J. 1986. *The Chimpanzees of Gombe: Patterns of Behavior*. Cambridge, MA: Harvard University Press.

Peterson, D. 2006. *Jane Goodall: The Woman Who Redefined Man*. New York: Houghton Mifflin.

Snowdon, C. T. 2017. Learning from monkey talk. *Science* 355: 1120–1122.

Stanford, C. B. 2001. *The Hunting Apes*. Princeton, NJ: Princeton University Press.

Strier, K. B. 2017. *Primate Behavioral Ecology*, 5th ed. New York: Routledge.

PART II

THE PAST

Evidence for the Present

Living organisms have resulted from millions of years of natural selection and other evolutionary forces. This living record has provided natural historians and biologists, Charles Darwin first and foremost, with important information about how evolution works and what forces are behind it. Fundamental as it is, however, the living record provides a limited picture of evolution, a record of just the *surviving* lineages. The other fundamental part of the evolutionary picture is found in the past, thanks to the fossil record, which portrays the lineages and extinct species that gave rise to living species. The focus of the remainder of this book—the fossil record—is the basis for documenting and interpreting biological history. Because fossils are the only source of evidence for what past organisms were like, where they lived, and how they behaved, living *and* past records are essential for understanding evolution—one is incomplete without the other.

Part II begins with a look at what fossils are and how they can be interpreted. Once this window onto the past has been opened, we will explore the diversity and abundance of primate species, starting with the first true primates (strepsirrhines), followed by the origins and evolution of the first higher primates (haplorrhines); then the appearance, evolution, and diversity of the first apes (hominoids); and, beginning around 6–7 mya, the origins and evolution of primitive, humanlike ancestors (hominins).

◀ The past record of evolution comes from fossils. This record shows us what ancestral species looked like. For example, a 6-million-year sequence of fossils from the Middle Awash River Valley in Ethiopia illustrates human evolution from *Ardipithecus*—the first bipeds—who lived 6 mya, to the earliest *Homo sapiens*, who lived more than 100,000 years ago. Just as important, the thousands of fossil remains of plants and animals found in this setting reveal details of the environment and ecology related to this lineage, whose evolution led to all of us now living around the globe.

The past record of evolution comes from fossils. For example, this 65-million-year-old *Tyrannosaurus rex* fossil reveals that enormous carnivorous reptiles once roamed the plains of western North America. The fossil remains of plants and animals found around the world provide details of the environment and ecology of Earth through time, including the conditions that led to the evolution of modern humans.

8

Fossils and Their Place in Time and Nature

BIG QUESTIONS

1. **What are fossils?**

2. **What do fossils tell us about the past?**

3. **What methods do anthropologists and other scientists use to study fossils?**

Although Charles Darwin's theory of evolution was based mostly on his observations of living species, Darwin certainly knew about fossils. His extensive reading must have included the works of the ancient Greek historian Herodotus, who had recognized the shells preserved in rock as the remains of organisms. Darwin was no doubt familiar with discoveries of fossils in the Americas. He even had a hand in prospecting for fossils in Argentina, noting in his journal that "the great size of the bones . . . is truly wonderful." He likely heard about discoveries in the United States, such as by the American president Thomas Jefferson (1743–1826), an avid fossil collector who reported on an extinct ground sloth found in Virginia (**Figure 8.1**). Darwin definitely knew the work of the French paleontologist Georges Cuvier (discussed in chapter 2), who had meticulously studied and published on the fossils of

FIGURE 8.1

Megalonyx jeffersonii **Fossil Claws** In 1796, Thomas Jefferson (inset) discovered the bones of an extinct ground sloth. The paper he presented on his finding to the American Philosophical Society helped launch the field of vertebrate paleontology in America.

many different plants and animals around Paris, and had read *Principles of Geology*, the book by the eminent English geologist Charles Lyell.

Though Darwin and these other figures made important contributions to scientific and anthropological thought, none of these people fully appreciated the importance of fossils as a record of the past. Cuvier recognized the fact that fossils are the remains of once-living organisms. Darwin saw the significance of the similarity in features between living ground sloths and the extinct forms in Argentina. But the larger role of fossils in reconstructing the history of life and a time frame in which to place that history was not at the forefront of either Cuvier's or Darwin's thinking. In science, it sometimes takes one person with just the right combination of background, experience, and intellect to put together various lines of evidence and draw conclusions from this evidence that result in a breakthrough. The breakthrough that set the stage for fossils as a fundamental source of information about the past came not from a respected scientist but from an engineering surveyor with a remarkable attentiveness to detail and pattern. Unlike many of the great scientists of the eighteenth and nineteenth centuries, the Englishman William Smith (1769–1839) was born into a family of very modest means. At 18, he apprenticed as a surveyor, and he eventually worked for a coal-mining and canal-construction company. In the mines, he observed that layers of rock—**strata**—were always positioned the same way relative to each other. He deduced this pattern from the colors and other physical properties of each stratum. He also realized that each stratum contained a unique collection of fossils representing long-extinct life-forms. From these observations, he hypothesized that the

FIGURE 8.2

1815 Geologic Map of England, Wales, and Part of Scotland, by William Smith Using fossils and the physical characteristics of geologic strata, William Smith created this map of the British Isles, which measures some 2 m (6 ft) by 3 m (10 ft). Smith's methods laid the groundwork for how geologists and paleontologists understand Earth's landscape, reconstruct geologic history, and study the evolution of life worldwide.

relative positions of strata and the kinds of fossils found in the layers were the same throughout England. He called his hypothesis the *principle of faunal succession,* and he tested it with a research program that correlated strata and fossils throughout Britain.

Smith was fired from his job in 1799, likely because of his distractions from his surveying work. Despite going into abject poverty and spending time in debtors' prison, he continued recording data across the country, ultimately producing in 1815 the first geologic map of the British Isles (**Figure 8.2**). What motivated him? Like the other scientists we have studied, Smith was motivated by questions about the natural world around him. And he believed that fossils provided an important record of past life and of time's passage. Although his passion was to produce a geologic map, he recognized the importance of fossils in the creation of a time frame for

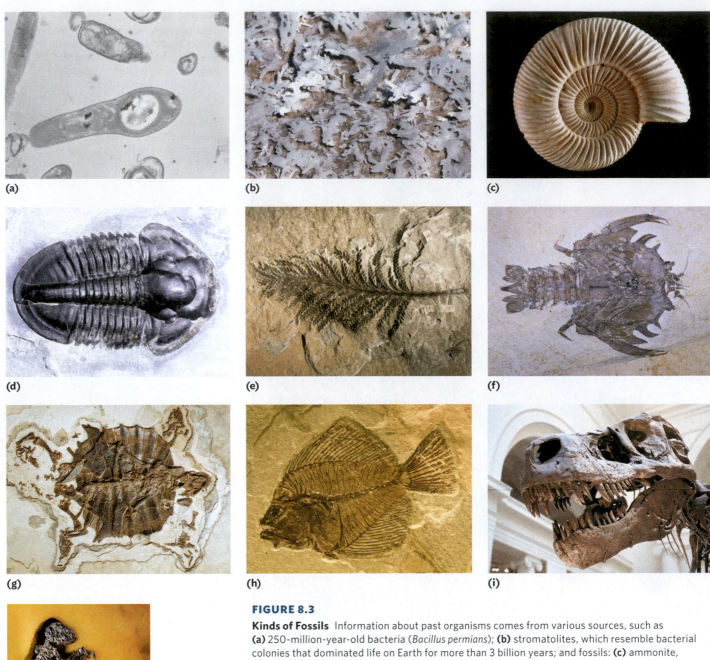

FIGURE 8.3

Kinds of Fossils Information about past organisms comes from various sources, such as **(a)** 250-million-year-old bacteria (*Bacillus permians*); **(b)** stromatolites, which resemble bacterial colonies that dominated life on Earth for more than 3 billion years; and fossils: **(c)** ammonite, **(d)** trilobite, **(e)** fern, **(f)** crab, **(g)** soft-shelled turtle, **(h)** fish, **(i)** *Tyrannosaurus* skeleton, and **(j)** Eocene primate, *Darwinius masillae*. Fossils like these have been found all over the world.

once-living organisms. The scientific world grew to realize what an important thing he had accomplished, and in the last years of his life Smith was recognized by the leading scientists of the time. Owing to his pursuit of answers to questions regarding the natural world, fossils became a means of documenting the evolution of life on Earth and a means of reconstructing geologic time.

Fossils are the very heart of the study of evolution. They provide us with the only direct physical evidence of past life and its evolution, from the simple bacterial organisms that lived more than 3 bya to the complex organisms that evolved later (**Figure 8.3**). The scientific study of fossils centers around two components: time and environment. Placement of fossils in time allows us to document *phylogeny*, or biological change and evolutionary relationships (see chapter 6). Placement of fossils in their environmental contexts helps us understand the factors that shaped the evolution of the organisms the fossils represent.

In this chapter, you will learn about the study of fossils, or paleontology, and the vast chronology within which scientists place the fossil record. You will also learn how paleontologists—the scientists who study fossils—determine how long ago organisms lived and what their environments were like. Paleontologists are the timekeepers of the past.

8.1 Fossils: Memories of the Biological Past

WHAT ARE FOSSILS?

Fossils (Latin *fossilis,* meaning "dug up") are the remains of once-living organisms. More specifically, they are the remains of organisms that have been wholly or partially transformed into rock through a long process of chemical replacement. In the replacement process, the minerals in bones and teeth, such as calcium and phosphorus, are very gradually replaced with rock-forming minerals such as iron and silica.

TAPHONOMY AND FOSSILIZATION

Fossils can derive from any body part, but bones and teeth are by far the most common sources, providing more than 99% of the fossil record. **Taphonomy**—the study of what happens to an organism's remains—describes the multiple circumstances that must (and must not) occur for a dead organism to become a fossil (**Figure 8.4**). An organism will *not* become a fossil, for example, if its remains are left exposed on the ground surface for any length of time. If the remains are exposed for an extended period after death, scavengers such as dogs, wolves, or birds may eat the soft tissues. Maggots will quickly consume flesh. Once the flesh is gone, the bones of the skeleton will weather, break, or disappear. Because of the unlikelihood of a quick natural burial (that is, one not performed by humans), very few once-living organisms end up as fossils.

If an organism is buried soon after its death, such as under soil sediments deposited by water, the remains will be at least partly protected from scavengers. To become fossilized, however, the remains must stay in an oxygen-free (anoxic) environment, where scavengers cannot access the body and where bacterial activity and decomposition are limited.

Even in this ideal burial environment, other factors can lead to the decay or alteration of the remains. For example, groundwater or acidic soils can dissolve bones and teeth, and ground pressure or geologic activity can distort the appearance of any potential fossils.

TYPES OF FOSSILS

Fossils are found in various types of rock, but most commonly in **sedimentary rock**, which is produced by water and wind carrying and then dropping tiny bits of rock, sand, and soil over time. In South Africa, for example, sediments were

sedimentary rock Rock formed when the deposition of sediments creates distinct layers, or strata.

A hominin collapses and dies on shore.

After the soft-tissue remains of the hominin decay, only the skeleton is left.

The water level of the lake rises, and the lake sediments settle and cover the hominin's bones and footprints.

The hominin's footprints are left in the mud.

The bones fossilize in the thick layer of sediment at the bottom of the lake, while sediments continue to be deposited as layers. The lake dries, and other geologic processes occur. A volcanic eruption, for example, spews ash over the region, providing more layers. The fossil is now embedded in a geologic stratum.

TIME

Erosion exposes deep strata in a geologic column, revealing the fossil skeleton and footprints.

A physical anthropologist examines the fossilized hominin remains. The bones provide material for study. The ancient soils (paleosols) provide material for environmental reconstruction.

FIGURE 8.4

What Is in a Fossil? The Making of the Biological Past

washed, blown, or dropped into caves. Coincidentally, as the sediments built up, carnivores dropped the remains of animals, including early hominins, in the caves (**Figure 8.5**). Sediments subsequently buried the remains and filled the caves, preserving fossils for millions of years.

Fossilization has also occurred when volcanic activity has buried animal remains in volcanic ash. Occasionally, volcanic ash preserves footprints, such as the spectacular tracks left by three hominins around 3.5 mya at Laetoli, Tanzania (**Figure 8.6**).

Though fossils do not contain the original biological materials that were present in life, even fossils that are millions of years old preserve vestiges of the

(a) 2 mya

(b) Before excavation

(c) During excavation

FIGURE 8.5

South African Cave Taphonomy These cutaway figures show key aspects of the taphonomy of hominin remains in South African cave sites, 2 mya and today. Through the careful study of bone accumulations, the South African paleontologist Charles Kimberlin Brain realized that the early hominin bones found in the caves, as well as the bones of many other kinds of animals, were likely there due to carnivore activity. **(a)** Carnivores such as leopards often take their prey into trees to feed. If such a tree hangs over an opening of a cave, the remains of the prey may fall into it when the animal has finished its meal. As the cave fills with bones and sediment, the remains become a part of the depositional process and are fossilized over time. **(b)** Paleontologists discover the strata with the fossils preserved from hundreds of thousands of years of deposition. One of the most famous hominin finds, the Taung child, was found in a South African cave (discussed further in chapter 10). **(c)** The excavation of Swartkrans Cave in South Africa has provided important hominin fossils. The grid over the excavation is used to map fossils and artifacts.

(a)

(b)

FIGURE 8.6

Ancient Footprints at Laetoli **(a)** Fossilized footprints of our human ancestors in Laetoli, Tanzania, provide information about **(b)** bipedal locomotion in early hominins. What information about locomotion can anthropologists learn from footprints? (Figure 8.6b: "The Fossil Footprint Makers of Laetoli," © 1982 by Jay H. Matternes)

original tissue. DNA within this tissue can be used to identify genetic information. Also, chemicals within original bone tissue or tooth tissue may be used for dietary reconstruction. Chemical constituents of bone, for example, have been extracted from early hominins from South Africa and Europe. Chemical analysis shows that early hominins ate a range of foods, including meat and plants.

LIMITATIONS OF THE FOSSIL RECORD: REPRESENTATION IS IMPORTANT

To form a complete picture of life in the past, we need fossils that represent the full range of living things from the past to the present. Representation, then, is the crucial factor in creating a fossil record. The fuller and more representative the collection of fossils from specific animals and plants in any site or region, the richer will be our understanding of the various populations of these animals and plants within that site or region.

Some fossil species are remarkably well represented. Paleontologists have found thousands of fossils from some 55 mya, for example, representing many different kinds of early primates and animals of the period. By contrast, many taxa are known from very limited fossil records, such as for the earliest apes of Africa (from around 20 mya). Key stages in the record of past life are missing because (1) paleontologists have searched for fossils in only some places—they simply have not discovered all the fossil-bearing rocks around the world; (2) fossils have been preserved in some places and not in others; and (3) rock sequences containing fossils are not complete in all places.

The Fayum Depression in Egypt helps illustrate these limitations. There, paleontologists have examined an unusually rich record of early primate evolution from about 37 mya to 29 mya (primate evolution is the subject of chapter 9). Hundreds of early primate fossils have been found in the Fayum geologic strata. The record ends at about 29 mya, however, when the rock stops bearing fossils. Did primates stop living there at 29 mya? Probably not. Rather, the geologic activity necessary for fossilization—the depositing of sediments—probably stopped after 29 mya. Without deposition and the burial of organisms, no new fossils were created.

Elsewhere in Africa, geologic strata dating to the same time period as the Fayum are exceedingly rare or they do not contain fossils. Primates might have lived in those areas, but sedimentation or fossilization or both simply did not occur.

Similarly, the record of early hominin evolution in Africa is mostly restricted to the eastern and southern portions of the continent. In all likelihood, early hominins inhabited all of Africa, certainly by 4 mya, but they were not preserved as fossils throughout the continent (early hominin evolution is the subject of chapter 10).

When fossil records are especially well represented over time, they help us discuss aspects of evolutionary theory, such as the timing and tempo of change. These records can indicate whether evolution is the gradual process that Charles Darwin wrote about in his *On the Origin of Species* or if its pace can speed up or slow down.

Fully interpreting the information in fossils means knowing both where the fossils were found and their ages. Without being able to place fossils in time, anthropologists cannot trace the evolution of past life (**Figure 8.7**).

8.2 Just How Old Is the Past?

TIME IN PERSPECTIVE

Most of us have limited perspectives on time. We tend to think about yesterday, today, and tomorrow or perhaps next week. Long expanses of time might extend to our earliest memories. Because most of us alive today were born after World War II, that conflict seems like part of the distant past. "Ancient" history might mean the beginning of the American Revolution in 1775 or Columbus's arrival at the Americas in 1492.

For scientists who deal with the distant past—such as geologists, paleontologists, biological anthropologists, and archaeologists—recent centuries constitute a tiny portion of time. Indeed, when put in the context of Earth's age (4.6 billion years) or the existence of life on Earth (at least 3.8 billion years), several centuries are not even an eyeblink in time. An appreciation of the history of life and (more immediately for this book) of primate and human evolution must be grounded in an understanding of the deep time involved. That is, to reconstruct and interpret evolutionary changes, it is crucial to place each fossil in time, answering the question: *How old is it?* Without an answer to that question for each and every fossil, it is not possible to order the fossils in chronological sequence. Simply, without a chronological sequence, there is no fossil record.

Throughout Part II of this book, our normally narrow perspective on time broadens to include the vast record of natural history. The following discussion is a first step toward that broader sense of time.

8.7

WHAT DID THEY LOOK LIKE?

BRINGING FOSSILS TO LIFE THROUGH RECONSTRUCTION

→

CONTEXT

Among the amazingly well-pre-served fossil hominins discovered beneath the ruins of Dmanisi, a medieval town in the countryside of the nation of Georgia, was the skull of a teenage boy, called D-2700. Dating to 1.7 mya, this skull is the first evidence of the genus *Homo* (*Homo erectus*) outside Africa. Soon after the fossil's discovery, the eminent French paleoartist and sculptor Elisabeth Daynès was asked to reconstruct the teenager's physical appearance—what he might have looked like in life. Her reconstruction provides us with a picture of one of the earliest occupants of Eurasia.

THE PROCESS: FROM DEATH TO LIFE

Producing a reconstruction of the living form for any fossil is difficult, and finishing just one can take up to 4 months. The process involves an interplay of art and science—for example, it requires an extensive knowledge of bones and of muscle and other soft tissue. Some of the process is guesswork, but most is based on knowledge of living forms and experience with creating reconstructions.

First, strips of clay are placed to mimic muscle size. The sticks mark approximations for the depth of the tissue over the bone. Second, tissue approximations are made, and then the tedious job begins of applying clay and molding the exterior surface. One of the huge challenges in producing a realistic reconstruction is the eyes. Without lifelike eyes, it is hard to make a model seem alive and compelling.

Finally, after the skin is placed over the muscles and other tissues, detailed painting creates skin texture, skin color, and facial expression. For this reconstruction, Daynès chose a whimsical smile, with the eyes focusing on something amusing. We can never know what the real hominin's facial expressions were like, but the individual had to be depicted as expressing emotion. While the Dmanisi boy does not look like anyone you would know, you undoubtedly recognize his humanness.

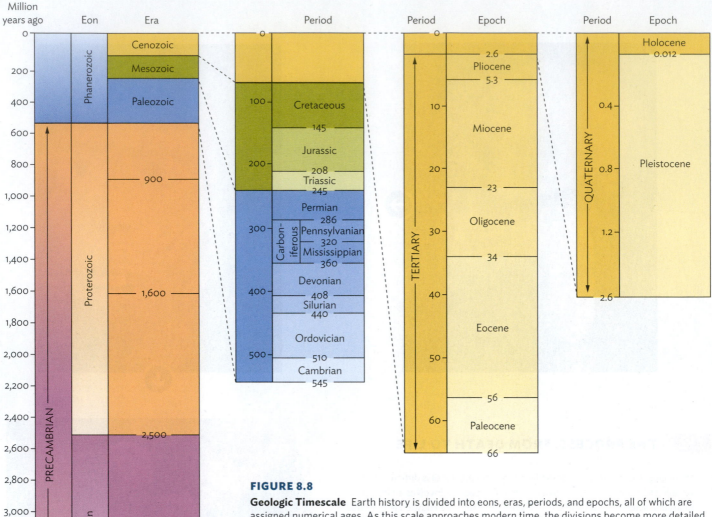

FIGURE 8.8

Geologic Timescale Earth history is divided into eons, eras, periods, and epochs, all of which are assigned numerical ages. As this scale approaches modern time, the divisions become more detailed numerically. According to this scale, which eon, era, period, and epoch are we in?

GEOLOGIC TIME: EARTH HISTORY

The evolutionary history of life on Earth involves deep time, as represented by the geologic timescale (**Figure 8.8**). By placing all past life-forms—as represented by fossils—on that scale, paleontologists record the major changes and events in the evolution of plants and of animals (**Figure 8.9**). Paleontologists order the evolution of major life-forms, as geologists order Earth history, in a series of three **eras**— the **Paleozoic**, the **Mesozoic**, and the **Cenozoic**—each subdivided by a series of **epochs**. Collectively, these eras and their epochs cover the past 545 million years. During this long expanse, an incredible amount of change—biological and geologic—has occurred.

In the upcoming chapters, we will look at some of the biological evolution during the current eon (the Phanerozoic), especially in the Cenozoic era. It is during the Cenozoic era that we see the first appearance and proliferation of primates, including humans in the later Cenozoic. Some of the most profound geologic changes have taken place within the Mesozoic and Cenozoic eras, or within the past 245 million years. At the beginning of this time frame, the supercontinent

Paleozoic The first major era of geologic time, 545–245 mya, during which fish, reptiles, and insects first appeared.

Mesozoic The second major era of geologic time, 245–66 mya, characterized by the emergence and extinction of dinosaurs.

FIGURE 8.9

Evolution of Life Earth's geologic timescale demonstrates the evolution of major organisms. As shown in this chart, modern humans are one of the most recent organisms to have developed; our roots go much deeper, however, as our ancestors appeared millions of years ago.

that we call **Pangaea**—the original continent from which our continents derive—began a process of separation, which is still ongoing (**Figure 8.10**). By the time true primates appeared, 145 million years later, the Atlantic Ocean had formed, separating North America from Europe, and South America from Africa. The gaps between North America and Europe and between South America and Africa continue to widen as the continental (**tectonic**) plates drift apart.

Cenozoic The era lasting from 66 mya until the present, encompassing the radiation and proliferation of mammals such as humans and other primates.

epochs Divisions of *periods* (which, in turn, are the major divisions of *eras*) in geologic time.

Pangaea A hypothetical single landmass, forming the origin for all continents.

tectonic Referring to various structures on Earth's surface, such as the continental plates.

(a) Paleozoic (about 350 mya)

(b) Late Jurassic (about 150 mya)

(c) Late Cretaceous (about 70 mya)

(d) Current positions

FIGURE 8.10

Movement of Continents Earth's continents have been moving for hundreds of millions of years and continue to drift. In the Paleozoic (545–245 mya), all the land on Earth formed **(a)** a single mass, which we call Pangaea. Beginning in the Late Jurassic (208–145 mya), this supercontinent began to break up into **(b)** separate continents. The initial split seems to have occurred in the northern part of Pangaea, creating the North Atlantic; the southern part, including South America, Africa, Antarctica, and Australia, remained closed. In the Late Cretaceous (145–66 mya), most of the continents were **(c)** separate and the Atlantic Ocean was complete; however, the continents had yet to reach their **(d)** present-day positions.

RELATIVE AND NUMERICAL AGE

The events just described and the idea that Earth could be hundreds of millions of years old seemed preposterous to most scholars living even a few hundred years ago. Before the eighteenth century, not many people could fathom that time stretched more than several thousand years before the present, beyond what geologists call "historical" time, the time since written records began. In 1654, the archbishop of Armagh, Ireland, James Ussher (1581–1656), added up all the generations of religious patriarchs listed in the Old Testament of the Bible and reported that Earth was created at midday on Sunday, October 23, 4004 BC. Ussher's pronouncement became the definitive answer to the question raised by many—*How old is planet Earth?*

Other scholars turned to nonhistorical sources of information, determining that a geologic past began long before the historical past. Niels Stensen (also known by his Latinized name, Nicolaus Steno; 1638–1686), a Dane serving as the court physician to the grand duke of Tuscany, studied the geologic formations around Florence, Italy, and the fossils they contained. Hypothesizing that the fossilized shark teeth that he found far under the ground were prehistoric, Stensen concluded that in a series of geologic layers—the stratigraphic sequence—higher rocks are younger than lower rocks.

This layer deposited first, parallel to the Earth's surface.

This layer deposited later, on top of the previous layer.

This layer deposited even later.

This layer must be younger than the others because it cuts across all three.

(a)

TIME

Steno's law of superposition laid the foundation for relative dating, which states the relative age of one event (such as the formation of a geologic stratum) or object (such as a fossil or an artifact) with respect to another (**Figure 8.11**). That is, the event recorded or object found on the bottom is the oldest, the event or object immediately above it is next oldest, and so forth. By contrast, the numerical age of an event or object is expressed in absolute years, such as 2,000 years ago, 1.3 billion years, 4004 BC, or AD 2014. Developed long before numerical dating, relative dating can be accomplished through several methods.

RELATIVE METHODS OF DATING: WHICH IS OLDER, YOUNGER, THE SAME AGE?

Stratigraphic Correlation Geologic correlation of strata from multiple locations in a region—that is, matching up strata based on physical features, chemical compositions, fossils, or other properties—helps place the passage of time in a larger context. This highly sophisticated method, first developed by William Smith, involves matching up physical and chemical characteristics of strata with the fossils found in those strata. Chemical characteristics make **stratigraphic correlation** possible across vast regions. For example, any volcanic eruption produces ash with an individual and highly specific chemical signature. The eruption's force, together with powerful winds, can spread the ash over hundreds or even thousands of kilometers, as when Krakatoa, an island volcano in Indonesia that erupted in 1883, sent ash as far as 6,000 km (3,700 mi) away (**Figure 8.12**). When an ash layer exists above or below a fossil, that fossil can be judged younger or older than the ash, depending on their relative positions. Such correlations, from various lines of evidence, involving millions of places around the world, have resulted in the geologic timescale.

Chemical Dating Soils around the world have specific chemical compositions, reflecting their local geologic histories. For example, some soils contain fluorine. Once a bone is buried in fluorine-bearing soil, the bone begins to absorb the element. A bone that has been buried for a long time will have more fluorine in it than will a bone that has been buried for a short time.

Fluorine dating, one of the first **chemical dating** methods, was proposed by the English chemist James Middleton in 1844 (**Figure 8.13**). The Croatian paleontologist Dragutin Gorjanović-Kramberger applied fluorine dating to human and animal remains found in Krapina, Croatia, in the late 1890s and early 1900s.

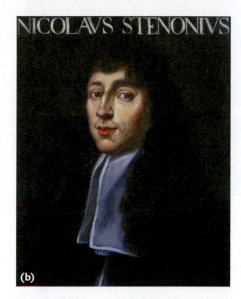

NICOLAVS STENONIVS

(b)

FIGURE 8.11

Steno's Law of Superposition **(a)** This law, formulated by **(b)** Niels Stensen (also known as Nicolaus Steno), states that the youngest geologic strata are at the top and the oldest strata are on the bottom. In which situations would this law not apply?

Steno's law of superposition The geologic principle that the lower the stratum, or layer, the older its age; the oldest layers are at the bottom, and the youngest are at the top.

stratigraphic correlation The process of matching up strata from several sites through the analysis of chemical, physical, and other properties.

fluorine dating A relative (chemical) dating method that compares the accumulation of fluorine in animal and human bones from the same site.

chemical dating Dating methods that use predictable chemical changes that occur over time.

FIGURE 8.12

Krakatoa The eruption of Krakatoa in 1883 (which made front page news in contemporary papers) was one of the most violent volcanic explosions in recorded history. The ash layer that resulted provided a frame of reference for dating materials found above and below it. Anything found under the layer of ash existed before 1883; everything on top existed after 1883.

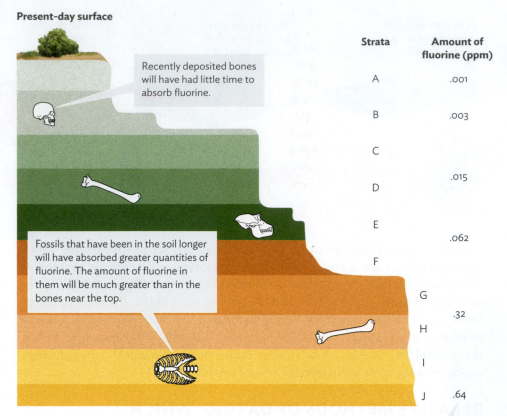

FIGURE 8.13

Fluorine Dating Buried bones absorb fluorine from the surrounding soil over time, enabling their relative dating.

biostratigraphic dating A relative dating method that uses the associations of fossils in strata to determine each layer's approximate age.

Hypothesizing that the bones buried in strata at the site had absorbed fluorine, he wanted to determine if the human bones, all representing humans called *Neandertals* (see chapter 10), were the same age as the animal bones. The animal bones were from long-extinct, Pleistocene forms of rhinoceroses, cave bears, and cattle. Some scientists believed that the Krapina Neandertals were not ancient, however, but had been living at the site in recent times only. They considered the Neandertals simply different from people living in Croatia in the late nineteenth and early twentieth centuries. If Gorjanović-Kramberger could show that the two sets of bones—human and animal—contained the same amount of fluorine, he could prove that the Neandertals were ancient and, in fact, had lived at the same time as the extinct animals. When the simple chemical analysis revealed that the Neandertal bones and the animal bones had very similar amounts of fluorine, this pioneering study demonstrated human beings' deep roots.

Biostratigraphic (Faunal) Dating Gorjanović-Kramberger recognized that different strata include different kinds of fossils. He regarded these findings as chronologically significant. That is, the forms of specific animals and plants change over time, so the forms discovered within individual layers can help determine relative ages. **Biostratigraphic dating** draws on the first appearance of an organism in the

(a)   (b)

FIGURE 8.14

Irish Elk (a) The skeleton of this giant deer shows how large the animal was; it stood more than 2.1 m (7 ft) tall at the shoulder. The man standing next to the skeleton was 1.85 m (6 ft, 1 in). **(b)** A reconstruction depicts the Irish elk.

fossil record, that organism's evolutionary development over time, and the organism's extinction. Pliocene and Pleistocene African rodents, pigs, and elephants and Eurasian mammals of all kinds have been especially useful for biostratigraphic dating because they show significant evolutionary change. By determining when certain animals lived, scientists have developed biostratigraphic markers, or **index fossils**, for assessing age. For example, giant deer—sometimes called Irish elk—provide useful information based on their extinction (**Figure 8.14**). That is, because the species appears to have died out in northern Europe around 10,600 yBP, the presence of Irish elk fossils in a northern European site indicates that the site predates 10,600 yBP.

Mammoths—relatives of modern elephants—first lived and evolved in Africa, then spread to Europe, Asia, and North America around 2.5 mya. Mammoths went extinct in Africa but continued to evolve elsewhere. After 2.5 mya, their molars became increasingly complex. Paleontologists have determined how these teeth changed from the species' emergence to its complete extinction. Therefore, when paleontologists discover fossilized mammoth teeth, they can determine the relative age of the site simply by looking at the molars. Likewise, changes in molar shape and size have helped paleontologists develop relative ages for Pliocene–Pleistocene pigs in East Africa and South Africa (**Figure 8.15**).

Material culture can provide information for **cultural dating**. The first evidence of material culture—simple stone tools—dates to about 3.3 mya (see chapter 10). Although individually distinctive in appearance, these simple tools are not especially useful for bracketing small amounts of time, mainly because their forms changed so slowly. For example, a stone tool from 2.6 mya produced by a hominin is very much like one from 1.8 mya produced by a hominin. However, the presence of a certain kind of tool, such as one of these early stone tools, enables

index fossils Fossils that are from specified time ranges, are found in multiple locations, and can be used to determine the age of associated strata.

The youngest molars are the tallest and longest.

Over time, the molars increased in height and length.

The oldest pig molars are relatively thin and short.

FIGURE 8.15

Fossil Pig Molars Changes in the size and shape of these teeth can be used for biostratigraphic dating in a method developed by the American paleontologists Jack Harris and Tim White. This figure shows the strata investigated by paleontologists, showing oldest (far right) to youngest (far left) strata. Note the increase in size of the molars over time.

In addition, fossil pig molars found in conjunction with layers of volcanic ash may be used for absolute dating, if paleontologists can determine the age of the ash. (On techniques for doing this, see "The Revolution Continues: Radiopotassium Dating" later in this chapter.) Because the teeth and the volcanic layer are associated chronologically, the teeth can then be used as time markers when found at other sites. ("Pig Dating: Stratigraphic Correlations," © 1985 by Jay H. Matternes)

paleontologists to say that the site (and its occupants) dates to a certain age or within a range (**Figure 8.16**).

Beginning in the later Pleistocene, stone tools and other components of material culture changed more rapidly. The various regional cultures in Europe collectively known as the Upper Paleolithic provide a number of "time-specific" artifacts, such as the small sculpture known as Lion Man. The first of these artifacts was found in

FIGURE 8.16

Cultural Artifacts Among the remains of material culture that can be used to determine the time periods of archaeological sites are **(a)** an Oldowan chopper, **(b)** an Oldowan flake tool, **(c)** an Acheulean hand axe (France), **(d)** a hand axe from Olorgesailie (Kenya), **(e)** a hand axe from the Galería at Atapuerca (Spain), **(f)** a Mousterian Levallois flake tool, **(g)** Mousterian tools, **(h)** Solutrean tools, **(i)** an Upper Paleolithic point, **(j)** a Neolithic flake tool, **(k)** a Neolithic axe head, **(l)** Neolithic scrapers, **(m)** a Mayan pot, **(n)** Clovis points, **(o)** a post-Neolithic spade, **(p)** a Native American stone maul, **(q)** an Inuit fishing spear, **(r)** a Ford Model T, and **(s)** an Apple iPhone.

FIGURE 8.17

Lion Man The discovery of another sculpture like this one, made of mammoth ivory and about 30 cm (11.8 in) high, would provide a relative date for the archaeological site. The site would be at least 30,000 years old.

a cave in Germany in 1939, neglected for 30 years in part because of World War II, and only recently restored (**Figure 8.17**).

In the Holocene, artifacts such as ceramics became even more time-specific. In fact, ceramics were invented during this period, and their forms changed rapidly (**Figure 8.18**).

ABSOLUTE METHODS OF DATING: WHAT IS THE NUMERICAL AGE?

The Radiometric Revolution And The Dating Clock When we say that the American Civil War took place after the American Revolution, we have provided relative ages for the two wars. That is, we have related the ages without specifying them. When we say that the American Civil War began in 1861 and the American Revolution began in 1775, we have provided numerical ages. That is, we have pinpointed the wars' beginnings in terms of years, a measure of scaled time. We know these dates thanks to written records; individuals recorded all sorts of events associated with both wars (**Figure 8.19**). Since the time that Niels Stensen and his contemporaries began studying geologic features and fossils, scientists have been recording relative ages. By doing so, they have established the sequence of events in the geologic timescale—proving that the Eocene came before the Miocene, for example, and that ceramics were invented long after Neandertals lived in Europe. However, unlike historians, who often work with records containing dates, premodern

(a)

(b)

(c)

(d)

(e)

FIGURE 8.18

Ceramics Like stone tools, sculptures, or other artifacts, ceramics can be used to provide relative dates for a site. Changes in size, material, shape, and decoration are well documented for series of ceramics in some locations. When a newly discovered ceramic piece belongs to a known temporal series, archaeologists determine where it falls in the chronology. Examples include **(a)** an Amratian vase, ca. 4000–3100 BC; **(b)** a vase created by Aristonothos from Greece, ca. 650 BC; **(c)** an Egyptian Ptolemaic alabaster jar, ca. 300 BC; **(d)** an Anasazi black-on-white jar, ca. 1000–1300; and **(e)** a water pitcher commemorating the 1796 US presidential election.

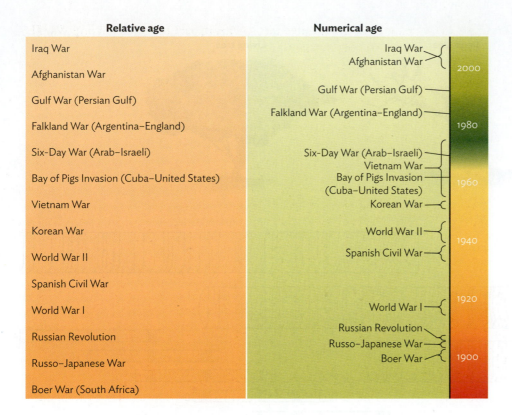

Relative age	Numerical age
Iraq War	Iraq War / Afghanistan War
Afghanistan War	— 2000
Gulf War (Persian Gulf)	Gulf War (Persian Gulf)
Falkland War (Argentina–England)	Falkland War (Argentina–England) — 1980
Six-Day War (Arab–Israeli)	Six-Day War (Arab–Israeli)
Bay of Pigs Invasion (Cuba–United States)	Vietnam War
	Bay of Pigs Invasion (Cuba–United States) — 1960
Vietnam War	Korean War
Korean War	World War II — 1940
World War II	Spanish Civil War
Spanish Civil War	
World War I	— 1920
	World War I
Russian Revolution	Russian Revolution
Russo–Japanese War	Russo–Japanese War
Boer War (South Africa)	Boer War — 1900

FIGURE 8.19

Relative versus Numerical Age Wars of the twentieth and twenty-first centuries can be ordered relatively or numerically. The relative chart simply shows the order of events and does not specify when these events occurred or how long they lasted. The numerical chart provides dates and gives at least a rough sense of the wars' starting points and durations.

geologists, paleontologists, and anthropologists had no means of providing numerical dates. Geologists could only group geologic events; paleontologists could only group species' lives; and anthropologists could only group peoples' lives and cultural events.

In the 1920s, the American astronomer A. E. Douglass (1867–1962) developed the first method for numerically dating objects and events, specifically ones including or involving wood. In studying sunspots and their impact on climate, Douglass noted that in temperate and very cold regions, tree growth stopped in the winter and reactivated in the spring. This intermittence resulted in layers of growth, visible as a concentric ring pattern in the cross section of a tree. Douglass's **dendrochronology**, or tree-ring method of dating, involved counting the number of rings, each of which represented 1 year of growth (**Figure 8.20**). Tree-ring dating was first used on tree sections found in archaeological sites in the American Southwest. It works, however, only when wood is as excellently preserved as it is in the arid Southwest, and thus it can be applied only in limited regions of the world.

Widely applicable numerical dating became possible in the nuclear age, after World War II (1939–1945). In 1949, the American chemist Willard Libby (1908–1980) discovered **radiocarbon dating**, an accomplishment for which he won a Nobel Prize. Scientists now had a means of determining the numerical age of past life-forms via the decay of radioactive elements.

The radiocarbon method, sometimes called the *carbon-14 method,* involves dating carbon **isotopes**. Isotopes are variants of an element based on the number of neutrons in the atom's nucleus. Some isotopes of an element are stable—in theory, they will last for an infinite amount of time, at least with respect to maintaining the same number of neutrons. Stable isotopes are called non-radioactive isotopes. Other isotopes are unstable—over time, they decay radioactively, transforming themselves into stable isotopes of either the same element or another element. Unstable isotopes are called radioisotopes, or radioactive isotopes. Carbon has

dendrochronology A chronometric dating method that uses a tree-ring count to determine numerical age.

radiocarbon dating The radiometric dating method in which the ratio of ^{14}C to ^{12}C is measured to provide an absolute date for a material generally younger than 50,000 years.

isotopes Two or more forms of a chemical element that have the same number of protons but vary in the number of neutrons.

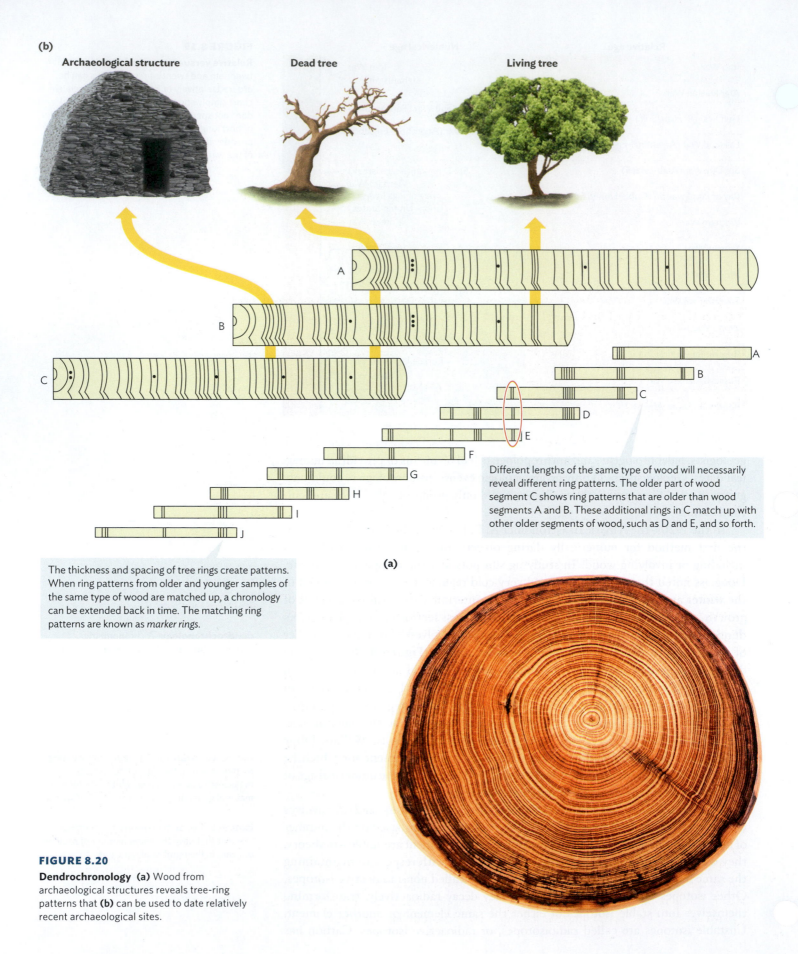

(b)

Archaeological structure Dead tree Living tree

A

B

C

A
B
C
D
E
F
G
H
I
J

Different lengths of the same type of wood will necessarily reveal different ring patterns. The older part of wood segment C shows ring patterns that are older than wood segments A and B. These additional rings in C match up with other older segments of wood, such as D and E, and so forth.

The thickness and spacing of tree rings create patterns. When ring patterns from older and younger samples of the same type of wood are matched up, a chronology can be extended back in time. The matching ring patterns are known as *marker rings*.

(a)

FIGURE 8.20

Dendrochronology (a) Wood from archaeological structures reveals tree-ring patterns that **(b)** can be used to date relatively recent archaeological sites.

TABLE 8.1 Isotopes Used in Radiometric Dating

PARENT → DAUGHTER	HALF-LIFE (YEARS)	MATERIAL IN WHICH THE ISOTOPES OCCUR
$^{14}C \rightarrow {}^{14}N$	5,730	Anything organic (that is, anything that has carbon), such as wood, shell, bone
$^{238}U \rightarrow {}^{206}Pb$	4.5 billion	Uranium-bearing minerals (zircon, uraninite)
$^{40}K \rightarrow {}^{40}Ar$	1.3 billion	Potassium-bearing minerals (mica, feldspar, hornblende)
$^{40}Ar \rightarrow {}^{39}Ar$	1.3 billion	Potassium-bearing minerals (mica, feldspar, hornblende)
$^{235}U \rightarrow {}^{207}Pb$	713 million	Uranium-bearing minerals (zircon, uraninite)

one radioisotope, identified as ^{14}C (carbon-14) because it has an atomic mass of 14 (six protons and eight neutrons) in its nucleus. Carbon has two stable isotopes, ^{12}C (carbon-12) and ^{13}C (carbon-13), which have an atomic mass of 12 (six protons and six neutrons) and 13 (six protons and seven neutrons), respectively. The radiocarbon method focuses on what happens to the radioisotope, ^{14}C. Over 5,730 years, half of the ^{14}C decays into ^{14}N. Over the next 5,730 years, another half of the ^{14}C decays again into ^{14}N, and so on, until eventually most of the radioisotope will have decayed. The number representing the time it takes for half of the radioisotope to decay is called the **half-life** (**Table 8.1**).

All living plants and animals (including you) absorb about the same amount of ^{14}C in their tissues, through the ingestion of very small amounts of atmospheric carbon dioxide (CO_2). During the life of a plant or animal, the ratio of ^{14}C to ^{12}C remains relatively constant. Once the organism dies, it stops absorbing ^{14}C and the ^{14}C begins to decay, but the ^{12}C does not decay. This means that the ratio of ^{14}C to ^{12}C changes over time—the longer since the death of the plant or animal, the greater the amount of ^{12}C relative to ^{14}C (**Figure 8.21**).

The great advantage of the radiocarbon dating method is that it has a precise baseline for the start of the clock—the death of the organism. The disadvantage for dating major events in primate and human evolution is that ^{14}C has a fairly short half-life, rendering its dates most accurate for only the past 50,000 yBP. Dates can be determined for another 25,000 years or so beyond that, but they are less precise owing to the very small amount of ^{14}C left.

The Revolution Continues: Radiopotassium Dating All organic materials contain carbon and thus can be dated through the radiocarbon method. By contrast, nonorganic materials such as rocks contain other elements that can be radiometrically dated. Because the radioisotopes of these elements have very long half-lives, the radiometric clock is considerably longer for these nonorganic materials than for carbon-based materials. **Igneous rock** (also called volcanic rock), for example, contains the radioisotope ^{40}K (potassium-40). ^{40}K decays very slowly from its unstable form to a stable gas, ^{40}Ar (argon-40)—its half-life is 1.3 *billion* years. It is usually not possible to date rocks much younger than 200,000 yBP, but ^{40}K's long half-life presents no limitation on the other end of the range. **Radiopotassium dating** certainly accommodates all of primate evolution.

The great strength of this method is the presence of volcanic rock in many places throughout the world. During a volcanic eruption, the heat is so extreme that it drives off all argon gas in the rock. The ^{40}K solid that is in the rock sealed by lava then begins to decay to ^{40}Ar gas, and the gas accumulates, trapped within

igneous rock Rock formed from the crystallization of molten magma, which contains the radioisotope ^{40}K; used in potassium–argon dating.

radiopotassium dating The radiometric dating method in which the ratio of ^{40}K to ^{40}Ar is measured to provide an absolute date for a material older than 200,000 years.

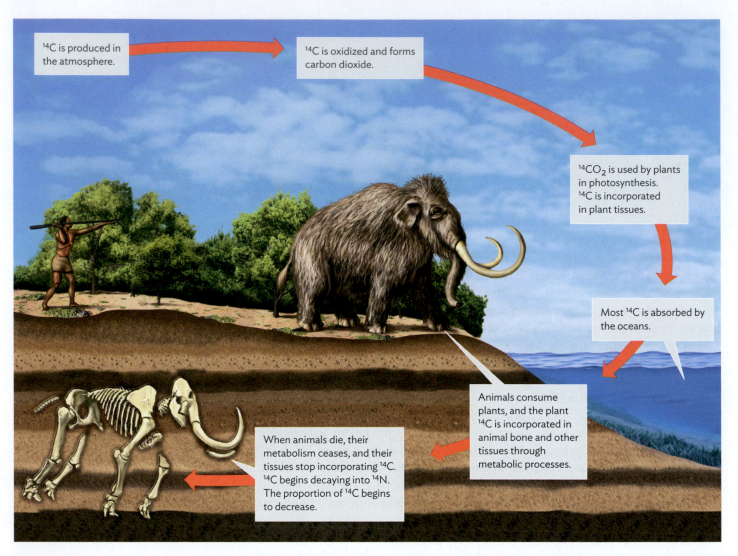

The following labels appear within the figure:

¹⁴C is produced in the atmosphere.

¹⁴C is oxidized and forms carbon dioxide.

¹⁴CO₂ is used by plants in photosynthesis. ¹⁴C is incorporated in plant tissues.

Most ¹⁴C is absorbed by the oceans.

Animals consume plants, and the plant ¹⁴C is incorporated in animal bone and other tissues through metabolic processes.

When animals die, their metabolism ceases, and their tissues stop incorporating ¹⁴C. ¹⁴C begins decaying into ¹⁴N. The proportion of ¹⁴C begins to decrease.

FIGURE 8.21

Radiocarbon Dating This dating method was the first generation of radioisotope methods. Such dating methods remain among the most important for the determination of numerical dates.

the rock's crystalline structure. To date that rock—which could be millions of years old—a scientist measures, with sophisticated instruments, the amount of gas (^{40}Ar) relative to the amount of nongas (^{40}K) in the rock. The more gas there is, the older the rock.

The radiopotassium dating method was first used to date the volcanic rock associated with an early hominin skull found by the British archaeologist Mary Leakey (1913–1996) in the lowest strata of Olduvai Gorge, in Tanzania, in 1959. At that time, scientists assumed that hominins had been around for perhaps a half-million years but not longer. When the associated volcanic rock at Olduvai proved to be 1.8 million years old, that dating nearly quadrupled the known time frame for hominin evolution. Since then, radiometric methods have helped paleontologists fine-tune the chronologies of primate and human evolution.

In the 1990s, scientists developed an alternative method of radiopotassium dating, whereby they measure the ratio of ^{40}Ar gas to ^{39}Ar gas. In the argon–argon method, volcanic rock is bombarded with "fast" neutrons in a nuclear reactor. Like ^{40}K, ^{39}K is present in the volcanic rock, and the two isotopes, ^{40}K and ^{39}K, occur in the same amounts relative to one another, no matter how old the rock may be. The neutron bombardment converts the ^{39}K to ^{39}Ar. Because ^{39}Ar serves as a proxy for ^{40}K, the ratio of ^{40}Ar to ^{39}Ar reveals the rock's absolute age. This method's advantages over the potassium–argon method are that it requires less rock and the potassium does not have to be measured. Now routinely being used by paleontologists and geologists to date early hominins, the method has made it possible to date hundreds of hominin (and other) fossils from 5 mya to *Homo sapiens'* origin, more than 100,000 yBP. Note, though, that radiopotassium can be used to date only igneous rock, not sedimentary rock.

Fission track dating is based on the radioactive decay of naturally occurring ^{238}U (uranium-238; **Figure 8.22**). When the isotope decays, fragments produced in the decay, or fission, process leave a line, or track, measuring just a few atoms wide on the rock crystal. Thus, the greater the number of tracks, the older the material being dated. This method can date materials from the past several million years and has been used for dating volcanic ash and obsidian (volcanic glass).

Non-Radiometric Absolute Dating Methods Several other, non-radiometric methods provide absolute dates. Among these methods, **amino acid dating** is the most useful in more recent settings (**Figure 8.23**). This method is based on the decay of protein molecules after an organism's death. Amino acids, the compounds that make up proteins (among the subjects of chapter 3), come in two forms, L-isomers and D-isomers, respectively known as left-handed amino acids and right-handed amino acids. Basically, this distinction means that when a protein is viewed under high-power magnification with a specialized light called **polarized light**, the molecules bend light to the left (and are called L-isomers) or to the right (D-isomers). Most living organisms' tissues are composed of L-isomers. Once an organism dies, these L-isomers begin to transform to D-isomers. The longer the organism has been dead, the greater the number of D-isomers, so the fossil's date is based on the ratio of L to D.

The limitation of amino acid dating is that the rate of the chemical decomposition resulting in the shift from L to D—a process called **racemization**—is largely determined by the temperature of the region. A region with a higher average temperature will promote a faster rate of chemical decomposition than will a region with a cooler average temperature. Therefore, the method is dependent on the local climate and is not broadly comparable across large regions. The age range for amino acid dating is generally 100,000–40,000 yBP but has been extended to 200,000 yBP in tropical settings and to nearly 3 mya in cooler settings. The method has provided useful dates for a variety of sites, but it is best known in human evolutionary studies for dating Border Cave in South Africa (145,000–70,000 yBP) and the human occupation during the Pleistocene in Britain.

Paleomagnetic dating is based on changes in Earth's magnetic field. In essence, movement of the planet's liquid (iron alloy) outer core creates an electric current that results in the magnetic field (**Figure 8.24**). When the magnetic field shifts, the magnetic north and south poles shift. The poles' shifts have been well documented. In the past 6 million years, for example, there have been four "epochs" of polar changes, or four different well-dated periods. Because certain metal grains align themselves with Earth's magnetic field as they settle and help form sedimentary rock, geologists can examine the orientation of these fragments to determine the planet's polarity at the time of the rock's formation. In addition, when molten igneous rock is produced, each new layer records the polarity, which can later be determined from the hard igneous rock.

FIGURE 8.22
Fission Track Dating Fission track dating uses the number of tracks left behind by isotope decay. Here, tracks are visible in an apatite crystal.

fission track dating An absolute dating method based on the measurement of the number of tracks left by the decay of ^{238}U.

amino acid dating An absolute dating method for organic remains, such as bone or shell, in which the amount of change in the amino acid structure is measured.

L form   D form

L/D

Time →

FIGURE 8.23
Amino Acid Dating Amino acid dating is based on changes in the form of amino acid molecules (from L to D) over time. Marine shell, depicted here, is one type of material that is dated.

FIGURE 8.24

Paleomagnetic Dating Paleomagnetic dating derives from changes in Earth's polarity.

Earth's magnetic field today

The alternating layers in this schematic of a section of rock represent changes in polarity over time.

Mya	Era	Period	Epoch	Polarity N R
0		Quater-nary	Holocene	
			Pleistocene	
5			Pliocene	
10	Cenozoic	Tertiary	Miocene	
15				
20				
25				

The black and white bars (N = normal, R = reversal) represent polarity changes, each of which is assigned beginning and ending dates. This chart shows the polarity changes over the past 25 million years.

polarized light A kind of light used in amino acid dating because it allows amino acid changes to be observed and measured.

racemization The chemical reaction resulting in the conversion of ʟ amino acids to ᴅ amino acids for amino acid dating.

paleomagnetic dating An absolute dating method based on the reversals of Earth's magnetic field.

electron spin resonance dating An absolute dating method that uses microwave spectroscopy to measure electrons' spins in various materials.

thermoluminescence dating A dating method in which the energy trapped in a material is measured when the object is heated.

Electron spin resonance dating relies on the measurement of radioisotope concentrations (for example, of uranium) that have accumulated in fossils over periods of time. Once buried, remains such as bones and teeth absorb radioisotopes and record the radioactivity in the surrounding burial environment. The older the fossil, the greater the concentration, and this method can date material from a few thousand to more than a million years old.

Thermoluminescence dating is based on the amount of the sun's energy trapped in material such as sediment, stone, or ceramic (**Figure 8.25**). When such an object is heated—as in an early hominin's campfire—the energy it contains is released as light. The next time that same material is heated—as in the laboratory to derive a date—the amount of light released reveals the amount of time since the material was first heated. This method can date materials back to about 800,000 yBP.

Scientists must consider various factors when choosing an absolute dating method, among them the material involved and the time range in which the fossilized organism likely lived. Some methods date the fossil, and some date the *context* of the fossil. Radiocarbon, for example, can be used to date either the remains of the once-living organism or an associated organic substance, such as wood. To determine the age of a human skeleton, the bones can be dated directly. If, however, it can be proved that the deceased was buried at the same time a fire was lit nearby, the firepit can be dated.

GENETIC DATING: THE MOLECULAR CLOCK

The DNA in living organisms is an important source of information for retrospectively dating key events in their species' evolution, including divergence from closely related species and phylogenetic relationships with other organisms. In light of the well-founded assumption that a species accumulates genetic differences in general and mutations in particular over time at a more or less constant rate, it should be possible to develop a chronology showing the amount of time that has passed since two species diverged in their evolution. Simply put, more closely related species should have more similar DNA than less closely related species have. In the 1960s, the American geneticist Morris Goodman and others developed the molecular clock for dating the divergences of the major primate taxa. This record indicates that Old World monkeys first diverged from all other primates about 25 mya; gibbons diverged about 18 mya; orangutans, about 14 mya; and gorillas, about 12 mya; and the split occurred between chimpanzees and hominins about 9 mya (**Figure 8.26**). Molecular anthropologists and paleoanthropologists studying the respective genetic and fossil records find a general consistency in the dates for the origins of the major primate groups. As geneticists and anthropologists learn more about the primate genome, this method of retrospective dating is becoming increasingly refined. For example, studies of the human genome are revealing the rate of the appearance of mutations in newborn infants. These findings suggest a slower mutation rate than previously thought, making the split between chimpanzees and the first hominins 8–10 mya. This revision of the molecular clock is also more consistent with the dates for the earliest hominins, which exceed the divergence dates provided by Goodman many years ago (see chapter 10).

FIGURE 8.25

Thermoluminescence Dating
Thermoluminescence dating is related to the amount of light released when an object with stored energy is heated.

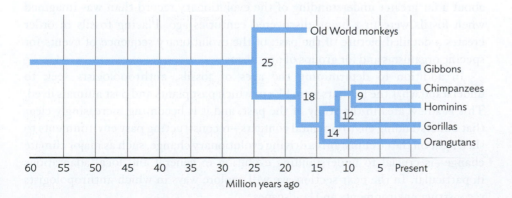

Old World monkeys

25

18

9

Gibbons

Chimpanzees

Hominins

12

Gorillas

14

Orangutans

60   55   50   45   40   35   30   25   20   15   10   5   Present

Million years ago

FIGURE 8.26

Genetic Dating: Divergence of Higher Primates Modern primates diverged from a common ancestor millions of years ago. A "molecular clock" helps determine the time since the divergence of monkey and ape species. This system assumes that species accumulate genetic differences over time at a regular rate.

How Old Is It?

Fossils are the primary source of information for documenting the evolution of past life. Paleontologists have developed various means for determining a fossil's age.

METHOD	BASIS	MATERIAL	DATE RANGE
Relative Age			
Law of superposition	Older is lower	Just about anything	Just about any time
Stratigraphic correlation	Like strata from different regions are related to the same event	Rocks and fossils	Just about any time
Biostratigraphic (faunal) dating	Evolution of animals	Bones and teeth	Just about any time
Chemical dating	Fossils absorb chemicals, such as fluorine, in soil	Bones	Less than 100,000 yBP
Cultural dating	Artifacts are time-specific	Technology generally	Less than 2.5 mya
Numerical Age			
Dendrochronology	Tree growth	Specific tree types	Less than 12,000 yBP
Radiocarbon dating	Carbon-14	Anything organic	AD 1950 to 50,000 yBP
Radiopotassium dating	Potassium-40	Volcanic rocks	More than 200,000 yBP
Amino acid dating	Racemization	Bones, shells	Less than 3 mya
Fission track dating	Fission tracks on rock crystal	Volcanic rock	Up to 3 mya
Paleomagnetic dating	Shifts in Earth's magnetic field	Sedimentary and igneous rocks	Less than 5 mya
Electron spin resonance dating	Concentrations of radioisotopes	Bones, teeth	Several thousand years to more than 1 mya
Thermoluminescence dating	Trapped energy	Sediment, stone, ceramics	Less than 800,000 yBP

In summary: Anthropologists and other scientists who deal with deep time have various methods and research tools for answering questions about when past organisms were alive. Some of these methods and tools directly date fossils, and others date the fossils' geologic contexts. Relative and absolute dating have brought about a far greater understanding of the evolutionary record than was imagined when fossils were first being discovered centuries ago. Placing fossils in order creates a detailed picture of the past: of the evolutionary sequence of events for specific organisms and for groups of organisms.

In addition to determining the ages of fossils, anthropologists seek to understand what the habitats were like in which past plants and past animals lived. This is a new area in the study of the past, and it is becoming increasingly clear that understanding environmental contexts—reconstructing past environments to shed light on the circumstances driving evolutionary change, such as major climate change—is crucial to understanding evolution in general and local adaptations in particular. In the next section, we will explore ways in which anthropologists reconstruct environments and landscapes.

8.3 Reconstruction of Ancient Environments and Landscapes

For much of the history of paleontology, the focus has been on evolutionary relationships (phylogeny). In studying the origins and morphological evolution of the various life-forms, paleontologists have asked questions such as *Which (now fossilized) species gave rise to primates? To the first apes? To the first hominins? To the first modern humans?* Phylogenetic questions remain central to the study of evolution, but the evolution of past organisms is not truly meaningful unless it is correlated with the circumstances under which the organisms lived and the processes that underlay their evolutionary changes. Scientists need to ask additional questions; for example, *Which conditions drove natural selection and other processes that account for the appearance, evolution, radiation, and extinction of past primates and humans?* This question pertains especially to the ecology of the setting the primates lived in— their habitat. Using models derived from the study of living animals, paleontologists can look at the bones of extinct animals and determine how they functioned during life and in what kinds of habitats they functioned. For example, as discussed in chapter 6, the long arms and short legs of apes are now well understood to be part of the species' adaptation to life in the trees—the apes are skilled at suspensory forms of locomotion. Therefore, when paleontologists find fossil apes with long arms, such as the Miocene ape *Oreopithecus,* they can infer that these primates lived in a habitat where trees were the dominant form of vegetation (**Figure 8.27**).

THE DRIVING FORCE IN SHAPING ENVIRONMENT: TEMPERATURE

Temperature is perhaps the single most important feature of climate. Therefore, if scientists can reconstruct the temperature for a particular geologic stratum, they come very close to characterizing a past climate. Scientists cannot measure temperature in the past, but they can identify and study the effects of different

(a)   (b)

FIGURE 8.27

Life in the Trees (a) The skeleton and body reconstruction of *Oreopithecus* show that the ape's long arms were adapted to a suspensory form of locomotion. **(b)** Gibbons have a similar body style, adapted to life in the trees. What differences in skeletal anatomy would you expect in a primate that lived primarily on open grassland?

FIGURE 8.28

Foraminifera The chemical composition of these microorganisms found in sediments on the ocean floor provides information on past climates.

foraminifera Marine protozoans that have variably shaped shells with small holes.

temperatures on biology and geologic chemistry. Hot climates leave very different biological and chemical signatures from those left by cold climates.

Because of this close linkage of temperature with biology and chemistry, paleoclimatologists have reconstructed temperature changes for much of the Cenozoic (and before). Some of the best information on climate history—and especially temperature—is based on the study of **foraminifera** and other ocean-dwelling microorganisms (**Figure 8.28**). These microorganisms' tiny shells are preserved in sediments on the ocean floor worldwide, and their chemical compositions tell important stories about temperature change over time. While the microorganisms are alive, they ingest two of the three stable isotopes of oxygen, ^{18}O (oxygen-18) and ^{16}O (oxygen-16), from the ocean water. Atmospheric temperature directly affects the water's temperature, which in turn affects the amount of ^{18}O in the water. When temperature declines, the amount of ^{18}O in the water, and therefore in the microorganisms, increases. When temperature increases, the amount of ^{18}O decreases. Geologists have taken core samples of sediments from the ocean floor and have tracked the ^{18}O content in the microorganisms within those sediments, producing a record of global temperature change (**Figure 8.29**).

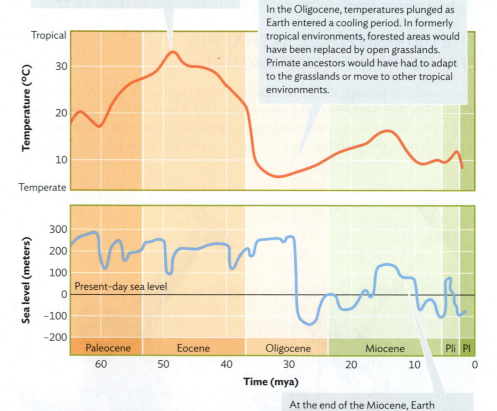

During the Eocene, temperature increased. This change might have led to the growth of tropical forests, which were ideal habitats for the tree-dwelling ancestors of modern primates.

In the Oligocene, temperatures plunged as Earth entered a cooling period. In formerly tropical environments, forested areas would have been replaced by open grasslands. Primate ancestors would have had to adapt to the grasslands or move to other tropical environments.

At the end of the Miocene, Earth entered another cooling period. Again, dramatic changes in habitat and climate occurred. The reduced forests and increased grasslands might have accounted, in part, for the evolution of bipedal locomotion.

FIGURE 8.29

Global Temperature and Climate Changes Changes in temperature during the Cenozoic have been documented by measuring ^{18}O in foraminifera shells. A decrease in ^{18}O indicates an increase in temperature; conversely, an increase in ^{18}O indicates a decrease in temperature. Note: "Pli" refers to Pliocene and "Pl" refers to Pleistocene.

Based on the isotope signatures of ancient sediments, we know that temperatures were high in the Paleocene, preceding the appearance of true primates, and that they peaked in the Early Eocene. This warm period was followed by a gradual decline in temperature throughout the Eocene. At the boundary between the Eocene and Oligocene, about 34 mya, temperature sharply declined, then rose, then sharply declined again. Moderate ups and downs followed in the Oligocene and into the Middle Miocene. After a sharp decline about 17–15 mya, temperatures leveled off for the remainder of the Miocene. Climate was drier and more seasonal about 10–5 mya, coinciding with the appearance of early hominins.

One of the most profound temperature changes, and thus dramatic alterations of climate and habitat, began at the end of the Miocene, about 6 mya (**Figure 8.30**). Sea levels are at their highest during warm periods; during cold periods, more water is tied up in ice and glaciers than during warm periods. This cold period likely added a permanent ice sheet on the continent of Antarctica; so much water was tied up in glacial ice that the Mediterranean Sea was nearly dry. During the Pleistocene (2.6 mya–12,000 yBP), periods of massive glaciation, or glacials, were followed by periods of relative warmth, or interglacials. Studies of such cold-and-warm patterns indicate that the time we live in, the Holocene, is not a separate epoch but simply another interglacial. More severely cold weather might be just around the corner following the current warming trend (see chapter 13).

FIGURE 8.30

Antarctica During the latter part of the Miocene, glaciers advanced, tying up a great deal of water that once filled the Mediterranean Sea. Antarctica was covered by a massive ice sheet, as seen in this satellite image.

CHEMISTRY OF ANIMAL REMAINS AND ANCIENT SOILS: WINDOWS ONTO DIETS AND HABITATS

Chemical analysis of the bones and teeth in fossils provides important information about past animals' diets and habitats. The reconstruction of diets and habitats is based on the plants those animals ate. Edible plants use either C_3 photosynthesis or C_4 photosynthesis. The type of photosynthesis determines how the plant extracts and uses carbon from atmospheric carbon dioxide (CO_2). In East Africa, to take one example, C_3 **plants** include trees, bushes, and shrubs associated with a relatively wet, wooded environment; C_4 **plants** are associated with open grasslands typical of tropical savannas. Because C_3 and C_4 plants extract and use carbon differently, the two stable isotopes of carbon in the plants (^{12}C and ^{13}C) have different ratios. C_3 plants have lower ratios of ^{13}C to ^{12}C than do C_4 plants (**Figure 8.31**). That is, the values for the stable isotope ratios are lower for C_3 plants than for C_4 plants.

When animals eat the plants, those ratios are transmitted to the body tissues (including bones and teeth) through digestion and metabolism. Thus, scientists can determine which kind of plant the animal ate based on the ratio of ^{13}C to ^{12}C in the animal's remains. The amounts of ^{13}C and ^{12}C are determined by placing a very tiny piece of bone or of tooth in an instrument called a *mass spectrometer*.

Similarly, the soils in which edible plants grow express different ratios of ^{13}C to ^{12}C. The plant's residue after decay preserves the stable carbon isotopes. Worldwide,

C_3 plants Plants that take in carbon through C_3 photosynthesis, which changes carbon dioxide into a compound having three carbon atoms; tending to be from more temperate regions, these plants include wheat, sugar beets, peas, and a range of hardwood trees.

C_4 plants Plants that take in carbon through C_4 photosynthesis, which changes carbon dioxide into a compound with four carbon atoms; these plants tend to be from warmer regions with low humidity and include corn, sugarcane, millet, and prickly pear.

(a)   (b)

FIGURE 8.31

C$_3$ and C$_4$ Plants C$_3$ and C$_4$ plants exhibit different ratios of ^{13}C to ^{12}C. **(a)** C$_3$ plants, such as wheat, and **(b)** C$_4$ plants, such as corn, have separate photosynthetic pathways that use CO$_2$ differently.

the ratios in the soils, like those in the animals, tend to be lower in forested settings than in grasslands.

Numerous remains of Miocene apes and Pliocene and Pleistocene hominins and other animals have been found in Kenya (discussed further in chapters 9 and 10). The study of the isotopic compositions of these fossils has greatly informed scientists' environmental reconstructions. Today, the Serengeti grasslands of Tanzania and Kenya are dominated by C$_4$ grasses (**Figure 8.32**). It has long been assumed that the first hominins and their immediate apelike ancestors lived in such a setting. New evidence from the study of the ancient soils (paleosols) and animal bones in Kenya and elsewhere indicates an environment with relatively low ^{13}C to ^{12}C ratios (C$_3$ plant dominance). This means that if C$_4$ grasses typical of an open grassland were present, they were quite minimal. However, sometime after 6 mya, C$_4$ plants became dominant for a range of mammals, indicating a marked shift in ecology. Recent work at the Lemudong'o archeological site in Kenya, by the American anthropologist Stanley Ambrose and colleagues, shows that at about 6 mya, the animals then living there, unlike the ones there today, lived among large trees and water. In particular, birds of prey that roost in large trees (such as the strigid owl) and the large number of colobine monkeys argue for a woodland habitat at 6 mya. Paleosols and fauna dating to about 5.6 mya at early hominin sites in the Middle Awash River Valley of Ethiopia show a similar record of open woodland or wooded grasslands around lake margins. The combined evidence from the study of paleosols and animal fossils indicates that the earliest hominins lived in wooded settings, probably for some time after 5 mya (discussed further in chapter 10). This knowledge is crucial because it helps us understand

FIGURE 8.32

Serengeti Plain, East Africa These grasslands are mostly composed of C$_4$ grasses.

the environmental context in which our humanlike ancestors rose—and that rise is fundamental to who we are as biological organisms.

This chapter presented several key concepts for understanding the past, primarily the importance of fossils as windows onto the past. Once placed in time, fossils document and enable us to interpret change over time—they become the central record of evolution. In the upcoming chapters, we will apply this knowledge about fossils and how to evaluate them as we examine nonhuman and human primate evolution. We will look at the origin and evolution of primates, from their very beginning some 55 mya to the dawn of human evolution. Primates are part of a great adaptive radiation of mammals, a radiation that continues to the present day. Understanding primate evolution provides the context for understanding who we are as biological organisms.

ANSWERING THE BIG QUESTIONS

1. What are fossils?

- Fossils are the remains of once-living organisms, wholly or partially transformed into rock. The most common types of fossils are bones and teeth.

2. What do fossils tell us about the past?

- Fossils provide an essential historical record for documenting and understanding the biological evolution of surviving and nonsurviving lineages.
- Fossils provide information on chronology and geologic time.
- Fossils and their geologic settings reveal past diets and environments, important contexts for understanding how past organisms evolved.

3. What methods do anthropologists and other scientists use to study fossils?

- Geologic time provides the grand scale of the evolution of life. Both relative and absolute (numerical) dates place fossils and past events in chronological sequence on that scale.
- Relative and absolute dates can be determined through various methods. Radioactive decay is central to some of the best methods of determining absolute dates.
- Past climates and habitat in general can be reconstructed via the stable isotopes of oxygen.
- Ancient animals' diets and their habitats can be reconstructed through the stable isotopes of carbon. This record reveals the increasing dominance of open grasslands in later Miocene and Pliocene times, the period when early hominins evolved.

STUDY QUIZ

1. Which burial environment would best promote fossilization?

a. Burial soon after death by sediments or volcanic ash
b. Burial after defleshing of bones by scavengers and insects
c. Burial in groundwater or acidic soils
d. Burial in a geologically active area with high ground pressure

2. Relative methods of dating can tell us

a. the approximate numerical age of a fossil.
b. the exact numerical age of a fossil.
c. whether a fossil is older or younger than another fossil or artifact.
d. the amount of organic material remaining in a fossil.

3. Radiometric and non-radiometric absolute dating methods both

a. provide only a relative date.
b. provide a numerical date.
c. measure the radioactive decay of an unstable isotope.
d. determine past climate history through stable isotope analysis.

4. What must be considered when choosing a radiometric dating method?

a. The half-life of an isotope limits its usefulness to a certain date range.
b. No radiometric dating methods can date organic materials.
c. No radiometric dating methods can date nonorganic materials.
d. Fossils must be associated with another fossil to give a relative date.

KEY TERMS

amino acid dating
biostratigraphic dating
C_3 plants
C_4 plants
Cenozoic
chemical dating
cultural dating
dendrochronology
electron spin resonance dating
epochs
eras
fission track dating
fluorine dating
foraminifera
half-life
igneous rock
index fossils
isotopes
Mesozoic
paleomagnetic dating
Paleozoic
Pangaea
polarized light
racemization
radiocarbon dating
radiopotassium dating
sedimentary rock
Steno's law of superposition
strata
stratigraphic correlation
taphonomy
tectonic
thermoluminescence dating

STUDY QUIZ (CONTINUED)

5. **Stable isotope analysis of carbon in a fossilized tooth would be most useful for determining the**

   a. relative age of the tooth compared to another fossil.
   b. absolute age of the tooth.
   c. temperature of the animal's environment.
   d. types of plants consumed by the animal during life.

EVOLUTION REVIEW

The Fossil Record

SYNOPSIS The evolution of life on Earth has occurred on a geologic timescale that is almost unfathomable, with the first single-celled organisms appearing around 3.5 *billion* years ago and the first multicellular organisms appearing around 1.2 *billion* years ago. The evolution of the order Primates is more recent, occurring over the past 50 million years, and the evolution of our own branch (that is, hominins) more recent still, from approximately 7 mya to the present. The physical evidence, primarily bones and teeth, of these evolutionary processes constitutes the fossil record. Advances in scientific dating techniques and the ability to reconstruct ancient environments have greatly expanded paleontologists' and biological anthropologists' understanding of the timing of major evolutionary events, the tempo at which evolution occurs, and the environmental pressures operating on species in deep time. This knowledge sets the stage for the "big questions" regarding primate and hominin evolution that will be addressed in the subsequent chapters.

Q1. Identify the two main components around which paleontology, or the scientific study of the fossil record, is built. How does each of these components contribute to our understanding of biological evolution?

Q2. Identify the main difference between methods of relative dating and methods of absolute dating. Provide one example of the use of a relative dating technique and one example of the use of an absolute dating technique in addressing research questions about human evolution.

Q3. By definition, our knowledge of the fossil record will always be incomplete, but scientists are nonetheless able to test hypotheses regarding the evolution of our own and other species. Summarize the process by which an organism's remains become fossilized. What are some factors that can influence fossil discoveries and our knowledge of the fossil record?

   HINT Think about events that can occur before, during, and after fossilization of an organism's remains.

Q4. Describe the process by which genetic dating can be accomplished via the molecular clock. How do biological anthropologists use both genetic dating and the fossil record to clarify evolutionary relationships and the timing of evolutionary events? How do the data sources for genetic dating and the fossil record differ from one another?

   HINT Think about the kinds of organisms studied for genetic dating compared to those found in the fossil record.

Q5. Explain why the record of material culture (stone tools, for example) is important for documenting the age of fossil sites. What are the problems associated with the use of material culture for determining chronology?

ADDITIONAL READINGS

Klein, R. G. 2009. *The Human Career: Human Biological and Cultural Origins,* 3rd ed. Chicago: University of Chicago Press.

Lanham, U. 1973. *The Bone Hunters.* New York: Columbia University Press.

Lee-Thorp, J. A., M. Sponheimer, and N. J. van der Merwe. 2003. What do stable isotopes tell us about hominid dietary and ecological niches in the Pliocene? *International Journal of Osteoarchaeology* 13: 104–113.

Marshak, S. 2019. *Earth: Portrait of a Planet,* 6th ed. New York: Norton.

Mayor, A. 2001. *The First Fossil Hunters: Paleontology in Greek and Roman Times.* Princeton, NJ: Princeton University Press.

Taylor, R. E. 1995. Radiocarbon dating: The continuing revolution. *Evolutionary Anthropology* 4: 169–181.

Winchester, S. 2001. *The Map That Changed the World: William Smith and the Birth of Modern Geology.* New York: HarperCollins.

Wolpoff, M. H. 1999. *Paleoanthropology,* 2nd ed. New York: McGraw-Hill.

Also known as the "dawn ape," this fossil primate was an early ancestral catarrhine. *Aegyptopithecus* lived approximately 32–29 mya, before the divergence of hominoids (apes) and Old World monkeys. Like many catarrhines, this primate was likely an arboreal quadruped that regularly consumed leaves and fruit.

9

Primate Origins and Evolution

THE FIRST 50 MILLION YEARS

BIG QUESTIONS

1. **Why become a primate?**

2. **What were the first primates?**

3. **What were the first higher primates?**

4. **What evolutionary developments link past primate species and living ones?**

Remember Georges Cuvier, the Frenchman (introduced in chapter 2) who recognized that fossils are the remains of now-extinct animals and of plants? I bring him up again because of his central role in the study of primate evolution. The field would not have been the same had he not lived in the late eighteenth and early nineteenth centuries, when the scientific method, as we know it, began to take shape. As a child, Cuvier read scientific works of the eighteenth-century biology luminaries Linnaeus (also introduced in chapter 2) and the Comte de Buffon (Georges-Louis Leclerc; 1707–1788), and their works sparked in him a lifelong interest in natural history. He went on to attend college at the University of Stuttgart in Germany, and like many other bright college graduates at the time, he was recruited as a private tutor for a wealthy family, in his case in Normandy, France. While living with his host family,

FIGURE 9.1

Cuvier and *Adapis* In describing the fossil remains of an animal he mistakenly thought was an ungulate, or artiodactyl (hoofed mammal), Cuvier (here seated) named the specimen *Adapis*, Latin for "toward sacred bull." Later scholars realized that these remains were the first primate fossil ever recorded by a scientist.

as luck would have it, he met France's leading naturalist and anatomist, Étienne Geoffroy Saint-Hilaire (1772–1844). Professor Geoffroy must have been impressed with young Cuvier because he hired Cuvier as his assistant in comparative anatomy at the new National Museum of Natural History in Paris. Cuvier became interested in the mammal fossils around Paris, and his encyclopedic knowledge of anatomy enabled him to recognize similarities between animals represented by fossils and living animals.

Among the hundreds of fossil bones and fossil teeth that he studied was a tiny skull, which he found in a gypsum quarry at nearby Montmartre. Dating to the Eocene, this specimen was unlike any skull Cuvier had ever seen. Was the animal it had come from living or extinct? When he published his description of the fossil in 1822, he did not recognize the animal he called *Adapis parisiensis* as a primate (**Figure 9.1**).

By the late nineteenth century, other French paleontologists had realized that Cuvier's fossil was that of an early primate, a finding that has been substantiated time and time again during the twentieth century, making *Adapis* the first primate fossil described by a scientist. Cuvier, the founder of paleontology, had good reasons for not recognizing this animal as a primate. For one thing, *no* fossil record of primates existed then—just about everything discussed in this chapter was found long after Cuvier's time. For another, taxonomists had very little understanding of living primate variation, and they had not yet defined the order much beyond Linnaeus's classification scheme (discussed in chapter 2).

Although Cuvier's assessment was wrong, his meticulous description of the *Adapis* fossil was very important. Stories like this happen often in science: the original discoverer may not recognize the finding for what it is, mostly because there is no context or prior discovery. Nevertheless, the discovery provides later scientists with important evidence. In this case, Cuvier's pioneering detailed description began the long process of documenting primate evolution, a process that continues today. Moreover, Cuvier set the bar high for future paleontologists by demonstrating the value of thorough description. Most important, Cuvier's careful work planted the seeds for asking key questions about primate origins.

In the two centuries since Cuvier, many thousands of fossils of ancient primates have been discovered in Europe, Asia, Africa, North America, and South America (**Figure 9.2**), providing a record—relatively complete for some time periods, frustratingly incomplete for others—of the origins and evolution of the earliest primates and their descendants. In this chapter, we address the big questions by examining the fossil record for evidence of three key developments: the emergence of the first primates, the origins of higher primates (anthropoids), and the origins and evolution of the major anthropoid groups (monkeys, apes, and humans). The time frame for this chapter is expansive—more than 60 million years! We start in the Early Paleocene, somewhere around 66 mya (about 10 million years or so before the emergence of the first true primate), and end in the Late Miocene, around 5.3 mya, at the dawn of human evolution. The record indicates that primates were highly successful and, like other mammals, underwent a cycle of adaptive radiations, followed by extinctions, and then new radiations of surviving lineages. These survivors are the primates occupying Earth today, including human beings (**Figure 9.3**).

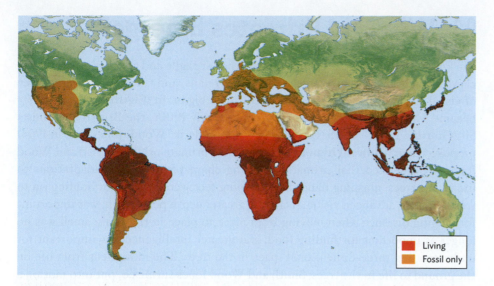

FIGURE 9.2

Living and Extinct Primates As this map indicates, fossils of extinct primate species have been found on every continent except Australia and Antarctica. Climate changes over millions of years probably explain why primates were once distributed more extensively throughout the world than are modern, living primates.

Living
Fossil only

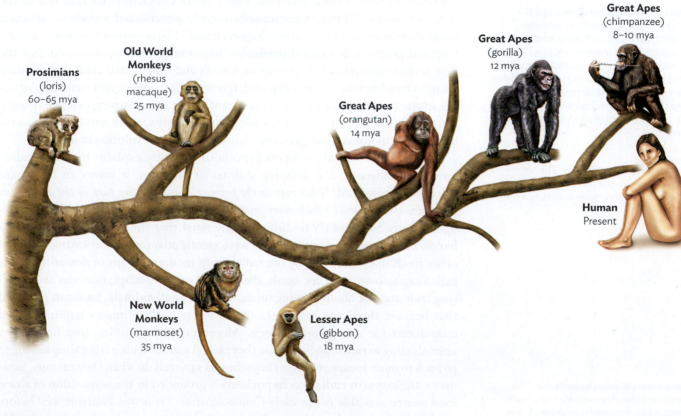

Prosimians
(loris)
60–65 mya

Old World Monkeys
(rhesus macaque)
25 mya

Great Apes
(orangutan)
14 mya

Great Apes
(gorilla)
12 mya

Great Apes
(chimpanzee)
8–10 mya

Human
Present

New World Monkeys
(marmoset)
35 mya

Lesser Apes
(gibbon)
18 mya

FIGURE 9.3

Primate Family Tree The variety of primates today is the result of millions of years of primate evolution. The different lineages represented by great apes, lesser apes, Old World monkeys, New World monkeys, and prosimians reflect divergences in primate evolution. For example, New World monkeys split off around 35 mya, and Old World monkeys diverged approximately 25 mya. The lineage leading to modern humans, however, diverged from the chimpanzee lineage much more recently, somewhere between 8 and 10 mya.

9.1 Why Did Primates Emerge?

FIGURE 9.4

Primate Characteristics Primates differ from other mammals thanks to a unique combination of traits, such as forward-facing eyes, a postorbital bar or fully enclosed eye orbit, a large cranial vault, a reduced snout, and a versatile dentition. In the postcranial skeleton, primates usually have divergent big toes and divergent thumbs, grasping hands and grasping feet, and nails instead of claws on their fingers and their toes.

visual predation hypothesis The proposition that unique primate traits arose as adaptations to preying on insects and small animals.

angiosperm radiation hypothesis The proposition that certain primate traits, such as visual acuity, occurred in response to the availability of fruit and flowers after the spread of angiosperms.

We know *what* primates are. For example, they are agile and adept at grasping, the claws of their ancestors have been replaced by nails, and they have a high degree of visual acuity, a reduced sense of smell, and a big brain (**Figure 9.4**). *Why* they became what they are is far less clear. In the early 1900s, the British anatomists Sir Grafton Elliot Smith (1871–1937) and Frederic Wood Jones (1879–1954) proposed their **arboreal hypothesis** to explain primate origins. Smith and Wood Jones hypothesized that primates' defining characteristics were adaptations to life in the trees: grasping hands and grasping feet were crucial for holding on to tree branches; advanced vision, including greater depth perception, was important for judging distance when moving from place to place in the trees; smell was no longer as important for finding food; and greater intelligence was important for understanding three-dimensional space in the trees. The movement from life on the ground to life in the trees, Smith and Wood Jones surmised, put into motion a series of selective pressures that resulted in the ancestral primate.

The arboreal hypothesis continues to profoundly influence the way anthropologists think about primate origins and evolution. But in the early 1970s, the American biological anthropologist Matt Cartmill challenged the arboreal hypothesis. He pointed out that lots of mammals are arboreal (squirrels, for example), but except for primates none have evolved the entire set of characteristics that define the order Primates. (These characteristics include generalized structure, arboreal adaptation, and care of young; see chapters 6 and 7.) To account for primate origins, Cartmill proposed his **visual predation hypothesis**. He hypothesized that the first primate specialized in preying on insects and other small creatures, hunting them in tree branches or in forest undergrowth. Cartmill argued that the shift to life in the trees was not the most important factor in explaining primate origins. Rather, the catching of small prey—using both a highly specialized visual apparatus and the fine motor skills of grasping digits—set primate evolution in motion.

Although the visual predation hypothesis elegantly explains the visual adaptations, intelligence, and grasping abilities of primates, it leaves an important question unanswered: *What role do the primate characteristics play in the acquisition and consumption of fruit, which many primates eat?* The American biological anthropologist Robert Sussman (1941–2016) hypothesized that the visual acuity, grasping hands, and grasping feet of primates were mostly adaptations for eating fruit and other foods made available by the radiation of modern groups of flowering plants called *angiosperms*. In other words, the original primate adaptation was about getting fruit and not about preying on insects and small animals. Sussman reasoned that because there was little light in the forest, early primates required visual adaptations for seeing small objects. Moreover, their grasping toes helped the animals cling to tree branches while they picked and ate fruit, rather than having to go back to more secure and larger branches, as squirrels do when they eat nuts. Sussman's **angiosperm radiation hypothesis** is grounded in the acquisition of a new food source available in the early Cenozoic: fruit. Fruit was available well before the Cenozoic, but adaptations to long-existing resources can take a considerable amount of time and involve numerous factors in influencing natural selection.

In reality, elements of all three hypotheses may have provided the evolutionary opportunities that resulted in primate origins. Indeed, primates' most special feature is their adaptive versatility, especially in an arboreal setting. Primates have evolved strategies and anatomical features that enhance their ability to adapt to new and novel circumstances. That evolution constitutes primates' story of origin.

(a)

1 cm

0.39 in

(b)

FIGURE 9.5

Plesiadapis These primatelike mammals were an ancestral lineage leading to true primate ancestors. **(a)** As this *Plesiadapis* skull illustrates, plesiadapiforms did not possess primates' postorbital bar. And while primates have a versatile dentition, plesiadapiforms had very specialized anterior (front) teeth, which were separated from the posterior (rear) teeth by a large gap. In addition, *Plesiadapis* and other plesiadapiforms had much smaller brains than those of true primate ancestors. **(b)** This reconstruction of *Plesiadapis* reflects its similarities to and differences from modern primates.

9.2 The First True Primate: Visual, Tree-Dwelling, Agile, Smart Primates in the Paleocene?

We know *generally when* the first primates appeared—almost certainly in the early Cenozoic era. But just how early in the Cenozoic is debated by the paleontologists who study early primate evolution. They have reached no consensus as to whether the first primates appeared in the Paleocene epoch, which began 66 mya, or in the following epoch, the Eocene, which began 56 mya. The Paleocene candidate for the first primates is a highly diverse, highly successful group of primitive mammals called the **plesiadapiforms**, which lived in western North America, western Europe, Asia, and possibly Africa. The oldest plesiadapiforms are from North America, indicating the possibility that the origins of order Primates is in the New World. These animals represent an adaptive radiation that flourished over a 10-million-year period, beginning at the start of the Paleocene.

Despite their amazing diversity and geographic spread, by about 56 mya most of the plesiadapiforms had gone extinct. Were they primates? Perhaps not. The problem with attributing them to the order Primates is that they lack the key characteristics that define primates today. That is, they lacked a postorbital bar and convergent eye orbits; their digits were not especially well adapted for grasping tree branches (they lacked opposability) and lacked nails (they had claws); their teeth were highly specialized (some even had three cusps on their upper incisors, as opposed to the single cusp of most primates today); and their brains were tiny (**Figure 9.5**). Moreover, some plesiadapiforms lacked the petrosal bulla, a part of the temporal bone that contains the middle-ear bones and is present in all primates. Because of their potential relationship with

plesiadapiforms Paleocene organisms that may have been the first primates, originating from an adaptive radiation of mammals.

the first true primates, the American paleontologist Philip Gingerich has called them **Proprimates**, a separate order from Primates.

EOCENE EUPRIMATES: THE FIRST TRUE PRIMATES

Far better contenders for the earliest primates are the **euprimates** (meaning "true primates"), which first appeared at the start of the Eocene, as early as 56 mya. Euprimates consisted of two closely related, highly successful groups: the **adapids** and the **omomyids**. Their fossils are found in the western United States, western Europe, Africa, and Asia and are the most common early primate fossils—accounting for about 40% of all species from the Early Eocene, or about 200 species (**Figure 9.6**). Given the vast number of their fossils that have been collected—on the order of 100,000—anthropologists have an excellent picture of their physical description and their adaptive circumstances.

(a)

(c)

(b)

Notharctus

(d)

FIGURE 9.6

Omomyids and Adapids These two main groups of euprimates are related to tarsiers and lemurs, respectively. Unlike plesiadapiforms, omomyids and adapids are considered true primate ancestors because they possess many primate traits. **(a, b)** Omomyids, such as *Shoshonius* (shown here), had large eyes and large eye orbits on the front of the skull, grasping hands and grasping feet, and a reduced snout. Like tarsiers, these earliest primates were nocturnal. **(c, d)** Adapids, including Cuvier's *Adapis,* also had forward-facing eyes. However, adapids like *Adapis* and *Notharctus* (shown here) were diurnal and had longer snouts than omomyids.

Were they primates? Almost certainly. Unlike the plesiadapiforms, adapids and omomyids had clear primate characteristics: the postorbital bar and convergent eye orbits, long digits with opposability for grasping, digits with nails (not claws), nonspecialized teeth, and a large brain relative to body size. These features indicate that vision was essential to their adaptation, they were agile and tree-dwelling, their diet was not as specialized as that of the plesiadapiforms, and they were smarter than the earlier animals. Their body sizes were small but highly varied. Adapids were about the same size as some modern lemurs. One of the largest, *Notharctus*, weighed about 7 kg (15 lb). *Adapis*, known from many skulls and other parts of the skeleton, weighed a little more than 1 kg (2 lb). The adapids' incisors were flat and vertical, similar to those of many living anthropoids (**Figure 9.7**). In addition, like anthropoids, adapids had pronounced sexual dimorphism in body size and canine size, some had lower jaws with two fused halves, and some had relatively short foot bones.

The omomyids differed from the adapids in that they had large and projecting central lower incisors, small canines, and wide variation in the other teeth. Unlike most adapids (and sometimes like living tarsiers), omomyids had a short skull, a short and narrow snout, and large eye orbits. Their large eye orbits held huge eyes adapted for night vision. Like the adapids, the omomyids consisted of widely diverse species and have left behind a great number of fossils, facts that speak to their high degree of success throughout the Eocene epoch.

From what primitive mammalian group did the adapids and omomyids evolve? Most of the plesiadapiforms are unlikely ancestors for the euprimates because they either went extinct before the Eocene or were too specialized to have given rise to

Notharctus A genus of adapids from the Eocene; they were one of the largest adapids.

Adapis A genus of adapids from the Eocene.

FIGURE 9.7

Incisor Variation **(a)** In modern lemur species, the lower incisors form a dental comb that projects horizontally from the mandible. **(b)** This feature was absent, however, in adapids, whose more vertical incisors resembled those of living monkeys and living apes.

FIGURE 9.8

Carpolestes simpsoni (a) Fossilized remains such as these suggest that this species of plesiadapiforms is a link between primatelike mammalian ancestors and the earliest true primate ancestors. (b) In this reconstruction of the full skeleton, the fossilized remains are highlighted. (c) This reconstruction depicts what *Carpolestes* might have looked like in life.

(a)   (b)   (c)

Carpolestes A plesiadapiform genus from the Paleocene, probably ancestral to the Eocene euprimates.

Eocene primates. However, one plesiadapiform, *Carpolestes,* whose skeleton was found in Wyoming's Bighorn Basin, had a number of characteristics that would be expected in a transitional animal leading to what were clear primates later in time. *Carpolestes* had a grasping foot, made possible by an opposable big toe; it had long, grasping fingers; and it had a nail on the end of the first digit of the foot (**Figure 9.8**). This animal may be the link between the Proprimates of the Paleocene and the euprimates of the Eocene.

The extinction of the plesiadapiforms at the end of the Paleocene and the appearance of euprimates at the beginning of the Eocene coincided with a profound period of global warming. A rapid temperature increase around 55 mya created tropical conditions virtually everywhere around the world. The resulting creation of new habitats triggered an adaptive radiation of modern-appearing primates, the euprimates. In particular, the high global temperatures and high global humidity led to an expansion of evergreen tropical forest, the environment that made possible the growth of many mammalian groups, including the primates.

THE ANTHROPOID ANCESTOR: EUPRIMATE CONTENDERS

Like the Paleocene Proprimates preceding them, many of the euprimates went extinct, likely owing to a major change in climate involving a cooling trend, causing a change in habitat at the end of the Eocene. Some of them may have provided the ancestral base for strepsirrhines and haplorrhines. Based on the kind of skull and tooth evidence described earlier, Philip Gingerich has made the case that adapids represent the ancestral group for living lemurs and anthropoids, with lemurs evolving a tooth comb (missing in adapids) and anthropoids not evolving the tooth comb. Their flat incisors, general similarity with anthropoids, and great diversity suggest that adapids had an evolutionary relationship with anthropoids. However, some (or even all) of adapids' anthropoid-like features could simply be unevolved (primitive) traits of all primates. If that is the case, then an ancestral–descendant link between adapids and later primates would be difficult to prove.

The American anthropologist Frederick Szalay sees a strong resemblance between omomyid fossils and living tarsiers, and a greater similarity between tarsiers and anthropoids than between lemurs and anthropoids. Therefore, he regards the omomyids as more likely candidates for the ancestry of anthropoids than lemurs. However, the anatomical similarities between omomyids and tarsiers are more suggestive than definitive. No single characteristic links these Eocene primates with anthropoids. While the adapids or omomyids may be ancestral to anthropoids, the lack of clear transitional fossils between these archaic primates and later primates makes it unclear what the anthropoid ancestor was more than 40 mya.

Clues to the characteristics of the early haplorrhines are seen in a remarkably well-preserved skeleton of an early primate, dating to 55 mya and known as *Archicebus* (**Figure 9.9**). Discovered in an ancient lake bed in the Jingzhou area of Hubei Province, China, by a team led by the Chinese paleontologist Xijun Ni, this primate combines features of anthropoids and tarsiers. The presence of this primate in China at such an early date indicates that haplorrhines may have originated in Asia. Although *Archicebus* may not have been the first haplorrhine, it emerged very close to the split between strepsirrhines and haplorrhines. The bones of its heel and ankle resemble those of monkeys. Its skull resembles that of tarsiers, with small eye orbits and a short snout. In addition, the cusps on the molars are high and pointed, similar to what is seen in tarsiers. This mosaic of features suggests that haplorrhines originated at 55 mya, on the boundary between the Paleocene and the Eocene. It also suggests that the first haplorrhines were diurnal (and therefore had these small eye orbits), arboreal (and therefore had these foot, hand, and limb structures), and primarily insectivorous (as tarsiers are today). And, in contrast to their great evolutionary significance, the earliest-known primates appear to have been tiny. *Archicebus* is estimated to have been even smaller than the mouse lemur (the smallest primate today), weighing only about 28 g (1 oz) and easily fitting into the palm of your hand.

FIGURE 9.9

Archicebus This skeleton and reconstruction of *Archicebus* show its combination of anthropoid and tarsier features. Its heels and ankles resemble those of monkeys, whereas its small eyes and short snout resemble those of tarsiers.

THE FIRST ANTHROPOIDS

During the Eocene, a group of primates called **basal anthropoids**, whose fossils have been found in Asia and Africa, had the kinds of characteristics that would be expected in an anthropoid ancestor or even the earliest anthropoid. One of the most interesting basal anthropoids is the remarkably tiny *Eosimias* (meaning "dawn monkey"), found in Jiangsu Province, China, and dating to about 42 mya. It is one of a number of eosimiids found in southern and eastern Asia. Based on their observations of the teeth and the skeleton, especially of the foot bones, the American anthropologists Daniel Gebo and Christopher Beard regard *Eosimias* as the first true anthropoid. Especially convincing about their argument is the strong similarity between the shape and overall appearance of the tarsal (ankle) bones of *Eosimias* and the tarsal bones of fossil and living anthropoids. That is, *Eosimias*'s short calcaneus, or heel bone, was like that of an anthropoid (**Figure 9.10**). The heel bones are especially similar to the heel bones of South American monkeys, revealing that this primate moved in trees

Eosimias A genus of very small basal anthropoids from the Eocene.

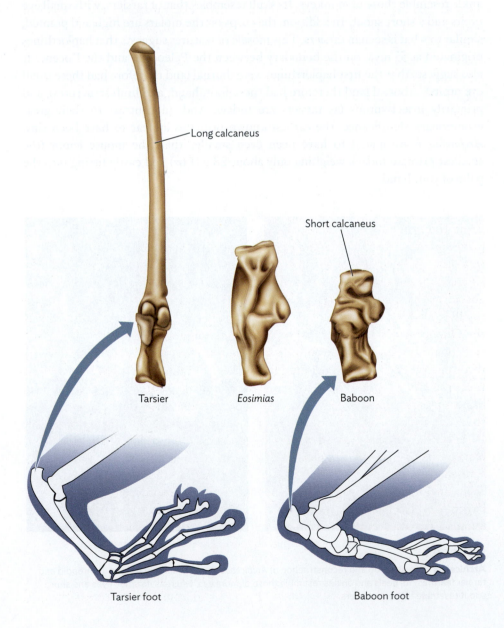

Long calcaneus

Short calcaneus

Tarsier

Eosimias

Baboon

Tarsier foot

Baboon foot

FIGURE 9.10

Calcaneal Variation Evidence for patterns of locomotion in *Eosimias* comes from some of the postcranial remains, especially bones of the ankle and foot. *Eosimias*'s calcaneus was more like that of an anthropoid (such as the baboon) than like that of a prosimian (such as the tarsier).

like a monkey. In addition, the upper canine and upper jaw would have given it a monkeylike face.

Another, somewhat later basal anthropoid is from the Fayum Depression in Egypt. Called *Biretia* by the American paleontologists Erik Seiffert and Elwyn Simons (1930–2016), it dates to the Late Eocene, at about 37 mya. The presence of anthropoid characteristics in the teeth, such as the two-cusped (bicuspid) lower premolars, indicates that this animal, too, represents the beginnings of higher primates (**Figure 9.11**). If it is the first higher primate, then either anthropoid ancestry began in Africa or the earlier primates from Asia emigrated to Africa and evolved into the African anthropoids. Based on the limited evidence, it is not possible to say conclusively whether Asia or Africa is the ancestral home of the higher primates, the anthropoids. However, *Eosimias* and *Biretia* have the attributes that would be expected in an anthropoid ancestor. Given the earlier date for *Eosimias*, Asia could be the ancestral home for the higher primates. If so, then Asian basal anthropoids gave rise to the higher primates of Africa.

This discussion should make clear that the origin of anthropoids is murky. To understand the geographic (Asia versus Africa) and environmental contexts in which anthropoids arose, anthropologists are looking to the increasing fossil record of basal anthropoids and their remarkable diversity. Regardless of their geographic origins, the diversity of basal anthropoids found in both Asia and Africa suggests the beginnings of a tremendous radiation of a highly successful group of mammals.

9.3 Early Anthropoids Evolve and Thrive

Beginning in the Oligocene epoch and coinciding with a period of widespread plant and animal extinctions, an episode of rapid global cooling occurred. With this shift in climate came new habitats and newly diverse primate taxa. The fossil record representing the evolution of these taxa is as remarkable in the Oligocene as the fossil record is in the Eocene. However, whereas Eocene primate fossils have been found in a wide variety of settings around the world, most of the Oligocene primate fossils have come from one region, the Fayum Depression. Spanning about 8 million years of evolution, roughly 37–29 mya, the fossil record consists of a wide and abundant variety of plants and of animals. From these remains, scientists have constructed a detailed picture of the environment in northeast Africa (**Figure 9.12**). In sharp contrast to the desert landscape of the Fayum today—it is among the harshest and driest places in the world—the Late Eocene–Early Oligocene landscape was much like today's Southeast Asia; namely, wet, warm, and tropical. The Fayum was long the focus for all organisms in the region. In addition to diverse primates, all sorts of animals lived there, including the ancestors of rodents (the earliest porcupines are from the Fayum), bats, hippopotamuses, elephants, crocodiles, and various birds. Plants are also represented by a diverse array of tropical taxa, such as mangroves, water lilies, climbing vines, figs, palms, and cinnamon. It must have been an amazing place.

The Fayum primates included various strepsirrhines and at least three groups of primitive (but unmistakable) higher primates: **oligopithecids, parapithecids,**

FIGURE 9.11

Biretia Its fossilized remains suggest that this animal was an anthropoid ancestor. For example, its lower premolars, with their two cusps, are structured like those of anthropoids.

Biretia A basal anthropoid genus found in the Fayum Depression, Egypt, that may be ancestral to later anthropoids.

oligopithecids The earliest anthropoid ancestors in the Oligocene, found in the Fayum, Egypt.

parapithecids Anthropoid ancestors from the Oligocene, found in the Fayum, Egypt.

FIGURE 9.12

The Fayum Climatological and environmental reconstructions have provided a glimpse of what the Fayum Depression in Egypt was like when some of the earliest primates lived, at the end of the Eocene and the beginning of the Oligocene.

propliopithecids Anthropoid ancestors from the Oligocene, found in the Fayum, Egypt.

Parapithecus A genus of later parapithecids from the Oligocene, found in the Fayum, Egypt.

Aegyptopithecus A propliopithecid genus from the Oligocene, probably ancestral to catarrhines; the largest primate found in the Fayum, Egypt.

and **propliopithecids** (**Figure 9.13**). The oligopithecids were the earliest, dating to about 35 mya. The later parapithecids, such as their namesake genus, ***Parapithecus***, are among these early anthropoids, and they retained some primitive characteristics. For example, parapithecids had three premolars. This condition may directly link parapithecids to platyrrhines (which also have three premolars), but having three premolars is more likely the ancestral condition that precedes the divergence of platyrrhines and catarrhines.

The propliopithecids consisted of several genera, but ***Propliopithecus*** and ***Aegyptopithecus***, both dating to between 32 and 29 mya, are the most common of

31 mya

LOWER OLIGOCENE

UPPER EOCENE

37 mya

Aegyptopithecus zeuxis, Propliopithecus chirobates, Apidium phiomense, Parapithecus grangeri, Parapithecus fraasi

Propliopithecus ankeli, Propliopithecus haeckeli, Apidium moustafai, Apidium bowni

Oligopithecus savagei

Catopithecus browni
Biretia fayumensis

FIGURE 9.13

Primate Ancestors in the Fayum The earliest primate ancestor found in Fayum deposits is *Biretia fayumensis.* Various species of early prosimians and anthropoids have been recovered from Fayum deposits spanning the Oligocene.

this group of primates. The propliopithecids had a more derived dental formula of 2/1/2/3, one less premolar than the parapithecids had. In this and other respects, they were more catarrhine-like than the parapithecids. *Aegyptopithecus,* the largest of the Fayum primates (it weighed 6–8 kg [13–18 lb], or about the weight of a fox), is the best-known Fayum primate (**Figure 9.14**). *Aegyptopithecus* had a sagittal crest on the top of the skull where a large temporalis muscle was attached (see Figure 6.32 in chapter 6). Its brain was small compared to those of later catarrhines. The front and hind limbs were of relatively equal size, suggesting that the animal was a slow-moving, arboreal quadruped, similar to the modern howler monkey. Its overall appearance indicates that *Aegyptopithecus* was a primitive catarrhine—and a likely contender for the common ancestor of all later catarrhines.

I mentioned that not all early primates of the Oligocene are from the Fayum. Although the record of early catarrhines is best and mostly richly represented at

FIGURE 9.14

Aegyptopithecus Shaded red in this reconstruction are the postcranial skeletal fossils of *Aegyptopithecus* that have been found in Fayum deposits. These recovered elements provide important information regarding the animal's mobility and form of locomotion: arboreal quadrupedalism.

Saadanius An early catarrhine Oligocene genus from a group of primates that gave rise to later catarrhines.

the Fayum, at least one fossil representing an ancestor of monkeys, apes, and humans has been recovered from the modern country of Saudi Arabia (see locater map on p. 253). During the Oligocene, before the formation of the Red Sea, the continent of Africa and the Arabian Peninsula formed a single landmass. The remarkable radiation of primates in the Fayum suggests that similar habitats in Arabia supported similar kinds of primates. In their search for Oligocene fossils, the paleontologist Iyad Zalmout and colleagues found most of a skull of an early catarrhine, now known as *Saadanius*. Dating to about 28 mya and postdating *Aegyptopithecus*, this primate shared a number of features with the Fayum catarrhines, such as dental formula (2/1/2/3); upper molars with low, rounded cusps; and shape of the face. However, it differs from Fayum primates in having the middle-ear anatomy typical of later catarrhine primates. In addition, a plethora of Early Oligocene primates has been recovered from northern China, Mongolia, and Pakistan, including a diversity of both strepsirrhines and haplorrhines, with the former dominating over the latter.

Consistent with the fossil record, the molecular evidence shows that the first anthropoids originated in the Late Oligocene, likely between 30 and 25 mya (see chapter 8, "Genetic Dating: The Molecular Clock"). The discovery of two fossil

CONCEPT CHECK

When Were They Primates? Anatomy through Time

Primates have a number of anatomical characteristics that reflect both an adaptation to life in the trees and related behaviors. Contenders for primate status in the Paleocene generally lack these characteristics; two groups of closely related Eocene mammals—adapids and omomyids— have these characteristics.

CHARACTERISTIC	PALEOCENE (66–56 MYA)	EOCENE (56–34 MYA)	PRESENT
Increased vision	No	Yes	Yes
Partially or fully enclosed eye orbits	No	Yes	Yes
Convergent eyes	No	Yes	Yes
Small incisors and large canines	No	Yes	Yes
Nails at ends of digits	No	Yes	Yes
Mobile, grasping digits	No	Yes	Yes
Short snout	No	Yes	Yes
Reduced smell	No	Yes	Yes
Increased brain size	No	Yes	Yes

primates in Tanzania documents the split that led to the emergence of modern apes and modern monkeys by 25 mya. In the Rukwa Rift Basin of western Tanzania, the American paleoanthropologist Nancy Stevens and her team discovered the earliest ape and earliest Old World monkey, named *Rukwapithecus fleaglei* and *Nsungwepithecus gunnelli*, respectively. *Rukwapithecus* is represented by part of a mandible and teeth, and its second molar shares features with the second molars of later fossil apes. *Nsungwepithecus* is represented by part of a mandible and just one molar. While the bilophodont cusps of that molar are not fully modern, they are clearly cercopithecoid. As a representation of the split between apes and monkeys, this fossil record is modest, but it shows that ancestral apes and monkeys were present in East Africa at about the time most authorities expected.

The presence of the later Oligocene catarrhine in the Arabian Peninsula and East Africa underscores the strong likelihood that the ancestry of fossil and modern catarrhines is broadly based in the African–Arabian landmass during the later Oligocene.

9.4 Coming to America: Origin of New World Higher Primates

Aegyptopithecus, the earliest definitive catarrhine, clearly evolved from some anthropoid in the Old World, almost certainly in Africa. But where did the other anthropoids, the platyrrhines, come from? The first South American primate is a primitive monkey called ***Perupithecus***, represented by fossil molars from Santa Rosa, Peru, dating possibly as early as 36 mya. This primate is clearly more primitive than the next oldest platyrrhine fossil, ***Branisella***, found near Salla, Bolivia, in geologic deposits dating to the very late Oligocene, about 26 mya. *Branisella*'s link with living species of platyrrhines is especially convincing owing to its having three premolars and, especially, three upper molars with a four-cusp chewing surface strongly similar to that of the upper molars in living New World monkeys, such as the owl monkey (**Figure 9.15**). The fossil record for South America is generally sparse after the Late Oligocene, but it shows the general patterns of platyrrhine evolution. The fossil platyrrhines bear a striking resemblance to living platyrrhines, represented by cebids and atelids.

HOW ANTHROPOIDS GOT TO SOUTH AMERICA

One important question about the origins of platyrrhines is just how their ancestors got from Africa to South America. Four alternative hypotheses have emerged to explain primates' presence in South America (**Figure 9.16**). First, platyrrhines evolved from a North American anthropoid, then migrated to South America in the Late Oligocene. Second, platyrrhines evolved from an African anthropoid and migrated across the Atlantic to South America. Third, platyrrhines evolved from an anthropoid in Africa that migrated south (mainly) on land to Antarctica and then to Patagonia, at the southern tip of South America. Fourth, Old World and New World anthropoids evolved independently from different lineages in Africa and South America, respectively.

No evidence supports the first hypothesis—there were no anthropoids in North America during the Eocene or Oligocene. There were various euprimates, but none resembled the platyrrhines in South America during the Late Oligocene.

Perupithecus The earliest genus of a platyrrhine, dating to the Early Oligocene.

Branisella A South American genus from the Oligocene, ancestral to platyrrhines.

Low, rounded cusps

FIGURE 9.15

Branisella In the dental remains of this first definitive platyrrhine, the low, rounded cusps of its molars suggest that *Branisella* was frugivorous (fruit-eating).

One hypothesis suggests that the ancestors migrated south from North America, evolving into the platyrrhine species of the Oligocene.

A second hypothesis suggests that after originating in Africa, the ancestors migrated across the Atlantic Ocean to South America.

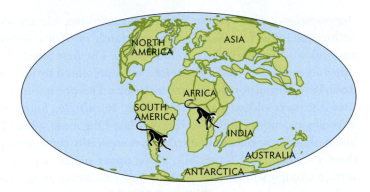

A third hypothesis suggests that the African ancestors reached South America not only by water but also by land; they migrated to the southern tip of Africa, crossed Antarctica, and eventually reached the southern tip of South America.

A fourth hypothesis suggests that platyrrhines and catarrhines originated independently.

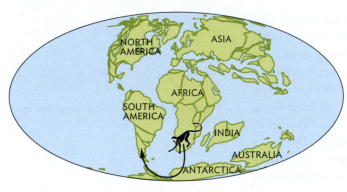

FIGURE 9.16

Platyrrhine Origins Many researchers believe the ancestors of New World monkeys originated in North America. Others believe they originated in Africa and then migrated to South America. As Africa and South America separated in the Mesozoic, how would ancestors in Africa have reached South America?

Evidence supports the second hypothesis. There were early anthropoids in Africa (Fayum) beginning in the Late Eocene, and they predated platyrrhines but looked remarkably similar to the earliest platyrrhines in South America (for example, they had three premolars). This resemblance indicates that platyrrhines originated in Africa *before* their appearance in South America. In addition, fossils indicate other similarities between animals in Africa and in South America.

The strong similarities between Old World and New World higher primates also support the third hypothesis. Migration across Antarctica would be impossible today, of course. However, migration over this major landmass would have been possible through much of the Eocene, when the climate there was much warmer and drier than it is today.

Given the strong anatomical resemblance between African higher primates and South American higher primates, it is highly unlikely that anthropoids evolved independently in Africa and South America (**Figure 9.17**). DNA evidence showing

(a)   (b)

FIGURE 9.17

Old World and New World Monkeys The physical resemblance between **(a)** Old World monkeys and **(b)** New World monkeys suggests that platyrrhines originated in Africa, rather than North America. Their mode of reaching South America, however, is still highly debated.

a strong relationship between Old World and New World higher primates is even stronger proof against the fourth hypothesis. In other words, these two groups did not evolve independently: they both originated in Africa.

On the face of it, it might seem unlikely that primates migrated from Africa to South America via the Atlantic, especially in view of the wide and prohibitive expanse of open sea separating the west coast of Africa from the east coast of South America. At the time, however, areas of the ocean might have been shallow and dotted with series of islands. Moreover, primates might have crossed from Africa to South America via ocean currents, on natural rafts consisting of accumulated vegetation.

9.5 Apes Begin in Africa and Dominate the Miocene Primate World

After the Oligocene, the strength and completeness of the higher primate fossil record derives from rich Miocene geologic deposits in East Africa, especially in the present-day countries of Kenya and Uganda (**Figure 9.18**). Just before this time, a warming trend in the Late Oligocene provided the conditions for a shift in habitats and the appearance of a new and widespread radiation of a group of catarrhine primates called the **proconsulids**, mostly dating to roughly 22–17 mya

proconsulids Early Miocene apes found in East Africa.

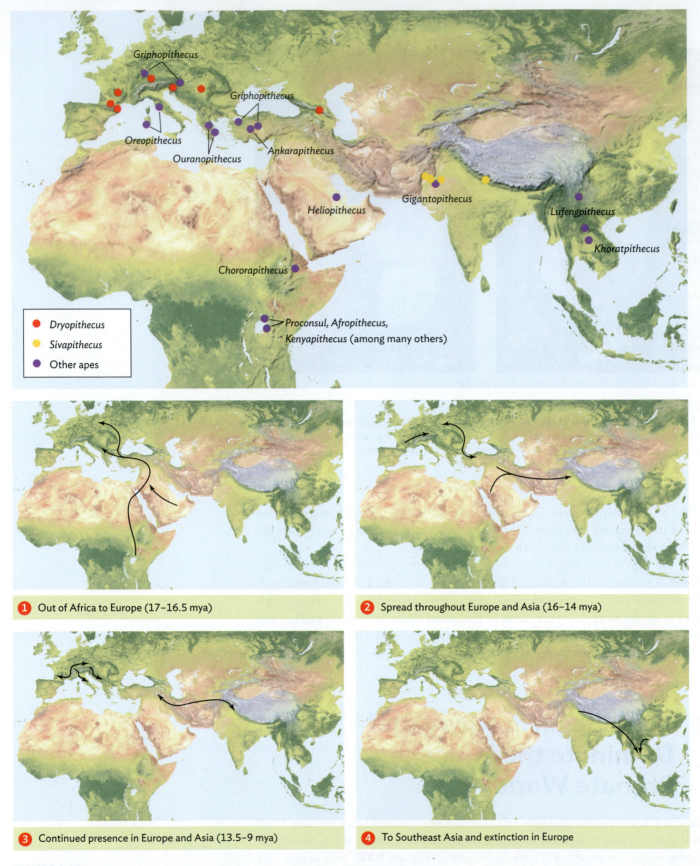

FIGURE 9.18

Miocene Ape Fossil Localities A wide variety of ape fossils have been found in Miocene deposits in Africa, Asia, and Europe. These fossils provide a record of evolution and location during this dynamic period of hominoid evolution. The first proconsulids—*Proconsul, Afropithecus,* and *Kenyapithecus*— arose in East Africa. During the next 10–11 million years, these and related apes migrated from Africa to Europe and western Asia (map 1), diversified in Europe and western Asia (map 2), then continued to diversify in Europe and western Asia (map 3) and eventually into eastern Asia (map 4).

(**Figure 9.19**). Recall that the last of the Oligocene primate fossils, in Egypt and Saudi Arabia, date to about 29–28 mya. This means that about a 6-million-year gap exists between the Late Oligocene catarrhines (28 mya) and the first Miocene proconsulids (22 mya). As a consequence, the immediate ancestors of proconsulids are a mystery. However, the strong anatomical similarity in skulls and in teeth between Oligocene catarrhines from the Fayum and the Arabian Peninsula and the proconsulids of the Miocene indicates a likely ancestral–descendant relationship between the earlier and later groups. For example, all of these primates have a dental formula of 2/1/2/3, and their upper incisors are broad and flat.

The proconsulids are represented by a diversity of taxa—as many as 10 genera and 15 species—from the Early and Middle Miocene. In fact, the diversity of the extinct apes in the Miocene is much greater than that of living apes today. For example, proconsulids ranged from the tiny *Micropithecus*, the size of a small New World monkey, to the namesake genus, *Proconsul*, a species of which, *Proconsul major,* was about the size of a modern male chimpanzee, weighing about 50 kg (110 lb). *Proconsul* is the best known of the Early to Middle Miocene apes from Africa, in part thanks to a nearly complete skeleton discovered on Rusinga Island, in western Kenya's Lake Victoria, in the late 1940s (**Figure 9.20**). Reflecting the proconsulids' biological diversity, their fossils have been found in a range of settings, representing different climates and environments, from open woodlands to tropics. Reflecting these different habitats, their diets varied considerably.

The skulls and teeth of the Miocene proconsulids were clearly like those of apes in overall appearance. The molars have the Y-5 pattern, and the cusps are wide and rounded for eating fruit. There are well-developed honing surfaces on the backs of the upper canines and the fronts of the lower third premolars. Comparisons of tooth wear in living apes and in extinct Miocene apes suggest that some of the extinct apes ate leaves and some ate nuts and fruit, but that most of them routinely ate ripe fruit.

In contrast to the skulls and teeth, the rest of the skeleton of Miocene apes is generally like that of monkeys (**Figure 9.21**). Unlike the living apes, these primitive apes had front and hind limbs that were equally long and that lacked specializations for knuckle-walking or arm-swinging that we see in today's apes. Moreover, like Old World monkeys, *Proconsul* had wrist bones (carpals) that articulated directly with the ulna, one of the two forearm bones. This direct articulation, a primitive characteristic, indicates relatively limited wrist mobility, whereas living apes have highly mobile wrists for arm-swinging and arm-hanging. Proconsulids' elbows could straighten only so far, whereas living apes' elbows can extend completely. Proconsulids' feet combined primitive and derived features—some of the anklebones were slender, like monkeys', but the big toes were large, like apes'. The whole package suggests that *Proconsul,* unlike living apes, walked on the tops of tree branches on all fours. Because these creatures lacked a number of anatomical features that living hominoids share, they can be used as a model of the animals that gave rise to the last common ancestor of all later hominoids.

Micropithecus A genus of very small proconsulids from the Miocene, found in Africa.

Proconsul A genus of Early Miocene proconsulids from Africa, ancestral to catarrhines.

9.6 Apes Leave Africa: On to New Habitats and New Adaptations

The presence of ape fossils in Europe and Asia from about 17 mya (but not before) suggests that apes originated in Africa and then spread to Europe and Asia. The migration of primates (and other animals) from Africa to Europe

9.19

EOCENE–OLIGOCENE–MIOCENE HABITATS AND THEIR PRIMATES

Primate evolution began with primitive primates in the Eocene, setting the stage for the origin of all hominoids. Euprimates of the Eocene had the basic characteristics of living primates, such as convergent eye orbits and grasping digits. In the past 20 million years, primates diversified in appearance and behavior. These changes included the shift, for some, from life in the trees to life on the ground, and eventually the beginning of bipedalism in the Late Miocene. (Based on Fleagle, J. G. *Primate Adaptation and Evolution*, 2nd ed. 1999. San Diego: Academic Press.)

Convergent eyes and grasping hands

Eocene 56–34 mya

Large eyes for nocturnal vision

Scenes from the Late Eocene in the Paris Basin.
Top: The diurnal *Adapis* is feeding on leaves.
Bottom: Several taxa of omomyids (*Pseudoloris, Necrolemur, Microchoerus*). Note the large eyes, a nocturnal adaptation, typical of both ancient and modern prosimians that are active at night.

Oligocene 34–23 mya

Quadrupedal, monkeylike primate with superb arboreal skills

Scenes from the Early Oligocene of the Fayum, Egypt. These anthropoid ancestors include *Aegyptopithecus*, *Propliopithecus*, and *Apidium*. These primates were adept arborealists, using their hands and feet for climbing and feeding.

Miocene 23–5.3 mya

Quadrupedal, apelike primate. Note the lack of a tail, an ape characteristic.

Scene from the Early Miocene of Rusinga Island, Kenya. Apes first appeared during this period, and these are the first apes (two species of *Proconsul*, *Dendropithecus*, *Limnopithecus*). These and other taxa form the ancestry of all later apes and hominins. Note the range of habitats occupied by these primates within the forest, including some in the middle and lower canopies and some on the forest floor. These primates show a combination of monkeylike and apelike features, in the skeleton and skull, respectively.

(a)

(c)

(b)

FIGURE 9.20

Proconsul This Miocene ape genus was first found in Kenya in 1909—it was the first fossil mammal ever discovered in that region of Africa. *Proconsul* literally means "before Consul"; *Consul* was the name given to chimpanzees that performed in European circuses. *Proconsul,* then, is considered an ancestor to apes, including chimpanzees. **(a)** The first skull of the genus was found in 1948 and was nearly complete. The cranial remains helped researchers determine that *Proconsul* was possibly an ancestor to apes. **(b)** Other fossil finds have helped researchers determine what *Proconsul*'s full skeleton was like. Note that it lacked a tail, like all modern apes. Here, areas shaded red represent the parts of the skeleton that have been discovered. **(c)** An artist's reconstruction illustrates *Proconsul*'s rainforest habitat and arboreal nature. (Figure 9.20c: "*Proconsul heseloni* Habitation," © 1992 by Jay H. Matternes)

and Asia was made possible by a land bridge created 23–18 mya by a drop in sea levels and the joining of the African–Arabian tectonic plate with Eurasia. After their dispersal into Europe and Asia, apes became more diverse than ever before, thus representing an extraordinary adaptive radiation, among the most successful among higher primates.

APES IN EUROPE: THE DRYOPITHECIDS

By 13 mya, the early apes had successfully adapted to a wide range of new habitats. During this time, Europe was covered by a dense, subtropical forest that provided a rich variety of foods, especially fruit. ***Dryopithecus***, the best-known genus within a group of great apes called **dryopithecids**, lived in the area of Europe that is now the countries of France and Spain. Larger than earlier apes—about the size of a chimpanzee—it was first discovered and described by the eminent French paleontologist Édouard Lartet (1801–1871) in 1856 in St. Gaudens, southern France.

Dryopithecus A genus of dryopithecid apes found in southern France and northern Spain.

dryopithecids Early Miocene apes found in various locations in Europe.

Shoulder joint
mobility limited

Deep
ribcage

Limited elbow
extension

Arms and legs
same length

Small hands

Highly mobile
shoulder joint

Shallow rib cage

High degree of
elbow extension

Arms longer
than legs

Large hands

FIGURE 9.21

Proconsulid Body Plan The body plan of primitive, Miocene apes (left) differs from that of modern apes (right). The Miocene apes had a more monkeylike body, with smaller hands, a more restricted hip joint, and a more flexible spine. Modern apes have highly mobile shoulder joints and fully extendable elbow joints, enabling them to brachiate, or swing from branch to branch; the Miocene apes, by contrast, probably were arboreal quadrupeds, not needing the great mobility in their shoulders and their wrists. For the purposes of comparison, this Miocene ape, *Proconsul,* and this lesser ape, the modern gibbon, have been drawn the same size. In reality, *Proconsul* was about half the size of a gibbon.

(a)   (b)

FIGURE 9.22

Dryopithecus **(a)** The mandible of *Dryopithecus*, a Miocene ape genus from Europe, like that of **(b)** a modern gorilla, includes the Y-5 molar pattern and low, rounded cusps. Both also have large canines, plus the diastema between the canine and the first premolar.

sivapithecids Early Miocene apes found in Asia.

Sivapithecus A genus of Miocene sivapithecids, proposed as ancestral to orangutans.

Khoratpithecus A genus of Miocene apes from Asia, likely ancestral to orangutans.

Gigantopithecus A genus of Miocene pongids from Asia; the largest primate that ever lived.

Dryopithecus and its contemporary taxa are known from other European regions, such as Spain, Greece, Germany, and Hungary.

Dryopithecus resembled living apes in many ways: its canines were sharp and tusklike; its cheek teeth were long and had very simple chewing surfaces, well-adapted for chewing fruit (**Figure 9.22**); and microscopic studies of cross sections of the teeth enamel indicate that these apes grew slowly. Their brains were larger than those of earlier primates, similar to those of modern chimpanzees. Their long forelimbs, grasping feet, and long, grasping hands were powerful and adapted for gibbon-like arboreal, suspensory behavior, which are modern apes' main forms of locomotion.

APES IN ASIA: THE SIVAPITHECIDS

In Asia, the **sivapithecids** were the counterpart of Europe's dryopithecids. The best-known sivapithecid is *Sivapithecus*, an ape ancestor that thrived about 12–8 mya. Whereas chimpanzees and gorillas have thin-enameled teeth, *Sivapithecus* had thick-enameled teeth, adapted for eating hard, tough-textured foods such as seeds and nuts. Its robust jawbones were similarly adapted.

Because hominins also have thick-enameled teeth, primatologists once thought *Sivapithecus* was the ancestor of hominins. This hypothesis was rejected in 1979, when the anthropologists David Pilbeam and Ibrahim Shah discovered a partial *Sivapithecus* skull (**Figure 9.23**). *Sivapithecus* skulls are strikingly similar to those of living orangutans, with concave faces, narrow nasal bones, oval eye orbits from top to bottom, projecting premaxillas (the *premaxilla* is the area of the face below the nose), large upper central incisors, and tiny lateral incisors. Even more similar to living orangutans, however, is the newly discovered ***Khoratpithecus***, a hominoid of the Late Miocene (9–6 mya) in Thailand and Myanmar. Various features of this primate's teeth and lower jaw—for example, broad front teeth, and canines with a flat surface on the tongue side—indicate that this Miocene primate is a potential ancestor of living orangutans.

Closely related to *Sivapithecus, Khoratpithecus,* and other Asian Miocene apes, ***Gigantopithecus*** is a very interesting pongid (great ape) from India, northern Vietnam, and southern China, dating to about 8–0.3 mya (**Figure 9.24**). Appropriately named for its massive body, *Gigantopithecus* is the biggest primate that has

FIGURE 9.23

Sivapithecus Originally found in the Siwalik Hills of modern-day India and Pakistan, this Miocene ape (center) has been proposed as ancestral to the orangutan (right). *Sivapithecus*'s facial features, for example, are far closer to the orangutan's than to those of other great apes, such as the chimpanzee (left). *Sivapithecus* has three species, any of which may be a direct ancestor to the orangutan; however, recent finds of another Miocene ape genus have called this ancestry into question.

FIGURE 9.24

Gigantopithecus Bamboo was probably among the plant foods eaten by this enormous, herbivorous Miocene ape. Climate change and competition with other primate species likely brought about this ape's extinction.

ever lived, and would have stood at nearly 3 m (10 ft) tall and weighed as much as 300 kg (660 lb)! Its massiveness would have limited this fossil primate to the ground for all its activities. Like some of the other Miocene apes, it had thick-enameled teeth and large, thick-boned jaws, adapted for eating very hard foods, likely nuts, seeds, fruits, leaves, and stems. Until recently, the evolutionary links to other great apes have been made solely on the basis of morphology of the fossil teeth and bones. However, a new analysis (reported in 2019) of protein sequences in a *Gigantopithecus* molar dating to 1.9 mya from Chuifeng Cave, China, reveals a clear phylogenetic affinity with the modern orangutan, also an Asian great ape (see chapter 6). This research, the first of its kind, clearly confirms the long-held hypothesis that the divergence of *Gigantopithecus* from *Pongo* is part of the radiation of the great apes during the Miocene.

DEAD END IN APE EVOLUTION: THE OREOPITHECIDS

Around the same time *Gigantopithecus* emerged, a group of apes called **oreopithecids** lived in Europe. They appear in the fossil record around 8 mya and disappear around 7 mya. *Oreopithecus*, the best known of this group, has been found on the island of Sardinia and in coal mines in Tuscany, Italy. (Oreopithecids were also present in Africa at the same time as the proconsulids on that continent.) Its Miocene habitat was dense, tropical forests, and its teeth were highly specialized for eating leaves (**Figure 9.25**). Also known as the "Swamp Ape," *Oreopithecus* was a medium-size primate, weighing an estimated 30–35 kg (66–77 lb), but it had a tiny brain. Its relatively long arms indicate that it was adept at some form of suspensory locomotion, similar to that of a modern gibbon. Some of its hand adaptations foreshadow developments in hominin evolution.

oreopithecids Miocene apes that were found in Europe.

Oreopithecus A genus of oreopithecids found in Italy that was extinct within a million years of its appearance.

FIGURE 9.25

Oreopithecus The high, shearing crests on its molars suggest that this Miocene ape was folivorous. Like *Gigantopithecus*, this ancestral ape likely became extinct due to climate change.

CLIMATE SHIFTS AND HABITAT CHANGES

During the period in which *Oreopithecus* and other later Miocene apes disappeared, Europe, Asia, and Africa experienced dramatic changes in climate and ecology. Several factors coincided to cause these changes: a shift in tectonic plates, which created the Alps, the Himalayas, and the East African mountain chains; changes in ocean currents; and reforming of the polar ice caps. In Europe and then Africa, the once-lush tropical forests changed to cooler, drier mixed woodlands and grasslands. As a result, tropical foods disappeared, including the apes' favored diet, fruit. In Asia, a decrease in rainfall, reduced forests, and decreased fruit availability likely contributed to the extinction of *Sivapithecus*.

CONCEPT CHECK

The First Apes: A Remarkable Radiation

The apes' evolutionary glory days were in the Miocene epoch (23–5.3 mya), beginning in Africa and then spreading into Europe and Asia. Some survived well into the Pleistocene, as late as 0.3 mya. Out of this remarkable adaptive radiation came the ancestors of living apes and of humans. All of these fossil primates had characteristics seen in living apes, especially in the teeth and the skull (Y-5 lower molars, 2/1/2/3 dental formula, broad incisors, large honing canines), but most were monkeylike in the postcranial skeleton (front and back limbs equally long).

GROUP	CHARACTERISTICS	AGE	LOCATION
Proconsulids	Large range in size Tropics to open woodlands Thin enamel (E.g., *Proconsul*)	22–17 mya	Africa (Kenya, Uganda)
Dryopithecids	Some size range Tropics Thin enamel (E.g., *Dryopithecus*)	14–9 mya	Europe (France, Spain, Germany, Greece, elsewhere)
Sivapithecids	Some size range Tropics Thick enamel Skull like orangutan's (e.g., *Sivapithecus*) or massive body size (e.g., *Gigantopithecus*)	14–0.3 mya	Asia (Pakistan, India, China, Thailand, Vietnam)
Oreopithecids	Large body Tiny brain Specialized molars for eating leaves Suspensory locomotion (E.g., *Oreopithecus*)	9–7 mya	Europe (Italy), earlier form in East Africa (Kenya)

MIOCENE APE SURVIVORS GIVE RISE TO MODERN APES

A handful of ape taxa survived these dramatic disruptions in habitat. *Khoratpithecus,* for example, thrived for a time and gave rise to the orangutan of Southeast Asia. The origins of the great apes of Africa and hominins are far less clear. In fact, only one small set of fossils—named *Chororapithecus* by their discoverer, the Japanese paleoanthropologist Gen Suwa—resembles similar parts of living great apes. Teeth representing three individuals, found in Ethiopia and dating to about 10.5 mya, are remarkably similar to the modern gorilla's teeth. Their existence suggests that Late Miocene African pongids may have been the common ancestor of African apes and hominins. However, the fossil record in Africa between 13 mya and 5 mya is extremely sparse, leaving an 8-million-year gap until the first hominins' appearance, about 6 mya (discussed further in chapter 10). Therefore, the link between Late Miocene African apes and later hominoids is unknown.

9.7 Apes Return to Africa?

Ape fossils from the Late Miocene might be so scarce in East Africa because apes simply were not living there, at least not in great numbers, at that time. Somewhere other than Africa may be the source of the common ancestor of living African apes and humans. The Canadian primate paleontologist David Begun suggests that Late Miocene Europe might yield that ancestor. He speculates that the similarities in dentition and skull between the Greek dryopithecid *Ouranopithecus,* on the one hand, and African apes and early hominins, on the other, indicate an ancestral–descendant relationship between European great apes and African hominins. Begun argues that the climate changes in Europe prompted Late Miocene apes to move from Europe back to Africa, essentially following the tropical forests, and the foods these forests provided, as forests and foods disappeared behind them. Some of the pongids adapted to forested settings, some lived in woodlands, and eventually one group, hominins, became committed to life on the ground. However, the record of hominoid evolution in Africa and the clear presence of the earliest hominins in Africa strongly favors an African origin of today's apes and humans. Thus, it is likely that the European pongids went extinct in the late Miocene.

Ouranopithecus A genus of Miocene dryopithecids found in Greece.

9.8 Monkeys on the Move

At the same time as the evolution and proliferation of ape taxa, an expansion and adaptive radiation of monkeys occurred, both in the New World (see "How Anthropoids Got to South America" earlier) and in the Old World. Primates recognizable as cercopithecoids—they have the distinctive bilophodont molars of Old World monkeys—first appeared during the Early Miocene in North Africa and East Africa. These primitive primates are generally called **victoriapithecids**. *Victoriapithecus,* a prominent genus of the group, is just the kind of primate that would be expected for the ancestor of Old World monkeys.

Beginning in the Late Miocene, especially in the Pliocene and Pleistocene, and continuing to the present day, monkey taxa have proliferated enormously. While

victoriapithecids Miocene primates from Africa, possibly ancestral to Old World monkeys.

ape species were far more prevalent and diverse during the Early and Middle Miocene, far outnumbering the living groups, monkey species are far more diverse since the end of the Miocene. Today's monkey taxa are for the most part the descendants of the fossil species from the Pliocene and Pleistocene. By contrast, most of the ape and apelike taxa from the Miocene went extinct and left no descendants.

The rise in number and diversity of monkey species and the decline in ape species were not due to competition between the two groups. Rather, the origin and diversification of monkeys reflect habitat changes. The climates and environments of the Early Miocene seem to have favored the adaptive radiation of apes, with most taxa then going extinct as climates and environments changed. The climates and environments of the Late Miocene, and into the Pliocene and Pleistocene, seem to have favored the adaptive radiation of monkeys.

The Pliocene and Pleistocene fossil monkeys are divided into the same two subfamilies as Old World monkeys: cercopithecines and colobines. The cercopithecines are represented by three major groups: macaques; mangabeys, baboons, and geladas; and guenons. The fossil monkeys were widespread, as living species of monkeys are. The fossil monkeys and their living descendants are similar in many respects, such as skeletal and dental anatomy. For example, the fossil and living monkeys have virtually identical teeth (large, projecting canines) and cranial morphology.

Some of the Pliocene and Pleistocene monkeys were quite large. For example, *Theropithecus oswaldi,* one of the best-known fossil species of Old World monkeys from East, North, and South Africa in both the Pliocene and the Pleistocene, may have weighed as much as 80 kg (176 lb), the weight of a modern female gorilla (**Figure 9.26**). Males had enormous canines and would have been avoided by early hominins because they were so dangerous.

The colobines included three geographic groups of species: European, Asian, and African. These species differed in many ways from their living descendants, in part reflecting their greater geographic distribution and the diverse environments they occupied. One clear evolutionary trend in many monkey species is a

Theropithecus A genus of fossil and living Old World monkeys found in Africa; it was more diverse in the past than it is today and was one of the first monkey genera to appear in the evolutionary record.

(a)　　　　　(b)

FIGURE 9.26

Theropithecus **(a)** Of the same genus as living gelada baboons, fossil *Theropithecus* species have been found in many areas of Africa. *Theropithecus* ate predominantly grasses. **(b)** Like their living counterparts, fossil *Theropithecus* species were likely terrestrial quadrupeds, as their front and hind limbs were of similar length; however, the fossil species were substantially larger than the living gelada baboons.

decrease in body size. In other words, around the world during the later Pleistocene there were widespread extinctions of large animals, including primates. These extinctions might have been caused by human hunting, climate change, competition with other mammals, or a combination of these factors (discussed further in chapter 14).

All of primate evolution is a dynamic story, peaking at different times and different places with key events, such as the origins of all the major groups of higher primates (**Figure 9.27**). The record becomes even more fascinating in the Late Miocene, with the appearance of a new primate that is similar to but different from other primates. The first 50 million years of primate evolution, from the beginning of the Eocene to the last several million years of the Miocene, set the stage for the appearance of this new taxon—a primitive, humanlike primate. This ancestor's origin begins the 7-million-year history of the appearance, rise, and dominance of humans. That story begins in the next chapter.

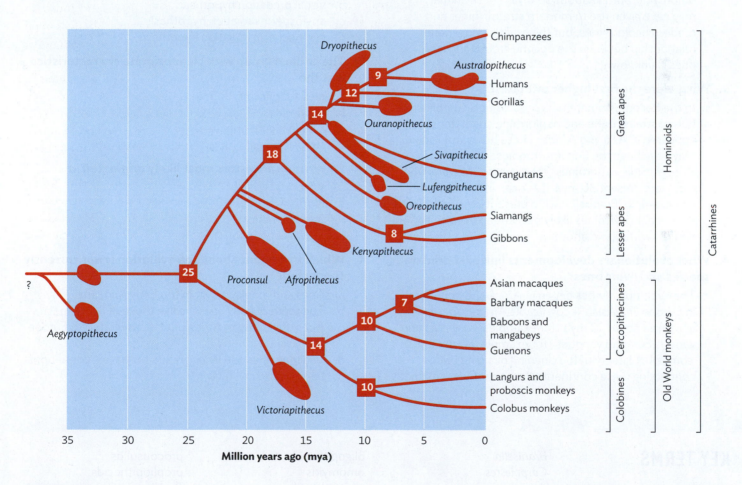

FIGURE 9.27

Catarrhine Origins This phylogeny represents catarrhine evolution. The numbers set in squares represent the estimated times of divergence (in mya). Balloons refer to approximate time ranges for fossil taxa. Old World monkeys and hominoids share a common ancestor; however, approximately 25 mya, Old World monkeys and hominoids split, each creating a separate evolutionary lineage. This last common ancestor, though, has not been discovered. Within the hominoid lineage, branching has occurred many times, including the branch leading to the lesser apes, around 18 mya, and most recently the branch leading to humans, approximately 9–8 mya. The Old World monkey lineage has also branched several times, most notably when colobines and cercopithecines split, approximately 14 mya.

ANSWERING THE BIG QUESTIONS

1. Why become a primate?

- According to the predominant theory, primate origins represent the radiation of a primitive mammalian ancestor that adapted to life in the trees. Other theories suggest that the origins may be more closely linked to preying on insects or eating fruit.

2. What were the first primates?

- The first radiation of primates included the appearance of two primitive primate groups, adapids and omomyids, both at about 55 mya. These animals may have given rise to modern strepsirrhines and modern haplorrhines, but the exact phylogenetic relationship between the Eocene groups and later ones is unknown.

3. What were the first higher primates?

- In the Eocene, primate taxa possessing a combination of strepsirrhine and haplorrhine characteristics appeared in Asia and Africa. These basal anthropoids may have been the first anthropoids.
- Recognizable catarrhines (for example, *Aegyptopithecus*) were present 30 mya in Africa, and platyrrhines (for example, *Branisella*) were present 26 mya in South America. Platyrrhines likely descended from an early African anthropoid ancestor.

4. What evolutionary developments link past primate species and living ones?

- The evolution of apes began in Africa and continued in Europe and Asia. Recognizable African apes first appeared about 22 mya (for example, *Proconsul*) and various Eurasian varieties (for example, *Sivapithecus*) somewhat later with the opening of a land bridge connecting these continents. Most apes went extinct in the later Miocene, although a few survived, giving rise to modern apes and humans.
- Monkeys underwent a massive adaptive radiation in the Pliocene and Pleistocene, providing the foundation for the evolution of modern species.

STUDY QUIZ

1. The _____ specifically links the evolution of primates to flowering plants.

a. arboreal hypothesis
b. visual predation hypothesis
c. angiosperm radiation hypothesis
d. gymnosperm radiation hypothesis

2. The earliest group with clear primate characteristics was the

a. plesiadapiforms.
b. euprimates.
c. Fayum higher primates.
d. strepsirrhines.

3. Platyrrhine ancestors most likely originated in

a. Africa.
b. North America.
c. South America.
d. Madagascar.

4. Which statement about ape evolution is *not* currently supported?

a. Apes and monkeys split in the Early Miocene.
b. The teeth of early apes are like those of living apes.
c. Apes originated in Africa but later migrated to Europe and Asia.
d. Miocene apes and living great apes have a continuous fossil record in Africa.

KEY TERMS

adapids
Adapis
Aegyptopithecus
angiosperm radiation hypothesis
arboreal hypothesis
basal anthropoids
Biretia

Branisella
Carpolestes
dryopithecids
Dryopithecus
Eosimias
euprimates
Gigantopithecus
Khoratpithecus
Micropithecus
Notharctus

oligopithecids
omomyids
oreopithecids
Oreopithecus
Ouranopithecus
parapithecids
Parapithecus
Perupithecus
plesiadapiforms
Proconsul

proconsulids
propliopithecids
Propliopithecus
Proprimates
Saadanius
sivapithecids
Sivapithecus
Theropithecus
victoriapithecids
visual predation hypothesis

STUDY QUIZ (CONTINUED)

5. **Which statement about Old World monkey evolution is *not* currently supported?**
   a. Fully modern bilophodont molars first appear in the victoriapithecids.
   b. Many monkey species decreased in body size.
   c. Old World monkeys became more diverse than apes in the Late Miocene.
   d. Ape diversity decreased due to direct competition with Old World monkeys.

EVOLUTION REVIEW

Primate Social Organization and Behavior: The Deep Roots of the Order Primates

SYNOPSIS The origin of our own taxonomic order, the order Primates, extends more than 50 million years into the past. Various hypotheses—based on characteristics seen in both living and extinct primates, such as arboreal adaptations and visual acuity—have been proposed to explain why the first true primates arose deep in the past. The evolutionary history of the order Primates can be described as somewhat tumultuous. Fluctuations in climate and other environmental pressures during the Eocene, Oligocene, and Miocene epochs affected the survival and adaptive radiations of various fossil primate taxa to differing degrees. Fossils of primate ancestors are found across Africa, Asia, and Europe in the Old World and North and South America in the New World. The locations and characteristics of these fossils clarify the timeline of major evolutionary events that shaped the order Primates and illustrate that the geographic extent of primates in the past was much larger than the distribution of nonhuman primate species living today.

Q1. Describe the three hypotheses for explaining primate origins, discussed at the beginning of this chapter. Do you think the environmental pressures associated with each of these hypotheses are mutually exclusive, or could all of these factors have influenced the origins and adaptability of the earliest primates?

Q2. Identify the four alternative hypotheses for explaining the presence of primates in South America. Summarize the evidence that supports each of these four hypotheses. Based on this evidence, assess how plausible each hypothesis is in explaining the origins of the New World primates.

Q3. Explain the role of climate fluctuations in the origins and evolution of the first true primates, the earliest anthropoids, the Early Miocene apes (proconsulids), and the surviving ape species of the Late Miocene.

HINT Focus on the ways that warming and cooling episodes affected habitable land areas, caused habitat changes, and affected availability of different food sources.

Q4. There is much less diversity among living ape species than among the many fossil ape taxa of the Early Miocene and Middle Miocene. In contrast, there is much greater diversity among living monkey species than among the fossil monkey taxa of the Late Miocene. Discuss the kinds of selective pressures operating in the Late Miocene, Pliocene, and Pleistocene that favored an adaptive radiation of monkeys and contributed to decreased diversity among apes.

Q5. A bumper sticker reads, "If humans evolved from monkeys, then why are there still monkeys?" Using your knowledge of biological evolution in general, and the timeline of primate origins and evolution outlined in this chapter more specifically, counter the faulty logic behind this bumper sticker.

HINT See Figure 9.27 for a timeline of the key events in primate evolution.

ADDITIONAL READINGS

Beard, C. 2004. *The Hunt for the Dawn Monkey: Unearthing the Origins of Monkeys, Apes, and Humans*. Berkeley: University of California Press.

Cachel, S. 2015. *Fossil Primates*. Cambridge, UK: Cambridge University Press.

Fleagle, J. G. 2013. *Primate Adaptation and Evolution*, 3rd ed. San Diego: Academic Press.

Miller, E. R., G. F. Gunnell, and R. D. Martin. 2005. Deep time and the search for anthropoid origins. *Yearbook of Physical Anthropology* 48: 60–95.

Rose, K. D. 1994. The earliest primates. *Evolutionary Anthropology* 3: 159–173.

Ross, C. F. 2000. Into the light: The origin of Anthropoidea. *Annual Review of Anthropology* 29: 147–194.

Often referred to as the "cradle of humankind," Olduvai Gorge is a ravine in East Africa's Great Rift Valley from which many hominin fossils have been recovered, providing insight into our evolutionary roots. Geologic activity and erosion have exposed some of the deepest and oldest layers of sediment, enabling paleoanthropologists to find fossils from strata that are nearly 2 million years old.

Olduvai
Gorge

TANZANIA

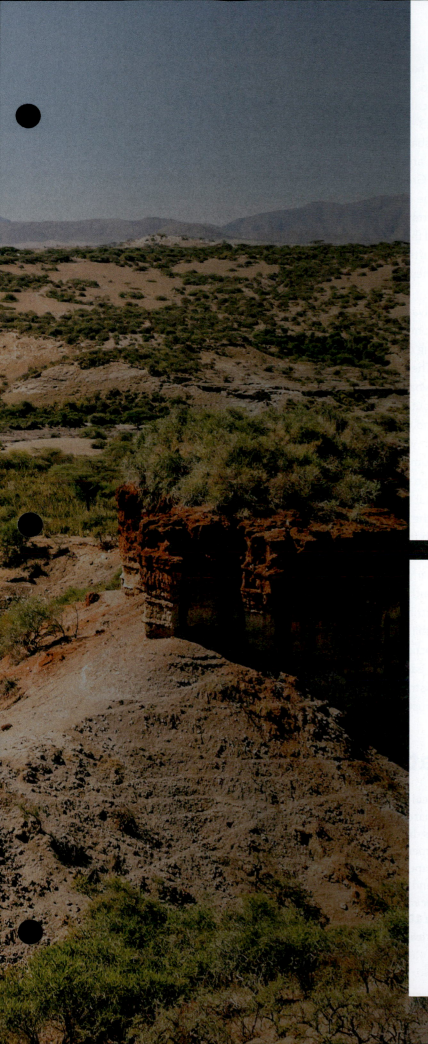

10

Early Hominin Origins and Evolution

THE ROOTS OF HUMANITY

BIG QUESTIONS

1. **What is a hominin?**
2. **Why did hominins evolve from an apelike primate?**
3. **What were the first hominins?**
4. **What was the evolutionary fate of the first hominins?**

Imagine yourself walking across the hot, desolate, and altogether inhospitable landscape of East Africa's Great Rift Valley. Further imagine that you have spent the better part of the past three decades—all your adult life—searching for early hominin fossils. Over those years, you have found evidence, such as stone tools, that early humans had lived in this place hundreds of thousands—even millions—of years ago. Still, you have found no fossils—at least, none worth getting especially excited about. On this particular day, you see part of a bone sticking out of the ground, just like others you have seen over and over before. This one turns out to be different, though. Instead of being an animal of some sort, this fossil has primitive

FIGURE 10.1

Mary and Louis Leakey This wife-and-husband team conducted some of the earliest excavations in Olduvai Gorge.

human teeth—you have found a hominin, your first! In an instant, all your searching has been vindicated.

That scene describes exactly what happened to the English-born anthropologist Mary Leakey (1913–1996) one sunny morning in July 1959 (**Figure 10.1**). She, along with her husband, the Kenyan anthropologist Louis Leakey (1903–1972), had searched high and low for early human bones in Olduvai Gorge, Tanzania, a side branch of the Great Rift Valley that runs 50 km (31 mi) long. Since beginning their searches in the early 1930s, they had found ancient stone tools and ancient animal remains scattered about the landscape—lots of them. However, they wanted more. They wanted the remains of the people who had made the tools and had eaten the animals. Year after year, field season after field season, disappointment after disappointment, they searched for the bones and teeth that would represent our ancestors' roots.

What had motivated these two individuals to work so hard for so little payoff under such awful conditions? Simple. They were motivated by questions. In fact, the Leakeys were asking one of the most fundamental questions of all time: *Who were the first humans?* The Leakeys demanded answers about human origins, and they were willing to do what had to be done to get those answers.

They started out with a pretty simple hunch about early hominins. Other scientists had found old things in Olduvai Gorge—ancient bones and tools, both in association with very old geologic strata—that strongly suggested the place would yield early hominin remains. Based on these findings, the Leakeys decided to investigate the gorge's geologic strata (**Figure 10.2**). Their work took a lot of time and resources, but it paid off well, laying the essential groundwork for our current understanding of the first humans and their place in evolution. In fact, the bits of bone and the teeth found in 1959 turned out to be a crucially important hominin skull (*Australopithecus boisei*; **Figure 10.3**). Not only did this discovery expand the territory in which early hominins were known to have lived—at that point, they were known just from South Africa—but it added a whole new dimension to their variability and geographic distribution. The Leakeys' pioneering work in East Africa was built around questions still central to paleoanthropology.

This chapter focuses on the fossil record of early human evolution. This record sheds light on the earliest humanlike ancestors. In order of origin and evolution, they are the pre-australopithecines (before the genus *Australopithecus*), which lived 7–4 mya, and the australopithecines, which lived 4–1 mya.

10.1 What Is a Hominin?

The morphological characteristics—and behaviors inferred from these characteristics—shared by living humans and their ancestors, but not shared by apes, reveal what is distinctive about hominins. For example, living humans speak (use language), depend fully on complex material culture, and have advanced cognition—living apes do not have these characteristics. But speech, complex material culture, and advanced cognition evolved in the human line long after the first hominins appeared in Africa (7–6 mya), so these characteristics do not define a hominin (**Figure 10.4**). Speech likely developed only in the past 2 million years, and some authorities argue for its development late in that period. Evidence for

Present-day surface

Naisuisiu

Ndutu — OH 11

Masek — OH 23

Bed IV — OH 12, OH 28, OH 22

0.7

Bed III

Bed II — OH 9, OH 13

1.7

Bed I — OH 5, OH 10, OH 20, OH 24, OH 8, OH 7

1.9 mya

Basalt layer/no fossils

FIGURE 10.2

Geologic Strata at Olduvai One key aspect of excavations at Olduvai is the exposed strata, dating back millions of years. The strata include volcanic rock, which can be radiometrically dated to provide accurate ages for each layer. Any Olduvai hominin (OH) fossils found in these layers can then be dated according to the stratum in which they were found. The ages of fossil hominins recovered from Olduvai Gorge help anthropologists reconstruct humans' family tree.

material culture, in the form of primitive stone tools, dates to at least 2.6 mya. As discussed in chapter 1, a hominin is much better understood as having two obligate behaviors—bipedal locomotion and nonhoning chewing—and the suite of associated physical characteristics that manifest these behaviors. The evidence is very clear: bipedal locomotion and nonhoning chewing preceded speech and material culture by several million years. Like large brains, speech and material culture help define humans today but were not attributes of the earliest hominins.

BIPEDAL LOCOMOTION: GETTING AROUND ON TWO FEET

In the 1800s, when the entire human fossil record was a very small fraction of what it is today, numerous authorities believed that the beginning of bipedalism was not the hallmark event distinguishing humans from apes. Rather, these scientists

FIGURE 10.3

Australopithecus boisei This fossil (OH 5) is one of the most famous ever recovered from Olduvai Gorge. The almost complete cranium is of an adult male. Its robust features and large molars caused anthropologists to classify it as a robust australopithecine.

FIGURE 10.4

What Makes Us Human? Humans and apes differ in a number of key ways. For example, humans have and apes lack **(a)** bipedalism, **(b)** nonhoning chewing, **(c)** dependence on material culture, **(d)** speech, **(e)** hunting and cooperation, and **(f)** domestication of plants and animals. This suite of characteristics helps define what it means to be human.

HUMAN–APE DIFFERENCES
HUMANS HAVE, APES LACK:

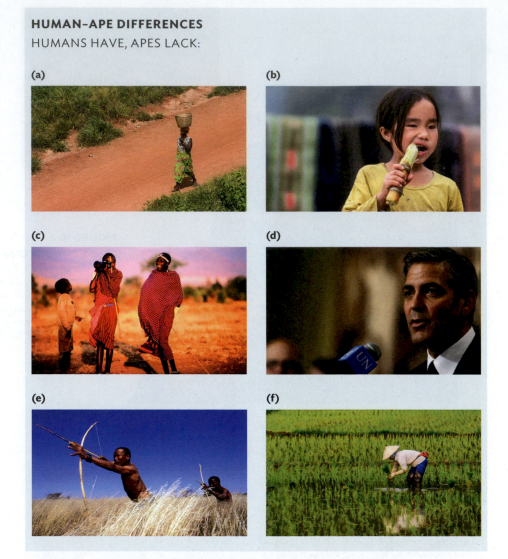

believed that the most important initial evolutionary change was an increase in brain size, reflecting advanced (human) intelligence. They speculated that only with advanced intelligence would language, tool use, and the other behaviors that collectively define humanness have become possible. The focus on intelligence to the exclusion of other attributes helped bring about the rapid and uncritical acceptance of some purported early hominin ancestors that later turned out to be fake.

Since then, the large early hominin fossil record has proved that bipedalism—and not human intelligence—was the foundational behavior of the Hominini (humans and humanlike ancestors), preceding most attributes associated with humans and with human behavior by *millions* of years. More than any other characteristic, the shift from walking and running with four limbs (arms and legs) to walking and running with two limbs (legs) distinguishes hominins from the apes (and other nonhuman primates).

Seven distinguishing characteristics in the skeleton are associated with bipedalism (**Figure 10.5**; see also "What Is a Primate?" in chapter 6): (1) the foramen magnum is positioned on the bottom of the skull; (2) the spine has an *S*-shaped curve; (3) the ilium is short from front to back; (4) the legs are long relative to the body trunk and arms; (5) the knees are angled inward; (6) the foot has a

1. **Position of the foramen magnum:** In humans, the foramen magnum is on the bottom of the skull, closer to the teeth. In apes, the foramen magnum is in a posterior position. This difference reflects the fact that the human head sits on top of the body trunk, whereas the ape head sits on the front of the trunk.

2. **Shape of the spine:** In humans, the spine has an S-shape. In apes, it is straighter, almost C-shaped. The distinctive S-shape in humans is created by the concave curvature of the thoracic vertebrae, in front, and the concave curvature of the lumbar vertebrae, in the back. This arrangement, especially of the lumbar vertebrae, serves to position the body trunk's center of gravity above the pelvis, providing more stability during walking and running.

3. **Shape of the pelvis:** The human pelvis has a very different shape from the ape pelvis. Especially distinctive is the short ilium in the bipedal human. This morphology is an essential element of the stability of the pelvis during standing, walking, and running (discussed further in chapter 6).

4. **Length of the leg:** The relatively long leg of the bipedal human provides increased efficiency during stride. In hominins, the leg is generally longer relative to the arm than it is in apes. The long arm of the ape reflects its suspensory use in trees.

5. **Valgus knee:** The knees in the biped angle inward to give it a knock-kneed appearance. The angle formed by the long axis of the femur shaft and the horizontal at the knee—called the bicondylar angle—provides an angle greater than 90 degrees. This angle is significantly greater in humans than in most apes. The valgus knees place the feet together and beneath the center of gravity. By doing so, they provide stability in walking and running, especially when only one foot is on the ground during locomotion.

6. **Longitudinal foot arch:** The biped has a distinctive arch that runs from the front to the back of the bottom surface of the foot. This form gives increased leverage as the body pushes forward and serves as a shock absorber when the feet make contact with the ground during walking and running. Apes have flat feet, which reflect the adaptation of their feet for grasping.

7. **Opposable big toe:** The first digit of the foot—the big toe—is opposable in apes but not in humans. This difference reflects the function of the foot in humans, which is solely (pun intended!) to support the body during walking and running. The ape toe has a dual function; it facilitates both terrestrial walking and grasping or manipulating objects. Humans have largely lost their ability to manipulate objects with their toes.

FIGURE 10.5

Seven Steps of Bipedalism This figure shows the seven key differences between a bipedal hominin and a quadrupedal pongid. The two skeletons are of a modern human and a modern gorilla. They are similar in overall form, reflecting their common ancestry. However, because the human is a biped and the gorilla is a quadruped, they have important anatomical differences. Anthropologists use these differences to identify patterns in fossils and to reconstruct their respective locomotor and related behavioral patterns.

Imagine yourself as a biological anthropologist who has just unearthed in East Africa a fossil skeleton of a hominoid dating to 4 or 5 mya. In examining your newly discovered skeleton, you would want to pay attention to these seven anatomical features. But you would need to be prepared for surprises, which you might encounter if your specimen is closer to or further away from the nearest ancestor of apes and humans.

FIGURE 10.6

Nonhoning versus Honing Chewing While humans have nonhoning chewing, primates such as gorillas (pictured here) have a honing complex, in which their very large canines cut food. The upper canines are sharpened against the lower third premolars.

longitudinal arch; and (7) the big toe (hallux) is not opposable. The position of the foramen magnum reflects the fact that the (bipedal) hominin carries its head atop its body, in contrast to the (quadrupedal) ape, which carries its head on the front of the body. The shortened ilium and pelvis generally reflect anatomical changes that coincided with the shift from quadrupedalism to bipedalism. Especially important is the reconfiguring of the gluteal muscles for stabilizing the hip in walking on two legs. Bipeds have distinctively long legs, which provide the ability to stride and to do so with minimal energy. The angling of the knees toward the midline of the body helps to place the feet below the body's center of gravity, thereby helping stabilize the biped when standing, walking, or running. The loss of opposability in the big toe reflects the use of this digit in helping propel the body forward during walking and running. The longitudinal arch acts as a kind of shock absorber, allowing the foot to sustain the demanding forces of body weight, especially during running and long-distance walking.

NONHONING CHEWING: NO SLICING, MAINLY GRINDING

The second of the two major differences between living apes and humans (and human ancestors) is the way that their dentitions process food (again, see "What Is a Primate?" in chapter 6). Apes and humans have evolved different dental characteristics, reflecting how each uses the canine and postcanine teeth (**Figure 10.6**). When apes grab on to food with their front teeth, the upper canines and lower third premolars cut and shred the food. Through evolution, apes' upper canines have become large, pointed, and projecting, with a sharp edge on the back (**Figure 10.7**). When the jaws are fully closed, each canine fits snugly in the diastema, the gap located between the canine and the third premolar on the lower jaw and the canine and the second incisor on the upper jaw. The sharp edge on the

FIGURE 10.7

Human and Nonhuman Dentition **(a)** Humans' nonhoning chewing complex is characterized by canines that are much shorter than **(b)** those found in nonhuman primates' honing complex, such as this gorilla's. In addition, humans lack the diastema that nonhuman primates such as gorillas have. What other differences do you see?

(a)

I1 I2 Honing wear on back C

(b)

Wear on tip I1 I2 C

FIGURE 10.8

Canine Wear (a) This gorilla's dentition reveals honing wear on the back of the upper canine, caused by the tooth's rubbing against the lower third premolar. **(b)** This human's dentition reveals wear on the upper canine's tip, which is the point of contact between the upper canine and the lower teeth when the jaws are closed.

back of the upper canine hones, or rubs against, a sharp edge on the front of the lower third premolar, or sectorial premolar. This honing action helps maintain a sharp, shearing edge on both the canine and the premolar. The shearing edge is essential for slicing up leaves and fruit before they are chewed by the back teeth and swallowed. Apes' lower third premolar is also distinctive in having one large, dominant cusp on the cheek side of the tooth and a tiny cusp on the tongue side of the tooth.

In contrast, living and past hominins have small, blunt, and nonprojecting canines and no diastema. Hominin canines wear on the tips instead of the backs (**Figure 10.8**). The cusps on both sides of the lower third premolars are similar in

CONCEPT CHECK

What Makes a Hominin a Hominin?

Hominins have a number of anatomical characteristics that reflect two fundamental behaviors: bipedal locomotion and nonhoning chewing.

BEHAVIOR	ANATOMICAL CHARACTERISTICS
Bipedalism	Foramen magnum on the bottom of the skull
	S-shaped spine
	Short pelvis from front to back
	Long legs
	Knees angled toward midline of the body
	Double-arched foot, including a well-developed longitudinal arch
	Nonopposable big toe
Nonhoning chewing	Blunt, nonprojecting canine
	Small canine relative to size of other teeth
	No diastema
	Wear on tips of canines and of third premolars
	Similar-sized cusps on both sides of lower third premolars

M. temporalis

M. masseter

Human

Gorilla

FIGURE 10.9

Masticatory Muscles Humans and other primates have powerful chewing muscles to process food. In humans, the temporalis muscle is vertically oriented, enabling a crushing ability. In nonhuman primates, this muscle is oriented horizontally, producing slicing motions.

size, or at least more similar in size than are the cusps in apes. Unlike apes, hominins do not hone their canines as they chew.

Apes' and humans' postcanine teeth have many similar anatomical characteristics. The third and fourth premolars, upper and lower, have two cusps each. Apes' and humans' upper molars have four cusps, and their lower molars have five cusps. Apes' and humans' back teeth crush and slice food, but with a different emphasis: humans crush food more than apes do. Apes use their molars more for slicing than crushing, reflecting their plant-heavy diet.

In apes and humans, grinding and slicing are facilitated by powerful chewing (or masticatory) muscles, especially the temporalis, masseter, and pterygoid muscles (**Figure 10.9**). Hominins place more emphasis on the front portion of these muscles, to provide greater vertical force in crushing food. Apes place more emphasis on the back portion of the masticatory muscles because slicing requires more horizontally oriented forces. As an additional aid in powerful crushing, hominins have evolved thick enamel on their teeth (**Figure 10.10**). Living apes have evolved thin enamel, reflecting diets dominated by plants and soft fruit. Among the hominoids, the only exception is the orangutan, which has evolved thick enamel—its diet includes tough foods that require heavy crushing.

Like bipedalism, hominins' nonhoning masticatory complex developed very early in the evolutionary record. Collectively, then, the key distinguishing features of hominins are located in the anatomical complexes associated with acquiring and transporting food (locomotion) and chewing food (mastication).

Thick enamel

Thin enamel

(a)　　　　　　　　(b)

FIGURE 10.10

Enamel Thickness Enamel is the outermost layer of the exposed part of a tooth and is the hardest substance in the human body, enabling the tooth to grind and slice all types of food. Species with diets heavy in hard foods, such as seeds and nuts, have thicker enamel, allowing more of the enamel to be eroded or worn before the softer layers underneath are exposed. In these cross sections of (a) a human tooth and (b) a chimpanzee tooth, note how much thicker the enamel is in the human.

10.2　Why Did Hominins Emerge?

The fossil record and genetic information continue to fill in the story of hominins' first appearance on the scene, in the Late Miocene epoch. But *why* did hominins evolve? Central to most arguments is bipedalism, a focal point in the study of human origins.

CHARLES DARWIN'S HUNTING HYPOTHESIS

Charles Darwin offered the first serious hypothesis about the first appearance of hominins. It was a simple but elegant adaptive model for explaining human origins. Drawing on the great British naturalist Thomas Huxley's anatomical research on the living apes of Africa (both Darwin and Huxley are discussed in chapter 2), Darwin concluded that because of the remarkable anatomical similarity between humans and African apes, Africa was hominins' likely place of origin (**Figure 10.11**). The characteristics that distinguish living humans from living apes, Darwin reasoned, derive from one key evolutionary event in their common ancestor; namely, the shift from life in the trees to life on the ground. He observed four characteristics that set living humans apart from living apes: (1) humans are bipedal, whereas apes are quadrupedal; (2) humans have tiny canines, whereas apes have large canines; (3) humans rely on tools in their adaptation, whereas apes do not; and (4) humans have big brains, whereas apes have small brains (**Figure 10.12**).

Building on these observations, Darwin asked what the advantages of bipedalism would be in a world where bipeds—early humans—ate mostly meat they acquired by killing animals with weapons. He concluded that bipedalism had freed the hands for carrying the weapons. To manufacture and use these tools, the early humans needed great intelligence. Once they had the tools, they did not need the big canines for hunting or for defense. Although he saw tool production

GIBBON.   ORANG.   *Skeletons of the* CHIMPANZEE.   GORILLA.   MAN.

FIGURE 10.11

Ape and Human Skeletons Thomas Huxley studied apes' and humans' anatomies. This illustration, from the frontispiece of Huxley's *Evidence as to Man's Place in Nature* (1863), shows the overall similarity in the skeletons of assorted primates (note that the gibbon here is twice its actual size). The major differences between the skeletons of apes and humans—limb proportions, pelvic shape, and spine curvature—are related to humans' bipedalism.

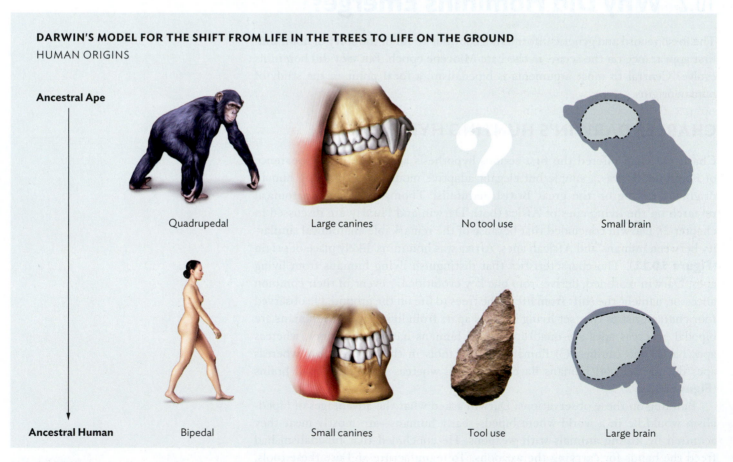

DARWIN'S MODEL FOR THE SHIFT FROM LIFE IN THE TREES TO LIFE ON THE GROUND
HUMAN ORIGINS

Ancestral Ape

Quadrupedal   Large canines   No tool use   Small brain

Ancestral Human   Bipedal   Small canines   Tool use   Large brain

FIGURE 10.12

Four Key Differences From Huxley's comparative studies of apes and humans, Darwin noted four differences between these two types of primates. In Darwin's time, there were no recorded instances of apes' making or using tools, so tools appeared a uniquely human phenomenon. Since then, however, apes have been seen making and using tools, such as when chimpanzees "fish" for termites with a rod and crack hard nuts with a "hammer and anvil" (see "Acquiring Resources and Transmitting Knowledge: Got Culture?" in chapter 7).

and tool use as essential factors in the development of human intelligence, Darwin believed that humans' large brains resulted mainly from the presence of language in humans.

Scientists now know that tool use and the increase in brain size began well after the appearance of bipedalism and the reduction in canine size. The earliest known tools for which we have good evidence date to about 2.6 mya, and evidence of brain expansion dates to sometime after 2 mya. Therefore, it now seems doubtful that canine reduction began with tool use. Although Darwin's hypothesis was refuted, it provided an essential first step toward an understanding of hominin origins.

Since Darwin, other hypotheses have emerged to answer the question of why there are hominins. The starting point for these hypotheses is the knowledge that, after 17 mya, a massive adaptive diversification of apes occurred in Africa, resulting in many different taxa (see "Apes Begin in Africa and Dominate the Miocene Primate World" in chapter 9). At some point later, this diversity declined considerably, perhaps due in part to competition between apes and to the rising number of monkey species that were also evolving in the Late Miocene epoch. Changes in climate and in habitat also likely influenced the decline in the number of ape taxa. Most important about the evolution of Miocene apes is that somewhere out of this ancestral group of ape species arose the animal that was more human than ape.

Darwin proposed that hunting was at the heart of the divergence. However, the archaeological record suggests that hunting began much later in human evolution. Hunting, at least in the sense of cooperation among individuals to kill an animal, likely did not begin until after 2 mya, at about the same time the brain began expanding. It now seems very likely that hunting played an important role in later human evolution but not in hominin origins.

PETER RODMAN AND HENRY MCHENRY'S PATCHY FOREST HYPOTHESIS

The American biological anthropologists Peter Rodman and Henry McHenry have proposed that human origins and bipedalism in particular may be related to the greater efficiency, in certain habitats, of walking on two feet rather than four. They suggest that bipedalism arose in areas where the forest was becoming fragmented, a process that began toward the end of the Miocene (**Figure 10.13**). Apes' quadrupedalism, they note, is not energy-efficient in Africa's patchy forests. As the forests became patchy and food became more dispersed, early hominins would have used their energy much more efficiently once bipedalism freed their hands to pick up food. The early hominins could then have fed in trees and on the ground, depending on the availability of resources.

OWEN LOVEJOY'S PROVISIONING HYPOTHESIS

The American biological anthropologist Owen Lovejoy has offered another alternative to Darwin's ideas about the arboreal-to-terrestrial shift and the origins of bipedalism. He has hypothesized that freeing the early hominins' hands was important in initiating bipedal locomotion but not for the reasons Darwin cited. Lovejoy observes that in many species of monkeys and apes, males compete for sexual access to females. However, the young are cared for by the mother without

FIGURE 10.13

East African Tree Cover Around the time that humans and bipedalism arose, East Africa had large amounts of discontinuous tree cover. Rodman and McHenry propose that the areas of open grassland, interspersed with some stands of trees, such as shown here, favored bipedalism over quadrupedalism.

any involvement of the father (see "What Is a Primate?" in chapter 6). Owing to the obligations of caregiving, such as the acquisition of food for her infant (and herself), the mother theoretically is not able to care for more than one infant at a time. Moreover, she is unreceptive to mating until the infant is able to find food on its own. In apes as in humans, the time from birth to the infant's independence can be rather long, upwards of 5 years in chimpanzees, for example. The downside of this extended care period is that it gives apes a reproductive disadvantage because so few offspring can be born to any female. Lovejoy hypothesizes that if infants and mothers were provided with more food, then they would not have to move around as much for resources. If males provisioned mothers and their offspring, then each mother would be able to care for two or more infants at a time. In other words, the mother could have more births—the time interval between births would be reduced.

Lovejoy makes the case that for early hominins, a monogamous father enhanced the survival of the mother and offspring by providing both food and protection from predators. This habitual provisioning required the male to have free hands for carrying food, so bipedalism arose. This model focuses on the selective and simultaneous advantages of monogamy and pair-bonding, of food provisioning, of cooperation, and of bipedalism, all rolled into one distinctively human behavioral package.

SEXUAL DIMORPHISM AND HUMAN BEHAVIOR

Among all the hypotheses about hominin origins, Lovejoy's hypothesis had a unique focus on differences in female and male body sizes and on the implications of behavior with a decidedly human bent. Through field and laboratory studies, anthropologists have observed that in terms of body size, many living primate species are highly dimorphic sexually: males are considerably larger than females. This difference has come about because the larger the male, the more equipped it will be to outcompete other males for sexual access to females. Through natural selection, then, males in many primate species have maintained relatively large bodies. Some authorities argue that early hominins were highly dimorphic, in which case competing males were likely not involved in caring for their offspring. However, if early hominins were not especially dimorphic, then male competition for mates probably was not part of early hominin social behavior. The American anthropologist Philip Reno and his associates have studied early hominin bones to determine relative sizes of females and males. Their analysis suggests relatively little sexual dimorphism in body size, especially in comparison with apes. Such reduced sexual dimorphism suggests that males were cooperative, not competitive. This cooperative behavior could have included pair-bonding—one male paired with one female—a behavior pattern necessary for the kind of provisioning required in Lovejoy's hypothesis. The hypothesis is controversial in a number of respects, including, for example, that it may be too reliant on models of behavior reflecting traditional gender roles and the Western emphasis on males. In general, attempting to reconstruct hominin behavior is one of the more difficult challenges anthropologists undertake, but it is one that continues to motivate scientific inquiry surrounding human evolution. Part of what makes this task so challenging is that hominin behavior is complex in all ways, and its origin is tied to multiple factors—a topic discussed throughout this book.

BIPEDALISM HAD ITS BENEFITS AND COSTS: AN EVOLUTIONARY TRADE-OFF

Although the mechanisms underlying the origin of bipedality are complex, all hypotheses about human origins agree that an apelike primate evolved into an early hominin through positive adaptation. Bipedalism's advantages over quadrupedalism included an increased ability to see greater distances (thanks to an upright posture), greater ease of transporting both food and children, the ability to run long distances, and the freeing of the hands for, eventually, remarkable skills and activities such as tool manufacture and tool use. However, the profound adaptive shift to bipedalism also had its costs. Standing upright yields a better view across the landscape, but it also brings exposure to predators. Standing or walking on two feet while simultaneously lifting or carrying heavy objects over long periods of time causes back injury, such as that associated with arthritis and with slipped intervertebral disks. Bipedalism also places an enormous burden on the circulatory system as it moves blood from the legs to the heart. The result of this burden is the development of varicose veins, a condition in which overwork causes the veins to bulge. Lastly, if one of a biped's two feet is injured, then that biped's ability to walk can be severely reduced. Unable to move about the landscape, an early hominin would have had limited chances of surviving and of reproducing. In short, bipedalism is a wonderful example of the trade-offs that occur in evolution. Only rarely do adaptive shifts, including one of the most fundamental human behaviors, come without some cost. Bipedality is an adaptive characteristic that came with considerable costs.

10.3 What Were the First Hominins?

Until the 1970s, the oldest hominin fossil dated to less than 4 mya. The earliest hominins were known from one genus, *Australopithecus*, found mostly in two key areas of Africa: in a series of limestone caves in South Africa and in sedimentary basins and associated river drainages in the Eastern Rift Valley (part of the Great Rift Valley) in Ethiopia, Kenya, and Tanzania (**Figure 10.14**). As we saw in the previous chapter, the latest African Miocene apes—the group of hominoids out of which the first hominins evolved—date to about 8 mya. Thus, the crucial time period during which hominins and the last common ancestor with apes (chimpanzees) split into separate lineages had been an unknown because of the 4-million-year gap in the fossil record (8–4 mya). Subsequently, however, hominins predating *Australopithecus* have been discovered in north-central and eastern Africa. These hominins have closed the gap between Late Miocene ape evolution and the first hominins, the pre-australopithecines.

Australopithecus An early hominin genus, representing as many as 10 species, found in East and South Africa 4–1 mya.

THE PRE-AUSTRALOPITHECINES (7–4 MYA)

Pre-australopithecine fossils are few in number and quite fragmentary, but they have provided critically important information about the origins and earliest evolution of the Hominini. The pre-australopithecines had a number of primitive attributes, and in some respects they were more apelike than humanlike. They represent the first recognizable ancestors of the lineage leading to humans.

***Sahelanthropus tchadensis* (7–6 mya)** The earliest pre-australopithecine is represented by most of a skull and other fossils found in central Africa, beginning in 2001,

- - - East African Rift Zone

FIGURE 10.14

African Hominins **(a)** Many hominin fossils have been found in East Africa and South Africa. **(b)** In East Africa, layers of geologic strata have been exposed through erosion and geologic activities. The volcanic rock in these strata allows the layers to be dated directly, providing age estimates for the fossils found in them. **(c)** In South Africa, by contrast, many fossils have been found in limestone caves, which cannot be dated directly. Age estimates for fossils found there are made through other methods.

Sahelanthropus tchadensis The earliest pre-australopithecine species found in central Africa with possible evidence of bipedalism.

by the French paleontologist Michel Brunet and his colleagues (**Figure 10.15**). Named *Sahelanthropus tchadensis* (meaning "genus named for the region of the southern Sahara Desert known as the Sahel") by its discoverers, this creature's fossils date to 7–6 mya. The finding's geographic location—the Toros-Menalla locality of the Djurab Desert in Chad—surprised many because it was 2,500 km (1,553 mi) from the Eastern Rift Valley, where all other early hominins in East Africa had been found for the past three-quarters of a century. The presence of early hominins in central Africa opened a third geographic "window" onto their evolution, the first two being later presences in East Africa and South Africa. In short, humans originated in Africa during the Late Miocene and Early Pliocene.

Cranial capacity, a rough measure of brain volume, is one important quantitative characteristic with which anthropologists determine the degree of humanness in individual fossil hominins. The fossil record of human evolution shows an increase in brain size, from the smallest in the oldest hominins (about 350 cubic

(a)

(b)

(c)

FIGURE 10.15

Sahelanthropus tchadensis **(a)** Among the first and few hominin fossils uncovered in central Africa, this skull belonged to a primate with a small and primitive brain like that of apes. Note the large browridge. **(b)** Left to right: Ahounta Djimdoumalbaye, Michel Brunet, and Mackaye Hassane Taisso examine the skull, which they found in Chad. **(c)** This artist's reconstruction depicts how *Sahelanthropus* might have appeared in life. Its many apelike features combined with bipedalism caused researchers to classify this creature as a pre-australopithecine, part of a group of very early hominin ancestors that bridge the gap between other hominin ancestors and apes.

centimeters, or cc) to the largest in *Homo sapiens* (about 1,450 cc). *Sahelanthropus* had a brain size of about 350 cc.

Its brain was primitive and like that of apes. Moreover, this hominin had a massive browridge, larger than that of modern gorillas. However, the two critical attributes that define the Hominini are present in *Sahelanthropus*—the primate was likely bipedal (based on the position of the foramen magnum at the base of the skull), and the canine–premolar chewing complex was nonhoning. This combination of primitive (more apelike) and derived (more humanlike) features is to be expected in the oldest hominin, especially in apes' and humans' common ancestor. Its great age and primitive characteristics indicate that *Sahelanthropus* existed very close—the closest of any fossil known—to the divergence of apes and hominins from the common ancestor.

Also found at the same site were the bones and teeth of nonprimate animals, fossils that create a picture of *Sahelanthropus*'s habitat. These remains—of hugely diverse animal species, including fish, crocodiles, amphibious mammals associated with aquatic settings, bovids (hoofed mammals), horses, elephants, primates, and rodents associated with forests and grasslands—indicate that *Sahelanthropus* lived in a forest near a lake.

Orrorin tugenensis* (6 mya)** Dating to around 6 mya, the fossils of at least five pre-australopithecines were found in the Tugen Hills, on the western side of Kenya's Lake Turkana. The discoverers, paleoanthropologists Brigitte Senut and Martin Pickford, named these hominins ***Orrorin tugenensis (the genus means "original man" in Tugen's local language). Among the 20 fossils were several partial femurs, each missing the knee but indicating that these hominins were bipedal. For example, the femur's neck, the area that is at the top of the bone and articulates with the hip, was relatively long (**Figure 10.16**). A hand phalanx found at the site was curved like a living ape's, suggesting that *Orrorin* spent time in the trees. Like those of *Sahelanthropus,* the canines had wear on the tips and were nonhoning. The animal bones at the site indicated that *Orrorin* lived in a forest.

Orrorin tugenensis A pre-australopithecine species found in East Africa that displayed some of the earliest evidence of bipedalism.

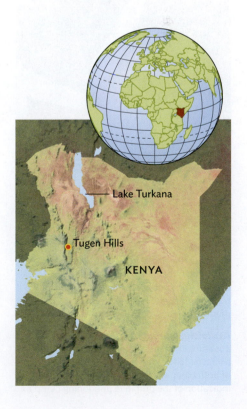

Lake Turkana

Tugen Hills

KENYA

FIGURE 10.16

Orrorin tugenensis The most important skeletal remain of this pre-australopithecine is a proximal, or upper, portion of the femur, which has a long femoral neck and a groove for the obturator externus muscle. These characteristics are the same as in humans and hominin ancestors, suggesting *Orrorin* was bipedal. By contrast, apes (such as the chimpanzee) have a short femoral neck and no groove.

Modern human   ***Orrorin***   **Chimpanzee**

Long neck — — Short neck

No obturator externus groove

Location of obturator externus groove

Ardipithecus kadabba An early pre-australopithecine species from the Late Miocene to the Early Pliocene; shows evidence of a perihoning complex, a primitive trait intermediate between apes and modern humans.

Ardipithecus ramidus A later pre-australopithecine species from the Late Miocene to the Early Pliocene; shows evidence of both bipedalism and arboreal activity but no indication of the primitive perihoning complex.

Ardipithecus kadabba **and** ***Ardipithecus ramidus*** **(5.8–4.4 mya)** At Aramis, one of a number of important paleontological sites in the fossil-rich Middle Awash Valley of Ethiopia's expansive Afar Depression (**Figure 10.17**), the American biological anthropologist Tim White and his colleagues recovered the most spectacular of the pre-australopithecines (or, for that matter, any other early hominin assemblage). They began exploring the Middle Awash in the early 1980s as a potential place for finding fossils. At Aramis, beginning in the early 1990s and continuing for the next 10 years, they collected fossils intensively. Their team grew to include 70 scientists from 18 countries. What drew the team back to the site, field season after field season, interrupted for some years by political unrest in the region, were the very strong signals for successful recovery of key fossils that would date from the period at or just after the origins of the human lineage. The team concluded that this would be the place to look for answers to questions about the transition from ape to hominin, from a primate that walked on all fours and used its arms to move in trees to a primate that walked on the ground. Eventually, the Middle Awash region yielded the longest continuous record of hominin evolution: more than 6 million years, dating from before the australopithecines through the appearance and evolution of early *Homo* to the first modern *H. sapiens* (discussed in chapters 11 and 12) and after.

The scientists of the Middle Awash project predicted that fossils they discovered from the Miocene and Early Pliocene at Aramis would reveal hominin ancestors having a mosaic of apelike and humanlike characteristics. These ancestors would have set the stage for all of later human evolution. And indeed, among their findings were two species of a new genus of hominin, *Ardipithecus,* including the earlier ***Ardipithecus kadabba*** and the later ***Ardipithecus ramidus*** (in the local Afar language, *ardi* means "ground" or "floor," *kadabba* means "oldest ancestor," and *ramid* means "root"), dating to 5.8–5.5 mya and 4.4 mya, respectively. The earlier *Ar. kadabba* is known mainly from teeth, and these fossils show that hominins' canines wore from the tips (not the sides) but had some honing or polishing on the sides of the third lower premolar (**Figure 10.18**).

The later *Ar. ramidus,* dubbed "Ardi" by its discoverers, is one of three or four fossil hominin discoveries of the many hundreds since the mid-nineteenth century

FIGURE 10.17

Middle Awash Valley, Ethiopia This hotbed of hominin fossil finds is located in the Afar Depression, an area of much geologic and tectonic activity. The Awash River flows through the depression, creating rich plant and animal life in the midst of an arid region. Because the Afar's floor consists of volcanic rock, radiometric dating methods can be used to provide age estimates for the fossils found in the geologic strata.

that have transformed our understanding of the earliest period of human evolution. In 2009, *Science,* a leading international journal for all scientific disciplines, devoted much of an issue to the description and interpretation of this hominin, calling the finding the "Breakthrough of the Year" (**Figure 10.19**). Anthropologists worldwide call it the breakthrough of the century.

Ardipithecus is remarkable, first of all, because it is represented by a huge assemblage of fossils. These fossils include the most complete early hominin skeleton found to date, along with bones and teeth of at least 35 other individuals, all bracketed to a depositional period of less than 10,000 years, an eyeblink in human evolution (**Figure 10.20**).

FIGURE 10.18

Ardipithecus kadabba The earlier form of this pre-australopithecine had an intermediate honing, or perihoning, complex in its dentition, while the later form lacked honing entirely. Shown here, the perihoning complex of an early form of *Ardipithecus* (right) is similar to chimpanzees' honing complex (left). Together, these forms suggest that *Ardipithecus* was an early hominin ancestor, as its dental morphology was intermediate between apes' and humans'. (Photo © 2003 Tim D. White/David L. Brill, humanoriginsphotos.com)

Breakthrough of the Year
Ardipithecus ramidus

FIGURE 10.19

Cover of *Science* Magazine The discovery of *Ardipithecus ramidus* was such a fundamental development that *Science* magazine called it the "Breakthrough of the Year" in 2009.

10.20

FROM DISCOVERY TO UNDERSTANDING
CONSTRUCTING A FUNDAMENTAL SCIENTIFIC THEORY

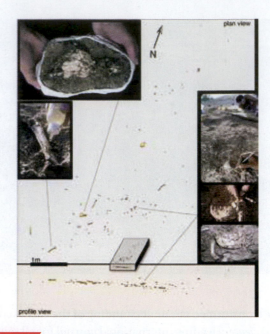

1 DISCOVERY

In the early 1980s, a multidisciplinary team of geologists, paleoanthropologists, and archaeologists first visited the region near the village of Aramis, in the Middle Awash Valley, identifying it as a place where Pliocene hominins could be found. Field teams collected intensively in the region from 1995 to 2005, in geologic deposits dating to 4.4 mya. During the 10-year collection period, scientists and field workers literally crawled across the landscape on their hands and knees in search of hominins and other fossils. This Herculean effort had an enormous payoff, producing one of the most important fossil records of early hominins ever found and an abundant record of plants and animals. The plant and animal fossils reveal that these early hominins inhabited a cool, wet forest.

2 RECOVERY

Once the fossils' locations had been recorded, it was important to remove the fossils as quickly as possible. The bones were soft and had to be treated with preservatives, and some had to be removed in plaster jackets. They were taken first to the field camp and eventually to the laboratory at the National Museum in Addis Ababa, Ethiopia, for detailed study. The 109 hominin fossils represented 36 individuals. Among them was a partial skeleton, field number ARA-VP-6/500. The oldest fossil hominin skeleton yet found, it predates Lucy's skeleton by more than a million years. The map plotting the fossils of this hominin shows that it was widely scattered and no bones were articulated. It took the researchers 3 years of hard work to recover the remains of this skeleton alone.

3 LAB WORK

Almost from the beginning of the discovery of fossils in this locality some years before, it was clear that they needed a new name. Tim White called it *Ardipithecus ramidus* (in the local Afar language, *ardi* means "ground" or "floor" and *ramid* means "root"). The partial skeleton, nicknamed "Ardi" by the field team, required years of cleaning, preparation, and reconstruction. For example, to assemble all the skull fragments into an accurate reconstruction, casts of each of the scores of pieces were made. The resulting images were combined with digital images to produce a composite picture (see the upper left corner of the facing page). Various indicators, including the size of the body, revealed that the hominin was a female adult, weighing 50 kg (110 lb) and standing 120 cm (4 ft) high.

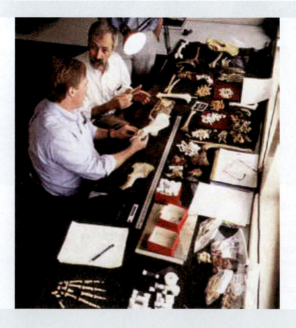

4 UNDERSTANDING ARDI: HEAD TO TOE

Skull and teeth The skull is very similar to those of other pre-australopithecines, such as *Sahelanthropus* (see p. 289), with its tiny brain (300–350 cc) and highly projecting face. It is probably like the skull of the nearest common ancestor of apes and humans. The teeth show none of the specializations seen in living apes, such as the big incisors and canines and sectorial complex of orangutans and chimpanzees. Wear on the teeth suggests that the hominin was omnivorous, eating nonabrasive foods and some hard foods. The canine shows no functional honing, and so these hominins processed their food like later hominins.

Upper limb and hand Especially striking about the upper limb and hand are their primitiveness. Compared with those of living humans, the forearm (radius and ulna) is extraordinarily long in relation to the upper arm. The elbow joint shows no evidence that these arms were used for suspension, however. The size and morphology of the hand indicate that the hominin did not knuckle-walk. Thus, knuckle-walking evolved in later apes. The fingers are quite long and had excellent grasping capability. Ardi walked on her palms when in the trees.

Pelvis The wide pelvis indicates full hominin status: Ardi walked bipedally when on the ground. In this respect, the pelvis is quite evolved, especially compared with the upper limb/hand and lower limb/feet. The lower part of the pelvis reveals evidence of muscles used in climbing.

Lower limb The lower limb and foot are adapted for bipedalism, but they also reveal characteristics that indicate significant time spent in the trees. For example, the foot has greatly elongated toes and a fully divergent big toe for grasping. No later hominin has this particular combination of features. While retaining its very primitive grasping capability, the foot also served in propelling the body forward when walking or running on the ground. Like the other parts of the skeleton, it is a mosaic of primitive and derived characteristics.

5 IMPLICATIONS FOR HUMAN EVOLUTION

This remarkable hominin skeleton, along with the other fossils found at Aramis, provides us with a new understanding of the origins and evolution of the human and ape lineages. This new understanding is made possible by this exceptionally complete fossil record and the unprecedented level and detail of multidisciplinary study, ranging from habitat reconstruction to the analysis of function and behavior of early hominins. The very primitive nature of this skeleton confirms that the divergence of the chimpanzee–human lineage was quite recent and provides insight into behavior and adaptation soon after the divergence. This fossil is the closest yet found to the common ancestor of chimpanzees and humans. Most important, all earlier models suggesting a chimpanzeelike ancestor for hominins are incorrect—the first hominin was not chimpanzeelike.

The Pre-australopithecines

The first hominins spanned a 3-million-year period in Africa, about 7–4 mya. They had both apelike characteristics and the features that define hominins.

HOMININ	DATE(S)	LOCATION	HOMININ	DATE(S)	LOCATION
Sahelanthropus tchadensis	7–6 mya	Djurab Desert, Chad	*Ardipithecus kadabba*	5.8–5.5 mya	Middle Awash Valley, Ethiopia

Key features:

Skull and teeth found

Tiny brain (350 cc)

Skull like apes', with massive browridge

Key features:

Skull, teeth, postcranial bones found

Small brain

Some tooth wear on outside of third premolar (perihoning)

Thin enamel

Curved foot phalanges

Femur and pelvis indicate capable of bipedalism

Less than 1 m (3.3 ft) tall

Lived in wooded setting

Orrorin tugenensis	6 mya	Tugen Hills, Kenya	*Ardipithecus ramidus*	4.4 mya	Middle Awash Valley, Ethiopia

Key features:

Skull, teeth, postcranial bones found

Small brain

No perihoning

Thin enamel (only hominin with thin enamel)

Curved foot phalanges

Femur and pelvis indicate capable of bipedalism

120 cm (3.9 ft) tall

Lived in wooded setting

Key features:

Postcranial bones found

Femurs indicate likely bipedalism

Hand phalanx like apes' (curved)

Less than 1 m (3.3 ft) tall

Second, the fossils provide us with a snapshot of these first hominins as a species: their behavior, their adaptation, and what life was like for them not long after the chimpanzee and human lineages had diverged from their common ancestor in the Late Miocene. This picture includes unprecedented ecological detail derived from the study of thousands of fossilized plant and animal remains from the site in conjunction with the study of the fossil hominin remains. The ecological context shows that these early hominins lived in a forest. This discovery provides compelling evidence that—contrary to the hypotheses of Darwin and other authorities and reaffirmed by most of the fossil record dating to the Pliocene and Pleistocene—the first hominins clearly did not evolve in the open grasslands (**Figure 10.21**). The forest context for pre-australopithecines had been suggested by paleoecological analyses of the settings for *Sahelanthropus* and *Orrorin,* but the ecological records from places where these pre-australopithecine fossils were found are not nearly as extensive as the ecological record for Aramis.

Like earlier species of *Ardipithecus,* the Aramis fossils have a primitive yet fully hominin masticatory complex, with short, nonprojecting canines and wear on the tips of the canines. The tooth enamel is not as thin as in extant apes, but it is thinner than in all later hominins. As noted by Owen Lovejoy and his colleagues, the lower limb and foot bones reveal that the big toe was opposable, more like that of an ape today and completely unlike a human's (**Figure 10.22**). Unlike an ape's foot, however, Ardi's foot lacked the flexibility required for grasping tree limbs and moving through trees. The musculature and construction of Ardi's foot were rigid, a hominin adaptation for using the foot to propel itself forward when walking bipedally. The phalanges of the feet and hands were curved, indicating grasping capabilities similar to those of apes. In addition, Ardi's wrist lacked the articulations and specialized adaptations of today's suspensory, knuckle-walking great apes. These details show that Ardi was adapted to life in the trees *and* to life on the ground. It was a part-time biped and a part-time quadruped. It did not evolve from an ape that was suspensory in the trees and a knuckle-walker on the ground. Instead, as suggested by reconstruction of its skeleton, Ardi moved on its palms and feet along tree branches and walked upright on the ground.

Ardi's intermediate form of bipedalism is part of the ancestry of later hominins, which became fully committed to life on the ground. Ardi evolved from some apelike ancestor, but the great apes and hominins took two entirely different behavioral and associated anatomical pathways, the former evolving suspensory locomotion and knuckle-walking and the latter evolving efficient bipedalism and losing all arboreal behavior.

The extensive fossil record for *Ardipithecus* is also being documented from other contexts in Ethiopia, extending the record back further in time at the site of Gona. There, teeth dating to 6.3 and 5.5 mya have been discovered. In addition, discovery of a partial postcranial skeleton dating from 4.8 to 4.3 mya shows that like the *Ardipithecus* from Aramis, the Gona hominin had a locomotor pattern involving bipedality and arboreal activity. These fossils, discovered by American paleoanthropologist Scott Simpson and his field team, reveal an adaptive proliferation of hominin species in the Late Miocene.

In summary, Ardi was clearly a primitive hominin, and its array of remarkable characteristics postdate the chimpanzee–human divergence. This record puts it on the evolutionary pathway to later hominins, the australopithecines, and us. Thus, *Ardipithecus* was one of a few surviving hominoid lineages in the adaptive radiation of Miocene apes. It retained an arboreal adaptation but shares critically important anatomical characteristics with all later hominins.

THE AUSTRALOPITHECINES (4–1 MYA)

The australopithecines are represented by hundreds of fossils, perhaps as many as 10 species. Some of the species are members of ancestral–descendant lineages (**Figure 10.23**). That is, we can link an ancestral species with its descendant species.

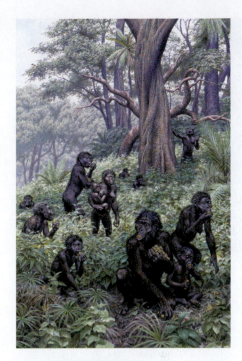

FIGURE 10.21

Origins of Bipedalism The earliest hominin ancestors, the pre-australopithecines, lived in a forested setting. Contrary to earlier hypotheses, bipedalism likely originated not in open grasslands, but in an environment with trees. Shown here is a reconstruction of *Ardipithecus* in its Late Miocene–Early Pliocene habitat in East Africa.

Gona

ETHIOPIA

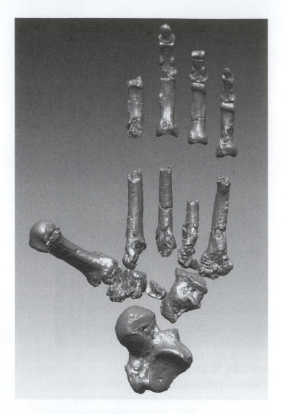

FIGURE 10.22

Ardipithecus Foot There is evidence that *Ardipithecus* was bipedal. However, its big toe (hallux) is divergent like apes', indicating that this pre-australopithecine was arboreal at least some of the time. Like its dentition, this anatomical evidence suggests *Ardipithecus* was an intermediate genus.

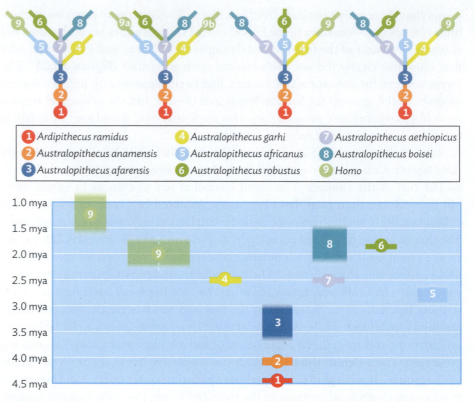

1. *Ardipithecus ramidus*
2. *Australopithecus anamensis*
3. *Australopithecus afarensis*
4. *Australopithecus garhi*
5. *Australopithecus africanus*
6. *Australopithecus robustus*
7. *Australopithecus aethiopicus*
8. *Australopithecus boisei*
9. *Homo*

FIGURE 10.23

Hominin Phylogenies The four alternative phylogenies at the top depict the possible ancestral-descendant relationships among the many australopithecine species. In each tree, *Ardipithecus* is at the base, leading to its descendant *Australopithecus anamensis*, one of the earliest australopithecines. In the second tree, the 9a and 9b indicate that the *Homo* genus may have been the product of both ancestors. The graph at the bottom illustrates the general pattern of hominin evolution, showing the extinction of the australopithecines, with one lineage leading to the genus *Homo*.

On the other hand, some species overlap in time, and some of the species and their evolutionary relationships remain unclear. Australopithecine variation is mostly in size and robusticity—ranging from relatively small and gracile to large and robust. As a group, the australopithecines had small brains, small canines, large premolars, and large molars (**Table 10.1**). The latest australopithecines' faces, jaws, and teeth were very large.

Australopithecus anamensis **(4 mya)** The oldest australopithecine species, *Australopithecus anamensis* (*anam* means "lake" in the Turkana language), was named and studied by the paleoanthropological team of Meave Leakey, Carol Ward, and Alan

Australopithecus anamensis The oldest species of australopithecine from East Africa and a likely ancestor to *Au. afarensis*.

TABLE 10.1 The Earliest Hominins Evolve

FEATURE	PRE-AUSTRALOPITHECINE	→	AUSTRALOPITHECINE
Teeth	Wear on tip of canine, but with modified honing	→	Nonhoning
Bones	Vestiges of apelike arboreal traits	→	Loss of traits
Brain	Small	→	Slight increase

FIGURE 10.24
Skull of *Australopithecus anamensis* This skull, from Woranso-Mille, Afar region, Ethiopia, has a protruding face and a long, narrow cranium.

Walker. *Au. anamensis* dates to about 4 mya and was found within Allia Bay and Kanapoi in the eastern side and to the south of Lake Turkana, Kenya. Other remains, including a partial skull found at Asa Issie, Middle Awash, Ethiopia, have been studied by the Ethiopian paleoanthropologist Yohannes Haile-Selassie and his colleagues (**Figure 10.24**). This hominin was broadly similar in physical appearance to *Ardipithecus,* enough to indicate a probable ancestral–descendant relationship between the two genera. Reflecting its relatively early place in australopithecine evolution, *Au. anamensis* has a number of primitive, apelike characteristics, including very large canines, parallel tooth rows in the upper jaw, and a lower third premolar with both a very large outer cusp and a very small inner cusp (**Figure 10.25**). The Asa Issie skull has a sagittal crest, a feature that is more

Chimpanzee

Au. anamensis

Modern human

FIGURE 10.25

Mandible of *Australopithecus anamensis* A human's mandible (right) widens at the rear, causing the two rows of teeth not to be parallel to each other. By contrast, this australopithecine's mandible (center) is like that of apes (left), *U*-shaped and with two parallel rows of teeth. Primitive features like this, combined with numerous hominin features, have led many researchers to conclude that *Au. anamensis* is the earliest australopithecine.

Australopithecus afarensis An early australopithecine from East Africa that had a brain size equivalent to a modern chimpanzee's and is thought to be a direct human ancestor.

Lucy One of the most significant fossils: the 40% complete skeleton of an adult female *Au. afarensis*, found in East Africa.

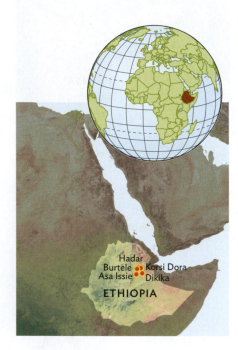

common in the late australopithecines. The fossils were recovered from settings that had been woodland contexts with access to water in the Pliocene.

Australopithecus afarensis **(3.6–3.0 mya)** Since the early 1970s, numerous fossils representing *Australopithecus afarensis* have been found in four main sites: Laetoli, in Tanzania, and Hadar, Korsi Dora, and Dikika, all in Ethiopia (*Afar* is the name of the local tribe on whose land the fossils were found in Ethiopia). *Au. afarensis* is the best-known australopithecine and is represented by dozens of individuals from Laetoli and Hadar and single individuals from Korsi Dora and Dikika, collectively dating to 3.6–3.0 mya. The most spectacular of the *Au. afarensis* fossils are three partial skeletons from Hadar, Korsi Dora, and Dikika. They represent, respectively, an adult female—nicknamed "**Lucy**" by its discoverers, American paleoanthropologist Donald Johanson and his field team, after the Beatles' song "Lucy in the Sky with Diamonds"—an adult male, and a 3-year-old child (**Figure 10.26**).

The completeness of these fossil remains gives us detailed insight into the biology of *Au. afarensis*. Lucy stood only a little more than 1 m (about 3.5 ft) and had somewhat short legs relative to the length of the arms and body trunk. Some authorities have argued that these short legs would have limited the stride in comparison with that of modern people. However, the male stood about 1.5–1.7 m (about 5.0–5.5 ft), and the features of the skeleton and limb bones indicate that the form of walking was likely quite similar to that of modern humans. This similarity suggests that Lucy's legs were not short because it had some form of limited bipedalism. Rather, Lucy simply was short. In addition to limb bones, a partial pelvis, ribs, and a scapula have been preserved from an adult male. In some respects, Lucy's

(a)   (b)   (c)

FIGURE 10.26

Australopithecus afarensis **(a)** As shown here, "Lucy" is a relatively complete skeleton, which helped researchers conclude that this species was bipedal. **(b)** More recently, the fossil remains of a 3-year-old child were recovered in Dikika and nicknamed "Lucy's baby." There are few children in the fossil record. **(c)** This adult male skeleton is from Korsi Dora. (Photo [c] Y. Haile-Selassie, Case Western Reserve University)

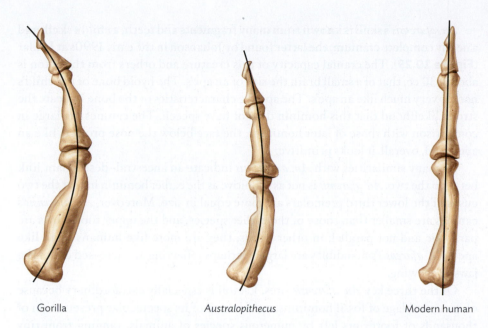

Gorilla   *Australopithecus*   Modern human

FIGURE 10.27

Finger and Toe Curvature Gorillas and other nonhuman primates have curved phalanges, which provide a better grip on tree branches and improve arboreal locomotion. In modern humans, this curvature has been lost in the hands and feet as humans are adapted to life on the ground. The phalanges of early hominins, including australopithecines, have an intermediate amount of curvature, which likely reflects an increasing adaptation to bipedalism but a retained ability to move through the trees.

skeleton is similar to that of a modern human. However, while the phalanges from Lucy's skeleton are the same length as modern humans', they are curved, like those of the pre-australopithecines. In addition, the curvature of the phalanges suggests some potential arboreal locomotion using the hands (**Figure 10.27**). The capability for arboreal activity may also be expressed in the morphology of the scapulae (shoulder joints) of the Dikika juvenile (nicknamed "Lucy's baby"), especially those traits indicating suspensory locomotion. That is, the shoulder joints in this child are angled more like an ape's than like a modern human's (**Figure 10.28**). Thus, *Au. afarensis* displays an interesting mosaic of apelike and humanlike anatomical features. Regardless of how paleoanthropologists interpret the shoulder joint morphology, *Au. afarensis* clearly was an efficient, habitual biped that spent most of its time on the ground.

(a) Adult

(b) Juvenile

Au. afarensis   Orangutan   Gorilla   Chimpanzee   Human

Supraspinous fossa
Glenoid fossa
Scapular spine
Infraspinous fossa
Lucy
Dikika

FIGURE 10.28

Shoulder Joint of *Australopithecus afarensis* The glenoid fossa of the shoulder joint of Lucy, an adult, and of the Dikika juvenile ("Lucy's baby") is oriented slightly upward, more like a modern ape than a modern human. The modern human's glenoid faces completely vertically. The angled glenoid fossa of *Au. afarensis* suggests climbing abilities.

FIGURE 10.29

Cranium of *Australopithecus afarensis* Although this species was bipedal, its brain size and canine size are more primitive and apelike. Other features of the dentition, however, are more homininlike, illustrating the creature's intermediate position between the pre-australopithecines and other, later australopithecines.

Au. afarensis's skull is known from many fragments and teeth, a child's skull, and a nearly complete cranium, the latter found by Johanson in the early 1990s at Hadar (**Figure 10.29**). The cranial capacity of this creature and others from the taxon is about 430 cc, that of a small brain the size of an ape's. The hyoid bone of the child's neck is very much like an ape's. The apelike characteristics of the bone indicate the strong likelihood that this hominin did not have speech. The canines are large in comparison with those of later hominins; the face below the nose projects like an ape's; and, overall, it looks primitive.

Its many similarities with *Au. anamensis* indicate an ancestral–descendant link between the two. *Au. afarensis* is not as primitive as the earlier hominin in that the two cusps of the lower third premolars are more equal in size. Moreover, *Au. afarensis*'s canines are smaller than those of the earlier species, and the upper tooth rows are parabolic and not parallel; in other words, they are more like humans' than like apes'. *Au. afarensis*'s mandibles are larger, perhaps reflecting an increased use of the jaws in chewing.

Of the three key *Au. afarensis* sites, Laetoli is especially extraordinary because of its assemblage of fossil hominins and because of its spectacular preservation of thousands of footprints left by numerous species of animals, ranging from tiny insects to giant elephants. Geologic evidence indicates the eruption of a nearby volcano, which spewed a thin layer of very fine ash across the landscape. Soon after the eruption, a light rain fell, causing the ash to turn into a thin, gooey layer of mud. Animals then traversed the landscape, among them three hominins that left tracks indicating they had simultaneously walked across the muddy terrain around 3.6 mya (**Figure 10.30**). The footprints are remarkable for having been preserved

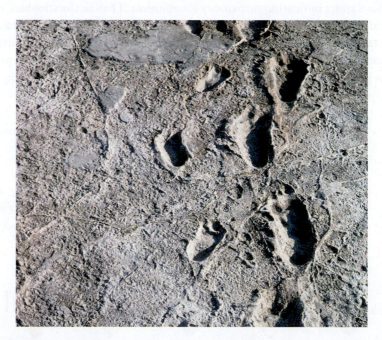

FIGURE 10.30

Laetoli Footprints These footprints, found in Tanzania, resolved any doubt as to whether *Au. afarensis* was bipedal. Shown here are three of the five sets of tracks found by paleoanthropologists. The tracks were made by bipedal hominins. On the right is a larger set of tracks: a child's footprints are superimposed in the larger footprints of an adult, indicating that the child had followed behind the adult, placing its feet exactly where the adult had just walked. To their left is a set of adult tracks. In addition to the hominin footprints, many other prints were found at the site, including those of large animals, such as elephants and giraffes, and those of small animals, including rabbits and birds.

for millions of years and with such clarity, a preservation made possible because the volcanic ash was wet carbonatite, which dries into a rock-hard substance. Biological anthropologists' study of these tracks reveals that the creatures were human-like and had three key characteristics of bipedalism: round heels, double arches (front-to-back and side-to-side), and nondivergent big toes.

In contrast to earlier hominins, which were mostly associated with some type of forested environment, *Au. afarensis* lived in various habitats, including forests, woodlands, and open country. These diverse environments indicate that hominins became more successful at this time, especially after 4 mya, in adapting to and exploiting new habitats. That *Au. afarensis*'s tooth wear is more varied than that of earlier australopithecines indicates *Au. afarensis* probably had a more diverse diet than its predecessors did.

One of the most important characteristics of the Laetoli footprints is the nondivergent big toe. This feature indicates that the hominin had very minimal grasping ability in its toes. In this lack of ability, *Au. afarensis* resembles living humans and differs from living apes. The nondivergent big toe is clear evidence that *Au. afarensis* used its feet primarily in terrestrial locomotion, quite unlike the hominin living a million years earlier, *Ar. ramidus*. However, at least one other taxon of Pliocene hominin was walking around the East African landscape on considerably more primitive feet than those of *Au. afarensis*. At the Burtele site, in the Afar region of Ethiopia dating to 3.4 mya, Yohannes Haile-Selassie and his paleoanthropology field team discovered the front half of a single right foot with a short but divergent opposable big toe. This foot belonged to a hominin that, at least in this one respect, was quite similar to *Ardipithecus*. Unlike the toe bones indicated in the Laetoli footprints, the second to fifth toe bones of the Burtele hominin are long and curved. This foot anatomy shows that the early hominin spent consider-able time in the trees. The other characteristics of the foot bones indicate that this hominin walked bipedally. During this period of time, then, there were at least two contemporary hominins, one a climber and the other much more a biped, spending its time on the ground. Perhaps the foot bones from Burtele are from *Ardipithecus*, which would then have survived into the period of early *Australopithecus*. In any case, this fossil shows the presence of considerably more diversity in early hominin locomotion than the consensus had previously indicated.

Australopithecus (Kenyanthropus) platyops (3.5 mya) *Australopithecus* (or *Kenyanthropus*) *platyops* is a lesser-known hominin from about the same time as *Au. afarensis* (**Figure 10.31**). The partial cranium was discovered by Meave Leakey and her colleagues at Lomekwi, on the western side of Kenya's Lake Turkana, in deposits that date to about 3.5 mya. Its habitat was mainly woodlands. Its face was unusually flat (*platyops*, from the Greek, means "flat face"), a derived feature in hominins, but retained some primitive characteristics.

Australopithecus deyiremeda (3.5–3.3 mya) *Australopithecus deyiremeda* is the most recent fossil discovery of this genus. Found in deposits dating between 3.5 and 3.3 mya by Haile-Selassie and his team at Burtele, the fossils represented by jaws and teeth are distinctive, including having surprisingly small teeth. Not until lat-er hominin evolution (for example, with the appearance of *Homo*) are the teeth as small. Especially important about this discovery is the fact that it dates to the same time as *Au. afarensis* and *Au. (Kenyanthropus) platyops*. This record makes clear the presence of hominin diversity, more so than had previously been anticipated when the much better known and better represented *Au. afarensis* was first discovered more than four decades ago. That is, the presence of three species of contemporary

Australopithecus (or Kenyanthropus) platyops An australopithecine from East Africa that had a unique flat face and was contemporaneous with *Au. afarensis*.

Australopithecus deyiremeda An australopithecine, overlapping in time with *Au. afarensis* in East Africa.

Lomekwi

KENYA

FIGURE 10.31

Australopithecus (Kenyanthropus) platyops A contemporary of *Au. afarensis*, this australopithecine was unique in having a flat face and small teeth. Its brain size, however, was similar to that of *Au. afarensis*.

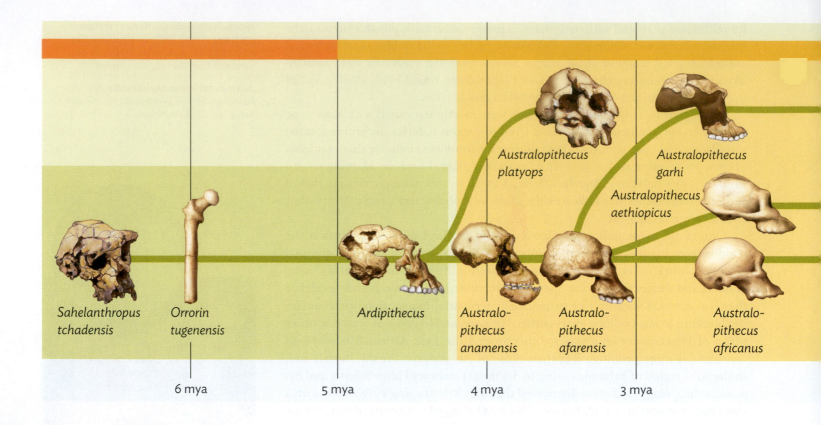

Australopithecus platyops

Australopithecus garhi

Australopithecus aethiopicus

Sahelanthropus tchadensis

Orrorin tugenensis

Ardipithecus

Australo- pithecus anamensis

Australo- pithecus afarensis

Australo- pithecus africanus

6 mya   5 mya   4 mya   3 mya

australopithecines presents a record of considerable diversity in the genus *Australopithecus*, much more so than what was known just a few years ago. It also underscores the importance of fieldwork and discovery in order to develop an understanding of early hominin evolution.

DIVERSIFICATION OF HOMININS: THE EMERGENCE OF MULTIPLE EVOLUTIONARY LINEAGES FROM *AUSTRALOPITHECUS* (3–1 MYA)

The presence of variable hominin species of the genus *Australopithecus*, some of which were overlapping in time, indicates that the australopithecines were highly diverse, including in their locomotion, mastication, and other key aspects. About 3 mya the picture of diversity, however, becomes even more complex with the appearance of new adaptive patterns associated with the origin and evolution of a new genus, the genus *Homo*. In addition to the anatomical differences, the key distinction between the lineages representing *Australopithecus* and *Homo* is that *Australopithecus* became extinct by about 1 mya (**Figure 10.32**), whereas the lineage represented by *Homo* survives to the present. Here, we look at the two emerging forms of early hominins, *Australopithecus* and *Homo*.

***Australopithecus garhi* (2.5 mya)** Soon after discovering *Au. afarensis* at Hadar, Johanson and White began to suspect that *Au. afarensis* was the most likely ancestor of the genus *Homo*. However, the ancestral–descendant linkage between the two taxa was difficult to identify, owing to the virtual lack of a hominin fossil record in East Africa dating to 3–2 mya, the time during which earliest *Homo* likely evolved (discussed further in chapter 11). In 1999, this picture changed dramatically when

Bouri

ETHIOPIA

FIGURE 10.32

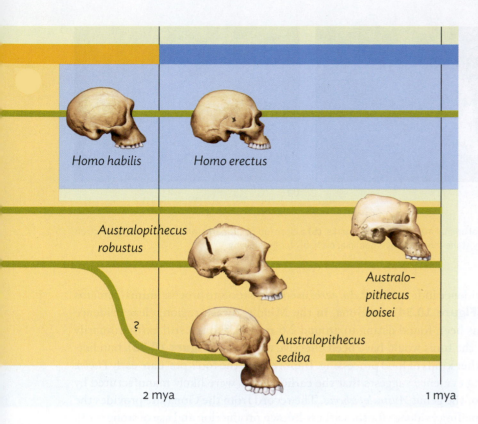

Hominin Lineages The evolutionary relationships among the various *Australopithecus* species suggest the appearance of two main lineages by 3 mya: one leading to modern *Homo sapiens* (top) and the other leading to a number of australopithecines (bottom). (This second lineage is shown here as separate lines in East Africa and South Africa.) The ancestor to australopithecine lineages is hypothesized to be *Au. afarensis*, which may be a descendant of *Ardipithecus* and *Au. anamensis*. Only the *Homo* lineage continued after 1 mya.

Homo habilis

Homo erectus

Australopithecus robustus

Australopithecus boisei

?

Australopithecus sediba

2 mya

1 mya

Australopithecus garhi A late australopithecine from East Africa that was contemporaneous with *Au. africanus* and *Au. aethiopicus* and was the likely ancestor to the *Homo* lineage.

Oldowan Complex The stone tool culture associated with *H. habilis* and, possibly, *Au. garhi*; characterized by the use of primitive chopper tools.

Lower Paleolithic The oldest part of the period during which the first stone tools were created and used, beginning with the Oldowan Complex.

the Ethiopian paleoanthropologist Berhane Asfaw and his associates discovered a new *Australopithecus* species, which they named ***Australopithecus garhi*** (*garhi* means "surprise" in the Afar language). Found in Bouri, in Ethiopia's Middle Awash region, it dated to about 2.5 mya.

Au. garhi is represented by bones, teeth, a partial skeleton, and a skull (**Figure 10.33**). Its teeth were larger than the earlier australopithecines'. Its third premolar's two cusps were almost equal in size. As in *Au. afarensis,* beneath the nose the face had a primitive projection, and the brain was small (450 cc). For the first time in hominin evolution, the ratio of arm (humerus) length to leg (femur) length was much more humanlike than apelike, resulting from the femur's lengthening. This more humanlike ratio indicates a decreased commitment to the arborealism of earlier australopithecines. These features combined—especially the chronological position at 2.5 mya and the cranial, dental, and postcranial features—suggest that *Au. garhi* was ancestral to *Homo*. Environmental reconstructions based on animal remains and other evidence indicate that this hominin lived on a lakeshore, as was typical of later australopithecines and early *Homo*.

The First Toolmakers and Users: *Australopithecus* or *Homo*? Paleoanthropologists have found very primitive stone tools from a number of sites in East Africa dating mostly to the Early Pleistocene, 2.6–1.6 mya. These stone tools are part of the **Oldowan Complex**, the first hominin culture and the earliest culture of the **Lower Paleolithic**, named by Louis and Mary Leakey from their work at Olduvai Gorge. It has long been thought that the first toolmakers may have been early *Homo*. Indeed, the Leakeys, the describers of the Oldowan Complex, assumed that the larger-brained early *Homo* found at Olduvai were the first hominins to make stone tools, rather than the contemporary smaller-brained australopithecines. However,

FIGURE 10.33

Australopithecus garhi This hominin may be the link between *Au. afarensis* and the *Homo* genus. That some of its traits are similar to those of *Au. afarensis* while others are similar to features of *Homo* suggests its intermediate status.

(a)

(b)

(c)

FIGURE 10.34

Tool Use and *Australopithecus garhi* Pictured here are **(a)** a partial animal mandible with cutmarks, **(b)** a close-up of cutmarks, and **(c)** a scanning electron micrograph of cutmarks showing a clear signature of cuts created by stone tools held by a hominin, probably for butchering.

equifinality The principle that a particular outcome can be produced by more than one process or combination of processes.

FIGURE 10.35

Oldowan-Complex Stone Tools at Gona A number of Oldowan tools were found at Gona, Ethiopia. Dating to 2.6 mya, these primitive tools were not found in association with hominin remains, so it is unclear which genera or species produced them. Among the remains were flaked pieces and "chopper" tools; these may have had various functions.

the new evidence indicates that *Au. garhi* used stone tools to process animal remains for food (**Figure 10.34**). At Gona, in the Middle Awash region, clear evidence of tools has been found dating to around 2.6 mya. Although still extraordinarily primitive, the tools would have been effective at cutting (**Figure 10.35**), butchering, and other kinds of food processing. Importantly, the tools pre-date early *Homo*. This dating evidence suggests that the earliest tools were likely manufactured by members of the genus *Australopithecus*. The record from the Gona site provides the most compelling evidence for the earliest-known production and use of stone tools.

The dominant Oldowan tools, "chopper" tools and flakes, discovered in these early hominin sites were used to remove and process the meat from various animals, mostly herbivores. At least two activities were involved: the use of flakes with sharp edges for cutting meat from bones, and the use of choppers and cobbles to break and smash the bones to access the protein-rich marrow. One of the sites best known for such findings is the FLK 22 site at Olduvai Gorge, where the Leakeys found the famous *Australopithecus boisei* cranium in the late 1950s.

Although virtually all of the record of early stone tool use dates to the Early Pleistocene, other sources of evidence indicate that first tool use may be considerably earlier than the stone tools themselves. That is, the discovery of animal bones that may have cutmarks on them from Dikika, Ethiopia, dating to 3.3 mya suggests the possibility that tool production and use may date to considerably earlier than 2.6 mya.

Until recently, paleoanthropologists have largely assumed that linear, puncture, and other kinds of marks on the bones from Dikika and other localities resulted from hominins cutting meat and getting access to protein-rich marrow by use of tools. However, paleoanthropologist Yonatan Sahle and his research team's detailed study of surface marks—including scratches, grooves, and punctures—on fossil animal bones from Bouri, Hadar, Maka, and other East African localities demonstrates a strong similarity between those marks and the marks on animal bones that have been made by crocodiles (**Figure 10.36**). Experiments with trampling animals and biting crocodiles that have been fed animal carcasses reveal that both circumstances produce marks on bones that mimic the marks that paleoanthropologists have seen on animal bones dating to millions of years ago in East Africa. Paleoanthropologists have recognized that it is important to sort out issues surrounding **equifinality** before drawing conclusions about the causes of marks on bones. Specifically, were the marks caused by crocodile chewing or stone tools wielded by early hominins? The overlap in the appearance of marks on bones needs to be fully sorted out before drawing definitive conclusions.

Other evidence for perhaps even earlier tool production and use comes from the discovery of stone objects dating to 3.3 mya from Lomekwi, West Turkana, Kenya. If these objects are stone tools, then they are the only ones of their kind at such an early date, pre-dating the record from the Gona site by 1 million years. The evidence for this record of early stone tool production and use, therefore, is preliminary, and not as compelling as the record from Gona.

Archaeologists have long assumed that the early stone tools from Olduvai and elsewhere were used for cutting animal tissues to obtain the meat. In some South African caves, bone tools found by paleoanthropologists show distinctively polished patterns of microscopic wear. Through experiments, the South African paleoanthropologist Lucinda Backwell and the French paleoanthropologist Francesco d'Errico have shown this kind of wear to be produced by digging in the ground, especially digging in termite mounds. Their finding supports the idea that early hominins ate insects (in addition to meat). While the idea of eating insects may be unappealing to our Western tastes, insects would have provided important proteins for our ancestors. Alternatively, the bone tools may have been used for digging up edible roots.

Archaeologists may not have found compelling evidence of tool production and use predating 2.6 mya at the Gona site because tools predating 2.6 mya were probably made from more ephemeral materials, such as wood and grass. In the kinds of environments in which the earliest hominins lived, these materials would not have survived. Other evidence exists, though, to suggest that australopithecines used tools. For example, australopithecines' hand bones have anatomical features associated with finer manipulation than that used by living apes. The paleoanthropologist Randall Susman has found evidence of a flexor muscle in the thumb of australopithecines that is very similar to a muscle in living humans but which is absent in apes. The flexor muscle makes possible the finer precision use of the thumb and other fingers for tool production and tool use. In addition, the internal structure of the hand bones in *Australopithecus* is similar to that of *H. sapiens*. In particular, the internal structure shows physical behavior involving forceful opposition of the thumb and fingers. This evidence, combined with the presence of stone tools and/or possibly cutmarks on animal remains in multiple settings, indicates that various species of *Australopithecus* incorporated material culture as a part of the behavioral repertoire for acquiring, processing, and consuming animal sources of protein.

EVOLUTION AND EXTINCTION OF THE AUSTRALOPITHECINES

In addition to *Au. garhi,* other australopithecine species lived in East Africa and South Africa. In East Africa, the species included earlier and later forms of robust australopithecines called ***Australopithecus aethiopicus*** (named for Ethiopia, the country where they were first found) and ***Australopithecus boisei*** (named for a benefactor who supported the discoverer's research), respectively. Some authorities refer to these hyper-robust australopithecines as the genus *Paranthropus*. The earlier hominin, *Au. aethiopicus,* from the west side of Lake Turkana, dates to about 2.5 mya and had a brain size of about 410 cc. The later hominin, *Au. boisei,* from Olduvai Gorge and around Lake Turkana, dates to 2.3–1.2 mya and had a brain size of about 510 cc. Compared with earlier australopithecines, these remarkably robust australopithecines had smaller front teeth, larger back teeth, and larger faces. Their most visually striking characteristic was a massive attachment area, on the skull, for the temporalis muscle, resulting in a well-developed sagittal crest. Both their

FIGURE 10.36

Tool Marks or Crocodile Damage? Extensive damage can be seen on this fossil animal bone from Maka, Middle Awash, Ethiopia, with microscopic images showing linear marks. The damage is likely due to crocodile biting and not stone tools. Similar marks are documented on an *Au. afarensis* humerus from the same site.

Australopithecus aethiopicus An early robust australopithecine from East Africa, with the hallmark physical traits of large teeth, a large face, and massive muscle attachments on the cranium.

Australopithecus boisei A later robust australopithecine from East Africa that was contemporaneous with *Au. robustus* and *Au. africanus* and had robust cranial traits, including large teeth, a large face, and heavy muscle attachments; formerly known as *Zinjanthropus boisei*.

(a)

(b)

FIGURE 10.37

Robust Australopithecines **(a)** *Australopithecus aethiopicus* and **(b)** *Australopithecus boisei* had a large sagittal crest; large, flaring zygomatic, or cheek, bones; and large teeth. The description of these australopithecines as robust, however, applies only to their crania and is likely related to a diet rich in hard foods. Neither of these bipedal species had a robust postcranial skeleton.

Australopithecus africanus A gracile australopithecine from South Africa that was roughly contemporaneous with *Au. aethiopicus*, *Au. garhi*, and *Au. boisei* and was likely ancestral to *Au. robustus*.

Australopithecus prometheus The earliest known australopithecine in South Africa; bore a strong resemblance to *Au. africanus*.

Australopithecus robustus A robust australopithecine from South Africa that may have descended from *Au. africanus* and had the robust cranial traits of large teeth, a large face, and heavy muscle attachments.

Australopithecus sediba A late species of australopithecine from South Africa that may have descended from *Au. africanus*, was a contemporary of *Au. robustus*, and expresses anatomical features found in *Australopithecus* and in *Homo*.

premolars and their molars were enormous. These big teeth with large chewing surfaces, combined with large chewing muscles, made robust australopithecines the ultimate grinders (**Figure 10.37**).

Australopithecines' greater cranial robusticity after about 2.5 mya indicates that they were increasingly focused on acquiring and eating foods that required more powerful chewing muscles than before. That is, they were eating harder foods. Robust australopithecines' presence in East Africa ended sometime before 1 mya, indicating that they became extinct at about that time.

The first evidence of hominins in South Africa was described by the paleoanthropologist and anatomist Raymond Dart (1893–1988). He named the species, initially found at Taung in the north-central part of the country, *Australopithecus africanus*. Found also at the limestone caves of Sterkfontein, *Au. africanus* dates to about 3–2 mya and had larger teeth than those of *Au. afarensis*. Further excavations of a fossil hominin from Sterkfontein by the paleoanthropologist Ron Clarke over a 20-year period revealed the nearly complete skeleton of an early hominin dating to 3.7 mya (**Figure 10.38**). The skeleton was dubbed "Little Foot," owing to the diminutive size of the foot bones. In addition, like *Au. afarensis*, this hominin had long arms relative to its legs. Clarke regarded this remarkable fossil as an australopithecine, calling it *Australopithecus prometheus*. However, other authorities see a strong anatomical resemblance with *Au. africanus* (**Figure 10.39**), and believe it is a member of that species. Regardless of what it is called, Little Foot represents the most complete skeleton of an australopithecine and the oldest evidence for hominins in South Africa, allowing anthropologists to extend back in time the early end of hominin evolution in this region of the African continent. Importantly, owing to its completeness, Little Foot provides a new perspective on early hominin anatomy and behavior that will be studied by paleoanthropologists for decades to come.

After about 2 mya, there were at least two descendant species of australopithecines in South Africa, *Australopithecus robustus* (sometimes called *Parathropus robustus*; **Figure 10.40**) and *Australopithecus sediba* (**Figure 10.41**), dating to 2.0–1.5 mya and 2.0 mya, respectively. *Au. robustus* is represented by fossils from the cave sites in Swartkrans, Kromdraai, and Drimolen. *Au. sediba*, discovered in 2008, is from the Malapa cave.

Australopithecus robustus, probably the longest-surviving species of the australopithecine lineage in South Africa, had large premolars, a big face, and a well-developed sagittal crest. These hominins were similar in many respects to their contemporary East African counterparts. Australopithecines' greater robusticity in South Africa and East Africa indicates a widespread adaptation involving an increased focus on foods that required heavy chewing. Anthropologists have long thought that this powerful masticatory complex—amply documented in later australopithecines—was well suited for chewing small, hard food items, such as nuts and seeds. Studies of microwear on tooth surfaces and stable carbon isotopes from fossils suggest, however, that while robust australopithecines in South and East Africa chewed tough foods, they were eating significant amounts of low-quality vegetation. In East Africa in particular, the evidence from stable carbon isotope ratios indicates that *Au. boisei* mostly ate savanna (C_4) grasses. In this way, *Au. boisei* was like other contemporary grass-consuming mammals (such as horses, pigs, and hippopotamuses) but strikingly different from all other hominins. This reliance on grasses—perhaps as much as 80% of their diet was grass—would have required heavy grinding by the jaws and teeth.

The contemporary of *Au. robustus, Au. sediba,* is represented by the partial skeleton of a young male that was about age 12 or 13 at the time of death, the partial skeleton of an adult female, and parts of at least two other individuals, including an infant. The cranial features are substantially different from those of *Au. robustus*. The American paleoanthropologist Lee Berger, who lives and works in South Africa, and his collaborators found that the face, jaws, and teeth are relatively small. The cheekbones (zygomatics) do not flair outward, unlike those of *Au. robustus*. In addition, the broad pelvis and its overall shape are more *Homo*-like. The small body and relatively long arms, however, are more like those of australopithecines.

FIGURE 10.38

Little Foot (*Australopithecus prometheus*) The earliest australopithecine from South Africa, this complete skeleton provides new and important perspective on anatomy and behavior in hominin evolution.

FIGURE 10.39

Australopithecus africanus This *Au. africanus* cranium was discovered in a series of limestone caves known as Sterkfontein. Located in South Africa, this site has been declared a UNESCO World Heritage Site. Unlike the robust australopithecines also discovered in South Africa, this *Au. africanus* cranium is gracile.

FIGURE 10.40

Australopithecus robustus Discovered in South Africa, this robust australopithecine shares many traits with East Africa's robust species. One of these traits, dietary specialization, might have led to the eventual extinction of both *Au. robustus* and the East African robust species, as they were not able to adapt to vegetation changes caused by climate change.

FIGURE 10.41

Australopithecus sediba Found in a cave in South Africa, this australopithecine is quite different from its contemporary, *Au. robustus*, in that its face and jaws are relatively gracile, at least as represented in this juvenile skull. The gracile nature of the skull may be due to the individual being a child; fully mature adult characteristics are not yet present. The very small brain is an australopithecine feature.

The Australopithecines

The australopithecines existed about 4–1 mya. Their fossils are from East Africa and South Africa. These creatures were still primitive in a number of ways, but they were more humanlike than apelike compared with the pre-australopithecines.

HOMININ	DATE(S)	LOCATION	HOMININ	DATE(S)	LOCATION
Australopithecus anamensis	4 mya	Lake Turkana, Kenya Awash Valley, Ethiopia	*Australopithecus platyops*	3.5 mya	Lomekwi, Kenya

Key features:

Skull fragments, teeth, postcrania found

Large outer cusp (like apes') on third premolar

Large canines

Parallel tooth rows in upper jaw (like apes')

Curved hand phalanx

Less than 1 m (3.3 ft) tall

Lived in wooded setting

Key features:

Skulls and teeth found

Flat face

Small brain (400–500 cc)

Contemporary with *Au. afarensis*, signaling split of australopithecine lineage into two

Lived in woodlands

HOMININ	DATE(S)	LOCATION	HOMININ	DATE(S)	LOCATION
Australopithecus afarensis	3.6–3.0 mya	Hadar, Ethiopia	*Australopithecus deyiremeda*	3.5–3.3 mya	Burtele, Ethiopia

Key features:

Skulls, teeth, postcrania (hundreds of pieces) found

Partial adult skeleton (Lucy)

Partial juvenile (3-year-old) skeleton

Small brain (430 cc)

Hyoid like apes'

Mandible larger in earlier Laetoli than in later Hadar

Smaller canines than in earlier species

Equal-size cusps on third premolar (like humans')

Parabolic tooth rows in upper jaw

Curved hand phalanges

Short legs

Footprints indicate bipedal foot pattern with no divergent big toe

Lived in wooded setting, but a more open one than associated with *Ardipithecus* or *Au. anamensis*

Key features:

Mandibles, maxillae, teeth found

Increased diversity of australopithecines—three contemporary species of *Australopithecus* in East Africa

Relatively small teeth

HOMININ	DATE(S)	LOCATION	HOMININ	DATE(S)	LOCATION
Australopithecus africanus	3.0–2.0 mya	Taung, South Africa	*Australopithecus garhi*	2.5 mya	Bouri, Ethiopia
		Sterkfontein, South Africa			
		Makapansgat, South Africa			

Key features:

Skulls, teeth, endocast (impression of brain), postcrania, two partial adult skeletons found

Small brain (450 cc)

Moderate-size teeth

Equal-size cusps on third premolar

Phalanges not curved

Adult partial skeleton has apelike leg-to-arm ratio (short legs, long arms)

Lived in open grasslands

Key features:

Skulls, teeth, postcrania found

Small brain (450 cc)

Equal-size cusps on third premolar

Teeth larger than in earlier *Au. afarensis*

Ratio of upper arm length to upper leg length more humanlike than apelike

Curved foot phalanx (like *Au. afarensis*'s)

Lived in grasslands, on lakeshore

Tool maker/user (animal butchering)

HOMININ	DATE(S)	LOCATION	HOMININ	DATE(S)	LOCATION
Australopithecus boisei	2.3–1.2 mya	Olduvai, Tanzania	*Australopithecus aethiopicus*	2.5 mya	Lake Turkana, Kenya
		Lake Turkana, Kenya			

Key features:

Skulls and teeth found

Small brain (510 cc)

Massive posterior teeth

Robust skull with sagittal crest

Lived in open grasslands

Key features:

Skull and teeth found

Small brain (410 cc)

Massive posterior teeth

Robust skull with sagittal crest

Lived in open grasslands

HOMININ	DATE(S)	LOCATION	HOMININ	DATE(S)	LOCATION
Australopithecus robustus	2.0–1.5 mya	Swartkrans, South Africa	*Australopithecus sediba*	2.0 mya	Malapa, South Africa
		Kromdraai, South Africa			
		Drimolen, South Africa			

Key features:

Skulls and teeth found

Small brain (530 cc)

Massive posterior teeth

Robust skull with sagittal crest

Lived in open grasslands

Key features:

Four partial skeletons (two adults, two juveniles)

Small brain (420 cc)

Relatively small teeth

Equal-size cusps on third premolars

Gracile face and jaws

Phalanges not curved

Short finger, long thumbs for precision grip

Long arms

Small, australopithecine-like skeleton

Homo-like pelvis

Lived in open grasslands

JULIET BROPHY, PHD

Louisiana State University

What do I do? I am a paleoanthropologist who specializes in the study of early human evolution in southern Africa. My research primarily involves analyzing fossil teeth. I developed a methodology to quantify the way we identify teeth in the family Bovidae (antelopes and buffalo) using a process called elliptical Fourier analysis. Bovids have dominated the southern African fauna for the past 4 million years, and their remains, in particular their teeth, are one of the most common fossils found at sites throughout the region. In addition, these animals are excellent environmental indicators. I identify the bovids at fossil sites and use them to reconstruct the past environments and behaviors of our early human ancestors. More recently, I adapted this methodology to analyze hominin teeth. I use the form (shape and size) of the crown outline of a hominin tooth to assess the taxonomic identity and to investigate evolutionary relationships.

What excites me most about my work? I thrive on the fact that I contribute to our endeavor to better understand human evolution. I love that I get to study teeth from species that lived so long ago. Tooth analyses are especially interesting to me because they can inform us about diet, special adaptations, evolutionary relationships, and taxonomic identity, to name just a few aspects of our ancestors' lives. I also love the interdisciplinary aspect of anthropology. I personally work very closely with an anatomist,

WATCH THE VIDEO

digital.wwnorton.
com/essanthro5

a statistician, and a computer scientist. Different backgrounds bring unique perspectives to scientific discussions. Lastly, paleoanthropology fascinates me because it is constantly changing as we find more specimens, develop new techniques, and ask new questions.

Why did I study biological anthropology? Accompanied by our father, my sister and I attended an archaeological field school in Belize the summer before I started college. When I was signing up for courses at orientation, many of the traditional ones (biology, chemistry, etc.) were full. Still wanting to fulfill my requirements, I decided to enroll in Introduction to Cultural Anthropology and Introduction to Biological Anthropology my first semester. I simply fell in love with the classes. Specifically, I found that I had to do my biological anthropology homework last or I would not get to the rest of my homework! I always wanted to research more. Then, I had a course with a professor whose passion for anthropology was utterly infectious. I took every course he and every other biological anthropologist offered at my university. In one of the textbooks, I saw a picture of my now favorite fossil, Mrs. Ples (a member of the species *Australopithecus africanus*). For some reason I have always been drawn to this skull from South Africa that dates to ~2.5 mya. I decided I was going to go to South Africa and study early human evolution. I started researching there in 2003, and I see Mrs. Ples just about every year. It seems ironic that I study teeth and Mrs. Ples is edentulous (has no teeth), but she plays an important role in both early human evolution and my path toward becoming a biological anthropologist.

Similarly, the hand has fingers with large, powerful muscles for grasping in arboreal settings, yet with a long thumb for precision gripping, perhaps for tool production and use. The brain was tiny, only about 420 cc, considerably smaller than the brains in any early *Homo*. The presence of features associated with *Homo* suggests that this australopithecine might have played a part in the ancestry of our genus. For example, genetic traits in the teeth of *Au. sediba* show strong affinities with other australopithecines in South Africa and with early and recent *Homo*. However, the presence of early *Homo* in East Africa well before *Au. sediba* indicates that the transition from *Australopithecus* to *Homo* first took place in East Africa. Nevertheless, this set of fossils from Malapa provides a record of complexity that challenges some of the earlier notions of the origins of *Homo*. Perhaps our genus originated at various times and places on the African continent.

As in East Africa, the australopithecines in South Africa went extinct by 1 mya. The reasons for this extinction are unclear. However, the lineage leading to *Homo* seems to have developed an increasingly flexible and generalized diet, whereas the later robust australopithecines' diets became less flexible and more specialized. This increasing focus on a narrower range of foods in the later robust australopithecines may have led to their extinction. Their brains show very little increase in size. The brains of South African *Au. africanus* and *Au. robustus* were only about 450 cc and 530 cc, respectively.

From the Late Miocene through the Pliocene and into the Pleistocene—about 6–1 mya—the earliest hominins began to evolve. These diverse hominins had increasingly specialized diets, and their cranial morphology reflected this specialization. However, they experienced no appreciable change in brain size or body size. Thus, evolution focused on mastication. Eventually, however, a new genus and species of hominin, ***Homo habilis***—having a larger brain and reduced chewing complex—made its appearance (**Table 10.2**). At that time, australopithecines were diverse, evolving, and a significant presence on the African landscape. This gracile hominin likely evolved from an australopithecine, and the ancestor may have been *Au. garhi*. This point in human evolution is critically important because it is the earliest record of a remarkable adaptive radiation, leading to the most prolific and widespread species of primate: us.

Homo habilis The earliest *Homo* species, a possible descendant of *Au. garhi* and an ancestor to *H. erectus*; showed the first substantial increase in brain size and was the first species definitively associated with the production and use of stone tools.

TABLE 10.2 **Trends from Late Australopithecine to Early *Homo***

FEATURE	LATE AUSTRALOPITHECINE	→	EARLY *HOMO*
Brain		Increase in size	
Face		Reduction in size	
Teeth		Reduction in size	

ANSWERING THE BIG QUESTIONS

1. What is a hominin?

- Hominins are defined by two obligate behaviors: bipedal locomotion and nonhoning chewing.

2. Why did hominins evolve from an apelike primate?

- The origin of hominins is closely tied to the origins of bipedal locomotion. This form of movement may have provided early hominins with a more efficient means of exploiting patchy forests, freeing the hands for feeding in trees and on the ground.

3. What were the first hominins?

- The pre-australopithecines were the earliest fossil hominins, dating to 7–4 mya. These hominins lived in forests.
- The pre-australopithecines gave rise to the australopithecines, dating to 4–1 mya.
- According to evidence from early stone tools of the Oldowan Complex, stable isotopes, dental microwear, and craniofacial anatomy, early hominins underwent a wide range of diet-related adaptations. The record generally reflects increasing specialization, with preferred foods narrowing from meat to grasses.
- The first hominins show considerable diversity in all anatomical characteristics, including both above and below the neck. Within the genus *Australopithecus*, some were highly terrestrial, whereas others were strongly committed to an arboreal lifestyle.

4. What was the evolutionary fate of the first hominins?

- The evolution of the australopithecine lineages resulted in generally increased robusticity of the chewing complex, no change in brain size, and eventual extinction. The change in the chewing complex reflected an increasing focus on eating hard or tough foods, especially plants.
- By 2.5 mya, at least one australopithecine lineage gave rise to the genus *Homo*. At least two other distinct australopithecine lineages, one in East Africa and one in South Africa, went extinct around 1 mya.

STUDY QUIZ

1. Which characteristic was present in the earliest hominins?

a. Communication through speech
b. Modification of stone to make tools
c. Bipedal locomotion
d. Increased brain size

2. Which skeletal characteristic is *not* associated with the hominin evolution of bipedalism?

a. A foramen magnum on the bottom of the skull
b. A shortened pelvis
c. Knees bent outward
d. An S-shaped spine

3. Which dental characteristic is *not* a hominin adaptation?

a. Nonhoning chewing
b. Small, blunt canines
c. Loss of the diastema
d. Thin tooth enamel

4. Pre-australopithecines are distinguished from apes both by bipedalism and by

a. adaptation for a savanna or grassland environment.
b. complete loss of adaptations for arboreal locomotion.
c. an intermediate or complete loss of the honing complex.
d. a significantly enlarged cranial capacity.

5. How did the australopithecine lineage leading to *Homo* adapt its diet to prevent extinction?

a. Consuming mostly low-quality vegetation
b. Relying on tough, hard foods
c. Focusing on a narrow range of foods
d. Developing a flexible and generalized diet

KEY TERMS

Ardipithecus kadabba
Ardipithecus ramidus
Australopithecus
Australopithecus aethiopicus
Australopithecus afarensis
Australopithecus africanus
Australopithecus anamensis
Australopithecus boisei
Australopithecus deyiremeda
Australopithecus garhi
Australopithecus (or *Kenyanthropus*) *platyops*
Australopithecus prometheus
Australopithecus robustus
Australopithecus sediba
equifinality
Homo habilis
Lower Paleolithic
Lucy
Oldowan Complex
Orrorin tugenensis
Sahelanthropus tchadensis

EVOLUTION REVIEW

The First Hominins

SYNOPSIS The earliest hominins arose during the transition from an arboreal lifestyle to a terrestrial lifestyle. For this reason, the fossils of these first hominin species (for example, *Ardipithecus ramidus*) have some anatomical features that reflect bipedalism and some features that reflect arborealism. Over the course of several million years, the arboreal traits, such as a grasping foot, disappear from the fossil record. Key anatomical changes that take place in later hominins include the remarkable increase in robusticity and size of the masticatory (chewing) apparatus. These changes disappear with the extinction of the hyper-robust australopithecines. Throughout the fossil record, especially after 2.6 mya, evidence of tool use is present. The use of tools may or may not have been fundamental to the success of the first hominins. Most authorities regard tool use and technology in general to be especially important for the appearance and evolution of the earliest members of our own genus, *Homo*.

Q1. Identify the two fundamental behaviors that first emerged in the pre-australopithecines and that reflected distinctive characteristics of the hominin evolutionary branch. Summarize the anatomical features present in early hominin species that are indicative of each of these behaviors.

Q2. Biological anthropologists often describe bipedalism as an adaptive trade-off, a characteristic with both benefits and costs associated with its evolution. Give two examples of the evolutionary benefits bipedalism provided to our early hominin ancestors. Also, give two examples of the evolutionary costs of bipedalism that are still encountered by humans today.

Q3. What factors explain the evolution of the robust faces and jaws of *Australopithecus*, especially in the Early Pleistocene?

HINT Focus on the adaptive advantages of robust faces and jaws, and then consider the environmental factors that may have caused the conditions that *Australopithecus* was adapting to.

Q4. Discuss the major anatomical differences between some of the earliest hominins (for example, *Ardipithecus ramidus*) and some of the latest australopithecines (for example, *Australopithecus garhi* and *Australopithecus boisei*). Also, contrast the cranial and dental morphology of the gracile and robust australopithecines. Which of these two groups do you think is more likely to be directly ancestral to the first members of the genus *Homo*?

Q5. What role might climate fluctuations have played in the appearance and evolution of the first hominins?

HINT Climate change in the Late Miocene caused tropical forests to shift to patchy forests and open grasslands and changed the kinds of foods that were available.

ADDITIONAL READINGS

Cartmill, M. and F. H. Smith. 2009. *The Human Lineage.* Hoboken, NJ: Wiley-Blackwell.

Conroy, G. C. and H. Pontzer. 2012. *Reconstructing Human Origins: A Modern Synthesis,* 3rd ed. New York: W. W. Norton.

Gibbons, A. 2006. *The First Human: The Race to Discover Our Earliest Ancestors.* New York: Doubleday.

Relethford, J. H. 2017. *50 Great Myths of Human Evolution: Understanding Misconceptions about Our Origins.* Chichester, UK: Wiley-Blackwell.

Simpson, S. W. 2010. The earliest hominins. Pp. 314–340 in C. S. Larsen, ed. *A Companion to Biological Anthropology.* Chichester, UK: Wiley-Blackwell.

Located on the outer margins of the city of Johannesburg, South Africa, the Rising Star Cave produced nearly 1,700 hominin fossils, far exceeding the number from any other site in the entire continent of Africa. The fossils found by excavators represent an early form of *Homo* combining both ancient and modern characteristics. Pictured here are field team members Marina Elliott and Becca Peixotto.

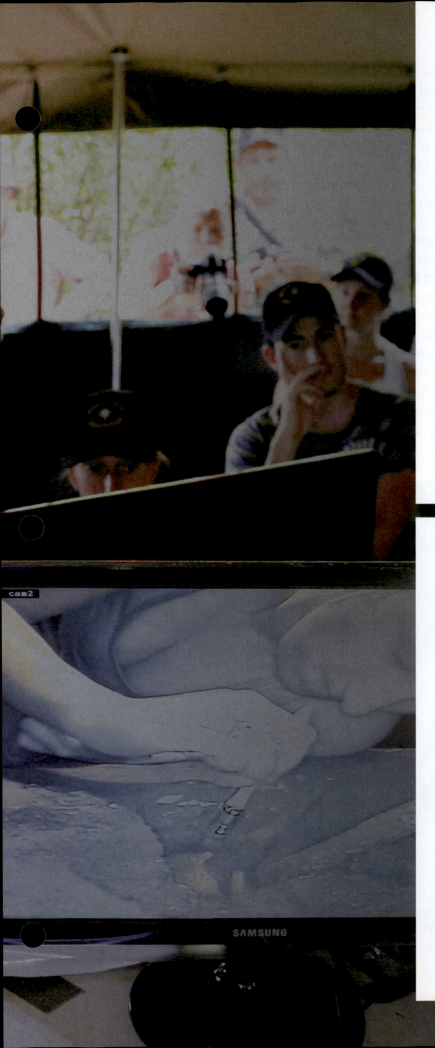

11

The Origins and Evolution of Early *Homo*

BIG QUESTIONS

1. What characteristics define the genus *Homo*?
2. What were the earliest members of the genus *Homo*?
3. What are the key evolutionary trends and other developments in early *Homo*?

Charles Darwin was struck by the great anatomical similarity of living humans and African apes. In 1871, writing about human origins without having seen a human fossil, he settled on Africa as the birthplace of the earliest hominins. But he was not the only leading scientist in the nineteenth century to think about human origins and where humans first evolved. Ernst Haeckel (1834–1919), Germany's preeminent anatomist and evolutionary biologist of the late nineteenth century, came up with an entirely different origins scenario. He reasoned that the Asian great ape, the orangutan, is more anatomically similar to humans than are the African great apes. Asia, not Africa, he concluded, must have been the hominins' ancestral homeland. In his extensive scholarly work about human origins and evolution, Haeckel went to great lengths to describe what the first hominin would have looked like. He even went so far as to propose a genus name for the ancestor: *Pithecanthropus,* meaning "ape-man."

Haeckel's books on early human evolution and its Asian origins profoundly inspired a precocious Dutch teenager, Eugène Dubois (1858–1940). Fascinated by Haeckel's ideas about evolution, Dubois devoured Darwin's *On the Origin of Species*. He enrolled in medical school at the University of Amsterdam at age 19 and received his medical degree at 26. In addition to being a well-trained physician, Dubois was a superb scientist and was hired as a lecturer in the university's anatomy department. At the same time, his interests in evolution deepened. He became convinced that to truly *study* human origins, he had to *find* human fossils. Within a year of being promoted to lecturer, he quit his job, gathered his resources, got hired as a physician for the Dutch colonial government, and moved with his wife and their baby to the Dutch East Indies (the modern country of Indonesia, which includes the islands of Sumatra and Borneo; **Figure 11.1**). His friends, neighbors, and associates thought he was reckless at best to risk his family's well-being as he looked for something that might never be found. Soon after landing in Sumatra in December 1887, Dubois assumed his new responsibilities as a physician at a military hospital, spending his money and free time in the pursuit of fossils. After trying to juggle medicine and fossil hunting, he talked the Dutch colonial government into letting him leave his day job as a physician to work for the Dutch as a full-time paleontologist. With the help of two civil engineers and a group of 50 convicts, he searched the island but found nothing. Meanwhile, he suffered from discomfort, fatigue, illness, and depression.

FIGURE 11.1

Dutch East Indies On the island of Java, one of the southernmost islands of what is now Indonesia, Dubois discovered the hominin fossil later identified as *Homo erectus*.

Desperate to avoid returning to Holland without having found fossils, Dubois pleaded with his superiors to let him shift his focus from Sumatra to nearby Java. The authorities accepted his assurances that Java would produce fossils. After his move to Java, Dubois heard about bones appearing out of the eroding banks of the Solo River, near the village of Trinil. Soon after commencing excavations in the late summer of 1891, he and his field crew discovered a human molar. Within a couple of months, they found a partial skull (**Figure 11.2**), and later in the following year they found a complete femur. The skull was extraordinary. It was clearly not from *Homo sapiens*—it had a low and long braincase, no forehead to speak of, and large browridges like apes'. Was the skull from an ape, a human, or something between the two? By measuring the braincase's volume, Dubois estimated that in life the brain had been about 1,000 cc, too big for a modern ape (a chimpanzee's brain is 400 cc) and too small for a modern human (the average human brain today is about 1,450 cc). He had found what he was looking for: the human ancestor. In fact, Dubois's anatomical study revealed that the femur was essentially identical to a modern human's—this primitive human ancestor was fully bipedal. Convinced that he had found what Haeckel had predicted, he called his fossil hominin **Pithecanthropus erectus**, meaning "upright-walking ape-man."

Dubois's ideas and the fossils he found met with mixed reactions, mostly negative. However, as the years went by, others found more hominin fossils in Java and elsewhere in Asia. It became clear to most anthropologists that Dubois's fossils from Java were early members of our genus but a different species, and these hominins are now called **Homo erectus**. Dubois's fossil turned out to not be from the earliest hominin or even from the earliest species of *Homo* (see chapter 10 and later in this chapter).

Dubois was wrong in thinking that evidence of the earliest human would be found in Southeast Asia, but he was working in a scientific vacuum. Without today's fossil record to guide him, he drew the best possible conclusion from the evidence available and made crucially important discoveries about the genus *Homo*'s evolution. The only scientist of the time who set out a research plan to test a hypothesis about early human ancestors, he sought fossil evidence to establish evolutionary relationships. In contrast to the great evolutionists of the nineteenth century—Darwin, Haeckel, Huxley, and others—he endeavored to use fossils, not living animals' comparative anatomy, to test his hypothesis. This revolutionary development in anthropology set the stage for paleoanthropology, the study of early human evolution.

This chapter focuses on the appearance and evolution of the earliest members of the genus *Homo*, of which there were at least four species, including *Homo habilis*, *Homo erectus*, *Homo naledi*, and *Homo floresiensis*. They were the hominins that began to develop the characteristic behaviors that we see in living humans, that increasingly employed intelligence and displayed adaptive flexibility, and that first depended on material culture. During early *Homo*'s evolution, hominins began to colonize areas of the world outside Africa. The earliest fossil evidence, from around 2.8–1.0 mya, indicates that early *Homo*—*H. habilis* and *H. erectus*—lived at the same time as other hominins, the later australopithecines (discussed in chapter 10). In some key respects, early *Homo* adapted very differently from the australopithecines.

FIGURE 11.2

Java Man Dubois originally named this hominin fossil *Pithecanthropus erectus*, though it was nicknamed "Java Man" after the island on which it was found. Dubois recovered the hominin remains, including this partial cranium.

Pithecanthropus erectus The name used by Eugène Dubois for his first fossil discovery, which later became known as *Homo erectus*.

Homo erectus An early species of *Homo* and the likely descendant of *H. habilis*; the first hominin species to move out of Africa into Asia and Europe.

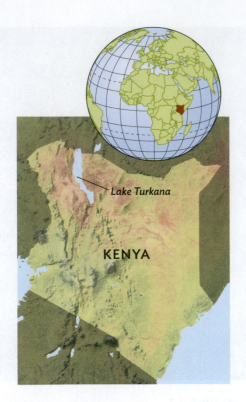

Lake Turkana

KENYA

11.1 *Homo habilis:* The First Species of the Genus *Homo*

THE PATH TO HUMANNESS: BIGGER BRAINS, TOOL USE, AND ADAPTIVE FLEXIBILITY

Modern humans are distinctive in having large brains and in depending on material culture for survival. Rather than relying on their bodies for the collection, processing, and eating of food, modern humans rely on tools and technology as part of their adaptive strategy. These attributes are what scientists looked for in the fossil record when they sought the first species of our genus. Which of the multiple hominin species in the Late Pliocene and Early Pleistocene showed brain size expansion? Which of the hominins with brain size expansion likely depended on tools and material culture for promoting adaptive success and behavioral flexibility?

Soon after the discovery of the massively robust australopithecine *Australopithecus boisei* (fossil OH 5 from Olduvai Gorge; see chapter 10), remains of a hominin having jaws, teeth, and a face that were relatively smaller and a brain that was relatively larger were found, also in Olduvai Gorge. Its describers—Louis Leakey, Phillip Tobias (1925–2012), and John Napier—recognized the significance of this combination of characteristics and named the new hominin ***Homo habilis*** (meaning "handy man"). *Homo habilis* is now known from Tanzania, Kenya, Ethiopia, Malawi, and South Africa—the same geographic distribution as that of the contemporary australopithecines (**Figure 11.3**). *Homo habilis* found on the eastern side of Kenya's Lake Turkana is sometimes called *Homo rudolfensis* (**Figure 11.4**). The major difference is that *H. rudolfensis* is somewhat bigger

(a)

(b)

(c)

FIGURE 11.3

Homo habilis Many fossils of this hominin species have been recovered from East Africa and South Africa. **(a)** This specimen, known as OH 24 or "Twiggy," was discovered in Tanzania in 1968. Dating to 1.8 mya, Twiggy had a larger brain and a less protruding face than those of australopithecines. **(b)** Slightly younger than Twiggy, this lower jaw, known as OH 7, was found in Tanzania in 1960 and dates to 1.75 mya. Given its small dental size, researchers estimated that the brain size would have been smaller than in other *H. habilis* fossils. **(c)** This cranium, KNM-ER 1813, was discovered in Kenya in 1973 and dates to 1.9 mya. Its brain capacity is somewhat smaller than that of other, later *H. habilis* specimens.

than *H. habilis*. Because they have the same general body plan and overall morphology (bigger brains, smaller faces), here the two species are discussed as one species, *H. habilis*.

As Leakey and his associates recognized, *H. habilis* differs in its anatomy from the robust australopithecines dating to about the same time in East Africa and South Africa. *Australopithecus boisei* had an enormous chewing complex—its back teeth, jaws, and face were very large—but it had a small brain. In sharp contrast, *H. habilis* had a smaller chewing complex and a larger brain. Combined, the reduced chewing complex and increased brain size gave *H. habilis*'s skull a more rounded, or globular, appearance. Most anthropologists agree these attributes indicate that *H. habilis* began the lineage leading to modern humans.

Still unconfirmed is the identity of *H. habilis*'s immediate ancestor. Tim White's morphological comparisons between *H. habilis* and the earlier australopithecines suggest that the ancestor of *H. habilis* was *Australopithecus garhi* because its face, jaws, and teeth are most similar to *H. habilis*'s. White suggests that the evolutionary transition and appearance of *Homo* was sometime around 3.0–2.5 mya. Consistent with this interpretation is the discovery of hominin fossils that combine australopithecine and *Homo* morphological characteristics. For example, from the site of Ledi-Geraru in the Afar region of Ethiopia, a partial mandible dating to 2.8 mya combines large teeth (*Australopithecus*) with *Homo*-like morphology. The discovery of a hominin with australopithecine characteristics meets the expectation of early *Homo*; that is, the hominins represented by the Ledi-Geraru mandible have only minor differences with the ancestral hominins.

HOMO HABILIS AND AUSTRALOPITHECUS: SIMILAR IN BODY PLAN

For many years, *H. habilis* was known from just skulls and teeth. Anthropologists had no idea what the rest of the skeleton looked like. Excavations at Olduvai Gorge in the 1980s by Donald Johanson and his field teams (**Figure 11.5**) led to

FIGURE 11.4

Homo habilis Owing to its larger size, this fossil hominin is believed by some researchers to be a separate species from *H. habilis*, called *Homo rudolfensis*.

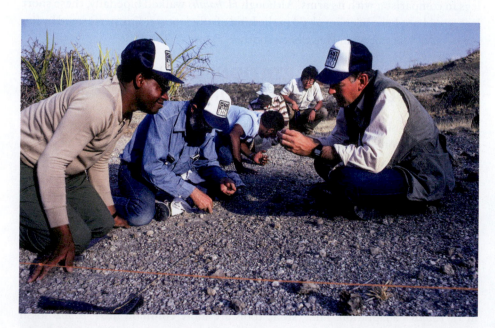

FIGURE 11.5

Excavating *Homo habilis* Donald Johanson and his team, including Prosper Ndessokia, Gerry Eck, Berhane Asfaw, and Gen Suwa, excavating a partial skeleton of *Homo habilis* in 1986.

Olduvai Gorge

TANZANIA

CONCEPT CHECK

Homo habilis: The First Member of Our Lineage

Homo habilis was the first hominin to have anatomical and behavioral characteristics that foreshadowed the evolution of *Homo sapiens:* greater intelligence, reliance on tools, and dietary and behavioral flexibility.

LOCATION/SITES	Africa (Olduvai Gorge, Lake Turkana, Afar, Omo, Uraha, Sterkfontein)	
CHRONOLOGY	2.8–1.8 mya	

BIOLOGY AND CULTURE (COMPARED WITH AUSTRALOPITHECINES)

FEATURE	EVIDENCE	OUTCOME
Tool use (Oldowan)	Skulls	Smaller face and smaller jaws
	Teeth	Reduced size
Intelligence	Brain size	Increase (to 650 cc)
Diet (scavenging, plant collecting)	Plants available, butchery of animals	Perhaps more generalized, increased access to animal sources of protein
	Body size	No significant change
Locomotion	Ratio of leg length to arm length	No significant change

the discovery of a very fragmentary but important skeleton of *H. habilis,* known as OH 62. The skeleton is from an individual that was short—about 1.1 m (3.5 ft)—like the australopithecines. Also like the australopithecines, this individual had short legs in comparison with its arms. Although *H. habilis* walked bipedally, these short legs would not have been involved in the kind of efficient striding performed by living people. The gait would have been shorter.

HOMO HABILIS'S ADAPTATION: INTELLIGENCE AND TOOL USE BECOME IMPORTANT

Homo habilis's short legs indicate that the species retained a primitive form of bipedalism, more australopithecine than human. Much more telling about *H. habilis*'s adaptation and evolution are skull and teeth morphology and evidence of the making and use of stone tools. Fossil skulls and fossil teeth reveal that this hominin ancestor had a larger brain, smaller chewing muscles, and smaller teeth than those of earlier and contemporary hominins, the australopithecines. Both the brain enlargement and the masticatory changes may be linked to the growing importance of tools. Anatomical evidence from the study of hand bones, such as the presence of muscles that would have provided the necessary precision grip, suggests that *H. habilis* and at least some of the australopithecines made and used tools. For several reasons, toolmaking and tool use were likely more important in *H. habilis*'s adaptation. First, stone tools are more common in *H. habilis* fossil sites than in *Australopithecus* fossil sites. Moreover, the presence of butchery marks produced by a hominin using stone tools indicates clear access to animal sources of protein. Second, *H. habilis*'s expanding brain size indicates that it was smarter than *Australopithecus,* with a kind of cognitive advancement almost certainly linked to toolmaking and tool use. That is, *H. habilis* and the lineage it founded became reliant on intelligence, toolmaking, and tool use as central means of adaptation. In contrast, the australopithecines became increasingly specialized, focusing on a narrower range of foods that required extremely heavy chewing. They may have made and used tools, but tools were not as fundamental to their survival and adaptation. *Homo habilis*'s behavioral advances laid the foundation for later hominins' success, including their rapid spread out of Africa and to other areas of the globe.

HABITAT CHANGES AND INCREASING ADAPTIVE FLEXIBILITY

Environmental reconstruction of the East African and South African landscapes at 2.5 mya provides some insight into early *Homo*'s adaptive shifts. This reconstruction indicates a spread of warm-season (C_4) grasses, increasing habitat diversity, and increasing food resources exploited by early hominins. Such information, along with skull and teeth morphology, suggests early *Homo*'s increasing dietary versatility. Tools may have played a central role in these early hominins' ability to exploit this increasingly diverse landscape. That is, stone tools were likely important for digging roots and tubers and for processing them for consumption. Such extremely primitive technology did not include the kinds of tools associated with later hominins that were clearly social, predatory hunters (discussed later; see "Evolution of *Homo erectus:* Biological Change, Adaptation, and Improved Nutrition"). Still, tools increased these early hominins' *capability* of eating a greater range of foods, most of it being plants or small animals, the latter acquired by luck, opportunity, and perhaps scavenging. This dietary shift to include more access to animal sources of protein may be what spelled adaptive success for early *Homo* and extinction for late *Australopithecus.*

11.2 *Homo erectus:* Early *Homo* Goes Global

Beginning around 1.8 mya, a new hominin appeared, *H. erectus,* which had anatomical characteristics that distinguished it from *H. habilis.* As discussed earlier, *H. erectus* was a descendant taxon of *H. habilis* and was among the earliest fossil hominins to be described in the scientific literature, having been found in the late nineteenth century by Eugène Dubois at Trinil in Java.

In the century since Dubois began his work in Java, many fossils with the same general attributes as the Trinil skull—large browridges, a long and low skull, and a bigger brain—have been found elsewhere in Asia, and also in Europe and Africa (**Figure 11.6**). These hominins collectively date to about 1.8 mya–300,000 yBP. During this fascinating and dynamic period of human evolution, hominins first left Africa, colonized vast areas of Asia and Europe, and underwent fundamental changes in culture and adaptation that shaped human biological variation. By any measure, this spread of hominins reflects their enormous success.

FIGURE 11.6

Homo erectus Sites Fossils of *H. erectus* have been discovered throughout Africa, Europe, and Asia.

- **Homo erectus** fossil finds
- **Homo erectus** archaeological sites (without hominin bones)

HOMO ERECTUS IN AFRICA (1.8–0.3 MYA)

The earliest record of *H. erectus* comes from Africa, less than 2 mya. At that time, the last australopithecines were still around in East Africa and South Africa, and comparing the fossils of each reveals great differences in anatomy and adaptation between *H. erectus* and the last australopithecines (**Figure 11.7**). Among the earliest and the most spectacular of the *H. erectus* fossils is an 80% complete juvenile skeleton from Nariokotome, on the western side of Lake Turkana (**Figure 11.8**)

The presence of a sagittal crest to anchor large chewing muscles reflects this species' hard diet of nuts and seeds.

The large premolars and molars enabled this species to grind hard nuts and seeds.

The lack of a sagittal crest indicates this species had smaller chewing muscles, reflecting a much softer diet.

This species had much smaller molars and thinner enamel, reflecting its softer diet.

Australopithecus boisei

Homo erectus

FIGURE 11.7

Australopithecus boisei* versus *Homo erectus While both of these genera were contemporaneous for a period of time in Africa, there are important differences in their cranial and dental morphologies.

FIGURE 11.9

Nariokotome Skull The skull of Nariokotome Boy has been invaluable for relating brain size and overall body size in *H. erectus*. Why is that relationship important for us to know?

FIGURE 11.8

Nariokotome Boy Researchers have debated the exact age of Nariokotome Boy, also known as Turkana Boy, but he was likely around 11 years old. Discovered in 1984, this *H. erectus* fossil is one of the most complete early hominin skeletons ever found.

This remarkably complete skeleton, dubbed "Nariokotome Boy," dates to about 1.6 mya. In contrast to *Australopithecus* and *H. habilis,* the Nariokotome hominin has several quintessentially modern anatomical features. One of the most striking modern characteristics is the combination of relatively short arms and long legs. That is, the *H. erectus* body plan is much more like that of a living human in its ratio of arm length to leg length. This change in limb proportions in *H. erectus* signals the beginning of a major alteration in the pattern of bipedal locomotion: *H. erectus* became completely committed to terrestrial life by adopting a fully modern stride. Life in the trees became a thing of the past.

Features of the pelvic bones and overall size indicate that the Nariokotome individual was likely a young adolescent male. He was quite tall, about 166 cm (65 in). Had he survived to adulthood, he would have grown to nearly 180 cm (71 in) in height. This change in height in comparison with *H. habilis* and the australopithecines indicates an enormous body size increase in this taxon. In addition, the Nariokotome skeleton's cranial capacity was about 900 cc (**Figure 11.9**). Even taking into account the body size increase (brain size and body size are roughly correlated), this expansion in brain size is large compared with similar changes in earlier hominins.

The Nariokotome skeleton is just one of many *H. erectus* fossils from East Africa. At Ileret, on the eastern side of Lake Turkana, the partial skull of a very small

(a)

(b)

FIGURE 11.10

Footprints from Ileret, Kenya **(a)** This exposed surface at Ileret reveals numerous animal and hominin footprints. **(b)** A site drawing shows just the hominin footprints. Note the orientations of the tracks, which show different individuals walking at different times and in different directions. Can you figure out how many hominins made these tracks?

FIGURE 11.11

Daka Partial Cranium The Daka *H. erectus* fossil from the Middle Awash Valley, Ethiopia, has large browridges, a characteristic of many other *H. erectus* specimens in Africa and elsewhere.

FIGURE 11.12

Gona Partial Cranium The skull is similar to other *Homo erectus* skulls with its pronounced supraorbital torus. The adult female has the smallest cranial capacity (598 cc) of any known African *H. erectus*.

H. erectus—possibly a female—was found in geologic strata dating to about 1.6 mya. The skull's diminutive size and small browridges indicate the very high degree of variation in *H. erectus*. Some *H. erectus* individuals had very large and robust bones, whereas others—such as the hominin from Ileret—were quite gracile.

Just as significant as the Ileret fossil is the presence of multiple sets of footprints on an Ileret landscape dating to around 1.5 mya (**Figure 11.10**). Recall the footprints from Laetoli discussed in chapter 10, representing *Australopithecus afarensis* and dating to around 3.5 mya. These footprints provide a kind of fossilized picture of behavior: evidence of how early human ancestors walked. They reveal that the Ileret *H. erectus* walked just like a modern human. In fact, these prints provide the first solid evidence of fully modern walking. We know this because the footprints have all the fundamentals that we see in our feet, namely, the double arch (the long one extending from your heel to the base of your toes and the shorter side-to-side one in back of your toes) and an **adducted** big toe (the big toe is close to the second toe), whereas in the Laetoli fossil the big toe and second toe are **abducted** (spread apart). Moreover, the Ileret footprints are big, as would be expected given the great heights of *H. erectus* compared to earlier hominins. The pelvis and leg bones of *H. erectus* had strongly indicated the modern form of walking. The Ileret footprints provided further proof that this hominin had a foot adapted for activities requiring travel, such as hunting and long-distance walking, behaviors likely first seen with *H. erectus*.

Other key *H. erectus* fossils from sites in Africa include a partial cranium found in Olduvai Gorge and dating to about 1.2 mya, a partial cranium and post-crania found at Daka and dating to 1 mya (**Figure 11.11**), a partial cranium and pelvis found at Buia and dating to about 1 mya, a partial cranium and a pelvis found at Gona and dating to 1.2 mya (**Figure 11.12**), and a cranium found at

Bodo and dating to about 600,000 yBP (**Figure 11.13**). The Daka, Gona, and Bodo hominin fossils are from the Middle Awash Valley (**Figure 11.14**), and the Buia cranium is from Eritrea. In contrast to the Nariokotome skull and the skull from Ileret, the skulls from Olduvai Gorge, Daka, Gona, Buia, and Bodo are very robust, having thick cranial bones and very large browridges. At just under 600 cc, the Gona cranium has the smallest brain size of any *H. erectus* in Africa. The Olduvai cranium's browridges are the largest of any known fossil hominin (**Figure 11.15**). This greater size can only partially be accounted for by the Nariokotome hominin's immaturity, because the other *H. erectus* hominins were fully mature adult males. The pelvis from Buia is strikingly similar to that of modern humans, suggesting that our pelvic anatomy had its beginnings in the early Pleistocene.

During the process of cleaning the facial bones of the Bodo skull, Tim White found a series of barely visible linear marks on the left cheek, around the left eye orbit and the nose, and elsewhere on the cranium (**Figure 11.16**). Microscopic analysis of the marks indicates that they were caused by a stone tool, perhaps as a contemporary hominin removed the soft tissue covering the facial bones. This activity may have been related to some ritual or to cannibalism. If so, it is the earliest evidence of body manipulation in human evolution.

FIGURE 11.13

Bodo Cranium This *H. erectus* fossil has different cranial features from other specimens of this species. Note the large browridges and thick cranial bones.

HOMO ERECTUS IN ASIA (1.8–0.3 MYA)

The earliest evidence of hominins outside of Africa is a series of primitive stone tools dating to 2.1 mya and excavated at Shangchen, China, by Chinese paleoanthropologist Zhaoyu Zhu and his field team. The tools were likely manufactured by *H. erectus*, but that is impossible to tell in the absence of associated hominin fossils. The earliest fossil evidence of *H. erectus* in Asia consists of five skulls, other bones,

HOMO ERECTUS AT 1 MILLION YEARS AGO:
THE DAKA LANDSCAPE OF THE MIDDLE AWASH, ETHIOPIA

The source of a continuous fossil record from before 6 mya to about 50,000 yBP, the Middle Awash Valley is among the most fossil-rich regions in the world. The Daka Member (*Daka* being an abbreviation of the place-name Dakanihylo and *Member* meaning "part") is among the most interesting areas of the Middle Awash. The area's rich fossil record of plants and animals dates to around 1 mya, the time of *Homo erectus*, and thus provides us access to the habitat there during this period of human evolution.

The American paleoanthropologist W. Henry Gilbert and his team have studied the thousands of fossils, ranging from the tiny ancestors of mice to the large animals. The record indicates a savanna/grasslands setting with wooded areas, ample water, and floodplains, unlike the dry desert of the region today.

This reconstruction shows what the Daka landscape might have looked like a million years ago, when *H. erectus* hunted and gathered there. The following animal taxa are represented:

1 *Felids* (ancestors of lions and domestic cats) are exclusively carnivorous. Their abundance indicates that the area included plenty of animals that served as prey for them.

2 *Cercopithecids* ([2a] *Theropithecus oswaldi* and [2b] *Cercopithecoides alemayehui*) suggest the presence of forests and permanent rivers with associated wetlands.

3 *Equids* (ancestors of asses) indicate a broad range of habitats.

4 *Giraffids* (ancestors of giraffes) indicate the presence of large acacia trees.

5 *Hippopotamids* (ancestors of hippopotamuses) indicate the continual availability of deep water and adjacent grasslands.

6 *Elephantids* (ancestors of elephants) are grazers and browsers and occupy a wide range of habitats.

7 *Rhinocerids* (at least two genera, ancestors of rhinoceroses) are typically associated with standing water (ponds) and grasslands.

8 *Suids* (ancestors of pigs) indicate the availability of water but with sometimes semiarid conditions.

9 *Murids* (ancestors of grass mice or rats) are especially common today in grasslands and savannas.

10 *Bovids* (ancestors of today's impalas, gazelles, sheep, ibex, oryx, kudu, and other bovines of the African landscape) are numerous and indicate the presence of woodlands and brush thickets, large streams, and water supply continually throughout the year. The fossil record indicates that the grasslands would have been full of herds of different bovid species.

11 *Hominins* (ancestors of *Homo sapiens*) at this point in their evolution are adaptable to a wide range of habitats but are exclusively terrestrial.

Very large
browridges

Thick cranial
bone

Large area for
muscle attachment
on the posterior, or
rear, of the cranium

FIGURE 11.15

Olduvai Cranium This *H. erectus* fossil, known as OH 9, has the largest browridges of any hominin species.

and many stone tools found in Dmanisi, Georgia (**Figure 11.17**). The date for this important site, 1.8 mya, indicates that *H. erectus* colonized western Asia very soon after it began to evolve in Africa (**Figure 11.18**). Compared with some members of the African *H. erectus,* these hominins' faces and jaws were smaller and their browridges were less developed—all *H. habilis*–like facial characteristics. However, in overall shape the Dmanisi hominins' mandible and face strikingly resemble those of both Nariokotome Boy and the Ileret skull from East Africa. Also, like those of

FIGURE 11.16

Ritual Defleshing? Viewed through a scanning electron microscope, cutmarks such as this one (arrows) indicate that stone tools were used to remove flesh from the Bodo skull. The arrows point to the groove left by the stone tool.

the Nariokotome skeleton, the leg bones are relatively long compared with the arm bones, at least as shown in the two partial skeletons—a child and an adult—found at the site. The oldest *H. erectus* from Dmanisi has a cranial capacity of only about 650 cc. The strong resemblance between the Dmanisi *H. erectus* and at least some of the East African *H. erectus* individuals indicates the relatedness of the Asian *H. erectus* and African *H. erectus*.

In far western Asia, field teams discovered a partial *H. erectus* cranium—fragments of frontal and parietal bones—of an adult male dating to much later (about 500,000 yBP) in a rock quarry near the village of Kocabaş, in the Büyük Menderes, a large valley system in western Turkey. Like many other *H. erectus* specimens from Africa and from Asia, the Kocabaş cranium has massive brow-ridges and a **sagittal keel**—a slight ridge that runs along the sagittal suture atop the skull. According to the American paleoanthropologist John Kappelman and his colleagues, the cranium's internal surface appears to have had a bone infection.

Since Dubois completed his fieldwork in the 1890s, *H. erectus* fossils have been found at a number of sites in Indonesia, especially in Java. Fossils from one of these sites, Sangiran, date to as early as 1.5–1.3 mya. This early date shows that *H. erectus* rapidly spread eastward from western Asia. Thus, once the taxon had first evolved, it colonized areas outside of Africa at a swift pace, perhaps within less than a few hundred thousand years. The emerging picture is of *H. erectus*'s

FIGURE 11.17

Dmanisi Extensive paleoanthropological investigations took place in the town of Dmanisi after early stone tools were discovered there in 1984. Since 1991, more than 20 hominin remains have been found, including skull 5 shown here. Discovered in 2005, the remarkable completeness of the skull—the most complete of Early Pleistocene *Homo*—helps paleoanthropologists to understand the full morphology of the cranium, mandible, and teeth of some of the earliest members of our genus. Skull 5 has the combined features typical of *H. erectus* in having a long, low cranium and relatively large browridges. The individual combines a small braincase (brain size is 546 cc) with a large face. The high level of cranial robusticity compared to the other individuals at Dmanisi indicates that skull 5 is likely a male. This skull and other remains from Dmanisi provide evidence for a single evolving lineage of early *Homo* and for continuity of evolution from at least 1.8 mya across Africa, Europe, and Asia.

FIGURE 11.18

First Migration *Homo erectus* was the first hominin species to migrate out of Africa and expand into Europe and Asia. This map illustrates the movement: **(1)** earliest *H. erectus* in East Africa (Lake Turkana; ~1.8 mya); **(2)** early expansion of *H. erectus* into western Asia (Dmanisi, Georgia; ~1.7 mya); **(3)** rapid eastward expansion of *H. erectus* into southeastern Asia (Sangiran, Indonesia; ~1.8–1.6 mya); **(4)** earliest butchered animal bones and stone tools attributed to *H. erectus* in northeastern Asia (Majuangou, China; ~1.7 mya); and **(5)** earliest fossil evidence of *H. erectus* in western Europe (Atapuerca, Spain; ~1.2 mya).

sagittal keel A slight ridge of bone found along the midline sagittal suture of the cranium, which is typically found on *H. erectus* skulls.

FIGURE 11.19

Sangiran *Homo erectus* Excavations in Indonesia have uncovered many hominin fossils, including Dubois's *H. erectus* and, shown here, the Sangiran 17 fossil. Note the long cranium, low forehead, and large browridges.

rapid, widespread movement throughout Asia. This rapid spread illustrates the hominin's high degree of adaptive success, a factor likely related to increasing intelligence, increasing reliance for survival on both material culture and tools, overall greater ability at acquiring food, and other resources in new and novel settings.

Dating to 800,000 yBP, the most complete skull from eastern Asia is the Sangiran 17 cranium. Like the African fossils, it has thick cranial bones and large browridges (**Figure 11.19**). Its cranial capacity is about 1,000 cc, and like other *H. erectus* skulls from Asia, Africa, and Europe, it has a sagittal keel.

Later *H. erectus* fossils from Java, dating to between 1 mya and 500,000 yBP, include fossil remains from Sangiran and Sambungmacan, plus the original Trinil skull found by Dubois. These fossils show many of the same physical characteristics as the earlier ones but also some changes, such as larger brains and smaller teeth. Some of the best information about the first hominins outside Africa comes from China. The earliest hominin fossil is a partial skull from Gongwangling, near the village of Lantian, Shaanxi Province. The skull dates to about 1.2 mya. Like the fossils from Java, this specimen has large, well-developed browridges and thick cranial bones. Its cranial capacity is about 800 cc. The skull postdates the earliest evidence of hominins in north China, from Majuangou, by nearly 500,000 years. Both the animal bones with butchery marks and the stone artifacts found by the Chinese geologist R. X. Zhu and his collaborators date to nearly 1.7 mya, making them the earliest specimens from Asia.

The site yielding the most impressive *H. erectus* remains in eastern Asia is the cave in Zhoukoudian, on Dragon Bone Hill, near the modern city of Beijing. After being discovered in the 1920s, the cave was excavated into the early 1940s (**Figure 11.20**). Deposits dating to 780,000–400,000 yBP contained, in fragments, the bones and teeth of 40–50 individuals, as well as many stone tools and food remains (**Figure 11.21**). Tragically, the entire collection of priceless bones was lost during World War II, late in 1941. Fortunately, shortly before the loss, the eminent German anatomist and anthropologist Franz Weidenreich (1873–1948) had thoroughly studied the bones and teeth, written detailed scientific reports, and made cast replicas, drawings, and photographs (**Figure 11.22**). This record has allowed scientists to continue studying the Zhoukoudian remains.

FIGURE 11.20

Zhoukoudian During excavations at this site in China between 1923 and 1927, *H. erectus* remains were discovered. Excavations continued until the early 1940s. Today, the place is a UNESCO World Heritage Site.

FIGURE 11.21

Cave at Zhoukoudian The cave in which *H. erectus*'s remains were discovered took millions of years to form. In addition to the remains, stone tools were found there.

Originally, a limestone mound stood where the cave is now.

Over time, groundwater dissolved the limestone, hollowing out a cave and an entry to it.

During the time of *H. erectus*, approximately 460,000 yBP, the cave was a habitable shelter.

FIGURE 11.22

Zhoukoudian Skull Although the original remains of this *H. erectus* fossil are lost, excellent casts, such as this reconstructed skull, enable modern anthropologists to study this important hominin.

HOMO ERECTUS IN EUROPE (1.2–0.4 MYA)

The earliest presence and subsequent evolution of *H. erectus* were somewhat later in Europe than in Africa and Asia. The earliest fossil evidence of *H. erectus* in western Europe is from the Sierra de Atapuerca in northern Spain—at the cave sites of Sima del Elefante, dating to about 1.2 mya, and Gran Dolina, dating to about 900,000 yBP. The earlier site is represented by a partial mandible and some teeth, along with animal bones showing cutmarks from butchering. The later site, excavated by the Spanish paleontologist Juan Luis Arsuaga and his colleagues, is among the most important in Europe, owing to the discovery of fragmentary bones and teeth of a half-dozen hominins, along with many stone tools and animal bones (**Figure 11.23**). Animal bones and hominin bones had been cut with stone

FIGURE 11.23

Gran Dolina In the mid-1990s, the excavation of this Spanish cave site uncovered fossil remains of at least six individual hominins along with hundreds of stone tools. In addition, ample evidence that both hominins and other animals were butchered here has led some researchers to suggest that these hominin ancestors practiced cannibalism. Gran Dolina is part of the Atapuerca archeological site, which, like Zhoukoudian (see Figure 11.19), is a UNESCO World Heritage Site.

tools and purposely broken. This evidence indicates that hominins processed and consumed animals and other hominins (these practices are discussed further in chapter 10).

The most complete skull from Gran Dolina is Atapuerca 3, consisting of the left facial bones, upper jaw, and teeth of a child. This specimen provides a rare glimpse at what juveniles looked like at this point in human evolution (**Figure 11.24**). Juvenile or not, the cranium indicates that Atapuerca 3 appeared more modern than other members of *H. erectus* but was clearly ancestral to later hominins in the Atapuerca region and elsewhere in Europe. Indeed, its bones and teeth are similar in a number of ways to those of hominins that lived in Europe later in the Pleistocene: *H. sapiens*. For example, like the later hominins, the Gran Dolina adults have a wide nasal aperture (opening for the nose).

The only other *H. erectus* remains in Europe are a partial cranium from Ceprano, Italy, dating to 800,000 yBP; the Mauer jaw—a mandible and most of its teeth—from near Heidelberg, Germany, dating to 500,000 yBP; and a tibia from Boxgrove, England, also dating to 500,000 yBP.

EVOLUTION OF *HOMO ERECTUS*: BIOLOGICAL CHANGE, ADAPTATION, AND IMPROVED NUTRITION

How did *H. erectus* differ from earlier *Homo* species, such as *H. habilis*? One of the most obvious differences is *H. erectus*'s remarkable body size and height. Moreover, the increase in body size occurred rapidly, perhaps in less than a couple of hundred thousand years. That is, at 1.8 mya *H. habilis* was about the size of an australopithecine, but by 1.6 mya another hominin, *H. erectus,* was considerably taller and heavier. The American biological anthropologists Henry McHenry and Katherine Coffing estimate that from *H. habilis* to *H. erectus,* males' heights increased by 33% (to 1.8 m, or 5.9 ft) and females' heights by 37% (to 1.6 m, or 5.3 ft). In other words, *H. habilis*—like the australopithecines—was quite short

FIGURE 11.24

Atapuerca 3 These remains, from Gran Dolina, are the subject of debate, as some researchers believe that the juvenile they came from belonged not to *H. erectus* but to a new species of hominin, *Homo antecessor.* Others believe that despite its more modern appearance, this hominin belonged to *H. erectus.*

(typically less than 1.2 m, or 4 ft), but *H. erectus* was considerably taller (more than 1.5 m, or 5 ft). Most of this increase took place 2.0–1.7 mya (**Table 11.1**).

What caused the rapid increase in body size from *H. habilis* to *H. erectus*? Various factors were likely involved, such as climate change and its impact on food supply. But the fundamental reason was likely increased access to animal food sources—protein—acquired from hunting. That some primitive stone tools date to at least 2.6 mya indicates that early hominins were able to cut meat and process it.

Cutmarks made with stone tools have been found on bones of animal prey in Kenya and Ethiopia, at the Olduvai Gorge and Bouri sites, respectively. Indeed, the pattern of cutmarks found at Bouri indicates that even some late australopithecines, ones that preceded *Homo,* were skilled in animal butchery.

As the American anthropologist Pat Shipman's work has shown, at Olduvai Gorge, stone-tool cutmarks overlay animal tooth marks. This finding suggests that at least some of the butchering-related behavior involved scavenging—eating animals killed by other animals—and not hunting (**Figure 11.25**). Other evidence of meat eating has been documented in the bone chemistry of early hominins and in wear on their teeth.

Meat eating likely started long before *H. erectus* appeared, but the technology available to earlier hominins and the minimal record of hunting prior to *H. erectus* suggest that meat was a minor part of this hominin's diet. Two things had to happen for early hominins to routinely acquire meat as a food source. First, to kill game, hominins had to become able to manufacture the right tools, especially stone tools that could be thrown or thrust accurately, such as spears. Second, hominins had to develop the social structure and behavioral strategy whereby groups of individuals—older adolescent and adult males, primarily—could efficiently track and kill game. Both developments were part of the increase in hominin intelligence at this time, as recorded by brain size expansion and more complex technology. Once

TABLE 11.1 **Trends from *Homo habilis* to *Homo erectus***

	HOMO HABILIS	→	HOMO ERECTUS
Teeth		Reduction in size	
Face and jaws		Reduction in size relative to size of braincase	
Brain		Increase in size	
Browridge		Increase in size	
Cranial bone		Increase in thickness	
Body		Increase in size	
Arms		Reduction in length	
Legs		Increase in length	

(a)   (b)

FIGURE 11.25

Hunters or Scavengers? (a) The cutmarks on this bone were made by stone tools, whereas **(b)** animal tooth marks and cutmarks are visible on the shaft of this antelope humerus. Cutmarks that occurred after animal tooth marks indicate that *H. erectus* scavenged for meat at least some of the time.

Acheulean Complex The stone tool culture associated with *H. erectus*; characterized by the use of handaxes and other types of stone tools. It was more refined than the earlier Oldowan Complex.

handaxe The most dominant tool in the Acheulean Complex, characterized by a sharp edge for both cutting and scraping.

hominins had developed the technological and social means of accessing animal food sources daily, they likely had increased access to high-quality protein. This increased access to protein, in turn, produced *H. erectus*'s bump in height—these hominins were taller than their ancestors because of improved nutrition that came about by acquiring food (especially protein) through hunting.

Such increasingly sophisticated technology and increased dependence on culture were important in human evolution generally. The culture associated with this period of evolution, beginning around 1.8 mya, is called the **Acheulean Complex**. Acheulean stone tools are more sophisticated than Oldowan tools, were produced from a wider variety of raw materials, and were fashioned into a greater range of tool types with a greater range of functions. This diversity suggests increased familiarity with the necessary resources and with their availability. Within this diversity, the dominant tool is the **handaxe** (**Figure 11.26**). The handaxe's sharp edge was used in cutting, scraping, and other functions.

In addition, the tools became increasingly refined; better made than before, they clearly required a great deal of learning and skill to produce. Acheulean tools are found in association with large animals, suggesting that these tools were used to kill large animals and butcher them. In Ethiopia's Middle Awash region, for

(a)

(b)

FIGURE 11.26

Handaxes and Other Tools **(a)** At Olorgesailie, an Acheulean site in Kenya, the remains of hundreds of butchered animals were found along with many handaxes and other tools. **(b)** This close-up shows the stone tools, with the handaxes in the middle.

KENYA

• Olorgesailie

example, tools are commonly associated with hippopotamus bones. In Olorgesailie, Kenya, the South African archaeologist Glynn Isaac (1937–1985) recovered many baboon bones in addition to those of hippopotamuses, elephants, and other animals. All these bones have cutmarks from stone tools. In addition, the tools from this and other Acheulean sites display microscopic patterns of wear that are the same as those seen in experimental studies where anthropologists have butchered animals. Clearly, *H. erectus* had killed, processed, and eaten the animals at

FIGURE 11.27

Butchering This artist's reconstruction shows how early *Homo* likely processed animals in groups using a variety of stone tools. (© 1995 by Jay H. Matternes)

these sites, well before 1 mya (**Figure 11.27**). This record, from Olorgesailie and sites like it, indicates that hunting was occurring by the Middle Pleistocene. If body size increase was tied to acquisition of animal protein via hunting, it was well in place by somewhat earlier than 1.5 mya.

In addition to the increase in body size, a key difference between *H. habilis* and *H. erectus* is the latter's much larger brain. From *H. habilis* to *H. erectus*, brain volume increased by 33% (from 650 cc to 950 cc). Some of the enlargement in brain size was due simply to the increase in body size generally. But even when accounting for the body size increase, there was still an increase in brain size. The increase in sophistication of technology and other cultural changes seen after 2 mya or so strongly suggests that this increase in brain size reflects an increase in intelligence and cognitive abilities generally. Simply put, the adaptation of *H. erectus* placed an emphasis on intelligence, and there was likely a selective advantage for the cognitively advanced behaviors that characterized this hominin.

Anthropologists are keenly interested in the nature of the energy intake that would have been required to grow these very brainy ancestors. That is, the brain is an energetically "expensive" tissue. What did these hominins eat that "paid" the high energetic cost of a large brain? While a number of factors are likely to have operated, improved nutritional quality is central to understanding how the cost of increasing brain size was paid. Nutrition improved as a result of meat consumption and the rich source of protein that it provided. The primatologist Richard Wrangham hypothesizes that *H. erectus* was adapted to eating cooked meat and other cooked foods. These rich sources of energy would help explain the increases in brain size and body size. Cooking increases the digestibility of meat and other foods, and furthermore, improves the quality of the energy that it gives the consumer.

Wrangham's **cooking hypothesis** is built on the premise that the cooking of food would have been an important practice in *H. erectus* in order for their bodies to take full advantage of animal sources of protein for growth and development. Archaeological evidence for the habitual use of fire and cooking is sparse but, nonetheless, highly significant. For example, at Koobi Fora, Kenya, archaeologists found fire-burned stone tools, soil, and bone fragments dating to 1.5 mya, which represent the earliest evidence of controlled use of fire in hominin evolution. Similarly, burned animal and plant remains in association with Acheulean tools dating to 1 mya have been found at Wonderwerk Cave in South Africa (**Figure 11.28**). Likewise, in later *H. erectus* contexts at Zhoukoudian, China, the record of burned tools, animal bones, stones, and seeds, as well as ash accumulations, reveals the presence of significant fire usage and likely cooking by 300,000 yBP. These findings indicate

cooking hypothesis The hypothesis that cooking food increases the efficiency of digestion and availability of nutrients required for brain and body growth and development, thus explaining the increase in brain and body size in *H. erectus* relative to earlier hominins.

FIGURE 11.28

Wonderwerk Cave, South Africa This site may contain early evidence for the controlled use of fire by early hominins.

CONCEPT CHECK

Homo erectus: Beginning Globalization

Homo erectus was the first hominin to inhabit territory all over the Old World. After first evolving in Africa, it spread rapidly to Asia and then to Europe. Increased intelligence, increased dependence on technology and on material culture, social hunting, and access to more protein and to better nutrition contributed to this early hominin's remarkable adaptive success.

LOCATION/SITES	Africa (Olduvai Gorge, Lake Turkana, Ileret, Bouri, Buia, Bodo, Gona, Olorgesailie); Asia (Dmanisi, Kocabaş, Trinil, Sangiran, Sambungmacan, Gongwangling, Majuangou, Zhoukoudian); Europe (Gran Dolina, Mauer, Boxgrove)

CHRONOLOGY	1.8 mya–300,000 yBP in Africa
	1.8 mya–300,000 yBP in Asia
	1.2 mya–400,000 yBP in Europe

BIOLOGY AND CULTURE (COMPARED WITH *HOMO HABILIS*)

FEATURE	EVIDENCE	OUTCOME
Tool use (Acheulian)	Skulls	Smaller face and smaller jaws
	Teeth	Reduced size
Fire and cooking	Ash in habitation sites	Smaller face and smaller jaws
Intelligence	Brain size	Increase (average 950 cc)
Hunting and increased meat protein	Butchered large animals	Increased body size
Possible cannibalism	Cutmarks	New ritual or dietary innovation
Growth	Tooth enamel	Slower growth, but not modern
Locomotion	Ratio of leg length to arm length	No significant change

that *H. erectus*, in at least some settings, had controlled use of and access to fire, with a particular focus on cooking their food.

Fire likely played a role in hominins' adaptation to regions of the globe where the temperature is cold for at least part of the year. The controlled use of fire may have facilitated an expansion to areas where people could live and the manner in which they prepared their food. Moreover, hominins most likely had to have made and controlled fire in order to live in temperate settings, such as Zhoukoudian, especially during cold periods of the year.

Most important, however, *H. erectus* used fire to cook food. Before using fire, hominins ate plants and animals raw. But cooking these foods made them easier to chew and, as a result, made the very powerful jaws and large teeth of *H. erectus*'s predecessors less necessary. Indeed, the jaws and teeth of these Middle Pleistocene hominins were smaller than those of earlier hominins. This size reduction was almost certainly related to the cultural innovations of the Middle Pleistocene, including both controlled use of fire and more advanced tool technology. These cultural developments were the harbingers of increasing environmental control and improved adaptive success, both of which form an ongoing theme of human evolution.

In this and other settings, another potential means of improving dietary quality and energy intake was food sharing. In this case, males would have hunted for meat and subsequently shared it with females and dependent children. Indeed, an extensive ethnographic record for living societies shows that food sharing happened in this manner universally. It is likely that this kind of provisioning was an essential element of increased access to high-quality nutrition. Thus, food sharing, meat eating, and cooking help explain the increase in brain size in human evolution, beginning especially with *H. erectus*.

PATTERNS OF EVOLUTION IN *HOMO ERECTUS*

Comparisons of all the *H. erectus* fossils from Africa, Asia, and Europe reveal important information about this early *Homo* species, both in general similarities across these continents and in the evolution of each form. *H. erectus* skulls are long, low, and wide at the base, and they have thick bone and large browridges. The African *H. erectus* tends to be the most robust, with the largest and thickest cranial bones. The Dmanisi and African forms are strongly similar—the sagittal keel, for example, is missing in Dmanisi and present only rarely in the African representatives. Morphological variations are likely related to differences in time and in geography, but the degree of variability is far smaller than that in other mammals.

Some authorities have interpreted the general similarity of *H. erectus* across Africa, Asia, and Europe and through time as representing evolutionary stasis. However, various morphological attributes show significant evolution in *H. erectus*, with earlier forms having considerably smaller brains than later forms. For example, the average Dmanisi skull is 650 cc, while the average Zhoukoudian skull is 1,200 cc. Overall, *H. erectus*'s brain size increased by some 30%. The American biological anthropologist Milford Wolpoff has also documented decreases in cranial bone thickness and browridge size. These characteristics indicate a decline in skull robusticity. Accompanying these changes is a reduction in tooth size, caused by the decreased demand on the face and jaws because of the increasing importance of technology and of cooking.

Hominins' increasing reliance on tools profoundly affected human biology. As tools began to perform the functions of the face and jaws in preparing food for consumption—that is, in cutting up, cooking, and processing meat and other food—there was a commensurate decline in the robusticity of these body parts, the anatomical area associated with mastication. In terms of both culture and biology, *H. erectus* evolved the contextual behavior—hunting, successful dispersal across large territory, adaptive success, and increasing dependence on and effective use of culture as a means of survival. The increased dependence on culture and the dominance of behaviors requiring technology for the acquisition and processing of food increased the diversity of environments occupied by *H. erectus*. The expansion of resources acquired and habitats occupied, coupled with the high degree of mobility, laid the basis for a high level of gene flow and the presence of a limited number of species. The next chapter tracks and interprets the evolution of the species that would become dominant, and ultimately, the only one surviving—*Homo sapiens*.

11.3 Expect the Unexpected in Hominin Evolution: Two Surprises in the *Homo* Lineage

HOMO IN SOUTH AFRICA: *HOMO NALEDI*

As you have gathered by now from reading this book and listening to your instructor's lectures, the record of human evolution is filled with both complexity and unexpected discoveries. At Rising Star Cave, located within a mile or so of the iconic Swartkrans, Sterkfontein, and Kromdraai australopithecine sites in the Blaaubank River valley in South Africa (see chapter 10), an all-female team recruited by paleoanthropologist Lee Berger—consisting of Marina Elliott, Becca Peixotto, Lindsay Hunter, Elen Feuerriegel, Hannah Morris, and Alia Gurtov—recovered a remarkable cache of early hominin remains beginning in 2013. The deep and tortuous cave system made recovery of the fossils highly challenging and certainly dangerous in the minds of anyone who has watched the videos of the recovery of the remains. Working in the Dinaledi chamber of the cave system during the period 2013–2014, Berger and his team found and described some 1,550 cranial, dental, and postcranial hominin fossils representing at least 15 individuals. Following the discovery of these *Homo naledi* fossils in the Dinaledi chamber, paleoanthropologists explored the nearby Lesedi chamber, where they recovered another 133 fossils representing three more *H. naledi* individuals (**Figure 11.29** and **Figure 11.30**). The Rising Star Cave collection contains individuals of all ages and both sexes, presenting an unprecedented opportunity to develop an understanding of population variation within a single hominin population of one locality.

Homo naledi A morphologically primitive hominin found in the later Pleistocene from cave deposits in South Africa.

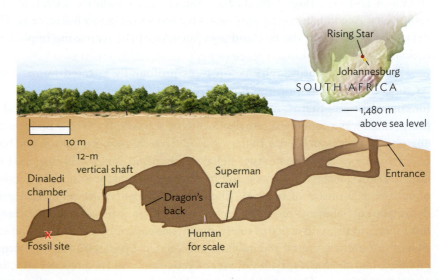

FIGURE 11.29

Rising Star Cave The Rising Star cave system includes at least two localities yielding hundreds of *H. naledi* fossils. On the left is a map of the area of the cave system producing the discoveries in the Dinaledi and Lesedi chambers. The complex passageways, shown in the cross-section profile of the Dinaledi chamber on the right, contain the site of the first discoveries of *H. naledi*.

FIGURE 11.30

Homo naledi **(a)** The remarkable collection of *H. naledi* fossils representing at least 18 individuals, including a relatively complete skeleton in the center of the image, reveals a hominin having a combination of primitive and derived characteristics. **(b)** The cranial morphology is similar to *Homo erectus*'s protruding supraorbital torus and elongated cranial vault, albeit with a tiny brain.

The extraordinarily large number of hominin fossils from Rising Star Cave makes this one of the largest collections of early hominins found at any one site in Africa. The challenge facing paleoanthropologists studying the Rising Star hominins focuses on understanding the biological variation of *H. naledi* and how it fits into an already complex landscape of human evolution.

The general morphology of the hominin fossils from Rising Star Cave is representative of early *Homo*, but specific details in the bones and teeth reveal a mixture of both primitive and derived characteristics. The skull is similar to *Homo erectus* in overall shape, such as the presence of a sagittal keel, a large browridge, thick cranial bones, and reduced tooth size. Some authorities suggest the cranial morphology indicates that the hominin is a variant of *H. erectus*. However, *H. naledi* has a number of distinctive characteristics, including primitive, australopithecine-like morphology. For example, the estimated brain size for *H. naledi* is quite small—only 560 cc for males and 475 cc for females. In addition, similar to australopithecines, the hand phalanges are curved, the femur neck is long, and the body size and brain size are smaller than those of most other Pleistocene hominins. The narrow range of skeletal and dental variation in the Rising Star fossils indicates that they represent one genus, one species, and one morphologically homogeneous population. Given the presence of a number of primitive characteristics, many paleoanthropologists predicted early dates for these hominins, perhaps even in the range of *Australopithecus* or *H. erectus*. However, the fossils were dated to a relatively recent range of 335,000–236,000 yBP, setting the hominins from Rising Star somewhat late in time, far later than many paleoanthropologists would have predicted.

There are some frustrating elements to the discovery of *H. naledi*, including the apparent lack of stone tools or other cultural associations and no animal remains

WATCH THE VIDEO
UNDERGROUND ASTRONAUTS
digital.wwnorton.com/essanthro5

or other evidence of diet. However, there are important lessons that were learned from the study of the Rising Star hominin remains. In particular, the massive size of a single hominin fossil collection covering a relatively constrained time frame allows paleoanthropologists to understand variation within a hominin population, something rarely achieved. Moreover, and most important, paleoanthropologists are aware that this closely related group of individuals represents a critical addition to understanding the enormous diversity of hominins in the Pleistocene—a diversity far greater than previously recognized.

EARLY *HOMO* IN SOUTHEAST ASIA: *HOMO FLORESIENSIS*

The other big surprise is the remarkable discovery made in 2014 on Flores Island, Indonesia, by paleontologists excavating at the Mata Menge site, which dates to 700,000 yBP. Expecting to find the remains of *H. erectus*—at a time during which *H. erectus* has been well documented in Africa, Asia, and Europe—paleontologist Gerrit van den Bergh and his field team found something new and different represented by a partial adult mandible and six isolated teeth representing at least two children. But, quite unlike all other hominins from Indonesia and the rest of Asia, Africa, and Europe dating to the Middle Pleistocene, the Mata Menge mandible (and, by inference, the rest of the skeleton) and teeth are *extraordinarily* small, perhaps representing an adult having half the body size of the other contemporary hominins that have been discussed in this chapter. The morphology of the teeth is similar in many respects to the much later but remarkably small **Homo floresiensis** (the "hobbit"), also from Flores Island and dating between 100,000 and 60,000 yBP (see chapter 12). The extremely small body size of the Mata Menge hominin (and of *H. floresiensis*) is unique. In life, the individual would have been only about 106 cm (3.5 ft) tall. The discovery of earlier and later dwarf hominins suggests the presence of a dwarf lineage of *Homo* specific to Flores Island. The *H. floresiensis* lineage represents descendants of *H. erectus* that settled on this island in the Middle Pleistocene, likely by 1 mya.

Importantly, the Mata Menge mandible and teeth add to the growing body of evidence showing considerable anatomical variation in the Middle Pleistocene, ranging from very small body size (Flores Island) to relatively large body size everywhere else. Although the taxonomic identity of the Mata Menge hominin is preliminary, it nevertheless underscores the important point made earlier in this chapter, and in this textbook in general, regarding the remarkable adaptability of humans and their ancestors. For Mata Menge and the later hominin descendant from Flores Island, the small body size was likely a result of their having lived on an island with limited food resources. We know that many species of animals living in island settings worldwide have reduced body size, owing to resource restrictions. Simply put, stunted size results from less caloric intake. Therefore, it seems that small body size has a selective advantage in these insular circumstances.

The origin and evolution of the genus *Homo* was once a fairly simple story. The story began with a hominin—*H. habilis*—appearing in East and South Africa in the Late Pliocene to Early Pleistocene and having a distinctly larger brain and smaller jaws and teeth than those of *Australopithecus*. This chapter has shown you that the evolution of the genus *Homo* is far more complex than was understood even a decade ago. The growing number of early fossil hominin discoveries presents us with a

Homo floresiensis Dubbed the "hobbit" for its diminutive size, a possible new species of *Homo* found in Liang Bua Cave on the Indonesian island of Flores.

landscape of ancestral biological diversity and sometimes highly localized variation not imagined until the past few years. As discussed in this chapter, much of the hominin fossil record reveals some common variation that defines an ancestral and descendant species: *H. habilis* and *H. erectus*. However, the discovery of at least two new hominin taxa—one in South Africa called *H. naledi* and one in Southeast Asia called *H. floresiensis*—presents us with new challenges for understanding pattern and change in the evolution of early hominins.

The growing diversity observed among early *Homo* reflects the discovery of more fossil hominins, presenting another common theme in the study of hominin evolution: the more fossils that are discovered, the more we appreciate the complexity of human evolution and the diversity of ancestry that it represents. It presents tough questions having no simple answers. On the other hand, that increasing record of fossils and their biological diversity is what makes this field so dynamic and so exciting for all of us who study it. And, one thing remains the same: it is the remarkable variation of earlier hominins presented in this chapter that lays the foundation for the evolution of modern people.

ANSWERING THE BIG QUESTIONS

1. What characteristics define the genus *Homo*?

- The genus *Homo* is defined by physical and behavioral attributes, including a relatively large brain, small face and jaws, and dependence on material culture for survival.
- The genus *Homo* is characterized by considerable anatomical and behavioral diversity, a fact that reflects adaptation to a wide variety of environmental and behavioral circumstances (for example, climate, migration to new settings, and availability of new resources).

2. What were the earliest members of the genus *Homo*?

- The earliest members of the genus *Homo* were *Homo habilis, Homo erectus, Homo naledi,* and *Homo floresiensis.*
- Fossils of *H. habilis* have been found in East Africa and South Africa and date to about 2.5–1.8 mya.
- *H. erectus,* a geographically and morphologically diverse species, dates to about 1.8 mya–300,000 yBP. Its fossil record is represented in Africa, Asia, and Europe.
- *H. naledi* fossils were recovered from the Rising Star Cave in South Africa and date to 335,000–236,000 yBP.
- *H. floresiensis* fossils are from Flores Island, Indonesia, and date to 700,000 yBP.

3. What are the key evolutionary trends and other developments in early *Homo*?

- Compared to the australopithecines, early *H. habilis* experienced an enlargement of the brain and a general gracilization of the chewing complex (face, jaws, and teeth). These developments were linked with increases in tool production and use, dietary diversity, and intelligence.
- Compared with *H. habilis, H. erectus* experienced a continued reduction in size of the chewing complex, increased brain and body size, and the first evidence of modern limb proportions.
- *H. erectus* developed an increasingly innovative and complex technology, including more elaborate tools, organized social hunting, and controlled use of fire.

These developments facilitated greater access to protein and improved nutrition, which likely explains the rapid increase in body and brain size around 2.0–1.7 mya. This increasing adaptive flexibility is a central theme of human evolution.

- *Homo* increasingly became a predator genus in the Early Pleistocene, and this change at least partly explains its remarkable and rapid geographic expansion. Successful predation was largely from hunting, but early *Homo* likely acquired food through hunting *and* scavenging.
- The increased intelligence and full commitment to material culture as an adaptive strategy of *H. erectus* set the stage for the emergence and evolution of *Homo sapiens.*
- Discoveries of a large group of hominin fossils unlike other taxa in South Africa (*H. naledi*) and a unique lineage of dwarf hominins from Southeast Asia (*H. floresiensis*) reveal newly discovered variation in Pleistocene hominins.

STUDY QUIZ

1. What anatomical feature did *H. habilis* share with earlier australopithecine species?

a. A small brain
b. A large chewing complex
c. A large face and large jaws
d. Short legs relative to arms

2. Where does *H. naledi* most likely fit into the human lineage?

a. An early taxon of genus *Homo*
b. A late taxon of genus *Homo*
c. A descendant of *H. erectus*
d. Actually an australopithecine

3. Which skeletal adaptation of *H. erectus* contributed to its fully modern walking?

a. Longer legs and shorter arms
b. A more abducted big toe
c. Loss of arches of the foot
d. Decreased body height

KEY TERMS

abducted (big toe)	adducted (big toe)	Homo erectus	Homo naledi
Acheulean Complex	cooking hypothesis	Homo floresiensis	Pithecanthropus erectus
	handaxe	Homo habilis	sagittal keel

STUDY QUIZ (CONTINUED)

4. Which of the following is *not* an *H. erectus* behavioral innovation?

a. Long-distance hunting and walking
b. Controlled use of fire for cooking
c. Production of symbolic material culture
d. Migration outside of Africa to Asia and Europe

5. The rapid increases in *H. erectus*'s body and brain size are most likely linked to which diet?

a. A high-fiber diet of fruits and vegetables
b. A high-fiber diet of grasses and seeds
c. A high-protein diet of raw meat
d. A high-protein diet of cooked meat

EVOLUTION REVIEW

The Origins of *Homo*

SYNOPSIS The earliest members of our genus, *Homo*, arose nearly 2.5 mya and were characterized by an increase in brain size and a stronger reliance on material culture for survival. Key anatomical changes in *Homo habilis*—such as a larger brain, a less robust jaw, and smaller teeth—highlight the growing importance of tool use and dietary diversity as adaptations in the genus *Homo*. *Homo erectus* became the first hominin species to spread out of Africa to Europe and Asia, a global dispersal made possible by anatomical and cultural adaptations, including increased brain size, larger body size, more complex tool technology, use of fire for cooking, and emergence of hunting behaviors. The first members of *Homo* exhibited a series of evolutionary trends that set the stage for the ongoing evolution of the genus and the eventual emergence of our own species, *Homo sapiens*. The surprising fossil assemblages recovered from Rising Star Cave in South Africa and from Flores Island in Indonesia reveal the remarkable diversity of hominin taxa in the Pleistocene. The fossils and the larger record discussed in this chapter suggest that the origins and evolution of later hominins derive from a diversity of taxa, all representing the genus *Homo*.

Q1. Name the three features outlined in this chapter that set the earliest member of our genus, *H. habilis*, apart from the australopithecines and that are defining characteristics of the genus *Homo*.

Q2. In some ways, the differences between *H. erectus* and *H. habilis* are more pronounced than those between *H. habilis* and the latest australopithecines. Provide three examples of anatomical characteristics in *H. erectus* that differ substantially from those observed in *H. habilis*. What are the evolutionary trends in these characteristics that are seen between these two species?

Q3. What are some of the roles that tool use and climate change may have played in shaping the adaptive flexibility (and evolutionary success) of *H. habilis* relative to the species of australopithecines living at the same time?

HINT Climate change in the Early Pleistocene led to the spread of a grassland environment and increased habitat and resource diversity.

Q4. Early *Homo* is characterized by substantial changes in body size, brain size, material culture, and dietary and behavioral flexibility compared to earlier hominin species. Rather than being unidirectional (for example, increased brain size leads to complex material culture but not the other way around), how might all of these changes reflect local adaptation?

HINT Consider the ways that certain behaviors emerging in *H. erectus* may have had anatomical, physiological, and nutritional effects, as well as the ways in which these effects may have further influenced behavioral flexibility.

Q5. *H. erectus* was the first hominin species to spread out of Africa to other areas of the globe. Use specific biological and cultural features and the concepts of survival, reproduction, and migration to explain why *H. erectus* was the first species capable of such a widespread existence. Explain the adaptive contexts for *H. naledi* and *H. floresiensis*.

ADDITIONAL READINGS

Begun, D. R., ed. 2013. *A Companion to Paleoanthropology.* Chichester, UK: Wiley-Blackwell.

Berger, L. R., J. Hawks, P. H. G. M. Dirks, M. Elliot, and E. M. Roberts. 2017. *Homo naledi* and Pleistocene hominin evolution in subequatorial Africa. *eLife* 6: e24234. DOI: 10.7554/eLife.24234.

Culotta, E. 2016. Likely hobbit ancestors lived 600,000 years earlier. *Science* 352: 1260–1261.

Dunsworth, H. and A. Walker. 2002. Early genus *Homo*. Pp. 419–435 in W. C. Hartwig, ed. *The Primate Fossil Record.* Cambridge, UK: Cambridge University Press.

McHenry, H. M. and K. Coffing. 2000. *Australopithecus* to *Homo*: Transformations in body and mind. *Annual Review of Anthropology* 29: 125–146.

Rightmire, G. P. 1990. *The Evolution of* Homo erectus. Cambridge, UK: Cambridge University Press.

Shapiro, H. L. 1974. *Peking Man: The Discovery, Disappearance and Mystery of a Priceless Scientific Treasure.* New York: Simon & Schuster.

Shipman, P. 2001. *The Man Who Found the Missing Link.* New York: Simon & Schuster.

In this reconstruction, a Neandertal child from Roc de Marsal in Dordogne, France, shows a mix of modern and archaic features. Neandertals and contemporary humans are central to our understanding of the origins and evolution of modern humans, including key aspects of human growth and development, evolution, and dispersal.

12

The Origins, Evolution, and Dispersal of Modern People

BIG QUESTIONS

1. What is so modern about modern humans?

2. What do *Homo sapiens* fossils reveal about modern humans' origins?

3. How has variation in fossil *H. sapiens* been interpreted?

4. What other developments took place in *H. sapiens'* evolution?

The Feldhofer Cave Neandertal was the first fossil hominin to receive serious attention from scientists. Prior to its discovery in 1856, answers to questions about the physical characteristics and behaviors of human ancestors were highly speculative. The uncovering of this skeleton signaled a change for anthropology. Feldhofer Cave is located in Neander Valley (in German, *Neander Tal*), which is near Düsseldorf, Germany. Workers happened upon the skeleton while removing clay deposits from the cave as part of a limestone quarrying operation. Sometimes accidental discoveries like this are reported; often, they are not. The world of anthropology got very lucky because these workers picked

FIGURE 12.1

Feldhofer Neandertal This Neandertal's DNA has been used recently to test hypotheses concerning the genetic relationship between modern humans and Neandertals.

up the skull and bones and took them to a local schoolteacher. As luck further had it, the teacher recognized these remains as human and passed them on to the anthropologist Hermann Schaaffhausen (1816–1893) at the University of Bonn. Schaaffhausen studied the remains, quickly reported his findings to the German Natural History Society, and published a description in a leading German scientific journal. He described a skull having some distinctive archaic features, different from those of modern humans. In particular, the skull was long and low, different from modern people's but with some similarities, such as in brain size (**Figure 12.1**). Moreover, the skeletal remains of extinct Pleistocene animals also found in the cave indicated that this human had lived at the same time as these animals. At the time these breathtaking announcements were made, many authorities believed that humans had appeared very recently in the history of life, certainly postdating extinct animals associated with the great Pleistocene Ice Age.[1]

Schaaffhausen and the Neandertal skeleton caught the attention of scientific leaders in Germany and around the world. One of these leaders was the top German anthropologist of the time, Rudolf Virchow (1821–1902; **Figure 12.2**). In addition to being a leading authority on evolutionary theory, archaeology, and cultural anthropology, Virchow started the discipline of cell pathology (diseases of cells). He helped found several national scientific organizations and periodicals. He was a medical activist, a political leader known across Germany, and the teacher of others who would become leaders in science and medicine. In short, his pronouncements about the Feldhofer Cave skeleton would be taken very seriously by scientists. After looking carefully at the remains, he summarily dismissed any notion that they belonged to an ancestor of living humans. He argued that their characteristics—a long, low skull and bowed, thick limb bones—were those of some modern human afflicted with rickets and arthritis. Others disagreed. Thomas Henry Huxley (see Figure 2.19) argued that this was a primitive, potentially ancestral human. But Virchow's assessment was convincing to most, setting the course for years. Later, scores of remains showing the same morphology as the Feldhofer Cave skeleton and dating to the same period of the Late Pleistocene were found. Eventually, Virchow's pathology hypothesis was rejected, and debate centered on the role of the Feldhofer Cave skeleton and others like it—a group of hominins we call *Neandertals*—in later human evolution.

FIGURE 12.2

Rudolf Virchow Virchow made an influential but wrong pronouncement about the Feldhofer Neandertal skeleton. Among his many achievements was being the first researcher to recognize leukemia, a cancer of the blood and of bone marrow.

---

[1] Excavations at the Feldhofer Cave in 1997 and 2000 produced more than 62 new bone fragments that are part of the original skeleton, part of at least one other adult, and part of a juvenile. Radiocarbon dates on these new bones indicate that this Neandertal site is about 40,000 years old.

In this chapter, we will look at *Homo sapiens'* evolution, from its origins in *Homo erectus* to its development into modern humans. Neandertals play a central role in this discussion, which is also based on rich records—of fossils, genetic variation, culture, and behavior—from around the world. First, though, we will explore which aspects of the fossil record indicate the first appearance of modern people. Then, we will examine those aspects to understand just how anthropologists interpret the variation across the bones and teeth of *H. sapiens*. This is a critically important period of human evolution, one that provides us with an emerging picture of the circumstances that gave rise to modern humans.

12.1 What Is So Modern about Modern Humans?

What exactly do biological anthropologists mean by *modern* when they are talking about members of the genus *Homo* and species *sapiens*? This question is important because the answer to it provides us with the baseline from which to assess the origins, evolution, and geographic distribution of modern people, *Homo sapiens*. Biological anthropologists define *modern* on the basis of a series of distinctive anatomical and behavioral characteristics that contrast in a number of key ways with *archaic* characteristics found in earlier hominins (**Figure 12.3**). Modern people—that is, people

(a)

Small, gracile browridges

Flat face

Flat, small cheekbones

Small teeth

(b)

Large browridges

Large, wide cheekbones

Large teeth

Projecting face

FIGURE 12.3

Modern Human Features **(a)** Anatomically, modern *Homo sapiens* possess a unique suite of traits that are absent in **(b)** archaic *H. sapiens*.

who essentially look like us—tend to have an anatomical profile consisting of a high and vertical forehead, a round and tall skull, a small browridge, a small face, small teeth, and a projecting chin (anthropologists call the latter a "mental eminence"). These characteristics, as an anatomical package, are largely exclusive to modern humans. Below the neck, modern humans, both past and present, have relatively more gracile, narrower bones than their predecessors. Fossil humans having these cranial and postcranial characteristics are considered modern *H. sapiens*.

The immediate ancestors of modern people—archaic *H. sapiens*—differ from modern *H. sapiens*. Compared to modern *H. sapiens,* archaic *H. sapiens* have a longer and lower skull, a larger browridge, a bigger and more projecting face, a wider nasal aperture (opening for the nose), a more projecting occipital bone (sometimes called an **occipital bun** when referring to Neandertals), larger teeth (especially the front teeth), and no chin. The postcranial bones of archaic *H. sapiens* are thicker than those of modern people.

Some hominin skeletons dating to the Upper Pleistocene have a mixture of archaic and modern features. The Skhul 5 skeleton from Israel, discussed later in this chapter, is an excellent example of a hominin with both archaic features, including a somewhat forward-projecting face and a pronounced browridge, and modern features, such as a distinctive chin and no occipital bun (see Figure 12.38, p. 378). Similarly, the Herto skulls from Ethiopia have a combination of archaic and modern features, although the modern features dominate over the archaic ones (see Figure 12.34, pp. 374–375). The modern characteristics of their skulls indicate that the Skhul and Herto hominins were on the verge of modernity or were very early modern *H. sapiens,* the earliest in western Asia and Africa, respectively.

12.2 Modern *Homo sapiens*: Single Origin and Global Dispersal, or Multiple Origins and Regional Continuity?

H. sapiens' evolution begins with the emergence of archaic forms some 500,000–350,000 yBP. These early *H. sapiens* provide the context for modern *H. sapiens'* evolutionary development, which took place at different times in different places. Modern *H. sapiens* first appeared in Africa, by 160,000 yBP, and in Europe, by about 35,000 yBP. The transition to fully modern *H. sapiens* was completed globally by about 25,000 yBP.

Two main hypotheses have emerged to explain modern people's origins (**Figure 12.4**). The Out-of-Africa hypothesis states that modern *H. sapiens* first evolved in Africa and then spread to Asia and Europe, replacing the indigenous archaic *H. sapiens* populations (Neandertals) living on these two continents. The Multiregional Continuity hypothesis regards the transition to modernity as having taken place regionally and without involving replacement. From this point of view, African archaic *H. sapiens* gave rise to African modern *H. sapiens,* Asian archaic *H. sapiens* gave rise to Asian modern *H. sapiens,* and European archaic *H. sapiens* gave rise to European modern *H. sapiens.* Both models seek to explain why today's human beings consist of just one genus and why that genus consists of just one species. The models differ, though, in accounting for that genus and species.

occipital bun A cranial feature of Neandertals in which the occipital bone projects substantially from the skull's posterior.

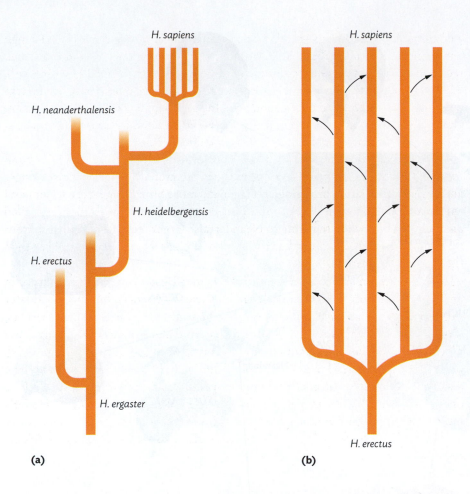

H. sapiens

H. neanderthalensis

H. heidelbergensis

H. erectus

H. ergaster

(a)

H. sapiens

H. erectus

(b)

FIGURE 12.4

Out-of-Africa versus Multiregional Continuity This important anthropological debate is about modern humans' origins. **(a)** This chart depicts one of the two hypotheses, Out-of-Africa, according to which modern humans originated in Africa and then migrated throughout the world. **(b)** This chart depicts the second hypothesis, Multiregional Continuity, according to which *Homo erectus* evolved into modern *Homo sapiens* in various geographic locations. The arrows represent continuous gene flow throughout human evolution. This hypothesis considers *H. ergaster* and *H. heidelbergensis* to be *H. erectus,* and *H. neanderthalensis* to be *H. sapiens.*

The Out-of-Africa model explains the single species of living humans by emphasizing a single origin of modern people and eventual replacement of archaic *H. sapiens* throughout Africa, Asia, and Europe. A simple story. The Multiregional Continuity model emphasizes the importance of gene flow across population boundaries—separate species of humanity never arose owing to the constant interbreeding of human groups throughout human evolution. Not such a simple story.

Fossil and genetic records provide a wealth of information about modern human origins. We will now consider these records and draw some conclusions from them. We will then be ready to reassess the two hypotheses and to draw further conclusions about the origins of us—living people.

12.3 What Do *Homo sapiens* Fossils Tell Us about Modern Human Origins?

The fossil remains of archaic *H. sapiens* have been found throughout Africa, Asia, and Europe. In Africa, archaic *H. sapiens* evolved into modern *H. sapiens* at least by 160,000 yBP, perhaps as early as 200,000 yBP. In Asia and Europe, the archaics consisted of an early group and a late group, which divided roughly around 130,000 yBP. To understand the biological changes involved in hominin groups' evolution, we need to compare some details of a number of key fossils.

FIGURE 12.5

Early Archaic *Homo sapiens* This map illustrates some of the sites in Africa, Asia, and Europe where the remains of early archaic *H. sapiens* have been found.

EARLY ARCHAIC *HOMO SAPIENS*

The earliest forms of *H. sapiens* emerged around 350,000 yBP. They have been found in Africa, Asia, and Europe (**Figure 12.5**). Their evolution is clearly from the earlier *H. erectus* populations. Anthropologists have documented this evolutionary transition in the three continental settings, noting, for example, the similarly massive browridges in archaic *H. sapiens* and in earlier *H. erectus*. Although quite primitive in key respects, all the fossils representing archaic *H. sapiens* and earlier *H. erectus* show continued reduction in skeletal robusticity, smaller tooth size, expansion in brain size, and increasing cultural complexity.

Archaic *Homo sapiens* in Africa (350,000–200,000 yBP) One of several individuals found in the Kabwe (Broken Hill) lead mine in Zambia (formerly Northern Rhodesia) has an enormous browridge, but the facial bones and the muscle attachment areas on the back of the skull for the neck muscles are quite small compared with those of *H. erectus* in Africa (**Figure 12.6**). The cranial capacity is about 1,300 cc. The skull is similar in appearance to those of early archaic hominins from Europe. Both

FIGURE 12.6

Kabwe This archaic *H. sapiens,* also known as "Broken Hill Man" or "Rhodesian Man," was among the first early human fossils discovered in Africa. Found by miners searching for metal deposits in caves, it was originally thought to be less than 40,000 years old.

the Zambian and the European skulls have *H. erectus*–like characteristics: a large face, a large browridge, and thick cranial bones. However, archaic *H. sapiens* skulls, like their Asian counterparts, are higher than *H. erectus* skulls, reflecting a brain expansion in the later hominins.

Early Archaic *Homo sapiens* in Asia and Europe (350,000–130,000 yBP) Some of the best-known fossils representing early archaic *H. sapiens* are from the Ngandong site on the island of Java (**Figure 12.7**). The skulls are represented by the braincases only—the faces are missing. Ngandong 11 has a brain size of about 1,100 cc, well within the range for early archaic *H. sapiens.* The skull is long and low, but compared with its *H. erectus* ancestor, the skull is somewhat higher, reflecting its larger brain. The browridge is massive, certainly of the magnitude of many *H. erectus* examples.

The Ngandong skulls share a number of features with skulls of other Asian early archaic *H. sapiens,* especially with those found at Narmada (in Madhya Pradesh, India) and Dali (in Shaanxi Province, People's Republic of China) (**Figure 12.8**). The crania are large and robust. The browridges are also quite large, although not as large as in *H. erectus.*

FIGURE 12.7

Ngandong Multiple skulls were found at the Ngandong site in Java, Indonesia, in the 1930s. The brain size of this early archaic *Homo sapiens* falls between that of *Homo erectus* and that of modern humans.

(a)

(b)

FIGURE 12.8

Asian Early Archaic *Homo sapiens* Like the Ngandong cranium, the crania found at **(a)** Narmada and **(b)** Dali are robust, with thick cranial bones. The cranial capacity, however, indicates the brain size was much larger than in *Homo erectus* but somewhat smaller than in modern humans.

In Europe, well-known early archaic *H. sapiens* fossils include a skull and other remains from Arago, France; a skull from Petralona, Greece; a skull from Steinheim, Germany (**Figure 12.9**); and a partial skull from Swanscombe, England. Their average cranial capacity is 1,200 cc. These early archaic *H. sapiens* exhibit larger brains and rounder, more gracile skulls than those of *H. erectus*.

Early Archaic *Homo sapiens'* Dietary Adaptations The earliest archaic *H. sapiens* had many of the same kinds of tools and material technology as the earlier *H. erectus,* but

(a)   (b)   (c)

FIGURE 12.9

European Early Archaic *Homo sapiens* Cranial remains from three prominent European sites—
(a) Arago, **(b)** Petralona, and **(c)** Steinheim—have somewhat larger cranial capacities than those of
other early archaic *H. sapiens*. Although these crania reflect a more modern appearance, they retain
primitive features such as larger browridges.

H. sapiens used more diverse tools to acquire and process food. Across the group,
the face, jaws, and back teeth (premolars and molars) show a general reduction in
size. The American biological anthropologist C. Loring Brace hypothesized that
selection for large back teeth lessened as tools became more important for processing food. Simply, with reduced selection, the teeth became smaller. Alternatively,
as technological innovation changed the way teeth were used, the teeth may have
been under *greater* selection for reduced size. Anthropologists have not reached a
consensus on the mechanisms behind the reduction in tooth size except to say that
cultural innovation and increased dependence on material culture likely played a
role in this fundamental biological change.

    However, while the importance of the back teeth diminished, the use of the
front teeth increased. That is, during this period of human evolution, the incisors
and canines underwent heavy wear. For example, in the Atapuerca 5 fossil from
Spain, the front teeth are worn nearly to where the gums would have been in life
(**Figure 12.10**). This evidence tells us that these hominins used their front teeth as
a tool, perhaps as a kind of third hand for gripping materials. In European archaic
H. sapiens, the front teeth show a size increase. The link between the heavy use of
the front teeth and an increase in the size of these teeth suggests the likelihood of
selection for large front teeth.

(a)

(b)

LATE ARCHAIC *HOMO SAPIENS*: THE NEANDERTALS

The hominins from this period show a continuation of trends begun with early
Homo, especially increased brain size, reduced tooth size, and decreased skeletal
robusticity. However, in Asia and Europe, a new pattern of morphology emerges,
reflecting both regional variation and adaptation to cold climates. As it pertains
especially to southwestern Asia and Europe, this new pattern defines the
Neandertals. Neandertal features include wide and tall nasal apertures; a projecting
face; an occipital bun; a long, low skull; large front teeth (some with especially
heavy wear); a wide, stocky body; and short limbs.

FIGURE 12.10

Atapuerca 5 **(a)** One of many human skeletal
remains found in Sima de los Huesos (meaning
"pit of bones") in Atapuerca, Spain, Atapuerca
5 represents a nearly complete adult male
skeleton. Its cranial capacity falls within the
range of other Pleistocene humans, but its
cranium is unusual in its degree of tooth
wear. Notice that the upper front tooth is
extremely worn—it has very little enamel left.
(b) A researcher works to reconstruct another
fossil skull from Sima de los Huesos.

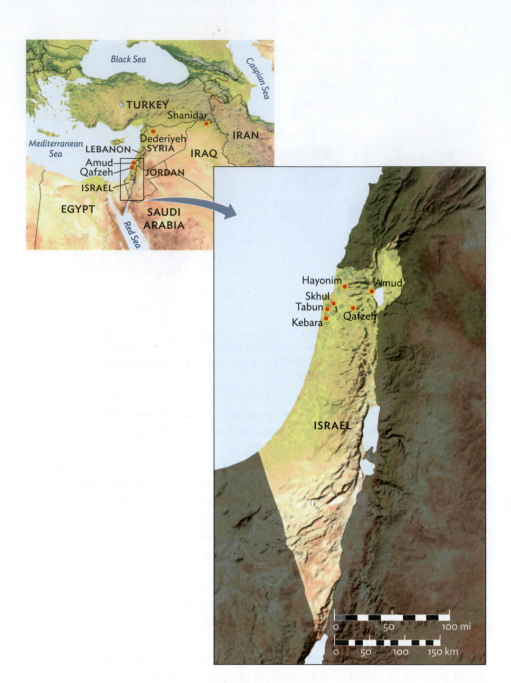

FIGURE 12.11

West Asian Late Archaic *Homo sapiens* This map illustrates where late archaic *Homo sapiens'* remains have been found in western Asia, along the eastern Mediterranean Sea.

FIGURE 12.12

Amud Neandertal The exceptionally large cranial capacity of the Amud Neandertal indicates that this hominin's brain was at least as large as a modern human's.

The fossil record of the late archaic *H. sapiens* is fascinating. For the first time in human evolution, a number of fairly complete skeletons exist, allowing new insights into the biology and behavior of these ancient humans. Moreover, the material culture includes new kinds of tools and reflects new behaviors that are modern in several important ways.

Late Archaic *Homo sapiens* in Asia (125,000–40,000 yBP) For Asian late archaic *H. sapiens,* the record is fullest from sites in southwestern Asia (**Figure 12.11**). Fossils from Israel form the core of discussions among anthropologists about modern people's emergence in western Asia. This record pertains in part to Neandertals from Amud, Kebara, and Tabun. The Amud Neandertals date to about 55,000–40,000 yBP and are best known from the complete skeleton of an adult male. He had an enormous brain, measuring some 1,740 cc, larger than earlier humans' and the largest for any fossil hominin (**Figure 12.12**). The Kebara Neandertals date to about 60,000 yBP and are represented by a complete mandible and body skeleton; the legs and cranium are missing (**Figure 12.13**). A nearly complete female Neandertal skeleton from Tabun was long thought to date to about the same time, but new thermoluminescence dating suggests that the skeleton may be as old as 170,000 yBP. Like the Amud male, she had a large brain.

The Amud and Tabun skulls have a number of anatomical characteristics that are strongly similar to those of contemporary populations of late archaic *H. sapiens* in Europe. For example, their eye orbits tend to be small and round, their nasal openings are tall and wide, and their faces project forward. However, these two skulls share a number of modern characteristics, such as the lack of the occipital bun and the presence of relatively small teeth.

Some of the most interesting Neandertals are from the Shanidar site in northern Iraq's Kurdistan region (**Figure 12.14**). The site was excavated from 1951 to 1960 by the archaeologist Ralph Solecki in collaboration with biological anthropologist T. Dale Stewart, and then again from 2015 to 2019 by the archaeologist Graeme Barker in collaboration with biological anthropologist Emma Pomeroy. The Neandertals discovered at this site—seven adults and three young children—have provided important insight into the lives, lifestyles, and cultural practices of late archaic *H. sapiens* living some 70,000 yBP. Shanidar 1, an older adult male dating to at least 45,000 yBP, is one of the most complete skeletons from the site (**Figure 12.15**). The face is that of a typical Neandertal, especially in its wide nasal aperture and forward facial projection. This individual's life history is written in his bones. A fracture on his upper face, well healed at the time of his death, may have been severe enough to cause blindness. Severe arthritis in his feet might have resulted from the constant stresses of traversing difficult, mountainous terrain.

Shanidar 1's upper incisors are severely worn, probably from his use of the front teeth as a tool for grasping and holding objects in the same or a similar way as the much earlier hominin from Atapuerca. This extra masticatory wear on the front

FIGURE 12.13

Kebara Neandertal The almost complete skeletal torso of this hominin was discovered in Kebara Cave, Israel. Even without a cranium and legs, this is one of the most complete Neandertal skeletons found to date.

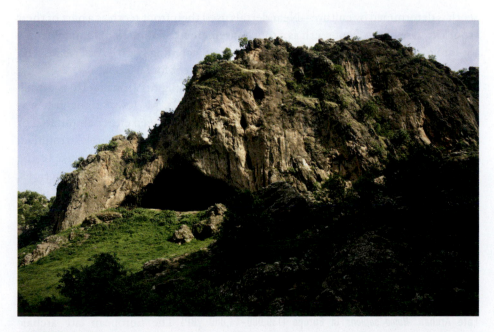

FIGURE 12.14

Shanidar This Iraqi cave site was excavated in the late 1950s by an American archaeological team. Evidence found with the Neandertal skeletons suggests that the Neandertals intentionally buried their dead and possibly performed some type of burial ceremony.

FIGURE 12.15

Shanidar 1 Neandertal The skeleton of this Neandertal tells a life story of injury owing to accidents and violence. The majority of Neandertal skeletons have injuries, a pattern involving especially head and neck trauma. By comparing Neandertals and modern humans, biological anthropologists gain insight into the physical risks Neandertals faced on a daily basis. Shanidar 1, an older adult male, had an especially tough life. **(a)** The skull reveals a healed fracture of his right supraorbital torus. **(b)** The atrophy of his right humerus (left humerus shown for comparison) may also have been due to injury. Regardless of cause, the lower right arm was likely amputated at its elbow joint. **(c)** With only the left arm fully usable, Shanidar 1 relied on his front teeth as a kind of hand, causing considerable wear on his incisors, both upper and lower.

(a)

(b)

(c)

teeth is determined by culture—Neandertals used their front teeth as a part of their "tool kit." Use of the front teeth as a tool has remained a hallmark of human behavior into recent times in a wide variety of cultures, including Native Americans who use their incisors to process plant material to prepare it for basketry.

Shanidar 1 may have had personal reasons for using his front teeth as a tool. When he was excavated by Solecki in the late 1950s, his lower right arm was missing. Stewart suggested that the lower arm may have been either amputated or accidentally severed right above the elbow. The humerus was severely atrophied, probably owing to disuse of the arm during adult life. The loss of the use of the arm meant that Shanidar 1 *had* to use his teeth to perform some simple functions, such as eating or making tools. His survival likely depended on the use of his front teeth.

Late archaic *H. sapiens* have only recently been found in eastern Asia, represented by two newly discovered hominin crania from the open-air site of Xuchang, China. The Xuchang crania show a number of striking similarities with western Asian Neandertals, especially with respect to their low cranial vaults, from top to bottom, enlarged cranial capacity, and relatively thin browridges.

Late Archaic *Homo sapiens* in Europe (130,000–44,000 yBP) The European late archaic *H. sapiens*—that is, the European Neandertals—are some of the best-known, most-studied fossil hominins in the world (**Figure 12.16**). Owing to the relative completeness of the fossil record, paleoanthropologists have been able to document and debate

FIGURE 12.16

Neandertal Sites This map illustrates the various locations of Neandertal (late archaic *Homo sapiens*) discoveries throughout southern and central Europe and the Middle East as well as the suggested boundaries of the Neandertal range.

the meaning of their physical characteristics. The Neandertal record begins in Eastern Europe, at the Krapina site in Croatia, which dates to 130,000 yBP (**Figure 12.17**). The record ends with fossils from Vindija, Croatia, dating to 44,000 yBP.

Like a number of Neandertal remains, the Krapina fossils were excavated more than a century ago. Not all such early excavations were carefully done. Fortunately, the excavator of the Krapina site—the Croatian paleontologist Dragutin Gorjanović-Kramberger (1856–1936)—was extraordinarily meticulous in conserving, curating and recording the fossils found in his excavation. During the period in which he excavated the site, 1899–1905, he kept detailed notes about where his workers found fossils and stone tools. Well ahead of his time, he was also especially careful in recording the stratigraphic locations of the several hundred bones and teeth found at the site.

The Krapina remains were recovered from a series of strata inside a rockshelter (not quite a cave—a rock overhang that provides protection from the elements). The remains are highly fragmentary, making it difficult to identify key physical characteristics. The most complete cranium, Krapina 3, has the typical Neandertal features: round eye orbits, wide space between the eye orbits, wide nasal aperture, and protruding midfacial region (**Figure 12.18**). The Krapina front teeth are the largest of any known fossil hominin. In fact, tooth size comparisons with earlier and later humans in Europe indicate that in these Neandertals, the size of the front

FIGURE 12.17

Krapina Croatian paleontologist Dragutin Gorjanović-Kramberger and his team discovered more than 800 Neandertal fossils at this site. This image shows one of several monuments in present-day Krapina marking where the fossils were found.

teeth had increased, and the size of the back teeth had decreased. The front teeth are some of the biggest in human evolution.

The Krapina bones are mostly in fragments. The American anthropologist Tim White has found that some of these fragments display a series of distinctive cutmarks in places where ligaments (the tissue that connects muscle to bone) were severed with stone tools. The location and pattern of cutmarks on the Krapina Neandertal bones are identical to those on animal bones found at the site. That strategically placed cutmarks appear on human and animal bones indicates that these people processed and ate animal *and* human tissue.

The Krapina Neandertals were not the only ones to practice cannibalism. From at least three other sites in Europe—the Moula-Guercy Cave in southeastern France, El Sidrón in northern Spain, and Goyet in Belgium—multiple individuals dating to 100,000 and 45,000 yBP display cutmark patterns very similar to those on animal remains (**Figure 12.19**). The cutmarks on cranial and postcranial bones involved removal of tissue and marrow extraction. Unlike other settings where the processed human and animal bones are mixed, the Neandertal remains at El Sidrón are not associated with animal remains, and they are located in a remote area of a complex system of caves.

Scientists cannot explain why cannibalism was practiced, but perhaps Neandertals ate human flesh to survive severe food shortages during their occupation of Ice Age Europe. Alternatively, perhaps cannibalism was performed for ritual functions.

Many Neandertal skeletons, including some of the best known from western Europe, are relatively late, post-dating 60,000 yBP. The skeleton from La Chapelle-aux-Saints, France, is especially well known because anthropologists used it as the prototype for all Neandertals in the early twentieth century. It has the characteristic Neandertal cranial morphology, including a wide nasal aperture, a projecting midface, an occipital bun, and a low, long skull (**Figure 12.20**).

FRANCE

La Chapelle-aux-Saints

Moula-Guercy Cave

(a)

(b)

FIGURE 12.19

Moula-Guercy Neandertal fossils from this French cave site show evidence of butchery and, possibly, cannibalism. **(a)** The French archaeologist Alban Defleur examines the fragmentary remains of at least six cannibalized Neandertals. **(b)** Using a scanning electron microscope, researchers were able to closely examine cutmarks from a stone tool on a Neandertal cranial bone.

The Neandertal Body Plan: Aberration or Adaptation? The La Chapelle-aux-Saints skeleton is one of the most complete Neandertals. The skeleton was first described in great detail by the eminent French paleoanthropologist Marcellin Boule (1861–1942) in the early 1900s. Boule's scientific writings tremendously influenced contemporary and later scientists' interpretations of Neandertal phylogeny, behavior, and place in human evolution generally, basically continuing the earlier opinions expressed by Virchow (discussed at the start of this chapter). Boule argued that the Neandertal cranial and postcranial traits were simply too primitive and too different from modern people's to have provided the ancestral basis for later human evolution (**Figure 12.21**). He concluded that the La Chapelle individual must have walked with a bent-kneed gait—as in chimpanzees that walk bipedally—and could not have been able to speak. Simply, in his mind, Neandertals represented some side branch of human evolution—they were too primitive, too stupid, and too aberrant to have evolved into modern humans.

Boule's interpretations led to the prevailing view at the time (still held by some authorities) that Neandertals were evolutionary dead ends, replaced by the emerging modern humans and representing distant cousins of humanity that were not able to survive. In rejecting this view, we should take a closer look at some topics Boule addressed in his study of the La Chapelle skeleton.

One very distinctive feature of Neandertal faces is the *enormous* nasal aperture (**Figure 12.22**). The great size of the nasal aperture in many Neandertal fossils indicates that these people had huge noses, in both width and projection. It is not just the big external nose that is so massive; the internal nasal structure is also distinctively large compared to that of modern humans. Such massive noses were

FIGURE 12.20
La Chapelle-aux-Saints Neandertal Like Shanidar 1, this skull and the associated skeleton show evidence of healed injuries and arthritis.

(a)

(b)

FIGURE 12.21

Neandertal Depictions **(a)** The La Chapelle-aux-Saints skeleton, here fleshed out by an illustrator in 1909, reinforced the notion that Neandertals were too stupid and too brutish to have evolved into modern humans. **(b)** More recent reconstructions show that Neandertals looked very similar to modern humans in many respects. In addition, estimates of brain size put them squarely within the modern human range.

FIGURE 12.22

Nasal Aperture The large nasal aperture of Neandertal crania, such as this cranium from Gibraltar, may have been an adaptation to cold.

one of the cranial characteristics that led Boule to believe that Neandertals were not related to later humans in an evolutionary sense. However, nasal features are more likely part of an adaptive complex reflecting life in cold climates during the Upper Pleistocene. The shape and size of any nose is an excellent example of the human face's highly adaptable nature, especially in relation to climate. One of the nose's important functions is to transform ambient air—the air breathed in from the atmosphere—into warm, humid air. Large noses, including those of Neandertals, have more internal surface area, thus providing an improved means of warming and moistening the cold, dry air that Neandertals breathed regularly. Moreover, the adaptation to cold climates may also involve increased metabolic demands for oxygen, as well as other energetic demands in lower temperatures and drier climates, a finding well documented in living humans. Alternatively, the large noses of Neandertals may simply be due to the fact that their faces are so large. The wide nasal aperture is similar to that in some earlier European hominins, such as in early archaic *Homo sapiens* from Atapuerca, Spain (see Figure 12.10). These attributes are not uniquely Neandertal (**Figure 12.23**), but they dominate the European Neandertal facial morphology and are best explained as being climatic adaptations.

Other features of Neandertal skeletons are consistent with adaptation to cold. For example, the infraorbital foramina—the small holes in the facial bones located beneath the eye orbits—are larger in European Neandertals than in modern people (**Figure 12.24**). The foramina's increased size is due to the blood vessels that tracked through them having been quite large. The larger blood vessels may have allowed greater blood flow to the face, preventing exposed facial surfaces from freezing.

Most distinctive about the cold-adaptation complex in Neandertals are the shape of the body trunk and the length of the arms and legs. Compared with modern humans, European Neandertals were stocky—the body was short, wide, and deep (**Figure 12.25**). Neandertals' limbs were shorter than those of earlier or later humans. This combination—stocky trunk and short limbs—is predicted

FIGURE 12.23

Modern Human Relatives? Some of the morphological traits associated with Neandertals can be found in modern humans, as illustrated by this photograph of the biological anthropologist Milford Wolpoff facing the reconstructed head of a European Neandertal. Might Neandertals have interbred with modern human ancestors, passing along some of these traits?

Low forehead

Large prominent nasal bones

Occipital bun

Large infraorbital foramen

Large nasal aperture

FIGURE 12.24

Cold-Adaptive Traits Large infraorbital foramina are among the Neandertal traits that likely were responses to a cold environment during the later Pleistocene. Note also the distinctive Neandertal traits—low forehead and projecting occipital bone (occipital bun).

by Bergmann's and Allen's rules (see "The Role of Climate in Human Adaptation: Living on the Margins" in chapter 5). That is, animals that live in cold climates are larger than animals that live in hot climates (Bergmann's rule). The larger body trunk reduces the amount of surface area relative to the body size. This helps promote heat retention. Moreover, animals that live in cold climates have shorter limbs than animals that live in hot climates (Allen's rule). This, too, promotes heat retention in cold settings.

The American biological anthropologist Christopher Ruff has refined these concepts in interpreting human body shape morphology. His research reveals that adaptation to heat or cold is not related to a person's height—some heat-adapted populations are quite tall, and some are quite short. Much more important is the width of the body trunk (usually measured at the hips), because the ratio of surface area to body mass is maintained regardless of height (**Figure 12.26**). This finding is borne out by a wide range of populations around the world today: populations living in the same climate all have body trunks of the same width, no matter how their heights vary. Populations living in cold climates always have wide bodies; populations living in warm climates always have narrow bodies. These dimensions are always constant in adaptation to heat or cold. In addition, the ratio of tibia (lower leg) length to femur (upper leg) length differs between people who live in hot climates and people who live in cold climates. Heat-adapted populations have long tibias relative to their femurs (their legs are long), but cold-adapted populations have short tibias relative to their femurs (their legs are short). Neandertals fit the predictions for cold adaptation: their body trunks are wide, and their tibias are short.

Neandertal Hunting: Inefficient or Successful? The French paleoanthropologists of the 1800s and early 1900s questioned Neandertals' humanness. They suggested that Neandertals were unintelligent, could not speak, and had a simplistic culture. Put in the vernacular, "Their lights were on, but nobody was home." Some paleoanthropologists continue to argue this point, viewing Neandertals

FIGURE 12.25

Neandertal Body Proportions A further adaptation to the cold appears in Neandertals' body proportions (left) compared with those of early modern humans (right). Neandertals' much stockier body build reduced heat loss and increased heat retention. Early modern humans' narrower trunk, narrower hips, and longer legs reflected the warmer environment in which these people lived.

Modern Inuit
(260 cm²/kg)

Modern Nilotic
(301 cm²/kg)

Modern Pygmy
(314 cm²/kg)

FIGURE 12.26

Body Size and Body Shape The refinement of Bergmann's and Allen's rules regarding body size, body shape, and temperature adaptations is illustrated by these body types. The ratio of body surface area to body mass (square centimeters per kilogram) is given below each type. The greater the ratio, the more that body shape and that body size are adaptations to high temperatures. Individuals living in cold environments, such as the modern Inuit, have a lower ratio than that of individuals living in hot environments, such as the modern Nilotic. Because of their short stature, modern Pygmies appear to contradict Bergmann's and Allen's rules. However, body surface ratio reveals that Pygmies are well adapted to hot environments.

Mousterian The stone tool culture in which Neandertals produced tools using the Levallois technique.

Middle Paleolithic The middle part of the Old Stone Age, associated with Mousterian tools, which Neandertals produced using the Levallois technique.

Levallois technique A distinctive method of stone tool production used during the Middle Paleolithic, in which the core was prepared and flakes removed from the surface before the final tool was detached from the core.

Upper Paleolithic The most recent part of the Old Stone Age, associated with early modern *Homo sapiens* and characterized by finely crafted stone and other types of tools with various functions.

as inefficient hunters and not especially well adapted to their environments. A growing body of archaeological and biological evidence, however, demonstrates that Neandertals were not clumsy mental deficients.

Neandertals were associated with the culture known as **Mousterian** or **Middle Paleolithic**. This culture's stone tool technology, lasting from about 300,000–30,000 yBP, includes a complex and distinctive type of flaking called the **Levallois technique**. This technique involves preparing a stone core and then flaking the raw materials for tools from this core (**Figure 12.27**). Contrary to the opinions of early anthropologists, this Neandertal technology was complex and required considerable hand–eye coordination. Moreover, anthropologists are learning that late Neandertals participated fully in the **Upper Paleolithic**—the earliest cultures associated mostly with early modern *H. sapiens* in Europe—producing stone tools that were modern in many respects and certainly as complex as those produced by early modern humans. Moreover, the size, shape, and articulations of the Neandertal hand reflect the kind of precise manual dexterity crucial for the fine crafting of tools (**Figure 12.28**).

A large stone of flint is chosen.

Small flakes are removed from the stone's perimeter using an antler or other tool.

One side of the stone has flakes removed from the entire surface, giving it the appearance of a tortoise shell.

A heavy, specific blow is directed at one end of the stone, removing a large flake. This flake is convex on one side and flat on the other.

This flake can now be used for scraping or cutting. Further flake removal will produce a more specialized tool.

FIGURE 12.27

Levallois Technique To produce their Mousterian tools, Neandertals used a specific technique to remove flakes from flint cores. The use of such a technique indicates that Neandertals could visualize the shape and size of a tool from a stone core, an advanced cognitive ability.

calculus Hardened plaque on teeth; caused by the minerals from saliva being continually deposited on tooth surfaces.

FIGURE 12.28

Mousterian Tools Neandertals made these tools out of flint. The use of such tools would have replaced the use of front teeth as tools, reducing the amount of anterior tooth wear in some later Neandertals.

If Neandertals were not effective hunters, then they might have been less successful adaptively than modern people. One way to measure hunting success is to determine how much meat Neandertals ate. The bones of butchered animals are abundant in Neandertal habitation sites, indicating that Neandertals hunted the animals and processed the carcasses for food. As suggestive as this evidence is, the mere presence of animal remains does not reveal how *important* animals were in the people's diet. To find out how important meat was in Neandertals' diets, anthropologists have applied the powerful tools of bone chemistry and stable isotope analysis. Measurement of stable isotopes of both nitrogen and carbon in the bones of Neandertals—from Scladina Cave (Belgium), Vindija Cave (Croatia), and Marillac (France)—indicates that Neandertals ate lots of meat, at or nearly at the level of carnivores living at the same time and place (**Figure 12.29**). The chemical signature of their diet, then, is a powerful indicator of Neandertals' effectiveness in acquiring and consuming animal protein. That is, it shows that Neandertals were successful hunters. This is not to say that Neandertals depended wholly on animals for food. Tooth **calculus**, the hard substance that your dental hygienist periodically scrapes off your teeth, contains a treasure trove of microscopic residue of plant and other food remains. Analysis of calculus in the El Sidrón Neandertal, for example, shows that they ate a diversity of plants, including mushrooms, moss, and pine nuts.

FIGURE 12.29

Neandertal Diet Measures of stable isotopes of both carbon and nitrogen, here labeled as ^{13}C and ^{15}N ratios, respectively, can be used to determine the relative amounts of different kinds of foods consumed. This graph shows the isotope values for a variety of herbivores and carnivores. Herbivores generally have lower isotope values than those of carnivores. Neandertals' isotope values (asterisk) are close to those of known carnivores, indicating that Neandertals ate plenty of meat.

Some foods were clearly cooked. In addition, these analyses have revealed that some Neandertals might have consumed some of these plants for medicinal purposes. The British archaeologist Karen Hardy and her associates have documented in calculus from El Sidrón the presence of bitter-tasting chemicals that are well-known appetite suppressants. The presence of residues of plants that lack nutritional value indicates that Neandertals might have self-medicated, but we cannot know for sure if they did.

Another indicator of their effective adaptation is the measurement of stress levels. The American biological anthropologist Debbie Guatelli-Steinberg and her associates found that enamel hypoplasias, the stress markers in teeth that reflect growth disruption due to poor diets or poor health, are present in Neandertals but at a frequency no different from that of modern humans. This finding, too, suggests that Neandertals dealt successfully with their environments.

Neandertals Buried Their Dead In many Neandertal sites, the remains have been found scattered about, commingled and concurrent with living areas. For example, the Krapina Neandertal fossils are fragmentary and were scattered throughout the site. That is, the deceased were treated no differently from food remains or anything else being discarded. In contrast, a significant number of skeletons have been found in pits. Excavation of some Neandertal sites in Europe and western Asia has shown that pits were dug, corpses were placed in the pits, and the pits were filled in. For example, the Neandertal skeletons from several key sites—Spy, Belgium; various sites in France, including La Chapelle-aux-Saints; Shanidar, Israel (several individuals); and Amud and Tabun, both in Israel—were all found in burial pits (**Figure 12.30**).

Was burial of the dead a religious or ceremonial activity having significant symbolic meaning for the living? Or was burial simply a means of removing bodies from living spaces? Most of the intentionally buried skeletons were in flexed (fetal-oriented) postures. The hands and arms were carefully positioned, and the

FIGURE 12.30

Intentional Burial Like the Shanidar skeletons (among others), the La Chapelle-aux-Saints skeleton, shown here, provides evidence of intentional burial. When this individual was found in a pit, it was the first suggestion that Neandertals cared for their dead in a way similar to modern humans' methods.

bodies were typically on their sides or backs. This vigilant treatment indicates that care was taken to place the bodies in the prepared pits. The skeletons' postures suggest, therefore, that these burials were not just disposals. They represented purposeful symbolic behavior linking those who died and those who were living.

Neandertals Talked Fundamental to human behavior is the ability to speak as part of the repertoire of communication. Conversation is a key way that we present information and exchange ideas. Because early anthropologists believed that Neandertals lacked the ability to speak, they argued that Neandertals were not related to modern people in an evolutionary sense. This idea has continued into more recent times. In the 1970s, the American linguist Philip Lieberman and the American anatomist Edmund Crelin, for example, reconstructed the Neandertal vocal tract. Because their reconstruction resembled a modern newborn infant's vocal tract, Lieberman and Crelin concluded that, like human babies, Neandertals could not express the full range of sounds necessary for articulate speech. Although interesting, their reconstruction of the Neandertal vocal tract was conjectural. Based on skulls alone, it necessarily lacked the anatomical parts (soft tissues) important for determining whether Neandertals had speech.

Indeed, one compelling line of evidence suggests that Neandertals were, in fact, able to speak. The Kebara Neandertal skeleton includes the hyoid bone, a part of the neck that can survive from ancient settings. Various muscles and ligaments attach it to the skull, mandible, tongue, larynx, and pharynx, collectively producing speech (**Figure 12.31**). The morphology of the Kebara Neandertal's hyoid is identical to that of a living human's. The Kebara people talked.

Even more convincing evidence that Neandertals spoke are findings from the study of microscopic wear patterns on the surfaces of incisors and canines, especially the study of the relationship with brain laterality. The human brain is distinctive in its laterality: the clearly defined left and right sides are an anatomical marker for the ability to speak. In right-handed humans, the left side of the brain is dominant. The left brain controls right-sided body movements, especially the use of the right hand and right arm. It also controls speech and language production.

FIGURE 12.31

Did Neandertals Speak? The Kebara skeleton's hyoid is identical to a modern human hyoid, indicating that Neandertals could speak.

Hyoid bone

Hyoid bone

In left-handed people, these connections are reversed. Therefore, evidence of handedness (a preference for the right or left hand) is itself evidence for brain laterality. In fossil hominins, hand preference can be determined by looking at scratches on the front teeth. The American biological anthropologist David Frayer and his associates have detected microscopic parallel scratches on the surfaces of upper incisors and canines of many fossil hominins, including Neandertals from Europe. It has long been thought that Neandertals (and lots of other hominins, including modern humans) used a "stuff-and-cut" method of meat processing before chewing the meat. This method consists of cutting a piece of meat by biting one end of it and holding the other end with the left hand, then holding a stone tool with the right hand to cut the meat. Often, cutting meat in this fashion inadvertently scratches the front teeth. When this happens, the scratches on the teeth have a highly distinctive pattern: they are parallel to each other, and they angle downward. When the stuff-and-cut method is performed experimentally, right-handed people end up with tooth scratches that angle downward to the right, and left-handed people end up with scratches that angle downward to the left.

Frayer and his research group examined the scratch patterns on the teeth of 17 Neandertals from different sites, finding that all but two of the Neandertals had scratch patterns consistent with right-handedness (**Figure 12.32**). The two exceptions had just the opposite, consistent with left-handedness. Similarly, in the early archaic *H. sapiens* from Sima de los Huesos at Atapuerca, dating to 500,000 yBP, all 12 individuals studied had the scratch pattern associated with handedness. The conclusion is simple: because Neandertals uniformly exhibited handedness, we know they had brain laterality. (As with modern humans today, most Neandertals and their predecessors had left-dominant brains and were right-handed.) And because they had brain laterality, we can conclude that Neandertals talked.

Genetic evidence also supports the notion that Neandertals spoke. The German geneticist Johannes Krause and his team successfully identified the *FOXP2* gene—a gene strongly implicated in the production of speech—from Neandertal bone samples from the El Sidrón site. Although it is not *the* gene for speech, it is part of a complex of genetic variation found in modern humans. Its presence in these late archaic *H. sapiens* indicates that Neandertals talked.

FIGURE 12.32

Handedness in Neandertals Shown here is an upper right first incisor of a Neandertal from the Vindija site in Croatia. The surface has more than 150 scratches produced by a stone tool rubbing against the tooth. Almost all the scratches are angled down toward the individual's right. The red lines highlight the main scratches. This Neandertal had a left-dominant brain, was right-handed, and possessed the ability to speak.

CONCEPT CHECK

Archaic *Homo sapiens*

Archaic *H. sapiens* are the first of our species, beginning some 350,000 yBP globally and evolving locally from earlier *H. erectus* populations. After 150,000 yBP, regional patterns of diversity emerge, followed by simultaneous occupation of Europe by late archaic *H. sapiens* (Neandertals) and early modern *H. sapiens* by 40,000 yBP.

LOCATIONS (SITES)*	Africa (Kabwe) Asia (Ngandong, Dali, Narmada, *Amud, Kebara,*† *Tabun, Shanidar, Teshik Tash*) Europe (Sima de los Huesos, Swanscombe, Steinheim, Petralona, Arago, *Feldhofer Cave,* Atapuerca, *Spy, Krapina, Vindija, Moula-Guercy, La Chapelle-aux-Saints, Scladina Cave, Marillac, Les Rochers-de-Villeneuve, Engis, El Sidrón, Monte Lessini*)
CHRONOLOGY	350,000–44,000 yBP
BIOLOGY	Mixture of *H. erectus* and *H. sapiens* characteristics 1,200 cc cranial capacity early 1,500 cc cranial capacity late Both skulls and skeletons more robust than those of modern humans Reduced tooth size, but most of reduction in premolars and molars (front teeth increase in size) Appearance of Neandertal morphology after 130,000 yBP in Middle East and Europe (long, low skull; wide, large nose; large front teeth with common heavy wear; forward-projecting face; no chin; wide body trunk; short limbs) Distinctive mitochondrial DNA (mtDNA) structure Distinctive nuclear DNA (nDNA) structure but sharing with living humans'
CULTURE AND BEHAVIOR	Some evidence of housing structures Large-game hunting Fishing and use of aquatic resources after 100,000 yBP More advanced form of Acheulean early Mousterian late (Europe) Increased use of various raw materials besides stone after 100,000 yBP Skilled tool production Burial of deceased after 100,000 yBP Symbolic behavior, including cave art Social care of sick and injured Speech likely

*Sites mentioned in text.
†Italics denote sites where Neandertal (late archaic *H. sapiens*) remains have been found.

Neandertals Used Representative Symbols Burial of the dead is only one of the countless contexts in which modern humans use symbolism. Think, for example, of all the signs, images, and codes you encounter every day, from the letters on this page to the jewelry you wear to your friend's tattoo. Decorative items such as perforated shells, some stained with pigments of various colors, have been well documented in the earlier Paleolithic in Africa and the Middle East, dating to 120,000–70,000 yBP. A number of anthropologists have suggested that Neandertals differed from modern *H. sapiens* in that they lacked symbolic behavior. This lack, in turn, is seen as a feature of Neandertals' purported cognitive inferiority to *H. sapiens*. However, the archaeologist João Zilhão and his colleagues have discovered clear evidence of symbolic behavior at two sites in Spain that date to 50,000 yBP. At Cueva de los Aviones and Cueva Antón, they found perforated marine shells similar to those in Africa and the Middle East that were painted with naturally occurring pigments, especially red, yellow, and orange. These shells were likely strung around an individual's neck. These body ornaments are evidence that Neandertals used symbolism at least 10,000 years before the appearance of modern *H. sapiens* in Europe. At three caves dating to more than 65,000 yBP in Spain, symbolic behavior is clearly illustrated involving the painted outline of a hominin hand, a painted stalactite, and a red linear motif. Indeed, Neandertals may be Europe's first artists. They used symbols to communicate ideas and expressions.

The key point of this discussion of Neandertal characteristics—relating to climate adaptation, material culture, efficiency in hunting strategies, access to animal protein, treatment of the deceased, and the use of speech and symbolism—is that Neandertals likely were not weird humanlike primates, less adaptable and less intelligent than modern humans. The record shows that their behaviors, both in form and in symbol, were similar to modern humans'. The size and robusticity of their long bones show that Neandertals were highly physically active, more so than living humans. Such cultural and biological features reflect Neandertals' success in adapting to environmental circumstances of the Upper Pleistocene, not evolutionary failure. The empirical evidence disproves arguments that Neandertals were less than human. The characterization of Neandertals as nonhuman or inferior to modern humans in behavior and adaptation, as presented in the press and in public folklore, is not supported by the large and growing paleoanthropological record. Simply, Neandertals were fully human.

EARLY MODERN *HOMO SAPIENS*

Modern *H. sapiens* from the Upper Pleistocene are represented in the fossil record throughout Africa, Asia, and Europe. During this time, hominins moved into other areas of the world. Later in this period, they spread into regions with extreme environments, such as the Arctic tundra of Siberia in northern Asia. It was a time of significant increases in population size, of increased ability through cultural means of adapting to new and difficult landscapes, and of the development of new technologies and subsistence strategies. (**Table 12.1** lists the four major Upper Paleolithic cultures of Europe and important events associated with each.)

TABLE 12.1 Timeline for Major Upper Paleolithic Cultures of Europe

The Aurignacian (45,000–30,000 yBP)

• Associated with the first anatomically modern humans in Europe

The Gravettian (30,000–20,000 yBP)

• The Perigordian in France

• Earliest art, in the form of carved figurines

• Lagar Velho burial in Portugal

The Solutrean (21,000–17,000 yBP)

• France and Spain during the last glacial peak

• Made very fine stone points

The Magdalenian (17,000–12,000 yBP)

• Successful hunters of reindeer and horses

• Spread out across Europe as conditions improved at the end of the Ice Age

• Made many of the spectacular paintings and carvings

(a)

(b)

(c)

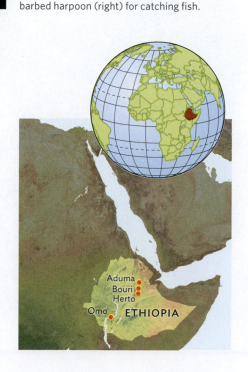

FIGURE 12.33

Chauvet Cave Art (a) Chauvet Cave is located half a mile from the Pont d'Arc, a natural bridge in France's Ardèche River valley. The extensive cave system contains more than 400 images of Late Pleistocene animals, especially lions, mammoths, and rhinoceroses. **(b)** Rhinos and lions are among the animals depicted in this Ardèche cave painting, which is about 30,000 years old. **(c)** Upper Paleolithic tools, such as these, include some of the forms seen in earlier periods of human evolution; however, new tools reflect the procurement of additional types of food, as is the case with the barbed harpoon (right) for catching fish.

The cultures of the later Pleistocene, grouped in the Upper Paleolithic, are also known from their stunning imagery, including hundreds of artistic works in caves throughout Europe but concentrated especially in France and Spain (**Figure 12.33**). This period of human evolution also includes the universal appearance of the modern anatomical characteristics discussed at the beginning of this chapter. That is, in comparison with early archaic *H. sapiens*, there is a clear trend of increasing brain size and decreasing face, tooth, and jaw size and robusticity (**Table 12.2**). In addition, the postcranial bones become more gracile. Modern humans' evolution started much earlier in Africa than in Europe and Asia.

Early Modern *Homo sapiens* in Africa (200,000–6,000 yBP) The African record for early *H. sapiens* is especially important because it includes the earliest evidence of modern people's anatomical characteristics. Crucially important fossil hominins from this time come from the Herto, Aduma, and Bouri sites in Ethiopia's Middle Awash Valley and from Omo in southern Ethiopia. The remains from Herto—partial skulls of two adults and of a child, dating to 160,000–154,000 yBP—show a cranial capacity of about 1,450 cc, close to the average for modern humans (**Figure 12.34**). In addition, many of the characteristics are essentially modern, including a

12.34

THE FIRST MODERN HUMANS:

BIOLOGY AND BEHAVIOR

BIOLOGY: ANATOMY OF THE FIRST MODERN HUMANS

Kabwe Skull

BEHAVIOR: HUNTING AND BUTCHERING

These early modern *Homo sapiens* were skilled hunters. They produced sophisticated stone tools (above) used for killing and butchering large game, such as hippopotamuses living along lake margins. At the Herto site, Tim White, Berhane Asfaw, Giday Wolde Gabriel, Yonas Beyene, and their team found more than 600 stone tools. These tools had multiple functions, mostly relating to the killing and butchering of animals for food.

Herto Reconstruction
© 2005 Jay H. Matternes

Herto Skull

	Skull characteristics	Kabwe 300,000 yBP	Herto 160,000 yBP
a	Braincase	Shorter	Taller
b	Forehead	Less vertical	More vertical
c	Browridge	Larger	Smaller
d	Face	Projecting	Retracted
e	Brain size	Smaller	Larger

Near the village of Herto, in the Middle Awash region of Ethiopia, the paleoanthropology team discovered hundreds of hominid skull fragments dating to about 160,000 yBP. When pieced together, the skull proved to be remarkably modern (see the drawing on the facing page). In contrast to earlier hominids, such as Kabwe (found in Zambia and dating to 300,000 yBP), Herto has a tall braincase, a vertical forehead, a small browridge, a retracted face, and a large brain. In combination, these are definitive characteristics of modern people. White and his team had found the first modern human.

HOMO SAPIENS' BIG BRAINS EVOLVE

Paleoanthropologists are learning that the stone tools used by the Herto people for butchering animals were also used for other purposes. The skull bones from a second adult display cutmarks made by stone tools on the face, front, side, and back, all created when flesh was removed from the skull (see the black-and-white photos at the right). This could have been done as part of some ancient ritual. The cutmarks are similar to ones found in skulls from New Guinea and from other places where the people were known to have practiced cannibalism.

FEATURE	ARCHAIC *H. SAPIENS*	→	EARLY MODERN *H. SAPIENS*
Brain	1,200 cc	Increase in size	1,500 cc
Face		Decrease in size and robusticity	
Teeth and jaws		Decrease in size	

relatively tall cranium, a vertical forehead, smaller browridges, smaller nose, and a nonprojecting face. Among the archaic features are significant browridges (though the trend is toward smaller) and a relatively long face. These remains may be from the earliest modern people in Africa or at least close to the earliest. German paleoanthropologist Günter Bräuer argues that modernization in Africa first took place in East Africa. The overall appearance of the remains indicates that modern people emerged in Africa long before their arrival in Europe and western Asia. The remains from Omo may be as old as 195,000 yBP. If so, they are the oldest evidence of anatomically modern humans. However, their dating is uncertain because the fossils were not positioned in the geologic context as clearly as the Herto fossils were.

Belonging to later contexts in East Africa are the partial skulls from Aduma, Bouri, and Olduvai Gorge dating to 105,000–32,000 yBP. Like the Herto skulls, these skulls have both premodern and modern characteristics. However, the most complete Aduma skull is modern in nearly every characteristic.

Skulls from two key locations in southern Africa—Klasies River Mouth Cave and Hofmeyr—provide important information about early modern *H. sapiens* that date to after 100,000 yBP. Among the fragmentary remains from the Klasies site, anthropologists have documented the presence of a chin, a distinctively modern characteristic, that dates to at least 90,000 yBP (**Figure 12.35**). A nearly complete skull from Hofmeyr, dating to 36,000 yBP, bears a striking resemblance to Pleistocene modern Europeans.

Throughout the Pleistocene and well into the Early Holocene, African hominins, although modern, retained some robusticity. For example, the skulls from Lothagam, Kenya, dating to the Holocene (ca. 9,000–6,000 yBP), are robust

SOUTH AFRICA

Hofmeyr

Klasies River Mouth

(a)

Chin

(b)

FIGURE 12.35

Klasies River Mouth Cave **(a)** Excavations at this site in South Africa revealed evidence of early modern *Homo sapiens*. **(b)** One of the most important features found on the cranial remains discovered here was a chin on a mandible.

compared with those of living East Africans' (**Figure 12.36**). During this period, a number of characteristics seen in the region's living populations were present, such as wide noses. At Wadi Kubbaniya and Wadi Halfa, both in the Nile River valley, populations had some very robust characteristics, such as flaring cheekbones and well-developed browridges. These features contrast sharply with the gracile facial features seen later in the Holocene and in living people (these features are discussed further in chapter 13).

Gobero

NIGER

Lothagam

KENYA

EGYPT

Wadi
Kubbaniya

Wadi Halfa

SUDAN

FIGURE 12.36

Lothagam Skull This Kenyan cranium illustrates early modern humans' rather robust nature. Note the projection both of the lower part of the front of the skull and of the mandible.

(a)

(b)

FIGURE 12.38

Skhul Cranium This skull possesses many characteristics associated with modern humans, including a chin, a less-projecting face, small and gracile cheeks, and a high, vertical forehead. The browridges are still distinct but are much reduced compared with those of archaic *Homo sapiens.*

FIGURE 12.37

Gobero Crania (a) This adult male cranium from Gobero, dating to about 9,500 yBP, is long and low and has a wide, flat face. **(b)** In contrast, this adult male cranium, from the same site but dating to about 6,500 yBP (the Middle Holocene), is high and has a narrow, gracile face. These differences could be due to local evolutionary change or the later arrival of a new population in the region having different craniofacial characteristics.

Zhoukoudian
Tianyuan Cave

CHINA

Similarly, the earlier Holocene skulls (ca. 9,500 yBP) found at Gobero, in the modern country of Niger, are long, low, and robust compared with later Holocene skulls from the same place (**Figure 12.37**). A later population of incipient pastoralists may have replaced the earlier hunter-gatherers. However, the reduction in robusticity more likely reflects craniofacial evolution that occurred in this setting (see chapter 13).

The record of later hominin adaptation in Africa is especially important owing to the presence of residential sites—called settlements—from diverse environmental contexts. Archaeological excavations at the Fincha Habera rockshelter located in a high-altitude, glaciated Late Pleistocene setting of Ethiopia clearly indicate that the hominin foragers were successfully adapted to both high-altitude and seasonal cold conditions.

Early Modern *Homo sapiens* in Asia (100,000–18,000 yBP) The earliest modern *H. sapiens* in Asia are best represented by fossils from western Asia, from the same region, in fact, as the Amud and Kebara Neandertals in Israel. The 90,000-year-old remains from Skhul have distinctively modern characteristics, suggesting that the people living there were modern *H. sapiens.* Among the most prominent remains from the site are several male skulls, of which Skhul 5 is the most complete. That the Skhul 5 cranium dates to before the Amud fossils indicates modern humans lived in the region before Neandertals (**Figure 12.38**).

Remains of the earliest modern people from eastern Asia are very scarce. Some of these remains are purported to be older than 60,000 yBP. For example, at Zhiren Cave in southern China, two molars and a partial mandible possibly dating to 100,000 yBP show a combination of archaic and modern features. The mandible is relatively thick, like that of other archaic *H. sapiens,* but it has a chin like that of modern *H. sapiens.* Although not a fully modern *H. sapiens,* it is certainly a hominin

(a)

(b)

FIGURE 12.39

Zhoukoudian Crania (a, b) Two views of a skull recovered from Zhoukoudian shows several modern human traits, but in general these crania are more robust than their modern Asian counterparts. In the older area of this site, the famous *Homo erectus* fossils were found prior to World War II.

that shows transitional characteristics leading to anatomical modernity. Other evidence for modern *H. sapiens* dates to 101,000–81,000 yBP from Huanglong Cave in central China. Although represented by just teeth, these remains' relatively simple morphology and small size provide evidence for the presence of distinctively modern people in East Asia by perhaps 100,000 yBP.

The earliest and most complete fossil remains, however, are a mandible and partial skeleton, dating to about 41,000 yBP, from Tianyuan Cave, China, and a skull dating to about 46,000 yBP from Tam Pa Ling Cave, Laos. Like the Zhiren Cave remains, these fossils have both archaic and modern features. For example, the Tam Pa Ling skull lacks a prominent supraorbital torus, a feature that is quite modern. Better known are three skulls from the Upper Cave at Zhoukoudian, China, dating to 29,000–24,000 yBP (**Figure 12.39**; this site is discussed further in chapter 11). The Upper Cave skulls are robust compared with living Asians', but the facial flatness is characteristic of native eastern Asians today. Similarly, the early modern people from Minatogawa, in Okinawa, Japan, dating to about 18,000 yBP, are gracile but retain thick cranial bones and large browridges, especially compared with those of the later Holocene populations in eastern Asia.

On the Margin of Modernity in Southeast Asia: *Homo floresiensis* and *Homo luzonensis* (100,000–50,000 yBP) The discovery of skeletal remains dating to 100,000–60,000 yBP from Liang Bua Cave on the island of Flores, Indonesia, has challenged long-standing conclusions about the evolution of modern people in far eastern and southeastern Asia. In 2003, scientists found a skeleton with highly unusual characteristics (**Figure 12.40**). Dubbed the "hobbit" by the popular press, this hominin had an extremely tiny brain (400 cc) and skull, and stood only slightly above 1 m (3.3 ft). Anthropologists disagree on how to interpret these and other characteristics. The Australian anthropologists Peter Brown and Michael Morwood and colleagues have regarded the skeleton as evidence for the long-term presence of an archaic species of hominin, distinct from modern people: *Homo floresiensis* (see Chapter 11).

FIGURE 12.40

Flores Woman A 2003 discovery on Flores Island, Indonesia, has become the source of much debate in anthropology. Some researchers believe this "hobbit" represents a group of early hominins that evolved in isolation in the far western Pacific region. Others believe this skeleton belonged to a modern human who had some developmental or genetic abnormality. (Reconstruction photo [left] © 2007 Photographer P. Plailly/E. Daynès/ Eurelios/Look at Sciences—Reconstruction Elisabeth Daynès, Paris)

The cranium is very small, especially compared with that of a modern human.

This artist's reconstruction shows what Flores Woman may have looked like in life.

Based on measurements of the long bones, the Flores individual would have been approximately 1.0 m (slightly more than 3 ft) tall, considerably shorter than the average modern human.

In their interpretation of this dwarf species' existence, a group of primitive humans became isolated earlier in human evolution, and their isolation led to a unique pattern of biological variation.

Alternatively, the Indonesian paleoanthropologist Teuku Jacob and colleagues have argued that this hominin was not part of a different species but a modern human who suffered from **microcephaly** or some other genetic or developmental abnormality. They point out that some cranial features of *H. floresiensis* are within the modern range of variation seen in living populations from the larger region. In addition, some of the creature's anatomical characteristics (such as a small or absent chin and rotated premolars) resemble those of populations now living in the immediate region.

There are strengths to both arguments for interpreting the remains of the hominin from Liang Bua. However, the discovery of an earlier dwarf hominin from Mata Menge, also from Flores and dating to 700,000 yBP (see chapter 11), argues for the validity of a new species having deep temporal roots in the region and the strong possibility for an earlier ancestor of this hominin, likely *H. erectus*. Moreover, the similarities in tooth and body size of the Mata Menge and Liang Bua hominins argue for an ancestral–descendant relationship. Regardless of their interpretation, the hominin from Liang Bua and its predecessor dwarf hominin from Mata Menge represent a highly unusual morphology at the extremes of hominin variation in the Middle to Late Pleistocene. Interestingly, the island today is occupied by people also having remarkably short stature. This similarity with earlier insular dwarf hominins on the island in the earlier and later Pleistocene suggests an ancestral–descendant relationship between the *H. floresiensis* lineage and the people living on Flores Island today. However, genomic analysis reveals no evidence for deep temporal ancestry between the fossil lineage and today's Flores Island inhabitants. These findings illustrate adaptation to life on the island in two independent evolutionary events.

Similarly, the Philippines contain a unique later Pleistocene record of hominin adaptation and variation. Excavations at Callao Cave on the island of Luzon in 2007 and 2010 yielded hand and foot phalanges and teeth; in 2019, two of these fossils were dated to 67,000 yBP and 50,000 yBP. Called *Homo luzonensis*, this hominin had extraordinarily small teeth, and its hand and foot phalanges were distinctively curved. This unusual curvature may be a primitive trait but more likely reflects a local adaptation to the considerable climbing required in this arboreal environment. These fossils reveal a broad suite of morphological traits reflecting dietary and behavioral adaptations that, like those of the Pleistocene hominins from Flores Island, suggest a remarkable range of variation in the earliest hominins to inhabit the region. Moreover, these hominins reveal anatomical features that are strikingly different from those of other taxa described in this chapter. Therefore, it is most likely that these features reflect evolutionary changes that characterize small, isolated populations.

Early Modern *Homo sapiens* in Europe (35,000–15,000 yBP) Early modern people are known from various places throughout Europe. The earliest modern *H. sapiens* in Europe is from Peştera cu Oase, Romania, and dates to 35,000 yBP. The Oase 2 skull from that site is distinctively modern, contrasting with Neandertals that lived during the same time. For example, Oase 2 has very reduced browridges and a generally gracile appearance. Almost as old are remains from Mladeč, Předmostí, and Dolní Věstonice, all in the Czech Republic, dating to 35,000–26,000 yBP. The half-dozen

microcephaly A condition in which the cranium is abnormally small and the brain is underdeveloped.

Homo luzonensis A diminutive, Late Pleistocene hominin from Luzon, Philippines, showing a mixture of primitive hand and foot phalanges and modern dentition.

FIGURE 12.41

Dolní Věstonice Skull (a, b) This cranium, from Dolní Věstonice, combines modern human and Neandertal characteristics.

Mladeč skulls (35,000 yBP) show remarkable variability, including a mix of Neandertal characteristics in some (occipital bun, low skull, large browridges, large front teeth, and thick bone) and modern characteristics in others (nonprojecting face, narrow nasal opening). The Předmostí and Dolní Věstonice skulls retain a few Neandertal characteristics, but they are clearly more modern in appearance than the Mladeč people (**Figure 12.41**). Some Neandertal features persist well into recent times in eastern Europe, especially in the facial region (**Figure 12.42**).

Western Europe has virtually no fossil record for the earliest modern people, those contemporary with the populations represented by the Mladeč and

High nasal angle

Inward angle of the suture at the bottom of the cheek

Pinching of the bottom portion of the nasal bones

Lateral location of cheeks

FIGURE 12.42

Neandertal Traits in Modern Humans The La Chapelle-aux-Saints Neandertal cranium (bottom; see also Figure 12.20) and a modern Croatian cranium (top) share four major facial similarities.

Předmostí fossils. The skeleton of a 5-year-old child from Lagar Velho, Portugal, dating to 24,000 yBP, has a number of archaic, Neandertal-like cranial and post-cranial features, such as its limb proportions and robusticity (**Figure 12.43**).

The best-known western European representatives of early modern people are the remains of a half-dozen individuals from Cro-Magnon, in Dordogne, France, and remains from the Grimaldi Caves, in the Italian Riviera region, all of these dating to about 30,000–25,000 yBP. The Cro-Magnon remains are often presented as the archetypical example of the earliest modern people, but in fact people varied considerably during this time. Collectively, though, both ensembles of skeletons from western Europe have distinctively modern features: vertical forehead, narrow nasal aperture, and small browridges (**Figure 12.44**). In addition, unlike Neandertals, their tibias are long and their body trunks are narrow. Like Neandertals, these people lived in cold climates of the Late Pleistocene, but their very different body morphology suggests adaptation to warmer climates. (The implications of these skeletal features for the origins of modern *H. sapiens* are discussed later in this chapter.)

Overall, comparisons of earlier with later early modern *H. sapiens* in Europe indicate a trend toward gracilization—the faces, jaws, and teeth became smaller, and the faces became less projecting. In addition, comparison of early and late Upper Paleolithic heights reconstructed from the long bones shows that the later early modern people were shorter. The decrease in the height of early modern people may have been caused, at the very end of the Pleistocene, by both a decrease in the quality of nutrition and resource stress. That is, during the last 20,000 years of the Pleistocene, food procurement intensified—more effort was put into acquiring and processing food for the same amount of caloric intake as before. This change may have occurred because human population size was increasing, placing increased pressure on food resources. An outcome of this change was a global

FIGURE 12.43

Lagar Velho This skeleton of a child was discovered at a rockshelter site in Portugal's Lapedo Valley.

(a)

(b)

FIGURE 12.44

Cro-Magnon (a, b) In 1868, a geologist discovered skeletons in a rockshelter in Cro-Magnon, France. These remains are anatomically modern, with a number of features distinct from Neandertals', including a high and vertical forehead, flat browridges, a much narrower nasal aperture, and an overall gracile skull.

increase in the range of foods eaten. Archaeological evidence shows that the later early modern humans hunted and collected smaller and less desirable (because not as protein-rich) foods, such as small vertebrates, fish, shellfish, and plants. As the American anthropologist Trenton Holliday has also shown, the late Upper Paleolithic people had wider body trunks and shorter legs than those of the early Upper Paleolithic people. The morphological shift indicates an adaptation to cold climates during the late Upper Paleolithic, a highly dynamic period of human adaptation and evolution.

MODERN BEHAVIORAL AND CULTURAL TRANSITIONS

Anthropologists are learning that various behavioral and cultural practices developed at different places and different times in the later Pleistocene, culminating in full modernity in *H. sapiens* globally. In many respects, the fossil record and the cultural record show that modern behaviors and practices began, biologically and culturally, in Africa. For example, fishing and the use of aquatic resources as an important part of diet are first documented at Katanda, in the Democratic Republic of the Congo, where early modern *H. sapiens* were exploiting huge catfish

---

CONCEPT CHECK

Early Modern *Homo Sapiens*

Early modern *H. sapiens* occurred first in Africa, and later in Asia and Europe. The peopling of Europe, Asia, and Africa by only modern *H. sapiens* was complete by 25,000 yBP.

LOCATIONS (SITES)*	Africa (Herto, Aduma, Bouri, Omo, Olduvai Gorge, Klasies River Mouth Cave, Lothagam, Wadi Kubbaniya, Wadi Halfa)
	Asia (Skhul 5, Zhiren, Tianyuan, Huanglong, Minatogawa, Zhoukoudian)
	Europe (Peștera cu Oase, Mladeč, Předmostí, Dolní Věstonice, Cro-Magnon, Grimaldi)
CHRONOLOGY	160,000 yBP in Africa
	100,000 yBP in eastern Asia
	90,000 yBP in western Asia
	35,000 yBP in Europe
BIOLOGY	Vertical forehead, high skull, rounder skull, reduced facial robusticity, smaller teeth, reduced midfacial projection, 1,500 cc cranial capacity
	Heat-adapted body morphology (small trunk, long limbs)
CULTURE AND BEHAVIOR	Upper Paleolithic or equivalent
	Increased visible symbolic behavior (cave art)
	Burial of deceased with grave goods
	Decreased hunting, increased fishing, aquatic foods, likely more plants, and reduced focus on big-game animals
	Technology changes reflect increased focus on fishing (e.g., bone harpoons)

*Sites mentioned in text.

FIGURE 12.45

Modern Human Tools Early modern humans used a variety of specialized tools shaped for specific purposes, including bone tools for hunting and fishing. These tools were found in fisher-hunter-gatherer archaeological contexts in Japan.

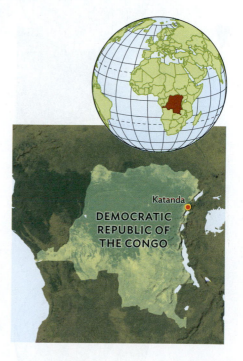

Katanda

DEMOCRATIC REPUBLIC OF THE CONGO

by at least 75,000 yBP. This development is part of a larger package of behaviors associated with modern humans, including more specialized kinds of hunting, wider employment of raw materials (such as bone) for producing tools, advanced blade technology, and trade (**Figure 12.45**). However, as discussed earlier (see "Neandertals Used Representative Symbols"), symbolic behavior and cognitive advancement were also present in Europe, albeit later than in Africa. The successful adaptation of symbolically advanced late archaic *H. sapiens*—the Neandertals—in Europe shows that the story of later evolving humans is complex. Neandertals were fundamentally no different from modern *H. sapiens,* especially in regard to a number of behaviors—burial of the dead, speech, and symbolism—that remain with us today.

12.4 How Has the Biological Variation in Fossil *Homo sapiens* Been Interpreted?

Earlier in this chapter, you read about the two key models that anthropologists use to explain modern *H. sapiens'* origins: the Out-of-Africa model and the Multiregional Continuity model. Now, having learned what the fossil record reveals about the variation in late archaic *H. sapiens,* you are in a better position to understand what this record reveals about the origins of modern humans and to address the question, *Which of the two models best explains modern* H. sapiens' *origins?*

The European fossil record from 40,000 to 30,000 yBP provides clues about modern *H. sapiens'* origins in Europe. The earliest modern *H. sapiens* were present as early as 35,000 yBP at Mladeč (Czech Republic) and at Peştera cu Oase (Romania). That the earliest modern *H. sapiens* had clear Neandertal features (such as the occipital bun) indicates interbreeding between Neandertals and early modern people. This finding argues against the Out-of-Africa model, which sees no gene flow between Neandertals and early modern humans. We will now see if the genetic record provides additional insight into modern *H. sapiens'* origins in Europe.

ANCIENT DNA: INTERBREEDING BETWEEN NEANDERTALS AND EARLY MODERN PEOPLE?

Analysis of mitochondrial DNA (mtDNA), the DNA inherited only via the mother, offers potential clues about the origins of modern people (mtDNA is among the topics of chapter 3). Comparisons of mtDNA from more than a dozen Neandertal skeletons—from Engis and Scladina in Belgium, Les Rochers-de-Villeneuve and La Chapelle-aux-Saints in France, Monte Lessini in Italy, El Sidrón in Spain, Feldhofer Cave in Germany, Mezmaiskaya in Russia, Teshik Tash in Uzbekistan, and Vindija Cave in Croatia—with that of early modern humans and living humans shows *similarity* among Neandertals and *dissimilarity* between Neandertals and modern humans. The German molecular geneticist Matthias Krings and his associates found, for example, that 27 mtDNA base pairs of a sequence of 378 base pairs from the Feldhofer Cave Neandertal differ completely from living Europeans'. In contrast, living human populations have an average of just eight differences among them. These genetic differences seem to support the hypothesis that no gene flow occurred between Neandertals and modern humans during the later Pleistocene and, importantly, that Neandertals contributed none of their genetic material to the modern human gene pool. Neandertals underwent extinction, pure and simple. However, the extinction hypothesis may not be the best one. That is, mtDNA is just a tiny part of the human genome and reflects only a very small fraction of the genetic code. The failure of one part of the genome to survive to the present does not mean that the entire genome became extinct. Moreover, it is possible that mtDNA lineages have been lost owing to genetic drift. Much more of the genome is needed to have a more complete picture.

Only recently has the remarkable scientific technology been available to document and characterize nuclear DNA (nDNA) in order to reconstruct the Neandertal genome. Such a reconstruction makes it possible to address the important question of the Neandertal contribution (if any) to the modern human genome. A breakthrough study led by Swedish geneticist Svante Pääbo used *high-throughput DNA sequencing*—a technology through which all of the genome can be sequenced from fossil bones—to answer this question. (Prior to the development of high-throughput sequencing, only segments of DNA were accessed.) The results using the new technology are breathtaking: Eurasians and Neandertals share between 1% and 4% of their nDNA, an indication of small but significant admixture. Given that Africans share no nDNA with Neandertals, the admixture occurred between early modern Europeans and Neandertals *after* early modern people expanded out of Africa and migrated to Europe. European and European-descended people living outside of Africa today have DNA that likely originated from Neandertals. In fact, people of European descent have on average 2% Neandertal DNA. In that sense, the Neandertals are still with us!

New studies of the Vindija Cave Neandertal genome show the presence of alleles that give us insights into modern human variation and the genetic and phenotypic contribution of Neandertals to modern human variation. For example, various research teams have revealed that Neandertal alleles contribute to skin and hair color in modern European populations, including both lighter and darker tones. This suggests that Neandertals, like modern humans, were variable in these phenotypes.

But there is much more to learn from the newly reconstructed Neandertal genome. For example, contributions of the Neandertal genome to key health and well-being indicators show genetic variants associated with low-density lipoprotein (LDL, or the so-called bad cholesterol). In addition, other health-related indicators are shared between Neandertals and modern *H. sapiens* in shaping the latter's immune system. French geneticist Hélène Quach and her research team have identified genetic variation associated with immune responses, especially those responses related to viruses and viral infections. These responses were introduced via admixture between Neandertals and Europeans, potentially representing a selective advantage.

THE DENISOVANS: THE OTHER LATE ARCHAIC *HOMO SAPIENS*

Not all early modern *H. sapiens* interbred with Neandertals exclusively. Beginning in 2010, analysis of mitochondrial and nuclear DNA recovered from a hominin hand bone, foot bone, and tooth dating to 40,000 yBP from Denisova Cave in southern Siberia revealed a hominin genome that is neither Neandertal nor modern human. In reconstructing the Denisovan genome, Svante Pääbo and team expected to find a genome that was either Neandertal or modern human. However, their analysis revealed a genome that shows some differences from Neandertals and modern humans. The only similarity they could find between the **Denisovans** and living people is from populations in Melanesia (New Guinea and Bougainville Island) and China. This finding suggests that genetic diversity in the Late Pleistocene is considerably more complex than previously thought and likely involved **introgression**, the mating between different hominin taxa (see chapter 4).

What has been especially vexing to paleoanthropologists, however, is the lack of a temporal and geographic context for the Denisovans. Moreover, based on the very scant fossil record, it has not been possible to say anything about what they looked like. How can we have a hominin that is represented by just a hand bone? But, temporal and genomic analyses of a hominin mandible found years earlier from the Baishiya Karst Cave near Xiahe, China, provide new insights into the identity of the Denisovans. In 2019, analyses by Fahu Chen and his research team gave a date of 160,000 yBP and new insights in the morphology of the lower face (**Figure 12.46**). The analyses of this fossil reveal that the Xiahe hominin is especially important because it is the earliest evidence for a hominin's adaptation to high altitude of 3,500 m (11,500 ft) above sea level and seasonally low temperatures (see chapter 5). Like the later Pleistocene contexts of high-altitude Ethiopia, this record from China further confirms the hypothesis that later Pleistocene hominins had successfully adapted to extreme environmental conditions involving both high altitude and cold conditions.

The emerging picture suggests that the Denisovans are archaic *H. sapiens* sharing a common origin with Neandertals. The genetic evidence strongly suggests that modern humans migrated from Africa and interbred with hominin species

Denisovans Extinct hominins, likely of the genus *Homo*; genetic evidence suggests they are related to Neandertals and modern *Homo sapiens*, perhaps sharing a common ancestor.

FIGURE 12.46

Baishiya Karst Cave Analysis of this partial mandible from Baishiya Karst Cave in Xiahe, China, reveals a broad geographic and temporal distribution of Denisovans in the Middle Pleistocene and signals the earliest evidence of high-altitude adaptation in hominin evolution.

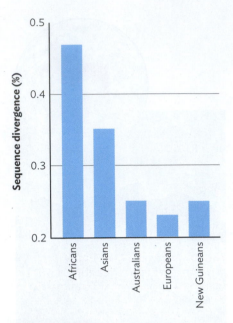

FIGURE 12.47

Genetic Diversity Patterns of genetic diversity have been used to assess the Out-of-Africa and Multiregional Continuity models of modern humans' origins. This graph shows genetic diversity within several major geographic groups, expressed as the average amount of genetic sequence divergence in percent. Note the much greater genetic diversity in Africans compared with other groups. (Source: R. L. Cann, M. Stoneking, and A. Wilson. 1987. Mitochondrial DNA and human evolution. *Nature* 325: 31–36.)

beyond just Neandertals. As the research continues, the picture of genetic variation and widening environmental contexts in humans on their evolutionary pathway toward modernity becomes increasingly complex.

LIVING PEOPLE'S GENETIC RECORD: SETTLING THE DEBATE ON MODERN HUMAN ORIGINS

Living people's genetic record helps settle the question about whether the Out-of-Africa model or the Multiregional Continuity model explains modern *H. sapiens'* origins. The American geneticist and molecular biologist Rebecca Cann and her collaborators have found that sub-Saharan African populations are more genetically diverse than populations from any other region of the world. That is, the genes of people living south of the Sahara Desert today are more variable in frequency than are the genes of people living in Europe, Asia, the Americas, and Australia (**Figure 12.47**). This pattern is also present in the phenotypic variation of anatomical characteristics (for example, cranial measurements).

Two explanations exist for Africa's greater genetic diversity. First, a population or group of populations that has been around a long time will have accumulated more mutations—hence, greater genetic variation—than will a population or group of populations that has been around a short time. Therefore, Africa's greater genetic diversity may mean that modern people have existed longer there than in Asia or Europe.

On the basis of their assessment of mutation rates, Cann's group came up with a figure of 200,000 yBP for the appearance of the first early modern *H. sapiens*, and this date is consistent with the earliest fossil record of modern *H. sapiens* in Africa. Calculations based on other sources of genetic material, such as from the Y chromosome, provide broadly similar results.

The second explanation for Africa's greater genetic diversity lies in its population structure compared with that of other continents. The American anthropological geneticist John Relethford observes that population size tremendously influences genetic diversity. As discussed in chapter 3, if the breeding population is small, then genetic drift is a potentially powerful force for altering gene frequencies. Over time, genetic drift reduces genetic diversity in a small population (such as might have been the case in Europe and Asia). For example, if a group of 10 people splits off from a group of 1,000 people, the two resulting groups will show very different patterns of gene frequency change. The smaller population will be less variable, whereas its parent population will be more variable. Relethford argues that because in the remote past Africa had a significantly larger breeding population size than other continents did, Africa now has greater genetic diversity.

12.5 Assimilation Model for Modern Human Variation: Neandertals Are Still with Us

The more modern characteristics of East African skeletons from the Upper Pleistocene (for example, Herto) provide compelling evidence that modern human variation originated in Africa and expanded from Africa to Europe and Asia. The fossil record and the genetic record indicate, however, that neither the Out-of-Africa model nor the Multiregional Continuity model adequately explains modern humans' origins. The Out-of-Africa model correctly accounts for the origin of modern human variation, but it incorrectly asserts that no gene flow occurred between Neandertals and modern *H. sapiens* once modern *H. sapiens* arrived in Europe. The Multiregional Continuity model is not correct about modern *H. sapiens'* regional development. However, it is correct about gene flow and the notion that Neandertals have contributed to modern *H. sapiens'* gene pool.

In other words, elements of both models explain the emergence and evolution of fully modern people worldwide in the Upper Pleistocene. That is, sometime within 200,000–100,000 yBP, a population of modern heat-adapted *H. sapiens* expanded outward from Africa to Europe and Asia. Once arriving in Europe, this population encountered the Neandertals—fellow members of their species who were as behaviorally and technologically complex as they. Cold-adapted people, the Neandertals had evolved from earlier *H. sapiens* populations in Europe—the early archaic *H. sapiens*—and they interbred with the newly arrived modern *H. sapiens*. Therefore, as proposed by Fred Smith, Anthony Falsetti, and Steven Donnelly in what is known as the **Assimilation model**, Neandertals' disappearance after 30,000 yBP or so likely resulted not from their extinction but from their assimilation by much larger, more genetically diverse populations of modern humans migrating into Europe from Africa during the Late Pleistocene (**Figure 12.48**). The Neandertal genetic

Assimilation model The hypothesis postulating the African origin of modern *Homo sapiens*, with contributions of Eurasian archaic *H. sapiens* during the migration process.

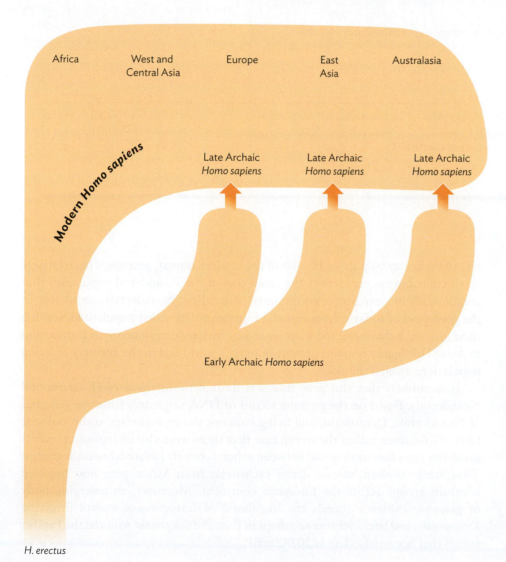

FIGURE 12.48

Assimilation Model According to this model, modern *Homo sapiens* evolved first in Africa from *Homo erectus*. Groups of *H. sapiens* then spread to Europe and Asia. Once in Europe and Asia, these modern *H. sapiens* interbred with late archaic *H. sapiens* (Neandertals) and Denisovans. This admixture is the biological foundation for modern *H. sapiens* living outside of Africa today. The narrow thickness of the vertical bars represents smaller population sizes of Neandertals, archaic East Asians, and archaic Australasians. The arrows show gene flow between archaic and early modern humans in specific regions. The taxonomic affiliation of Denisovans is unclear, but the genomic record indicates gene flow involving modern *H. sapiens*, Neandertals, and Denisovans in Europe during the later Pleistocene (Source: F. H. Smith. 2018. Assimilation model of modern human origins. Pp. 129–131 in W. Trevathan, ed. *International Encyclopedia of Biological Anthropology*. New York: John Wiley & Sons.)

Models for Explaining Modern *Homo sapiens'* Origins

With fossil and genetic records of human evolution now more complete than ever and continuing to grow, it is possible to weigh the strengths and weaknesses of hypotheses that explain the origins of modern *Homo sapiens*.

MODEL	FEATURES	PROPONENTS
Out-of-Africa	Modern biology, behavior, and culture originated in Africa.	Christopher Stringer
	Modern humans spread from Africa to Europe after 50,000 yBP.	
	Modern humans replaced all populations once arriving in Europe, with no gene flow.	
Multiregional Continuity	Modern humans evolved from earlier archaic populations in their respective regions (Africa, Europe, Asia).	Milford Wolpoff
	Throughout evolution, there is always significant gene flow on the borders of populations.	
	There is continuity of morphology in all regions of the globe.	
Assimilation	Modern humans first evolved in Africa, then spread to Europe and Asia.	Fred Smith, Erik Trinkaus, Anthony Falsetti, Steven Donnelly
	Once they arrived in Europe and Asia, modern humans underwent gene flow with Neandertals and Denisovans.	

record makes up only about 1%–4% of the modern human genome. This relatively small contribution may reflect the small size of the Neandertal population that anatomically modern people encountered. Regardless, Neandertals contributed to the gene pool of today's European and European-descended populations, leaving their genetic, behavioral, and adaptive legacy with modern humans in Europe and in Asia. This legacy remains present in today's world and in the ancestry of living populations around the globe.

It is unlikely that this gene flow was limited to just modern *H. sapiens* and Neandertals. Based on the growing record of DNA sequences from the genomes of Neandertals, Denisovans, and living humans, the evolutionary anthropologist Omer Gokcumen makes the strong case that there were also introgression events involving gene flow among and between other, formerly isolated, hominin groups. Thus, while modern humans derive exclusively from Africa, gene flow involved hominin groups across the European continent. Moreover, an emerging body of genomic evidence reveals the likelihood of introgression events involving Denisovans and later Pleistocene groups in East and Southeast Asia and the Pacific, events that occurred as late as 20,000 yBP.

12.6 Modern Humans' Other Migrations: Colonization of Australia, the Pacific, and the Americas

This chapter and the preceding one have emphasized the critical importance of migration and gene flow in human evolution. In the first wave out of Africa, *H. erectus* spread rapidly throughout Asia and Europe. In the second wave out of Africa, early modern *H. sapiens* assimilated with the descendants of *H. erectus* in Asia and Europe, especially the Neandertals and the Denisovans. The last 50,000 years of the Pleistocene saw fully modern people spreading not only into Asia and Europe but also to continents that had previously not been occupied by people. Prior to 50,000 yBP, humans occupied only three of the six inhabitable continents: Africa, Asia, and Europe. After 50,000 yBP, populations expanded from the southeastern fringes of Asia to Australia, eventually fanning out from west to east across the hundreds of islands that dot the Pacific Ocean. In the last few millennia of the Pleistocene, humans spread throughout the Americas (**Figure 12.49**). These migrations do not simply represent populations picking up and moving from one place to another. Rather, they represent adaptive radiations involving movement and adaptation to new settings. These adaptive radiations represent ongoing adaptations to unfamiliar environments and are no less a part of human evolution than are bipedalism, language use, and all the other key developments discussed in this chapter and in chapter 11. The spread of modern *H. sapiens* into Europe, Asia, and later into Australia and the Americas, and the associated adaptive radiations, were the end point of migrations of anatomically modern people out of Africa.

FIGURE 12.49

Modern Humans' Migrations Another major research question in biological anthropology focuses on modern humans' spread from and adaptive radiations in Asia, Australia, the Pacific, North America, and South America. This map shows modern humans' migration patterns and spread from southern Asia **(1a–6a)** and eastern Asia **(1b–3b)** beginning in the Late Pleistocene: **(1a)** earliest migration of modern *Homo sapiens* into Australia (Lake Mungo; ~40,000 yBP); **(2a)** earliest evidence of modern human occupation of New Guinea and adjacent islands (Bobongara; ~35,000 yBP); **(3a)** earliest evidence of modern human occupation of Tasmania (Warreen Cave; ~33,000 yBP); **(4a)** early expansion into Oceania (Mariana Islands; ~1500 BC); **(5a)** oceanic expansion into western Polynesia (Tonga and Samoa; ~1000 BC); **(6a)** expansion into eastern Polynesia (Cook Islands; ~AD 700); **(1b)** earliest evidence for expansion from Northeast Asia into North America (Beringia; ~15,500 yBP—or Clovis, New Mexico; ~12,000 yBP); **(2b)** proposed coastal route for colonization of the Pacific rim of North America, Central America, and South America (Monte Verde, Chile; ~14,500 yBP); **(3b)** migration of earliest Native Americans across North America.

What motivated these early modern people to move? Among the multiple reasons, four are most important: population increase, disappearance of food resources, increased competition with neighbors for remaining resources, and climate deterioration. That is, a population's resources—food especially—are available in finite quantities. As Relethford has shown through genetic studies, African populations expanded rapidly during the Late Pleistocene. These increases, as populations outgrew their carrying capacities, were the prime force stimulating anatomically modern people to move into Asia and Europe. Similarly, as population size expanded in Asia and Europe, humans continued to move and began to occupy vast regions of the globe.

Beginning in the very late Pleistocene, eastern Asia became the stepping-off point for migrations to previously unoccupied continents. Southeast Asia, the first rainforest occupation by anatomically modern humans some 60,000 yBP, served as the stepping-off point for the movements to Australia and across the Pacific as people eventually occupied most of the 20,000–30,000 islands between Australia and the Americas. Northeast Asia served as the stepping-off point for the spread to North America and South America.

DOWN UNDER AND BEYOND: THE AUSTRALIAN AND PACIFIC MIGRATIONS

In the Late Pleistocene, sea levels were considerably lower than they are today, by as much as 90 m (295 ft), exposing land surfaces now submerged by water and making them available for human occupation and movement between landmasses. Australia and New Guinea constituted a single landmass, which we call *Greater Australia* (**Figure 12.50**). The islands of Sulawesi, Borneo, and Java were connected to mainland Asia. But even at the peak of the Late Pleistocene's coldest period, when sea levels were at their lowest, a considerable distance of open water separated Greater Australia from Asia. At least 70 km (43.5 mi) of open water separated Sulawesi and Borneo from Australia. To traverse open water from southeastern

FIGURE 12.50

Land Bridge During the Late Pleistocene, temperatures were much cooler and a great amount of seawater was locked in glaciers. As a result, sea levels were at their lowest, exposing shallow land, such as the Sunda shelf in Southeast Asia. On this map, the exposed land is white. Some of it connected the islands of Southeast Asia (Borneo, Java, and Sumatra) with the Asian mainland, and some of it connected Australia with New Guinea and Tasmania. Despite the increased land area, traveling to Australia would have still required a sea voyage; however, there was much less distance between Southeast Asia and Australia. Modern researchers are unable to investigate evidence of the people who once inhabited the areas that are now under water.

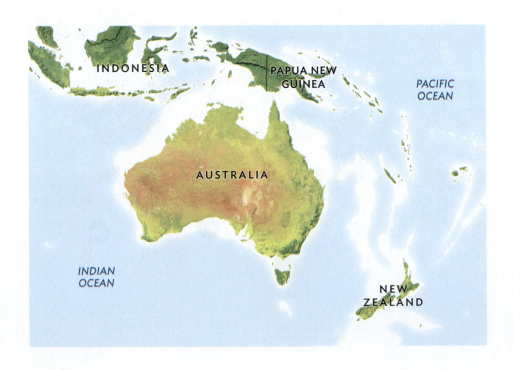

Asia to Australia, Late Pleistocene humans would have needed boating technology of some manner and equally sophisticated navigational skills. No evidence of such technology and skills has been found.

The earliest human biological record in Australia is from Lake Mungo, in southeastern Australia (New South Wales), dating to about 40,000 yBP. The two skulls from Lake Mungo, from an adult male and an adult female, have modern characteristics: the skulls are high and have rounded foreheads with small browridges. In overall appearance, the skulls resemble ones from Kow Swamp in Victoria's Murray River valley, which date to 13,000–9,000 yBP (**Figure 12.51**). However, the Kow Swamp skulls are more robust, with larger browridges, larger and more robust faces, and lower foreheads than the Lake Mungo skulls. These early Australians share features with *H. erectus* and later Indonesian hominins, especially in the facial skeleton, such as in the shape of the eye orbits. These anatomical similarities suggest a common genetic origin, thereby indicating regional continuity of human populations and their biological evolution. It is unclear how early the first arrival and occupation of Australia occurred, but consideration of the genetic, archaeological, and paleoanthropological record by American archaeologist James O'Connell and collaborators suggests that it was less than 50,000 yBP.

These early Australians also bear a strong similarity to native people who inhabit the continent today; the anatomical evidence indicates an ancestral–descendant relationship. However, mtDNA from the Lake Mungo and Kow Swamp skeletons differs substantially from that of living native Australians. Based on the mtDNA evidence alone, one might conclude that the ancient populations represented by the Lake Mungo and Kow Swamp skeletons were not ancestral to living native Australians, but this conclusion runs counter to a range of cultural and archaeological evidence. As with the Neandertal mtDNA lineages discussed earlier, a more likely explanation for the disparity between ancient and modern genes in Australia is that the mtDNA sequence in ancient anatomically modern people has not survived to the present. This Australian evidence is an important example of the very different evolutionary pathways that mtDNA and anatomical evolution can take. The fossil remains show continuity with modern native people of Australia, but the mtDNA lineage went extinct at some point after 40,000 yBP.

Southeast Asia is also the point of origin for populations that eventually dispersed throughout the Pacific Ocean. Most of the Pacific islands extending from east of New Guinea to Easter Island were not settled until well after 5,000 yBP. In fact, east of the Solomon Islands, settlement across the vast Pacific did not begin until after about 1500 BC, ending with humans' arrival on Easter Island around AD 600.

ARRIVAL IN THE WESTERN HEMISPHERE: THE FIRST AMERICANS

Nearly a century ago, the American biological anthropologist Aleš Hrdlička noted the remarkable similarity in the shapes of the upper incisors of East Asian and Native American peoples, past and present. He observed that East Asians and Native Americans have **shovel-shaped incisors** (**Figure 12.52**). In these incisors and many other dental features, the American anthropologists Albert Dahlberg and Christy Turner identified a common ancestry for East Asians and Native Americans. Common ancestry is supported by the fact that most Native Americans

FIGURE 12.51

Kow Swamp This Australian site has yielded skeletons much more robust than those discovered at Lake Mungo.

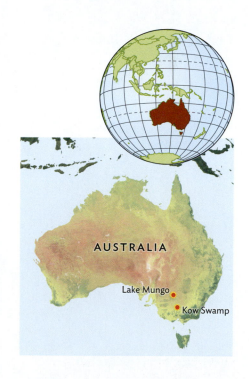

AUSTRALIA

Lake Mungo

Kow Swamp

shovel-shaped incisors A dental trait, commonly found among Native Americans and Asians, in which the incisors' posterior aspect has varying degrees of concavity.

FIGURE 12.52

Shovel-Shaped Incisors A dental characteristic often found in East Asians is the shoveled appearance of the back, or lingual side, of the incisors. That this trait has also been found in Native Americans likely reflects their descent from East Asians.

today have exclusively blood type O. Moreover, the alleles for this blood type are present with only limited variation. It is highly likely, therefore, that the founding population had these characteristics.

Additional clues about the peopling of the Americas appear in modern and ancient Native Americans' mtDNA. For 95% of living Native Americans throughout North America and South America, nearly all mtDNA falls into any one of four main haplogroups—A, B, C, or D. (As discussed in chapter 3, mtDNA is inherited just from the mother, so the haplogroup unit reflects the maternal line of inheritance.) Notably, the same pattern of four main haplogroups has been found in mtDNA recovered from ancient Native American skeletons. This sharing of haplogroups by modern people and ancient skeletons indicates a common founding ancestry for present and past Native Americans representing just four maternal lines with each having a common ancestor around 18,000–15,000 yBP. Moreover, Native Americans share haplogroups with northeastern Asians. The evidence indicates that the haplogroups were present in Asians who migrated to the Americas (**Figure 12.53**). The presence of all four groups throughout the Americas and the great similarity of the nucleotide sequences suggest that Native Americans share

FIGURE 12.53

Native American Mitochondrial DNA Studies of mtDNA haplogroups in Native Americans have yielded information about human migrations from Asia to the Americas. This map shows the relative amount of each haplogroup in various native groups (the Eskaleut, the Na-Dené, and the Amerind).

a common ancestry in a single founding population that arrived in the Americas from Asia via one migration. Consistent with the mtDNA evidence from skeletal remains is the emerging record provided by the sequencing of the genome from a Paleoindian young boy's skeleton from Anzick, Montana, dating to the Late Pleistocene (ca. 12,700 yBP). The strong similarity of the genome with that of Native people today indicates that the person and the population he represents was part of the earliest wave of migration giving rise to nearly all indigenous groups in North and South America. Research by the American anthropological geneticist Connie Mulligan and her colleagues suggests that the founding population consisted of only about 800 people who were reproductively isolated from Asian populations for some period of time before traveling on to North and South America.

This northeastern Asian origin indicates that in contrast to Australia's founding populations, who were adapted to tropical, wet climates, the Americas' founding populations were adapted to cold, dry climates. Both migrations indicate that these founding humans were adapted to extreme environments at the margins of human capabilities.

In contrast to the migrations to Australia and the Pacific, where the founders traveled across open seas, migrations to the Americas occurred via a land route or along the deglaciated Pacific coastline or via both routes. If it was a land route, then it was likely across the Bering Land Bridge (which we call *Beringea*), connecting Siberia and Alaska. Like those in the western Pacific Ocean, this land route was created when sea levels reached a low point during the later Pleistocene, exposing areas of land that are now submerged.

Genetic dating based on mutation rates of mtDNA and Y chromosomes, as well as single nucleotide polymorphisms (SNPs; see chapter 3) and the genomic record, indicates that the migration from Asia to the Americas likely took place by about 15,000 yBP. The genetic dating is consistent with the dates on the earliest archaeological sites in the Americas, such as from the Page–Ladson site in Florida, dating to 14,550 yBP. The genetic/genomic findings indicate that one early migration likely resulted in the ancestral population for most Native Americans of North America and South America today. The uniform distribution of haplotypes and genomic evidence across the Americas indicates that the migration was a remarkably rapid process and not a slow diffusion. Two other smaller and much later migrations from Asia yielded the founding populations of (1) Na-Dené speakers of northwestern North America and the Navajo and Apache of the southwestern United States and (2) the speakers of Eskimo–Aleut languages, respectively. In North America, the earliest well-documented archaeological record of habitation and material culture (especially stone artifacts) dates to around 11,500 yBP. The earliest people associated with this and other early cultures are called **Paleoindians**. They are well known from stone artifacts, especially large spear points associated with pre-Clovis, **Clovis**, and later **Folsom** cultures. The Paleoindians hunted various animals, but they are best known for hunting **megafauna**, the large Pleistocene game such as the mammoth, steppe bison, and reindeer (caribou) in North America, and processing the meat from these animals for food (**Figure 12.54**).

Pleistocene megafauna throughout the Americas became extinct by the Early Holocene, and some evidence suggests that in the Americas and Australia, humans hunted these large animals to extinction. It seems unlikely, however, that small numbers of humans could have killed so many animals in such a short time. These extinctions were more likely due, at least in part, to climate change at the end of the Pleistocene and the changes in habitats frequented by large mammals. If humans'

Paleoindians The earliest hominin inhabitants of the Americas; they likely migrated from Asia and are associated with the Clovis and Folsom stone tool cultures in North America and comparable stone tool cultures in South America.

Clovis The earliest Native American ("Paleoindian") culture of North America; technology known for large, fluted, bifacial stone projectile points used as spear points for big-game hunting.

Folsom Early Native American (immediately following Clovis) culture of North America; technology known for large, fluted, bifacial projectile points used as spear points for big-game hunting.

megafauna Large game animals hunted by pre-Holocene and Early Holocene humans.

(a)

(b)

FIGURE 12.54

Paleoindians **(a)** This first group of inhabitants in the Americas likely hunted a variety of megafauna, such as the mammoth shown here and a wide range of other animals. **(b)** The tools the Paleoindians hunted with included a specialized, fluted projectile point, which we call a *Folsom point*. An extraordinary amount of skill was required to make this tool.

hunting during the Late Pleistocene and Early Holocene was involved, then it played a very minor part.

While a continuity in genes has been demonstrated between Paleoindians and later Native peoples, there were distinctive anatomical changes between them, most of which reflect foods consumed. One very clear difference is reflected in craniofacial morphology. The Paleoindians' skulls were relatively long and narrow, and their faces were robust, with large attachment areas for the masticatory muscles. In contrast, many late prehistoric and living Native Americans have short, round skulls with gracile faces. For example, the Paleoindian skull from Kennewick, Washington, dating to 8,400 yBP, is long and narrow; the face and jaws are robust (**Figure 12.55**). These differences between the Paleoindians and modern Native Americans have been interpreted to mean either that the Paleoindians are not the living Native Americans' ancestors or, alternatively, that the Paleoindians are the living Native Americans' ancestors, but cranial morphology has changed because of evolutionary forces and other processes over the past 10,000 years in the Americas (discussed further in chapter 13).

In 2015, the Danish paleogeneticist Eske Willerslev and his team at the Natural History Museum of Denmark discovered that the genetic variation—autosomal, mtDNA, and Y-chromosomal—is strongly similar between Kennewick Man and recent Native Americans, which makes it highly unlikely that Paleoindians are not the ancestors of modern Native Americans. That is, the ancestral–descendant genetic relationship supports the hypothesis that the cranial morphology evolved *in situ* and was shaped by later processes, such as those involving use of the face and jaws in mastication. This record is consistent with studies of Paleoindians from the Yucatán Peninsula in Mexico showing a different morphology in Paleoindians than in later populations, yet with clear genetic links between the earlier and later populations. Overall, this important record—fossil and genetic—shows that Paleoindians have a different cranial morphology from that of modern Native Americans, but with clear genetic ties between the two. In summary: Like all other populations you have read about in this book, populations native to the Americas have evolved. The migrational stasis and period of isolation in Beringea played a major role in determining the genetic composition of Native American populations from the time of the initial migration into the Americas to recent times. The record of genetic continuity at all levels—hemispheric, continental, regional, and local—is striking to the scientists who study the genetic record.

Modern humans' emergence and subsequent dispersal around the globe marks a remarkable period of population expansion, behavioral and biological diversification, and assimilation. The geographic biological diversity in the world today was likely well in place by the end of the Pleistocene. The rapid expansion of human population size resulted in increased types of foods eaten. The adoption and increased use of fish and aquatic life in general during the Late Pleistocene likely reflects humans' need for alternative foods as population size expanded. Such dietary expansion set the stage for one of the most dramatic adaptive shifts in human evolution, the shift from eating plants that were gathered and animals that were hunted to eating plants and animals that were domesticated. In the next chapter, we will look at this important transition's biological implications for humans over the past 10,000 years of our evolution.

FIGURE 12.55

Kennewick Man Discovered on the banks of the Columbia River, Kennewick Man represents the Paleoindians. This artist's reconstruction shows his likely facial appearance.

ANSWERING THE BIG QUESTIONS

1. **What is so modern about modern humans?**
   - Distinguishing characteristics of modern humans include small faces, jaws, and teeth; a vertical and high forehead; narrow nasal apertures and body trunks; and long legs.

2. **What do *Homo sapiens* fossils reveal about modern humans' origins?**
   - Early archaic *H. sapiens* evolved from *Homo erectus*.
   - In Africa, nearly modern people evolved 200,000–150,000 yBP. After 130,000 yBP, an archaic form of *H. sapiens* called Neandertals occupied western Asia and then Europe.
   - From about 40,000 to 30,000 yBP, multiple hominin groups occupied Europe: Neandertals, modern *H. sapiens*, and Denisovans.

3. **How has variation in fossil *H. sapiens* been interpreted?**
   - The Out-of-Africa model argues that modern *H. sapiens* migrated from Africa to Asia and Europe, replacing native late archaic *H. sapiens*, including Neandertals.
   - The Multiregional Continuity model argues that modern *H. sapiens* arose regionally in each of the three inhabited continents: Africa, Asia, and Europe.
   - Physical characteristics and DNA in fossils support the Assimilation model, which argues that Neandertals in Europe and Asia were assimilated through admixture with early modern *H. sapiens* (who originated in Africa) and did not go extinct.

4. **What other developments took place in *H. sapiens*' evolution?**
   - More advanced tools, diet diversification, and symbolism appeared first in Africa and later in Europe and Asia.
   - Neandertals were likely capable of articulate speech.
   - Neandertals and contemporary humans were the first species to intentionally bury their dead.
   - Fully modern humans migrated to Australia by 40,000 yBP and to North and South America by 15,000 yBP.

- Modern human populations globally have evolved in significant ways morphologically since the Late Pleistocene, as established by the ancient DNA record.
- Gene flow occurred among early modern humans, Neandertals, and Denisovans in Europe and Asia.

STUDY QUIZ

1. **What distinguishes early archaic *Homo sapiens* from *Homo erectus*?**
   a. Presence in Asia and Europe
   b. Loss of large browridges
   c. Development of a projecting chin
   d. Reduction in skeletal robusticity

2. **What aspect of Neandertal culture supports their intelligence?**
   a. Their simpler Mousterian stone tools
   b. Inefficient hunting techniques
   c. No communicating by speech
   d. Symbolic burial rituals

3. **Modern *H. sapiens* most likely evolved**
   a. from archaic *H. sapiens* already living in Africa, Asia, and Europe.
   b. in Africa and replaced archaic *H. sapiens* in Asia and Europe.
   c. in Asia and Europe and replaced archaic *H. sapiens* in Africa.
   d. in Africa and assimilated archaic *H. sapiens* in Asia and Europe.

4. **How did modern *H. sapiens* reach North and South America?**
   a. They crossed the Pacific Ocean from Australia.
   b. They migrated from Southeast Asia via the Pacific islands.
   c. They migrated from Northeast Asia along the Bering Land Bridge.
   d. They traveled from southern Africa through Antarctica.

KEY TERMS

Assimilation model
calculus
Clovis
Denisovans
Folsom
Homo luzonensis
introgression
Levallois technique
megafauna
microcephaly
Middle Paleolithic
Mousterian
occipital bun
Paleoindians
shovel-shaped incisors
Upper Paleolithic

STUDY QUIZ (CONTINUED)

5. ***Homo floresiensis* has *not* been proposed to be**
    a. a modern human with a developmental abnormality.
    b. within the range of variation of local human populations.
    c. an isolated descendant of an earlier hominin species.
    d. a descendant of modern humans.

EVOLUTION REVIEW

The Origins of Modern People

SYNOPSIS Since some of the earliest discoveries of hominin fossils, such as that of the Neandertal skull found in Germany in 1856, biological anthropologists have uncovered an amazing amount of information about our evolutionary past. Fossil discoveries, as well as the application of new technologies in genetic research, have helped clarify the relationship between anatomically modern humans and our evolutionary cousins, the Neandertals. These results have also helped determine the most likely scenario for the origin and subsequent global dispersal of our own species, *Homo sapiens*, from approximately 200,000 yBP to the present. The remarkable discoveries made and rigorous scientific study performed by paleoanthropologists continue to inform our understanding of what it means to be human.

Q1. Provide two examples of anatomical features that biological anthropologists consider to be "modern" when defining modern humans as a species (*H. sapiens*). Also, identify two ways in which these "modern" features contrast with the morphological characteristics present in earlier members of the genus *Homo*.

Q2. As discussed in chapter 5, modern human variation is highly influenced by environmental factors. Describe three cranial and postcranial features of Neandertal skeletons that are likely adaptations to the cold climates of Upper Pleistocene Europe.

Q3. Many early descriptions and modern popular depictions portray Neandertals as particularly primitive in comparison to modern humans. Summarize the aspects of Neandertal behavior and culture that strongly counter the assumption that they were simplistic, cognitively deficient evolutionary failures.

Q4. Contrast the Out-of-Africa and Multiregional Continuity models for explaining the origins of anatomically modern *H. sapiens*. Using both fossil and genetic evidence, outline how neither model by itself adequately explains modern human origins but how elements of both contribute to the Assimilation model.

HINT Consider the genetic evidence from both fossil specimens and living human populations.

Q5. More than 1.5 million years after *H. erectus* became the first hominin species to migrate out of Africa, modern *H. sapiens* also spread from Africa to Europe and Asia and from there to Australia and the Americas. What kinds of environmental pressures contributed to the dispersal of modern *H. sapiens* across all regions of the globe? What do the migrations of modern humans into Australia (at least 40,000 yBP) and the Americas (at least 15,000 yBP) tell us about the range of human variation and adaptability in the past? How does this compare to the diversity we see in human populations today?

ADDITIONAL READINGS

Bräuer, G. 2008. The origin of modern anatomy: By speciation or intraspecific evolution? *Evolutionary Anthropology* 17: 22–37.

Disotell, T. R. 2012. Archaic human genomics. *Yearbook of Physical Anthropology* 55: 24–39.

Meltzer, D. J. 2009. *First Peoples in a New World: Colonizing Ice Age America.* Berkeley: University of California Press.

Nowell, A. 2010. Defining behavioral modernity in the context of Neandertal and anatomically modern human populations. *Annual Review of Anthropology* 39: 437–452.

Relethford, J. H. 2001. *Genetics and the Search for Modern Human Origins.* New York: Wiley-Liss.

Ruff, C. B. 1993. Climatic adaptation and hominid evolution: The thermoregulatory imperative. *Evolutionary Anthropology* 2: 53–60.

Waters, M. R. 2019. Late Pleistocene exploration and settlement of the Americas by modern humans. *Science* 365: eaat5447.

Weaver, T. D. 2009. The meaning of Neandertal skeletal morphology. *Proceedings of the National Academy of Sciences USA* 106: 16028–16033.

Wolpoff, M. H. and R. Caspari. 1997. *Race and Human Evolution: A Fatal Attraction.* New York: Simon & Schuster.

Once humans began practicing agriculture, three of the main crops they cultivated were corn, wheat, and rice, among many others. The movement from procuring wild food to producing domesticated food has had many varied outcomes for modern *Homo sapiens*, including changes in health, well-being, and lifestyle. These developments in the human condition beginning around 10,000 yBP provided the context for the challenges facing our world today and in the future.

13

Our Past 10,000 Years

AGRICULTURE, POPULATION, BIOLOGY

BIG QUESTIONS

1. When, where, and why did agriculture first develop?
2. How did agriculture affect human living circumstances?
3. How did agriculture affect human biological change?
4. What does our evolutionary future look like?

One of my greatest disappointments as a child was when my dentist told me my teeth were crooked and had to be straightened. My dentist was able to fix the problem by removing a lower third premolar on each side of my mandible, making room for other teeth to grow without crowding taking place. Most of my friends were not so lucky: the problems with their teeth required years of treatment, which involved painful throbbing in their mouths after each orthodontic visit (in which the braces were tightened as in some kind of medieval torture). In addition, they suffered a tinny-metallic flavor no matter what was eaten, food stuck in their wiring, and, perhaps worst of all, dietary restrictions (no popcorn, no gum, no caramel, nothing sweet and sticky)—in short, none of the wonderful comforts of "civilization" (**Figure 13.1**).

"Relax, Billy, they're just braces, even I had them when I was your age."

(a)

(b)

FIGURE 13.1

Braces **(a)** The straightening of teeth has become so common that orthodontics in the United States is a multibillion-dollar industry. **(b)** Among the types of braces used are the standard, stainless-steel wires and apparatus shown here. ([a] www.CartoonStock.com)

Tooth crowding and *malocclusion*—improper fit of the upper and lower teeth, sometimes called underbite or overbite—are commonplace around much of the world today. Millions of people have crowded, misaligned teeth. This phenomenon has not always been the case, however. It has occurred mostly within the past 10,000 years—the Holocene. What happened?

This development, not present for most of human evolution, came about because of changes in *what* humans ate and *how* they prepared their food for consumption. Namely, they switched from a diet of wild plants and wild animals to a diet partly based on domesticated plants and domesticated animals. In other words, in many areas of the world humans gave up, at least in part, hunting and gathering for agriculture (farming). They shifted from *foraging* for their food to *producing* their food. Moreover, pottery—invented first by hunter-gatherers 10,000 years earlier in Late Pleistocene China—took on a new function; namely, as vessels for boiling grains into soft mushes. As a result of this technology, foods became much softer than ever before. These changes in what was eaten and how it was prepared reduced the stresses on humans' chewing muscles. This reduced stress, like that on any muscle, also reduced the underlying bone. Basically, we have smaller jaws now because our ancestors began eating softer foods. (Remember Wolff's law, discussed in chapter 5: bone develops where it is needed and recedes where it is unnecessary.)

Tooth size is under stronger genetic control than is bone size, and as a result, tooth size is less affected by the environment. As a consequence, humans' teeth had much less room to grow, resulting in the remarkable increase in crowded and poorly occluded teeth (**Figure 13.2**). The malocclusion epidemic, part of recent human evolution, is one of many outcomes of our species' dietary change and but one example of our very dynamic biology. Of greater importance for health and well-being in our current world, though, is the rapidly growing size and density of the human population. Population growth is one of a number of factors that provide the environmental and cultural conditions conducive to the evolution and spread of pathogens that cause infectious disease. The spread of these pathogens can, in turn, cause deadly global pandemics, making them one of humankind's most significant modern challenges.

(a)   (b)

FIGURE 13.2

Malocclusion Two major forms of malocclusion can be corrected with orthodontic treatments, including braces. **(a)** An overbite occurs when the maxillary teeth extend farther forward than the mandibular teeth. **(b)** An underbite occurs when the mandibular teeth extend farther forward than the maxillary teeth. While malocclusion appears in some archaeological skeletal remains, it became common only after humans adopted agriculture.

13.1 The Agricultural Revolution: New Foods, New Adaptations, New Challenges

Up until roughly 10,000 yBP, humans acquired all their food through hunting and gathering. They hunted, trapped, fished, and otherwise collected animals big and small, terrestrial and aquatic; and they collected a huge variety of plants. During the later Pleistocene, they began to intensively exploit fish and shellfish in oceans, lakes, and streams. In the final centuries of that epoch, at the key environmental transition from the Pleistocene's cold and dry climate to the Holocene's warm and wet climate, people began to control the growth cycles of animals and plants through a process called **domestication.** Eventually, humans replaced nearly all the wild animals and plants in their diets with domesticated animals and plants. This dramatic change in lifeway—in which people at the end of the Pleistocene and in the Early Holocene began raising the animals and grew the plants they ate—is associated with the period called the **Neolithic**.

By any measure, the invention and adoption of agriculture in human prehistory ranks as one of the most transformative developments in the record of hominin evolution. It was the foundation for the profoundly important adaptive transition from foraging to farming. I rank agriculture up there with bipedalism and speech as being fundamental to who today's humans are as organisms. As will be discussed in this chapter, this shift had important and long-lasting implications for *Homo sapiens* as an evolving species. For example, many diseases in humans today are linked in one way or another to this extraordinary change in lifeway. The transition from foraging to farming laid the foundation for population size to increase to its current remarkable level, resulting in an increasingly crowded world. This transition has had, and will continue to have, enormous implications for the health and well-being of all who inhabit the world today and for the foreseeable future. These implications reflect the basic tenets of biology and evolution that were introduced at the beginning of this book and which you examined in the first days of your biological anthropology class.

But for now, let's return to the beginning of human evolution. For 99.8% of the 7 million years of human evolution, hominins ate plants and animals of all kinds,

domestication The process of converting wild animals or wild plants into forms that humans can care for and cultivate.

Neolithic The Late Pleistocene–Early Holocene culture, during which humans domesticated plants and animals.

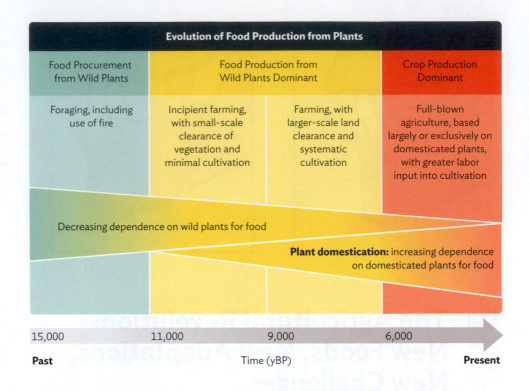

FIGURE 13.3

Adoption of Agriculture As this chart illustrates, humans did not simply abandon foraging and adopt agriculture. Initially, they foraged for wild plants to supplement their farming of cultivated plants. Over time, they depended less on wild plants and more on domesticated plants.

but not until very recently did they *grow* them. Domesticated plants became an integral part of food production across much of the globe, all within just the last 10,000 years or so, but that quickness is relative to the geologic timescale. Rather than happening overnight, the shift from foraging to farming took place over centuries and likely involved many successes and failures as the process unfolded for different human populations around the world (**Figure 13.3**). But compared with evolutionary changes that took place over thousands, hundreds of thousands, or even millions of years, the transitional process of domestication—the dietary changes, biological adaptations, and resulting health changes—was quite rapid.

Authorities agree on where and when domestication took place, based on the study of plant and animal remains found in archaeological sites in various places around the world. In addition, breakthroughs in plant and animal genetics and genomics provide new insights on the origins of domesticated species. That is, the domesticated descendants of formerly wild plants and animals have undergone genetic changes from their ancestral forms, and these genetic changes have been documented via breeding experiments and by the extraction and study of plant and animal DNA. The changes were brought about by humans' selecting food products that were beneficial to them. For example, they probably selected many plants with soft outer coatings and large seed yields. In a very real sense, humans practiced artificial selection, as opposed to natural selection. The resulting changes proved very deleterious for some of the species being domesticated. In wheat, the part holding all the edible sections is called the *rachis*, and at some point humans selected wheat with a hard rachis for storage and later consumption. This practice, in turn, selected for plants with a hard rachis. After many generations, the wheat was unable to reproduce itself because humans had selected for plants that could not reproduce without human involvement (annual planting manually).

The American archaeologist and zooarchaeologist Melinda Zeder regards one important outcome for humans to be the increased security and predictability of food access. This was a mutualistic relationship with their plant and animal

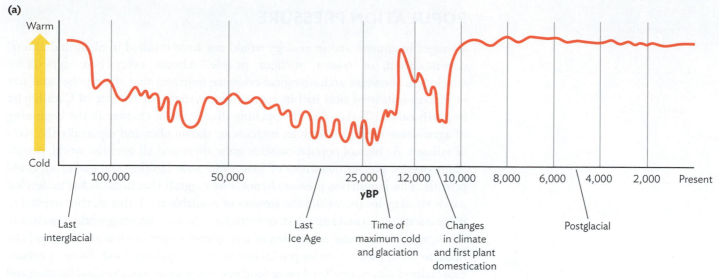

(a)

Warm

Cold

| 100,000 | 50,000 | 25,000 | 12,000 | 10,000 | 8,000 | 6,000 | 4,000 | 2,000 | Present |

yBP

Last interglacial

Last Ice Age

Time of maximum cold and glaciation

Changes in climate and first plant domestication

Postglacial

(b)

(c)

FIGURE 13.4

Temperature Changes and Plant Domestication **(a)** Over the past 120,000 years, as this timeline shows, Earth's temperature has fluctuated substantially. Around 11,000 yBP, a rapid warming trend created new habitats favorable for plant domestication. **(b)** The first grains were the wild ancestors of the domesticated varieties we know today. The wild ancestor of maize (right) is teosinte (left). **(c)** Domestication began with humans' harvesting of wild plants using Late Paleolithic technology, such as this tool, an antler handle with stone microblades inserted into it.

"partners" in that plants and animals experienced increased reproductive fitness, range expansion, and productivity.

While authorities agree on where and when this dramatic, worldwide change in food acquisition took place, they disagree on its cause. They are learning, however, that the change likely did not have only one cause. At least two factors probably brought about this agricultural revolution. First, the environment changed radically, going from cooler, drier, and highly variable during the very late Pleistocene to warmer, wetter, and more stable during the Holocene, beginning around 10,000–12,000 yBP (**Figure 13.4**). This abrupt environmental change taking place globally brought about new conditions—local climates and local ecologies—suited to the domestication of plants and of animals. Second, almost everywhere, agriculture was developing and human population was increasing.

POPULATION PRESSURE

Changes in climate and in ecology would not have resulted in plant and animal domestication, of course, without people. Almost everywhere agriculture developed, abundant archaeological evidence indicates that the number and size of human-inhabited sites had increased. For example, at the site of Çatalhöyük in south-central Turkey (see the opening discussion in chapter 1), the beginning of agriculture coincided with an increase in the number and especially the sizes of villages. As human population sizes grew there and all over the world, people likely needed greater quantities of food than what hunting and gathering could provide. This population pressure hypothesis suggests that humans *had* to develop a new strategy for increasing the amount of available food; that is, they needed to domesticate plants and animals in order to feed the ever-growing world population. Thus, agriculture came into being as a response to population pressure and the need to have another, more productive way of acquiring food. Domestication, especially of plants, produced more food per unit area of land than had hunting and gathering—more people could be fed from the same amount of land. In addition, agriculture provided food that could be stored for long periods. As an adaptive solution to population increase, domestication shows yet another example of humans' remarkable flexibility under new and challenging circumstances.

REGIONAL VARIATION

Plant and animal domestication processes and outcomes were not simply the result of a one-time event, first occurring in one place and then spreading globally. Rather, domestication—in particular, plant domestication—started in at least 11 independent regions around the world (**Figure 13.5**). From these primary centers, the practice spread through a process of diffusion in some areas and through the movement of agricultural people in others. It evolved slowly in some areas and quickly in others. Eventually, every inhabitable continent except Australia saw the change. In some regions, newly domesticated plants replaced earlier ones. For example, in the American Midwest, native seed crops—goosefoot, sumpweed, and sunflowers—were farmed about 6,000–1,000 yBP. Later, corn replaced these crops, probably owing to its greater productivity and potential for feeding more people than before.

Archaeological evidence and genetic studies of domesticated plants indicate that prior to becoming agricultural at the end of the Pleistocene, people living in southwestern Asia began to intensively harvest the grains of wheat's and barley's wild ancestors. These grains provided food for the growing populations that were beginning to live in small, settled communities for at least part of the year. For the other part of the year, people were likely out and about, hunting and gathering. Within 1,000 or so years after this combined practice of exploiting wild grains and foraging, sometime around 11,500 yBP, people began to manipulate the growth cycles of plants. This manipulation was purposeful and probably based on the simple observation that some seeds falling to the ground grew into new plants. People figured out what circumstances were conducive to the plants' growth, such as adequate water and protection from animals that might eat the plants. It would have been important for the people harvesting these plants to realize that if the seeds were placed in the ground, they would sprout new plants that could grow to full maturity. These mature plants could then be harvested, just as the plants' wild ancestors were harvested generations before.

(a)

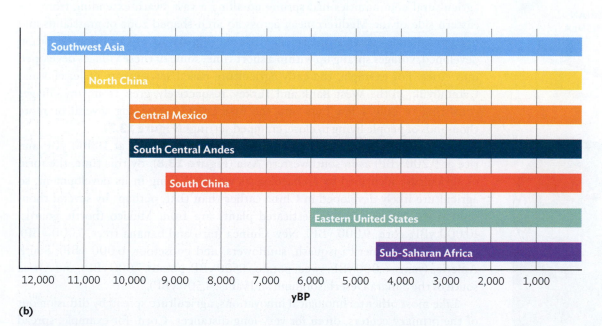

(b)

FIGURE 13.5

Worldwide Plant Domestication **(a)** This map shows the 11 separate centers of plant domestication. At each location, different types of domesticated plants were cultivated, including maize in Central America, sunflowers in eastern North America, cotton in South America, millet and sorghum in Africa, wheat in the Middle East, and banana trees in New Guinea. **(b)** This chart illustrates the approximate times of plant and animal domestication in the major regions of the world.

FIGURE 13.6

Southwestern Asia and the Fertile Crescent Southwestern Asia, especially the region known by anthropologists as the Fertile Crescent, has numerous archaeological sites that date between 11,500 and 8,000 yBP and contain evidence of early agriculture.

The archaeological record suggests that farming first started in southwestern Asia, specifically in modern-day Turkey, around 10,500 yBP. By 8,000 yBP, early agricultural communities had sprung up along a vast swath extending from the eastern side of the Mediterranean across an arch-shaped zone of grasslands and open woodlands known as the Fertile Crescent (**Figure 13.6**). Once domestication developed, villages sprang up within a short time; some of these villages developed into cities. For example, the early agriculture-based settlements of Jericho and Çatalhöyük, in the West Bank and Turkey, respectively, grew from tiny villages consisting of only a few huts into the first cities, containing several or more thousands of people living in close, cramped settings (**Figure 13.7**).

Plant domestication was nearly as early in China (millet at 11,000 yBP and rice at 9,200 yBP) as in southwestern Asia (**Figure 13.8**). By this time, the form of agriculture identified by archaeologists was well along in its development, so agriculture likely developed in China earlier than that, perhaps by several thousand years. Other early domesticated plants are from Mexico (bottle gourds, 10,000 yBP; corn, 9,000 yBP), New Guinea (taro and banana trees, 7,000 yBP), eastern North America (squash, sunflowers, and goosefoot, 6,000 yBP), South America (yams, 6,000 yBP; sweet potato, 4,500 yBP; potato, 7,000 yBP), and Africa south of the Sahara Desert (sorghum and yams, 4,500 yBP).

Like most other technological innovations, agriculture spread by diffusion out of the primary centers, often for very long distances. Corn, for example, spread from its primary center in Mexico (probably in the lowland tropics) to the American Southwest. Eventually, corn agriculture spread eastward across North America and reached the Atlantic coast by about 1,000 yBP. The spread occurred not through people carrying corn but through people describing their agricultural successes to neighbors, those neighbors telling their neighbors, and so forth, until the idea spread for thousands of miles over a series of generations. For some areas of North America, the adoption and intensive use of corn occurred very rapidly, perhaps within a few generations.

(a)

(b)

FIGURE 13.7

Çatalhöyük One of the earliest agricultural communities in Southwest Asia, Çatalhöyük eventually grew into a city with a large sedentary population. **(a)** This reconstruction shows how closely spaced the houses and other buildings were in the burgeoning city. **(b)** Skeletal remains have been discovered at the Çatalhöyük site, such as this Neolithic adult male. An obsidian knife can be seen on his left shoulder. Skeletons such as these provide an immense amount of information about life in this early city. (Photo courtesy of Scott Haddow.)

Another important area of the world where anthropologists have studied the origins and diffusion of agriculture consists of both far western Asia and Europe. From southwestern Asia, the domestication of wheat and barley spread to Greece by 8,000–7,000 yBP, and then throughout Europe. The idea of agriculture spread through cultural contact and the exchange of knowledge. New analyses by Ayça Omrak and her paleogenetics team of the ancient DNA of Neolithic skeletons in western Anatolia (modern Turkey) and in Europe, however, reveals sharing of significant elements of the genome. These genetic similarities in Neolithic Anatolians and Europeans signal significant gene flow from Anatolia to Europe. This indicates that the movement of early farmers from western Asia to Europe was widespread enough to result in the patterns of genetic diversity seen today in Europe and European-descent populations.

FIGURE 13.8

Rice There are more than 20 varieties of wild rice and two types of domesticated rice. The first variety of domesticated rice was established in southern Asia approximately 9,200 yBP. The second variety of domesticated rice was established in western Africa approximately 2,000 yBP.

Animals were also domesticated around the world, beginning with dogs between 30,000 and 15,000 or so years ago. By 8,000 yBP, goats, sheep, cattle, and pigs were domesticated. These animals were an important food source in Asia and later in Europe, but domesticated plants likely provided the majority of calories and were far more fundamental to the growing human populations' survival at the regional and the global scales. For Neolithic Southwest Asia, American archaeologist Benjamin Arbuckle suggests that not only is animal husbandry highly labor-intensive and resource-expensive, but also, prior to domestication, hunting as a social act was a central element of community life and not easily abandoned. Regardless of the reasons for considerably greater focus on the role of domesticated plants than domesticated animals in diet, the record reveals human adaptation and change that is largely explained by the central importance of domesticated plants.

SURVIVAL AND GROWTH

The importance of domestication for human evolutionary history cannot be overestimated. Domestication fueled humans' remarkable population growth in the Holocene, and it formed the foundation for the rise of complex societies, cities, and increasingly sophisticated technology. Archaeologists are learning that domesticated plants served as both a food staple and a source of drink, especially alcoholic drink. In China, for example, chemical analysis of residue inside ceramic vessels shows that perhaps as early as 8,000 yBP, grapes and rice were fermented for wine.

The arrival of European explorers and colonists in the Americas had an enormous impact on the kinds of domesticated plants consumed by world populations. That is, beginning with Columbus's voyages, different plants were transported and grown throughout the world. Corn, for example, was taken back to Europe by early explorers. By the middle of the 1500s, its use as a food had spread widely, and it had become an important part of diets, especially in Africa.

Today, domesticated plants remain crucially important for sustaining human populations. Two-thirds of calorie and protein intake comes from the key cereal grains domesticated in the earlier Holocene, especially wheat, barley, corn, and rice. Rice has fed more people since its domestication than any other plant. It now accounts for *half* the food consumed by the 1.7 billion people in the world whose diets include rice and for more than 20% of all calories consumed by humans today. Rice and these other cereal grains are now aptly called **superfoods**.

superfoods Cereal grains, such as rice, corn, and wheat, that make up a substantial portion of the human population's diet today.

13.2 Agriculture: An Adaptive Trade-Off

Most people assume that the adoption of agriculture—farming—was a highly positive development in human history. Indeed, agriculture's potential for supporting large numbers of people living in a concentrated setting and for creating surplus and, thus, wealth for some laid the foundation for the great civilizations of the past—such as in China, South America, and Mexico—and those of today. Beginning with the earliest cities in the Early Holocene, no complex society anywhere in the world would have been possible without an agricultural economic base. Writing, art, business, technology, and just about every other feature of modern life came about because of agriculture. However, the rise of complex societies, of civilizations, and of technologically sophisticated ways of acquiring both food and other resources also brought about a number of profound, and largely negative, consequences for humankind, consequences that continue today and into the foreseeable future.

POPULATION GROWTH

Probably the single most visible characteristic associated with the shift from foraging to farming is the increase in population size. Called the *Neolithic demographic transition*, this shift from a low birthrate in hunter-gatherers to a high birthrate in farmers resulted in a rapid increase in the world's population. The greater number of births was brought about by earlier weaning—that is, the period of time during which the infant's nutrition came from breastfeeding was shortened (and remains so). The availability of grains cooked into soft mushes and fed to infants made it possible to wean infants from breast milk earlier in their lives. With this development, spacing between births was reduced, and mothers were able to produce more offspring.

The world's first major demographic transition spurred a remarkable increase in human population in most of the places that made the transition to farming. This pattern of population growth continues to the present day, and continues to place increased demands on the environment.

The growth of human population over the past 10,000 years is truly staggering. The world population around 10,000 yBP was probably no more than 10 million people. By 2,000 yBP, population had likely increased to 250 million or 300 million. By AD 1850, population had increased to 1 billion, and today it is approaching 8 billion (**Figure 13.9**). Increasing population leads to competition for resources. As towns and cities began to compete for increasingly limited resources (for example, arable land for crops), organized warfare developed. Interpersonal violence has a long history in human evolution, going back at least to Neandertals

WATCH THE VIDEO

FIRST WARFARE

digital.wwnorton.com/essanthro5

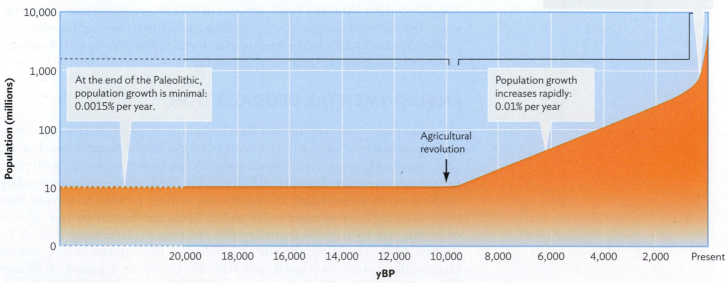

Modern-day rates continue to rise:

Eighteenth century	0.3%
Nineteenth century	0.6%
Present	2.0%

At the end of the Paleolithic, population growth is minimal: 0.0015% per year.

Population growth increases rapidly: 0.01% per year

Agricultural revolution

(Y-axis: Population (millions) — 10,000; 1,000; 100; 10; 0)

(X-axis: yBP — 20,000; 18,000; 16,000; 14,000; 12,000; 10,000; 8,000; 6,000; 4,000; 2,000; Present)

FIGURE 13.9

World Population Size This graph shows the trend in human population size on a global scale. Until 10,000 yBP and the advent of agriculture, population remained constant, numbering perhaps as many as 10 million people. After the agricultural revolution, however, population skyrocketed.

(a)

(b)

(c)

FIGURE 13.10

Interpersonal Conflict Skeletons from all regions of the world provide evidence of warfare and of organized violence, especially after the adoption of agriculture and the creation of towns and then cities. **(a)** Cranial depression fractures, such as this one on the frontal bone of the Neolithic early farmer remains from Çatalhöyük, Turkey, are the result of blunt-force trauma. **(b)** These skeletons are the remains of victims of battle in Iran in the ninth century BC. They were discovered on the floors of buildings that had been burned during the conflict. (Photo: Penn Museum image no. 78138) **(c)** This cranium received its puncture wound (square hole) during a late medieval massacre, the Battle of Towton, in England.

in the Late Pleistocene. But the level and volume of violence among pre-Holocene hominins was nothing compared with that of the early civilizations in Southwest Asia, Central America, and South America or with the medieval wars in Europe, where thousands of people were killed in organized warfare and interpersonal conflict (**Figure 13.10**). As the study of human remains shows, organized violence has likely been present in small societies as well.

ENVIRONMENTAL DEGRADATION

The consequences of environmental degradation, like those of extreme population growth, are well documented by historians and ecologists for recent human history. This degradation actually has a much more ancient origin, beginning with plant and animal domestication around 10,000 yBP. For much of the region surrounding the Mediterranean, especially the Levant (see map on p. 408), landscapes have been substantially transformed and degraded. Dense settlement based on agrarian economies has contributed to soil erosion, making it increasingly difficult to produce food. Around 8,000 yBP, a number of large towns in the eastern Mediterranean were abandoned, probably due mostly to a period of climate drying. Contributing to the abandonment, however, was human activity, such as overgrazing of livestock, which resulted in damaging erosion. Moreover, the amount of fuel, especially wood, needed to support the community resulted in the destruction of native vegetation and the desiccation of landscapes (**Figure 13.11**).

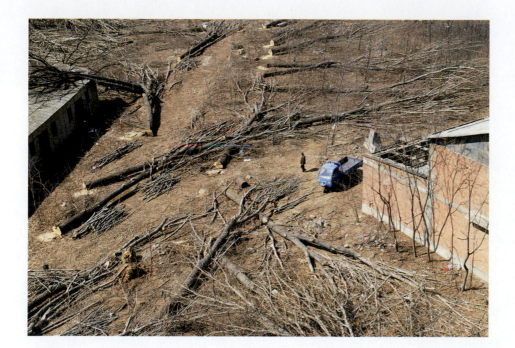

FIGURE 13.11

Human Impact With the domestication of plants and of animals, humans began having a greater impact on the world. Soil erosion, deforestation, and overgrazing have contributed to many environmental problems. Excessive tree cutting, such as shown here in China, can lead to greater soil erosion and to desertification.

Likewise, the recent collapse of coastal ecosystems worldwide clearly had its start in overfishing—especially of large vertebrates (for example, whales) and shellfish—beginning thousands of years ago. Simply, the dramatically altered ecosystems worldwide have caused biodiversity to crash, a development that appears to be accelerating. The American anthropologist Jeffrey McKee argues that one primary force behind the reduction in biodiversity is expanding human population size. He predicts that if left unchecked, the population will outstrip the arable land available to produce the plants and animals consumed by humans. Thus, the increased food supply that resulted from the agricultural revolution in the Holocene could, in the not-too-distant future, lead to a food crisis.

CONCEPT CHECK

The Good and Bad of Agriculture

Agriculture had many advantages for human adaptation, but there were also trade-offs.

ADVANTAGES

Support for feeding larger numbers of people

Creation of surplus food for leaner times

Long-term food storage, especially of grains, for later consumption

DISADVANTAGES

Increased demands on the environment (land degradation)

Pollution

Conflict between populations competing for the same lands

Loss of wild species through overhunting and displacement

Decline of biodiversity

Health costs and quality-of-life implications

13.3 How Did Agriculture Affect Human Biology?

A misperception shared by the public and anthropologists is that with the appearance of essentially modern *Homo sapiens* in the Late Pleistocene, human biological evolution ground to a halt. That is, many think that humans stopped evolving biologically once they became modern in the Upper Paleolithic. Unlike recent humans' cultural evolution (for example, increasing use of technology and development of the arts), humans' biological evolution since the closing days of the Pleistocene has gone largely unrecognized.

In the remainder of this chapter, we will examine the human biological changes that accompanied the agricultural revolution—changes linked directly or indirectly to the fundamental change, discussed earlier, in how humans have acquired resources, especially food. At the end of the chapter, we will revisit the question of why humans made this remarkable transition. Some very compelling reasons exist to believe that agriculture has contributed to *H. sapiens'* evolutionary success, at least as measured by humankind's remarkable population increase since then.

THE CHANGING FACE OF HUMANITY

As discussed at the beginning of this chapter, the foods we eat and the manner in which they are prepared tremendously influence our biology, our health, and our physical appearance. The relationship between food and morphology is well illustrated by the major anatomical changes throughout human evolution. As discussed in chapter 10, the massiveness of the late australopithecines' face and jaws was clearly linked to the hard foods those hominins ate, such as seeds. Generating the power to chew hard foods required large masticatory muscles (and their bony support). Thus, the well-developed sagittal crests of some later australopithecines—such as *Australopithecus aethiopicus*—are adaptations related to chewing. Over the course of human evolution after the australopithecines, the face and jaws have continually reduced in size and robusticity, reflecting a general decrease in the demand placed on the jaws and teeth as culture became increasingly complex and foodstuffs changed.

The reduction in size of the face and jaws is a general theme throughout human evolution, including during the Holocene and with the dietary adoption of domesticated plants. For example, in studying skulls from England that dated to the past couple of thousand years, Sir Arthur Keith (1866–1955) documented a clear reduction in the size of the face and jaws. He believed that this reduction came about from eating soft foods, such as cooked cereal grains. Other biological anthropologists have noted similar changes in many other places of the world. In Sudan's Nile Valley—the region known as Nubia—hunter-gatherers living during the time immediately preceding agriculture had long and narrow skulls, whereas their descendants had short and wide skulls.

Two Hypotheses To explain why the human skull changed shape in Nubia during the past 10,000 years, anthropologists in the 1800s and most of the 1900s offered an explanation based on old concepts of race (see chapter 5 for discussion of race). In Nubia, for example, they believed that the change occurred because short-headed people invaded territory occupied by long-headed people. These earlier anthropologists viewed head shape as unchanging and essentially a diagnostic racial marker.

They were correct that humans living in specific areas of the globe have physical characteristics in common. However, in the Holocene, anthropologists have learned that human facial and skull forms are highly plastic, as are other parts of the skeleton.

The American biological anthropologists David Carlson and Dennis Van Gerven have offered an alternative hypothesis, which explains differences in head shape in Nubia but can also be applied globally. Their **masticatory-functional hypothesis** states that change in skull form represents a response to decreased demands on the chewing muscles—temporalis and masseter—as people shifted from eating hard-textured wild foods to eating soft-textured agricultural foods, such as millet. (**Figure 13.12** lays out the hypothetical steps of this process.) To be sure, the millet grains eaten by ancient Nubians were not especially soft in their uncooked form. However, during the very late Pleistocene and beginning of the Holocene, early farmers used pottery vessels to cook grains (**Figure 13.13**). By *cooking*, I mean not a simple warm-up but cooking for hours until grains turned into soft mushes, rather easily chewed. The chewing of these mushes would have required far less powerful

masticatory-functional hypothesis The hypothesis that craniofacial shape change during the Holocene was related to the consumption of softer foods.

(a)

Taller

Shorter from front to back

FIGURE 13.12

Craniofacial Changes **(a)** The overall reduction in cranial size over the course of human evolution can be seen in Nubians' skeletal remains. Here, the dashed line indicates the craniofacial changes that have occurred between the Mesolithic foragers and the later agriculturalists. The skull has become shorter from front to back and, simultaneously, has gotten taller. **(b)** As presented in this flowchart, the Nubians' craniofacial changes resulted from alteration in diet associated with eating softer foods. In changing their diet, the Nubians were placing less demand on their chewing muscles. As a result, the associated bones changed—facial bones and jaws became smaller, and the cranial vault became rounder. The reduction in jaw size left less room for teeth, and the increased crowding resulted in malocclusion.

(b)

masticatory muscles. Because light use of muscle produces limited bone growth, the later Nubians, eating soft foods, had reduced faces.

Carlson and Van Gerven's explanation for much of the change in human head shape during the Holocene is strongly supported by evidence from living species, including nonhumans. For example, experimental research shows that primates fed soft foods have a relatively shorter skull with a smaller face and jaws than those of primates fed hard foods.

Implications For Teeth These changes in skull size and skull shape had enormous implications for our teeth. Today, the high numbers of people with orthodontic problems—malocclusions ranging from simple overbite to very poorly aligned teeth—contrast sharply with the few such problems found in ancient hominins and throughout much of prehistory. The American biological anthropologist James Calcagno has noted a number of exceptions, which may have influenced the size of our teeth, but malocclusions are rare prior to the modern era.

Why, then, do so many people around the globe have dental malocclusions? As with general skull shape, food plays an especially important role. Animals experimentally fed soft-textured foods develop far more occlusal abnormalities, such as crooked teeth, misaligned jaws, and chewing problems, than do animals fed hard-textured foods. The study of many thousands of human skulls has shown that tooth size and jaw size have reduced in the past 10,000 years but at different paces. Bone is highly subject to environmental factors, so a child fed softer foods than his or her parents ate will have appreciably reduced jaws. By contrast, teeth are controlled much more by genes, so over the course of evolution, teeth have reduced far less than jaws have. Simply, the greater reduction of the bones supporting the teeth has led to greater crowding of teeth. This disharmony underscores the complex nature of our biology, which involves an interplay between intrinsic (genetic) factors and extrinsic (environmental) factors.

Malocclusion is a clearly negative result of humans' eating soft foods. A positive result is that our teeth have very little wear because eating soft foods places less stress on the chewing surfaces.

FIGURE 13.13

Pottery Vessels, such as this terra-cotta pot, were an important invention. Such containers made possible both the storage of food for periods of time and the cooking of food into softer forms.

CONCEPT CHECK

Soft Food and Biological Change

The shift to agriculture and the eating of softer foods resulted in biological changes to the face, jaws, and teeth of modern people. Although not universal, some tendencies characterized the skulls and teeth of hunter-gatherers and of agriculturalists.

HUNTER-GATHERERS	AGRICULTURALISTS
Long cranial vault	Short skull
Large, robust mandible	Small, gracile mandible
Large teeth	Small teeth
Few malocclusions	Many malocclusions
Much tooth wear	Little tooth wear

BUILDING A NEW PHYSIQUE: AGRICULTURE'S CHANGES TO WORKLOAD AND ACTIVITY

One major debate in anthropology concerns the extent to which the agricultural revolution improved the quality of human life, including workload. Did people have to work more or work less to acquire food through agriculture rather than through hunting and gathering? The eminent American archaeologist Robert Braidwood (1907–2003) characterized the lifestyle of a typical hunter-gatherer as "a savage's existence, and a very tough one ... following animals just to kill them to eat, or moving from one berry patch to another." About the time Braidwood was writing this in the 1960s, the Canadian cultural anthropologist Richard Lee and the American biological anthropologist Irven DeVore organized

FIGURE 13.14

Leisure Time While foragers, such as this band of !Kung, must spend many hours searching for and hunting for food, their work does not preclude them from relaxing for periods of time. However, studies of numerous foraging groups have shown a great deal of variation in the workloads and amounts of leisure time of hunter-gatherers.

what turned out to be one of the most important conferences in the modern era of anthropology. They invited experts in different areas of anthropology from around the globe to determine the quality of life of hunter-gatherers, ancient and modern. A key component in assessing the quality of life was workload. If Braidwood was correct, then hunter-gatherers had to work very hard, basically spending all waking hours in the food quest, getting food wherever and whenever possible. However, Lee and others reported that hunter-gatherers might not have had it all that bad when it came to workload. In fact, in his research on the Ju/'hoansi (!Kung) of southern Africa, Lee found that these hunter-gatherers had a great deal of leisure time (**Figure 13.14**).

Lee's work in the 1960s set in motion the work of a whole generation of anthropologists, who addressed both his observations and his hypotheses. Science works this way, of course—old hypotheses are often rejected as new observations are made, and new observations generate new hypotheses. Indeed, the subsequent work showed that hunter-gatherers have quite diverse workloads. Anthropologists realized that workload depended highly on the local ecology and the kinds of foods being eaten. For example, in how they acquire plants and animals, people living in the tropics differ greatly from people living in the Arctic.

How do scientists know how hard or how easy a lifestyle was? Obviously, they cannot observe the behavior of dead people. But biological anthropology offers a way to reconstruct past behavior. Biomechanics, an area of great interest to biological anthropologists, provides enormous insight into the evolution of the body below the neck in relation to workload and to other activity. As with the bones of the face and of the jaws, the bones of the postcranial skeleton are highly plastic during the years of growth and development, all the way through to adulthood. The general shape and size of bones—the femur, in the leg, for example, or the humerus, in the arm—are determined by a person's genes. However, the finer details are subject to work and activity. Highly physically active people's bones tend to be larger and more developed than those of not so physically active people.

Borrowing from how engineers measure the strength of building materials—such as the I-beam used in the construction of a bridge or of a building—biological anthropologists have developed a means for assessing the robusticity of bone cross sections. Based on the simple premise that material located farther away from an axis running down the center of the bone is stronger than material placed closer

FIGURE 13.15

Cross-Sectional Geometry Using engineering principles, biological anthropologists can gain insight into activity patterns by examining the cross sections of long bones, such as the femur and the humerus. The shapes of long bones, like those of I-beams (building materials used for structural support), maximize both strength and the ability to resist bending by distributing mass away from the center of the section.

osteoarthritis Degenerative changes of the joints caused by a variety of factors, such as physical activity and mechanical stress.

to the axis (**Figure 13.15**), it has become possible to look at the degree of bone development and determine by empirical means how bone strength has changed over the course of human evolution to the present. Bone comparisons—from hunter-gatherers' to later agriculturalists' to modern peoples'—show a remarkable decline in size.

Measurement involves first getting a good image of the bone's cross section. Doing so might mean cutting the bone to physically expose the cross section, usually in the mid-diaphysis. If cutting is impossible, a cross section can be created by taking a CT (computed tomography) scan of the bone, just as a radiologist would as part of a medical examination. On the section, the biological anthropologist traces the bone's outer perimeter, or periosteal surface, and inner perimeter, or endosteal surface, with an electronic stylus hooked up to a computer loaded with engineering software that automatically calculates bone strength properties called second moments of area.

The American biological anthropologist Christopher Ruff has pioneered a method of assessing bone strength in long bones (e.g., humerus and femur) in order to document and interpret trends in a population's adaptations to the mechanical demands associated with physical activities such as heavy labor. The method utilizes cross-sectional geometric analyses—a technique developed by civil and mechanical engineers—to determine the strength of long bone shafts (called *diaphyses*). Ruff's research has uncovered one very clear trend in human evolution: bone strength in the genus *Homo* has declined dramatically, but especially so during the last 10,000 years with the transition from hunting and gathering to agriculture (**Figure 13.16**). In many settings where bone skeletal structural properties declined, there was also a decrease in the prevalence of **osteoarthritis**, a disorder of the skeletal joints that results from excessive stresses (for example, on the elbow and knee joints) and wear and tear due to high levels of physical activity (**Figure 13.17**).

In general, the reduction in human bone strength represents a dramatic skeletal adaptation in the recent Holocene following the transition to settled community life and to farming and industrialization. For most of us today, our bone strength is considerably lower than that of our ancestors living thousands of years ago. This change reflects the fact that our lifestyle is much less physically demanding as it pertains to activity, labor, and workload generally. Specifically,

Humerus

Hunter-gatherer
bone cross sections

Agriculturalist
bone cross sections

Femur

FIGURE 13.16

Activity Pattern Comparison Biological anthropologists have compared the biomechanical properties of cross-sections of femora and humeri from prehistoric hunter-gatherers and early agriculturalists in North America, Europe, and other settings in order to document and interpret biomechanical adaptations to labor and activity changes. In general, bone strength declined. The larger cross-sections in the hunter-gatherers indicate greater bone strength and resistance to mechanical stress than in the farmers.

our increasing reliance on material culture and increasing tool complexity have shifted labor from physical activity to mechanization, and this decline in mechanical demand has resulted in an increasingly gracile skeleton, especially in recent modern humans.

HEALTH AND THE AGRICULTURAL REVOLUTION

Population Crowding and Infectious Disease The population increase during the Holocene, discussed extensively earlier in the chapter, was linked with agriculture and increased food production. As the population increased, communities grew more committed to raising crops and became more sedentary, or settled, living in one place the entire year. Before then, the smaller number of people had moved around at least on a seasonal basis. The increase in size and density of the population, especially when the population remained in place, had enormous, negative effects on people's health. In short, humans began to live in conditions crowded and unsanitary enough to support pathogens and their successful evolution.

Consider the overcrowded cities around the globe today. In the urban slums of Bombay, India, or Rio de Janeiro, Brazil, or La Paz, Bolivia, or even within developed nations such as in the United States where sanitation is carefully regulated and monitored, the crowding sets up conditions for increased interpersonal contact and the spread of numerous infectious microorganisms and viruses (**Figure 13.18**).

FIGURE 13.17

Osteoarthritis Degenerative joint disease, or osteoarthritis, can occur in a variety of sites throughout the body, commonly in the vertebrae, hips, knees, and hands.

Normal joints and bones

Cervical spine

Lumbar spine

Hand

Hip

Knee

periosteal reaction An inflammatory response of a bone's outer covering due to bacterial infection or to trauma.

FIGURE 13.18

Overcrowding One negative effect of agriculture and the resulting increase in sedentism (the practice of living in one place for a long time) is overcrowding. In overcrowded slums, such as this one in Bombay, India, unsanitary conditions help increase the levels of infectious microorganisms and thus lead to disease outbreaks.

During the Holocene, especially in agricultural settings, crowding seems to have produced illnesses and injuries. Any kind of injury to the outer surface of bone can cause a **periosteal reaction**, or bone buildup, which is sometimes combined with an abnormal expansion of a bone's diameter. The reaction is often caused by localized infection, such as from the so-called staph bacteria, *Staphylococcus aureus*. The infection essentially stimulates new bone growth, hence the swollen appearance. Most periosteal reactions are nonspecific, so anthropologists cannot tell exactly what caused them. Anthropologists find, however, a general increase in

CONCEPT CHECK

Labor, Lifestyle, and Adaptation in the Skeleton

The human skeleton responds to activity, reflecting the person's lifestyle. Hunter-gatherers' skeletons and agriculturalists' skeletons vary in patterns that reveal different levels of activity, including that of workload; but the skeletons of hunter-gatherers tend to show higher levels of responses resulting from higher or more strenuous activity.

HUNTER-GATHERERS	AGRICULTURALISTS
Larger, more robust bones	Smaller, less robust bones
More osteoarthritis	Less osteoarthritis

periosteal reactions on the limb bones of skeletons from crowded settings in the Holocene. Such reactions are practically nonexistent in human groups pre-dating that time.

Some infections identified on bones from Holocene populations have a specific pattern that suggests a variety of bacterial infectious diseases that caused them. In the American Midwest and Southeast, for example, tibias are swollen and bowed, while crania have a distinctive uneven, pitted texture. Both kinds of bone deformation are caused by a group of diseases called **treponematoses**, which include venereal syphilis, nonvenereal syphilis (also called endemic syphilis), and yaws. Anthropologists, historians, and others debate the origin of venereal syphilis, some blaming native populations, some blaming Christopher Columbus and his ship crews, and some arguing for the appearance of a wholly new disease sometime after the initial European explorations of the New World. However, the pattern of bone changes in the New World prior to the late 1400s suggests the presence of a nonvenereal syphilis, one passed not by sexual contact but by casual contact, such as by a mother holding her child.

Many other bacterial infectious diseases likely affected Holocene populations worldwide. Bioarchaeologists have documented poor health conditions, including infectious disease and evidence of physiological stress, before the Europeans' arrival in North and South America. The skeletal indicators of tuberculosis, for example, are widespread in parts of the New World, Old World, and Australia, well before the time of European exploration. For much of the mid-twentieth century, many medical practitioners thought this microbial infection had been conquered; but today, 2–3 million people die annually from the disease.

Other modern diseases made possible by population-size increase, overcrowding, and human-to-human contact include, but are not limited to, cholera, pneumonia, plague, bacterial meningitis, and smallpox. Some of these diseases have an Old World origin, but the New World was hardly a disease-free paradise before their introduction.

The Consequences of Declining Nutrition: Tooth Decay All domesticated plants have nutritional drawbacks. Because they are carbohydrates, they promote **dental caries**, commonly known as tooth decay or "cavities" (**Figure 13.19**). Caries is a process in which the natural bacteria in your mouth—common culprits are *Streptococcus mutans* and *Lactobacillus acidophilus*—digest the carbohydrates there. One end product of this digestive process is lactic acid, which literally dissolves tooth enamel. In industrial societies today, dentists stabilize caries by removing diseased parts of teeth and filling the cavities with composite material to stop the spread of decay. In the ancient world, dentistry was mostly nonexistent, and cavities grew until the teeth fell out or, in some instances, people with cavities died from secondary infections.

Different domesticated plants promote tooth decay at varying rates. Rice does not seem to cause it to the same extent as other domesticated plants do. Corn causes it considerably. Once post–AD 800 populations in eastern North America adopted corn agriculture, the frequency of their dental caries rose dramatically (**Figure 13.20**).

Nutritional Consequences Due to Missing Nutrients: Reduced Growth and Abnormal Development The popular and the academic literatures suggest that agriculture has improved humans' nutrition. This conclusion makes sense given the huge worldwide investment in agriculture, even today. However, the assessment of superfoods' nutritional content argues otherwise.

treponematoses A group of related diseases (venereal syphilis, endemic syphilis, yaws) caused by the bacteria *Treponema*, which produces pathologic changes most often to the cranium and tibiae.

dental caries A disease process that creates demineralized areas in dental tissues, leading to cavities; demineralization is caused by acids produced by bacteria that metabolize carbohydrates in dental plaque.

(a)

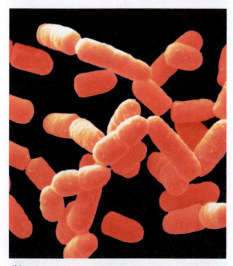

(b)

FIGURE 13.19

Dental Caries Cavities are more common in individuals with carbohydrate-rich diets. As a result of the digestion of carbohydrates, carious lesions form as the enamel of the teeth deteriorates. In extreme cases, the pulp of the teeth can be affected. **(a)** This cross-section of a mandibular molar affected by dental caries shows a large hole (red arrow) that extends into the interior of the tooth crown. **(b)** *Lactobacillus* is one of the two main bacteria that cause dental caries.

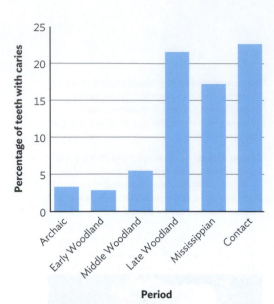

FIGURE 13.20

Changes in Oral Health This chart shows temporal changes in dental caries in eastern North America. During the Archaic, Early Woodland, and Middle Woodland periods, which pre-date AD 800, the region's native inhabitants were hunter-gatherers. During the Late Woodland, Mississippian, and Contact periods, which post-date AD 1000, the adoption of agriculture caused a large increase in dental caries.

hypoplasia A tooth-enamel deficiency usually appearing as a groove on the surface of the tooth and caused by growth disruption.

FIGURE 13.21

Enamel Hypoplasias These defects reflect stress episodes that occurred during tooth development. Individuals with multiple hypoplasias on each tooth underwent several stress episodes.

In most places where early populations relied on agriculture, there existed the potential for abnormal growth and development because of the nutritional limitations of domesticated plants. Dietary reconstructions of past societies by archaeologists and studies of living agrarian populations in different settings indicate that the diets of agriculturalists tend to overemphasize one plant or a couple of them, such as rice in Asia, wheat in Europe and temperate Asia, corn in the Americas, and millet or sorghum in Africa. Thus, many groups, especially in the later Holocene, received poor nutrition from an increasingly narrow range of foods. A well-balanced diet, as your parents and teachers have told you time and again, involves variety from all the food groups.

Domesticated plants have nutritional value, of course, but they also present a range of negative nutritional consequences. For example, corn is deficient in the amino acids lysine, isoleucine, and tryptophan, and a person who does not receive the right amount of even one amino acid will neither grow normally nor develop properly. In addition, vitamin B_3 (niacin) in corn is bound chemically, therefore making this essential nutrient unavailable to the body. Corn also contains phytate, a chemical that binds with iron and hampers the body's iron absorption. Also, grains such as millet and wheat contain very little iron. Rice is deficient in protein and thus inhibits vitamin A activity.

Numerous societies worldwide have developed strategies for improving these foods' nutritional content. For example, corn-dependent populations commonly treat corn with alkali, a weak solution of lye. This treatment increases the availability of niacin and improves the quality of the protein. Such treatments cannot, however, entirely make up for the negative consequences of dietary over-reliance on these plants.

One of the most obvious ways of assessing the impact of nutritional change in the Holocene is by looking at the growth of bones and of teeth. Like any other body tissues, bones and teeth grow to their full genetic potential only if they receive proper nutrition. Anthropologists are able to identify a few indicators of growth stress in skeletal and dental records from fossils, but these indicators are generally nonspecific; that is, they are not linked to a precise cause (for example, a particular vitamin that the person was deficient in). These stress indicators are also related to multiple factors that may or may not include nutrition. Nonnutritional factors often include infection or infectious disease. Yet, as studies of living populations have shown, nutrition and infection have a synergistic relationship: poor nutrition worsens the infection, and vice versa; essential nutrition is used to fight the infection and is taken away from the growth process. Despite such complications, anthropologists have found these indicators to be very informative about the history of stress both in individuals and in populations.

Deficiencies in dental enamel are one of the most important nonspecific stress indicators. Typically, the deficiencies appear as lines, pits, or grooves, any of which occur when the cells responsible for enamel production (called **ameloblasts**) are disrupted. Consequently, when the disturbance ends (the illness or the infection is over), a defect, or **hypoplasia**, is left (**Figure 13.21**). Defects of this kind are commonplace in earlier humans' teeth—indeed, researchers have found them in australopithecines—but they are rare through most of human evolution. Some hunter-gatherer populations have high frequencies, but hypoplasias became relatively common in Holocene populations. The high frequency in agriculturalists around the world was caused by two factors: decline in nutritional quality and increase in infectious disease. (Other dental defects, visible in teeth only with a microscope, reflect very short-term stress episodes, lasting several hours to several days. Virtually everyone has microscopic defects in the deciduous teeth, created as a result of birth stress.)

Nutritional Consequences of Iron Deficiency Other markers of stress and of deprivation in agricultural populations can be linked to specific causes. **Iron deficiency anemia**, a condition that plagues millions of people around the globe, results when the body receives limited iron. Iron is necessary for many body functions and is an essential element in hemoglobin, serving in the transport of oxygen to the body tissues. Iron—specifically, **heme iron**—enters the body easily through meat eating because the amino acids from the digestion of meat promote iron absorption. Iron from plants—**nonheme iron**—is not as readily available because various substances in plants inhibit iron absorption (see the earlier discussion on corn and its iron content). Citric acid found in various fruits, however, may promote iron absorption.

Some authorities believe that iron deficiency is rarely caused by dietary stress and is more often related to nondietary factors. Parasitic infections, for example, are a primary cause of iron deficiency anemia in many regions of the globe. One such infection, hookworm disease, is caused when someone inhales or ingests hookworm larvae. The worm (*Ancylostoma duodenale, Necator americanus*) extracts blood from its human host by using the sharp teethlike structures in its head to latch itself to the intestinal wall (**Figure 13.22**). When several hundred or more of these worms are present, severe blood loss—and therefore anemia—can result.

Abundant evidence of anemia exists among skeletons in numerous settings worldwide. In response to anemia, red blood cells increase in production, potentially leading to **porotic hyperostosis** in skulls and **cribra orbitalia** in eye orbits, in which these areas gain a porous appearance. These abnormalities were quite rare before the Holocene but then suddenly appeared, especially in agricultural groups.

iron deficiency anemia A condition in which the blood has insufficient iron; may be caused by diet, poor iron absorption, parasitic infection, and severe blood loss.

heme iron Iron found in meats, such as red meat, fish, and poultry; this type of iron is absorbed efficiently by the body.

nonheme iron Iron found in plants, such as lentils and beans; this type of iron is less efficiently absorbed by the body than is heme iron.

porotic hyperostosis The expansion and porosity of cranial bones due to anemia caused by an iron-deficient diet, parasitic infection, or genetic disease.

cribra orbitalia Porosity in the eye orbits due to anemia caused by an iron-deficient diet, parasitic infection, or genetic disease.

FIGURE 13.22

Hookworm Parasites, such as this hookworm, can cause iron deficiency. Today, hookworms are commonly found in subtropical regions of North Africa, India, and elsewhere.

CRAIG HADLEY, PHD

Emory University

What do I do? I am a biological anthropologist who studies the social determinants of health. My degrees are in biological anthropology and international nutrition, and I did postdoctoral work in demography and social epidemiology. My research examines why some populations are healthier than others, and I do this through fieldwork in East Africa and by analyzing large publicly available data sets. My fieldwork in Ethiopia is aimed at understanding how the material and cultural aspects of life affect people's health and well-being. I am specifically interested in exploring the relationship between food insecurity and mental and physical health. These efforts entail conducting large surveys of households and interviewing and measuring people. My work with large data sets increasingly examines how different forms of household wealth are related to different forms of health, be this physical, mental, or social well-being. In short, I try to bring an anthropological perspective to global health issues.

What excites me most about my work? I am interested in understanding what contributes to the variation we see in human health and well-being. Collecting and analyzing data, therefore, excites me because within those data, waiting to be uncovered or discovered, are answers or clues about the drivers of the human condition. The entire research process is exciting: from reading and thinking about problems and questions, to designing studies that test competing ideas, to doing the final analyses. It's always satisfying to learn something new about how the world works (or doesn't!).

Why did I study biological anthropology? I happened into an anthropology class by chance but quickly became fascinated by paleoanthropology and human origins. I then branched out and began to take courses on contemporary human populations, especially courses focusing on contemporary biological variation and health and well-being. I continued to study biological anthropology because it allowed me to combine my interests in evolutionary theory, population studies, statistics, human diversity, and global health. Biological anthropology offers an exciting and deeply relevant area of study, one that allows students to address big questions about the human experience while simultaneously developing a methodological tool kit that is relevant to many occupations.

Nutritional Consequences: Heights on the Decline In many regions where farming was adopted, adult heights declined appreciably. The fact that people simply stopped growing as tall has been documented in western Europe, the eastern Mediterranean, Nubia, southern Asia, the Ohio River valley, and central Illinois. The Peruvian biological anthropologist Lourdes Márquez and Mexican biological anthropologist Andrés del Ángel have found a general decline in height among the Maya of the first millennium AD, a time in which this ancient civilization experienced a deterioration in environment and in living circumstances. Thus, for some groups shorter height might have been the biological result of adopting agriculture, but for other groups it might have been an adaptation to reduced resources, as smaller bodies require less food. However, all the human populations whose height decreased because of stress also experienced elevated infectious disease loads, anemia, malnutrition, and other factors indicating that a smaller body does not confer an adaptive advantage. These people were smaller but not healthier.

13.4 If It Is So Bad for You, Why Farm?

This question brings us back to some points about evolution raised in earlier chapters. Namely, the key components of evolution are survival to the reproductive years and production of offspring. One documented fact about the Holocene is that human fertility greatly increased during this time. That women gave birth to more babies was likely made possible by the reduced spacing between births in agricultural groups. Simply put, because women were settled and not spending time moving about the landscape, they could bear children more frequently. Therefore, it is possible that a population with a reduced quality of life, as a result of disease and other negative health effects associated with an agricultural lifestyle, might still have very high fertility. This combination—of high fertility but poor nutrition and health—is, of course, present through much of the developing world, such as in Peru, Bangladesh, Mexico, Thailand, and many African countries.

We have seen the evidence—a huge record—showing that the adoption of agriculture resulted in the development and spread of infectious disease and a reduction in health generally (**Figure 13.23**). Agriculture's positive side is that it provides both more calories per unit of land and the resources for population increase. And evolution dictates that organisms, including humans, engage in behaviors that increase the potential for and outcome of reproduction.

FIGURE 13.23

New Pathogens The pattern of population concentration and increase that started in the Holocene, during the agricultural revolution, established the conditions for the appearance and evolution of old and new infectious diseases. In addition, the conditions have become ripe for the evolution of new pathogens, such as the viruses that cause Ebola virus disease and acquired immune deficiency syndrome (AIDS), and prions that cause mad cow disease. **(a)** The AIDS virus, known as human immunodeficiency virus (HIV), infiltrates human white blood cells, an essential part of the immune system. The virus forces the white blood cells to produce more virus particles (red). **(b)** The Ebola virus causes a hemorrhagic fever that can be life-threatening. The virus has a long, filamentous appearance, as shown in this electron micrograph.

13.5 Our Past Is Our Future

As a biological anthropologist, I am always asking and encouraging my students to apply what they've learned in this course to answering the big questions of the discipline: *How does our large and growing knowledge of the past inform our understanding of the present? What does the knowledge of key developments in human evolution and our biology over the past millions of years tell us about our collective future as a species?*

This final chapter has focused on a fundamental dietary and adaptive transition for our species, and one having important implications in nutrition, health, and many other aspects of who we are as *Homo sapiens.* The shift from a diet and lifeway based exclusively on hunting, gathering, and collecting of non-domesticated resources to one based exclusively on domesticated plants and animals has had, and will continue to have, profound consequences for our future. In many ways, the dramatic and remarkable foraging-to-farming transition that began just 10,000–12,000 years ago formed the cornerstone of *H. sapiens'* recent evolutionary success. At a very fundamental level, changes in how humans acquired food via farming in recent human evolution laid the foundation for our dramatic population increase and concentration in enormous urban aggregations (today, 50% of the nearly 8 billion humans on the planet live in cities). But the shift in the kinds of foods we consume and the lifestyle associated with it also came at a cost. Moving from a diet that was highly varied to one dominated by domesticated plant carbohydrates, fats, and various forms of processing formed the basis for one of our biggest collective challenges: an obesity epidemic now reaching virtually every corner of the world. The nutrition transition has also resulted in the prevalence of degenerative conditions, including but not limited to osteoporosis, cardiovascular disease, respiratory disease, diabetes, various cancers, and depression.

If that has not been enough of a challenge, we are experiencing increasing atmospheric temperatures globally, due in part to human activity. Within our lifetimes, this change will hamper food production, force major coastal urban centers to close, and disrupt society. This alarming development is the result of rising levels of "greenhouse gases" (carbon dioxide and methane, especially) in the atmosphere, brought about by the burning of fossil fuels, and it has been exacerbated by the increasing losses of vegetation and natural land cover. Concentrations of elevated heat, produced from roads and rooftops and other heat-storing materials, are producing abnormally high global temperatures. These circumstances, in addition to putting an unprecedented strain on food resources, are yielding what the United Nations has called a global "silent tsunami" of deaths due to infectious disease. For example, higher temperatures and loss of land cover increase the breeding of mosquitoes, which in turn help spread pathogens such as those associated with malaria.

If left unchecked, how might global warming affect future generations? Experts predict that the increasingly warm planet will see major shifts in precipitation patterns, resulting in desertification in areas of the globe that are currently productive. Those people most profoundly affected by the resulting decrease in the world food supply will be those already living in marginal circumstances, such as in vast areas of Africa, Asia, and Latin America. Overall, then, the ongoing environmental changes are threatening health by increased infectious disease, threats to food and water security, and population displacement as millions seek better living circumstances in especially threatened areas of the globe. Almost certainly, these circumstances will lead to biological change with long-term implications for many future generations.

13.6 Our Ongoing Human Evolution

Huge changes are occurring on our planet and in the human (and other) populations occupying it. These changes have real and impactful meaning for our future, including our evolution. But, is there evidence of ongoing biological change in general and of evolution in particular? In a word, *plenty*. Humans are among the most dominant evolutionary forces in comparison with the other living organisms. Indeed, abundant examples exist of humankind's role in other species' evolution. For example, even before the Swiss chemist Paul Müller received a Nobel Prize in 1948 for his discovery of the pesticide DDT, houseflies were reportedly becoming resistant to this chemical. By 1990, some 500 mosquito species had also developed resistance to DDT, dashing the hopes that malaria could be eradicated. Similarly, bacteria associated with horrific infections have evolved in response to human interventions, developing resistance to antibiotic medications, such as penicillin and tetracycline. Today, hospitals report that bacteria such as *Staphylococcus aureus* are almost always resistant to penicillin, and the list of resistant bacteria in these and other settings is growing at an alarming rate. The evolution of new, antibiotic-resistant strains of *Mycobacterium tuberculosis* is a big part of the dramatic rise in human deaths due to this bacterium—globally, 2–3 million people die from tuberculosis each year. Meanwhile, fish are evolving slower growth patterns and thinner bodies owing to overfishing.

These examples are just two of many that illustrate two fundamental points about evolution. The first is that it is ongoing today and will continue in some form well into the future. And the second is that, although biological anthropologists speculate on and debate evolution's causes in specific circumstances, we agree that as a general rule, evolution occurs as organisms are exposed to new opportunities and new challenges, often in unpredictable ways.

As you have learned in your course on biological anthropology, evolution is *opportunistic*. It is dynamic, nonlinear, and takes place in the context of ever-changing circumstances. The eighteenth- and nineteenth-century pioneers of evolutionary biology could not have predicted the dramatic changes that the peppered moth would undergo in the nineteenth and twentieth centuries. Even viruses—among the most genetically simple organisms—evolve, adapting to new circumstances and identifying new opportunities for reproduction.

Indeed, from an evolutionary standpoint, viruses have a remarkable record of evolvability and successful adaptation. Owing to their genetic structure—they only have simpler RNA, rather than more complex DNA—they quickly adapt to rapidly changing circumstances in their host targets, including humans. The sobering outcomes of their ready adaptation to human hosts were clearly illustrated by the 1918 influenza pandemic, which resulted in about 50 million deaths worldwide, and have been demonstrated again during more recent epidemics occurring in the twenty-first century. Specifically, the last two decades have seen several major occurrences of novel "coronaviruses"—so named for their crown-like spikes. These spikes are proteins that aid the coronavirus' entry into humans' host cells, allowing the virus to "hop" from animals to humans with devastating results.

The first major coronavirus epidemic of this millennium was the severe acute respiratory syndrome (SARS) outbreak in China in 2003, followed almost a decade later by the Middle East Respiratory Syndrome (MERS) outbreak in Saudi Arabia in 2012. But the most significant coronavirus outbreak in recent history is the one that, as of the time of this book's writing, we are currently experiencing across the globe. Beginning in 2019, the novel coronavirus SARS-CoV2, which causes coronavirus disease (COVID-19), found a new host population with the cross-over from bats to humans in China. Quickly adapting to humans, SARS-CoV2 began exploiting its new host, spreading globally and becoming a **pandemic**, as this highly contagious virus reproduced itself throughout much of the world.

pandemic An infectious disease that has become prevalent over an exceptionally large region, such as multiple countries, a continent, or the world.

What's behind the success of the SARS-CoV-2 virus? A big part of the answer lies in the fact that the single-stranded RNA in the virus is much less stable than the double-stranded DNA in a human being. That is, the virus has an adaptive advantage owing to the much greater mutation rate that occurs in its RNA than in the DNA the virus is targeting in the human host. It is estimated that mutation in the unstable RNA-based genes of the virus happens as much as a million times faster than in the stable DNA-based genes of its host. Thus, the virus is able to replicate fast, resulting in an infection characterized by symptoms associated with the upper respiratory system in the human host. Between February 2020 and February 2021—just one year following the virus' arrival in the United States—there were 28 million cases of COVID-19 infection and, tragically, more than 500,000 deaths. Globally, there were 112 million cases and 2.5 million deaths from COVID-19 infections in that time. The numbers of deaths and illnesses are staggering. Because of the vast number of viruses in every infected human host, the human body continues to be fertile ground for viral evolution and present opportunities for further mutations and further evolution.

Despite the evolutionary potency of viruses at a high cost for humans, the good news is that humans, too, are a success story in evolution and evolvability, as the experience of COVID-19 has demonstrated. Our capability to develop cultural solutions to challenges, including the adaptive behavioral measures of social distancing and the scientific innovation of vaccines, allowed us to combat the virus and have put us, as of this writing, on a path to ultimately overcoming it.

The COVID-19 pandemic has also provided some clear lessons regarding the manner and rate in which evolution works, as well as evolution's outcomes for human societies. One such lesson is that the challenges of viral infections are not evenly distributed across age and social groups. Most of us have an immune system that successfully mitigates the potential for infection. However, like most other systems in the body, the immune system declines over one's lifetime and can also be influenced by different biological and environmental factors. Thus, elderly individuals are more susceptible to infection and death than young individuals. More striking outcomes across the globe reveal additional health disparities with regard to social circumstance. Simply put, the less wealthy and those with limited access to medical care, nutrition, and overall well-being are more susceptible to infection and death. The starkness of how this fact has played out in our species' experience with COVID-19 is a powerful reminder that addressing these social inequities is of critical importance now and for the future of our planet.

What can we predict about the health, well-being, and the general picture for *H. sapiens* going forward? You can bet that humans will continue to consume energy, human population size will continue to increase, and the global climate will continue to challenge many aspects of life. If we are not successful at mitigating the negative outcomes of these developments, then humans and other organisms will continue to be faced with increasing challenges and likely new selective pressures. This chapter has painted a rather dark picture of our changing world—as we have more and more impact on the planet and its environment, we seem to be on a collision course with disaster. Just as humans have created, or contributed to, these environmental changes, we will need to develop means of slowing global warming, most likely by modifying technologies and lifestyles to limit the production of greenhouse gases. The warming trends have begun to melt massive ice sheets, resulting in rising sea levels and the alteration of weather patterns in major ways. These changes will create circumstances that are positive for some organisms (for example, pathogens in the Arctic) and negative for others (for example, agricultural crops, the growth of which will be adversely affected). Combined, these environmental stressors hinder ecosystems that societies rely on globally.

The field of biological anthropology is about both the evolutionary changes and the circumstances that created the context for evolution, such as the dramatic shifts in climate predicted in the near and distant future.

One key theme that I have emphasized throughout this book is that humans have an extraordinary capacity to adapt to novel circumstances, and an enormous component of this resilience is due to culture, especially technology and material culture. Some technology has negatively influenced the world, including the technology associated with industrialization and the burning of fossil fuels. At the same time, human technology has produced a growing global economy and ways of producing more food and increasing the population, which is living longer. Biological anthropology, with its integrative approach (involving evolution, adaptation, variation, and development) and its vast scale (covering the entire world, across all of time, and including all of its people and primates) is especially well positioned to tackle long-standing issues that require a comprehensive approach to understanding the natural world we live in and the issues that confront our fellow human beings globally. Although scientists expect some regions of the world to experience dramatic temperature changes relating to global warming, environmental disruption, food shortages, outbreaks of infectious disease (including the new pandemic viral infectious diseases), and other challenges, our evolvability remains a key advantage. The record of human evolution over the past 5 million years, and our capacity to utilize culture and other mechanisms discussed in this book, suggests that humans will develop means for dealing with such problems. Time will tell if humankind is indeed able to use culture, intelligence, and innovation to thrive in this changing world. That has been the story so far, and I believe it will continue. Your task is to pitch in and play a part in addressing the challenges going forward. All of us have the capability, made possible by the processes and outcomes of our shared evolution.

ANSWERING THE BIG QUESTIONS

1. **When, where, and why did agriculture first develop?**
   - During the Holocene epoch (the most recent 10,000 years), *Homo sapiens* included domesticated plants and animals in their diets for the first time.
   - The earliest agriculture occurred in the eastern Mediterranean (the Levant). It arose in at least 11 other centers independently around the world.
   - Plant and animal domestication may have arisen to feed the ever-increasing human population.

2. **How did agriculture affect human living circumstances?**
   - Agriculture (and associated population increases) resulted in population sedentism and crowding. This provided the conditions conducive to the spread and maintenance of infectious disease.
   - Nutrition shifted from a generalized diet to one focused on carbohydrates and poorer-quality protein.
   - In most settings, agriculture caused a decline in workload and activity.

3. **How did agriculture affect human biological change?**
   - Poorer-quality diets led to a decline in health as foragers became farmers.
   - The shift from hard foods to soft ones resulted in facial bones' reducing in size faster than the teeth. As a result, humans now have many more orthodontic issues requiring the artificial straightening of the teeth.
   - Decreased workload and activity resulted in a general tendency toward increased gracilization of the skeleton.
   - The decline in health did not affect human reproductive performance. Human population grew to perhaps several million by the close of the Pleistocene. Today, the human population is approaching *8 billion*.
   - The adoption of agriculture was an evolutionary trade-off: human health was adversely affected, but more individuals survived to reproductive age and produced offspring. The population explosion that resulted from the increased food supply represents the core of adaptive success.
   - Viruses are the most successful organismal group on Earth, causing increasing death rates and other challenges to the planet, including to *H. sapiens*.

4. **What do you think our evolutionary future looks like?**
   - Unlike the other Big Questions I posed throughout the text, this Big Question doesn't have an answer I can provide you. Time will tell what paths our evolutionary future will take. That said, based on everything you have learned about human evolution during this course, you are in an excellent position to consider what trends will likely significantly impact our species' future. Thinking like an anthropologist, what trends do you think will play the largest roles? (Hint: population size and crowding, diet and nutrition, and evolution of existing and newly emerging pathogens will likely play leading roles in shaping our future evolution.)

STUDY QUIZ

1. **Why did domestication of plants and animals occur in the Holocene?**
   a. The warmer, wetter environment supported agriculture.
   b. The cooler, drier environment supported agriculture.
   c. Wild populations of plants decreased.
   d. Wild populations of animals decreased.

2. **Plant domestication began in _____ and spread through _____.**
   a. a single location; conquest
   b. a single location; diffusion and migration
   c. multiple locations; conquest
   d. multiple locations; diffusion and migration

KEY TERMS

ameloblasts
cribra orbitalia
dental caries
domestication

heme iron
hypoplasia
iron deficiency anemia
masticatory-functional
    hypothesis

Neolithic
nonheme iron
osteoarthritis
pandemic
periosteal reaction

porotic hyperostosis
superfoods
treponematoses

STUDY QUIZ (CONTINUED)

3. During the agricultural revolution, the overuse of scant resources led to

   a.   environmental degradation and organized warfare.

   b.   cooperation and fair distribution of resources between settlements.

   c.   a return of most human populations to hunting and gathering.

   d.   a return of most domesticated plants and animals to the wild.

4. The masticatory-functional hypothesis states that with a diet of cooked, soft-textured foods, face and jaw size

   a.   increases, so teeth cannot fill the mouth.

   b.   decreases, so teeth become crowded.

   c.   decreases, so teeth develop caries.

   d.   does not change enough to affect tooth function.

5. Iron deficiency appears in the skeleton as

   a.   a periosteal reaction.

   b.   porotic hyperostosis.

   c.   enamel defects.

   d.   tooth crowding (malocclusion).

EVOLUTION REVIEW

The Origins and Biocultural Consequences of Farming

SYNOPSIS One of the most fundamental transitions in recent human evolution is the shift from hunting and gathering to agriculture. For 99.8% of the 7 million years of our evolutionary past, humans and our hominin ancestors were foragers. Only within the past 10,000 years or so have humans undertaken the process of plant and animal domestication and become farmers the world over. In fact, many of the issues we face and will encounter in the future—such as environmental degradation, population growth, nutritional stress, and infectious disease—can be traced, in part, to agriculture and its influence on human biocultural evolution.

The story of what it means to be human is one of adaptation, both biological and cultural. The ongoing evolution of our species will be shaped by newly emerging environmental and ecological pressures that will continue to test human adaptability and resilience.

Q1. Provide four examples of characteristics that indicate a decline in health among agriculturalists compared to their hunter-gatherer counterparts.

Q2. Explain how a combination of evolutionary and nonevolutionary factors has influenced the changes in cranial and facial form that accompanied the transition to agriculture. What kinds of complications have resulted from these changes? How do humans intervene to respond to these complications?

Q3. After the agricultural transition and subsequent increase in population size, what were the consequences, especially with regard to prevalence of infectious disease to the present day?

ADDITIONAL READINGS

Cohen, J. 2020. New coronavirus threat galvanizes scientists. *Science* 367: 492–493.

Gasperetti, M. A. and S. G. Sheridan. 2013. Cry havoc: Interpersonal violence at Early Bronze Age Bab edh-Dhra'. *American Anthropologist* 115: 388–410.

Holt, B., E. Whittey, M. Niskanen, V. Sládek, Margit Berner, and Christopher B. Ruff. 2018. Temporal and geographic variation in robusticity. Pp. 91–132 in C. B. Ruff, ed. *Skeletal Variation and Adaptation in Europeans: Upper Paleolithic to the Twentieth Century.* Hoboken, NJ: Wiley-Blackwell.

Katzenberg, M. A. and A. L. Waters-Rist. 2019. Stable isotope analysis. A tool for studying past diet, demography, and life history. Pp. 469–504 in M. A. Katzenberg and A. L. Grauer, eds. *Biological Anthropology of the Human Skeleton*, 3rd ed. Hoboken, NJ: John Wiley & Sons.

Larsen, C. S. 1995. Biological changes in human populations with agriculture. *Annual Review of Anthropology* 24: 185–213.

Ruff, C. B. 2019. Biomechanical analyses of archaeological human skeletons. Pp. 189–224 in M. A. Katzenberg and A. L. Grauer, eds. *Biological Anthropology of the Human Skeleton,* 3rd ed. Hoboken, NJ: John Wiley & Sons.

Smith, B. D. 1995. *The Emergence of Agriculture.* New York: Scientific American Library.

Walker, P. L. 2001. A bioarchaeological perspective on the history of violence. *Annual Review of Anthropology* 30: 573–596.

STUDY QUIZ ANSWERS

CHAPTER 1
1. c; 2. b; 3. a; 4. d; 5. a

CHAPTER 2
1. d; 2. c; 3. a; 4. b; 5. a

CHAPTER 3
1. c; 2. a; 3. d; 4. a; 5. d

CHAPTER 4
1. c; 2. b; 3. d; 4. b; 5. b

CHAPTER 5
1. c; 2. c; 3. d; 4. b; 5. d

CHAPTER 6
1. d; 2. a; 3. a; 4. b; 5. c

CHAPTER 7
1. a; 2. b; 3. d; 4. d; 5. d

CHAPTER 8
1. a; 2. c; 3. b; 4. a; 5. d

CHAPTER 9
1. c; 2. b; 3. a; 4. d; 5. d

CHAPTER 10
1. c; 2. c; 3. d; 4. c; 5. d

CHAPTER 11
1. d; 2. a; 3. a; 4. c; 5. d

CHAPTER 12
1. d; 2. d; 3. d; 4. c; 5. d

CHAPTER 13
1. a; 2. d; 3. a; 4. b; 5. b

APPENDIX: THE SKELETON

The skeleton is an essential part of the biology of living primates, human and nonhuman alike, and is discussed to one extent or another in many chapters of this book. Very likely, your instructor will want you to learn the essentials of primate osteology (that is, skeletal anatomy), including the names and parts of bones. This appendix provides a brief guide to that osteology, including the major bones and their parts. It presents a human skeleton, an ape (chimpanzee) skeleton, a monkey skeleton, a human skull, a human spine, human leg bones, and close-ups of the foot bones, hand bones, and pelvic bones of the human and the ape to illustrate important differences between the bipedal and quadrupedal primates.

For more details on osteology and anatomy, see Tim White and Pieter Folkens's *The Human Bone Manual* (Burlington, MA: Elsevier Academic Press, 2005) and Daris Swindler and Charles Wood's *An Atlas of Primate Gross Anatomy* (Seattle: University of Washington Press, 1973).

Phalanges

Metatarsals

Tarsals

Talus

Calcaneus

HUMAN FOOT

Talus

Calcaneus

CHIMPANZEE FOOT

Longitudinal arch   Transverse arch

HUMAN FOOT (MEDIAL VIEW)

Os coxae

Ilium

Sacroiliac joint

Sacrum

Acetabulum

Pubis

Ischium

HUMAN PELVIS

CHIMPANZEE PELVIS

Phalanges

Metacarpals

Carpals

HUMAN HAND

Phalanges

Metacarpals

Carpals

CHIMPANZEE HAND

Cranium

Mandible

Cervical
vertebrae (7)

Clavicle

Scapula

Sternum

Ribs

Thoracic
vertebrae (12)

Lumbar
vertebrae (5)

Ilium

Sacrum

Pubis

Ischium

Humerus

Ulna

Radius

Carpals (8)

Metacarpals (5)

Phalanges (14)

Femur

Patella

Tibia

Fibula

Tarsals (7)

Metatarsals (5)

Phalanges (14)

HUMAN SKELETON

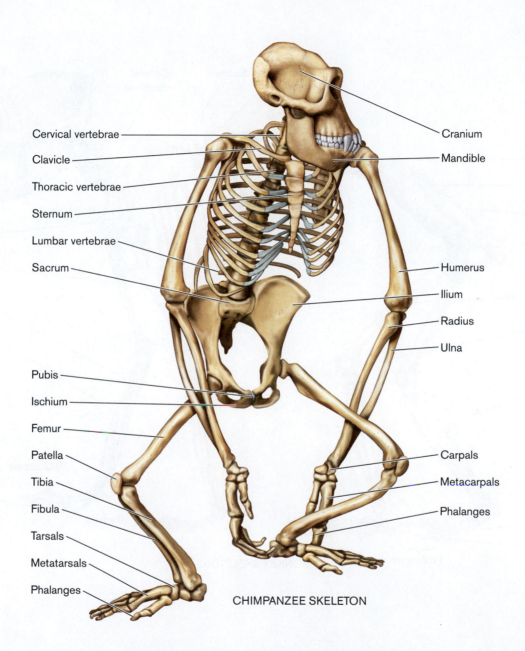

Cervical vertebrae

Clavicle

Thoracic vertebrae

Sternum

Lumbar vertebrae

Sacrum

Pubis

Ischium

Femur

Patella

Tibia

Fibula

Tarsals

Metatarsals

Phalanges

Cranium

Mandible

Humerus

Ilium

Radius

Ulna

Carpals

Metacarpals

Phalanges

CHIMPANZEE SKELETON

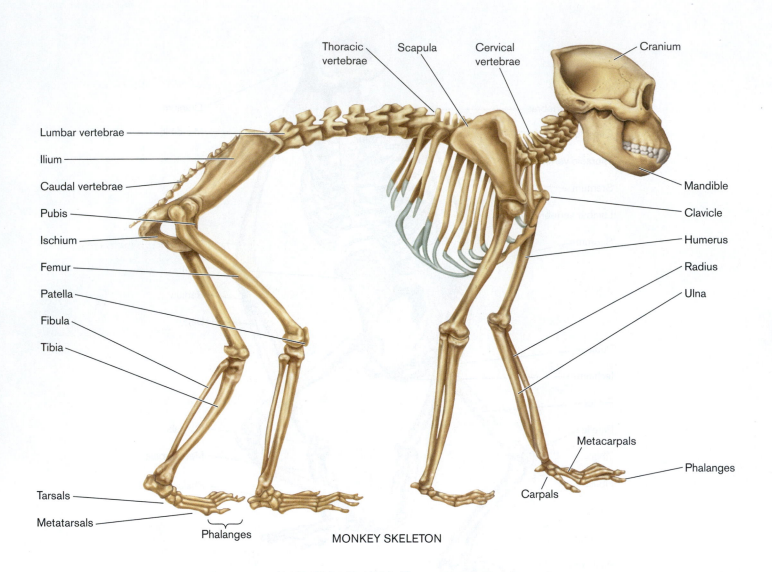

Thoracic vertebrae

Scapula

Cervical vertebrae

Cranium

Lumbar vertebrae

Ilium

Caudal vertebrae

Pubis

Ischium

Femur

Patella

Fibula

Tibia

Mandible

Clavicle

Humerus

Radius

Ulna

Metacarpals

Phalanges

Carpals

Tarsals

Metatarsals

Phalanges

MONKEY SKELETON

C1 (Atlas)
C2 (Axis)
C3
C4
C5
C6
C7
T1
T2
T3
T4
T5
T6
T7
T8
T9
T10
T11
T12
L1
L2
L3
L4
L5

Cervical curve

Thoracic curve

Lumbar curve

Pelvic curve

Spinous process
Vertebral arch
Vertebral foramen
Transverse process

Transverse foramen
Body (centrum)

Body (centrum)

Spinous process
Transverse process
Body (centrum)

Sacrovertebral joint
Sacrum (5 elements)
Coccyx (3–5 elements)

HUMAN SPINE

Frontal

Temporal

Nasal bones

Parietal

Eye orbit

Nasal aperture

Zygomatic

Maxilla

Mandible

HUMAN
SKULL

FRONTAL VIEW

Frontal

Sphenoid

Nasal

Zygomatic

Maxilla

Molars

Premolars

Incisors

Canine

Parietal

Temporal

Occipital

Mastoid
process

Mandible

LATERAL VIEW

Incisors (2)

Canine (1)

Premolars (2)

Zygomatic bone

Molars (3)

Temporal bone

Styloid process

Inferior nuchal line

Superior nuchal line

External occipital protuberance

Maxilla

Zygomatic bone

Palatine bone

Sphenoid

Foramen magnum

HUMAN SKULL

Mastoid process

Parietal

Occipital

BASILAR VIEW

Frontal

Coronal suture

Parietal

Sagittal suture

Lambdoidal suture

Occipital

SUPERIOR VIEW

Sagittal suture

Occipital

Mastoid process

Parietal

Lambdoidal suture

Nuchal line

POSTERIOR VIEW

HUMAN FEMUR

HUMAN TIBIA

6 mos.   3 yrs.   6 yrs.   11 yrs.   16 yrs.

GLOSSARY

abducted (big toe) A big toe, or great toe, that is spread apart from the second toe; compare with *adducted*. (Ch. 11)

abnormal hemoglobin Hemoglobin altered so that it is less efficient in binding to and carrying oxygen. (Ch. 4)

Acheulean Complex The stone tool culture associated with *H. erectus*; characterized by the use of handaxes and other types of stone tools. It was more refined than the earlier Oldowan Complex. (Ch. 11)

adapids Euprimates of the Eocene that were likely ancestral to modern lemurs and possibly ancestral to anthropoids. (Ch. 9)

Adapis A genus of adapids from the Eocene. (Ch. 9)

adaptations Changes in physical structure, function, or behavior that allow an organism or species to survive and reproduce in a given environment. (Ch. 2)

adaptive radiation The diversification of an ancestral group of organisms into new forms that are adapted to specific environmental niches. (Ch. 2)

adducted (big toe) A big toe, or great toe, that is close to the second toe; compare with *abducted*. (Ch. 11)

adenine One of the nitrogen bases that make up DNA and RNA; it pairs with thymine in DNA molecules and uracil in RNA molecules. (Ch. 3)

adenosine triphosphate (ATP) An important cellular molecule created by the mitochondria and carrying the energy necessary for cellular functions. (Ch. 3)

admixture The exchange of genetic material between two or more populations. (Ch. 4)

adult stage The third stage of life, involving the reproductive years and senescence. (Ch. 5)

Aegyptopithecus A propliopithecid genus from the Oligocene, probably ancestral to catarrhines; the largest primate found in the Fayum, Egypt. (Ch. 9)

aging The process of maturation. (Ch. 5)

allele One or more alternative forms of a gene. (Ch. 2)

Allen's rule The principle that an animal's limb lengths are heat-related; limbs are longer in hot environments and shorter in cold environments. (Ch. 5)

altruistic Relating to behavior that benefits others while being disadvantageous to the individual. (Ch. 7)

ameloblasts Cells that make tooth enamel. (Ch. 13)

amino acid dating An absolute dating method for organic remains, such as bone or shell, in which the amount of change in the amino acid structure is measured. (Ch. 8)

amino acids Organic molecules combined in a specific sequence by ribosomes to form a protein. (Ch. 3)

anatomical Pertaining to an organism's physical structure. (Ch. 1)

angiosperm radiation hypothesis The proposition that certain primate traits, such as visual acuity, occurred in response to the availability of fruit and flowers after the spread of angiosperms. (Ch. 9)

anthropogenic Relating to any effect caused by humans. (Ch. 4)

anthropology The study of humankind, viewed from the perspective of all people and all times. (Ch. 1)

antibodies Molecules that form as part of the primary immune response to the presence of foreign substances; they attach to foreign antigens. (Ch. 3)

anticodons Sequences of three nitrogen bases carried by tRNA; they match up with the complementary mRNA codons, and each designates a specific amino acid during protein synthesis. (Ch. 3)

antigens Specific proteins, on the surfaces of cells, that stimulate the immune system's antibody production. (Ch. 3)

arboreal Tree-dwelling, adapted to living in the trees. (Ch. 1)

arboreal adaptation Adaptation to life in the trees. (Ch. 6)

arboreal hypothesis The proposition that primates' unique suite of traits is an adaptation to living in trees. (Ch. 9)

archaeology The study of historic or prehistoric human populations through the analysis of material remains. (Ch. 1)

Ardipithecus kadabba An early pre-australopithecine species from the late Miocene to the early Pliocene; shows evidence of a perihoning complex, a primitive trait intermediate between apes and modern humans. (Ch. 10)

Ardipithecus ramidus A later pre-australopithecine species from the late Miocene to the early Pliocene; shows evidence of both bipedalism and arboreal activity but no indication of the primitive perihoning complex. (Ch. 10)

artifacts Material objects from past cultures. (Ch. 1)

Assimilation model The hypothesis postulating the African origin of modern *Homo sapiens*, with contributions of Eurasian archaic *H. sapiens* during the migration process. (Ch. 12)

Australopithecus An early hominin genus, representing as many as 10 species, found in East and South Africa from 4 to 1 mya. (Ch. 10)

Australopithecus aethiopicus An early robust australopithecine from East Africa, with the hallmark physical traits of large teeth, a large face, and massive muscle attachments on the cranium. (Ch. 10)

Australopithecus afarensis An early australopithecine from East Africa that had a brain size equivalent to a modern chimpanzee's and is thought to be a direct human ancestor. (Ch. 10)

Australopithecus africanus A gracile australopithecine from South Africa that was roughly contemporaneous with *Au. aethiopicus*, *Au. garhi*, and *Au. boisei* and was likely ancestral to *Au. robustus*. (Ch. 10)

Australopithecus anamensis The oldest species of australopithecine from East Africa and a likely ancestor to *Au. afarensis*. (Ch. 10)

Australopithecus boisei A later robust australopithecine from East Africa that was contemporaneous with *Au. robustus* and *Au. africanus* and had robust cranial traits, including large teeth, a large face, and heavy muscle attachments; formerly known as *Zinjanthropus boisei*. (Ch. 10)

Australopithecus deyiremeda An australopithecine, overlapping in time with *Au. afarensis* in East Africa. (Ch. 10)

Australopithecus garhi A late australopithecine from East Africa that was contemporaneous with *Au. africanus* and *Au. aethiopicus* and was the likely ancestor to the *Homo* lineage. (Ch. 10)

Australopithecus* (or *Kenyanthropus*) *platyops An australopithecine from East Africa that had a unique flat face and was contemporaneous with *Au. afarensis*. (Ch. 10)

Australopithecus prometheus The earliest known australopithecine in South Africa; bore a strong resemblance to *Au. africanus*. (Ch. 10)

Australopithecus robustus A robust australopithecine from South Africa that may have descended from *Au. africanus* and had the robust cranial traits of large teeth, a large face, and heavy muscle attachments. (Ch. 10)

Australopithecus sediba A late species of australopithecine from South Africa that may have descended from *Au. africanus*, was a contemporary of *Au. robustus*, and expresses anatomical features found in *Australopithecus* and in *Homo*. (Ch. 10)

autosomes All chromosomes, except the sex chromosomes, that occur in pairs in all somatic cells (not the gametes). (Ch. 3)

balanced polymorphism A situation in which selection maintains two or more phenotypes for a specific gene in a population. (Ch. 4)

basal anthropoids Eocene primates that are the earliest anthropoids. (Ch. 9)

basal metabolic rate (BMR) The rate at which an organism's body, while at rest, expends energy to maintain basic bodily functions; measured by the amount of heat given off per kilogram of body weight. (Ch. 5)

basal metabolic requirement The minimum amount of energy needed to keep an organism alive. (Ch. 5)

Bergmann's rule The principle that an animal's size is heat-related; smaller bodies are adapted to hot environments, and larger bodies are adapted to cold environments. (Ch. 5)

bilophodont (molar) Having two ridges, as the lower molars in Old World monkeys. (Ch. 6)

biocultural approach The scientific study of the interrelationship between what humans have inherited genetically and culturally. (Ch. 1)

biological anthropology The study of the evolution, variation, and adaptation of humans and their past and present relatives; sometimes called *physical anthropology*. (Ch. 1)

biostratigraphic dating A relative dating method that uses the associations of fossils in strata to determine each layer's approximate age. (Ch. 8)

bipedalism Walking on two feet. (Ch. 1)

Biretia A basal anthropoid genus found in the Fayum Depression, Egypt, that may be ancestral to anthropoids. (Ch. 9)

blending inheritance An outdated, refuted theory that the phenotype of an offspring was a uniform blend of the parents' phenotypes. (Ch. 2)

bone mass The density of bone per unit of measure. (Ch. 5)

brachiators Organisms that move by brachiation, or arm-swinging. (Ch. 6)

Branisella A South American genus from the Oligocene, ancestral to platyrrhines. (Ch. 9)

C₃ plants Plants that take in carbon through C_3 photosynthesis, which changes carbon dioxide into a compound having three carbon atoms; tending to be from more temperate regions, these plants include wheat, sugar beets, peas, and a range of hardwood trees. (Ch. 8)

C₄ plants Plants that take in carbon through C_4 photosynthesis, which changes carbon dioxide into a compound with four carbon atoms; these plants tend to be from warmer regions with low humidity and include corn, sugarcane, millet, and prickly pear. (Ch. 8)

calculus Hardened plaque on teeth; caused by the minerals from saliva being continually deposited on tooth surfaces. (Ch. 12)

canine–premolar honing complex The dental form in which the upper canines are sharpened against the lower third premolars when the jaws are opened and closed. (Ch. 6)

capillaries Small blood vessels between the terminal ends of arteries and the veins. (Ch. 4)

Carpolestes A plesiadapiform genus from the Paleocene, probably ancestral to the Eocene euprimates. (Ch. 9)

catastrophism The doctrine asserting that cataclysmic events (such as volcanoes, earthquakes, and floods), rather than evolutionary processes, are responsible for geologic changes throughout Earth's history. (Ch. 2)

Cenozoic The era lasting from 66 mya until the present, encompassing the radiation and proliferation of mammals such as humans and other primates. (Ch. 8)

chemical dating Dating methods that use predictable chemical changes that occur over time. (Ch. 8)

chromosomes The strands of DNA found in the nucleus of eukaryotes that contain hundreds or thousands of genes. (Ch. 2)

clade A group of organisms that evolved from a common ancestor. (Ch. 6)

cline A gradual change in a phenotypic characteristic from one geographic population to the next. (Ch. 5)

Clovis The earliest Native American ("Paleoindian") culture of North America; technology known for large, fluted, bifacial stone projectile points used as spear points for big-game hunting. (Ch. 12)

coding DNA Sequences of a gene's DNA (also known as exons) that are coded to produce a specific protein and are transcribed and translated during protein synthesis. (Ch. 3)

codominance The condition in which two different alleles are equally dominant; both alleles are fully expressed in a heterozygote's phenotype. (Ch. 3)

codons Sequences of three nitrogen bases carried by mRNA that are coded to produce specific amino acids in protein synthesis. (Ch. 3)

cognitive abilities The capacities of the brain to perceive, process, and judge information from the surrounding environment. (Ch. 5)

complementary bases The predictable pairing of nitrogen bases in the structure of DNA and RNA, such that adenine and thymine always pair together (adenine and uracil in RNA) and cytosine and guanine pair together. (Ch. 3)

cooking hypothesis The hypothesis that cooking food increases the efficiency of digestion and availability of nutrients required for brain and body growth and development, thus explaining the increase in brain and body size in *H. erectus* relative to earlier hominins. (Ch. 11)

cribra orbitalia Porosity in the eye orbits due to anemia caused by an iron-deficient diet, parasitic infection, or genetic disease. (Ch. 13)

crossing-over The process by which homologous chromosomes partially wrap around each other and exchange genetic information during meiosis. (Ch. 3)

cultural anthropology The study of modern human societies through the analysis of the origins, evolution, and variation of culture. (Ch. 1)

cultural dating Relative dating methods that are based on the time spans of material remains. (Ch. 8)

culture Learned behavior that is transmitted from person to person. (Ch. 1)

cytoplasm The jellylike substance inside the cell membrane that surrounds the nucleus and in which the organelles are suspended. (Ch. 3)

cytosine One of the nitrogen bases that make up DNA and RNA; it pairs with guanine. (Ch. 3)

data Evidence gathered to help answer questions, solve problems, and fill gaps in scientific knowledge. (Ch. 1)

deciduous dentition Also known as baby teeth or milk teeth, this is the first set of teeth, which form in utero and erupt shortly after birth. (Ch. 5)

deme   A local population of organisms that have similar genes, interbreed, and produce offspring. (Ch. 4)

demography   The study of a population's features and vital statistics, including birthrate, death rate, population size, and population density. (Ch. 2)

dendrochronology   A chronometric dating method that uses a tree-ring count to determine numerical age. (Ch. 8)

Denisovans   Extinct hominins, likely of the genus *Homo*; genetic evidence suggests they are related to Neandertals and modern *Homo sapiens*, perhaps sharing a common ancestor. (Ch. 12)

dental caries   A disease process that creates demineralized areas in dental tissues, leading to cavities; demineralization is caused by acids produced by bacteria that metabolize carbohydrates in dental plaque. (Ch. 13)

dental formula   The numerical description of a species' teeth, listing the number, in one quadrant of the jaws, of incisors, canines, premolars, and molars (in that order). (Ch. 6)

deoxyribonucleic acid (DNA)   A double-stranded molecule that provides the genetic code for an organism, consisting of phosphate, deoxyribose sugar, and four types of nitrogen bases. (Ch. 2)

derived characteristics   Characteristics present in only one or a few species of a group. (Ch. 6)

diaphyses   The main midsection, or shaft, portions of long bones; each diaphysis contains a medullary cavity. (Ch. 5)

diastema   A space between two teeth. (Ch. 6)

dietary plasticity   The ability of an organism to utilize a wide range of foods in meeting its nutritional requirements. (Ch. 6)

diploid cell   A cell that has a full complement of paired chromosomes. (Ch. 3)

directional selection   Selection for one allele over other alleles, causing allele frequencies to shift in one direction. (Ch. 4)

disruptive selection   Selection for both extremes of a phenotypic distribution; may eventually lead to a speciation event. (Ch. 4)

diurnal   Normally awake and active during daylight hours. (Ch. 6)

domestication   The process of converting wild animals or wild plants into forms that humans can care for and cultivate. (Ch. 13)

dominance   The ability to intimidate or defeat another individual in a pairwise, or dyadic, encounter. (Ch. 7)

dominant allele   An allele that is expressed in an organism's phenotype and that simultaneously masks the effects of another allele, if another one is present. (Ch. 2)

dryopithecids   Early Miocene apes found in various locations in Europe. (Ch. 9)

Dryopithecus   A genus of dryopithecid apes found in southern France and northern Spain. (Ch. 9)

electron spin resonance dating   An absolute dating method that uses microwave spectroscopy to measure electrons' spins in various materials. (Ch. 8)

empirical   Verified through observation and experiment. (Ch. 1)

endogamous   Characterized by endogamy, which is the practice (by a population or group) of breeding only within the population. (Ch. 4)

Eosimias   A genus of very small basal anthropoids from the Eocene. (Ch. 9)

epigenetic   Refers to chemical changes in the genome affecting how the underlying DNA is used in the production of proteins, but without altering the DNA sequences. (Ch. 3)

epiphyses   The end portions of long bones; once they fuse to the diaphyses, the bones stop growing longer. (Ch. 5)

epochs   Divisions of periods (which are, in turn, the major divisions of eras) in geologic time. (Ch. 8)

equifinality   The principle that a particular outcome can be produced by more than one process or combination of processes. (Ch. 10)

equilibrium   A condition in which a system is stable, balanced, and unchanging. (Ch. 4)

eras   Major divisions of geologic time that are divided into periods and further subdivided into epochs. (Ch. 8)

essential amino acids   Those amino acids that cannot be synthesized in the body and, thus, must be supplied by the diet. (Ch. 3)

ethnoprimatology   The study of ecological and cultural interactions between humans and primates. (Ch. 7)

eukaryotes   Multicelled organisms whose cells have a membrane-bound nucleus containing both the genetic material and specialized organelles. (Ch. 3)

euprimates   The first true primates from the Eocene: the tarsierlike omomyids and the lemurlike adapids. (Ch. 9)

evolutionary biology   A specialty within the field of biology; the study of the process of change in organisms. (Ch. 2)

evolutionary synthesis   A unified theory of evolution that combines genetics with natural selection. (Ch. 2)

evolvability   The capacity to evolve. (Ch. 1)

exogamous   Characterized by exogamy, which is the practice (by a population or group) of breeding outside the population. (Ch. 4)

fission track dating   An absolute dating method based on the measurement of the number of tracks left by the decay of ^{238}U. (Ch. 8)

fitness   Average number of offspring produced by parents with a particular genotype compared to the number of offspring produced by parents with another genotype. (Ch. 4)

fluorine dating   A relative (chemical) dating method that compares the accumulation of fluorine in animal and human bones from the same site. (Ch. 8)

Folsom   Early Native American (immediately after Clovis) culture of North America; technology known for large, fluted, bifacial projectile points used as spear points for big-game hunting. (Ch. 12)

foraminifera   Marine protozoans that have variably shaped shells with small holes. (Ch. 8)

forensic anthropology   The branch of biological anthropology pertaining to the recovery, analysis, and identification of human remains. (Ch. 1)

fossils   Physical remains of part or all of once-living organisms, mostly bones and teeth, that have become mineralized by the replacement of organic with inorganic materials. (Ch. 2)

founder effect   The accumulation of random genetic changes in a small population that has become isolated from the parent population due to the genetic input of only a few colonizers. (Ch. 4)

frameshift mutation   A change in a gene due to the insertion or deletion of one or more nitrogen bases, which causes the subsequent triplets to be rearranged and the codons to be read incorrectly during translation. (Ch. 4)

functional adaptations   Biological changes that occur during an individual's lifetime, increasing the individual's fitness in the given environment. (Ch. 5)

gametes   Sexual reproductive cells, ova and sperm, that have a haploid number of chromosomes and that can unite with a gamete of the opposite type to form a new organism. (Ch. 3)

gemmules   As proposed by Charles Darwin, the units of inheritance, supposedly accumulated in the gametes so they could be passed on to offspring. (Ch. 2)

gene   The basic unit of inheritance; a sequence of DNA on a chromosome, coded to produce a specific protein. (Ch. 2)

gene flow   Admixture, or the exchange of alleles between two populations. (Ch. 2)

gene pool   All the genetic information in a breeding population. (Ch. 4)

genetic drift   The random change in allele frequency from one generation to the next, with greater effect in small populations. (Ch. 2)

genetics   The study of specific genes and their function and transmission. (Ch. 2)

genome   The complete set of genetic information—chromosomal and mitochondrial DNA—for an organism or species that represents all the inheritable traits. (Ch. 1,. 3)

genomics   The study of an organism's entire set of genes, or genome. (Ch. 2)

genotype   The genetic makeup of an organism; the combination of alleles for a given gene. (Ch. 2)

genus   A group of related species. (Ch. 2)

geology   The study of Earth's physical history. (Ch. 2)

Gigantopithecus   A genus of Miocene pongids from Asia; the largest primate that ever lived. (Ch. 9)

glucose-6-phosphate dehydrogenase (G6PD)   An enzyme that aids in the proper functioning of red blood cells; G6PD deficiency, a genetic condition, leads to hemolytic anemia. (Ch. 4)

grade   A group of organisms sharing the same complexity and level of evolution. (Ch. 6)

growth velocity   The speed with which an organism grows in size, often measured as the amount of growth per year. (Ch. 5)

guanine   One of the nitrogen bases that make up DNA and RNA; it pairs with cytosine. (Ch. 3)

habitat   The specific area of the natural environment in which an organism lives. (Ch. 2)

habituate   Undertake the process of accustoming animals to human observers. (Ch. 7)

half-life   The time it takes for half of the radioisotopes in a substance to decay; used in various radiometric dating methods. (Ch. 8)

handaxe   The most dominant tool in the Acheulean Complex, characterized by a sharp edge for both cutting and scraping. (Ch. 11)

haplogroups   A large set of haplotypes, such as the Y chromosome or mitochondrial DNA, that may be used to define a population. (Ch. 3)

haploid cell   A cell that has a single set of unpaired chromosomes, half of the number of chromosomes as a diploid cell. (Ch. 3)

haplotypes   A group of alleles that tend to be inherited as a unit due to their closely spaced loci on a single chromosome. (Ch. 3)

Hardy–Weinberg law of equilibrium   A mathematical model in population genetics that reflects the relationship between frequencies of alleles and of genotypes; it can be used to determine whether a population is undergoing evolutionary changes. (Ch. 4)

heme iron   Iron found in meats, such as red meat, fish, and poultry; this type of iron is absorbed efficiently by the body. (Ch. 13)

hemoglobinopathies   A group of related genetic blood diseases characterized by abnormal hemoglobin. (Ch. 4)

hemolytic anemias   Conditions of insufficient iron in the blood due to the destruction of red blood cells resulting from genetic blood diseases, toxins, or infectious pathogens. (Ch. 4)

heteroplasmic   Regarding mitochondrial DNA or other organellar DNA, the quality of being different or varying among the parts of a single organism's body or even within cells of the same type, usually due to the mutation of the DNA in some organelles but not in others. (Ch. 3)

heterozygous   The condition in which the two alleles of a pair of alleles at a single locus on homologous chromosomes are different. (Ch. 3)

homeostasis   The maintenance of the internal environment of an organism within an acceptable range. (Ch. 5)

homeothermic   Maintaining a constant body temperature despite great variations in environmental temperature. (Ch. 5)

homeotic (Hox) genes   The genes responsible for differentiating the specific segments of the body, such as the head, tail, and limbs, during embryological development; also known as homeobox genes. (Ch. 3)

hominins   Humans and humanlike ancestors. (Ch. 1)

Homo erectus   An early species of *Homo* and the likely descendant of *H. habilis*; the first hominin species to move out of Africa into Asia and Europe. (Ch. 11)

Homo floresiensis   Dubbed the "hobbit" for its diminutive size, a possible new species of *Homo* found in Liang Bua Cave, on the Indonesian island of Flores. (Ch. 11)

Homo habilis   The earliest *Homo* species, a possible descendant of *Au. garhi* and an ancestor to *H. erectus*; showed the first substantial increase in brain size and was the first species definitively associated with the production and use of stone tools. (Ch. 10)

Homo luzonensis   A diminutive, Late Pleistocene hominin from Luzon, Philippines, showing a mixture of primitive hand and foot phalanges and modern dentition. (Ch. 12)

Homo naledi   A morphologically primitive hominin found in the later Pleistocene from cave deposits in South Africa. (Ch. 11)

homologous   Refers to chromosomes that occur in matching pairs in the genome. (Ch. 3)

homoplasmic   Regarding nuclear DNA, the quality of being identical in each cell type (except red blood cells) within an organism. (Ch. 3)

homozygous   The condition in which the two alleles of a pair of alleles at a single locus on homologous chromosomes are the same. (Ch. 3)

Huntington's chorea   A rare genetic disease in which the central nervous system degenerates and the individual loses control over voluntary movements, with the symptoms often appearing between ages 30 and 50. (Ch. 4)

hybridization   The process of interbreeding between members of different species. (Ch. 2)

hypercholesterolemia   The presence of high levels of cholesterol in an organism's blood; this condition may result from the dietary consumption of foods that promote high cholesterol or through the inheritance of a genetic disorder. (Ch. 5)

hypoplasia   A tooth-enamel deficiency usually appearing as a groove on the surface of the tooth and caused by growth disruption. (Ch. 13)

hypothermia   A condition in which an organism's body temperature falls below the normal range, which may lead to the loss of proper body functions and, eventually, death. (Ch. 5)

hypotheses   Testable statements that potentially explain specific phenomena observed in the natural world. (Ch. 1)

hypoxia   A condition characterized by less than the usual sea-level amount of oxygen in the air or in the body. (Ch. 5)

igneous rock   Rock formed from the crystallization of molten magma, which contains the radioisotope ^{40}K; used in potassium–argon dating. (Ch. 8)

index fossils   Fossils that are from specified time ranges, are found in multiple locations, and can be used to determine the age of associated strata. (Ch. 8)

induced mutations   Mutations in DNA resulting from exposure to toxic chemicals or to radiation. (Ch. 4)

infanticide   The killing of a juvenile. (Ch. 7)

intrauterine   Within the uterus. (Ch. 5)

introgression   Gene flow from closely related groups that were formerly reproductively isolated. (Ch. 4, 12)

iron deficiency anemia   A condition in which the blood has insufficient iron; may be caused by diet, poor iron absorption, parasitic infection, and severe blood loss. (Ch. 13)

isotopes   Two or more forms of a chemical element that have the same number of protons but vary in the number of neutrons. (Ch. 8)

karyotype   The complete set of chromosomes for an individual organism or a species. The karyotype is typically presented as a photograph of an individual's chromosomes that have been arranged in homologous pairs and put in numerical order by size. (Ch. 3)

Khoratpithecus A genus of Miocene apes from Asia, likely ancestral to orangutans. (Ch. 9)

kin selection Natural selection in favor of altruistic behaviors that increase the fitness of the donor's relatives. (Ch. 7)

Klinefelter's syndrome A chromosomal trisomy in which males have an extra X chromosome, resulting in an XXY condition; affected individuals typically have reduced fertility. (Ch. 4)

lactation The production and secretion of milk from a female mammal's mammary glands, providing a food source to the female's young. (Ch. 5)

Lamarckism First proposed by Lamarck, the theory of evolution through the inheritance of acquired characteristics in which an organism can pass on features acquired during its lifetime. (Ch. 2)

language A set of written or spoken symbols used by humans to refer to things (people, places, concepts, etc.) other than themselves. (Ch. 1)

law of independent assortment Mendel's second law, which asserts that the inheritance of one trait does not affect the inheritance of other traits. (Ch. 3)

law of segregation Mendel's first law, which asserts that the two alleles for any given gene (or trait) are inherited, one from each parent; during gamete production, only one of the two alleles will be present in each ovum or sperm. (Ch. 3)

Levallois technique A distinctive method of stone tool production used during the Middle Paleolithic, in which the core was prepared and flakes removed from the surface before the final tool was detached from the core. (Ch. 12)

life history The timing and details of growth events and development events from conception through senescence and death. (Ch. 5)

linguistic anthropology The study of the construction, use, and form of language in human populations. (Ch. 1)

locus The location on a chromosome of a specific gene. (Ch. 3)

loph An enamel ridge connecting cusps on a tooth's surface. (Ch. 6)

Lower Paleolithic The oldest part of the period during which the first stone tools were created and used, beginning with the Oldowan Complex. (Ch. 10)

Lucy One of the most significant fossils: the 40% complete skeleton of an adult female *Au. afarensis*, found in East Africa. (Ch. 10)

macroevolution Large-scale evolution, such as a speciation event, that occurs after hundreds or thousands of generations. (Ch. 4)

macronutrients Essential chemical nutrients, including fats, carbohydrates, and proteins, that a body needs to live and to function normally. (Ch. 5)

masticatory-functional hypothesis The hypothesis that craniofacial shape change during the Holocene was related to the consumption of softer foods. (Ch. 13)

material culture The part of culture that is expressed as objects that humans use to manipulate environments. (Ch. 1)

matriline Lineage or inheritance that can be traced from mother to daughter or to son; mitochondrial DNA is matrilineal DNA. (Ch. 3)

megafauna Large game animals hunted by pre-Holocene and early Holocene humans. (Ch. 12)

meiosis The production of gametes through one DNA replication and two cell (and nuclear) divisions, creating four haploid gametic cells. (Ch. 3)

melanin A brown pigment that determines the darkness or lightness of a human's skin color due to its concentration in the skin. (Ch. 5)

melanocytes Melanin-producing cells located in the skin's epidermis. (Ch. 5)

menarche The onset of menstruation in an adolescent female. (Ch. 5)

Mendelian inheritance The basic principles associated with the transmission of genetic material, forming the basis of genetics, including the law of segregation and the law of independent assortment. (Ch. 2)

menopause The cessation of the menstrual cycle, signifying the end of a female's ability to bear children. (Ch. 5)

Mesozoic The second major era of geologic time, 245–66 mya, characterized by the emergence and extinction of dinosaurs. (Ch. 8)

messenger RNA (mRNA) The molecules that are responsible for making a chemical copy of a gene needed for a specific protein—that is, for the transcription phase of protein synthesis. (Ch. 3)

methylation The attachment of a methyl group, a simple chemical, to DNA at certain sites throughout the genome. (Ch. 3)

microcephaly A condition in which the cranium is abnormally small and the brain is underdeveloped. (Ch. 12)

microevolution Small-scale evolution, such as changes in allele frequency, that occurs from one generation to the next. (Ch. 4)

micronutrients Essential substances, such as minerals or vitamins, needed in very small amounts to maintain normal body functioning. (Ch. 5)

Micropithecus A genus of very small proconsulids from the Miocene, found in Africa. (Ch. 9)

microsatellites Also called *short tandem repeats* (STRs); sequences of repeated base pairs of DNA, usually no more than two to six. If repeated excessively, they are often associated with neurologic disorders, such as Huntington's chorea. (Ch. 3)

Middle Paleolithic The middle part of the Old Stone Age, associated with Mousterian tools, which Neandertals produced using the Levallois technique. (Ch. 12)

mitochondria Energy-producing (ATP-producing) organelles in eukaryotic cells; mitochondria possess their own independent DNA. (Ch. 3)

mitosis The process of cellular and nuclear division that creates two identical diploid daughter cells. (Ch. 3)

monogamous Pertaining to a social group that includes an adult male, an adult female, and their offspring. (Ch. 7)

monosomy The condition in which only one of a specific pair of chromosomes is present in a cell's nucleus. (Ch. 3)

morphology Physical shape and appearance. (Ch. 1)

motor skills Complex movements and actions that require the control of nerves and muscles. (Ch. 5)

Mousterian The stone tool culture in which Neandertals produced tools using the Levallois technique. (Ch. 12)

mutagens Substances, such as toxins, chemicals, or radiation, that may induce genetic mutations. (Ch. 4)

mutation A random change in a gene or chromosome, creating a new trait that may be advantageous, deleterious, or neutral in its effects on the organism. (Ch. 2)

natural selection The process by which some organisms, with features that enable them to adapt to the environment, preferentially survive and reproduce, thereby increasing the frequency of those features in the population. (Ch. 2)

Neolithic The late Pleistocene–early Holocene culture, during which humans domesticated plants and animals. (Ch. 13)

nocturnal Normally awake and active during the night. (Ch. 6)

noncoding DNA Sequences of a gene's DNA (also known as introns) that are not coded to produce specific proteins and are excised before protein synthesis. (Ch. 3)

nondisjunctions Failures of chromosomes to properly segregate during meiosis, creating some gametes with abnormal numbers of chromosomes. (Ch. 3)

nonheme iron Iron found in plants, such as lentils and beans; this type of iron is less efficiently absorbed by the body than is heme iron. (Ch. 13)

nonhoning canine An upper canine tooth that, as part of a nonhoning chewing mechanism, is not sharpened against the lower third premolar. (Ch. 1)

nonmineralized (bone) Bone reduced to its organic component. (Ch. 5)

nonsynonymous point mutation A point mutation that creates a triplet coded to produce a different amino acid from that of the original triplet. (Ch. 4)

Notharctus   A genus of adapids from the Eocene; they were one of the largest adapids. (Ch. 9)

nucleotide   The building block of DNA and RNA, composed of a sugar, a phosphate group, and one of four nitrogen bases. (Ch. 3)

nucleus   A membrane-bound structure in eukaryotic cells that contains the genetic material. (Ch. 3)

nutrition transition   Change in diet involving a shift from a traditional diet of low-fat foods, cereals, and fiber to a Western diet of high-fat, high-carbohydrate, animal-sourced foods. (Ch. 5)

occipital bun   A cranial feature of Neandertals in which the occipital bone projects substantially from the skull's posterior. (Ch. 12)

Oldowan Complex   The stone tool culture associated with *H. habilis* and, possibly, *Au. garhi*; characterized by the use of primitive chopper tools. (Ch. 10)

olfactory bulb   The portion of the anterior brain that processes odor-detection signals. (Ch. 6)

oligopithecids   The earliest anthropoid ancestors in the Oligocene, found in the Fayum, Egypt. (Ch. 9)

omnigenic   Refers to complex traits that involve various parts of the genome and the interconnections among those parts. (Ch. 3)

omomyids   Euprimates of the Eocene that were likely ancestral to modern tarsiers. (Ch. 9)

opposable thumb   As found in primates, a thumb that can touch each of the four fingertips, enabling a grasping ability. (Ch. 6)

oreopithecids   Miocene apes that were found in Europe. (Ch. 9)

Oreopithecus   A genus of oreopithecids found in Italy that was extinct within a million years of its appearance. (Ch. 9)

Orrorin tugenensis   A pre-australopithecine species found in East Africa that displayed some of the earliest evidence of bipedalism. (Ch. 10)

osteoarthritis   Degenerative changes of the joints caused by a variety of factors, especially physical activity and mechanical stress. (Ch. 13)

osteoblasts   Cells responsible for bone formation. (Ch. 5)

osteoclasts   Cells responsible for bone resorption. (Ch. 5)

osteoporosis   The loss of bone mass, often due to age, causing the bones to become porous, brittle, and easily fractured. (Ch. 5)

Ouranopithecus   A genus of Miocene dryopithecids found in Greece. (Ch. 9)

paleobotanist   A scientist who studies ancient plant remains. (Ch. 13)

Paleoindians   The earliest hominin inhabitants of the Americas; they likely migrated from Asia and are associated with the Clovis and Folsom stone tool cultures in North America and comparable tools in South America. (Ch. 12)

paleomagnetic dating   An absolute dating method based on the reversals of Earth's magnetic field. (Ch. 8)

paleontology   The study of extinct life-forms through the analysis of fossils. (Ch. 2)

Paleozoic   The first major era of geologic time, 545–245 mya, during which fish, reptiles, and insects first appeared. (Ch. 8)

pandemic   An infectious disease that has become prevalent over an exceptionally large region, such as multiple countries, a continent, or the world. (Ch. 2, 13)

Pangaea   A hypothetical single landmass, forming the origin for all continents. (Ch. 8)

parapithecids   Anthropoid ancestors from the Oligocene, found in the Fayum, Egypt. (Ch. 9)

Parapithecus   A genus of later parapithecids from the Oligocene, found in the Fayum, Egypt. (Ch. 9)

parental investment   The time and energy parents expend for their offspring's benefit. (Ch. 6)

patriline   Lineage or inheritance that can be traced from father to son via the Y chromosome. (Ch. 3)

peptide bond   A chemical bond that joins amino acids into a protein chain. (Ch. 3)

periosteal reaction   An inflammatory response of a bone's outer covering due to bacterial infection or trauma. (Ch. 13)

personal genomics   The branch of genomics focused on sequencing individual genomes. (Ch. 3)

Perupithecus   The earliest genus of a platyrrhine, dating to the Early Oligocene. (Ch. 9)

phenome   The total set of phenotypic traits in an organism. (Ch. 3)

phenotype   The physical expression of the genotype; it may be influenced by the environment. (Ch. 2)

phylogeny   The evolutionary relationships of a group of organisms. (Ch. 6)

physical anthropology   The original term for *biological anthropology*. (Ch. 1)

Pithecanthropus erectus   The name used by Eugène Dubois for his first fossil discovery, which later became known as *Homo erectus*. (Ch. 11)

pleiotropy   The phenomenon of a single gene having multiple effects. (Ch. 3)

plesiadapiforms   Paleocene organisms that may have been the first primates, originating from an adaptive radiation of mammals. (Ch. 9)

point mutations   Replacements of a single nitrogen base with another base, which

may or may not affect the amino acid for which the triplet codes. (Ch. 4)

polarized light   A kind of light used in amino acid dating because it allows amino acid changes to be observed and measured. (Ch. 8)

polyandrous   Pertaining to a social group that includes one reproductively active female, several adult males, and their offspring. (Ch. 7)

polygenic   Refers to one phenotypic trait that is affected by two or more genes. (Ch. 3)

polygynous   Pertaining to a social group that includes one adult male, several adult females, and their offspring. (Ch. 7)

polymorphism   The presence of two or more alleles at a locus and such that the frequency of the alleles is greater than 1% in the population. (Ch. 3)

polypeptide   Also known as a protein, a chain of amino acids held together by multiple peptide bonds. (Ch. 3)

population genetics   A specialty within the field of genetics that focuses on the changes in gene frequencies and the effects of those changes on adaptation and evolution. (Ch. 2)

porotic hyperostosis   The expansion and porosity of cranial bones due to anemia caused by an iron-deficient diet, parasitic infection, or genetic disease. (Ch. 13)

positive selection   The process by which advantageous genetic variants quickly increase in frequency in a population. (Ch. 4)

postnatal stage   The second stage of life, beginning with birth, terminating with the shift to the adult stage, and involving substantial increases in height, weight, and brain growth and development. (Ch. 5)

power grip   A fistlike grip in which the fingers and thumb wrap around an object in opposite directions. (Ch. 6)

preadaptation   An organism's use of an anatomical feature in a way unrelated to the feature's original function. (Ch. 6)

precision grip   A grip in which the tips of the fingers and thumb come together, enabling fine manipulation. (Ch. 6)

prehensile tail   A tail that acts as a kind of a hand for support in trees; common in New World monkeys. (Ch. 6)

prenatal stage   The first stage of life, beginning with the zygote in utero, terminating with birth, and involving multiple mitotic events and the differentiation of the body into the appropriate segments and regions. (Ch. 5)

primates   A group of mammals in the order Primates that have complex behavior, varied forms of locomotion, and a unique suite of traits, including large brains, forward-facing eyes, fingernails, and reduced snouts. (Ch. 1)

primitive characteristics   Characteristics present in multiple species of a group. (Ch. 6)

Proconsul   A genus of early Miocene proconsulids from Africa, ancestral to catarrhines. (Ch. 9)

proconsulids   Early Miocene apes found in East Africa. (Ch. 9)

prokaryotes   Single-celled organisms with no nuclear membranes or organelles and with their genetic material as a single strand in the cytoplasm. (Ch. 3)

propliopithecids   Anthropoid ancestors from the Oligocene, found in the Fayum, Egypt. (Ch. 9)

Propliopithecus   An Oligocene propliopithecid genus. (Ch. 9)

Proprimates   A separate order of early primate ancestors from the Paleocene, such as the plesiadapiforms, but lacking key attributes of the order Primates. (Ch. 9)

racemization   The chemical reaction resulting in the conversion of L-amino acids to D-amino acids for amino acid dating. (Ch. 8)

radiocarbon dating   The radiometric dating method in which the ratio of ^{14}C to ^{12}C is measured to provide an absolute date for a material younger than 50,000 years. (Ch. 8)

radiopotassium dating   The radiometric dating method in which the ratio of ^{40}K to ^{40}Ar is measured to provide an absolute date for a material older than 200,000 years. (Ch. 8)

recessive allele   An allele that is expressed in an organism's phenotype if two copies are present but is masked if the dominant allele is present. (Ch. 2)

recombination   The exchange of genetic material between homologous chromosomes, resulting from a crossover event. (Ch. 3)

regulatory genes   Those genes that determine when structural genes and other regulatory genes are turned on and off for protein synthesis. (Ch. 3)

regulatory proteins   Proteins involved in the expression of control genes. (Ch. 3)

replication   The process of copying nuclear DNA prior to cell division, so that each new daughter cell receives a complete complement of DNA. (Ch. 3)

reproductive isolation   Any circumstance that prevents two populations from interbreeding and exchanging genetic material, such as when two populations are separated by a large body of water or a major mountain range. (Ch. 4)

rhinarium   The naked surface around the nostrils, typically wet in mammals. (Ch. 6)

ribonucleic acid (RNA)   A single-stranded molecule involved in protein synthesis, consisting of a phosphate, ribose sugar, and one of four nitrogen bases. (Ch. 3)

ribosomal RNA (rRNA)   A fundamental structural component of a ribosome. (Ch. 3)

ribosomes   The organelles attached to the surface of the endoplasmic reticulum, located in the cytoplasm of a cell; they are the site of protein synthesis. (Ch. 3)

rigidity (bone)   The strength of bone to resist bending and torsion. (Ch. 5)

Saadanius   An early catarrhine Oligocene genus from a group of primates that gave rise to later catarrhines. (Ch. 9)

sagittal keel   A slight ridge of bone found along the midline sagittal suture of the cranium, which is typically found on *H. erectus* skulls. (Ch. 11)

Sahelanthropus tchadensis   The earliest pre-australopithecine species found in central Africa with possible evidence of bipedalism. (Ch. 10)

scientific law   A statement of fact describing natural phenomena. (Ch. 1)

scientific method   An empirical research method in which data are gathered from observations of phenomena, hypotheses are formulated and tested, and conclusions are drawn that validate or modify the original hypotheses. (Ch. 1)

sectorial (premolar)   Adapted for cutting. (Ch. 6)

secular trend   A phenotypic change over time, due to multiple factors; such trends can be positive (e.g., increased height) or negative (e.g., decreased height). (Ch. 5)

sedimentary rock   Rock formed when the deposition of sediments creates distinct layers, or strata. (Ch. 8)

senescence   An organism's biological changes in later adulthood. (Ch. 5)

sex chromosomes   The pair of chromosomes that determine an organism's biological sex. (Ch. 3)

sexual dimorphism   A difference in a physical attribute between the males and females of a species. (Ch. 5)

sexual selection   The frequency of traits that change due to the attractiveness of those traits to members of the opposite sex. (Ch. 7)

shovel-shaped incisors   A dental trait, commonly found among Native Americans and Asians, in which the incisors' posterior aspect has varying degrees of concavity. (Ch. 12)

sickle-cell anemia   A genetic blood disease in which the red blood cells become deformed and sickle-shaped, decreasing their ability to carry oxygen to tissues. (Ch. 4)

single nucleotide polymorphisms (SNPs)   Variations in the DNA sequence due to the change of a single nitrogen base. (Ch. 3)

sivapithecids   Early Miocene apes found in Asia. (Ch. 9)

Sivapithecus   A genus of Miocene sivapithecids, proposed as ancestral to orangutans. (Ch. 9)

skin reflectance   The amount of light reflected from the skin that can be measured and used to assess skin color. (Ch. 5)

social learning   The capacity to learn from other humans, enabling the accumulation of knowledge across many generations. (Ch. 1)

sociality   The tendency within certain animal populations for individuals to form social groups and cooperative communities. (Ch. 7)

sociolinguistics   The science of investigating language's social contexts. (Ch. 1)

somatic cells   Diploid cells that form the organs, tissues, and other parts of an organism's body. (Ch. 3)

species   A group of closely related organisms having the potential to interbreed and produce offspring. (Ch. 2)

spontaneous mutations   Random changes in DNA that occur during cell division. (Ch. 4)

stabilizing selection   Selection against the extremes of a phenotypic distribution, decreasing the genetic diversity for a trait in the population. (Ch. 4)

Steno's law of superposition   The geologic principle that the lower the stratum, or layer, the older its age; the oldest layers are at the bottom, and the youngest are at the top. (Ch. 8)

strata   Layers of rock, representing various periods of deposition. (Ch. 8)

stratigraphic correlation   The process of matching up strata from several sites through the analysis of chemical, physical, and other properties. (Ch. 8)

stressors   Factors that can cause stress in an organism, potentially affecting the body's proper functioning and its homeostasis. (Ch. 5)

structural genes   Genes coded to produce particular products, such as an enzyme or hormone, rather than regulatory proteins. (Ch. 3)

structural proteins   Proteins that form an organism's physical attributes. (Ch. 3)

sun protection factor (SPF)   The rating calculated by comparing the length of time needed for protected skin to burn to the length of time needed for unprotected skin to burn. (Ch. 5)

superfoods   Cereal grains, such as rice, corn, and wheat, that make up a substantial portion of the human population's diet today. (Ch. 13)

synonymous point mutation   A neutral point mutation in which the substituted nitrogen base creates a triplet coded to produce the same amino acid as that of the original triplet. (Ch. 3)

systematics   The study and classification of living organisms to determine their evolutionary relationships with one another. (Ch. 2)

taphonomy The study of the deposition of plant or animal remains and the environmental conditions affecting their preservation. (Ch. 8)

taxa Plural of *taxon*, which is any unit in biological classification (taxonomy), such as genus, species, class, order, family, and the like. (Ch. 6)

taxonomy The classification of organisms into a system that reflects degrees of relatedness. (Ch. 2)

tectonic Referring to various structures on Earth's surface, such as the continental plates. (Ch. 8)

terrestrial Life-forms, including humans, that live on land versus living in water or in trees. (Ch. 1)

thalassemia A genetic blood disease in which hemoglobin is improperly synthesized, causing red blood cells to have a much shorter life span. (Ch. 4)

theory A set of hypotheses that have been rigorously tested and validated, leading to their establishment as a generally accepted explanation of specific phenomena. (Ch. 1)

thermoluminescence dating A relative dating method in which the energy trapped in a material is measured when the object is heated. (Ch. 8)

Theropithecus A genus of fossil and living Old World monkeys found in Africa; it was more diverse in the past than it is today and was one of the first monkey genera to appear in the evolutionary record. (Ch. 9)

thymine One of four nitrogen bases that make up DNA; it pairs with adenine. (Ch. 3)

tooth comb Anterior teeth (incisors and canines) that have been tilted forward, creating a scraper. (Ch. 6)

total daily energy expenditure (TDEE) The number of calories used by an organism's body during a 24-hour period. (Ch. 5)

transcription The first step of protein synthesis, involving the creation of messenger RNA (mRNA) based on the DNA template. (Ch. 3)

transfer RNA (tRNA) The molecules that are responsible for transporting amino acids to the ribosomes during protein synthesis. (Ch. 3)

translation The second step of protein synthesis, involving the transfer of amino acids by transfer RNA (tRNA) to the ribosomes, which are then added to the protein chain. (Ch. 3)

translocations Rearrangements of chromosomes due to the insertion of genetic material from one chromosome to another. (Ch. 3)

transposable elements Mobile pieces of DNA that can copy themselves into entirely new areas of chromosomes. (Ch. 4)

treponematoses A group of related diseases (venereal syphilis, endemic syphilis, yaws) caused by the bacteria *Treponema*, which causes pathologic changes most often to the cranium and tibiae. (Ch. 13)

triplets Sequences of three nitrogen bases each in DNA, known as codons in mRNA. (Ch. 3)

trisomy The condition in which an additional chromosome exists with the homologous pair. (Ch. 3)

type 2 diabetes A disease in which the body does not produce enough insulin or the cells do not use the available insulin, causing a buildup of glucose in the cells. (Ch. 5)

uniformitarianism The concept that processes that occurred in the geologic past are still at work today. (Ch. 2)

Upper Paleolithic The most recent part of the Old Stone Age, associated with early modern *Homo sapiens* and characterized by finely crafted stone and other types of tools with various functions. (Ch. 12)

uracil One of four nitrogen bases that make up RNA; it pairs with adenine. (Ch. 3)

vasoconstriction The decrease in blood vessels' diameter due to the action of a nerve or of a drug; it can also occur in response to cold temperatures. (Ch. 5)

vasodilation The increase in blood vessels' diameter due to the action of a nerve or of a drug; it can also occur in response to hot temperatures. (Ch. 5)

victoriapithecids Miocene primates from Africa, possibly ancestral to Old World monkeys. (Ch. 9)

visual predation hypothesis The proposition that unique primate traits arose as adaptations to preying on insects and small animals. (Ch. 9)

Wolff's law The principle that bone is placed in the direction of functional demand; that is, bone develops where needed and recedes where it is not needed. (Ch. 5)

Y-5 Hominoids' pattern of lower molar cusps. (Ch. 6)

zygote The cell that results from a sperm's fertilization of an ovum. (Ch. 3)

GLOSSARY OF PLACE NAMES

Primary research and/or findings are noted for each place.

CHAPTER 1

Çatalhöyük, Turkey—Clark Larsen research

CHAPTER 2

Galápagos Islands—Charles Darwin trip and observations

CHAPTER 6

New World (primates)
Old World (primates)
Taï National Park, Ivory Coast, West Africa—primate behavior and conservation

CHAPTER 7

Gombe National Park, Tanzania—Jane Goodall research

CHAPTER 9

Bighorn Basin, Wyoming—*Carpolestes*
The Fayum Depression, Egypt—*Aegyptopithecus*, *Parapithecus*, *Biretia*, oligopithecids, parapithecids, propliopithecids
Jingzhou, Hubei Province, China—*Archicebus*
Paris Basin, France—*Adapis*
Rukwa Rift Basin, Tanzania—*Rukwapithecus fleaglei*, *Nsungwepithecus gunnelli*
Rusinga Island, Lake Victoria, Kenya—*Proconsul*
Salla, Bolivia—*Branisella*
Santa Rosa, Peru—*Perupithecus*
Saudi Arabia—*Saadanius*
St. Gaudens, France—*Dryopithecus*
Tuscany, Italy—*Oreopithecus*

CHAPTER 10

Afar Depression, Ethiopia—*Ardipithecus*
Allia Bay, Kenya—*Australopithecus anamensis*
Aramis, Middle Awash Valley, Ethiopia—*Ardipithecus kadabba* and *Ardipithecus ramidus*
Asa Issie, Middle Awash Valley, Ethiopia—*Australopithecus anamensis*
Awash Valley, Ethiopia—*Ardipithecus* and *Australopithecus garhi*
Bouri, Middle Awash Valley, Ethiopia—*Australopithecus garhi*
Burtele, Ethiopia—*Australopithecus deyiremeda*

Dikika, Ethiopia—*Australopithecus afarensis* and evidence of cutmarks on bones
Djurab Desert, Chad—*Sahelanthropus tchadensis*
Drimolen, South Africa—*Australopithecus robustus*
Eastern Rift Valley, Africa—*Australopithecus*
Gona, Middle Awash Valley, Ethiopia—*Australopithecus garhi* tools
Hadar, Ethiopia—*Australopithecus afarensis*
Kanapoi, Kenya—*Australopithecus anamensis*
Korsi Dora, Ethiopia—*Australopithecus afarensis*
Kromdraai, South Africa—*Australopithecus robustus*
Laetoli, Tanzania—*Australopithecus afarensis*
Lake Turkana, Kenya—*Australopithecus anamensis*, *Orrorin tugenensis*, *Australopithecus (Kenyanthropus) platyops*, and *Australopithecus aethiopicus*
Lomekwi, Kenya—*Australopithecus (Kenyanthropus) platyops* and Oldowan-like cobble tools
Makapansgat, South Africa—*Australopithecus africanus*
Malapa, South Africa—*Australopithecus sediba*
Olduvai Gorge, Tanzania—various australopithecines
Sterkfontein, South Africa—*Australopithecus africanus*
Swartkrans, South Africa—*Australopithecus robustus*
Taung, South Africa—*Australopithecus africanus*
Tugen Hills, Kenya—*Orrorin tugenensis*

CHAPTER 11

Atapuerca, Spain—*Homo erectus*
Bodo, Middle Awash Valley, Ethiopia—*Homo erectus* and evidence of cutmarks on bones
Bouri, Middle Awash Valley, Ethiopia—*Homo erectus* and evidence of animal butchery
Boxgrove, England—*Homo erectus*
Buia, Eritrea—*Homo erectus*
Ceprano, Italy—*Homo erectus*
Dmanisi, Georgia—*Homo erectus*
Gona, Middle Awash Valley, Ethiopia—complete pelvis of *Homo erectus*
Gongwangling, China—*Homo erectus*

Gran Dolina, Spain—*Homo erectus*, evidence of animal butchery, and cutmarks on *H. erectus* bones
Ileret, Kenya—*Homo erectus*
Lake Turkana, Kenya—*Homo habilis* and *Homo erectus*
Ledi-Geraru, Afar region, Ethiopia—transitional hominin between australopithecines and *Homo*
Majuangou, China—*Homo erectus*
Mauer, Germany—*Homo erectus*
Nariokotome, Kenya—*Homo erectus*
Olduvai Gorge, Tanzania—*Homo habilis*, *Homo erectus*, and *Homo rudolfensis*
Olorgesailie, Kenya—Acheulean tools
Omo, Ethiopia—*Homo habilis*
Rising Star Cave, South Africa—*Homo naledi*
Sambungmacan, Java, Indonesia—*Homo erectus*
Sangiran, Java, Indonesia—*Homo erectus*
Sima del Elefante, Spain—*Homo erectus*
Sterkfontein, South Africa—*Homo habilis*
Trinil, Java, Indonesia—*Homo erectus*
Uraha, Malawi—*Homo habilis*
Zhoukoudian, China—*Homo erectus* and evidence of fire

CHAPTER 12

Aduma, Middle Awash Valley, Ethiopia—early modern *Homo sapiens*
Amud, Israel—Neandertal and evidence of intentional burial
Arago, France—early archaic *Homo sapiens*
Atapuerca, Spain—early archaic *Homo sapiens*
Bouri, Middle Awash Valley, Ethiopia—early modern *Homo sapiens*
Clovis, New Mexico—Paleoindian sites
Cro-Magnon, France—early modern *Homo sapiens*
Cueva Antón, Spain—Neandertal
Cueva de los Aviones, Spain—Neandertal
Dali, China—early archaic *Homo sapiens*
Denisova, Russia—Denisovan
Dolní Věstonice Czech Republic—early modern *Homo sapiens*
El Sidrón, Spain—Neandertal
Engis, Belgium—Neandertal
Feldhofer Cave, Germany—Neandertal
Flores, Indonesia—*Homo floresiensis*
Folsom, New Mexico—Paleoindian sites
Gobero, Niger—early modern *Homo sapiens*

Grimaldi Caves, Italy—early modern *Homo sapiens*

Herto, Middle Awash Valley, Ethiopia—early modern *Homo sapiens*

Hofmeyr, South Africa—early modern *Homo sapiens*

Kabwe (Broken Hill), Zambia—early archaic *Homo sapiens*

Katanda, Democratic Republic of the Congo—early modern *Homo sapiens*

Kebara, Israel—Neandertal

Kennewick, Washington—controversial Paleoindian find

Klasies River Mouth Cave, South Africa—early modern *Homo sapiens*

Kow Swamp, Victoria, Australia—early modern *Homo sapiens*

Krapina, Croatia—Neandertal and possible evidence of cannibalism

La Chapelle-aux-Saints, France—Neandertal and evidence of intentional burial

Lagar Velho, Portugal—early modern *Homo sapiens*

Lake Mungo, New South Wales, Australia—early modern *Homo sapiens*

Les Rochers-de-Villeneuve, France—Neandertal

Liang Bua Cave, Flores, Indonesia—*Homo floresiensis*

Lothagam, Kenya—early modern *Homo sapiens*

Luzon, Philippines—*Homo luzonensis*

Marillac, France—Neandertal

Mezmaiskaya, Russia—Neandertal

Minatogawa, Japan—early modern *Homo sapiens*

Mladeč, Czech Republic—early modern *Homo sapiens*

Monte Lessini, Italy—Neandertal

Moula-Guercy, France—Neandertal and possible evidence of cannibalism

Narmada, India—early archaic *Homo sapiens*

Ngandong, Java, Indonesia—early archaic *Homo sapiens*

Omo, Ethiopia—early modern *Homo sapiens*

Peştera cu Oase, Romania—early modern *Homo sapiens*

Petralona, Greece—early archaic *Homo sapiens*

Předmostí, Czech Republic—early modern *Homo sapiens*

Scladina Cave, Belgium—Neandertal

Shanidar, Kurdistan, Iraq—Neandertal, evidence of care of the sick, and evidence of intentional burial

Sima de los Huesos, Sierra de Atapuerca, Spain—early archaic *Homo sapiens*

Skhul, Israel—early modern *Homo sapiens*

Spy, Belgium—Neandertal

Steinheim, Germany—early archaic *Homo sapiens*

Swanscombe, England—early archaic *Homo sapiens*

Tabun, Israel—Neandertal and evidence of intentional burial

Teshik Tash, Uzbekistan—Neandertal

Tianyuan Cave, China—early modern *Homo sapiens*

Vindija Cave, Croatia—Neandertal

Wadi Halfa, Egypt—early modern *Homo sapiens*

Wadi Kubbaniya, Egypt—early modern *Homo sapiens*

Zhoukoudian (Upper Cave), China—early modern *Homo sapiens*

CHAPTER 13

Çatalhöyük, Turkey—evidence of early cities

Fertile Crescent—early agricultural communities

Jericho, West Bank—evidence of early cities

Levant—early plant domestication

BIBLIOGRAPHY

Abbate, E., A. Albianelli, A. Azzaroli, M. Benvenuti, B. Tesfamariam, P. Bruni, N. Cipriani, R. J. Clarke, G. Ficcarelli, R. Macchiarelli, G. Napoleone, M. Papini, L. Rook, M. Sagri, T. M. Tecle, D. Torre, and I. Villa. 1998. A one-million-year-old *Homo* cranium from the Danakil (Afar) depression of Eritrea. *Nature* 393: 458–460.

Abbate, E., B. WoldeHaimanot, Y. Libsekal, T. M. Tecle, and L. Rook. 2004. A step towards human origins: The Buia *Homo* one-million-years ago in the Eritrean Danakil Depression (East Africa). *Rivista Italiana di Paleontologia e Stratigrafia*, special issue, 110: 1–144.

Achilli, A., U. A. Perego, H. Lancioni, A. Olivieri, and F. Gandini. 2013. Reconciling migration models to the Americas with the variation of North American native mitogenomes. *Proceedings of the National Academy of Sciences USA* 110: 14308–14313.

Adger, N. 2007. *Climate Change 2007: Climate Change Impacts, Adaptation and Vulnerability.* Washington, DC: Intergovernmental Panel on Climate Change.

Aerts, P. 1998. Vertical jumping in *Galago senegalensis*: The quest for an obligate mechanical power amplifier. *Philosophical Transactions of the Royal Society of London B* 353: 1607–1620.

Agarwal, S. C. and S. D. Stout, eds. 2003. *Bone Loss and Osteoporosis: An Anthropological Perspective.* New York: Kluwer Academic/Plenum Press.

Aiello, L. C. 2010. Five years of *Homo floresiensis*. *American Journal of Physical Anthropology* 142: 167–179.

Ainsworth, C. and D. MacKenzie. 2001. Coming home. *New Scientist* 171(2298): 28–33.

Alba, D. M. 2012. Fossil apes from the Valles-Penedes basin. *Evolutionary Anthropology* 21: 254–269.

Alberts, S. C., J. Altmann, D. K. Brockman, M. Cords, L. M. Fedigan, A. Pusey, T. S. Stoinski, K. B. Strier, W. F. Morris, and A. M. Bronikowski. 2013. Reproductive aging patterns in primates reveal that humans are distinct. *Proceedings of the National Academy of Sciences USA* 110: 13440–13445.

Alemseged, Z., F. Spoor, W. H. Kimbel, R. Bobe, D. Geraads, D. Reed, and J. G. Wynn. 2006. A juvenile early hominin skeleton from Dikika, Ethiopia. *Nature* 443: 296–301.

Allison, A. C. 2004. Two lessons from the interface of genetics and medicine. *Genetics* 166: 1591–1599.

Alvarez, W. 1997. *T. rex and the Crater of Doom.* Princeton, NJ: Princeton University Press.

Alvesalo, K. and P. M. A. Tigerstedt. 1974. Heritabilities of human tooth dimensions. *Hereditas* 77: 311–318.

Ambrose, S. H., L. J. Hlusko, D. Kyule, A. Deino, and M. Williams. 2003. Lemudong'o: A new 6 Ma paleontological site near Narok, Kenya Rift Valley. *Journal of Human Evolution* 44: 737–742.

Ambrose, S. H. and J. Krigbaum. 2003. Bone chemistry and bioarchaeology. *Journal of Anthropological Archaeology*, special issue, 22(3): 191–304.

Ankel-Simons, F. 2007. *Primate Anatomy: An Introduction.* Amsterdam, Netherlands: Elsevier.

Anonymous. 2012. Genomics beyond genes. *Science* 338: 1528.

Antón, S. C. and C. C. Swisher III. 2004. Early dispersals of *Homo* from Africa. *Annual Review of Anthropology* 33: 271–296.

Arbib, M. A., K. Liebal, and S. Pika. 2008. Primate vocalization, gesture, and the evolution of human language. *Current Anthropology* 49: 1053–1076.

Arcadi, A. C. 2018. *Wild Chimpanzees: Social Behavior of an Endangered Species.* Cambridge, UK: Cambridge University Press.

Armelagos, G. J. and K. N. Harper. 2005. Genomics of the origins of agriculture, part one. *Evolutionary Anthropology* 14: 68–77.

Aron, J. L. and J. A. Patz. 2001. *Ecosystem Change and Public Health: A Global Perspective.* Baltimore: Johns Hopkins University Press.

Arsuaga, J.-L. 1997. Sima de los Huesos. *Journal of Human Evolution* 33: 105–421.

Arsuaga, J.-L. 2010. Terrestrial apes and phylogenetic trees. *Proceedings of the National Academy of Sciences USA* 107(suppl. 2): 8910–8917.

Arsuaga J. L., J.-M. Carretero, C. Lorenzo, A. Gomez-Olivencia, and A. Pablos. 2015. Postcranial morphology of the middle Pleistocene humans from Sima de los Huesos, Spain. *Proceedings of the National Academy of Sciences USA* 112: 11524–11529.

Arsuaga, J. L., I. Martínez, L. J. Arnold, A. Aranburu, A. Gracia-Téllez, et al. 2014. Neandertal roots: Cranial and chronological evidence from Sima de los Huesos. *Science* 344: 1358–1364.

Arsuaga, J.-L., I. Martínez, C. Lorenzo, A. Gracia, A. Muñoz, O. Alonso, and J. Gallego. 1999. The human cranial remains from Gran Dolina lower Pleistocene site (Sierra de Atapuerca, Spain). *Journal of Human Evolution* 37: 431–457.

Ascenzi, A., I. Biddittu, P. F. Cassoli, A. G. Segre, and E. Segre-Naldini. 1996. A calvarium of late *Homo erectus* from Ceprano, Italy. *Journal of Human Evolution* 31: 409–423.

Asfaw, B., W. H. Gilbert, Y. Beyene, W. K. Hart, P. R. Renne, G. WoldeGabriel, E. S. Vrba, and T. D. White. 2002. Remains of *Homo erectus* from Bouri, Middle Awash, Ethiopia. *Nature* 416: 317–320.

Asfaw, B., T. White, O. Lovejoy, B. Latimer, S. Simpson, and G. Suwa. 1999. *Australopithecus garhi:* A new species of early hominid from Ethiopia. *Science* 284: 629–635.

Atsalis, S. and S. W. Margulis. 2006. Sexual and hormonal cycles in geriatric *Gorilla gorilla gorilla*. *International Journal of Primatology* 27: 1663–1687.

Ayala, F. J. 2007. Darwin's greatest discovery: Design without designer. *Proceedings of the National Academy of Sciences USA* 104: 8567–8573.

Backwell, L. R. and F. d'Errico. 2001. Evidence of termite foraging by Swartkrans early hominids. *Proceedings of the National Academy of Sciences USA* 98: 1358–1363.

Bajpai, S., R. F. Kay, B. A. Williams, D. P. Das, V. V. Kapur, and B. N. Tiwari. 2008. The oldest Asian record of Anthropoidea. *Proceedings of the National Academy of Sciences USA* 105: 11093–11098.

Baker, C. 2006. *The Evolution Dialogues.* Washington, DC: American Association for the Advancement of Science.

Balter, M. 2005. Are humans still evolving? *Science* 309: 234–237.

Balter, M. 2006. Radiocarbon dating's final frontier. *Science* 313: 1560–1563.

Balter, M. 2007. Seeking agriculture's ancient roots. *Science* 316: 1830–1835.

Balter, M. 2008. Going deeper into the Grotte Chauvet. *Science* 321: 904–905.

Balter, M. 2010. Candidate human ancestor from South Africa sparks praise and debate. *Science* 328: 154–155.

Balter M. 2014. Ancient infant was ancestor of today's Native Americans. *Science* 343: 716–717.

Barker, D. J. P. 1996. The origins of coronary heart disease in early life. Pp. 155–162 in C. J. K. Henry and S. J. Ulijaszek, eds. *Long-Term Consequences of Early Environment: Growth, Development and the Lifespan Developmental Perspective.* Cambridge, UK: Cambridge University Press.

Barker, D. J. P. 1998. *In utero* programming of chronic disease. *Clinical Science* 95: 115–128.

Barker, D. J. P. 1998. *Mothers, Babies, and Health in Later Life.* Edinburgh and New York: Churchill Livingstone.

Barker, D. J. P. 2001. *Fetal Origins of Cardiovascular and Lung Disease.* Oxford, UK: Taylor & Francis.

Barker, D. J. P. 2004. The developmental origins of chronic adult disease. *Acta Paediatrica* 93(suppl. 446): 26–33.

Barker, D. J. P. and D. T. Lackland. 2003. Prenatal influences on stroke mortality in England and Wales. *Stroke* 34: 1598–1602.

Barnosky, A. D., P. L. Koch, R. S. Feranec, S. L. Wing, and A. B. Shabel. 2004. Assessing the causes of late Pleistocene extinctions on the continents. *Science* 306: 70–75.

Barsh, G. S. 2003. What controls variation in human skin color? *PLoS Biology* 1: 19–22.

Bartlett, T. Q. 2009. *The Gibbons of Khao Yai: Seasonal Variation in Behavior and Ecology.* Upper Saddle River, NJ: Pearson Prentice Hall.

Bar-Yosef, O. 2006. *Kebara Cave, Mt. Carmel, Israel.* Cambridge, MA: Harvard University Press.

Bar-Yosef, O. and A. Belfer-Cohen. 1989. The origins of sedentism and farming communities in the Levant. *Journal of World Prehistory* 3: 477–498.

Bar-Yosef, O. and B. Vandermeersch. 1993. Modern humans in the Levant. *Scientific American* 268(4): 94–100.

Barzun, J. 1965. *Race: A Study in Superstition.* New York: Harper & Row.

Bass, W. M. 1984. Time interval since death: A difficult decision. Pp. 136–147 in T. A. Rathbun and J. E. Buikstra, eds. *Human Identification: Case Studies in Forensic Anthropology.* Springfield, IL: Charles C. Thomas.

Baumgartner, R. J., M. J. Van Kranendonk, D. Wacey, M. L. Florentini, M. Saunders, et al. 2019. Nano-porous pyrite and organic matter in 3.5-billion-year-old stromatolites record primordial life. *Geology* 47: 1039–1043.

Bayon, G., B. Dennielou, J. Etoubleau, E. Ponzevera, S. Toucanne, and S. Bermell. 2012. Intensifying weathering and land use in Iron Age central Africa. *Science* 335: 1219–1222.

Beall, C., K. Song, R. C. Elston, and M. C. Goldstein. 2004. Higher offspring survival among Tibetan women with high oxygen saturation genotypes residing at 4,000 m. *Proceedings of the National Academy of Sciences USA* 101: 14300–14304.

Beall, C. and A. T. Steegmann Jr. 2000. Human adaptation to climate: Temperature, ultraviolet radiation, and altitude. Pp. 163–224 in S. Stinson, B. Bogin, R. Huss-Ashmore, and D. O'Rourke, eds. *Human Biology: An Evolutionary and Biocultural Perspective.* New York: Wiley-Liss.

Beall, C. M. 2001. Adaptations to altitude: A current assessment. *Annual Review of Anthropology* 30: 423–456.

Beall, C. M. 2006. Andean, Tibetan, and Ethiopian patterns of adaptation to high-altitude hypoxia. *Integrative and Comparative Biology* 46: 18–24.

Beall, C. M. 2014. Adaptation to high altitude: Phenotypes and genotypes. *Annual Review of Anthropology* 43: 251–272.

Beard, C. 2004. *The Hunt for the Dawn Monkey: Unearthing the Origins of Monkeys, Apes, and Humans.* Berkeley: University of California Press.

Beard, K. C. 2002. Basal anthropoids. Pp. 133–149 in W. C. Hartwig, ed. *The Primate Fossil Record.* Cambridge, UK: Cambridge University Press.

Beard, K. C., T. Qi, M. R. Dawson, B. Wang, and C. Li. 1994. A diverse new primate fauna from middle Eocene fissure-fillings in southeastern China. *Nature* 368: 604–609.

Beattie, O. and J. Geiger. 2000. *Frozen in Time: The Fate of the Franklin Expedition.* New York: Sterling Publishing.

Beck, T. J., C. B. Ruff, R. A. Shaffer, K. Betsinger, D. W. Trone, and S. K. Brodine. 2000. Stress fracture in military recruits: Gender differences in muscle and bone susceptibility factors. *Bone* 27: 437–444.

Begun, D. R. 2002. European hominoids. Pp. 339–368 in W. C. Hartwig, ed. *The Primate Fossil Record.* Cambridge, UK: Cambridge University Press.

Begun, D. R. 2003. Planet of the apes. *Scientific American* 289(2): 74–83.

Begun, D. R. 2010. Catarrhine cousins: The origin and evolution of monkeys and apes of the Old World. Pp. 295–313 in C. S. Larsen, ed. *A Companion to Biological Anthropology.* Chichester, UK: Wiley-Blackwell.

Begun, D. R. 2013. The Miocene hominoid radiations. Pp. 398–416 in D. R. Begun, ed. *A Companion to Paleoanthropology.* Chichester, UK: Wiley-Blackwell.

Begun, D. R., ed. 2013. *A Companion to Paleoanthropology.* Chichester, UK: Wiley-Blackwell.

Behrensmeyer, A. K. and A. P. Hill. 1980. *Fossils in the Making: Vertebrate Taphonomy and Paleoecology.* Chicago: University of Chicago Press.

Beleza, S., A. M. Santos, B. McEvoy, I. Alves, C. Martinho, E. Cameron, M. D. Shriver, E. J. Parra, and J. Rocha. 2012. The timing of pigmentation lightening in Europeans. *Molecular Biology and Evolution* 30: 24–35.

Bellisari, A. 2013. *The Obesity Epidemic in America.* Long Grove, IL: Waveland Press.

Bellwood, P. 2005. *First Farmers: The Origins of Agricultural Societies.* Malden, MA: Blackwell.

Benefit, B. R. and M. L. McCrossin. 1995. Miocene hominoids and hominid origins. *Annual Review of Anthropology* 24: 237–256.

Benn Torres, J., M. B. Doura, S. O. Y. Keita, and R. A. Kittles. 2012. Y chromosome lineages in men of West African descent. *PLoS One* 7: e29687.

Bennett, E. A., I. Crevecoeur, B. Viola, A. P. Derevianko, M. V. Shunkov, et al. 2019. Morphology of the Denisovan phalanx closer to modern humans than to Neandertals. *Science Advances* 5: eaaw3950.

Bennett, M. R., J. W. K. Harris, B. G. Richmond, B. R. Braun, E. Mbua, P. Kiura, D. Olago, M. Kibunjia, C. Omuombo, A. K. Behrensmeyer, D. Huddart, and S. Gonzalez. 2010. Early hominin foot morphology based on 1.5-million-year-old footprints from Ileret, Kenya. *Science* 323: 1197–1201.

Benton, M. J. 2003. *When Life Nearly Died: The Greatest Mass Extinction of All Time.* London: Thames & Hudson.

Benyshek, D. C., J. F. Martin, and C. S. Johnson. 2001. A reconsideration of the origins of the type 2 diabetes epidemic among Native Americans and the implications for intervention policy. *Medical Anthropology* 20: 25–64.

Berger, L. R. 2013. The mosaic nature of *Australopithecus sediba*. *Science* 340: 163–164.

Berger, L. R., D. J. de Ruiter, S. E. Churchill, P. Schmid, K. J. Carlson, P. H. G. M. Dirks, and J. M. Kibii. 2010. *Australopithecus sediba*: A new species of *Homo*-like australopith from South Africa. *Science* 328: 195–204.

Berger, L. R., J. Hawks, D. J. de Ruiter, S. E. Churchill, P. Schmid, et al. 2015. *Homo naledi*, a new species of the genus *Homo* from the Dinaledi chamber, South Africa. *eLife* 4: e09560. DOI: 10.7554/eLife.09560.

Berger, L. R., J. Hawks, P. H. G. M. Dirks, M. Elliot, and E. M. Roberts. 2017. *Homo naledi* and Pleistocene hominin evolution in subequatorial Africa. *eLife* 6: e24234. DOI: 10.7554/eLife.24234.

Berger, L. R. and W. S. McGraw. 2007. Further evidence for eagle predation of, and feeding damage on, the Taung child. *South African Journal of Science* 103: 495–498.

Berger, S. L., T. Kouzarides, R. Shiekhatter, and A. Shilatifard. 2009. An operational definition of epigenetics. *Genes and Development* 23: 781–783.

Berger, T. D. and E. Trinkaus. 1995. Patterns of trauma among the Neandertals. *Journal of Archaeological Science* 22: 841–852.

Bermejo, M., J. D. Rodriguez-Teijeiro, G. Illera, A. Barroso, C. Vila, and P. D. Walsh. 2006. Ebola outbreak killed 5000 gorillas. *Science* 314: 1564.

Bermúdez de Castro, J. M., M. Martinón-Torres, E. Carbonell, S. Sarmiento, A. Rosas, J. van der Made, and M. Lozano. 2004. The Atapuerca sites and their contribution to the knowledge of human evolution in Europe. *Evolutionary Anthropology* 13: 25–41.

Berna, F., P. Goldberg, L. K. Horwitz, J. Brink, S. Holt, M. Bamford, and M. Chazan. 2012. Microstratigraphic evidence of in situ fire in the Acheulean strata of Wonderwerk Cave, Northern Cape Province, South Africa. *Proceedings of the National Academy of Sciences USA* 109: 1215–1220.

Berra, T. M. 2008. Charles Darwin's paradigm shift. *The Beagle: Records of the Museums and Art Galleries of the Northern Territory* 24: 1–5.

Berra, T. M. 2009. *Charles Darwin: The Concise Story of an Extraordinary Man*. Baltimore: Johns Hopkins University Press.

Beyene, Y., S. Katoh, G. WoldeGabriel, W. K. Hart, K. Uto, M. Sudo, M. Kondo, M. Hyodo, P. R. Renne, G. Suwa, and B. Asfaw. 2013. The characteristics and chronology of the earliest Acheulean at Konso, Ethiopia. *Proceedings of the National Academy of Sciences USA* 110: 1584–1591.

Bhattacharjee, J. K., G. R. Janssen, and T. G. Gregg. 2006. Human genealogy: How wide and deep do our genetic connections go? *American Biology Teacher* 68: 69–71.

Billman, B. R., P. M. Lambert, and B. L. Leonard. 2000. Cannibalism, warfare, and drought in the Mesa Verde region during the twelfth century A.D. *American Antiquity* 65: 145–178.

Bininda-Emonds, O. R. P., M. Cardillo, K. E. Jones, R. D. E. MacPhee, R. M. D. Beck, R. Greyner, S. A. Price, R. A. Vos, J. L. Gittleman, and A. Purvis. 2007. The delayed rise of present-day mammals. *Nature* 446: 507–512.

Bischoff, J. L., R. W. Williams, R. U. J. Rosenbauer, A. Aramburu, J. L. Arsuaga, N. García, and G. Cuenca-Bescós. 2007. High-resolution U-series dates from the Sima de los Huesos hominids yields 600 kyrs: Implications for the evolution of the early Neanderthal lineage. *Journal of Archaeological Science* 34: 763–770.

Bitty E. A., S. G. Bi, J.-C. K. Bene, P. K. Kouassi, and W. S. McGraw. 2015. Cocoa farming and primate extirpation inside Cote d'Ivoire's protected areas. *Tropical Conservation Science* 8: 95–113.

Blakey, M. L. 1999. Scientific racism and the biological concept of race. *Literature and Psychology* 45: 29–43.

Bloch, J. I. and D. M. Boyer. 2002. Grasping primate origins. *Science* 298: 1606–1610.

Bloch, J. I., M. T. Silcox, D. M. Boyer, and E. J. Sargis. 2007. New Paleocene skeletons and the relationship of plesiadapiforms to crown-clade primates. *Proceedings of the National Academy of Sciences USA* 104: 1159–1164.

Blumenbach, J. F. 1775. *De Generis Humani Varietate Nativa*. Göttingen, Germany: Rosenbuschii.

Blumenbach, J. F. 1790–1828. *Decades suae craniorum diversarum Gentium, illustratae*. Göttingen, Germany: I. C. Dietrich.

Boas, F. 1912. Changes in bodily form of descendants of immigrants. *American Anthropologist* 14: 530–563.

Bocherens, H. 2009. Neanderthal dietary habits: Review of the isotopic evidence. Pp. 241–250 in J.-J. Hublin and M. P. Richards, eds. *The Evolution of Hominin Diets: Integrating Approaches to the Study of Palaeolithic Subsistence*. New York: Springer.

Boesch, C. and M. Tomasello. 1998. Chimpanzee and human cultures. *Current Anthropology* 39: 591–614.

Bogin, B. 1999. *Patterns of Human Growth*, 2nd ed. Cambridge, UK: Cambridge University Press.

Bogin, B., H. Azcorra, H. J. Wilson, A. Vazquez-Vazquez, M.L. Avila-Escalante, M. T. Castillo-Burgette, I. Varela-Silva, and F. Dickinson. 2014. Globalization and children's diets: The case of Maya of Mexico and Central America. *Anthropological Review* 77: 11–32.

Bogin, B. and B. H. Smith. 2012. Evolution of the human life cycle. Pp. 515–586 in S. Stinson, B. Bogin, and D. O'Rourke, eds. *Human Biology: An Evolutionary and Biocultural Perspective*, 2nd ed. Hoboken, NJ: Wiley-Blackwell.

Bogin, B., P. Smith, A. B. Orden, M. I. Varela Silva, and J. Louky. 2002. Rapid change in height and body proportions of Maya American children. *American Journal of Human Biology* 14: 753–761.

Böhme, M., N. Spassov, J. Fuss, A. Tröscher, A. S. Deane, et al. 2019. A new Miocene ape and locomotion in the ancestor of great apes and humans. *Nature* 575: 489–493.

Bond, M., M. F. Tejedor, K. E. J. Campbell, L. Chornogubsky, N. Novo, and F. Goin. 2015. Eocene primates of South America and the African origins of New World monkeys. *Nature* 520: 538–541.

Bouchard, C. 2007. The biological predisposition to obesity: Beyond the thrifty genotype scenario. *International Journal of Obesity* 31: 1337–1339.

Bouzouggar, A., N. Barton, M. Vanhaeren, F. d'Errico, S. Collcutt, T. Higham, E. Hodge, S. Parfitt, E. Rhodes, J.-L. Schwenninger, C. Stringer, E. Turner, S. Ward, A. Moutmir, and A. Stambouli. 2007. 82,000-year-old shell beads from North Africa and implications for the origins of modern human behavior. *Proceedings of the National Academy of Sciences USA* 104: 9964–9969.

Bowen, M. 2005. *Thin Ice: Unlocking the Secrets of Climate in the World's Highest Mountains*. New York: Henry Holt.

Bowler, P. J. 2003. *Evolution: The History of an Idea*. Berkeley: University of California Press.

Bowler, P. J. 2005. Variation from Darwin to the modern synthesis. Pp. 9–27 in B. Hallgrimson and B. K. Hall, eds. *Variation: A Central Concept in Biology*. Burlington, MA: Elsevier Academic Press.

Bowler, P. J. 2009. Darwin's originality. *Science* 323: 223–226.

Bown, T. M. and K. D. Rose. 1987. Patterns of dental evolution in early Eocene anaptomorphine primates (Omomyidae) from the Bighorn Basin, Wyoming. *Paleontological Society Memoirs* 23: 1–162.

Boyd, R., P. L. Richerson, and J. Henrich. 2011. The cultural niche: Why social learning is essential for human adaptation. *Proceedings of the National Academy of Sciences USA* 108(suppl. 2): 10918–10925.

Boyle, E. A., Y. I. Li, and J. K. Pritchard. 2017. An expanded view of complex traits:

From polygenic to omnigenic. *Cell* 169: 1177–1186.

Brace, C. L. 2002. The concept of race in physical anthropology. Pp. 239–253 in P. N. Peregrine, C. R. Ember, and M. Ember, eds. *Physical Anthropology: Original Readings in Method and Practice*. Upper Saddle River, NJ: Prentice Hall.

Brace, C. L. 2005. *"Race" Is a Four-Letter Word: The Genesis of a Concept*. New York: Oxford University Press.

Brace, C. L., S. L. Smith, and K. D. Hunt. 1991. What big teeth you had grandma! Human tooth size, past and present. Pp. 33–57 in M. A. Kelley and C. S. Larsen, eds. *Advances in Dental Anthropology*. New York: Wiley-Liss.

Bradley, R. S. 1999. *Paleoclimatology*. San Diego: Academic Press.

Brain, C. K. 1981. *The Hunters or the Hunted? An Introduction to African Cave Taphonomy*. Chicago: University of Chicago Press.

Brain, C. K. 1993. *Swartkrans: A Cave's Chronicle of Early Man*. Transvaal Museum Monographs 8. Pretoria, South Africa: Transvaal Museum.

Bräuer, G. 2008. The origin of modern anatomy: By speciation or intraspecific evolution? *Evolutionary Anthropology* 17: 22–37.

Braun, D. R., V. Aldeias, W. Archer, J. R. Arrowsmith, N. Baraki, et al. 2019. Earliest known Oldowan artifacts at >2.58 Ma from Ledi-Geraru, Ethiopia, highlight early technological diversity. *Proceedings of the National Academy of Sciences USA* 116: 11712–11717.

Bribiescas, R. G. 2006. *Men: Evolutionary and Life History*. Cambridge, MA: Harvard University Press.

Bridges, P. S. 1996. Skeletal biology and behavior in ancient humans. *Evolutionary Anthropology* 4: 112–120.

Briggs, A. W., J. M. Good, R. E. Green, J. Krause, T. Maricic, U. Stenzel, C. Lalueza-Fox, P. Rudan, D. Brajković, Ž. Kućan, I. Gušić, R. Schmitz, V. B. Doronichev, L. V. Golovanova, M. de la Rasilla, J. Fortea, A. Rosas, and S. Pääbo. 2009. Targeted retrieval and analysis of five Neandertal mtDNA genomes. *Science* 325: 318–321.

Brooke, J. L. and C. S. Larsen. 2014. The nurture of nature: Genetics, epigenetics, and environment in human biohistory. *American Historical Review* 119: 1500–1513.

Brown, K. 2002. Tangled roots? Genetics meets genealogy. *Science* 295: 1634–1635.

Brown, K. A. 2001. Identifying the sex of human remains by ancient DNA analysis. *Ancient Biomolecules* 3: 215–226.

Brown, P. 1992. Recent human evolution in East Asia and Australasia. *Proceedings of the Royal Society of London B* 337: 235–242.

Brown, P., T. Sutikna, M. J. Morwood, R. P. Soejono, Jatmiko, E. Wayhu Saptomo, and Rokus Awe Due. 2004. A new small-bodied hominin from the late Pleistocene of Flores, Indonesia. *Nature* 431: 1055–1061.

Brown, R. A. and G. J. Armelagos. 2001. Apportionment of racial diversity: A review. *Evolutionary Anthropology* 10: 34–40.

Brunel, S., E. A. Bennett, L. Cardin, D. Garraud, H. B. Emam, et al. 2020. Ancient genomes from present-day France unveil 7,000 years of its demographic history. *Proceedings of the National Academy of Sciences USA* 117: 12791–12798.

Bruner, E. and G. Manzi. 2007. Landmark-based shape analysis of the archaic *Homo* calvarium from Ceprano (Italy). *American Journal of Physical Anthropology* 132: 355–366.

Brunet, M., F. Guy, D. Pilbeam, H. T. Mackaye, A. Likius, D. Ahounta, A. Beauvilain, C. Blondel, H. Bocherens, J. R. Boisserie, L. De Bonis, Y. Coppens, J. Dejax, C. Denys, P. Duringer, V. Eisenmann, G. Fanone, P. Fronty, D. Geraads, T. Lehmann, F. Lihoreau, A. Louchart, A. Mahamat, G. Merceron, G. Mouchelin, O. Otero, P. P. Campomanes, M. P. De Leon, J. C. Rage, M. Sapanet, M. Schuster, J. Sudre, P. Tassy, X. Valentin, P. Vignaud, L. Viriot, A. Zazzo, and C. Zollikofer. 2002. A new hominid from the upper Miocene of Chad, Central Africa. *Nature* 418: 145–151.

Brutsaert, T. D., M. Kiyamu, G. E. Revollendo, J. L. Isherwood, F. S. Lee, M. Rivera-Ch, F. Leon-Velarde, S. Ghosh, and A. W. Bigham. 2019. Association of *EGLN1* gene with high aerobic capacity of Peruvian Quechua at high altitude. *Proceedings of the National Academy of Sciences USA* 116: 24006–24011.

Brutsaert, T. D., E. Parra, M. Shriver, A. Gamboa, J.-A. Palacios, M. Rivera, I. Rodriguez, and F. Leon-Velarde. 2004. Effects of birthplace and individual genetic admixture on lung volume and exercise phenotypes of Peruvian Quechua. *American Journal of Physical Anthropology* 123: 390–398.

Bufford, J. D. and J. E. Gern. 2005. The hygiene hypothesis revisited. *Immunology and Allergy Clinics of North America* 25: 247–262.

Buikstra, J. E. 1988. *The Mound-Builders of Eastern North America: A Regional Perspective*. Amsterdam, Netherlands: Elfde Kroon-Voordracht.

Buikstra, J. E. 2010. Paleopathology: A contemporary perspective. Pp. 395–411 in C. S. Larsen, ed. *A Companion to Biological Anthropology*. Chichester, UK: Wiley-Blackwell.

Burger, J., M. Kirchner, B. Bramanti, W. Haak, and M. G. Thomas. 2007. Absence of the lactase-persistence-associated allele in early Neolithic Europeans. *Proceedings of the National Academy of Sciences USA* 104: 3736–3741.

Burke, A. 2004. The ecology of Neanderthals. *International Journal of Osteoarchaeology*, special issue, 14(3–4): 155–342.

Bustamente, C. D. and B. M. Henn. 2010. Shadows of early migrations. *Nature* 468: 1044–1045.

Butynski, T. M., J. Kingdon, and J. Kalina, eds. 2013. *Primates of Africa*. Vol. 2: *The Mammals of Africa*. London: Bloomsbury.

Caballero, B. and B. M. Popkin. 2002. *The Nutrition Transition: Diet and Disease in the Developing World*. London: Academic Press.

Calcagno, J. M. and A. Fuentes. 2012. What makes us human? Answers from evolutionary anthropology. *Evolutionary Anthropology* 21: 182–194.

Calcagno, J. M. and K. R. Gibson. 1991. Selective compromise: Evolutionary trends and mechanisms in hominid tooth size. Pp. 59–76 in M. A. Kelley and C. S. Larsen, eds. *Advances in Dental Anthropology*. New York: Wiley-Liss.

Caldecott, J. and L. Miles, eds. 2005. *World Atlas of Great Apes and Their Conservation*. Berkeley: University of California Press.

Callaway, E. 2011. The Black Death decoded. *Nature* 478: 444–446.

Callaway, E. 2015. Crowdsourcing digs up an early human species. *Nature* 525: 297–298.

Cameron, D. W. 2004. *Hominid Adaptations and Extinctions*. Sydney: University of New South Wales Press.

Campbell, C. J., A. Fuentes, K. C. MacKinnon, M. Panger, and S. K. Bearder, eds. 2006. *Primates in Perspective*. New York: Oxford University Press.

Campbell, M. C. and S. A. Tishkoff. 2010. The evolution of human genetic and phenotypic variation in Africa. *Current Biology* 20: R106-R173.

Candela, P. B. 1942. The introduction of blood-group B into Europe. *Human Biology* 14: 413–443.

Cann, R. L., M. Stoneking, and A. Wilson. 1987. Mitochondrial DNA and human evolution. *Nature* 325: 31–36.

Caramelli, D., C. Lalueza-Fox, C. Vernesi, M. Lari, A. Casoli, F. Mallegni, B. Chiarelli, I. Dupanloup, J. Bertranpetit, G. Barbujani, and G. Bertorelle. 2003. Evidence for a genetic discontinuity between Neandertals and 24,000-year-old anatomically modern Europeans. *Proceedings of the National Academy of Sciences USA* 100: 6593–6597.

Carbonell, E., J. M. Bermúdez de Castro, J. M. Parés, A. Pérez-González, G. Cuenca-Bescós, A. Ollé, M. Mosquera, R. Huguet, J. van der Made, A. Rosas, R. Sala, J. Vallverdú, N. García,

D. E. Granger, M. Martinón-Torres, X. P. Rodríguez, G. M. Stock, J. M. Vergès, E. Allué, F. Burjachs, I. Cáceres, A. Canals, A. Benito, C. Diez, M. Lozano, A. Mateos, M. Navazom, J. Rodríguez, J. Rosell, and J. L. Arsuaga. 2008. The first hominin of Europe. *Nature* 452: 465–469.

Carey, N. 2012. *The Epigenetics Revolution: How Modern Biology Is Rewriting Our Understanding of Genetics, Disease, and Inheritance.* New York: Columbia University Press.

Carlson, D. S. and D. P. Van Gerven. 1977. Masticatory function and post-Pleistocene evolution in Nubia. *American Journal of Physical Anthropology* 46: 495–506.

Carlson, E. A. 2004. *Mendel's Legacy: The Origins of Classical Genetics.* Cold Spring Harbor, NY: Cold Spring Harbor Laboratory Press.

Carlson, K. J., D. Stout, T. Jashashvili, D. J. de Ruiter, P. Tafforeau, K. Carlson, and L. R. Berger. 2011. The endocast of MH1, *Australopithecus sediba. Science* 333: 1402–1407.

Carmody, R. N., G. S. Weintraub, and R. W. Wrangham. 2011. Energetic consequences of thermal and nonthermal food processing. *Proceedings of the National Academy of Sciences USA* 108: 19199–19203.

Carmody, R. N. and R. W. Wrangham. 2009. The energetic significance of cooking. *Journal of Human Evolution* 57: 379–391.

Carroll, M. W., D. A. Matthews, J. A. Hiscox, M. J. Elmore, G. Pollakis, et al. 2015. Temporal and spatial analysis of the 2014–2015 Ebola virus outbreak in West Africa. *Nature* 524: 97–101.

Carroll, S. B. 2005. *Endless Forms Most Beautiful: The New Science of Evo Devo.* New York: Norton.

Carroll, S. B. 2006. *The Making of the Fittest: DNA and the Ultimate Forensic Record of Evolution.* New York: Norton.

Carroll, S. B. 2009. *Remarkable Creatures: Epic Adventures in the Search for the Origins of Species.* Boston: Houghton Mifflin Harcourt.

Cartmill, M. 1974. Rethinking primate origins. *Science* 184: 436–443.

Cartmill, M. 1975. *Primate Origins.* Minneapolis, MN: Burgess.

Cartmill, M. 1992. New views on primate origins. *Evolutionary Anthropology* 1: 105–111.

Cartmill, M. 1996. *A View to a Death in the Morning: Hunting and Nature through History.* Cambridge, MA: Harvard University Press.

Cartmill, M. 2002. Explaining primate origins. Pp. 42–52 in P. N. Peregrine, C. R. Ember, and M. Ember, eds. *Physical Anthropology: Original Readings in Method and Practice.* Upper Saddle River, NJ: Prentice Hall.

Cartmill, M., P. T. Ellison, C. S. Larsen, C. B. Ruff, and E. J. E. Szathmáry, eds. 2018. Centennial anniversary issue of AJPA. *American Journal of Physical Anthropology*, special issue, 165(4): 611–954.

Cartmill, M. and F. H. Smith. 2009. *The Human Lineage.* Hoboken, NJ: Wiley-Blackwell.

Caspari, R. 2003. From types to populations: A century of race, physical anthropology, and the American Anthropological Association. *American Anthropologist* 105: 65–76.

Caspari, R. 2009. 1918: Three perspectives on race and human variation. *American Journal of Physical Anthropology* 139: 5–15.

Caspari, R. 2010. Deconstructing race: Racial thinking, geographic variation, and implications for biological anthropology. Pp. 104–123 in C. S. Larsen, ed. *A Companion to Biological Anthropology.* Malden, MA: Wiley-Blackwell.

Caspi, A., K. Sugden, T. E. Moffitt, A. Taylor, I. W. Craig, H. Harrington, J. McClay, J. Mill, J. Martin, A. Braithwaite, and R. Poulton. 2003. Influence of life stress on depression: Moderation by a polymorphism in the 5-HTT gene. *Science* 301: 386–389.

Cavalli-Sforza, L. L. and F. Cavalli-Sforza. 1995. *The Great Human Diasporas.* Cambridge, UK: Perseus.

Centers for Disease Control and Prevention. 2008. State-specific incidence of diabetes among adults—participating states, 1995–1997 and 2005–2007. *MMWR Weekly* 57(43): 1169–1173.

Cerling, T. E., J. M. Harris, S. H. Ambrose, M. G. Leakey, and N. Solounis. 1997. Dietary and environmental reconstruction with stable isotope analyses of herbivore tooth enamel from the Miocene locality at Fort Ternan, Kenya. *Journal of Human Evolution* 33: 635–650.

Cerling, T. E., J. Quade, Y. Wang, and J. R. Bowman. 1989. Carbon isotopes in soils and paleosols as ecologic and paleo-ecologic indicators. *Nature* 341: 138–139.

Chaimanee, Y., O. Chavasseau, K. C. Beard, A. A. Kyaw, A. N. Soe, C. Sein, V. Lazzari, L. Marivaux, B. Marandat, M.Swe, M. Rugbumrung, T. Lwin, X. Valentin, Zin-Maung-Maung-Thein, and J.-J. Jaeger. 2012. Late middle Eocene primate from Myanmar and the initial anthropoid colonization of Africa. *Proceedings of the National Academy of Sciences USA* 109: 10293–10297.

Chaimanee, Y., D. Jolly, M. Benammi, P. Tafforeau, D. Duzer, I. Moussa, and J.-J. Jaeger. 2003. A middle Miocene hominoid from Thailand and orangutan origins. *Nature* 422: 61–65.

Chaimanee, Y., V. Suteethorn, P. Jintasakul, C. Vidthayanon, B. Marandat, and J.-J. Jaeger. 2004. A new orangutan relative from the late Miocene of Thailand. *Nature* 427: 439–441.

Chaimanee, Y., C. Yamee, P. Tian, K. Khaowiset, B. Marandat, P. Tafforeau, C. Nemoz, and J.-J. Jaeger. 2006. *Khoratpithecus piriyai*, a late Miocene hominoid of Thailand. *American Journal of Physical Anthropology* 131: 311–323.

Chalmers, J. and K. C. Ho. 1970. Geographical variations in senile osteoporosis: The association with physical activity. *Journal of Bone and Joint Surgery* 52-B: 667–675.

Chaplin, G. 2004. Geographic distribution of environmental factors influencing human skin coloration. *American Journal of Physical Anthropology* 120: 292–302.

Chaplin, G. and N. G. Jablonski. 2009. Vitamin D and the evolution of human depigmentation. *American Journal of Physical Anthropology* 139: 451–461.

Chatters, J. C. 2001. *Ancient Encounters: Kennewick Man and the First Americans.* New York: Touchstone.

Chatters, J. C., D. J. Kennett, Y. Asmerom, B. M. Kemp, V. Polyak, A. N. Blank, P. A. Beddows, E. Reinhardt, J. Arroyo-Cabrales, D. A. Bolnick, R. S. Malhi, B. J. Culleton, P. L. Erreguerena, D. Rissolo, S. Morell-Hart, and T. W. Stafford Jr. 2014. Late Pleistocene human skeleton and mtDNA link Paleoamericans and modern Native Americans. *Science* 344: 750–754.

Check, E. 2006. How Africa learned to love the cow. *Nature* 444: 994–996.

Cheney, D. L. and R. M. Seyfarth. 1990. *How Monkeys See the World: Inside the Mind of Another Species.* Chicago: University of Chicago Press.

Cheney, D. L. and R. M. Seyfarth. 2007. *Baboon Metaphysics: The Evolution of a Social Mind.* Chicago: University of Chicago Press.

Childe, V. G. 1925. *The Dawn of European Civilization.* London: Kegan Paul.

Churchill, S. E. 1998. Cold adaptation, heterochrony, and Neandertals. *Evolutionary Anthropology* 7: 46–61.

Churchill, S. E. 2001. Hand morphology, manipulation, and tool use in Neandertals and early modern humans of the Near East. *Proceedings of the National Academy of Sciences USA* 98: 2953–2955.

Churchill, S. E., T. W. Holiday, K. J. Carlson, T. Jashashvili, M. E. Macias, S. Mathews, T. L. Sparling, P. Schmid, D. J. de Ruiter, and L. R. Berger. 2013. The upper limb of *Australopithecus sediba. Science* 340: 1233477. DOI: 10.1126/science.1233477.

Churchill, S. E. and F. H. Smith. 2000. Makers of the early Aurignacian of Europe. *Yearbook of Physical Anthropology* 43: 61–115.

Ciochon, R. L. and G. F. Gunnell. 2002. Chronology of primate discoveries in

Myanmar: Influences on the anthropoid origins debate. *Yearbook of Physical Anthropology* 45: 2–35.

Ciochon, R. L. and G. F. Gunnell. 2002. Eocene primates from Myanmar: Historical perspective on the origin of Anthropoidea. *Evolutionary Anthropology* 11: 156–168.

Clark, J. D., Y. Beyene, G. WoldeGabriel, W. K. Hart, P. R. Renne, H. Gilbert, A. Defleur, G. Suwa, S. Katoh, K. R. Ludwig, J.-R. Boisserie, B. Asfaw, and T. D. White. 2003. Stratigraphic, chronological and behavioural contexts of Pleistocene *Homo sapiens* from Middle Awash, Ethiopia. *Nature* 423: 747–752.

Clark, J. D. and S. A. Brandt. 1984. *From Hunters to Farmers: The Causes and Consequences of Food Production in Africa*. Berkeley: University of California Press.

Clark, J. D., J. de Heinzelin, K. D. Schick, W. K. Hart, T. D. White, G. WoldeGabriel, R. C. Walter, G. Suwa, B. Asfaw, E. Vrba, and Y. H.-Selassie. 1994. African *Homo erectus:* Old radiometric ages and young Oldowan assemblages in the Middle Awash valley, Ethiopia. *Science* 264: 1907–1910.

Clarke, R. J. 2019. Excavation, reconstruction and taphonomy of the StW 573 *Australopithecus prometheus* skeleton from Sterkfontein Caves, South Africa. *Journal of Human Evolution* 127: 41–53.

Clarke, R. J. and K. Kuman. 2019. The skull of StW 573, a 3.67 Ma *Australopithecus prometheus* skeleton from Sterkfontein Caves, South Africa. *Journal of Human Evolution* 134: 102634.

Clarke, R. J. and P. V. Tobias. 1995. Sterkfontein Member 2 foot bones of the oldest South African hominid. *Science* 269: 521–524.

Clarke T. K., M. K. Lipton, A. M. Fernandez-Pujals, J. Starr, G. Davies, et al. 2016. Common polygenic risk for autism spectrum disorder (ASD) is associated with cognitive ability in the general population. *Molecular Psychiatry* 21: 419–425.

Clarkson, C., Z. Jacobs, B. Marwick, R. Fullagar, L. Wallis, et al. 2017. Human occupation of northern Australia by 65,000 years ago. *Nature* 547: 306–310.

Clutton-Brock, J. 1999. *A Natural History of Domesticated Mammals*. Cambridge, UK: Cambridge University Press.

Cohen, J. 2020. New coronavirus threat galvanizes scientists. *Science* 367: 492–493.

Cohen, J. M. 1992. *The Four Voyages of Christopher Columbus*. New York: Penguin.

Cohen, M. N. 1977. *The Food Crisis in Prehistory*. New Haven, CT: Yale University Press.

Cohen, M. N. 1989. *Health and the Rise of Civilization*. New Haven, CT: Yale University Press.

Cohen, M. N. 2002. Were early agriculturalists less healthy than food-collectors? Pp. 180–191 in P. N. Peregrine, C. R. Ember, and M. Ember, eds. *Archaeology: Original Readings in Method and Practice*. Upper Saddle River, NJ: Prentice Hall.

Cohen, M. N. and G. J. Armelagos, eds. 1984. *Paleopathology at the Origins of Agriculture*. Orlando, FL: Academic Press. Reprinted 2013, University Press of Florida, Gainesville.

Cohen, M. N. and G. Crane-Kramer, eds. 2007. *Ancient Health: Skeletal Indicators of Economic and Political Intensification*. Gainesville: University Press of Florida.

Colbert, E. 2007. *Field Notes from a Catastrophe: A Frontline Report on Climate Change*. London: Bloomsbury.

Collins, D. N. 2003. *Nature Encyclopedia of the Human Genome*. London: Nature.

Collins, F. S., M. Morgan, and A. Patrinos. 2003. The human genome project: Lessons from large scale biology. *Science* 300: 286–290.

Conroy, G. C. 1990. *Primate Evolution*. New York: Norton.

Conroy, G. C. and H. Pontzer. 2012. *Reconstructing Human Origins: A Modern Synthesis*, 3rd ed. New York: Norton.

Cook, D. C. 2006. The old physical anthropology and the New World: A look at the accomplishments of an antiquated paradigm. Pp. 27–71 in J. E. Buikstra and L. A. Beck, eds. *Bioarchaeology: The Contextual Analysis of Human Remains*. Burlington, MA: Academic Press.

Cook, L. M., R. L. H. Dennis, and G. S. Mani. 1999. Melanic morph frequency in the peppered moth in the Manchester area. *Proceedings of the Royal Society of London B* 266: 293–297.

Cook, L. M., G. S. Mani, and M. E. Varley. 1986. Postindustrial melanism in the peppered moth. *Science* 231: 611–613.

Coon, C. S., S. M. Garn, and J. B. Birdsell. 1950. *Races: A Study of the Problems of Race Formation in Man*. Springfield, IL: Charles C. Thomas.

Cooper, C., G. Campion, and L. J. Melton III. 1992. Hip fractures in the elderly: A world-wide projection. *Osteoporosis International* 2: 285–289.

Cordain, L., B. A. Watkins, G. L. Florant, M. Kelher, L. Rogers, and Y. Li. 2002. Fatty acid analysis of wild ruminant tissues: Evolutionary implications for reducing diet-related chronic disease. *European Journal of Clinical Nutrition* 56: 1–11.

Costa, D. L. and R. H. Steckel. 1997. Long-term trends in health, welfare, and economic growth in the United States. Pp. 47–89 in R. H. Steckel and R. Floud, eds. *Health and Welfare during Industrialization*. Chicago: University of Chicago Press.

Covert, H. H. 2002. The earliest fossil primates and the evolution of prosimians: Introduction. Pp. 13–20 in W. C. Hartwig, ed. *The Primate Fossil Record*. Cambridge, UK: Cambridge University Press.

Cowgill, L. W., E. Trinkaus, and M. A. Zeder. 2007. Shanidar 10: A middle Paleolithic immature distal lower limb from Shanidar Cave, Iraqi Kurdistan. *Journal of Human Evolution* 53: 213–223.

Cox, S. L., C. B. Ruff, R. M. Maier, and I. Mathieson. 2019. Genetic contributions to variation in human stature in prehistoric Europe. *Proceedings of the National Academy of Sciences USA* 116: 21484–21492.

Crawford, M. H. 1998. *The Origins of Native Americans: Evidence from Anthropological Genetics*. Cambridge, UK: Cambridge University Press.

Crews, D. E. 2003. *Human Senescence: Evolutionary and Biocultural Perspectives*. Cambridge, UK: Cambridge University Press.

Crews, D. E. and B. Bogin. 2010. Growth, development, senescence, and aging: A life history perspective. Pp. 124–152 in C. S. Larsen, ed. *A Companion to Biological Anthropology*. Chichester, UK: Wiley-Blackwell.

Critser, G. 2003. *Fat Land*. New York: Penguin.

Culotta, E. 2016. Likely hobbit ancestors lived 600,000 years earlier. *Science* 352: 1260–1261.

Daegling, D. J. 2010. Understanding skull function from a mechanicobiological perspective. Pp. 501–515 in C. S. Larsen, ed. *A Companion to Biological Anthropology*. Chichester, UK: Wiley-Blackwell.

Dagasto, M. 2002. The origin and diversification of anthropoid primates: Introduction. Pp. 125–132 in W. C. Hartwig, ed. *The Primate Fossil Record*. Cambridge, UK: Cambridge University Press.

Dahlberg, A. A. 1963. Analysis of the American Indian dentition. Pp. 147–177 in D. R. Brothwell, ed. *Dental Anthropology*. New York: Pergamon Press.

DARA and the Climate Vulnerable Forum. 2012. *Climate Vulnerability Monitor, 2nd Edition: A Guide to the Cold Calculus of a Hot Planet*. Madrid, Spain: Fundación DARA Internacional.

Darwin, C. 1859. *On the Origin of Species*. London: John Murray.

Darwin, C. 1871. *The Descent of Man and Selection in Relation to Sex*. Reprinted 1900. Akron, OH: Werner.

Davies, A. G. and J. F. Oates. 1994. *Colobine Monkeys: Their Ecology, Behaviour and Evolution*. Cambridge, UK: Cambridge University Press.

Dawkins, R. 2004. *The Ancestor's Tale: A Pilgrimage to the Dawn of Civilization*. Boston: Houghton Mifflin.

Deacon, T. W. 1997. What makes the human brain different? *Annual Review of Anthropology* 26: 337–357.

Dean, C., M. G. Leakey, D. Reid, F. Schrenk, G. T. Schwartz, C. Stringer, and A. Walker. 2001. Growth processes in teeth distinguish modern humans from *Homo erectus* and earlier hominins. *Nature* 414: 628–631.

Dear, P. 2006. *The Intelligibility of Nature: How Science Makes Sense of the World.* Chicago: University of Chicago Press.

De Bonis, L., G. D. Koufos, and P. Andrews. 2001. *Hominoid Evolution and Climatic Change in Europe.* Vol. 2: *Phylogeny of the Neogene Hominoid Primates of Eurasia.* Cambridge, UK: Cambridge University Press.

Defleur, A., T. White, P. Valensi, L. Slimak, and É. Crégut-Bonnoure. 1999. Neanderthal cannibalism at Moula-Guercy, Ardèqche, France. *Science* 286: 128–131.

De Heinzelin, J., J. D. Clark, K. D. Schick, and W. H. Gilbert, eds. 2000. *The Acheulean and the Plio-Pleistocene Deposits of the Middle Awash Valley, Ethiopia.* Annales—Sciences Géologiques 104. Tervuren, Belgium: Musée Royal de L'Afrique Centrale.

De Heinzelin, J., J. D. Clark, T. White, W. Hart, P. Renne, G. WoldeGabriel, Y. Beyene, and E. Vrba. 1999. Environment and behavior of 2.5-million-year-old Bouri hominids. *Science* 284: 625–629.

Deino, A., P. R. Renne, and C. C. Swisher III. 1998. ^{40}Ar/^{39}Ar dating in paleoanthropology and archeology. *Evolutionary Anthropology* 6: 63–75.

De la Torre, I. 2019. Searching for the emergence of stone tool making in eastern Africa. *Proceedings of the National Academy of Science USA* 116: 11567–11569.

Delson, E. 1992. Evolution of Old World monkeys. Pp. 217-222 in J. S. Jones, R. D. Martin, D. Pilbeam, and S. Bunney, eds. *Cambridge Encyclopedia of Human Evolution.* Cambridge, UK: Cambridge University Press.

Delson, E., I. Tattersall, J. A. Van Couvering, and A. S. Brooks. 2000. *Encyclopedia of Human Evolution and Prehistory*, 2nd ed. New York: Garland.

Demeter, F., L. L. Shackelford, A.-M. Bacon, P. Duringer, K. Westaway, T. Sayavongkhamdy, J. Braga, P. Sichanthongtip, P. Khamdalavong, J.-L. Ponche, H. Wang, C. Lundstrom, E. Patole-Edouma, and A.-M. Karpoff. 2012. Anatomically modern human in southeast Asia (Laos) by 46 ka. *Proceedings of the National Academy of Sciences USA* 109: 14375–14380.

Demment, M. W., M. M. Young, and R. L. Sensenig. 2003. Providing micronutrients through food-based solutions: A key to human and national

development. *Journal of Nutrition* 133: 3879S–3885S.

Denham, T. P., S. G. Haberle, C. Lentfer, R. Fullagar, J. Field, M. Therin, N. Porch, and B. Winsborough. 2003. Origins of agriculture at Kuk Swamp in the highlands of New Guinea. *Science* 301: 189–193.

D'Errico, F., C. Henshilwood, G. Lawson, M. Vanhaeren, A.-M. Tillier, M. Soressi, F. Bresson, B. Maureille, A. Nowell, J. Lakarra, L. Backwell, and M. Julien. 2003. Archaeological evidence for the emergence of language, symbolism, and music—an alternative multidisciplinary perspective. *Journal of World Prehistory* 17: 1–70.

Derry, G. 2002. *What Science Is and How It Works.* Princeton, NJ: Princeton University Press.

De Ruiter, D. J., M. F. Laird, M. Elliott, P. Schmid, J. Brophy, J. Hawks, and L. R. Berger. 2019. *Homo naledi* cranial remains from the Lesidi chamber of the Rising Star Cave system. *Journal of Human Evolution* 132: 1–14.

Détroit, F., A. S. Mujares, J. Corny, G. Daver, C. Zanolli, E. Dizon, E. Robles, R. Grün, and P. J. Piper. 2019. A new species of *Homo* from the Late Pleistocene of the Philippines. *Nature* 568: 181–186.

DeVore, I. 1963. A comparison of the ecology and behavior of monkeys and apes. Pp. 301–339 in S. L. Washburn, ed. *Classification and Human Evolution.* Chicago: Aldine.

DeVore, I. 1965. *Primate Behavior: Field Studies of Monkeys and Apes.* New York: Holt, Rinehart and Winston.

Diamond, J. 2004. The astonishing micropygmies. *Science* 306: 2047–2048.

Diamond, J. 2005. Geography and skin color. *Nature* 435: 283–284.

Diamond, J. and P. Bellwood. 2003. Farmers and their languages: The first expansions. *Science* 300: 597–603.

Dirks, P. H. G. M., E. M. Roberts, H. Hilbert-Wolf, J. D. Kramers, J. Hawks, et al. 2017. The age of *Homo naledi* and associated sediments in the Rising Star Cave, South Africa. *eLife* 6: e24231. DOI: 10.7554/eLife.24231.

Disotell, T. R. 2012. Archaic human genomics. *Yearbook of Physical Anthropology* 55: 24–39.

Dixon, R. A. and C. A. Roberts. 2001. Modern and ancient scourges: The application of ancient DNA to the analysis of tuberculosis and leprosy from archaeologically derived human remains. *Ancient Biomolecules* 3: 181–194.

Dominguez-Rodrigo, M. and T. R. Pickering. 2003. Early hominid hunting and scavenging: A zooarchaeological review. *Evolutionary Anthropology* 12: 275–282.

Dore, K. M., E. P. Riley, and A. Fuentes, eds. 2017. *Ethnoprimatology: A Practical Guide to*

Research at the Human-Nonhuman Primate Interface. Cambridge, UK: Cambridge University Press.

Dorit, R. L. 2012. Rereading Darwin. *American Scientist* 100: 21–23.

Drapeau, M. S. M. and M. A. Steeter. 2006. Modeling and remodeling responses to normal loading in the human lower limb. *American Journal of Physical Anthropology* 129: 403–409.

Drapeau, M. S. M. and C. V. Ward. 2007. Forelimb segment length: Proportions in extant hominoids and *Australopithecus afarensis. American Journal of Physical Anthropology* 132: 327–343.

Dressler, W. W., K. S. Oths, and C. C. Gravlee. 2005. Race and ethnicity in public health research: Models to explain health disparities. *Annual Review of Anthropology* 34: 231–252.

Dronamraju, K. R. and P. Arese. 2006. *Malaria: Genetic and Evolutionary Aspects.* New York: Springer.

Ducrocq, S. 1998. Eocene primates from Thailand: Are Asian anthropoideans related to African ones? *Evolutionary Anthropology* 7: 97–104.

Dufour, D. 2010. Nutrition, health, and function. Pp. 194–206 in C. S. Larsen, ed. *A Companion to Biological Anthropology.* Chichester, UK: Wiley-Blackwell.

Dunavan, C. P. 2005. Tackling malaria. *Scientific American* 293(6): 76–83.

Dunbar, R. 1977. Feeding ecology of gelada baboons: A preliminary report. Pp. 252–273 in T. H. Clutton-Brock, ed. *Primate Ecology: Studies of Feeding and Ranging Behaviour in Lemurs, Monkeys and Apes.* London: Academic Press.

Dunsworth, H. and A. Walker. 2002. Early genus *Homo.* Pp. 419–435 in W. C. Hartwig, ed. *The Primate Fossil Record.* Cambridge, UK: Cambridge University Press.

Duren, D. L., R. J. Sherwood, A. C. Choh, S. A. Czerwinski, W. C. Chumlea, M. Lee, S. S. Sun, E. W. Demerath, R. M. Siervogel, and B. Towne. 2007. Quantitative genetics of cortical bone mass in healthy 10-year-old children from the Fels Longitudinal Study. *Bone* 40: 464–470.

Eaton, S. B., S. B. Eaton III, and L. Cordain. 2002. Evolution, diet, and health. Pp. 7–17 in P. S. Ungar and M. F. Teaford, eds. *Human Diet: Its Origin and Evolution.* Westport, CT: Bergin & Garvey.

Eckhardt, R. B. 2003. Polymorphisms: Past and present. *Human Biology* 75: 559–575.

Edgar, H. J. H. and K. L. Hunley, eds. 2009. Race reconciled: How biological anthropologists view human variation. *American Journal of Physical Anthropology*, special symposium issue, 139(1): 1–107.

Edgar, H. J. H. and K. L. Hunley. 2009. Race reconciled? How biological anthropologists view human variation. *American Journal of Physical Anthropology* 139: 1–4.

Eimerl, S. and I. DeVore. 1965. *The Primates*. New York: Time-Life.

Ellis, E. C., J. O. Kaplan, D. Q. Fuller, S. Vavrus, K. K. Goldewijk, and P. H. Verburg. 2013. Used planet: A global history. *Proceedings of the National Academy of Sciences USA* 110: 7978–7985.

Ellison, P. 2001. *On Fertile Ground: A Natural History of Human Reproduction*. Cambridge, MA: Harvard University Press.

Ellison, P. T. 1994. Advances in human reproductive ecology. *Annual Review of Anthropology* 23: 255–275.

Ellison, P. T. and M. T. O'Rourke. 2000. Population growth and fertility regulation. Pp. 553–586 in S. Stinson, B. Bogin, R. Huss-Ashmore, and D. O'Rourke, eds. *Human Biology: An Evolutionary and Biocultural Perspective*. New York: Wiley-Liss.

Elton, S. 2006. Forty years on and still going strong: The use of hominin-cercopithe-cid comparisons in palaeoanthropology. *Journal of the Royal Anthropological Institute* 12: 19–38.

El Zaatari, S., F. E. Grine, P. S. Ungar, and J.-J. Hublin. 2011. Ecogeographic variation in Neandertal dietary habits: Evidence from occlusal molar microwear texture analysis. *Journal of Human Evolution* 61: 411–424.

ENCODE Project Consortium. 2012. An integrated encyclopedia of DNA elements in the human genome. *Nature* 489: 57–74.

Epstein, P. R. and D. Ferber. 2011. *Changing Planet, Changing Health: How the Climate Crisis Threatens Our Health and What We Can Do about It*. Berkeley: University of California Press.

Ericson, P. A. 1997. Morton, Samuel George (1799–1851). Pp. 689–691 in F. Spencer, ed. *History of Physical Anthropology: An Encyclopedia*. New York: Garland.

Erikson, D. L., B. D. Smith, A. C. Clarke, D. H. Sandweiss, and N. Tuross. 2005. An Asian origin for a 10,000-year-old domesticated plant in the Americas. *Proceedings of the National Academy of Sciences USA* 102: 18315–18320.

Eriksson, J. G., T. Forsen, J. Tuomilehto, C. Osmond, and D. J. P. Barker. 2000. Early growth, adult income, and risk of stroke. *Stroke* 31: 869–874.

Eshleman, J. A., R. S. Malhi, and D. G. Smith. 2003. Mitochondrial DNA studies of Native Americans: Conceptions and misconceptions of the population history of the Americas. *Evolutionary Anthropology* 12: 7–18.

Estrada, A., P. A. Garber, A. B. Rylands, C. Roos, E. Fernandez-Duque, et al. 2017. Impending extinction crisis of the world's primates: Why primates matter. *Science Advances* 3: e1600946. DOI: 10.1126/sciadv.1600946.

Estrada-Mena, B., F. J. Estrada, R. Ulloa-Arvizu, M. Guido, R. Méndez, R. Coral, T. Canto, J. Granados, R. Rubí-Castellanos, H. Rangel-Villalobos, and A. Garcia-Carrancá. 2010. Blood group O alleles in Native Americans: Implications in the peopling of the Americas. *American Journal of Physical Anthropology* 142: 85–94.

Eveleth, P. B. and J. M. Tanner. 1990. *Worldwide Variation in Human Growth*, 2nd ed. Cambridge, UK: Cambridge University Press.

Fagan, B. M. 2004. *The Great Journey: The Peopling of Ancient North America*. Gainesville: University Press of Florida.

Falk, D. 2000. *Primate Diversity*. New York: Norton.

Falk, D. 2010. Evolution of the brain, cognition, and speech. Pp. 258–271 in C. S. Larsen, ed. *A Companion to Biological Anthropology*. Chichester, UK: Wiley-Blackwell.

Falk, D., C. Hildebolt, K. Smith, M. J. Morwood, T. Sutikna, P. Brown, Jatmiko, E. W. Saptomo, B. Brunsden, and F. Prior. 2005. The brain of LB1, *Homo floresiensis*. *Science* 308: 242–245.

Faria, N. R., R. do Socorro da Silva Azevedo, M. U. G. Kraemer, R. Souza, M. S. Cunha, et al. 2016. Zika virus in the Americas: Early epidemiological and genetic findings. *Science* 352: 345–349.

Feathers, J. K. 1996. Luminescence dating and modern human origins. *Evolutionary Anthropology* 5: 25–36.

Feldman, M. W., R. C. Lewontin, and M.-C. King. 2003. Race: A genetic melting-pot. *Nature* 424: 374.

Fiala, N. 2008. Meeting the demand: An estimation of potential future greenhouse gas emissions from meat production. *Ecological Economics* 67: 412–419.

Field, J. S., M. D. Petraglia, and M. M. Lahr. 2006. The southern dispersal hypothesis and the South Asian archaeological record: Examination of dispersal routes through GIS analysis. *Journal of Anthropological Archaeology* 26: 88–108.

Finlayson, C. 2004. *Neanderthals and Modern Humans: An Ecological and Evolutionary Perspective*. New York: Cambridge University Press.

Fiorato, V., A. Boylston, and C. Knüsel, eds. 2000. *Blood Red Roses: The Archaeology of a Mass Grave from the Battle of Towton AD 1461*. Oxford, UK: Oxbow.

Fiorenza, L., S. Benazzi, J. Tausch, O. Kullmer, T. G. Bromage, and F. Schrenk. 2011. Molar macrowear reveals Neanderthal eco-geographic dietary variation. *PLoS One* 6: 1–11.

Fischman, J. 2005. Dmanisi find. *National Geographic Research* 207: 18–27.

Fiske, S. J., S. A. Crate, C. L. Crumley, K. Galvin, H. Lazrus, et al. 2014. *Changing the Atmosphere: Anthropology and Climate Change*. Final report on the AAA Global Climate Task Force. Arlington, VA: American Anthropological Association.

Flannery, K. V. 1969. Origins and ecological effects of early domestication in Iran and the Near East. Pp. 73–100 in P. J. Ucko and G. W. Dimbleby, eds. *The Domestication of Plants and Animals*. Chicago: Aldine.

Fleagle, J. G. 2000. A century of the past: One hundred years in the study of primate evolution. *Evolutionary Anthropology* 9: 87–100.

Fleagle, J. G. 2013. *Primate Adaptation and Evolution*, 3rd ed. San Diego: Academic Press.

Fleagle, J. G. and R. F. Kay, eds. 1994. *Anthropoid Origins*. New York: Plenum Press.

Fleagle, J. G. and M. F. Tejedor. 2002. Early platyrrhines of southern South America. Pp. 161–173 in W. C. Hartwig, ed. *The Primate Fossil Record*. Cambridge, UK: Cambridge University Press.

Formenty, P., C. Boesch, M. Wyers, C. Steiner, F. Donati, F. Dind, F. Walker, and B. Le Guenno. 1999. Ebola virus outbreak among wild chimpanzees living in a rain forest of Côte d'Ivoire. *Journal of Infectious Diseases* 179: S120–S126.

Foster, E. A., M. A. Jobling, P. G. Taylor, P. Donnelly, P. de Knijff, R. Mieremet, T. Zerjal, and C. Tyler-Smith. 1998. Jefferson fathered slave's last child. *Nature* 396: 27–28.

Fragaszy, D., P. Izar, E. Visalberghi, E. B. Ottoni, and M. G. De Oliveira. 2004. Wild capuchin monkeys (*Cebus libidinosus*) use anvils and stone pounding tools. *American Journal of Primatology* 64: 359–366.

Frayer, D. W., M. Lozano, J. M. Bermúdez de Castro, E. Carbonell, J.-L. Arsuaga, J. Radovčić, I. Fiore, and L. Bondioli. 2012. More than 500,000 years of right-handedness in Europeans. *Laterality* 17: 51–69.

Freed, S. A. 2012. *Anthropology Unmasked: Museum, Science, and Politics in New York City*. Vol. 1: *The Putnam-Boas Era*. Wilmington, OH: Orange Frazer Press.

Freeman, A. S. and J. E. Byers. 2006. Divergent induced responses to an invasive predator in marine mussel populations. *Science* 313: 831–833.

Freeman, H. and R. D. Cox. 2006. Type-2 diabetes: A cocktail of genetic discovery. *Human Molecular Genetics* 15: R202–R209.

Frisancho, A. R. 1975. Functional adaptation to high-altitude hypoxia. *Science* 187: 313–319.

Frisancho, A. R. 1993. *Human Adaptation and Accommodation*. Ann Arbor: University of Michigan Press.

Fuentes, A. 1999. Re-evaluating primate monogamy. *American Anthropologist* 100: 890–907.

Fuller, D. Q., T. Denham, M. Arroyo-Kalin, L. Lucas, C. J. Stevens, et al. 2014. Convergent evolution and parallelism in plant domestication revealed by an expanding archaeological record. *Proceedings of the National Academy of Sciences USA* 111: 6147–6152.

Fuller, D. Q., L. Qin, Y. Zheng, Z. Zhao, X. Chen, L. A. Hosoya, and G.-P. Sun. 2009. The domestication process and domestication rate in rice: Spikelet bases from the Lower Yangtze. *Science* 323: 1607–1610.

Futuyma, D. J. 2005. *Evolution*. Sunderland, MA: Sinauer Press.

Gage, T. B. 1998. The comparative demography of primates: With some comments on the evolution of life histories. *Annual Review of Anthropology* 27: 197–221.

Gage, T. B. 2010. Demographic estimation: Indirect techniques for anthropological populations. Pp. 179–193 in C. S. Larsen, ed. *A Companion to Biological Anthropology*. Chichester, UK: Wiley-Blackwell.

Galik, K., B. Senut, M. Pickford, D. Gommery, J. Treil, A. J. Kuperavage, and R. B. Eckhardt. 2004. External and internal morphology of the BAR 1002'00 *Orrorin tugenensis* femur. *Science* 305: 1450–1453.

Gao, X., S. Zhang, Y. Zhang, and F. Chen. 2017. Evidence of hominin use and maintenance of fire at Zhoukoudian. *Current Anthropology* 58(suppl. 16): S267–S277.

Garcia, R. S. 2003. The misuse of race in medical diagnosis. *Chronicle of Higher Education* May 9: B15.

Garrett, L. 1994. *The Coming Plague: Newly Emerging Diseases in a World Out of Balance*. New York: Farrar, Straus, and Giroux.

Garruto, R. M., C.-T. Chin, C. A. Weitz, J.-C. Liu, R.-L. Liu, and X. He. 2003. Hematological differences during growth among Tibetans and Han Chinese born and raised at high altitude in Qinghai, China. *American Journal of Physical Anthropology* 122: 171–183.

Gasperetti, M. A. and S. G. Sheridan. 2013. Cry havoc: Interpersonal violence at Early Bronze Age Bab edh-Dhra'. *American Anthropologist* 115: 388–410.

Gasperetti, M. A., and S. G. Sheridan. 2013. *Postcranial Adaptation in Nonhuman Primates*. DeKalb: Northern Illinois University Press.

Gebo, D. L., ed. 1993. *Postcranial Adaptation in Nonhuman Primates*. DeKalb: Northern Illinois University Press.

Gebo, D. L. 2002. Adapiformes: Phylogeny and adaptation. Pp. 21–43 in

W. C. Hartwig, ed. *The Primate Fossil Record*. Cambridge, UK: Cambridge University Press.

Gebo, D. L. 2010. Locomotor function across primates: The postcranial skeleton. Pp. 530–544 in C. S. Larsen, ed. *A Companion to Biological Anthropology*. Chichester, UK: Wiley-Blackwell.

Gebo, D. L., M. Dagosto, K. C. Beard, and T. Qi. 2000. The smallest primates. *Journal of Human Evolution* 38: 585–594.

Gebo, D. L., M. Dagasto, K. C. Beard, T. Qi, and J. Wang. 2000. The oldest known anthropoid postcranial fossils and the early evolution of higher primates. *Nature* 404: 276–278.

Gebo, D. L., M. Dagosto, X. Ni, and K. C. Beard. 2012. Species diversity and postcranial anatomy of Eocene primates from Shanghuang, China. *Evolutionary Anthropology* 21: 224–238.

Gebo, D. L., L. MacLatchy, R. Kityo, A. Deino, J. Kingston, and D. Pilbeam. 1997. A hominoid genus from the early Miocene of Uganda. *Science* 276: 401–404.

Gibbard, P. L., M. J. Head, M. J. C. Walker, and Subcommission on Quaternary Stratigraphy. 2010. Formal ratification of the Quaternary system/period and the Pleistocene series/epoch with a base at 2.58 ma. *Journal of Quaternary Science* 25: 96–102.

Gibbons, A. 2006. *The First Human: The Race to Discover Our Earliest Ancestors*. New York: Doubleday.

Gibbons, A. 2007. European skin turned pale only recently, gene suggests. *Science* 316: 364.

Gibbons, A. 2007. Food for thought: Did the first cooked meals help fuel the dramatic evolutionary expansion of the human brain? *Science* 316: 1558–1560.

Gibbons, A. 2008. The birth of childhood. *Science* 322: 1040–1043.

Gibbons, A. 2009. A new kind of ancestor: *Ardipithecus* unveiled. *Science* 326: 36–43.

Gibbons, A. 2010. Close encounters of a prehistoric kind. *Science* 328: 680–684.

Gibbons, A. 2011. A new view of the birth of *Homo sapiens*. *Science* 331: 392–394.

Gibbons, A. 2012. Turning back the clock: Slowing the pace of prehistory. *Science* 338: 189–191.

Gibson, R. 1990. *Principles of Human Nutrition*. Oxford, UK: Oxford University Press.

Gilbert, C. C., W. S. McGraw, and E. Delson. 2009. Plio-Pleistocene eagle predation on fossil cercopithecids from the Humpata Plateau, southern Angola. *American Journal of Physical Anthropology* 139: 421–429.

Gilbert, W. H. and B. Asfaw. 2008. Homo erectus: *Pleistocene Evidence from the Middle Awash, Ethiopia*. Berkeley: University of California Press.

Gilby, I. C., L. E. Eberly, L. Pintea, and A. E. Pusey. 2006. Ecological and social influences on the hunting behaviour of wild chimpanzees, *Pan troglodytes schweinfurthii*. *Animal Behaviour* 72(1): 169–180.

Gillespie, J. H. 2004. *Population Genetics: A Concise Guide*, 2nd ed. Baltimore: Johns Hopkins University Press.

Gingerich, P. D. 1976. *Cranial Anatomy and Evolution of Early Tertiary Plesiadapidae (Mammalia, Primates)*. Papers on Paleontology 15. Ann Arbor: University of Michigan Museum of Paleontology.

Gingerich, P. D. 1976. Paleontology and phylogeny: Patterns of evolution at the species level in early tertiary mammals. *American Journal of Science* 276: 1–28.

Gingerich, P. D. 1980. *Early Cenozoic Paleontology and Stratigraphy of the Bighorn Basin, Wyoming*. Papers on Paleontology 24. Ann Arbor: University of Michigan Museum of Paleontology.

Gingerich, P. D. 1990. Mammalian order Proprimates. *Journal of Human Evolution* 19: 821–822.

Gingerich, P. D. 2011. Primates in the Eocene. Pp. 67–68 in T. Lehmann, and S. F. K. Schaal, eds. *The World of Time of Messell: Puzzles in Palaeobiology, Palaeoenvironment, and the History of Early Primates*. Frankfurt am Main, Germany: Senckenberg Gesellschaft für Naturforschung.

Gingerich, P. D. and G. F. Gunnell. 2005. Brain of *Plesiadapis cookei* (Mammalia, Proprimates): Surface morphology and encephalization compared to those of Primates and Dermoptera. *Contributions of the Museum of Paleontology, University of Michigan* 31: 185–195.

Glass, B., M. S. Sacks, E. Jahn, and C. Hess. 1952. Genetic drift in a religious isolate: An analysis of the causes of variation in blood group and other gene frequencies in a small population. *American Naturalist* 86: 145–159.

Gluckman, P. D., M. A. Hanson, and A. S. Beedle. 2007. Early life events and their consequences for later disease: A life history and evolutionary perspective. *American Journal of Human Biology* 19: 1–19.

Godfrey, K. 2006. The developmental origins hypothesis: Epidemiology. Pp. 6–32 in P. D. Gluckman and M. A. Hanson, eds. *Developmental Origins of Health and Disease*. Cambridge, UK: Cambridge University Press.

Godfrey, L. R. and W. L. Jungers. 2002. Quaternary fossil lemurs. Pp. 97–121 in W. C. Hartwig, ed. *The Primate Fossil Record*. Cambridge, UK: Cambridge University Press.

Goebel, T., M. R. Waters, and D. H. O'Rourke. 2008. The late Pleistocene dispersal of modern humans in the Americas. *Science* 319: 1497–1502.

Gokcumen, O. 2020. Archaic hominin introgression into modern human genomes. *American Journal of Physical Anthropology* 71(suppl. 70): 60–73.

Goldberg, K. E. 1982. *The Skeleton: Fantastic Framework*. Washington, DC: U.S. News.

Golden, B. E. 2009. Diseases of nutrient deficiencies. Pp. 141–162 in W. G. Pond, B. L. Nichols, and D. L. Brown, eds. *Adequate Food for All: Culture, Science, and Technology of Food in the 21st Century*. Boca Raton, FL: CRC Press.

Goodall, J. 1986. *The Chimpanzees of Gombe: Patterns of Behavior*. Cambridge, MA: Harvard University Press.

Goodman, A. H. 1994. Cartesian reductionism and vulgar adaptationism: Issues in the interpretation of nutritional status in prehistory. Pp. 163–177 in K. D. Sobolik, ed. *Paleonutrition: The Diet and Health of Prehistoric Americans*. Occasional Paper 22. Carbondale: Southern Illinois University at Carbondale, Center for Archaeological Investigations.

Goodman, A. H. 2005. Three questions about race, human biological variation and racism. *Anthropology News* 46(6): 18–19.

Goodman, A. H. and T. L. Leatherman. 1998. *Building a New Biocultural Synthesis: Political-Economic Perspectives on Human Biology*. Ann Arbor: University of Michigan Press.

Goodman, A. H., Y. T. Moses, and J. L. Jones. 2012. *Race: Are We So Different?* New York: Wiley-Blackwell.

Goodman, M., C. A. Porter, J. Czelusniak, S. L. Page, H. Schneider, J. Shoshani, G. Gunnell, and C. P. Groves. 1998. Toward a phylogenetic classification of primates based on DNA evidence complemented by fossil evidence. *Molecular Phylogenetics and Evolution* 9: 585–598.

Gore, A. 2006. *An Inconvenient Truth: The Planetary Emergency of Global Warming and What We Can Do about It*. New York: Rodale Press.

Goren-Inbar, N., N. Alperson, M. E. Kislev, O. Simchoni, Y. Melamed, A. Ben-Nun, and E. Werker. 2004. Evidence of hominin control of fire at Gesher Benot Ya'aqov, Israel. *Science* 304: 725–727.

Gosman, J. H. and S. D. Stout. 2010. Current concepts in bone biology. Pp. 465–484 in C. S. Larsen, ed. *A Companion to Biological Anthropology*. Chichester, UK: Wiley-Blackwell.

Gould, S. J. 1982. Darwinism and the expansion of evolutionary theory. *Science* 216: 380–387.

Gould, S. J. 1989. *Wonderful Life: The Burgess Shale and the Nature of History*. New York: Norton.

Gould, S. J. 1992. *Ever since Darwin: Reflections on Natural History*. New York: Norton.

Gould, S. J. 1996. *The Mismeasure of Man*. New York: Norton.

Grant, P. R. and B. R. Grant. 2002. Adaptive radiation of Darwin's finches. *American Scientist* 90: 130–139.

Graves, J. L., Jr. 2004. *The Race Myth*. New York: Dutton.

Gravlee, C. C., H. R. Bernard, and W. R. Leonard. 2003. Heredity, environment, and cranial form: A reanalysis of Boas's immigrant data. *American Anthropologist* 105: 125–138.

Grayson, D. K. 2001. The archaeological record of human impacts on animal populations. *Journal of World Prehistory* 15: 1–68.

Grayson, D. K. and D. J. Meltzer. 2003. A requiem for North American overkill. *Journal of Archaeological Science* 30: 585–593.

Green, B. B., N. S. Weiss, and J. R. Daling. 1988. Risk of ovulatory infertility in relation to body weight. *Fertility and Sterility* 50: 721–726.

Green, R. E., J. Krause, A. W. Briggs, T. Maricic, U. Stenzel, et al. 2010. A draft sequence of the Neandertal genome. *Science* 328: 710–722.

Green, R. E., J. Krause, S. E. Ptak, A. W. Briggs, M. T. Ronan, J. F. Simons, L. Du, M. Egholm, J. M. Rothberg, M. Paunovic, and S. Pääbo. 2006. Analysis of one million base pairs of Neanderthal DNA. *Nature* 444: 330–336.

Green, R. E., A.-S. Malaspinas, J. Krause, A. W. Briggs, P. L. F. Johnson, C. Uhler, M. Meyer, J. M. Good, T. Maricic, U. Stenzel, K. Prüfer, M. Siebauer, H. A. Burbano, M. Ronan, J. M. Rothberg, M. Egholm, P. Rudan, D. Brajković, Ž. Kućan, I. Gušić, M. Wikström, L. Laakkonen, J. Kelso, M. Slatkin, and S. Pääbo. 2008. A complete Neandertal mitochondrial genome sequence determined by high-throughput sequencing. *Cell* 134: 416–426.

Greene, B. 2008. Put a little science in your life. *New York Times* June 1: 14.

Greene, M. 2005. *Jane Goodall: A Biography*. Westport, CT: Greenwood.

Gremillion, K. J. 2004. Seed processing and the origins of food production in eastern North America. *American Antiquity* 69: 215–233.

Grieco, E. M. and R. C. Cassidy. 2001. Overview of race and Hispanic origin. Pp. 1–11 in *Census 2000 Brief*, C2KBR/01-1. Washington, DC: U.S. Census Bureau, U.S. Department of Commerce.

Grine, F. E., R. M. Bailey, K. Harvati, R. P. Nathan, A. G. Morris, G. M. Henderson, I. Ribot, and A. W. G. Pike. 2007. Late Pleistocene human skull from Hofmeyr, South Africa, and modern human origins. *Science* 315: 226–229.

Gross, B. L. and Z. Zhao. 2014. Archaeological and genetic insights into the origins of domesticated rice. *Proceedings of the National Academy of Sciences USA* 111: 6190–6197.

Grove, L. 1962. *Now It Can Be Told: The Story of the Manhattan Project*. New York: Harper.

Grün, F. and B. Blumberg. 2006. Environmental obesogens: Organotins and endocrine disruption via nuclear receptor signaling. *Endocrinology* 147: S50–S55.

Grün, R. 1993. Electron spin resonance dating in paleoanthropology. *Evolutionary Anthropology* 2: 172–181.

Grün, R. 2006. Direct dating of human fossils. *Yearbook of Physical Anthropology* 49: 2–48.

Guatelli-Steinberg, D. 2010. "Growing planes": Incremental growth layers in the dental enamel of human ancestors. Pp. 485–500 in C. S. Larsen, ed. *A Companion to Biological Anthropology*. Chichester, UK: Wiley-Blackwell.

Guatelli-Steinberg, D., C. S. Larsen, and D. L. Hutchinson. 2004. Prevalence and the duration of linear enamel hypoplasia: A comparative study of Neandertals and Inuit foragers. *Journal of Human Evolution* 47: 65–84.

Guatelli-Steinberg, D., D. J. Reid, T. A. Bishop, and C. S. Larsen. 2005. Anterior tooth growth periods in Neandertals were comparable to those of modern humans. *Proceedings of the National Academy of Sciences USA* 102: 14197–14202.

Guatelli-Steinberg, D., A. Stinespring-Harris, D. J. Reid, C. S. Larsen, D. L. Hutchinson, and T. M. Smith. 2014. Chronology of linear enamel hypoplasia formation in the Krapina Neanderthals. *Paleoanthropology* 2014: 431–445. DOI: 10.4207/PA.2014.ART84.

Gulick, S. P. S., T. J. Bralower, J. Ormö, B. Hall, K. Grice, et al. 2019. The first day of the Cenozoic. *Proceedings of the National Academy of Sciences USA* 116: 19342–19351.

Gunnell, G. F. and K. D. Rose. 2002. Tarsiiformes: Evolutionary history and adaptation. Pp. 45–82 in W. C. Hartwig, ed. *The Primate Fossil Record*. Cambridge, UK: Cambridge University Press.

Gunnell, G. F. and M. T. Silcox. 2010. Primate origins—the early Cenozoic fossil record. Pp. 275–294 in C. S. Larsen, ed. *A Companion to Biological Anthropology*. Chichester, UK: Wiley-Blackwell.

Haeckel, E. 1874. *The Evolution of Man*. 2 vols. Akron, OH: Werner.

Haeckel, E. 1889. *The History of Creation: Or the Development of the Earth and Its Inhabitants by the Action of Natural Causes*. New York: D. Appleton.

Haile-Selassie, Y. 2001. Late Miocene hominids from the late Awash, Ethiopia. *Nature* 412: 178–181.

Haile-Selassie, Y., B. Asfaw, and T. D. White. 2004. Hominid cranial remains from upper Pleistocene deposits at Aduma, Middle Awash, Ethiopia. *American Journal of Physical Anthropology* 123: 1–10.

Haile-Selassie, Y., B. M. Latimer, M. Alene, A. L. Deino, L. Gibert, S. M. Melillo, B. Z. Saylor, G. R. Scott, and C. O. Lovejoy. 2010. An early *Australopithecus afarensis* postcranium from Woranso-Mille, Ethiopia. *Proceedings of the National Academy of Sciences USA* 107: 12121–12126.

Haile-Selassie, Y., S. M. Melillo, A. Vazzana, S. Benazzi, and T. M. Ryan. 2019. A 3.8-million-year-old hominin cranium from Woranso-Mille, Ethiopia. *Nature* 573: 214–219.

Haile-Selassie, Y., G. Suwa, and T. D. White. 2004. Late Miocene teeth from Middle Awash, Ethiopia, and early hominid dental evolution. *Science* 303: 1503–1505.

Haile-Selassie, Y. and G. WoldeGabriel, eds. 2009. Ardipithecus kadabba: *Late Miocene Evidence from the Middle Awash, Ethiopia*. Berkeley: University of California Press.

Hallgrímsson, B. and B. K. Hall. 2005. *Variation: A Central Concept in Biology*. Burlington, MA: Elsevier Academic Press.

Halligan, J. J., M. R. Waters, A. Perrotti, I. J. Owens, J. M. Feinberg, et al. 2016. Pre-Clovis occupation 14,550 years ago at the Page-Ladson site, Florida, and the peopling of the Americas. *Science Advances* 2: e1600375.

Hamada, Y. and T. Udono. 2002. Longitudinal analysis of length growth in the chimpanzee. *American Journal of Physical Anthropology* 118: 268–284.

Hammond, A. S., S. Almécija, Y. Libsekal, L. Rook, and R. Macchiarelli. 2018. A partial *Homo* pelvis from the Early Pleistocene of Eritrea. *Journal of Human Evolution* 123: 109–128.

Hardy, K., S. Buckley, M. J. Collins, A. Estalrrich, D. Brothwell, L. Copeland, A. García-Tabernero, S. García-Vargas, M. de la Rasilla, C. Lalueza-Fox, R. Huguet, M. Bastir, D. Santamaría, M. Madella, J. Wilson, Á Fernández Cortés, and A. Rosas. 2012. Neanderthal medics? Evidence for food, cooking, and medicinal plants entrapped in dental calculus. *Naturwissenschaften* 99: 617–626.

Harlow, H. F. and M. K. Harlow. 1965. Social deprivation in monkeys. *Scientific American* 207(5): 136–146.

Harmand, S., J. E. Lewis, C. S. Feibel., C. J. Lepre, S. Prat, et al. 2015. 3.3-Million-year-old stone tools from Lomekwi 3, West Turkana, Kenya. *Nature* 521: 310–315.

Harper, G. J. and D. E. Crews. 2000. Aging, senescence, and human variation. Pp. 465–505 in S. Stinson, B. Bogin, R. Huss-Ashmore, and D. O'Rourke, eds. *Human Biology: An Evolutionary and Biocultural Perspective*. New York: Wiley-Liss.

Harris, E. E. 2014. *Ancestors in Our Genome: The New Science of Human Evolution*. Oxford, UK: Oxford University Press.

Harris, E. E. and D. Meyer. 2006. The molecular signature of selection underlying human adaptations. *Yearbook of Physical Anthropology* 49: 89–130.

Harris, J. M. and T. D. White. 1979. Evolution of the Plio-Pleistocene African Suidae. *Transactions of the American Philosophical Society* 69(2): 1–128.

Harrison, G. A. 1982. Lifestyles, well-being and stress. *Human Biology* 54: 193–202.

Harrison, G. A. 1993. *Human Adaptation*. Oxford, UK: Oxford University Press.

Harrison, G. G. and S. Hamide. 2009. Overweight, obesity, and related diseases. Pp. 129–139 in W. G. Pond, B. L. Nichols, and D. L. Brown, eds. *Adequate Food for All: Culture, Science, and Technology of Food in the 21st Century*. Boca Raton, FL: CRC Press.

Harrison, T. 2002. Late Oligocene to middle Miocene catarrhines from Afro-Arabia. Pp. 311–338 in W. C. Hartwig, ed. *The Primate Fossil Record*. Cambridge, UK: Cambridge University Press.

Harrold, F. B. 1980. A comparative analysis of Eurasian Paleolithic burials. *World Archaeology* 12: 195–211.

Hart, D. and R. W. Sussman. 2009. *Man the Hunted: Primates, Predators, and Human Evolution*, expanded ed. Jackson, TN: Westview Press.

Hartwig, W. C., ed. 2002. *The Primate Fossil Record*. Cambridge, UK: Cambridge University Press.

Haslam, M., A. Hernandez-Aguilar, V. Ling, S. Carvalho, I. de la Torre, A. DeStefano, A. Du, B. Hardy, J. Harris, L. Marchant, T. Matsuzawa, W. McGrew, J. Mercader, R. Mora, M. Petraglia, H. Roche, E. Visalberghi, and R. Warren. 2009. Primate archaeology. *Nature* 460: 339–344.

Havill, L. M., M. C. Mahaney, L. A. Cox, P. A. Morin, G. Joslyn, and J. Rogers. 2005. A quantitative trait locus for normal variation in forearm bone mineral density in pedigreed baboons maps to the ortholog of human chromosome 11q. *Journal of Clinical Endocrinology and Metabolism* 90: 3638–3645.

Hawkes, K. 2003. Grandmothers and the evolution of human longevity. *American Journal of Human Biology* 15: 380–400.

Hawkes, K., J. F. O'Connell, N. G. Blurton Jones, H. Alvarez, and E. L. Charnov. 1998. Grandmothering, menopause, and the evolution of human life histories. *Proceedings of the National Academy of Sciences USA* 95: 1336–1339.

Hawks, J. 2012. Longer time scale for human evolution. *Proceedings of the National Academy of Sciences USA* 109: 15532–15532.

Hawks, J., M. Elliott, P. Schmid, S. E. Churchill, D. J. de Ruiter, et al. 2017. New fossil remains of *Homo naledi* from the Lesedi chamber, South Africa. *eLife* 6: e24232. DOI: 10.7554/eLife.24232.

Hawks, J., E. T. Wang, G. M. Cochran, H. C. Harpending, and R. K. Moyzis. 2007. Recent acceleration of human adaptive evolution. *Proceedings of the National Academy of Sciences USA* 104: 20753–20758.

Hay, R. L. and M. D. Leakey. 1982. The fossil footprints of Laetoli. *Scientific American* 246(2): 50–57.

Head, M. J., P. Gibbard, and A. Salvador A. 2008. The Tertiary: A proposal for its formal definition. *Episodes* 31: 248–250.

Heaton, J. L., T. R. Pickering, K. J. Carlson, R. H. Crompton, T. Jashashvili, et al. 2019. The long limb bones of the StW 573 *Australopithecus* from Sterkfontein Member 2: Descriptions and proportions. *Journal of Human Evolution* 133: 167–197.

Heeney, J. L., A. G. Dalgleish, and R. A. Weiss. 2006. Origins of HIV and the evolution of resistance to AIDS. *Science* 313: 462–466.

Henry, A. G., A. S. Brooks, and D. R. Piperno. 2011. Microfossils in calculus demonstrate consumption of plants and cooked foods in Neanderthal diets (Shanidar III, Iraq; Spy I and II, Belgium). *Proceedings of the National Academy of Sciences USA* 108: 486–491.

Henshilwood, C. S., F. d'Errico, K. L. van Niekerk, Y. Coquinot, Z. Jacobs, S.-E. Lauritzen, M. Menu, and R. García-Moreno. 2011. A 100,000-year-old ochre-processing workshop at Blombos Cave, South Africa. *Science* 334: 219–222.

Hernandez-Aguilar, R. A., J. Moore, and T. R. Pickering. 2007. Savanna chimpanzees use tools to harvest the underground storage organs of plants. *Proceedings of the National Academy of Sciences USA* 104: 19210–19213.

Higham, T., C. B. Ramsey, I. Karavanic, F. H. Smith, and E. Trinkaus. 2006. Revised direct radiocarbon dating of the Vindija G1 upper Paleolithic Neandertals. *Proceedings of the National Academy of Sciences USA* 103: 553–557.

Hill, W. C. O. 1972. *Evolutionary Biology of the Primates*. London: Academic Press.

Hlubik, S., F. Berna, C. Feibel, D. Braun, and J. W. K. Harris. 2017. Researching the nature of fire at 1.5 Mya on the site of FxJj20 AB, Koobi Fora, Kenya, using high-resolution spatial analysis and FTIR spectrometry. *Current Anthropology* 58(suppl. 16): S243–S257.

Hlusko, L., N. Do, and M. C. Mahaney. 2007. Genetic correlations between mandibular molar cusp areas in baboons. *American Journal of Physical Anthropology* 132: 445–454.

Hodges, G. 2015. First Americans. *National Geographic* 227(1): 124–137.

Holden, C. 2004. The origin of speech. *Science* 303: 1316–1319.

Holliday, T. W. 1997. Body proportions in late Pleistocene Europe and modern human origins. *Journal of Human Evolution* 32: 423–447.

Holloway, R. L., D. C. Broadfield, and M. S. Yuan. 2004. *The Human Fossil Record*. Vol. 3: *Brain Endocasts—The Paleoneurological Evidence*. Hoboken, NJ: Wiley-Liss.

Holman, D. J., M. A. Grimes, J. T. Achterberg, E. Brindle, and K. A. O'Conner. 2006. The distribution of postpartum amenorrhea in rural Bangladeshi women. *American Journal of Physical Anthropology* 129: 609–619.

Holt B., E. Whittey, M. Niskanen, V. Sládek, Margit Berner, and Christopher B. Ruff. 2018. Temporal and geographic variation in robusticity. C. B. Ruff, ed. *Skeletal Variation and Adaptation in Europeans: Upper Paleolithic to the Twentieth Century*. Hoboken, NJ: Wiley-Blackwell.

Hubbe, A., M. Hubbe, I. Karmann, F. W. Cruz, and W. A. Neves. 2013. Insights into Holocene megafauna survival and extinction in southeastern Brazil from new AMS ^{14}C dates. *Quaternary Research* 79: 152–157.

Hudjashov, G., T. Kivisild, P. A. Underhill, P. Endicott, P. Sanchez, J. J. Sanchez, A. A. Lin, P. Shen, P. Oefner, C. Renfrew, R. Villems, and P. Forster. 2007. Revealing the prehistoric settlement of Australia by Y chromosome and mtDNA analysis. *Proceedings of the National Academy of Sciences USA* 104: 8726–8730.

Huijbrets, B., P. De Wachter, L. S. N. Obiang, and M. E. Akou. 2003. Ebola and the decline of gorilla *Gorilla gorilla* and chimpanzee *Pan troglodytes* populations in Minkebe Forest, north-eastern Gabon. *Oryx* 37: 437–443.

Hunley, K. L., G. S. Cabana, D. A. Merriwether, and J. C. Long. 2007. A formal test of linguistic and genetic coevolution in native Central and South America. *American Journal of Physical Anthropology* 132: 622–631.

Hunley, K. L., J. E. Spence, and D. A. Merriwether. 2008. The impact of group fissions on genetic structure in native South America and implications for human evolution. *American Journal of Physical Anthropology* 135: 195–205.

Huss-Ashmore, R. 2000. Theory in human biology: Evolution, ecology, adaptability, and variation. Pp. 1–25 in S. Stinson, B. Bogin, R. Huss-Ashmore, and D. O'Rourke, eds. *Human Biology: An Evolutionary and Biocultural Perspective*. New York: Wiley-Liss.

Huss-Ashmore, R., J. Schall, and M. Hediger. 1992. *Health and Lifestyle Change*. Philadelphia: Museum Applied Science Center for Archaeology, University of Pennsylvania.

Huxley, R. 2007. *The Great Naturalists*. New York: Thames & Hudson.

Ice, G. H. and G. D. James. 2012. Stress and human biology. Pp. 459–512 in S. Stinson, B. Bogin, and D. O'Rourke, eds. *Human Biology: An Evolutionary and Biocultural Perspective*, 2nd ed. Hoboken, NJ: Wiley-Blackwell.

Institute of Vertebrate Paleontology and Paleoanthropology. 1980. *Atlas of Primitive Man in China*. Beijing, China, and New York: Science Press of the People's Republic of China and Van Nostrand Reinhold.

Irish, J. D., D. Guatelli-Steinberg, S. S. Legge, D. J. de Ruiter, and L. R. Berger. 2013. Dental morphology and the phylogenetic "place" of *Australopithecus sediba*. *Science* 340. DOI: 10.1126/science.1233062.

Irvine, W. 1955. *Apes, Angels, and Victorians*. New York: McGraw-Hill.

Isaac, G. L. 1977. *Olorgesailie: Archeological Studies of a Middle Pleistocene Lake Basin in Kenya*. Chicago: University of Chicago Press.

Itan, Y., B. L. Jones, C. J. E. Ingram, D. M. Swallo, and M. G. Thomas. 2010. A worldwide correlation of lactase persistence phenotype and genotypes. *BMC Evolutionary Biology* 10: 36.

Jablonka, E. and M. J. Lamb. 2005. *Evolution in Four Dimensions: Genetic, Epigenetic, Behavioral, and Symbolic Variation in the History of Life*. Cambridge, MA: MIT Press.

Jablonski, N. 2002. Fossil Old World monkeys: The late Neogene radiation. Pp. 255–299 in W. C. Hartwig, ed. *The Primate Fossil Record*. Cambridge, UK: Cambridge University Press.

Jablonski, N. G. 2004. The evolution of human skin and skin color. *Annual Review of Anthropology* 33: 585–623.

Jablonski, N. G. 2006. *Skin: A Natural History*. Berkeley: University of California Press.

Jablonski, N. G. and G. Chaplin. 2000. The evolution of skin coloration. *Journal of Human Evolution* 39: 57–106.

Jablonski, N. G. and G. Chaplin. 2002. Skin deep. *Scientific American* 287(4): 50–55.

Jablonski, N. G. and G. Chaplin. 2010. Human skin pigmentation as an adaptation to UV radiation. *Proceedings of the National Academy of Sciences USA* 107(suppl. 2): 8962–8968.

Jablonski, N. G., M. G. Leakey, C. Kiarie, and M. Anton. 2002. A new skeleton of *Theropithecus brumpti* (Primates: Cercopithecidae) from Lomekwi, West Turkana, Kenya. *Journal of Human Evolution* 43: 887–923.

Jacob, T., E. Indriati, R. P. Soejono, K. Hsu, D. W. Frayer, R. B. Eckhardt, A. J. Kuperavage, A. Thorne, and M. Henneberg. 2006. Pygmoid Australomelanesian *Homo sapiens* skeletal remains from Liang Bua, Flores: Population affinities and pathological abnormalities. *Proceedings of the National Academy of Sciences USA* 103: 13421–13426.

Jaeger, J.-J., K. C. Beard, Y. Chaimanee, M. Salem, M. Benammi, O. Hlal, P. Coster, A. A. Bilal, P. Duringer, M. Schuster, X. Valentin, B. Marandat, L. Marivaux, E. Metais, O. Hammuda, and M. Brunet. 2010. Late middle Eocene epoch of Libya yields earliest known radiation of African anthropoids. *Nature* 467: 1095–1098.

Jaeger, J.-J. and L. Marivaux. 2005. Shaking the earliest branches of anthropoid primate evolution. *Science* 310: 244–245.

James, G. 2010. Climate related morphological variation and physiological adaptations in *Homo sapiens*. Pp. 153–166 in C. S. Larsen, ed. *A Companion to Biological Anthropology*. Chichester, UK: Wiley-Blackwell.

Janmaat, K. R. L., S. D. Ban, and C. Boesch. 2013. Chimpanzees use long-term spatial memory to monitor large fruit trees and remember feeding experiences across seasons. *Animal Behaviour* 86: 1183–1205.

Janmaat, K. R. L., L. Polansky, S. D. Ban, and C. Boesch. 2014. Wild chimpanzees plan their breakfast time, type, and location. *Proceedings of the National Academy of Sciences USA* 111: 16343–16348.

Jantz, L. M. and R. L. Jantz. 1999. Secular change in long bone length and proportion in the United States, 1800–1970. *American Journal of Physical Anthropology* 110: 57–67.

Jantz, R. L. and M. K. Spradley. 2014. Cranial morphometric evidence for early Holocene relationships and population structure. Pp. 472–491 in D. W. Owsley and R. L. Jantz, eds. *Kennewick Man: The Scientific Investigation of an Ancient American Skeleton*. College Station: Texas A&M University Press.

Johnston, W. R. 2015. Statistics on the 2014–2015 West Africa Ebola outbreak. http://www.johnstonarchive.net/policy/westafrica-ebola.html.

Jolly, A. 1985. *The Evolution of Primate Behavior*. New York: Macmillan.

Jones, M. 2003. Ancient DNA in pre-Columbian archaeology: A review. *Journal of Archaeological Science* 30: 629–635.

Jungers, W. L., S. G. Larson, W. Harcourt-Smith, M. J. Morwood, T. Sutikna, R. Due Awe, and T. Djubiantono. 2009. Descriptions of the lower limb skeleton of *Homo floresiensis*. *Journal of Human Evolution* 57: 538–554.

Kaestle, F. A. 1995. Mitochondrial DNA evidence for the identity of the descendants of the prehistoric Stillwater Marsh populations. Pp. 73–80 in C. S. Larsen and R. L. Kelly, eds. *Bioarchaeology of the Stillwater Marsh:*

Prehistoric Human Adaptation in the Western Great Basin. Anthropological Papers of the American Museum of Natural History 77. New York: American Museum of Natural History.

Kaestle, F. A. 2010. Paleogenetics: Ancient DNA in anthropology. Pp. 427–441 in C. S. Larsen, ed. *A Companion to Biological Anthropology.* Chichester, UK: Wiley-Blackwell.

Kaestle, F. A. and K. A. Horsburgh. 2002. Ancient DNA in anthropology: Methods, applications, and ethics. *Yearbook of Physical Anthropology* 45: 92–130.

Kaestle, F. A., R. A. Kittles, A. L. Roth, and E. J. Ungvarsky. 2006. Database limitations on the evidentiary value of forensic mitochondrial DNA evidence. *American Criminal Law Review* 43: 53–88.

Kaestle, F. A., J. G. Lorenz, and D. G. Smith. 1999. Molecular genetics and the Numic expansion: A molecular investigation of the prehistoric inhabitants of Stillwater Marsh. Pp. 167–183 in B. E. Hemphill and C. S. Larsen, eds. *Prehistoric Lifeways in the Great Basin Wetlands: Bioarchaeological Reconstruction and Interpretation.* Salt Lake City: University of Utah Press.

Kaifu, Y., H. Baba, F. Aziz, E. Indriati, F. Schrenk, and T. Jacob. 2004. Taxonomic affinities and evolutionary history of the early Pleistocene hominids of Java: Dento-gnathic evidence. *American Journal of Physical Anthropology* 128: 709–726.

Kalaydjieva, L., B. Morar, R. Chaix, and H. Tang. 2005. A newly discovered founder population: The Roma/Gypsies. *BioEssays* 27: 1084–1094.

Kappeler, P. M. and C. P. van Schaik. 2006. *Cooperation in Primates and Humans: Mechanisms and Evolution.* New York: Springer.

Kappelman, J. 1993. The attraction of paleomagnetism. *Evolutionary Anthropology* 2: 89–99.

Kappelman, J., M. C. Alcicek, N. Kazanci, M. Schultz, M. Ozkul, and S. Sen. 2008. First *Homo erectus* from Turkey and implications for migrations into temperate Eurasia. *American Journal of Physical Anthropology* 135: 110–116.

Karavanic, I. and F. H. Smith. 1998. The middle/upper Paleolithic interface and the relationship of Neanderthals and early modern humans in the Hrvatsko Zagorje, Croatia. *Journal of Human Evolution* 34: 223–248.

Katz, D. C., M. N. Grote, and T. D. Weaver. 2017. Changes in human skull morphology across the agricultural transition are consistent with softer diets in preindustrial farming groups. *Proceedings of the National Academy of Sciences USA* 114: 9050–9055.

Katzenberg, M. A. and A. L. Waters-Rist. 2019. Stable isotope analysis. A tool for studying past diet, demography, and life history. Pp. 469–504 in M. A. Katzenberg and A. L. Grauer, eds. *Biological Anthropology of the Human Skeleton*, 3rd ed. Hoboken, NJ: John Wiley & Sons.

Kay, R. F. 2015. New World monkey origins. *Science* 347: 1068–1069.

Kay, R. F., C. Ross, and B. A. Williams. 1997. Anthropoid origins. *Science* 275: 797–804.

Keesing, F., L. K. Belden, P. Daszak, A. Dobson, C. D. Harvell, R. D. Holt, P. Hudson, A. Jolles, K. E. Jones, C. E. Mitchell, S. S. Myers, T. Bogich, and R. S. Ostfeld. 2010. Impacts of biodiversity on the emergence and transmission of infectious diseases. *Nature* 468: 647–652.

Keith-Lucas, T., F. J. White, L. Keith-Lucas, and L. G. Vick. 1999. Changes in behavior in free-ranging *Lemur catta* following release in a natural habitat. *American Journal of Primatology* 47: 15–28.

Kelley, E. A. and R. W. Sussman. 2007. An academic genealogy on the history of American field primatologists. *American Journal of Physical Anthropology* 132: 406–425.

Kelley, J. 2002. The hominoid radiation in Asia. Pp. 369–384 in W. C. Hartwig, ed. *The Primate Fossil Record.* Cambridge, UK: Cambridge University Press.

Kelly, R. L. 2003. Maybe we know when people first came to North America; and what does it mean if we do? *Quaternary International* 109–110: 133–145.

Kemp, B. M., R. S. Malhi, J. McDonough, D. A. Bolnick, J. A. Eshleman, O. Rickards, C. Martinez-Labarga, J. R. Johnson, J. G. Lorenz, E. J. Dixon, T. E. Fifield, T. H. Heaton, R. Worl, and D. G. Smith. 2007. Genetic analysis of early Holocene skeletal remains from Alaska and its implications for the settlement of the Americas. *American Journal of Physical Anthropology* 132: 605–621.

Kemper, S. 2013. No alpha males allowed. *Smithsonian* 44(5): 38–43.

Kenneally, C. 2007. *The First Word: The Search for the Origins of Language.* New York: Viking.

Kennedy, G. 2003. Palaeolithic grandmothers? Life history theory and early *Homo. Journal of the Royal Anthropological Institute* 9: 549–572.

Kennedy, G. 2005. From the ape's dilemma to the weanling's dilemma: Early weaning and its evolutionary context. *Journal of Human Evolution* 48: 123–145.

Kennedy, K. A. R. 2000. *God-Apes and Fossil Men: Paleoanthropology in South Asia.* Ann Arbor: University of Michigan Press.

Kennedy, K. A. R., A. Sonakia, J. Chiment, and K. K. Verma. 1991. Is the Narmada hominid an Indian *Homo erectus? American Journal of Physical Anthropology* 86: 475–496.

Kettlewell, H. B. D. 1973. *The Evolution of Melanism.* Oxford, UK: Oxford University Press.

Kevles, B. H. 2006. *The Reluctant Mr. Darwin: An Intimate Portrait of Charles Darwin and the Making of His Theory of Evolution.* New York: Norton.

Keyser, A. W. 2000. The Drimolen skull: The most complete australopithecine cranium and mandible to date. *South African Journal of Science* 96: 189–197.

Khoury, M. J., R. Millikan, J. Little, and M. Gwinn. 2004. The emergence of epidemiology in the genomics age. *International Journal of Epidemiology* 33: 936–944.

Kim, U.-K., E. Jorgenson, H. Coon, M. Leppert, N. Risch, and D. Drayna. 2003. Positional cloning of the human quantitative trait locus underlying taste sensitivity to phenylthiocarbamide. *Science* 299: 1221–1225.

Kimbel, W. H. and L. K. Delezene. 2009. "Lucy" redux: A review of research on *Australopithecus afarensis. Yearbook of Physical Anthropology* 52: 2–48.

Kimbel, W. H., D. C. Johanson, and Y. Rak. 1994. The first skull and other new discoveries of *Australopithecus afarensis* at Hadar, Ethiopia. *Nature* 368: 449–451.

Kimbel, W. H., C. A. Lockwood, C. V. Ward, M. G. Leakey, Y. Rak, and D. C. Johanson. 2006. Was *Australopithecus anamensis* ancestral to *A. afarensis*? A case of anagenesis in the hominin fossil record. *Journal of Human Evolution* 51: 134–152.

Kimbel, W. H., Y. Rak, and D. C. Johanson. 2004. *The Skull of* Australopithecus afarensis. New York: Oxford University Press.

King, T. E., G. R. Bowden, P. L. Balaresque, S. M. Adams, M. E. Shanks, and M. A. Jobling. 2007. Thomas Jefferson's Y chromosome belongs to rare European lineage. *American Journal of Physical Anthropology* 132: 584–589.

Kirch, P. V. 2005. Archaeology and global change: The Holocene record. *Annual Review of Anthropology* 30: 409–440.

Kirk, S. F., T. L. Penney, and T.-L. F. McHugh. 2011. Characterizing the obesogenic environment: The state of the evidence with directions for future research. *Obesity Reviews* 11: 109–117.

Kitchen, D. M. 2003. Alpha male black howler monkey responses to loud calls: Effect of numeric odds, male companion behaviour and reproductive investment. *Animal Behaviour* 67: 125–139.

Klaus, H. D., C. S. Larsen, and M. E. Tam. 2009. Economic intensification and degenerative joint disease: Life and labor on the postcontact north coast of Peru. *American Journal of Physical Anthropology* 139: 204–221.

Klein, R. G. 2009. *The Human Career: Human Biological and Cultural Origins*, 3rd ed. Chicago: University of Chicago Press.

Klepinger, L. L. 2006. *Fundamentals of Forensic Anthropology*. Hoboken, NJ: Wiley-Liss.

Klitz, W., C. Brautbar, A. M. Schito, L. F. Barcellos, and J. R. Oksenberg. 2001. Evolution of the CCR5 Delta32 mutation based on haplotype variation in Jewish and Northern European population samples. *Human Immunology* 62: 530–538.

Koch, M., S. Wedmann, C. Labandeira, and J. Hamlin. 2011. Fossil bugs (Insecta: Heteroptera) of Messel and the Green River Formation (USA)—Are there any connections? Pp. 89–90 in T. Lehmann and S. F. K. Schaal, eds. *The World of Time of Messel: Puzzles in Palaeobiology, Palaeoenvironment, and the History of Early Primates*. Frankfurt am Main, Germany: Senckenberg Gesellschaft für Naturforschung.

Koenigswald, W., J. Habersetzer, and P. D. Gingerich. 2011. Morphology and evolution of the distal phalanges in primates. Pp. 91–94 in T. Lehmann and S. F. K. Schaal, eds. *The World at the Time of Messel: Puzzles in Palaeobiology, Palaeoenvironment, and the History of Early Primates*. Frankfurt am Main, Germany: Senckenberg Gesellschaft für Naturforschung.

Kolbert, E. 2007. *Field Notes from a Catastrophe: A Frontline Report on Climate Change*. London: Bloomsbury.

Kolman, C. J. 2006. Anthropological applications of ancient DNA: Problems and prospects. *American Antiquity* 71: 365–380.

Komlos, J., ed. 1994. *Stature, Living Standards, and Economic Development: Essays in Anthropometric History*. Chicago: University of Chicago Press.

Kordos, L. and D. R. Begun. 2002. Rudabanya: A late Miocene subtropical swamp deposit with evidence of the origin of the African apes and humans. *Evolutionary Anthropology* 11: 45–57.

Kramer, A. 2002. The natural history and evolutionary fate of *Homo erectus*. Pp. 140–154 in P. N. Peregrine, C. R. Ember, and M. Ember, eds. *Physical Anthropology: Original Readings in Method and Practice*. Upper Saddle River, NJ: Prentice Hall.

Krause, J., C. Lalueza-Fox, L. Orlando, W. Enard, R. E. Green, H. A. Burbano, J.-J. Hublin, C. Hänni, J. Fortea, M. de la Rasilla, J. Bertranpetit, A. Rosas, and S. Pääbo. 2007. The derived *FOXP2* variant of modern humans was shared with Neandertals. *Current Biology* 17: 1908–1912.

Krause, J., L. Orlando, D. Serre, B. Viola, B. Prufer, M. P. Richards, J.-J. Hublin, C. Hanni, A. P. Derevianko, and S. Pääbo.

2007. Neanderthals in central Asia and Siberia. *Nature* 449: 902–904.

Krause, K. W. 2009. Pathology or paradigm shift? Human evolution, *ad hominem* science, and the anomalous hobbits of Flores. *Skeptical Inquirer* 33(4): 31–39.

Krech, S., III. 1999. *The Ecological Indian: Myth and History*. New York: Norton.

Krogman, W. M. and M. Y. Iscan. 1986. *The Human Skeleton in Forensic Medicine*, 2nd ed. Springfield, IL: Charles C. Thomas.

Kunimatsu, Y., M. Nakatsukasa, Y. Sawada, T. Sakai, M. Hyodo, H. Hyodo, T. Itaya, H. Nakaya, H. Saegusa, A. Maxurier, M. Saneyoshi, H. Tsujikawa, A. Yamamoto, and E. Mbua. 2007. A new late Miocene great ape from Kenya and its implications for the origins of African great apes and humans. *Proceedings of the National Academy of Sciences USA* 104: 19220–19225.

Kuzawa, C. W. 1998. Adipose tissue in human infancy and childhood: An evolutionary perspective. *Yearbook of Physical Anthropology* 41: 177–209.

Laird, M. F., L. Schroeder, H. Garvin, J. E. Scott, and M. Dembo. 2017. The skull of *Homo naledi. Journal of Human Evolution* 104: 100–123.

Laitman, J. T. and I. Tattersall. 2001. *Homo erectus newyorkensis*: An Indonesian fossil rediscovered in Manhattan sheds light on the middle phase of human evolution. *Anatomical Record* 262: 341–343.

Lake, A., T. B. Townshend, and S. Alvanides. 2010. *Obesogenic Environments*. Hoboken, NJ: Wiley-Blackwell.

Lamason, R. L., M.-A. P. K. Mohideen, J. R. Mest, A. C. Wong, H. L. Norton, et al. 2005. SLC24A5, a putative cation exchanger, affects pigmentation in zebrafish and humans. *Science* 310: 1782–1786.

Lambert, D. M. and L. Huynen. 2010. Face of the past reconstructed. *Nature* 463: 739–740.

Lambert, D. M. and C. D. Millar. 2006. Ancient genomics is born. *Nature* 444: 275–276.

Lambert, J. E. 1999. Seed handling in chimpanzees (*Pan troglodytes*) and redtail monkeys (*Cercopithecus ascanius*): Implications for understanding hominoid and cercopithecine fruit-processing strategies and seed dispersal. *American Journal of Physical Anthropology* 109: 365–386.

Lambert, J. E., C. A. Chapman, R. W. Wrangham, and N. L. Conklin-Brittain. 2004. Hardness of cercopithecine foods: Implications for the critical function of enamel thickness in exploiting fallback foods. *American Journal of Physical Anthropology* 125: 363–368.

Lambert, P. M., ed. 2000. *Bioarchaeological Studies of Life in the Age of Agriculture:*

A View from the Southeast. Tuscaloosa: University of Alabama Press.

Lambert, P. M. 2002. The archaeology of war: A North American perspective. *Journal of Archaeological Research* 10: 207–241.

Lambert, P. M. 2009. Health versus fitness: Competing themes in the origins and spread of agriculture. *Current Anthropology* 50: 603–608.

Lander, E. S. 2011. Initial impact of the sequencing of the human genome. *Nature* 470: 187–197.

Langdon, J. H. 2005. *The Human Strategy: An Evolutionary Perspective on Human Anatomy*. New York: Oxford University Press.

Langergraber, K. E., K. Prüfer, C. Rowney, C. Boesch, C. Crockford, K. Fawcett, E. Inoue, M. Inoue-Muruyama, J. C. Mitani, M. N. Muller, M. M. Robbins, G. Schubert, T. S. Stoinski, B. Viola, D. Watts, R. M. Wittig, R. W. Wrangham, K. Zuberbühler, S. Pääbo, and L. Vigilant. 2012. Generation times in wild chimpanzees and gorillas suggest earlier divergence times in great ape and human evolution. *Proceedings of the National Academy of Sciences USA* 109: 15716–15721.

Lanham, U. 1973. *The Bone Hunters*. New York: Columbia University Press.

Larsen, C. S. 1994. In the wake of Columbus: Native population biology in the postcontact Americas. *Yearbook of Physical Anthropology* 37: 109–154.

Larsen, C. S. 1995. Biological changes in human populations with agriculture. *Annual Review of Anthropology* 24: 185–213.

Larsen, C. S. 1997. *Bioarchaeology: Interpreting Behavior from the Human Skeleton*. Cambridge, UK: Cambridge University Press.

Larsen, C. S. 2000. *Skeletons in Our Closet: Revealing Our Past through Bioarchaeology*. Princeton, NJ: Princeton University Press.

Larsen, C. S. 2002. Bioarchaeology: The lives and lifestyles of past people. *Journal of Archaeological Research* 10: 119–166.

Larsen, C. S. 2003. Animal source foods and human health during evolution. *Journal of Nutrition* 133: 1S–5S.

Larsen, C. S. 2003. Equality for the sexes in human evolution? Early hominid sexual dimorphism and implications for mating systems and social behavior. *Proceedings of the National Academy of Sciences USA* 100: 9103–9104.

Larsen, C. S., ed. 2010. *A Companion to Biological Anthropology*. Chichester, UK: Wiley-Blackwell.

Larsen, C. S., ed. 2015. *The Antiquity and Origin of Native North Americans*, 2nd ed. New York: Garland.

Larsen, C. S., D. L. Hutchinson, M. J. Schoeninger, and L. Norr. 2001. Food and stable isotopes in La Florida: Diet and nutrition before and after contact. Pp. 53–81 in C. S. Larsen, ed. *Bioarchaeology of Spanish Florida: The Impact of Colonialism*. Gainesville: University Press of Florida.

Larsen, C. S., C. J. Knüsel, S. D. Haddow, M. A. Pilloud, M. Milella, et al. 2019. Bioarchaeology of Neolithic Çatalhöyük reveals fundamental transitions in health, mobility, and lifestyle in early farmers. *Proceedings of the National Academy of Sciences USA* 116: 12615–12623.

Larsen, C. S., R. M. Matter, and D. L. Gebo. 1998. *Human Origins: The Fossil Record*, 3rd ed. Prospect Heights, IL: Waveland Press.

Larsen, C. S. and T. C. Patterson. 1997. Americas: Paleoanthropology. Pp. 69–74 in F. Spencer, ed. *History of Physical Anthropology: An Encyclopedia*. New York: Garland.

Larsen, C. S. and P. L. Walker. 2010. Bioarchaeology: Health, lifestyle, and society in recent human evolution. Pp. 379–394 in C. S. Larsen, ed. *A Companion to Biological Anthropology*. Chichester, UK: Wiley-Blackwell.

Larsen, E. 2005. Developmental origins of variation. Pp. 113–129 in B. Hallgrímson and B. K. Hall, eds. *Variation: A Central Concept in Biology*. Burlington, MA: Elsevier Academic Press.

Larson, G., U. Albarella, K. Dobney, P. Rowley-Conway, J. Schibler, A. Tresset, J.-D. Vigne, C. J. Edwards, A. Schlumbaum, A. Dinu, A. Balacsecu, G. Dolman, A. Tagliacozzo, N. Manaseryan, P. Miracle, L. Van Wijngaarden-Bakker, M. Masseti, D. G. Bradley, and A. Cooper. 2007. Ancient DNA, pig domestication, and the spread of the Neolithic into Europe. *Proceedings of the National Academy of Sciences USA* 104: 15276–15281.

Larson, G., D. R. Piperno, R. G. Allaby, M. D. Purugganan, L. Andersson, et al. 2014. Current perspectives and the future of domestication studies. *Proceedings of the National Academy of Sciences USA* 111: 6139–6146.

Larson, S. 2010. Did australopiths climb trees? *Science* 338: 478–479.

Lassek, W. D. and S. J. C. Gaulin. 2006. Changes in body fat distribution in relation to parity in American women: A covert form of maternal depletion. *American Journal of Physical Anthropology* 131: 295–302.

Latham, R. 1982. *The Travels of Marco Polo*. New York: Viking.

Lau, E. M., C. Cooper, C. Wickham, S. Donnan, and D. J. Barker. 1990. Hip fracture in Hong Kong and Britain. *International Journal of Epidemiology* 19: 1119–1121.

Leakey, M. 1984. *Disclosing the Past: An Autobiography*. Garden City, NY: Doubleday.

Leakey, M. G., C. S. Feibel, I. McDougall, and A. Walker. 1995. New four-million-year-old hominid species from Kanapoi and Allia Bay, Kenya. *Nature* 376: 565–571.

Leakey, M. G., F. Spoor, F. H. Brown, P. N. Gathogo, C. Kiarie, L. M. Leakey, and I. McDougall. 2001. New hominin genus from eastern Africa shows diverse middle Pliocene lineages. *Nature* 410: 433–440.

Leakey, M. G., F. Spoor, M. C. Dean, C. S. Feibel, S. C. Antón, C. Kiarie, and L. N. Leakey. 2012. New fossils from Koobi Fora in northern Kenya confirm taxonomic diversity in early *Homo*. *Nature* 488: 201–204.

Lebatard, A.-E., D. L. Bourlès, P. Duringer, M. Jolivet, R. Braucher, J. Carcaillet, M. Schuster, N. Arnaud, P. Moniè, F. Lihoreau, A. Likius, H. T. Mackaye, P. Vignaud, and M. Brunet. 2008. Cosmogenic nuclide dating of *Sahelanthropus tchadensis* and *Australopithecus bahrelghazali*: Mio-Pliocene hominids from Chad. *Proceedings of the National Academy of Sciences USA* 105: 3226–3231.

Lee, S.-H. and M. H. Wolpoff. 2003. The pattern of evolution in Pleistocene human brain size. *Paleobiology* 29: 186–196.

Lee-Thorp, J. 2002. Hominid dietary niches from proxy chemical indicators in fossils: The Swartkrans example. Pp. 123–141 in P. S. Ungar and M. F. Teaford, eds. *Human Diet: Its Origin and Evolution*. Westport, CT: Bergin & Garvey.

Lee-Thorp, J. and M. Sponheimer. 2006. Distributions of biogeochemistry to understanding hominin dietary ecology. *Yearbook of Physical Anthropology* 49: 131–148.

Lee-Thorp, J. A., M. Sponheimer, and N.J. van der Merwe. 2003. What do stable isotopes tell us about hominid dietary and ecological niches in the Pliocene? *International Journal of Osteoarchaeology* 13: 104–113.

Leidy, L. E. 1994. Biological aspects of menopause: Across the lifespan. *Annual Review of Anthropology* 23: 231–253.

Lemons, D. and W. McGinnis. 2006. Genomic evolution of Hox gene clusters. *Science* 313: 1918–1922.

Leonard, W. R. 2002. Food for thought: Dietary change was a driving force in human evolution. *Scientific American* 287(6): 106–115.

Leonard, W. R. 2012. Human nutritional evolution. Pp. 251–324 in S. Stinson, B. Bogin, and D. O'Rourke, eds. *Human Biology: An Evolutionary and Biocultural Perspective*, 2nd ed. Hoboken, NJ: Wiley-Blackwell.

Lepre, C. J., and D. V. Kent. 2015. Chronostratigraphy of KNM-ER 3733 and other Area 104 hominins from Koobi Fora. *Journal of Human Evolution* 86: 99–111.

Levy, S. 1994. *The Antiobiotic Paradox: How Miracle Drugs Are Destroying the Miracle*. New York: Plenum Press.

Lewin, R. 1988. *Bones of Contention: Controversies in the Search for Human Origins*. New York: Touchstone.

Lewis, S. L. and M. A. Maslin. 2015. Defining the Anthropocene. *Nature* 519: 171–180.

Lewontin, R. C. 1972. The apportionment of human diversity. *Evolutionary Biology* 6: 381–398.

Libby, W. F. 1952. *Radiocarbon Dating*. Chicago: University of Chicago Press.

Lieberman, D. E. 2007. Homing in on early *Homo*. *Nature* 449: 291–292.

Lieberman, L., R. C. Kirk, and A. Littlefield. 2003. Perishing paradigm: Race—1931–99. *American Anthropologist* 105: 110–113.

Lieberman, L. S. 2006. Evolutionary and anthropological perspectives on optimal foraging in obesogenic environments. *Appetite* 47: 3–9.

Little, B. B., P. H. Buschang, M. E. P. Reyes, S. K. Tan, and R. M. Malina. 2006. Craniofacial dimensions in children in rural Oaxaca, southern Mexico: Secular change, 1968–2000. *American Journal of Physical Anthropology* 131: 127–136.

Little, M. A. 2010. Franz Boas's place in American physical anthropology and its institutions. Pp. 55–85 in M. A. Little and K. A. R. Kennedy, eds. *Histories of American Physical Anthropology in the Twentieth Century*. Lanham, MD: Rowman & Littlefield.

Little, M. A. and P. W. Leslie. 1999. *Turkana Herders of the Dry Savanna: Ecology and Biobehavioral Response of Nomads to an Uncertain Environment*. Oxford, UK: Oxford University Press.

Little, M. A. and R. W. Sussman. 2010. History of biological anthropology. Pp. 13–38 in C. S. Larsen, ed. *A Companion to Biological Anthropology*. Chichester, UK: Wiley-Blackwell.

Liu, W., C.-Z. Jin, Y.-Q. Zhang, Y.-J. Cai, S. Xing, X.-J. Wu, X.-J. Cheng, H. Cheng, R. L. Edwards, W.-S. Pan, D.-G. Qin, Z.-S. An, E. Trinkaus, and X.-Z. Wu. 2010. Human remains from Zhirendong, south China, and modern human emergence in east Asia. *Proceedings of the National Academy of Sciences USA* 107: 19201–19206.

Liu, W., M. Martinon-Torress, Y.-J. Cai, S. Xing, and H.-W. Tong. 2015. The earliest unequivocally modern humans in southern China. *Nature* 526: 696–700.

Livingstone, F. B. 1958. Anthropological implications of sickle cell gene distribution in West Africa. *American Anthropologist* 60: 533–562.

Livingstone, F. B. 1962. On the non-existence of human races. *Current Anthropology* 3: 279.

Livingstone, F. B. 1967. *Abnormal Hemoglobins in Human Populations*. Chicago: Aldine.

Livingstone, F. B. 1971. Malaria and human polymorphisms. *Annual Review of Genetics* 5: 33–64.

Livingstone, F. B. 1973. *Data on the Abnormal Hemoglobins and Glucose-6-Phosphate Dehydrogenase Deficiency in Human Populations, 1967–1973*. Technical Reports 3, Contributions in Human Biology 1. Ann Arbor: Museum of Anthropology, University of Michigan.

Livingstone, F. B. 1985. *Frequencies of Hemoglobin Variants: Thalassemia, the Glucose-6-Phosphate Dehydrogenase Deficiency, G6PD Variants, and Ovalocytosis in Human Populations*. Oxford, UK: Oxford University Press.

Lock, M. and P. Kaufert. 2001. Menopause, local biologies, and cultures of aging. *American Journal of Human Biology* 13: 494–504.

Lockwood, C. A., W. H. Kimbel, and D. C. Johanson. 2000. Temporal trends and metric variation in the mandibles and dentition of *Australopithecus afarensis*. *Journal of Human Evolution* 39: 23–55.

Londo, J. P., Y.-C. Chiang, K.-H. Hung, T.-Y. Chiang, and B. A. Schaal. 2006. Phylogeography of Asian wild rice, *Oryza rufipogon*, reveals multiple independent domestications of cultivated rice, *Oryza sativa*. *Proceedings of the National Academy of Sciences USA* 103: 9578–9583.

Long, J. C. and R. A. Kittles. 2003. Human genetic diversity and the nonexistence of biological races. *Human Biology* 75: 449–471.

Long, J. C., J. Li, and M. E. Healy. 2009. Human DNA sequences: More variation and less race. *American Journal of Physical Anthropology* 139: 23–34.

Loomis, W. F. 1967. Skin-pigment regulation of vitamin-D biosynthesis in man. *Science* 157: 501–506.

Lordkipanidze, D., T. Jashashvili, A. Vekua, M. S. Ponce de Leon, C. P. E. Zollikofer, G. P. Rightmire, H. Pontzer, R. Ferring, O. Oms, M. Tappen, M. Bukhsianidze, J. Agusti, R. Kahlke, G. Kiladze, B. Martinez-Navarro, A. Mouskhelishvili, M. Nioradze, and L. Rook. 2007. Postcranial evidence from early *Homo* from Dmanisi, Georgia. *Nature* 449: 305–310.

Lordkipanidze, D., M. S. Ponce de Leon, A. Margvelashvili, Y. Rak, G. P. Rightmire, A. Vekua, and P. E. Zollikofer. 2013. A complete skull from Dmanisi, Georgia, and evolutionary biology of early *Homo*. *Science* 342: 326–331.

Louwe Kooijmans, L. P., Y. Smirnov, R. S. Solecki, P. Villa, and T. Weber. 1989. On the evidence for Neandertal burial. *Current Anthropology* 30: 322–326.

Lovejoy, C. O., G. Suwa, S. W. Simpson, J. H. Matternes, and T. D. White. 2009. The great divides: *Ardipithecus ramidus* reveals the postcrania of our last common ancestors with African apes. *Science* 326: 100–106.

Lwanga, J. S., T. T. Struhsaker, P. J. Struhsaker, T. M. Butynski, and J. C. Mitani. 2011. Primate population dynamic over 32.9 years at Ngogo, Kibale National Park, Uganda. *American Journal of Primatology* 73: 997–1011.

Lyell, C. 1830–33. *Principles of Geology*. 3 vols. London: John Murray.

Lynch, M. and B. Walsh. 1998. *Genetics and Analysis of Quantitative Traits*. Sunderland, MA: Sinauer.

Macdougall, D. 2008. *Nature's Clocks: How Scientists Measure the Age of Almost Everything*. Berkeley: University of California Press.

Maddox, B. 2002. *Rosalind Franklin: The Dark Lady of DNA*. New York: HarperCollins.

Madrigal, L., B. Ware, R. Miller, G. Saenz, M. Chavez, and D. Dykes. 2001. Ethnicity, gene flow and population subdivision in Limon, Costa Rica. *American Journal of Physical Anthropology* 114: 99–108.

Madrigal, L. and J. Willoughby. 2010. Ongoing evolution in humans. Pp. 207–221 in C. S. Larsen, ed. *A Companion to Biological Anthropology*. Chichester, UK: Wiley-Blackwell.

Malone, N., A. H. Wade, A. Fuentes, E. P. Riley, M. Remis, and C. J. Robinson. 2014. Ethnoprimatology: Critical interdisciplinarity and multispecies approaches in anthropology. *Critique of Anthropology* 34: 8–29.

Malthus, T. R. 1798. *An Essay on the Principle of Population*. Reprinted 2004, ed. Philip Appleman. New York: Norton.

Manson, J. H., S. Perry, and A. R. Parish. 1997. Nonconceptive sexual behavior in bonobos and capuchins. *International Journal of Primatology* 18: 767–786.

Maples, W. R. and M. Browning. 1994. *Dead Men Do Tell Tales*. New York: Doubleday.

Marcus, G. F. and S. E. Fisher. 2003. *FOXP2* in focus: What can genes tell us about speech and language. *Trends in Cognitive Sciences* 7: 257–262.

Marks, J. 1994. Black. White. Other. *Natural History* 103(12): 32–35.

Marks, J. 1995. *Human Biodiversity: Genes, Race, and History*. New York: Aldine de Gruyter.

Marks, J. 1996. Science and race. *American Behavioral Scientist* 40: 123–133.

Marlar, R. A., B. L. Leonard, B. M. Billman, P. M. Lambert, and J. E. Marlar. 2000. Biochemical evidence of cannibalism at a prehistoric Puebloan site in southwestern Colorado. *Nature* 407: 74–78.

Marquez, S., K. Mowbray, G. J. Sawyer, T. Jacob, and A. Silvers. 2001. New fossil hominid calvaria from Indonesia—Sambungmacan 3. *Anatomical Record* 262: 344–368.

Marshak, S. 2019. *Earth: Portrait of a Planet*, 6th ed. New York: Norton.

Marshall, G. A. 1968. Racial classifications: Popular and scientific. Pp. 149–166 in M. Mead, T. Dobzhansky, E. Tobach, and R. E. Light, eds. *Science and the Concept of Race*. New York: Columbia University Press.

Martin, D. L. and D. W. Frayer, eds. 1997. *Troubled Times: Violence and Warfare in the Past*. Amsterdam, Netherlands: Gordon and Breach.

Martin, D. L., R. P. Harrod, and V. R. Perez, eds. 2012. *The Bioarchaeology of Violence*. Gainesville: University Press of Florida.

Martin, L. 1985. Significance of enamel thickness in hominoid evolution. *Nature* 314: 260–263.

Martin, N., L. Eaves, and D. Loesch. 1982. A genetic analysis of covariation between finger ridge counts. *Annals of Human Biology* 9: 539–552.

Martin, R. A. 2004. *Missing Links: Evolutionary Concepts and Transitions through Time*. Sudbury, MA: Jones and Bartlett.

Martin, R. D. 1990. *Primate Origins and Evolution: A Phylogenetic Reconstruction*. London: Chapman & Hall.

Martin, R. D. 1993. Primate origins: Plugging the gaps. *Nature* 363: 223–234.

Masters, J., M. Gamba, and F. Génin. 2013. What's in a name? Higher level taxonomy of the prosimian primates. Pp. 3–9 in J. Masters and F. Genin, eds. *Leaping Ahead: Advances in Prosimian Biology*. New York: Springer.

Matsu'ura, S., M. Kondo, T. Danhara, S. Sakata, H. Iwano, et al. 2020. Age control of the first appearance datum for Javanese *Homo erectus* in the Sangiran area. *Science* 367: 210–214.

Mayor, A. 2001. *The First Fossil Hunters: Paleontology in Greek and Roman Times*. Princeton, NJ: Princeton University Press.

Mayr, E. 1942. *Systematics and the Origin of Species*. New York: Columbia University Press.

Mayr, E. 1970. *Populations, Species, and Evolution*. Cambridge, MA: Harvard University Press.

Mayr, E. 2004. 80 years of watching the evolutionary scenery. *Science* 305: 46–47.

McBrearty, S. and A. S. Brooks. 2000. The revolution that wasn't: A new interpretation of the origin of modern human behavior. *Journal of Human Evolution* 39: 453–563.

McCalman, I. 2009. *Darwin's Armada: Four Voyages and the Battle for the Theory of Evolution*. New York: Norton.

McCarthy, J. J., O. F. Canziani, N. A. Leary, D. J. Dokken, and K. S. White. 2001. *Climate Change 2001: Impacts, Adaptations, and Vulnerability*. Cambridge, UK: Cambridge University Press.

McCorriston, J. 2000. Wheat domestication. Pp. 158–174 in K. Kiple and C. Ornelas, eds. *Cambridge World History of Food and Nutrition*. New York: Cambridge University Press.

McDade, T. W., J. Rutherford, L. Adair, and C. W. Kuzawa. 2009. Early origins of inflammation: Microbial exposures in infancy predict lower levels of C-reactive protein in adulthood. *Proceedings of the Royal Society of London B* 277: 1129–1137.

McDougall, I., F. H. Brown, and J. G. Fleagle. 2005. Stratigraphic placement and age of modern humans from Kibish, Ethiopia. *Nature* 433: 733–736.

McGovern, P. E. 2003. *Ancient Wine: The Search for the Origins of Viniculture*. Princeton, NJ: Princeton University Press.

McGraw, W. S. 2010. Primates defined. Pp. 222–242 in C. S. Larsen, ed. *A Companion to Biological Anthropology*. Chichester, UK: Wiley-Blackwell.

McGraw, W. S., and L. R. Berger. 2014. Raptors and primate evolution. *Evolutionary Anthropology* 22: 280–293.

McGraw, W. S., C. Cooke, and S. Shultz. 2006. Primate remains from African crowned eagle (*Stephanoaetus coronatus*) nests in Ivory Coast's Taï Forest: Implications for primate predation and early hominid taphonomy in South Africa. *American Journal of Physical Anthropology* 131: 151–165.

McGraw, W. S. and K. Zuberbühler. 2008. Socioecology, predation, and cognition in a community of West African monkeys. *Evolutionary Anthropology* 17: 254–266.

McGraw, W. S., K. Zuberbühler, and R. Noe, eds. 2007. *Monkeys of the Taï Forest: An African Primate Community*. Cambridge, UK: Cambridge University Press.

McGrew, W. C. 1998. Culture in nonhuman primates. *Annual Review of Anthropology* 27: 301–328.

McGrew, W. C., L. F. Marchant, and T. Nishida. 1996. *Great Ape Societies*. Cambridge, UK: Cambridge University Press.

McHenry, H. M. 2002. Introduction to the fossil record of human ancestry. Pp. 401–405 in W. C. Hartwig, ed. *The Primate Fossil Record*. Cambridge, UK: Cambridge University Press.

McHenry, H. M. and K. Coffing. 2000. *Australopithecus* to *Homo*: Transformations in body and mind. *Annual Review of Anthropology* 29: 125–146.

McKee, J. K. 1996. Faunal evidence and Sterkfontein Member 2 foot bones of early hominid. *Science* 271: 1301.

McKee, J. K. 2003. *Sparing Nature: The Conflict between Human Population Growth and Earth's Biodiversity*. New Brunswick, NJ: Rutgers University Press.

McKee, J. K., F. E. Poirier, and W. S. McGraw. 2005. *Understanding Human Evolution*, 4th ed. Upper Saddle River, NJ: Pearson Prentice Hall.

McKee, J. K., P. W. Sciulli, C. D. Fooce, and T. A. Waite. 2003. Forecasting global biodiversity threats associated with human population growth. *Biological Conservation* 115: 161–164.

McPherron, S. P., Z. Alemseged, C. W. Marean, J. G. Wynn, D. Reed, D. Geraads, R. Bobe, and H. A. Béarat. 2010. Evidence for stone-tool-assisted consumption at Dikika, Ethiopia. *Nature* 466: 857–860.

Meltzer, D. J. 1993. Pleistocene peopling of the Americas. *Evolutionary Anthropology* 1: 157–169.

Meltzer, D. J. 2009. *First Peoples in a New World: Colonizing Ice Age America*. Berkeley: University of California Press.

Mercader, J., H. Barton, J. Gillespie, J. Harris, S. Kuhn, R. Tyler, and C. Boesch. 2007. 4,300-year-old chimpanzee sites and the origins of percussive stone technology. *Proceedings of the National Academy of Sciences USA* 104: 3043–3048.

Mercader, J., M. Panger, and C. Boesch. 2002. Excavation of a chimpanzee stone tool site in the African rainforest. *Science* 296: 1452–1455.

Merriwether, D. A. 2007. Mitochondrial DNA. Pp. 817–830 in D. H. Ubelaker, ed. *Handbook of North American Indians*. Washington, DC: Smithsonian Institution Press.

Meyer, C., C. Lohr, D. Gronenborn, and K. W. Alt. 2015. The massacre mass grave of Schöneck-Kilianstädten reveals new insights into collective violence in Early Neolithic Central Europe. *Proceedings of the National Academy of Sciences USA* 112: 11217–11222.

Meyer, M., J.-L. Arsuaga, C. de Filippo, S. Nagel, A. Aximu-Petri, B. Nickel, I. Martínez, A. Gracia, J. M. Bermúdez de Castro, E. Carbonell, B. Viola, J. Kelso, K. Prüfer, and S. Pääbo. 2016. Nuclear DNA sequences from the Middle Pleistocene Sima de los Huesos hominins. *Nature* 531: 504–507.

Mielke, J. H., L. W. Konigsberg, and J. H. Relethford. 2011. *Human Biological Variation*, 2nd ed. New York: Oxford University Press.

Miller, E. R., G. F. Gunnell, and R. D. Martin. 2005. Deep time and the search for anthropoid origins. *Yearbook of Physical Anthropology* 48: 60–95.

Minugh-Purvis, N. 2002. Neandertal growth: Examining developmental adaptations in earlier *Homo sapiens*. Pp. 154–173 in P. N. Peregrine, C. R. Ember, and M. Ember, eds. *Physical Anthropology: Original Readings in Method and Practice*. Upper Saddle River, NJ: Prentice Hall.

Mitani, J. C., J. Call, P. Kappeler, R. Palombit, and J. Silk, eds. 2012. *The Evolution of Primate Societies*. Chicago: University of Chicago Press.

Mittermeier, R. A. 2000. Foreword. Pp. xv– xxiii in P. Tyson, ed. *The Eighth Continent: Life, Death, and Discovery in the Lost World of Madagascar*. New York: HarperCollins Publishers.

Moffat, A. S. 2002. New fossils and a glimpse of evolution. *Science* 295: 613–615.

Molleson, T. 1994. The eloquent bones of Abu Hureya. *Scientific American* 271(2): 70–75.

Montagu, A. 1964. Natural selection and man's relative hairlessness. *Journal of the American Medical Association* 187: 356–357.

Monteiro, C. A., E. C. Moura, W. L. Conde, and B. M. Popkin. 2004. Socioeconomic status and obesity in adult populations of developing countries: A review. *Bulletin of the World Health Organization* 82: 940–946.

Moore, J. A. 1999. *Science as a Way of Knowing: The Foundations of Modern Biology*. Cambridge, MA: Harvard University Press.

Moorehead, A. 1969. *Darwin and the Beagle*. New York: Penguin Books.

Morris, C. D. 2015. Where it hurts: 2014 year in review. *American Anthropologist* 117: 540–552.

Morris, L. N. 1971. *Human Populations, Genetic Variation, and Evolution*. San Francisco: Chandler.

Morris, L. N. 1971. Overview. Pp. 409–426 in L. N. Morris, ed. *Human Populations, Genetic Variation, and Evolution*. San Francisco: Chandler.

Morwood, M., T. Sutikna, and R. Roberts. 2005. The people time forgot: Flores find. *National Geographic Research* 207(4): 4–12.

Mote, P. W. and G. Kaser. 2007. The shrinking glaciers of Kilimanjaro: Can global warming be blamed? *American Scientist* 95: 318–325.

Motulsky, A. G. 1961. Glucose-6-phosphate dehydrogenase deficiency, haemolytic disease of the newborn, and malaria. *Lancet* 1: 1168–1169.

Moura, A. C. A. and P. C. Lee. 2004. Capuchin stone tool use in Caatinga dry forest. *Science* 306: 1909.

Mowry, C. B., C. McCann, R. Lessnau, and E. Dierenfeld. 1997. Secondary compounds in foods selected by free-ranging primates on St. Catherines Island, GA. *Proceedings of the Second Conference of the Nutrition Advisory Group, American Zoo and Aquarium Association on Wildlife Nutrition, Fort Worth, Texas*. Unpaginated.

Moya-Soya, S., M. Kohler, and L. Rook. 1999. Evidence of hominid-like precision grip capability in the hand of the Miocene ape *Oreopithecus*. *Proceedings of the National Academy of Sciences USA* 96: 313–317.

Muehlenbein, M. P., ed. 2010. *Human Evolutionary Biology*. Cambridge, UK: Cambridge University Press.

Muehlenbein, M. P., D. P. Watts, and P. Whitten. 2004. Dominance rank and fecal testosterone levels in adult male chimpanzees (*Pan troglodytes schweinfurthii*) at Ngogo, Kibale National Park, Uganda. *American Journal of Primatology* 64: 71–82.

Mukherjee, S. 2017. *The Gene: An Intimate History*. New York: Scribner.

Mukhopadhyay, C. and R. C. Henze. 2003. How real is race? Using anthropology to make sense of human diversity. *Phi Delta Kappan* 84: 669–678.

Mulligan, C. J. 2015. Anthropological genetics: Social and behavioral epigenetics. *American Anthropologist* 117: 738–739.

Mulligan, C. J., A. Kitchen, and M. M. Miyamoto. 2008. Updated three-stage model for the peopling of the Americas. *PLoS One* 3(9): e3199.

Myers, S. S. and J. A. Patz. 2009. Emerging threats to human health from global environmental change. *Annual Review of Environmental Resources* 34: 223–252.

Napier, J. 1993. *Hands*, rev. R. H. Tuttle. Princeton, NJ: Princeton University Press.

Napier, J. R. and P. H. Napier. 1967. *A Handbook of Living Primates: Morphology, Ecology and Behaviour of Nonhuman Primates*. London, UK: Academic Press.

National Academy of Sciences. 1998. *Teaching about Evolution and the Nature of Science*. Washington, DC: National Academies Press. DOI: 10.17226/5787.

National Academy of Sciences. 2019. *Climate Change and Ecosystems*. Washington, DC: National Academies Press. DOI: 10.17226/25504.

Nelson, S. V. 2003. *The Extinction of Sivapithecus: Faunal and Environmental Changes Surrounding the Disappearance of a Miocene Hominoid in the Siwaliks of Pakistan*. Boston: Brill Academic Publishers.

Neufeld, A. H. and G. C. Conroy. 2004. Human head hair is not fur. *Journal of Human Evolution* 13: 89.

Neumann, G., T. Noda, and Y. Kawaoka. 2009. Emergence and pandemic potential of swine-origin H1N1 influenza virus. *Nature* 459: 931–939.

Newman, J. 2006. Allergies: A modern epidemic. *National Geographic* 209(5): 116–135.

Ni, X., D. L. Gebo, M. Dagosto, J. Meng, P. Tafforeau, J. J. Flynn, and K. C. Beard. 2013. The oldest known primate skeleton and early haplorhine evolution. *Nature* 498: 60–64.

Nickels, M. K. 2010. Science education and physical anthropology. Pp. 547–560 in C. S. Larsen, ed. *A Companion to Biological Anthropology*. Chichester, UK: Wiley-Blackwell.

Niewoehner, W. A., A. Bergstrom, D. Eichele, M. Zuroff, and J. T. Clark. 2003. Manual dexterity in Neanderthals. *Nature* 422: 395.

Nitecki, M. H. and D. V. Nitecki. 1994. *Origins of Anatomically Modern Humans*. New York: Plenum Press.

Noonan, J. P., G. Coop, S. Kudaravalli, D. Smith, J. Krause, J. Alessi, F. Chen, D. Platt, S. Pääbo, J. K. Pritchard, and E. M. Rubin. 2006. Sequencing and analysis of Neanderthal genomic DNA. *Science* 314: 1113–1118.

Nordin, M. and V. H. Frankel. 2001. *Basic Biomechanics of the Musculoskeletal System*. Philadelphia: Lippincott Williams & Wilkins.

Novembre, J., A. P. Galvani, and M. Slatkin. 2005. The geographic spread of the CCR5 Delta32 HIV-resistance allele. *PLoS Biology* 3: 1954–1962.

Nowak, R. M. 1999. *Walker's Primates of the World*. Baltimore: Johns Hopkins University Press.

Nowell, A. 2010. Defining behavioral modernity in the context of Neandertal and anatomically modern human populations. *Annual Review of Anthropology* 39: 437–452.

O'Connell, J. F. and J. Allen. 1998. When did humans first arrive in greater Australia and why is it important to know? *Evolutionary Anthropology* 6: 132–146.

Ogden, C. L., C. D. Fryar, M. D. Carroll, and K. M. Flegal. 2004. Mean body weight, height, and body mass index, United States 1960–2002. *Advance Data from Vital and Health Statistics* 337: 1–17.

Olsen, C. L., P. K. Cross, and L. J. Gensburg. 2003. Down syndrome: Interaction between culture, demography, and biology in determining the prevalence of a genetic trait. *Human Biology* 75: 503–520.

Omrak, A., T. Günther, C. Valdiosera, E. M. Svensson, H. Malmström, et al. 2015. Genomic evidence establishes Anatolia as the source of the European Neolithic gene pool. *Current Biology* 26: 270–275.

1000 Genomes Project Consortium. 2015. A global reference for human genetic variation. *Science* 526: 68–74.

Oota, H., W. Settheetham-Ishida, D. Tiwawech, T. Ishida, and M. Stoneking. 2001. Human mtDNA and Y-chromosome variation is correlated with matrilocal versus patrilocal residence. *Nature Genetics* 29: 20–21.

Oppenheim, A., C. L. Jury, D. Rund, T. J. Vulliamy, and L. Luzzatto. 1993. G6PD Mediterranean accounts for the high prevalence of G6PD deficiency in Kurdish Jews. *Human Genetics* 91: 293–294.

O'Roak, B. J., L. Vives, W. Fu, J. D. Egertson, I. B. Stanaway, I. G. Phelps, G. Carville, A. Kumar, C. Lee, K. Ankenman, J. Munson, J. B. Hiatt, E. H. Turner, R. Levy, D. R. O'Day, N. Krumm, B. P. Coe, B. K. Martin, E. Borenstein, D. Nickerson, H. C. Mefford, D. Doherty, M. J. Akey, R. Bernier, E. E. Eichler, and J. Shendure. 2012. Multiplex targeted sequencing identifies recurrently mutated genes in autism spectrum disorders. *Science* 338: 1619–1622.

O'Rourke, D. H. 2010. Human molecular genetics: The DNA revolution and variation. Pp. 88–103 in C. S. Larsen, ed. *A Companion to Biological Anthropology*. Chichester, UK: Wiley-Blackwell.

O'Rourke, D. H., M. G. Hayes, and S. W. Carlyle. 2000. Ancient DNA studies in physical anthropology. *Annual Review of Anthropology* 29: 217–242.

Ouattara, K., A. Lemasson, and K. Zuberbühler. 2009. Campbell's monkeys use affixation to alter call meaning. *PLoS One* 4(11): e7808. DOI: 10.1371/journal.pone.0007808.

Overpeck, J. T. and J. E. Cole. 2006. Abrupt change in Earth's climate system. *Annual Review of Environmental Resources* 31: 1–31.

Owsley, D. W., and R. L. Jantz. 2014. *Kennewick Man: The Scientific Investigation of an Ancient American Skeleton*. College Station: Texas A&M University Press.

Oxenham, M. 2006. Biological responses to change in prehistoric Viet Nam. *Asian Perspectives* 45: 212–239.

Oxenham, M. and N. Tayles, eds. 2006. *Bioarchaeology of Southeast Asia*. Cambridge, UK: Cambridge University Press.

Pakendorf, B., I. N. Novgorodov, V. L. Osakovskij, and M. Stoneking. 2007. Mating patterns amongst Siberian reindeer herders: Inferences from mtDNA and Y-chromosomal analyses. *American Journal of Physical Anthropology* 133: 1013–1027.

Palumbi, S. R. 2001. Humans as the world's greatest evolutionary force. *Science* 293: 1786–1790.

Panger, M. A., A. S. Brooks, B. G. Richmond, and B. Wood. 2002. Older than the Oldowan? Rethinking the emergence of hominin tool use. *Evolutionary Anthropology* 11: 235–245.

Papathanasiou, A. 2001. *A Bioarchaeological Analysis of Neolithic Alepotrypa Cave, Greece*. British Archaeological Reports Series 961. Oxford, England: Archaeopress.

Parish, A. R., and F. B. de Waal. 2006. The other "closest living relative": How bonobos (*Pan paniscus*) challenge traditional assumptions about females, dominance, intra- and intersexual interactions, and hominid evolution. *Annals of the New York Academy of Sciences* 907: 97–113.

Parker, I. 2007. Swingers. *New Yorker* 83(21): 49–61.

Parmesan, C. 2006. Ecological and evolutionary responses to recent climate change. *Annual Review of Ecology, Evolution and Systematics* 37: 637–669.

Partridge, T. C., D. E. Granger, M. W. Caffee, and R. L. Clarke. 2003. Lower Pliocene hominid remains from Sterkfontein. *Science* 300: 607–612.

Patterson, K. D. 2000. Lactose intolerance. Pp. 1057–1062 in K. F. Kiple and K. C. Ornelas, eds. *The Cambridge World History of Food*. New York: Cambridge University Press.

Patz, J. A., D. Campbell-Lendrum, T. Holloway, and J. A. Foley. 2005. Impact of regional climate change on human health. *Nature* 438: 310–317.

Patz, J. A., M. Hulme, C. Rosenzweig, T. D. Mitchell, R. A. Goldberg, A. K. Githeko, S. Lele, A. J. McMichael, and D. Le Seuer. 2002. Regional warming and malaria resurgence. *Nature* 99: 12506–12508.

Penkman, K. E. H., R. C. Preece, D. R. Bridgland, D. H. Keen, T. Meijer, S. A. Parfitt, T. S. White, and M. J. Collins. 2011. A chronological framework for the British Quaternary based on *Bithynia* opercula. *Nature* 476: 446–449.

Pennisi, E. 2006. The dawn of stone age genomics. *Science* 314: 1068–1071.

Pennisi, E. 2009. Tales of a prehistoric human genome. *Science* 323: 866–871.

Pennisi, E. 2013. More genomes from Denisova Cave show mixing of early human groups. *Science* 340: 799.

Perry, S. E. 2006. What cultural primatology can tell anthropologists about the evolution of culture. *Annual Review of Anthropology* 35: 171–190.

Peters, J. 1999. Urbanism and health in industrialised Asia. Pp. 158–172 in L. M. Schell and S. J. Ulijaszek, eds. *Urbanism, Health and Human Biology in Industrialised Countries*. Cambridge, UK: Cambridge University Press.

Peterson, D. 2006. *Jane Goodall: The Woman Who Redefined Man*. New York: Houghton Mifflin.

Peterson, J. 2002. *Sexual Revolutions: Gender and Labor at the Dawn of Agriculture*. Walnut Creek, CA: Altamira.

Peyrégne, S., V. Slon, F. Mafessoni, C. de Filippo, M. Hajdinjak, et al. 2019. Nuclear DNA from two early Neandertals reveals 80,000 years of genetic continuity in Europe. *Science Advances* 5: eaaw5873.

Pickford, M. and B. Senut. 2001. The geological and faunal context of late Miocene hominid remains from Lukeino, Kenya. *Comptes Rendus* 332: 145–152.

Pietrusewsky, M. 2006. The initial settlement of remote Oceania: The evidence from physical anthropology. Pp. 320–347 in T. Simanjuntak, I. H. E. Pojoh, and M. Hisyam, eds. *Austronesian Diaspora and the Ethnogenesis of People in Indonesian Archipelago*. Jakarta, Indonesia: Indonesian Institute of Sciences, LIPI Press.

Pietrusewsky, M. and M. T. Douglas. 2002. *Ban Chiang: A Prehistoric Village Site in Northeast Thailand*. Vol. 1: *The Human Skeletal Remains*. Philadelphia: University of Pennsylvania Press.

Pilbeam, D. R. 1982. New hominoid skull material from the Miocene of Pakistan. *Nature* 295: 232–234.

Pilbeam, D. R. 1996. Genetic and morphological records of the hominoidea and hominid origins: A synthesis. *Molecular Phylogenetics and Evolution* 5: 155–168.

Pilbeam, D. R. 2002. Perspectives on the Miocene Hominoidea. Pp. 303–310 in W. C. Hartwig, ed. *The Primate Fossil Record*. Cambridge, UK: Cambridge University Press.

Pinhasi, R., and J. T. Stock, eds. 2011. *Human Bioarchaeology of the Transition to Agriculture*. Chichester, UK: Wiley-Blackwell.

Pionnier-Capitan, M., C. Bemilli, P. Bodu, G. Célérier, J.-G. Ferrié, P. Fosse, M. Garcià, and J.-D. Vigne. 2011. New evidence for Upper Palaeolithic small domestic dogs in South-Western Europe. *Journal of Archaeological Science* 38: 2123–2140.

Piperata, B. A. 2007. Nutritional status of Ribeirinhos in Brazil and the nutritional transition. *American Journal of Physical Anthropology* 133: 868–878.

Piperno, D. R., A. U. Ranere, I. Holst, J. Iriarte, and R. Dickau. 2009. Starch grain and phytolith evidence for early ninth millennium B.P. maize from the Central Balsas River Valley, Mexico. *Proceedings of the National Academy of Sciences USA* 106: 5019–5024.

Plummer, T. 2004. Flaked stones and old bones: Biological and cultural evolution at the dawn of technology. *Yearbook of Physical Anthropology* 47: 118–164.

Pollan, M. 2003. The (agri)cultural contradictions of obesity. *New York Times Magazine* October 12: 41–48.

Pollitzer, W. S. 1958. The Negroes of Charleston; a study of hemoglobin types, serology, and morphology. *American Journal of Physical Anthropology* 16: 241–263.

Pollitzer, W. S. 1999. *The Gullah People and Their African Heritage*. Athens: University of Georgia Press.

Ponce de León, M. S., L. Golovanova, V. Doronichev, G. Romanova, T. Akazawa, O. Kondo, H. Ishida, and P. E. Zollikofer. 2008. Neanderthal brain size at birth provides insights into the evolution of human life history. *Proceedings of the National Academy of Sciences USA* 105: 13764–13768.

Pond, W. G., B. L. Nichols, and D. L. Brown. 2009. *Adequate Nutrition for All: Culture, Science, and Technology of Food in the 21st Century*. Boca Raton, FL: CRC Press.

Popkin, B. M. 1998. The nutrition transition and its health implications in lower-income countries. *Public Health Nutrition* 1: 5–21.

Popkin, B. M. 2004. The nutrition transition: An overview of world patterns of change. *Nutrition Reviews* 62: S140–S143.

Popkin, B. M. 2019. Rural areas drive the global weight gain. *Nature* 569: 200–201.

Porter, L. M. and P. A. Garber. 2004. The Goeldi's monkey: A primate paradox? *Evolutionary Anthropology* 13: 104–115.

Porter, L. M., S. M. Sterr, and P. A. Garber. 2007. Habitat use and ranging behavior of *Callimico goeldii*. *International Journal of Primatology* 28: 1035–1058.

Portugal, F. H. and J. S. Cohen. 1977. *A Century of DNA: A History of the Discovery of the Structure and Function of the Genetic Substance*. Cambridge, MA: MIT Press.

Powell, J. F. 2005. *The First Americans: Race, Evolution, and the Origin of Native Americans*. Cambridge, UK: Cambridge University Press.

Prabhakar, S., J. P. Noonan, S. Pääbo, and E. M. Rubin. 2006. Accelerated evolution of conserved noncoding sequences in humans. *Science* 314: 786.

Premack, D. 2007. Human and animal cognition: Continuity and discontinuity. *Proceedings of the National Academy of Sciences USA* 104: 13861–13867.

Price, P. W. 1996. *Biological Evolution*. Fort Worth, TX: Saunders.

Price, T. D. 2009. Ancient farming in eastern North America. *Proceedings of the National Academy of Sciences USA* 106: 6427–6428.

Proffit, W. R. 1998. Prevalence of malocclusion and orthodontic treatment need in the United States: Estimates from the NHANES III survey. *International Journal of Adult Orthodontics* 13: 97–106.

Proffit, W. R., H. W. Fields, and D. Sarver. 2013. *Contemporary Orthodontics*, 5th ed. St. Louis: Elsevier Mosby.

Pruetz, J. D. and P. Bertolani. 2007. Savannah chimpanzees, *Pan troglodytes verus*, hunt with tools. *Current Biology* 17: 412–417.

Pushkina, D. and P. Raia. 2007. Human influence on distribution and extinctions of the late Pleistocene Eurasian megafauna. *Journal of Human Evolution* 54: 769–782.

Quammen, D. 2006. *The Reluctant Mr. Darwin: An Intimate Portrait of Charles Darwin and the Making of His Theory of Evolution*. New York: Norton.

Quammen, D. 2007. Deadly contact: How animals and humans exchange disease. *National Geographic* 212(4): 79–105.

Raghaven, M., M. Steinrücken, K. Harris, S. Schiffels, S. Rasmussen, et al. 2015. Genomic evidence for the Pleistocene and recent population history of Native Americans. *Science* 349: aab3884. DOI: 10.1126/science.aab3884.

Rankin-Hill, L. M. 1997. *A Biohistory of 19th-Century Afro-Americans: The Burial Remains of a Philadelphia Cemetery.* Westport, CT: Bergin & Garvey.

Rasmussen, D. T. 2002. Early catarrhines of the African Eocene and Oligocene. Pp. 203–220 in W. C. Hartwig, ed. *The Primate Fossil Record.* Cambridge, UK: Cambridge University Press.

Rasmussen, D. T. 2002. The origin of primates. Pp. 5–9 in W. C. Hartwig, ed. *The Primate Fossil Record.* Cambridge, UK: Cambridge University Press.

Rasmussen, M., S. L. Anzick, M. R. Waters, P. Skoglund, M. DeGiorgio, et al. 2014. The genome of a late Pleistocene human from a Clovis burial site in western Montana. *Nature* 506: 225–229.

Rasmussen, M., X. Guo, Y. Wang, K. E. Lohmueller, S. Rasmussen, et al. 2011. An Aboriginal Australian genome reveals separate human dispersals into Asia. *Science* 334: 94–98.

Rasmussen, M., M. Sikora, A. Albrechtsen, T. S. Korneliussen, J. V. Moreno-Mayer, et al. 2015. The ancestry and affiliations of Kennewick Man. *Nature* 523: 455–458.

Reich, D., N. Patterson, D. Campbell, A. Tandon, S. Mazieres, et al. 2012. Reconstructing Native American population history. *Nature* 488: 370–374.

Reilly, P. R. 2006. *The Strongest Boy in the World: How Genetic Information Is Reshaping Our Lives.* Cold Spring Harbor, NY: Cold Spring Harbor Laboratory Press.

Relethford, J. H. 1995. Genetics and modern human origins. *Evolutionary Anthropology* 4: 53–63.

Relethford, J. H. 1997. Hemispheric difference in human skin color. *American Journal of Physical Anthropology* 104: 449–457.

Relethford, J. H. 1998. Genetics of modern human origins and diversity. *Annual Review of Anthropology* 27: 1–23.

Relethford, J. H. 2001. Absence of regional affinities of Neandertal DNA with living humans does not reject multiregional evolution. *American Journal of Physical Anthropology* 115: 95–98.

Relethford, J. H. 2001. *Genetics and the Search for Modern Human Origins.* New York: Wiley-Liss.

Relethford, J. H. 2002. Apportionment of global human genetic diversity based on craniometrics and skin color. *American Journal of Physical Anthropology* 118: 393–398.

Relethford, J. H. 2004. Global patterns of isolation by distance based on genetic and morphological data. *Human Biology* 76: 499–513.

Relethford, J. H. 2007. Population genetics and paleoanthropology. Pp. 621–641 in

W. Henke and I. Tattersall, eds. *Handbook of Paleoanthropology.* Vol. 1: *Principles, Methods and Approaches.* Berlin, Germany: Springer.

Relethford, J. H. 2009. Race and global patterns of phenotypic variation. *American Journal of Physical Anthropology* 139: 16–22.

Relethford, J. 2010. The study of human population genetics. Pp. 74–87 in C. S. Larsen, ed. *A Companion to Biological Anthropology.* Chichester, UK: Wiley-Blackwell.

Relethford, J. H. 2012. *Human Population Genetics.* Hoboken, NJ: Wiley-Blackwell.

Relethford, J. H. 2017. *50 Great Myths of Human Evolution: Understanding Misconceptions about Our Origins.* Chichester, UK: Wiley-Blackwell.

Relethford, J. H. and D. A. Bolnick. 2018. *Reflections of Our Past: How Human History Is Revealed in Our Genes,* 2nd ed. New York, NY: Routledge.

Remis, M. J. 2000. Preliminary assessments of the impacts of human activities on gorillas (*Gorilla gorilla gorilla*) and other wildlife at Dzanga-Sangha Reserve, Central African Republic. *Oryx* 34: 56–64.

Remis, M. J. 2001. Nutritional aspects of western lowland gorilla diet during seasonal fruit scarcity at Bai Hokou, Central African Republic. *International Journal of Primatology* 22: 807–835.

Renfrew, C. and K. Boyle. 2000. *Archaeogenetics: DNA and the Population Prehistory of Europe.* Cambridge, UK: McDonald Institute Monographs.

Reno, P. L., R. S. Meindl, M. A. McCollum, and C. O. Lovejoy. 2003. Sexual dimorphism in *Australopithecus afarensis* was similar to that of modern humans. *Proceedings of the National Academy of Sciences USA* 100: 9404–9409.

Repcheck, J. 2003. *The Man Who Found Time: James Hutton and the Discovery of the Earth's Antiquity.* Cambridge, MA: Perseus Publishing.

Reynolds, V. 2005. *The Chimpanzees of the Budongo Forest: Ecology, Behavior, and Conservation.* New York: Oxford University Press.

Richard, A. F. 1985. *Primates in Nature.* New York: W. H. Freeman.

Richards, G. D. 2006. Genetic, physiologic and ecogeographic factors to variation in *Homo sapiens: Homo floresiensis* reconsidered. *Journal of Evolutionary Biology* 19: 1744–1767.

Richards, M. 2003. The Neolithic invasion of Europe. *Annual Review of Anthropology* 32: 135–162.

Richards, M. P., R. Jacobi, J. Cook, P. B. Pettitt, and C. B. Stringer. 2005. Isotope evidence for the intensive use of marine foods by late upper Paleolithic humans. *Journal of Human Evolution* 49: 390–394.

Richards, M., P. Pettitt, E. Trinkaus, F. Smith, M. Paunovic, and I. Karavanic. 2000. Neanderthal diet and Vindija and Neanderthal predation: The evidence from stable isotopes. *Proceedings of the National Academy of Sciences USA* 97: 7663–7666.

Richards, M. P. and E. Trinkaus. 2009. Isotopic evidence for the diets of European Neanderthals and early modern humans. *Proceedings of the National Academy of Sciences USA* 106: 16034–16039.

Richmond, B. G. 2007. Biomechanics of phalangeal curvature. *Journal of Human Evolution* 53: 678–690.

Richmond, B. G., D. R. Begun, and D. S. Strait. 2001. Origin of human bipedalism: The knuckle-walking hypothesis revisited. *Yearbook of Physical Anthropology* 44: 70–105.

Richmond, B. G. and W. L. Jungers. 2008. *Orronin tugenensis* femoral morphology and the evolution of hominin bipedalism. *Science* 319: 1662–1665.

Ridley, M. 2004. *Evolution,* 3rd ed. Malden, MA: Blackwell Science.

Ridley, M. 2006. *Francis Crick: Discoverer of the Genetic Code.* New York: HarperCollins.

Riehl, S., M. Zeidi, and N. J. Conard. 2013. Emergence of agriculture in the foothills of the Zagros Mountains of Iran. *Science* 341: 65–67.

Rightmire, G. P. 1990. *The Evolution of* Homo erectus. Cambridge, UK: Cambridge University Press.

Rightmire, G. P. 1998. Human evolution in the middle Pleistocene: The role of *Homo heidelbergensis. Evolutionary Anthropology* 6: 218–227.

Rightmire, G. P. 2009. Middle and later Pleistocene hominins in Africa and southwest Asia. *Proceedings of the National Academy of Sciences USA* 106: 16046–16050.

Rightmire, G. P. 2010. Origins, evolution, and dispersal of early members of the genus *Homo.* Pp. 341–356 in C. S. Larsen, ed. *A Companion to Biological Anthropology.* Chichester, UK: Wiley-Blackwell.

Riley, E. P. 2007. The human-macaque interface: Conservation implications of current and future overlap and conflict in Lore Lindu National Park, Sulawesi, Indonesia. *American Anthropologist* 109: 473–484.

Riley, E. P., and A. Fuentes. 2011. Conserving social-ecological systems in Indonesia: Human-nonhuman primate interconnections in Bali and Sulawesi. *American Journal of Primatology* 73: 62–74.

Robbins, A. M., M. M. Robbins, N. Gerald-Steklis, and H. D. Steklis. 2006. Age-related patterns of reproductive success among female mountain gorillas. *American Journal of Physical Anthropology* 131: 511–521.

Robbins, L. H. 1974. *The Lothagam Site: A Late Stone Age Fishing Settlement in the Lake Rudolph Basin, Kenya.* Publications of the Museum, Michigan State University, Anthropological Series 1(2). East Lansing: Michigan State University.

Roberts, M. B., C. B. Stringer, and S. A. Parfitt. 1994. A hominid tibia from middle Pleistocene sediments at Boxgrove, UK. *Nature* 369: 311–313.

Roberts, R. G. and M. I. Bird. 2012. *Homo* "incendius." *Nature* 485: 586–587.

Rodman, P. S. 1999. Whither primatology? The place of primates in contemporary anthropology. *Annual Review of Anthropology* 28: 311–339.

Roebroeks, W., M. J. Sier, T. Kellberg Nielsen, D. De Loecker, J. M. Parés, C. E. S. Arps, and H. J. Mucher. 2012. Use of red ochre by early Neandertals. *Proceedings of the National Academy of Sciences USA* 109: 1889–1894.

Roff, D. A. 1992. *The Evolution of Life Histories: Theory and Analysis.* New York: Chapman and Hall.

Rogers, A. R., R. J. Bohlender, and C. D. Huff. 2017. Early history of Neanderthals and Denisovans. *Proceedings of the National Academy of Sciences USA* 114: 9859–9863. DOI: 10.1073/pnas.1706426114.

Rolland, N. 2004. Was the emergence of home bases and domestic fire a punctuated event? A review of the middle Pleistocene record in Eurasia. *Asian Perspectives* 43: 248–280.

Rosas, A., C. Martínez-Maza, M. Bastir, A. García-Tabernero, C. Lalueza-Fox, R. Huguet, J. E. Ortiz, R. Julià, V. Soler, T. de Torres, E. Martínez, J. C. Cañaveras, S. Sánchez-Moral, S. Cuezva, J. Lario, D. Santamaría, M. de la Rasilla, and J. Fortea. 2006. Paleobiology and comparative morphology of a late Neandertal sample from El Sidrón, Asturias, Spain. *Proceedings of the National Academy of Sciences USA* 103: 19266–19271.

Rose, K. D. 1994. The earliest primates. *Evolutionary Anthropology* 3: 159–173.

Rose, K. D. 2006. *The Beginning of the Age of Mammals.* Baltimore: Johns Hopkins University Press.

Roseman, C. C. 2004. Detecting interregionally diversifying natural selection on modern human cranial form using matched molecular and morphometric data. *Proceedings of the National Academy of Sciences USA* 101: 12824–12829.

Rosenberg, K. and W. Trevathan. 2002. Birth, obstetrics and human evolution. *British Journal of Obstetrics and Gynaecology* 109: 1199–1206.

Rosenberg, K. R. 1992. The evolution of modern human childbirth. *Yearbook of Physical Anthropology* 35: 89–124.

Rosenberg, K. R. and W. Trevathan. 2003. The evolution of human birth. *Scientific American* 13(2): 81–85.

Rosenzweig, C., D. Karoly, M. Vicarelli, P. Neofotis, Q. Wu, G. Casassa, A. Menzel, T. Root, N. Estrella, B. Seguin, P. Tryjanowski, C. Liu, S. Rawlins, and A. Imeson. 2008. Attributing physical and biological impacts to anthropogenic climate change. *Nature* 453: 353–358.

Ross, C. F. 2000. Into the light: The origin of anthropoidea. *Annual Review of Anthropology* 29: 147–194.

Ross, C. F. and R. F. Kay, eds. 2004. *Anthropoid Origins: New Visions.* New York: Kluwer Academic/Plenum.

Rossie, J. B., X. Ni, and K. C. Beard. 2006. Cranial remains of an Eocene tarsier. *Proceedings of the National Academy of Sciences USA* 103: 4381–4385.

Rougier, H., I. Crevecoeur, C. Beauval, C. Posth, D. Flas, et al. 2016. Neandertal cannibalism and Neandertal bones used as tools in northern Europe. *Scientific Reports* 6: 29005. DOI: 10.1038/srep29005.

Rougier, H., S. Milota, R. Rodrigo, M. Gherase, L. Sarcină, O. Moldovan, J. Zilhão, S. Constantin, R. G. Franciscus, C. P. E. Zolliker, M. Ponce de León, and E. Trinkaus. 2007. Peştera cu Oase 2 and the cranial morphology of early modern Europeans. *Proceedings of the National Academy of Sciences USA* 104: 1165–1170.

Rowe, N. 1996. *The Pictorial Guide to the Living Primates.* Charlestown, RI: Pogonias.

Roy, S. R., A. M. Schiltz, A. Marotta, Y. Shen, and A. H. Liu. 2003. Bacterial DNA in house and farm barn dust. *Journal of Allergy Clinical Immunology* 112: 571–578.

Rubin, G. M. 2001. Comparing species. *Nature* 409: 820–821.

Rudwick, M. J. S. 1997. *Georges Cuvier, Fossil Bones, and Geological Catastrophes: New Translations and Interpretations of the Primary Texts.* Chicago: University of Chicago Press.

Rudwick, M. J. S. 2005. *Bursting the Limits of Time: The Reconstruction of Geohistory in the Age of Revolution.* Chicago: University of Chicago Press.

Ruff, C. B. 1991. Climate and body shape in hominid evolution. *Journal of Human Evolution* 21: 81–105.

Ruff, C. B. 1993. Climatic adaptation and hominid evolution: The thermoregulatory imperative. *Evolutionary Anthropology* 2: 53–60.

Ruff, C. B. 1994. Morphological adaptation to climate in modern and fossil hominids.

Yearbook of Physical Anthropology 37: 65–107.

Ruff, C. B. 2002. Variation in human body size and shape. *Annual Review of Anthropology* 31: 211–232.

Ruff, C. B. 2005. Mechanical determinants of bone form: Insights from skeletal remains. *Journal of Musculoskeletal and Neuronal Interactions* 5: 202–212.

Ruff, C. B. 2006. Gracilization of the modern human skeleton. *American Scientist* 94: 508–514.

Ruff, C. B. 2019. Biomechanical analyses of archaeological human skeletons. Pp. 189–224 in M. A. Katzenberg and A. L. Grauer, eds. *Biological Anthropology of the Human Skeleton,* 3rd ed. Hoboken, NJ: John Wiley & Sons.

Ruff, C. B. and M. L. Burgess. 2015. How much more would KNM-WT 15000 have grown? *Journal of Human Evolution* 80: 74–82.

Ruiz-Pesini, E., D. Mishmar, M. Brandon, V. Procaccio, and D. C. Wallace. 2004. Effects of purifying and adaptive selection on regional variation in human mtDNA. *Science* 303: 223–226.

Ryan, T. M. and C. N. Shaw. 2015. Gracility of the modern *Homo sapiens* skeleton is the result of decreased mechanical loading. *Proceedings of the National Academy of Sciences USA* 112: 372–377.

Sabeti, P. C., S. F. Schaffner, B. Fry, J. Lohmueller, P. Varilly, O. Shamovsky, A. Palma, T. S. Mikkelsen, D. Altshuler, and E. S. Lander. 2006. Positive natural selection in the human lineage. *Science* 312: 1614–1620.

Samson, M., F. Libert, B. J. Doranz, J. Rucker, C. Liesnand, et al. 1996. Resistance to HIV-1 infection in Caucasian individuals bearing mutant alleles of the CCR-5 chemokine receptor gene. *Nature* 382: 722–725.

Sandgathe, D. M. 2017. Identifying and describing pattern and process in the evolution of hominin use of fire. *Current Anthropology* 58(suppl. 16): S360–S370.

Sankararaman, S., S. Mallick, M. Dannemann, K. Prüfer, J. Kelso, S. Pääbo, N. Patterson, and D. Reich. 2014. The genomic landscape of Neanderthal ancestry in present-day humans. *Nature* 507: 354–357.

Santé-Lhoutellier, V., T. Astruc, P. Marinova, E. Greve, and P. Gatellier. 2008. Effect of meat cooking on physicochemical state and in vitro digestibility of myofibrillar proteins. *Journal of Agricultural Food Chemistry* 56: 1488–1494.

Sapolsky, R. M. 2004. Of mice, men, and genes. *Natural History* 113(May): 21–24, 31.

Sapolsky, R. M. 2004. Social status and health in humans and other animals. *Annual Review of Anthropology* 33: 393–418.

Sapolsky, R. M. 2005. The influence of social hierarchy on primate health. *Science* 308: 648–652.

Sapolsky, R. M. 2006. Social cultures among nonhuman primates. *Current Anthropology* 47: 641–656.

Sardi, M. L., P. S. Novellino, and H. M. Pucciarelli. 2006. Craniofacial morphology in the Argentine Center-West: Consequences of the transition to food production. *American Journal of Physical Anthropology* 130: 333–343.

Sattenspiel, L. and D. A. Herring. 2010. Emerging themes in anthropology and epidemiology: Geographic spread, evolving pathogens, and syndemics. Pp. 167–178 in C. S. Larsen, ed. *A Companion to Biological Anthropology*. Chichester, UK: Wiley-Blackwell.

Saunders, M. A., M. F. Hammer, and M. W. Nachman. 2002. Nucleotide variability in *G6pd* and the signature of malarial selection in humans. *Genetics* 162: 1849–1861.

Savolainen, P., Y. Zhang, J. Luo, J. Lundeberg, and T. Leitner. 2002. Genetic evidence for an East Asian origin of domestic dog. *Science* 298: 1610–1613.

Scheinfeldt, L. B., S. Soi, and S. A. Tishkoff. 2010. Working toward a synthesis of archaeological, linguistic, and genetic data for inferring African population history. *Proceedings of the National Academy of Sciences USA* 107(suppl. 2): 8931–8938.

Schmitz, R. W. 1997. Neandertal (Feldhofer Grotte). Pp. 710–711 in F. Spencer, ed. *History of Physical Anthropology: An Encyclopedia*. New York: Garland.

Schmitz, R. W., D. Serre, G. Bonani, S. Feine, F. Hillgruber, H. Krainitzki, S. Pääbo, and F. H. Smith. 2002. The Neandertal type site revisited: Interdisciplinary investigations of skeletal remains from the Neander Valley, Germany. *Proceedings of the National Academy of Sciences USA* 99: 13342–13347.

Schoenemann, P. T. 2006. Evolution of the size and functional areas of the human brain. *Annual Review of Anthropology* 35: 379–406.

Schoeninger, M. J. 2010. Diet reconstruction and ecology using stable isotope ratios. Pp. 445–464 in C. S. Larsen, ed. *A Companion to Biological Anthropology*. Chichester, UK: Wiley-Blackwell.

Schroeder, L., J. E. Scott, H. M. Garvin, M. F. Laird, M. Dembo, D. Radovčić, L. R. Berger, D. J. de Ruiter, and R. R. Ackermann. 2017. Skull diversity in the *Homo* lineage and the relative position of *Homo naledi*. *Journal of Human Evolution* 104: 124–135. DOI: 10.1016/j.jhevol.2016.09.014.

Schultz, A. H. 1969. *The Life of Primates*. New York: Universe.

Schurr, T. G. 2000. Mitochondrial DNA and the peopling of the New World. *American Scientist* 88: 246–253.

Schurr, T. G. 2004. The peopling of the New World. *Annual Review of Anthropology* 33: 551–583.

Schurr, T. G. and S. T. Sherry. 2004. Mitochondrial DNA and Y chromosome diversity and the peopling of the Americas: Evolutionary and demographic evidence. *American Journal of Human Biology* 16: 420–439.

Schwartz, J. H. 1999. *Sudden Origins: Fossils, Genes, and the Emergence of Species*. New York: Wiley.

Schwartz, J. H. and I. Tattersall. 2000. The human chin revisited: What is it and who has it? *Journal of Human Evolution* 38: 367–409.

Schwartz, J. H. and I. Tattersall. 2002. *The Human Fossil Record*. Vol. 1: *Terminology and Craniodental Morphology of Genus* Homo *(Europe)*. New York: Wiley-Liss.

Schwartz, J. H. and I. Tattersall. 2003. *The Human Fossil Record*. Vol. 2: *Craniodental Morphology of Genus* Homo *(Africa and Asia)*. New York: Wiley-Liss.

Schwartz, J. H. and I. Tattersall. 2005. *The Human Fossil Record*. Vol. 4: *Craniodental Morphology of Early Hominids (Genera* Australopithecus, Paranthropus, Orrorin*) and Overview*. Hoboken, NJ: Wiley-Liss.

Scott, E. C. 2004. *Evolution vs. Creationism: An Introduction*. Westport, CT: Greenwood Press.

Scott, G. R. and C. G. Turner II. 1997. *The Anthropology of Modern Human Teeth: Dental Morphology and Its Variation in Recent Human Populations*. Cambridge, UK: Cambridge University Press.

Scrimshaw, N. S. and E. B. Murray. 1988. The acceptability of milk and milk products in populations with a high prevalence of lactose intolerance. *American Journal of Clinical Nutrition* 48(suppl.): 1083–1159.

Seager, R., Y. Kushnir, C. Herweijer, and N. Naik. 2005. Modeling of tropical forcing of persistent droughts and pluvials over western North America. *Journal of Climate* 18: 4068–4091.

Segalen, L., J. A. Lee-Thorp, and T. Cerling. 2007. Timing of C_4 grass expansion across sub-Saharan Africa. *Journal of Human Evolution* 53: 549–559.

Seiffert, E. R. 2006. Revised age estimates for the later Paleogene mammal faunas of Egypt and Oman. *Proceedings of the National Academy of Sciences USA* 103: 5000–5005.

Seiffert, E. R. 2012. Early primate evolution in Afro-Arabia. *Evolutionary Anthropology* 21: 239–253.

Seiffert, E. R., E. L. Simons, W. C. Clyde, J. B. Rossie, Y. Attia, T. M. Bown, P. Chatrath, and M. E. Mathison. 2005. Basal anthropoids from Egypt and the antiquity of Africa's higher primate radiation. *Science* 310: 300–304.

Selinus, O. 2005. *Essentials of Medical Geology: Impacts of the Natural Environment on Public Health*. Amsterdam, Netherlands: Elsevier Academic Press.

Semaw, S. 2000. The world's oldest stone artefacts from Gona, Ethiopia: Their implications for understanding stone technology and patterns of human evolution between 2.6–1.5 million years ago. *Journal of Archaeological Science* 27: 1197–1214.

Semaw, S., P. Renne, J. W. K. Harris, C. S. Feibel, R. L. Bernor, N. Fesseha, and K. Mowbray. 1997. 2.5-Million-year-old stone tools from Gona, Ethiopia. *Nature* 385: 333–336.

Semaw, S., M. J. Rogers, S. W. Simpson, N. E. Levin, J. Quade, et al. 2020. Co-occurrence of Acheulian and Oldowan artifacts with *Homo erectus* cranial fossils from Gona, Afar, Ethiopia. *Science Advances* 6: eaaw4694.

Semino, O., G. Passarino, P. J. Oefner, A. A. Lin, S. Arbuzova, L. E. Beckman, G. De Benedictis, P. Francalacci, A. Kouvatsi, S. Limborska, M. Marcikiae, A. Mika, B. Mika, D. Primorac, A. S. Santachiara-Benerecetti, L. L. Cavalli-Sforza, and P. A. Underhill. 2000. The genetic legacy of Paleolithic *Homo sapiens sapiens* in extant Europeans: A Y chromosome perspective. *Science* 290: 1155–1159.

Senut, B., M. Pickford, D. Gommery, P. Mein, K. Cheboi, and Y. Coppens. 2001. First hominid from the Miocene (Lukeino Formation, Kenya). *Comptes Rendus de l'Académie des Sciences—Series IIA—Earth and Planetary Science* 332: 137–144.

Sereno, P. C., E. Garcea, H. Jousse, C. M. Stojanowski, J.-F. Saliège, A. Maga, O. A. Ide, J. K. Knudson, A. M. Mercuri, T. W. Stafford, T. G. Kaye, C. Giraudi, I. M. N'siala, E. Cocca, H. M. Moots, D. B. Dutheil, and J. P. Stivers. 2008. Lakeside cemeteries in the Sahara: 5,000 years of Holocene population and environmental change. *PLoS One* 3(8): e2995. DOI: 10.1371/journal.pone.0002995.

Serre, D., A. Langaney, M. Chech, M. Teschler-Nicola, M. Paunovic, P. Mennecier, M. Hofreiter, G. Possnert, and S. Pääbo. 2004. No evidence of Neandertal mtDNA contribution to early modern humans. *PLoS Biology* 2(3): e57. DOI: 10.1371/journal.pbio.0020057.

Shackelford, L. L. 2007. Regional variation in the postcranial robusticity of late upper Paleolithic humans. *American Journal of Physical Anthropology* 133: 655–668.

Shah, S. 2016. *Pandemic: Tracking Contagions, from Cholera to Ebola and Beyond*. New York: Sarah Crichton Books.

Shang, H., H. Tong, S. Zhang, F. Chen, and E. Trinkaus. 2007. An early modern human from Tianyuan Cave, Zhoukoudian, China. *Proceedings of the National Academy of Sciences USA* 104: 6573–6578.

Shapiro, H. L. 1962. *The Pitcairn Islanders.* New York: Simon & Schuster.

Shapiro, H. L. 1974. *Peking Man: The Discovery, Disappearance and Mystery of a Priceless Scientific Treasure.* New York: Simon & Schuster.

Sharpe, T. 2015. The birth of the geological map. *Science* 347: 230–231.

Shea, J. J. 2003. Neandertals, competition, and the origin of modern human behavior in the Levant. *Evolutionary Anthropology* 12: 173–187.

Shea, J. J. 2006. Interdisciplinary approaches to the evolution of hominid diets. *Evolutionary Anthropology* 15: 204–206.

Shen, G., X. Gao, B. Gao, and D. E. Granger. Age of Zhoukoudian *Homo erectus* determined with ^{26}Al/^{10}Be burial dating. *Nature* 458: 198–200.

Shen, G., T.-L. Ku, H. Cheng, R. L. Edwards, Z. Yuan, and Q. Wang. 2001. High-precision U-series dating of Locality 1 at Zhoukoudian, China. *Journal of Human Evolution* 41: 679–688.

Shen, G., W. Wang, Q. Wang, J. Zhao, K. Collerson, C. Zhou, and P. V. Tobias. 2002. U-series dating of Liujiang hominid site in Guangxi, Southern China. *Journal of Human Evolution* 43: 817–830.

Shendure, J. and J. M. Akey. 2015. The origins, determinants, and consequences of human mutations. *Science* 349: 1478–1483.

Shipman, P. 2001. *The Man Who Found the Missing Link.* New York: Simon & Schuster.

Shipman, P. 2002. Hunting the first hominid. *American Scientist* 90: 25–27.

Shipman, P. 2002. *The Evolution of Racism: Human Differences and the Use and Abuse of Science.* Cambridge, MA: Harvard University Press.

Shipman, P. 2003. We are all Africans. *American Scientist* 91: 496–499.

Shirley, N. R., R. J. Wilson, and L. M. Jantz. 2011. Cadaver use at the University of Tennessee's Anthropological Research Facility. *Clinical Anatomy* 24: 372–380.

Sholtis, S. and K. Weiss. 2005. Phenogenetics: Genotypes, phenotypes, and variation. Pp. 499–523 in B. Hallgrimson and B. K. Hall, eds. *Variation: A Central Concept in Biology.* Burlington, MA: Elsevier Academic Press.

Shoshani, J., C. P. Groves, E. L. Simons, and G. F. Gunnell. 1996. Primate phylogeny: Morphological vs. molecular results. *Molecular Phylogenetics and Evolution* 5: 102–154.

Shreeve, J. 1994. Terms of estrangement. *Discover* 15(11): 56–63.

Shreeve, J. 2015. Mystery man. *National Geographic* 228(4): 30–56.

Shriver, M. D., E. J. Parra, S. Dios, C. Bonilla, H. Norton, C. Jovel, C. Pfaff, C. Jones, A. Massac, N. Cameron, A. Baron, T. Jackson, G. Argyropoulos, L. Jin, C. J. Hoggart, P. M. McKeigue, and R. Kittles. 2003. Skin pigmentation, biogeographical ancestry and admixture mapping. *Human Genetics* 112: 387–399.

Shultz, S., R. Noe, W. S. McGraw, and R. I. M. Dunbar. 2004. A community-level evaluation of the impact of prey behavioural and ecological characteristics on predator diet composition. *Proceedings of the Royal Society of London B* 271: 725–732.

Sicherer, S. H., A. Muñoz-Furlong, and H. A. Sampson. 2003. Prevalence of peanut and tree nut allergy in the United States is determined by means of a random digit dial telephone survey: A 5-year follow-up study. *Journal of Allergy Clinical Immunology* 112: 1203–1207.

Sievert, L. L. 2006. *Menopause: A Biocultural Perspective.* Newark, NJ: Rutgers University Press.

Sigmon, B. A. and J. S. Cybulski, eds. 1981. Homo erectus: *Papers in Honor of Davidson Black.* Toronto: University of Toronto Press.

Simons, E. L. 1972. *Primate Evolution: An Introduction to Man's Place in Nature.* New York: Macmillan.

Simons, E. L. 1990. Discovery of the oldest known anthropoidean skull from the Paleogene of Egypt. *Science* 247: 1567–1569.

Simons, E. L. 1995. Skulls and anterior teeth of *Catopithecus* (Primates: Anthropoidea) from the Eocene. *Science* 268: 1885–1888.

Simons, E. L. and P. C. Ettel. 1970. *Gigantopithecus. Scientific American* 222(1): 77–85.

Simons, E. L. and T. Rasmussen. 1994. A whole new world of ancestors: Eocene anthropoideans from Africa. *Evolutionary Anthropology* 3: 128–139.

Simons, E. L., E. R. Seiffert, T. M. Ryan, and Y. Attia. 2007. A remarkable female cranium of the early Oligocene anthropoid *Aegyptopithecus zeuxis* (Catarrhini, Propliopithecidae). *Proceedings of the National Academy of Sciences USA* 104: 8731–8736.

Simpson, G. G. 1944. *Tempo and Mode of Evolution.* New York: Columbia University Press.

Simpson, G. G. 1967. *The Meaning of Evolution.* New Haven, CT: Yale University Press.

Simpson, S. W. 1996. *Australopithecus afarensis* and human evolution. Pp. 3–28 in C. R. Ember, M. Ember, and P. Peregrine, eds. *Research Frontiers in Anthropology.* Needham, MA: Simon & Schuster.

Simpson, S. W. 2002. *Australopithecus afarensis* and human evolution. Pp. 103–123 in P. N. Peregrine, C. R. Ember, and M. Ember, eds. *Physical Anthropology: Original Readings in Method and Practice.* Upper Saddle River, NJ: Prentice Hall.

Simpson, S. W. 2010. The earliest hominins. Pp. 314–340 in C. S. Larsen, ed. *A Companion to Biological Anthropology.* Chichester, UK: Wiley-Blackwell.

Simpson S. W. 2013. Before *Australopithecus*: The earliest hominins. Pp. 417–433 in D. R. Begun, ed. *A Companion to Paleoanthropology.* Chichester, UK: Wiley-Blackwell.

Simpson, S. W., L. Kleinsasser, J. Quade, N. E. Levin, W. C. McIntosh, N. Dunbar, S. Semaw, and M. J. Rogers. 2015. Late Miocene hominin teeth from the Gona Paleoanthropological Research Project. *Journal of Human Evolution* 81: 68–82.

Simpson, S. W., J. Quade, N. E. Levin, R. Butler, G. Dupont-Nivet, M. Everett, and S. Semaw 2008. A female *Homo erectus* pelvis from Gona, Ethiopia. *Science* 322: 1089–1092.

Skinner, M. M., N. B. Stephens, Z. J. Tsegai, A. C. Foote, N. H. Nguyen, et al. 2015. Human-like hand use in *Australopithecus africanus. Science* 347: 395–399.

Skoglund, P. and I. Mathieson. 2018. Ancient genomics of modern humans: The first decade. *Annual Review of Genomics and Human Genetics* 19: 381–404.

Skov, L., M. C. Macià, G. Sveinbjörnsson, F. Mafessoni, E. A. Lucotte, et al. 2020. The nature of Neanderthal introgression revealed by 27,566 Icelandic genomes. *Nature* 582: 78–83.

Slocombe, K. E. and K. Zuberbühler. 2006. Food-associated cells in chimpanzees: Responses to food types or food preferences? *Animal Behaviour* 72: 989–999.

Slon, V., C. Hopfe, C. L. Weiss, F. Mafessoni, M. de la Rasilla, et al. 2017. Neandertal and Denisovan DNA from Pleistocene sediments. *Science* 356: 605–608.

Smail, J. K. 2002. Remembering Malthus: A preliminary argument for a significant reduction in global human numbers. *American Journal of Physical Anthropology* 118: 292–297.

Smith, B. D. 1992. *Rivers of Change: Essays on Early Agriculture in North America.* Washington, DC: Smithsonian Institution Press.

Smith, B. D. 1995. *The Emergence of Agriculture.* New York: Scientific American Library.

Smith, B. D. 2001. Documenting plant domestication: The consilience of biological and archaeological approaches. *Proceedings of the National Academy of Sciences USA* 98: 1324–1326.

Smith, B. D. and M. A. Zeder. 2013. The onset of the Anthropocene. *Anthropocene* 4: 8–13.

Smith, B. H. 1989. Dental development as a measure of life history in primates. *Evolution* 43: 683–688.

Smith, B. H. 1991. Dental development and the evolution of life history in the Hominidae. *American Journal of Physical Anthropology* 86: 157–174.

Smith, B. H. 1993. The physiological age of KNM-WT 15000. Pp. 195–220 in A. Walker and R. Leakey, eds. *The Nariokotome* Homo erectus *Skeleton*. Cambridge, MA: Harvard University Press.

Smith, B. H. 1994. Ages of eruption of primate teeth: A compendium for aging individuals and comparing life histories. *Yearbook of Physical Anthropology* 37: 177–231.

Smith, F., I. Janković, and I. Karavanić. 2005. The assimilation model, modern human origins in Europe, and the extinction of Neandertals. *Quaternary International* 137: 7–19.

Smith, F. H. 2002. Migrations, radiations and continuity: Patterns in the evolution of middle and late Pleistocene humans. Pp. 437–456 in W. C. Hartwig, ed. *The Primate Fossil Record*. Cambridge, UK: Cambridge University Press.

Smith, F. H. 2010. Species, population, and assimilation in later human evolution. Pp. 357–378 in C. S. Larsen, ed. *A Companion to Biological Anthropology*. Chichester, UK: Wiley-Blackwell.

Smith, F. H. 2018. Assimilation model of modern human origins. Pp. 129–131 in W. Trevathan, ed. *International Encyclopedia of Biological Anthropology*. New York: John Wiley & Sons.

Smith, F. H., A. B. Falsetti, and S. M. Donnelly. 1989. Modern human origins. *Yearbook of Physical Anthropology* 32: 35–68.

Smith, G. J. D., D. Vijaykrishna, J. Bahl, S. J. Lycett, M. Worobey, O. G. Pybus, S. K. Ma, C. L. Cheung, J. Raghwani, S. Bhatt, J. S. M. Peiris, Y. Guan, and A. Rambaut. 2009. Origins and evolutionary genomics of the 2009 swine-origin H1N1 influenza A epidemic. *Nature* 459: 1122–1125.

Smith, S. L. 2004. Skeletal age, dental age, and the maturation of KNM-WT 15000. *American Journal of Physical Anthropology* 125: 105–120.

Smith, T. M., A. J. Olejniczak, L. B. Martin, and D. J. Reid. 2005. Variation in hominoid molar enamel thickness. *Journal of Human Evolution* 48: 575–592.

Smith, T. M., A. J. Olejniczak, D. J. Reid, R. J. Ferrell, and J.-J. Hublin. 2006. Modern human molar enamel thickness and enamel-dentine junction shape. *Archives of Oral Biology* 51: 974–995.

Smuts, B. B., D. L. Cheney, R. M. Seyfarth, R. W. Wrangham, and T. T. Struhsaker, eds. 1987. *Primate Societies*. Chicago: University of Chicago Press.

Snodgrass, J. J., M. V. Sorensen, L. A. Tarskaia, and W. R. Leonard. 2007. Adaptive dimensions of health research among indigenous Siberians. *American Journal of Human Biology* 19: 165–180.

Snowdon, C. T. 2017. Learning from monkey talk. *Science* 355: 1120–1122.

Soficaru, A., C. Petrea, A. Doboş, and E. Trinkaus. 2007. The human cranium from the Peştera Cioclovina Uscată, Romania. *Current Anthropology* 48: 611–619.

Spencer, F. 1990. *Piltdown: A Scientific Forgery*. London: Oxford University Press.

Spencer, F., ed. 1997. *History of Physical Anthropology: An Encyclopedia*. New York: Garland.

Spencer, F. 1997. Piltdown. Pp. 821–825 in F. Spencer, ed. *History of Physical Anthropology: An Encyclopedia*. New York: Garland.

Speth, J. D. 2005. News flash: Negative evidence convicts Neanderthals of gross mental incompetence. *World Archaeology* 36: 519–526.

Sponheimer, M., B. H. Passey, D. J. de Ruiter, D. Guatelli-Steinberg, T. E. Cerling, and J. A. Lee-Thorp. 2006. Isotopic evidence for dietary variability in the early hominin *Paranthropus robustus*. *Science* 314: 980–981.

Spoor, F., M. G. Leakey, P. N. Gathogo, F. H. Brown, S. C. Anton, I. McDougall, C. Kiarie, F. K. Manthi, and L. N. Leakey. 2007. Implications of new early *Homo* fossils from Ileret, east of Lake Turkana, Kenya. *Nature* 448: 688–691.

Stafford, N. 2007. The other greenhouse effect. *Nature* 448: 526–528.

Stanford, C. B. 1995. Chimpanzee hunting behavior and human evolution. *American Scientist* 83(3): 256–263.

Stanford, C. B. 2001. *The Hunting Apes*. Princeton, NJ: Princeton University Press.

Stanton, W. 1960. *The Leopard's Spots: Scientific Attitudes toward Race in America, 1815–59*. Chicago: University of Chicago Press.

Steadman, D. W. 2003. *Hard Evidence: Case Studies in Forensic Anthropology*. Upper Saddle River, NJ: Prentice Hall.

Stearns, S. C. 1992. *The Evolution of Life Histories*. New York: Oxford University Press.

Stearns, S. C., S. G. Byars, D. R. Govindaraju, and D. Ewbank. 2010. Measuring selection in contemporary human populations. *Nature Reviews Genetics* 11: 611–622.

Steckel, R. H., J. C. Rose, C. S. Larsen, and P. L. Walker. 2002. Skeletal health in the Western Hemisphere from 4000 B.C. to the present. *Evolutionary Anthropology* 11: 142–155.

Steegmann, A. T., Jr. 2007. Human cold adaptation: An unfinished agenda. *American Journal of Human Biology* 19: 218–227.

Steele, D. G. and J. F. Powell. 1993. Paleobiology of the first Americans. *Evolutionary Anthropology* 2: 138–146.

Steinfeld, H., P. Gerber, T. Wassenaar, V. Castel, M. Rosales, and C. de Haan. 2006. *Livestock's Long Shadow: Environmental Issues and Options*. Rome, Italy: Food and Agriculture Organization of the United Nations.

Stevens, N. J., E. R. Seiffert, P. M. O'Connor, E. M. Roberts, M. D. Schmitz, C. Krause, E. Gorscak, S. Ngasala, T. L. Hieronymus, and J. Temu. 2013. Palaeontological evidence for an Oligocene divergence between Old World monkeys and apes. *Nature* 497: 611–614.

Stevenson, J. C., M. A. Grimes, and P. M. Stevenson. 2004. Reproductive measures, fitness, and migrating Mennonites: An evolutionary analysis. *Human Biology* 76: 667–687.

Stewart, T. D. 1953. An anthropologist looks at Lincoln. *Smithsonian Report for 1952*: 419–437.

Stewart, T. D. 1977. The Neanderthal skeletal remains from Shanidar Cave, Iraq: A summary of findings to date. *Proceedings of the American Philosophical Society* 121: 121–165.

Stewart, T. D. 1979. *Essentials of Forensic Anthropology*. Springfield, IL: Charles C. Thomas.

Stiner, M. C. 2001. Thirty years on the "Broad Spectrum Revolution" and paleolithic demography. *Proceedings of the National Academy of Sciences USA* 98: 6993–6996.

Stini, W. A. 1995. Osteoporosis in biocultural perspective. *Annual Review of Anthropology* 24: 397–421.

Stinson, S. 2000. Growth variation: Biological and cultural factors. Pp. 425–463 in S. Stinson, B. Bogin, R. Huss-Ashmore, and D. O'Rourke, eds. *Human Biology: An Evolutionary and Biocultural Perspective*. New York: Wiley-Liss.

Stinson, S., B. Bogin, R. Huss-Ashmore, and D. O'Rourke, eds. 2000. *Human Biology: An Evolutionary and Biocultural Perspective*. New York: Wiley-Liss.

Stinson, S., B. Bogin, and D. O'Rourke, eds. 2012. *Human Biology: An Evolutionary and Biocultural Perspective*, 2nd ed. Hoboken, NJ: Wiley-Blackwell.

Stinson, S., B. Bogin, D. O'Rourke, and R. Huss-Ashmore. 2012. Human biology: An evolutionary and biocultural perspective. Pp. 3–22 in S. Stinson, B. Bogin, and D. O'Rourke, eds. *Human Biology: An Evolutionary and Biocultural Perspective*, 2nd ed. Hoboken, NJ: Wiley-Blackwell.

Stocker, T. F., D. Qin, G. K. Plattner, M. Tignor, S. K. Allen, J. Boschung, A. Nauels, Y. Xia, V. Bex, and P. M. Midgley, eds. 2013. *Climate Change 2013: The Physical Science Basis. Contribution of*

Working Group I to the Fifth Assessment Report of the Intergovernmental Panel on Climate Change. New York: Cambridge University Press.

Stocking, G., ed. 1974. *The Shaping of American Anthropology, 1883–1911: A Franz Boas Reader*. New York: Basic Books.

Stokstad, E. 2003. The vitamin D deficit. *Science* 302: 1886–1888.

Stokstad, E. 2004. Forest loss makes monkeys sick. *Science* 305: 1230–1231.

Stone, A. C. 2000. Ancient DNA from skeletal remains. Pp. 351–371 in M. A. Katzenberg and S. R. Saunders, eds. *Biological Anthropology of the Human Skeleton*. New York: Wiley-Liss.

Stone, L., P. F. Lurquin, and L. L. Cavalli-Sforza. 2007. *Genes, Culture, and Human Evolution: A Synthesis*. Malden, MA: Blackwell.

Stoneking, M. 1993. DNA and recent human evolution. *Evolutionary Anthropology* 2: 60–73.

Storz, J. F. 2010. Genes for high altitudes. *Science* 329: 40–41.

Stott, R. 2003. *Darwin and the Barnacle: The Story of One Tiny Creature and History's Most Spectacular Scientific Breakthrough*. New York: Norton.

Stott, R. 2012. *Darwin's Ghosts: The Secret History of Evolution*. New York: Spiegel & Grau.

Strachan, D. P. 1989. Hay fever, hygiene, and household size. *British Medical Journal* 299: 1259–1260.

Street, M., T. Terberger, and J. Orschiedt. 2006. A critical review of the German Paleolithic hominin record. *Journal of Human Evolution* 51: 551–579.

Strickland, S. S. and P. S. Shetty. 1998. *Human Biology and Social Inequality*. Cambridge, UK: Cambridge University Press.

Strier, K. B. 1994. Myth of the typical primate. *Yearbook of Physical Anthropology* 37: 233–271.

Strier, K. B. 2010. Primate behavior and sociality. Pp. 243–257 in C. S. Larsen, ed. *A Companion to Biological Anthropology*. Chichester, UK: Wiley-Blackwell.

Strier, K. B. 2017. *Primate Behavioral Ecology*, 5th ed. New York: Routledge.

Strier, K. B. and J. P. Boubli. 2006. A history of long-term research and conservation of northern muriquis (*Brachyteles hypoxanthus*) at the Estacao Biologica de Caratinga/RPPN-FMA. *Primate Conservation* 20: 53–63.

Strier, K. B., J. P. Boubli, F. B. Pontual, and S. L. Mendes. 2006. Human dimensions of northern muriqui conservation efforts. *Ecological and Environmental Anthropology* 2: 44–53.

Stringer, C. and R. McKie. 1998. *African Exodus: The Origins of Modern Humanity*. New York: Henry Holt.

Stringer, C. B., J. C. Finlayson, R. N. E. Barton, Y. Fernández-Jalvo, I. Cáceres, R. C. Sabin, E. J. Rhodes, A. P. Currant, J. Rodríguez-Vidal, F. G. Giles-Pacheco, and J. A. Riquelme-Cantal. 2008. Neanderthal exploitation of marine mammals in Gibraltar. *Proceedings of the National Academy of Sciences USA* 105: 14319–14324.

Strum, S. C. and L. F. Fedigan. 2000. *Primate Encounters: Models of Science, Gender, and Society*. Chicago: University of Chicago Press.

Susman, R. L. 1994. Fossil evidence for early hominid tool use. *Science* 265: 1570–1573.

Susman, R. L. 1998. Hand function and tool behavior in early hominids. *Journal of Human Evolution* 35: 23–46.

Susman, R. L. 2004. *Oreopithecus bambolii*: An unlikely case of hominidlike grip capability in a Miocene ape. *Journal of Human Evolution* 46: 105–117.

Susman, R. L. 2005. *Oreopithecus*: Still apelike after all these years. *Journal of Human Evolution* 49: 405–411.

Susman, R. L., J. T. Stern, and W. L. Jungers. 1984. Arboreality and bipedality in Hadar hominids. *Folia Primatologica* 43: 113–156.

Susser, E., J. B. Kirkbride, B. T. Heijmans, J. K. Kresovich, L. H. Lumey, and A. D. Stein. 2012. Maternal prenatal nutrition and health in grandchildren and subsequent generations. *Annual Review of Anthropology* 41: 577–610.

Sussman, R. W. 2014. *The Myth of Race: The Troubling Persistence of an Unscientific Idea*. Cambridge, MA: Harvard University Press.

Sussman, R. W. and P. A. Garber. 2007. Primate sociality. Pp. 636–651 in S. Bearder, C. J. Campbell, A. Fuentes, K. C. Mackinnon, and M. Panger, eds. *Primates in Perspective*. New York: Oxford University Press.

Sussman, R. W., P. A. Garber, and J. M. Cheverud. 2005. Importance of cooperation and affiliation in the evolution of primate sociality. *American Journal of Physical Anthropology* 128: 84–97.

Sutikna, T., M. W. Tocheri, M. J. Morwood, E. W. Saptomo, Jatmiko, et al. 2016. Revised stratigraphy and chronology for *Homo floresiensis* at Liang Bua in Indonesia. *Nature* 532: 366–369.

Suwa, G., R. T. Kono, S. Katoh, B. Asfaw, and Y. Beyene. 2007. A new species of great ape from the late Miocene epoch in Ethiopia. *Nature* 448: 921–924.

Suwa, G., R. T. Kono, S. W. Simpson, B. Asfaw, C. O. Lovejoy, and T. D. White. 2009. Paleobiological implications of the *Ardipithecus ramidus* dentition. *Science* 326: 94–99.

Swallow, D. 2003. Genetics of lactase persistence and lactose intolerance. *Annual Review of Genetics* 37: 197–219.

Swindler, D. R. 1998. *Introduction to the Primates*. Seattle: University of Washington Press.

Swisher, C. C., III, G. H. Curtis, and R. Lewin. 2000. *Java Man*. New York: Scribner.

Swisher, C. C., III, W. J. Rink, S. C. Anton, H. P. Schwarcz, G. H. Curtis, A. Suprijo, and S. Widiasmoro. 1996. Latest *Homo erectus* of Java: Potential contemporaneity with *Homo sapiens* in Southeast Asia. *Science* 274: 1870–1874.

Sykes, B. 2001. *The Seven Daughters of Eve: The Science That Reveals Our Genetic Ancestry*. New York: Norton.

Szalay, F. S., ed. 1975. *Approaches to Primate Paleobiology*. Contributions to Primatology 5. Basel, Switzerland: S. Karger.

Szalay, F. S. and E. Delson. 1979. *Evolutionary History of the Primates*. New York: Academic Press.

Szalay, F. S., A. L. Rosenberger, and M. DaGosto. 1987. Diagnosis and differentiation of the order Primates. *Yearbook of Physical Anthropology* 30: 75–105.

Tabor, E., ed. 2007. *Emerging Viruses in Human Populations*. Amsterdam, Netherlands: Elsevier.

Takai, M., F. Anaya, N. Shigehara, and T. Setoguchi. 2000. New fossil materials of the earliest New World monkey, *Branisella boliviana*, and the problem of platyrrhine origins. *American Journal of Physical Anthropology* 111: 263–281.

Tamm, E., T. Kivisild, M. Reidla, M. Metspalu, D. G. Smith, C. J. Mulligan, C. M. Bravi, O. Rickards, C. Martinez-Labarga, E. K. Khusnutdinova, S. A. Fedorova, M. V. Golubenko, V. A. Stepanov, M. A. Gubina, S. I. Zhadanov, L. P. Ossipova, L. Damba, M. I. Voevoda, J. E. Dipierri, R. Villems, and R. S. Malhi. 2007. Beringian standstill and spread of Native American founders. *PLoS One* 9: e829.

Tang, H., T. Quertermous, B. Rodriguez, S. L. R. Kardia, X. Zhu, A. Brown, J. S. Pankow, M. A. Province, S. C. Hunt, E. Boerwinkle, N. J. Schork, and N. J. Risch. 2005. Genetic structure, self-identified race/ethnicity, and confounding in case-control association studies. *American Journal of Human Genetics* 76: 268–275.

Tanner, J. M. 1978. *Fetus into Man: Physical Growth from Conception to Maturity*. Cambridge, MA: Harvard University Press.

Tanno, K.-I. and G. Wilcox. 2006. How fast was wild wheat domesticated? *Science* 311: 1886.

Tattersall, I. 1995. *The Fossil Trail*. New York: Oxford University Press.

Tattersall, I. 2007. Madagascar's lemurs: Cryptic diversity or taxonomic inflation. *Evolutionary Anthropology* 16: 12–23.

Taubes, G. 2008. The bacteria fight back. *Science* 321: 356–361.

Taylor, R. E. 1995. Radiocarbon dating: The continuing revolution. *Evolutionary Anthropology* 4: 169–181.

Taylor, R. E. 2002. Dating archaeological materials. Pp. 15–35 in P. N. Peregrine, C. R. Ember, and M. Ember, eds. *Archaeology: Original Readings in Method and Practice*. Upper Saddle River, NJ: Prentice Hall.

Taylor, R. E. and M. J. Aitken. 1997. *Chronometric Dating in Archaeology*. New York: Plenum Press.

Teaford, M. F., P. S. Ungar, and F. E. Grine. 2002. Paleontological evidence for the diets of African Plio-Pleistocene hominins with special reference to early *Homo*. Pp. 143–166 in P. S. Ungar and M. F. Teaford, eds. *Human Diet: Its Origin and Evolution*. Westport, CT: Bergin & Garvey.

Teleki, G. 1973. *The Predatory Behavior of Wild Chimpanzees*. Bucknell, PA: Bucknell University Press.

Templeton, A. 2002. Out of Africa again and again. *Nature* 416: 45–51.

Templeton, A. 2005. Haplotype trees and modern human origins. *Yearbook of Physical Anthropology* 48: 33–59.

Teshler-Nicola, M., ed. 2006. *Early Modern Humans at the Moravian Gate: The Mladeč Caves and Their Remains*. New York: Springer.

Thalmann, O., B. Shapiro, P. Cui, V. J. Schuenemann, and S. K. Sawyer. 2013. Complete mitochondrial genomes of ancient canids suggest a European origin of domestic dogs. *Science* 342: 871–874.

Theunissen, B., L. T. Theunissen, and E. Perlin-West. 2006. *Eugène Dubois and the Ape-Man from Java: The History of the First Missing Link and Its Discoverer*. Berlin, Germany: Springer.

Thompson, J. L., G. E. Krovitz, and A. J. Nelson. 2003. *Patterns of Growth and Development in the Genus* Homo. Cambridge, UK: Cambridge University Press.

Thompson, L. 2010. Climate change: The evidence and our options. *Behavior Analyst* 33: 153–170.

Thompson, L. G., H. H. Brecher, E. Mosley-Thompson, D. R. Hardy, and B. G. Mark. 2009. Glacier loss on Kilimanjaro continues unabated. *Proceedings of the National Academy of Sciences USA* 106: 19770–19775.

Thompson, L. G., E. Mosley-Thompson, M. E. Davis, K. A. Henderson, H. H. Brecher, V. S. Zagorodnov, T. A. Mashiotta, P.-N. Lin, V. N. Mikhalenko, D. R. Hardy, and J. Beer. 2002. Kilimanjaro ice core records: Evidence of Holocene climate change in tropical Africa. *Science* 298: 589–593.

Thomson, K. 2011. Jefferson's old bones. *American Scientist* 99: 200–203.

Thorne, A. G. and M. H. Wolpoff. 2003. The multiregional evolution of humans. *Scientific American* 2: 46–53.

Thuiller, W. 2007. Climate change and the ecologist. *Nature* 448: 550–552.

Tianyuan, L. and D. A. Etler. 1992. New middle Pleistocene hominid crania from Yunxian in China. *Nature* 357: 404–407.

Tidwell, J. 2004. Requiem for a primate. *Zoogoer* 33(5): 8–15.

Tishkoff, S. A., F. A. Reed, A. Ranciaro, B. F. Voight, C. C. Babbitt, J. S. Silverman, K. Powell, H. M. Mortensen, J. B. Hirbo, M. Osman, M. Ibrahim, S. A. Omar, G. Lema, T. B. Nyambo, J. Ghori, S. Bumpsted, J. K. Pritchard, T. B. Wray, and P. Deloukas. 2006. Convergent adaptation of human lactase persistence in Africa and Europe. *Nature Genetics* 39: 31–40.

Tishkoff, S. A., R. Varkonyi, N. Cahinhinan, S. Abbes, G. Argyropoulos, G. Destro-Bisol, A. Drousiotou, B. Dangerfield, G. Lefranc, J. Loiselet, A. Piro, M. Stoneking, A. Tagarelli, G. Tagarelli, E. H. Touma, S. Williams, and A. G. Clark. 2001. Haplotype diversity and linkage disequilibrium at human *G6PD*: Recent origin of alleles that confer malarial resistance. *Science* 293: 455–462.

Tobias, P. V. 1967. *The Cranium and Maxillary Dentition of* Zinjanthropus (Australopithecus) boisei. Cambridge, UK: Cambridge University Press.

Tobias, P. V. 1997. Dart, Raymond A. (1893–1988). Pp. 314–315 in F. Spencer, ed. *History of Physical Anthropology: An Encyclopedia*. New York: Garland.

Tobias, P. V. 1997. Taung. Pp. 1022–1025 in F. Spencer, ed. *History of Physical Anthropology: An Encyclopedia*. New York: Garland.

Tocheri, M. W. 2019. Unknown human species found in Asia. *Nature* 568: 176–177.

Tocheri, M. W., C. M. Orr, S. G. Larson, T. Sutikna, Jatmiko, E. W. Saptomo, R. A. Due, T. Djubiantono, M. J. Morwood, and W. L. Jungers. 2007. The primitive wrist of *Homo floresiensis* and its implications for hominin evolution. *Science* 317: 1743–1745.

Tomasello, M. and J. Call. 1994. Social cognition in monkeys and apes. *Yearbook of Physical Anthropology* 37: 273–305.

Toth, N. and K. Schick, eds. 2007. *The Oldowan: Case Studies into the Earliest Stone Age*. Bloomington, IN: Stone Age Institute.

Trevathan, W. 2015. Primate pelvic anatomy and implications for birth. *Philosophical Transactions of the Royal Society of London B* 370: 20140065. DOI: 10.1098/rstb.2014.0065.

Trinkaus, E. 1983. *The Shanidar Neandertals*. New York: Academic Press.

Trinkaus, E. 2005. Early modern humans. *Annual Review of Anthropology* 34: 207–230.

Trinkaus, E. 2006. Modern human versus Neandertal evolutionary distinctiveness. *Current Anthropology* 47: 597–620.

Trinkaus, E. 2007. European early modern humans and the fate of the Neandertals. *Proceedings of the National Academy of Sciences USA* 104: 7367–7372.

Trinkaus, E., O. Moldovan, Ş. Milota, A. Bilgăr, S. Sarcina, S. Athreya, S. Bailey, R. Rodrigo, G. Mircea, T. Higham, C. Ramsey, and J. van der Plicht. 2003. An early modern human from the Peştera cu Oase, Romania. *Proceedings of the National Academy of Sciences USA* 100: 11231–11236.

Trinkaus, E. and P. Shipman. 1993. Neandertals: Images of ourselves. *Evolutionary Anthropology* 1: 194–201.

Trinkaus, E. and P. Shipman. 1994. *The Neandertals: Of Skeletons, Scientists, and Scandal*. New York: Vintage.

Trinkaus, E. and J. Svoboda. 2006. *Early Modern Human Evolution in Central Europe: The People of Dolní Věstonice and Pavlov*. New York: Oxford University Press.

Tubiello, F. N. and G. Fischer. 2007. Reducing climate change impacts on agriculture: Global and regional effects of mitigation, 2000–2080. *Technological Forcasting and Social Change* 74: 1030–1056.

Tung, T. A. 2011. *Bioarchaeology of Wari Imperialism*. Gainesville: University Press of Florida.

Turner, C. G., II. 1991. *The Dentition of Arctic Peoples*. New York: Garland.

Ubelaker, D. H. 2010. Issues in forensic anthropology. Pp. 412–426 in C. S. Larsen, ed. *A Companion to Biological Anthropology*. Chichester, UK: Wiley-Blackwell.

Ubelaker, D. H. and H. Scammell. 1992. *Bones: A Forensic Detective's Casebook*. New York: Edward Burlingame.

Ugan, A. 2005. Does size matter? Body size, mass collecting, and their implications for understanding prehistoric foraging behavior. *American Antiquity* 70: 75–89.

Ulijaszek, S. J. 2008. Seven models of population obesity. *Angiology* 59: S34–S38.

Ulijaszek, S. J., F. E. Johnston, and M. A. Preece. 1998. *The Cambridge Encyclopedia of Human Growth and Development.* Cambridge, UK: Cambridge University Press.

Ulijaszek, S. J. and H. Lofink. 2006. Obesity in biocultural perspective. *Annual Review of Anthropology* 35: 337–360.

Ulijaszek, S. J. and L. M. Schell. 1999. The future of urban environments. Pp. 311–322 in L. M. Schell and S. J. Ulijaszek, eds. *Urbanism, Health and Human Biology in Industrialised Countries.* Cambridge, UK: Cambridge University Press.

Underdown, S. and S. J. Oppenheimer. 2016. Do patterns of covariation between human pelvis shape, stature, and head size alleviate the obstetric dilemma. *Proceedings of the National Academy of Sciences USA* 113: E258. DOI: 10.1073/pnas.1517524113.

Ungar, P. and P. Lucas. 2010. Tooth form and function in biological anthropology. Pp. 516–529 in C. S. Larsen, ed. *A Companion to Biological Anthropology.* Chichester, UK: Wiley-Blackwell.

Ungar, P. S., F. E. Grine, and M. F. Teaford. 2006. Diet in early *Homo*: A review of the evidence and a new model of adaptive versatility. *Annual Review of Anthropology* 35: 209–228.

Ungar, P. S. and M. Sponheimer. 2011. The diets of early hominins. *Science* 334: 190–193.

Ungar, P. S. and M. F. Teaford. 2002. *Human Diet: Its Origin and Evolution.* Westport, CT: Bergin & Garvey.

United Nations Human Settlements Programme. 2005. *2005 Annual Report.* Nairobi, Kenya: UN-HABITAT.

U.S.–Venezuela Collaborative Research Project and N. S. Wexler. 2004. Venezuelan kindreds reveal that genetic and environmental factors modulate Huntington's disease age of onset. *Proceedings of the National Academy of Sciences USA* 101: 3498–3503.

Vahakangas, K. 2004. Ethical aspects of molecular epidemiology of cancer. *Carcinogenesis* 25: 465–471.

Van Arsdale, A. P. 2019. Population demography, ancestry, and the biological concept of race. *Annual Review of Anthropology* 48: 227–241.

Van Arsdale, A. P. and M. H. Wolpoff. 2012. A single lineage in early Pleistocene *Homo*: Size variation continuity in early Pleistocene *Homo* crania from East Africa and Georgia. *Evolution* 67: 841–850.

Van den Bergh, G. D., Y. Kaifu, I. Kurniawan, R. T. Kono, A. Brumm, E. Setiyabudi, F. Aziz, and M. J. Morwood. 2016. *Homo floresiensis*-like fossils from the early Middle Pleistocene of Flores. *Nature* 534: 245–248.

Van Schaik, C. P., M. Ancrenaz, G. Borgen, B. Galdikas, C. D. Knott, I. Singleton, A.

Suzuki, S. S. Utami, and M. Merrill. 2003. Orangutan cultures and the evolution of material culture. *Science* 299: 102–105.

Van Schaik, C. and C. D. Knott. 2001. Geographic variation in tool use on Neesia fruits in orangutans. *American Journal of Physical Anthropology* 114: 331–342.

Varea, C., C. Bernis, P. Montero, S. Arias, A. Barroso, and B. Gonzalez. 2000. Secular trend and intrapopulational variation in age at menopause in Spanish women. *Journal of Biosocial Science* 32: 383–393.

Vekua, A., D. Lordkipanidze, G. P. Rightmire, J. Agusti, R. Ferring, G. Maisuradze, A. Mouskhelishvili, M. Nioradze, M. P. de Leon, M. Tappen, M. Tvalchrelidze, and C. Zollikofer. 2002. A new skull of early *Homo* from Dmanisi, Georgia. *Science* 297: 85–89.

Veltman, J. A. and H. G. Brunner. 2012. De novo mutations in human genetic disease. *Nature Reviews Genetics* 13: 565–575.

Vignaud, P., P. Duringer, H. T. Mackaye, A. Likius, C. Blondel, J.-R. Boisserie, L. de Bonis, V. Eisenmann, M.-E. Etienne, D. Geraads, F. Guy, T. Lehmann, F. Lihoreau, N. Lopez-Martinez, C. Mourer-Chauvire, O. Otero, J.-C. Rage, M. Schuster, L. Viriot, A. Zazzo, and M. Brunet. 2002. Geology and paleontology of the upper Miocene Toros-Menalla hominid locality, Chad. *Nature* 418: 152–155.

Villa, P. 1992. Cannibalism in prehistoric Europe. *Evolutionary Anthropology* 1: 93–104.

Villa, P. and W. Roebroeks. 2014. Neandertal demise: An archaeological analysis of the modern human superiority complex. *PLoS ONE* 9: e96424.

Villanea, F.A., D. A. Bolnick, C. Monroe, R. Worl, R. Cambra, A. Leventhal, and B. M. Kemp. 2013. Brief communication: Evolution of a specific O allele (O1v^{G542A}) supports unique ancestry of Native Americans. *American Journal of Physical Anthropology* 151: 649–657.

Villmoare, B., W. H. Kimbel, C. Seyoum, C. J. Campisano, E. N. DiMaggio, J. Rowan, D. R. Braun, J. R. Arrowsmith, and K. E. Reed. 2015. Early *Homo* at 2.8 Ma from Ledi-Geraru, Afar, Ethiopia. *Science* 347: 1352–1359.

Visalberghi, E., D. Fragaszy, E. Ottoni, P. Izar, M. G. de Oliveira, and F. R. D. Andrade. 2007. Characteristics of hammer stones and anvils used by wild bearded capuchin monkeys (*Cebus libidinosus*) to crack open palm nuts. *American Journal of Physical Anthropology* 132: 426–444.

Visalberghi, E., M. Haslam, N. Spagnoletti, and D. Fragaszy. 2013. Use of stone

hammer tools and anvils by bearded capuchin monkeys over time and space: Construction of an archeological record of tool use. *Journal of Archeological Science* 40: 3222–3232.

Vogel, G. 2016. Experts fear Zika's effects may be even worse than thought. *Science* 352: 1375–1376.

Voland, E., A. Chasiotis, and W. Schiefenhövel, eds. 2005. *Grandmotherhood: The Evolutionary Significance of the Second Half of Female Life.* New Brunswick, NJ: Rutgers University Press.

Volpato, V., R. Macchiarelli, D. Guatelli-Steinberg, I. Fiore, L. Bondioli, and D. W. Frayer. 2012. Hand to mouth in a Neandertal: Right-handedness in Regourdou 1. *PLoS One* 7: e43949.

Von Cramon-Taubadel, N. 2017. Measuring the effects of farming on human skull morphology. *Proceedings of the National Academy of Sciences USA* 114: 8917–8919.

Von Koenigswald, G. H. R. 1952. *Gigantopithecus blacki* von Koenigswald, a giant fossil hominoid from the Pleistocene of southern China. *Anthropological Papers of the American Museum of Natural History* 43(4): 293–325.

Voris, H. K. 2000. Maps of Pleistocene sea levels in Southeast Asia: Shorelines, river systems and time durations. *Journal of Biogeography* 27: 1153–1167.

Wade, L. 2019. New species of ancient human unearthed. *Science* 364: 108.

Wadman, M., J. Couzin-Frankel, J. Kaiser, and C. Matacic. 2020. A rampage through the body. *Science* 368: 356–360.

Wagner, G. 1996. Fission-track dating in paleoanthropology. *Evolutionary Anthropology* 5: 165–171.

Wagner, G. A. 1999. *Age Determination of Young Rocks and Artifacts: Physical and Chemical Clocks in Quarternary Geology and Archaeology.* New York: Springer-Verlag.

Walker, A. and R. Leakey. 1993. *The Nariokotome* Homo erectus *Skeleton.* Cambridge, MA: Harvard University Press.

Walker, A. and P. Shipman. 1996. *The Wisdom of the Bones: In Search of Human Origins.* New York: Knopf.

Walker, A. and P. Shipman. 2005. *The Ape in the Tree: An Intellectual and Natural History of Proconsul.* Cambridge, MA: Belknap Press.

Walker, A. and M. Teaford. 1989. The hunt for *Proconsul. Scientific American* 260(1): 75–82.

Walker, C. S., Z. D. Cofran, M. Grabowski, D. Marchi, R. W. Cook, et al. 2019. Morphology of the *Homo naledi* femora from Lesedi. *American Journal of Physical Anthropology* 170: 5–23.

Walker, J., R. A. Cliff, and A. G. Latham. 2006. U-Pb isotopic age of the StW 573 hominid from Sterkfontein, South Africa. *Science* 314: 1592–1594.

Walker, P. L. 2001. A bioarchaeological perspective on the history of violence. *Annual Review of Anthropology* 30: 573–596.

Wallace, I. J., M. L. Burgess, and B. A. Patel. 2019. Phalangeal curvature in a chimpanzee raised like a human: Implications for inferring arboreality in fossil hominins. *Proceedings of the National Academy of Sciences USA* 117: 11223–11225.

Walsh, P. D. 2015. Protecting apes could backfire. *New York Times* September 27: 5.

Wang, E. T., G. Kodama, P. Baldi, and R. K. Moyzis. 2006. Global landscape of recent inferred Darwinian selection for *Homo sapiens*. *Proceedings of the National Academy of Sciences USA* 103: 135–140.

Ward, C., M. Leakey, and A. Walker. 1999. The new hominid species *Australopithecus anamensis*. *Evolutionary Anthropology* 7: 197–205.

Ward, C. V., A. S. Hammond, M. Plavcan, and D. R. Begun. 2019. A late Miocene hominid pelvis from Hungary. *Journal of Human Evolution* 136: 102645.

Ward, C. V., M. G. Leakey, and A. Walker. 2001. Morphology of *Australopithecus anamensis* from Kanapoi and Allia Bay, Kenya. *Journal of Human Evolution* 41: 255–368.

Ward, S. C. and D. L. Duren. 2002. Middle and late Miocene African hominoids. Pp. 385–397 in W. C. Hartwig, ed. *The Primate Fossil Record*. Cambridge, UK: Cambridge University Press.

Warden, S. J., S. M. Matilla Roosa, M. Kersh, A. L. Hurd, G. S. Fleisig, et al. 2014. Physical activity when young provides lifelong benefits to cortical bone size and strength in men. *Proceedings of the National Academy of Sciences USA* 111: 5337–5342.

Washburn, S. L. and I. DeVore. 1961. The social life of baboons. *Scientific American* 204: 62–72.

Wasik, B. R. and P. E. Turner. 2013. On the biological success of viruses. *Annual Review of Microbiology* 67: 519–541.

Waters, M. R. 2019. Late Pleistocene exploration and settlement of the Americas by modern humans. *Science* 365: eaat5447. DOI: 10.1126/science.aat5447.

Waters, M. R. and T. W. Stafford Jr. 2007. Redefining the age of Clovis: Implications for the peopling of the Americas. *Science* 315: 1122–1126.

Watson, J. D. 1980. *The Double Helix: A Personal Account of the Discovery of the Structure of DNA*. New York: Norton.

Watson, J. D. 2005. *Darwin: The Indelible Stamp*. Philadelphia: Running Press.

Watson, J. D. and F. H. C. Crick. 1953. Molecular structure of nucleic acids: A structure for deoxyribonucleic acid. *Nature* 171: 964–969.

Weaver, T. D. 2003. The shape of the Neandertal femur is primarily the consequence of a hyperpolar body form. *Proceedings of the National Academy of Sciences USA* 100: 6926–6929.

Weaver, T. D. 2009. The meaning of Neandertal skeletal morphology. *Proceedings of the National Academy of Sciences USA* 106: 16028–16033.

Webb, S. G. 2006. *The First Boat People*. Cambridge, UK: Cambridge University Press.

Weiner, J. 1994. *The Beak of the Finch: A Story of Evolution in Our Time*. New York: Knopf.

Weiner, J. S. and K. P. Oakley. 1954. The Piltdown fraud: Available evidence reviewed. *American Journal of Physical Anthropology* 12: 1–7.

Weinstein, K. J. 2007. Thoracic skeletal morphology and high-altitude hypoxia in Andean prehistory. *American Journal of Physical Anthropology* 134: 36–49.

Weiss, E., M. E. Kislev, and A. Hartmann. 2006. Autonomous cultivation before domestication. *Science* 312: 1608–1610.

Weiss, K. M. 1995. *Genetic Variation and Human Disease: Principles and Evolutionary Approaches*. Cambridge, UK: Cambridge University Press.

Weiss, K. M. 2010. Seeing the forest through the gene-trees. *Evolutionary Anthropology* 19: 210–221.

Weiss, K. M. and A. V. Buchanan. 2003. Evolution by phenotype: A biomedical perspective. *Perspectives in Biology and Medicine* 46: 159–182.

Weiss, K. M. and A. V. Buchanan. 2010. Evolution: What it means and how we know. Pp. 41–55 in C. S. Larsen, ed. *A Companion to Biological Anthropology*. Chichester, UK: Wiley-Blackwell.

Weiss, K. M. and D. M. Parker. 2013. Will you stop bugging me? Malaria and the evolutionary challenge that won't go away. *Evolutionary Anthropology* 22: 46–51.

Weiss, M. L. 2000. An introduction to genetics. Pp. 47–85 in S. Stinson, B. Bogin, R. Huss-Ashmore, and D. O'Rourke, eds. *Human Biology: An Evolutionary and Biocultural Perspective*. New York: Wiley-Liss.

Weiss, M. L. and J. Tackney. 2012. An introduction to genetics. Pp. 53–98 in S. Stinson, B. Bogin, and D. O'Rourke, eds. *Human Biology: An Evolutionary and Biocultural Perspective*, 2nd ed. Hoboken, NJ: Wiley-Blackwell.

Welker, F., J. Ramos-Madrigal, M. Kuhlwilm, W. Liao, P. Gutenbrunner, et al. 2019. Enamel proteome shows that *Gigantopithecus* was an early diverging pongine. *Nature* 576: 262–265.

Westaway, K. E., J. Louys, R. Due Awe, M. J. Morwood, G. J. Price, et al. 2017. An early modern human presence in Sumatra 73,000–63,000 years ago. *Nature* 548: 322–325.

Westaway, M. C., and D. Lambert. 2014. First Australians: Origins. Pp. 2787–2800 in C. Smith, ed. *Encyclopedia of Global Archaeology*. New York: Springer Science.

White, T. D. 2001. Once were cannibals. *Scientific American* 265(2): 58–65.

White, T. D. 2002. Earliest hominids. Pp. 407–417 in W. C. Hartwig, ed. *The Primate Fossil Record*. Cambridge, UK: Cambridge University Press.

White, T. D. 2006. Early hominid femora: The inside story. *Comptes Rendus Palevol* 5: 99–108.

White, T. D. 2006. Human evolution: The evidence. Pp. 65–81 in J. Brockman, ed. *Intelligent Thought: Science versus the Intelligent Design Movement*. New York: Vintage.

White, T. D., B. Asfaw, Y. Beyene, Y. Haile-Selassie, C. O. Lovejoy, G. Suwa, and G. WoldeGabriel. 2009. *Ardipithecus ramidus* and the paleobiology of early hominids. *Science* 326: 64–86.

White, T. D., B. Asfaw, D. DeGusta, H. Gilbert, G. D. Richards, G. Suwa, and F. C. Howell. 2003. Pleistocene *Homo sapiens* from Middle Awash, Ethiopia. *Nature* 423: 742–747.

White, T. D. and P. A. Folkens. 2005. *The Human Bone Manual*. Burlington, MA: Elsevier Academic.

White, T. D., C. O. Lovejoy, B. Asfaw, J. P. Carlson, and G. Suwa. 2015. Neither chimpanzee nor human, *Ardipithecus* reveals the surprising ancestry of both. *Proceedings of the National Academy of Sciences USA* 112: 4877–4884.

White, T. D., G. Suwa, and B. Asfaw. 1994. *Australopithecus ramidus*, a new species of early hominid from Aramis, Ethiopia. *Nature* 371: 306–312.

White, T. D., G. Suwa, W. K. Hart, R. C. Walter, G. WoldeGabriel, J. de Heinzelin, J. D. Clark, B. Asfaw, and E. Vrba. 1993. New discoveries of *Australopithecus* at Maka in Ethiopia. *Nature* 366: 261–265.

White, T. D., G. Suwa, S. Simpson, and B. Asfaw. 2000. Jaws and teeth of *Australopithecus afarensis* from Maka, Middle Awash, Ethiopia. *American Journal of Physical Anthropology* 111: 45–68.

White, T. D., G. WoldeGabriel, B. Asfaw, S. Ambrose, Y. Beyene, R. L. Bernor, J.-R. Boisserie, B. Currie, H. Gilbert, Y. Haile-Selassie, W. K. Hart, L.-J. Hlusko, F. C. Howell, R. T. Kono, T. Lehmann, A. Louchart, C. O. Lovejoy, P. R. Renne, H. Saegusa, E. S. Vrba, H. Wesselman, and G. Suwa. 2006. Asa Issie, Aramis and the origin of *Australopithecus*. *Nature* 440: 883–889.

White House Task Force on Childhood Obesity. 2010. *Solving the Problem of Childhood Obesity within a Generation: White House Task Force on Childhood*

Obesity Report to the President. Washington, DC: Executive Office of the President of the United States.

Whiten, A. 2005. The second inheritance system of chimpanzees and humans. *Nature* 435: 60–63.

Whiten, A., F. J. Ayala, M. W. Feldman, and K. N. Laland. 2017. The extension of biology through culture. *Proceedings of the National Academy of Sciences USA* 114: 7775–7781.

Whiten, A., J. Goodall, W. C. McGrew, T. Nishidas, V. Reynolds, Y. Sugiyama, C. E. G. Tutin, R. W. Wrangham, and C. Boesch. 1999. Cultures in chimpanzees. *Nature* 399: 682–685.

Whiten, A., K. Schick, and N. Toth. 2009. The evolution and social transmission of percussive technology: Integrating evidence from paleaeoanthropology and primatology. *Journal of Human Evolution* 57: 420–435.

Wild, E. M., M. Tescler-Nicola, W. Kutschera, P. Steier, E. Trinkaus, and W. Wanek. 2005. Direct dating of Early Upper Palaeolithic human remains from Mladeč. *Nature* 435: 332–335.

Wiley, A. S. and J. S. Allen. 2009. *Medical Anthropology: A Biocultural Approach*. New York: Oxford University Press.

Willcox, G. 2013. The roots of cultivation in southwestern Asia. *Science* 341: 39–40.

Williams, S. R. 2006. Menstrual cycle characteristics and predictability of ovulation in Bhutia women in Sikkim, India. *Journal of Physiological Anthropology* 25: 85–90.

Wilson, E. O. 1975. *Sociobiology: The New Synthesis*. Cambridge, MA: Harvard University Press.

Wilson, E. O., ed. 2006. *From So Simple a Beginning: Darwin's Four Great Books* [*The Voyage of the H.M.S. Beagle, The Origin of Species, The Descent of Man, The Expression of Emotions in Man and Animals*]. By Charles Darwin. New York: Norton.

Wilson, E. O. 2016. The global solution to extinction. *New York Times* March 13: 7.

Winchester, S. 2001. *The Map That Changed the World: William Smith and the Birth of Modern Geology*. New York: HarperCollins.

WoldeGabriel, G., Y. Haile-Selassie, P. R. Renne, W. K. Hart, S. H. Ambrose, B. Asfaw, G. Heiken, and T. White. 2001. Geology and paleontology of the Late Miocene Middle Awash valley, Afar rift, Ethiopia. *Nature* 412: 175–178.

WoldeGabriel, G., T. D. White, G. Suwa, P. Renne, J. de Heinzelin, W. K. Hart, and G. Heiken. 1994. Ecological and temporal placement of early Pliocene hominids at Aramis, Ethiopia. *Nature* 371: 330–333.

Wolfe, N. D., C. P. Dunavan, and J. Diamond. 2007. Origins of major human infectious diseases. *Nature* 447: 279–283.

Wolpoff, M. H. 1996. *Human Evolution*. New York: McGraw-Hill.

Wolpoff, M. H. 1999. *Paleoanthropology*, 2nd ed. New York: McGraw-Hill.

Wolpoff, M. H. 2006. "Neandertals on Our Family Tree." John Wesley Powell Memorial Lecture, Southwestern and Rocky Mountain Division of the American Association for the Advancement of Science, Denver, CO.

Wolpoff, M. H. and R. Caspari. 1997. *Race and Human Evolution: A Fatal Attraction*. New York: Simon & Schuster.

Wolpoff, M. H., B. Senut, M. Pickford, and J. Hawks. 2002. *Sahelanthropus* or "*Sahelpithecus*"? *Nature* 419: 581–582.

Wolpow, N. 2015. Meet the woman who helped discover a new species of human. *Refinery29*. https://www.refinery29.com/en-us/2015/09/93844/hannah-morris-homo-naledi-discovery.

Wood, A. R., T. Esko, J. Yang, S. Vedantam, T. H. Pers, et al. 2014. Defining the role of common variation in the genomic and biological architecture of adult human height. *Nature Genetics* 46: 1173–1186.

Wood, B. 1997. The oldest whodunnit in the world. *Nature* 385: 292–293.

Wood, B. 2002. Hominid revelations from Chad. *Nature* 418: 133–135.

Wood, B. 2006. A precious little bundle. *Nature* 443: 278–280.

Wood, B. 2010. Systematics, taxonomy, and phylogeny: Ordering life, past and present. Pp. 56–73 in C. S. Larsen, ed. *A Companion to Biological Anthropology*. Chichester, UK: Wiley-Blackwell.

Wrangham, R. 2017. Control of fire in the Paleolithic. *Current Anthropology* 58(suppl. 16): S303–S313.

Wrangham, R. and R. Carmody. 2010. Human adaptation to the control of fire. *Evolutionary Anthropology* 19: 187–199.

Wrangham, R. and D. Peterson. 1996. *Demonic Males: Apes and the Origins of Human Violence*. Boston: Houghton Mifflin.

Wrangham, R. W. 1999. Evolution of coalitionary killing. *Yearbook of Physical Anthropology* 42: 1–30.

Wrangham, R. W. 2009. *Catching Fire: How Cooking Made Us Human*. New York: Basic Books.

Wynn, T. 2002. Archaeology and cognitive evolution. *Behavioral and Brain Sciences* 25: 389–438.

Xia, W., S. He, A. Liu, and L. Xu. 2008. Epidemiological study of hip fracture in Beijing, China. *Bone* 43: S13.

Yong, E. 2015. 6 tiny cavers, 15 odd skeletons, and 1 amazing new species of ancient human. *Atlantic Monthly*. http://www.theatlantic.com/science/archive/2015/09/homo-naledi-rising-star-cave-hominin/404362/.

Yudell, M. 2014. *Race Unmasked: Biology and Race in the 20th Century*. New York: Columbia University Press.

Yudell, M., D. Roberts, R. DeSalle, and S. Tishkoff. 2016. Taking race out of human genetics. *Science* 351: 564–565.

Yusupova, G., L. Jenner, B. Rees, D. Moras, and M. Yusupov. 2006. Structural basis for messenger RNA movement on the ribosome. *Nature* 444: 391–394.

Zalasiewicz, J., C. N. Waters, A. D. Barnosky, A. Cearreta, M. Edgeworth, et al. 2015. Colonization of the Americas, "Little Ice Age" climate, and bomb-produced carbon: Their role in defining the Anthropocene. *Anthropocene Review* 2: 117–127.

Zalmout, I. S., W. J. Sanders, L. M. MacLatchy, G. F. Gunnell, Y. A. Al-Mufarreh, M. A. Ali, A.-A. H. Nasser, A. M. Al-Masari, S. A. Al-Sobhi, A. O. Nadhra, A. H. Matari, J. A. Wilson, and P. D. Gingerich. 2010. New Oligocene primate from Saudi Arabia and the divergence of apes and Old World monkeys. *Nature* 466: 360–365.

Zeder, M. A. 1994. After the revolution: Post-Neolithic subsistence strategies in northern Mesopotamia. *American Anthropologist* 96: 97–126.

Zeder, M. A. 1999. Animal domestication in the Zagros: A review of past and current research. *Paleorient* 25: 11–25.

Zeder, M. A. 2000. The goats of Ganj Dareh: Identification of the earliest directly dated domestic animals. *Science* 287: 2254–2257.

Zeder, M. A. 2006. Central questions in the domestication of plants and animals. *Evolutionary Anthropology* 15: 105–117.

Zeder, M. A. 2008. Domestication and early agriculture in the Mediterranean Basin: Origins, diffusion, and impact. *Proceedings of the National Academy of Sciences USA* 105: 11597–11604.

Zeder, M. A., D. G. Bradley, E. Emshwiller, and B. D. Smith. 2006. *Documenting Domestication: New Genetic and Archaeological Paradigms*. Berkeley: University of California Press.

Zhang, Y. and T. Harrison. 2017. *Gigantopithecus blacki*: A giant ape from the Pleistocene of Asia revisited. *American Journal of Physical Anthropology* 162(suppl. S63): 153–177.

Zhivotovsky, L. A., P. A. Underhill, C. Cinnioglu, M. Kayser, B. Morar, T. Kivisild, R. Scozzari, F. Cruciani, G. Destro-Bisol, G. Spedini, G. K. Chambers, R. J. Herrera, K. K. Yong, D. Gresham, I. Tournev, M. W. Feldman, and L. Kalaydjieva. 2004. The effective mutation rate at Y chromosome short tandem repeats, with application to human population-divergence time. *American Journal of Human Genetics* 74: 50–61.

Zhu, R. X., K. A. Hoffman, R. Potts, C. L. Deng, Y. X. Pan, B. Guo, C. D. Shi, Z. T. Guo, B. Y. Yuan, Y. M. Hou, and W. W. Huang. 2001. Earliest presence of humans in northeast Asia. *Nature* 413: 413–417.

Zhu, R. X., R. Potts, F. Xie, K. A. Hoffman, C. L. Deng, C. D. Shi, Y. X. Pan, H. Q. Wang, G. H. Shi, and N. Q. Wu. 2004. New evidence on the earliest human presence at high northern latitudes in northeast Asia. *Nature* 431: 559–562.

Zilhão, J., D. E. Angelucci, E. Badal-García, F. d'Errico, F. Daniel, L. Dayet, K. Douka, T. F. G. Higham, M. J. Martínez-Sánchez, R. Montes-Bernárdez, S. Murcia-Mascarós, C. Pérez-Sirvent, C. Roldán-García, M. Vanhaeren, V. Villaverde, R. Wood, and J. Zapata. 2010. Symbolic use of marine shells and mineral pigments by Iberian Neandertals. *Proceedings of the National Academy of Sciences USA* 107: 1023–1028.

Zilhão, J. and E. Trinkaus. 2002. *Portrait of the Artist as a Child: The Gravettian Human Skeleton from the Abrigo do Lagar Velho and Its Archeological Context*. Trabalhos de Arqueologia 22. Lisbon, Portugal: Instituto Portugues de Arqueologia.

Zimmer, C. 2006. A fin is a limb is a wing: How evolution fashioned its masterworks. *National Geographic* 210(5): 111–135.

Zimmer, C. 2006. *Smithsonian Intimate Guide to Human Origins*. Washington, DC: Smithsonian Books.

Zimmer, C. 2018. *She Has Her Mother's Laugh: The Powers, Perversions, and Potential of Heredity*. New York: Dutton.

Zimmet, P., K. G. M. M. Alberti, and J. Shaw. 2001. Global and society implications of the diabetes epidemic. *Nature* 414: 782–787.

Zollikofer, C. P. E. and M. S. Ponce de León. 2010. Reconsidering Neanderthal birth: Tabun mom, Kebara dad, Mezmaiskaya baby, and the consequences. *American Journal of Physical Anthropology* 141(suppl. 50): 252.

Zuberbühler, K. 2003. Referential signaling in non-human primates: Cognitive precursors and limitations for the evolution of language. *Advances in the Study of Behavior* 33: 265–307.

CREDITS

PHOTOS

Front Matter: Page ii: H Lansdown/Alamy Stock Photo; p. vi: John Nixon Photography; p. ix: Images & Stories/Alamy Stock Photo; p. x (top): Historia/Shutterstock; (bottom, author): John Nixon Photography; (ape): Anup Shah/Getty Images; (DNA): Benjamin Albiach Galen/Shutterstock; p. xi: Peter Scoones/Nature Picture Library; p. xii: Flashpop/Getty Images; p. xiii (top): Jean-Michel Labat/Science Source; (bottom): AF Archive/Alamy Stock Photo; p. xiv: Ton Bangkeaw/Shutterstock; p. xv: Doring Kindersley/UIG/Bridgeman Images; p. xvi (top) GranTotufo/Shutterstock; (bottom): Herman Verwey/Shutterstock; p. xvii: (reconstruction of child): Philippe Plailly/Science Source; (skull): Look at Sciences/Science Source; p. xviii: Johner Images/Getty Images; p. xxvii (right): Photo by John Hawks courtesy of Lee Berger and the University of Witwatersrand; (left): Xinhua/Alamy Stock Photo; p. xxxiv: Lesley A. Gregoricka.

Chapter 1: Pages 2–3: Images & Stories/Alamy Stock Photo; p. 6 (a): Bettmann/Getty Images; p. 6 (b): Pasquale Sorrentino/Science Source; (c): Leslie Moore; (d): Horacio Villalobos/Corbis/Getty Images; p. 8: AP Photo/Nati Harnik; p. 10 (a): Dr Francesco Coschino; p. 10 (b): Jochen Tack/Alamy; (c): Barbara Piperata; (d): AP Photo/Alan Marler; (e): Daniel Herard/Science Source; (f): Penelope Breese/Getty Images; p. 14 (top): © The Trustees of the British Museum; (bottom): Peter Davey/Flpa/imageBroker/Shutterstock; p. 15: Blend Images/Alamy Stock Photo; p. 17 (top): Science History Images/Alamy Stock Photo; (bottom): Tim Graham/Getty Images; p. 18 (top): Wolfgang Kaehler/Getty Images; (bottom): Getty Images.

Chapter 2: p. 21: Sukuman Rittem/Shutterstock; pp. 22–23: Historia/Shutterstock; p. 24 (a): Pictorial Press/Alamy Stock Photo; (b): Historia/Shutterstock; p. 25 (b): Tim Graham/Getty Images; (c): Miguel Castro/Science Source; (d): Kevin Schafer/Getty Images; (e) & (f): Tim Graham/Getty Images; p. 26: Classic Image/Alamy Stock

Photo; p. 27 (top): Pictorial Press/Alamy Stock Photo; (bottom): Stephen Marshak; p. 28 (top): Pictorial Press Ltd/Alamy Stock Photo; p. 28 (a): IanDagnall Computing/Alamy Stock Photo; (b): Omikron/Science Source; p. 29 (a): Science History Images/Alamy Stock Photo; (b): Dipper Historic/Alamy Stock Photo; p. 30: ART Collection/Alamy Stock Photo; p. 32 (a): Colport/Alamy Stock Photo; (b): General Photographic Agency/Getty Images; p. 33 (a): ART Collection/Alamy Stock Photo; p. 35 (a): Dan Sparham/Shutterstock; (b): Chronicle/Alamy Stock Photo; (c): Hulton Archive/Getty Images; p. 35 (bottom): FLHC 1B/Alamy Stock Photo; pp. 36–37 (background spread): Granger; p. 36 (top left and bottom right): Historia/Shutterstock; p. 36 (top right): Classic Image/Alamy Stock Photo; (center): Manfred Gottschalk/Alamy Stock Photo; p. 37 (top right): Andy Rain/EPA/Shutterstock; (center right): AMcCulloch/Alamy Stock Photo; (center left): Wikimedia/public domain; (bottom): Chronicle/Alamy Stock Photo; p. 38 (top): De Agostini Picture Library/Bridgeman Images; (a): From Catalogue of Ernst Benary, © Board of Trustees of the Royal Botanic Gardens, Kew; (b): Greg Mercer/Field Museum Library/Getty Images; p. 40: Universal History Archive/UIG/Shutterstock; p. 41 (a): Science History Images/Alamy Stock Photo; (b): David M. Phillips/Science Source; p. 42 (a): Courtesy of the Archives, California Institute of Technology; (b) & (c): Eye of Science/Science Source; 44 (b): Omikron/ Science Source; (c): Science History Images/Alamy Stock Photo.

Chapter 3: Pages 48–49: (chimp): Anup Shah/Getty Images; (author): John Nixon Photography; (DNA): Benjamin Albiach Galen/Shutterstock; p. 51 (b): Eye of Science/Science Source; (c): M. I. Walker/Science Source; p. 52 (top row): (a): M. I. Walker/Science Source; (b): Michael Abbey/Science Source; (c): Imaginechina/Alamy Stock Photo; (d, left): Michael Abbey/Science Source; (d, right): SPL/Science Source; (e): Jim Zuckerman/Getty Images; p. 52 (bottom row): (a): CNRI/Science Source; (b): Steve

Gschmeissner/Science Source; (c): Eye of Science/Science Source; p. 53 (a): Biophoto Associates/Science Source; (camel): Yuliya Honcharska/Shutterstock; (guinea pig): Eric Isselee/Shutterstock; (salamander): dpa picture alliance archive/Alamy Stock Photo; (housefly): Robin Brar/Shutterstock; (apple): Dionisvera /Shutterstock; (potato): Joe Gough/Shutterstock; (petunia): Roy Morsch/Getty Images; (algae): Gari Wyn Williams/Alamy; (lemur): Rosanne Tackaberry/Alamy Stock Photo; (monkey): Milan Zygmunt/Shutterstock; (orangutan): Gudkov Andrey/Shutterstock; p. 54 (top): Biophoto Associates/Science Source; (bottom): Keith R. Porter/Science Source; p. 57 (top right): Addenbrookes Hospital/Science Source; (a): L. Willatt/Science Source; (b): Biophoto Associates/Science Source; p. 59 (b): Steve Gschmeissner/Science Source; p. 63 (a): Clouds Hill Imaging Ltd./Getty Images; (b): Photo Researchers, Inc./Science Source; 68 (a): John Radcliffe Hospital/Science Source; (b): RGB Ventures/SuperStock/Alamy Stock Photo.

Chapter 4: Pages 80–81: Peter Scoones/Nature Picture Library; p. 83 (b): Sheli Jensen/Shutterstock; (c): Dennis Jacobsen/Alamy Stock Photo; 84 (a): Mira/Alamy Stock Photo; (b): Universal Images Group North America LLC/DeAgostini/Alamy Stock Photo; (c): Somchai Som/Shutterstock; (d): Roberto Nistri/Alamy Stock Photo; (e): Andre Mueller/Shutterstock; (f): *Papers in Palaeontology, 2021*, pp. 1–20], Wiley online library, 19 January 2021, "A new remarkably preserved fossil assassin bug (Insecta, Heteroptera, Reduviidae) from the Eocene Green River Formation of Colorado," Daniel R. Swanson, Sam W. Heads, Steven J. Taylor, Yinan Wang; p. 86: Album/Alamy Stock Photo; p. 90 (a): W. Perry Conway/Corbis; (b): makasana photo/Alamy Stock Photo; (c): Anthony Banister/Science Source; (d): Eye of Science/Science Source; p. 92: Stephen Frink Collection/Alamy Stock Photo; p. 93 (top): Michael Willmer Forbes Tweedie/Science Source; p. 93 (in chart top): Ian Redding/Alamy Stock Photo; (in chart bottom): DJTaylor/Shutterstock; p. 96:

Human Origins, Arizona State University; (center right): Human Origins Program at the National Museum of Natural History, Smithsonian Institution, photo by Chip Clark; (right): Human Origins Program at the National Museum of Natural History, Smithsonian Institution, photo by Chip Clark; p. 323 (left): Alan Walker; (right): FOSSIL CREDIT: National Museums of Kenya, Nairobi. PHOTO CREDIT: © 1985 David L. Brill, humanoriginsphotos.com; p. 324 (a): Image by Matthew Bennett, Bournemouth University, Bennett et al. "Early Hominin Foot Morphology Based on 1.5-Million-Year-Old Footprints from Ileret, Kenya" Science 27 February 2009: vol. 323 no. 5918 pp. 1197–1201. © 2009 AAAS; p. 324 (Daka Partial Cranium): FOSSIL CREDIT: National Museum of Ethiopia, Addis Ababa, PHOTO CREDIT: © 2001 David L. Brill, humanoriginsphotos.com; (Gona Partial Cranium): Dr. Scott Simpson; p. 325: FOSSIL CREDIT: National Museum of Ethiopia, Addis Ababa, PHOTO CREDIT: © 2001 David L. Brill, humanoriginsphotos.com; p. 328 (top): Courtesy of and © National Museum of Tanzania & Eric Delson (photo by C. Tarka); (bottom): PHOTO CREDIT: © Tim D. White, humanoriginsphotos.com; p. 329: Lordkipanidze et al. "A Complete Skull from Dmanisi, Georgia and the Evolutionary Biology of Early Homo." Science 8 October 2013: 342 (6156) 326-331. Copyright © 2013 AAAS; p. 330: Milford Wolpoff; p. 331: Philippe Plailly/Science Source; p. 332: ARTIFACT CREDIT: American Museum of Natural History, PHOTO CREDIT: © 1996 David L. Brill, humanoriginsphotos.com; p. 333 (all): Javier Trueba/ Madrid Scientific Films/Science Source; p. 336 (a & b): FOSSIL CREDIT: National Musuem of Tanzania, Dar es Salaam, PHOTO CREDIT: © 1985 David L. Brill, humanoriginsphotos.com; p. 337 (a and b): © Tim D. White, humanoriginsphotos.com; p. 338: © 1995 by Jay H. Matternes; p. 339: Courtesy of Michael Chazan; p. 340: ARTIFACT CREDIT: American Museum of Natural History, PHOTO CREDIT: © 1996 David L. Brill; humanoriginsphotos.com; p. 343 (a): photo by John Hawks, courtesy of Lee Berger and the University of Witwatersrand; (b): Xinhua/ Alamy Stock Photo.

Chapter 12: Pages 348–349 (reconstruction of child): Philippe Plailly/Science Source; (skull): Look at Sciences/Science Source; 350 (top): LVR-LandesMuseum, Bonn (bottom): National Library of Medicine; p. 354 (top left): Jeffrey H. Schwartz; (top center): Courtesy of Staatliches Museum fur Naturkunde; (top right): Milford Wolpoff; (right side top): Danita Delimont/Alamy Stock Photo; (right side bottom): Dr. W. Keith Kennedy; (bottom right): Milford Wolpoff; (bottom left): John Reader/Science Source; (left side bottom):

FOSSIL CREDIT: Musee De l'Homme, Paris, PHOTO CREDIT: © 1985 David L. Brill, humanoriginsphotos.com; (left side top): Javier Trueba/Madrid Scientific Films/Science Source; p. 355 (Kabwe): John Reader/Science Source; (Ngandong): Milford Wolpoff; p. 355 (a): Dr. W. Keith Kennedy; (b): Courtesy of and © of Eric Delson; p. 357 (Arago): FOSSIL CREDIT: Musee De l'Homme, Paris, PHOTO CREDIT: © 1985 David L. Brill, humanorigins.com; (Petralona): Milford Wolpoff; (Steinhem): Courtesy of Staatliches Museum fur Naturkunde; (Atapuerca and researcher): Javier Trueba/Madrid Scientific Films/Science Source; p. 358: Ira Block; p. 359 (Kebara): FOSSIL CREDIT: Tel Aviv University, Sackler School of Medicine, Department of Anatomy and Anthropology. PHOTO CREDIT: © 1995 David L. Brill, humanoriginsphotos.com; (cave): Georg Kristiansen/Alamy Stock Photo; 360 (all): © Dr. Erik Trinkaus; p.361: Tamisclao/Shutterstock; p. 362 (top): FOSSIL CREDIT: Geolosko-Paleontologi Musej, PHOTO CREDIT: © 1985 David L. Brill; humanoriginsphotos. com; p. 362 (a): © Tim D. White, humanoriginsphotos.com; (b): © 1999 Henry Gilbert, Berkeley; p. 363 (top): John Reader/Science Source; (bottom a): Granger; (b): Sculpture E.Daynes, Photo S.Entressangle/Lookat-Sciences/Science Source; p. 364 (top): John Reader/Science Source; (bottom): Milford Wolpoff; p.367 (both): ARTIFACT CREDIT: courtesy Denise de Soneville-Bordes, Centre Francois Bordes, Institut du Quaternaire, Batiment de Geologie, Universite de Bordeaux I PHOTO CREDIT: © 1985 David L. Brill, humanoriginsphotos.com; p. 369: Musee de l'Homme de Neandertal; p. 371 (left): Javier Trueba/MadridScientific Films/Science Source; (right): © Dr. Erik Trinkaus; p. 373 (a): Jeff Pachoud/Getty Images; (b): AP Photo/Jean Clottes; (c-1) ARTIFACT CREDIT: courtesy Denise de Sonneville-Bordes, Centre Francois Bordes, Institut du Quaternaire, Batiment de Geologie Universite de Bordeaux I. PHOTO CREDIT: © 1985 David L. Brill, humanoriginsphotos.com; (c-2): ARTIFACT CREDIT: Musee National de Prehistoire, Les Eyzies de Tayac, PHOTO CREDIT: © 1985 David L. Brill, humanoriginsphotos.com (c-3) ARTIFACT CREDIT: courtesy Denise de Sonneville-Bordes, Centre Francois Bordes, Institut du Quaternaire, Batiment de Geologie, Universite de Bordeaux I. PHOTO CREDIT: © 1985 David L. Brill, humanoriginsphotos.com; p. 374: Herto Reconstruction © 2005 Jay H. Matternes; Kabwe skull: Courtesy of Milford Wolpoff; butchering: ARTIFACT AND FOSSIL CREDIT: Paleoanthropology Laboratory, National Musuem of Ethiopia, PHOTO CREDIT: © Tim D. White, humanoriginsphotos.com; p. 375: Herto skull; FOSSIL CREDIT: Housed in

National Museum of Ethiopia, Addis Adaba, PHOTO CREDIT: Photo © 2001 David L. Brill, humanoriginsphotos.com; skulls with cutmakrs: ARTIFACT CREDIT & FOSSIL CREDIT: Paleoanthropology Laboratory, National Museum of Ethiopia, PHOTO CREDIT: Photo © 2003 Tim D. White, humanoriginsphotos.com; p. 377 (a): Ira Block; (b and bottom): Milford Wolpoff; p. 378 (a & b): Courtesy, Christopher Stojanowski, ASU; (Skhul): FOSSIL CREDIT: Peabody Museum, Harvard University, PHOTO CREDIT: © 1985 David L. Brill, humanoriginsphotos.com; p. 379 (a & b): The Natural History Museum/Alamy Stock Photo; p. 380 (map inset): Stringer/Reuters/Newscom; (Flores woman): Look at Sciences/Science Source; (skulls): Dr. Peter Brown; p. 382 (a & b): Courtesy of and © of Eric Delson; p. 383 (left): Photo by Milford Wolpoff. Wolpoff et al. 2004 "Why not the Neandertals?" World Archaeology 36 (4): 527–546. Copyright © 2004 Routledge; (right): Zilhão J. & Trinkaus E. (2002) 'Portrait of the Artist as a Child. The Gravettian Human Skeleton from the Abrigo do Lagar Velho and its Archaeological Context'. Instituto Português de Arqueologia. Photo by José Paulo Ruas; p. 384 (a & b): FOSSIL CREDIT: Musee De l'Homme, Paris, PHOTO CREDIT: © 1985 David L. Brill, humanoriginsphotos.com; (right): Courtesy of and © of Eric Delson; p. 385: Pictures From History/Newscom; p. 387: Dongju Zhang, Lanzhou University; p. 393 Milford Wolpoff; p. 394: Ira Block; p. 396 (b): Leland C. Bement; p. 397: James C. Chatters.

Chapter 13: Pages 400–401: Johner Images/ Getty Images; p. 402 (a): Cartoon by Ron Therien www.cartoonstock.com; (b): Corbis RF; p. 405 (b): Photo by John Doebly; p. 409 (a): blickwinkel/Alamy Stock Photo; (b): Scott Haddow; (bottom): Corbis RF; p. 412 (a): Bonnie Glencross; (b): Courtesy of Penn Museum; 412 (c): Image by D J Ortner © BARC, University of Bradford, UK; p. 413: China Photos/Getty Images; p. 416: funkyfood London - Paul Williams/Alamy Stock Photo; p. 417: John Warburton-Lee Photograph/Alamy Stock Photo; p. 420: Reuters/Alamy Stock Photo; p. 421 (a): Dr. Armen Taranyan/Science Source; p. 421 (b): Scimat/ Science Source; p. 422: Barry Stark. From Larsen. 1994. "In the wake of Columbus. Postcontact Native population biology of the Americas. Yearbook of Physical Anthropology" 37:109-154. © Wily-Liss; p. 423: David Scharf/Science Source; p. 425 (a): Eye of Science/Science Source; (b): Elena Ryabchikova/ Voisin/ Science Source; p. 424: Craig Hadley.

Timeline: (Ardipithecus skull): Brill Art & Art Renderings: FOSSIL CREDIT: Original in National Museum of Ethiopia, Addis

Ababa, DIGITAL RENDER CREDIT: © 2009 White, Suwa et al., humanorigins-photos.com; (Australopithecus gahri skull): Brill Art & Art Renderings: ARTIFACT CREDIT: Original in National Museum of Ethiopia, Addis Ababa, PHOTO CREDIT: © 1999 David L. Brill, humanoriginsphotos.com; (Naledi skull): John Hawks; (teeth): William K. Sacco; (Oldowan Chopper): Peter Bostrom/Lithic Casting; (prismatic blade core): Brill Art & Art Renderings ARTIFACT CREDIT: courtesy Denise de Sonneville-Bordes, Centre Francois Bordes, Institut du Quaternaire, Batiment de Geologie, Universite de Bordeaux PHOTO CREDIT: ©1985 David L. Brill, humanori-ginsphotos.com; (harpoon): Brill Art & Art Renderings: ARTIFACT CREDIT: courtesy R. Deffarge, Institut du Quaternaire, Batiment de Geologie, Universite de Bordeaux I, PHOTO CREDIT: © 1985 David L. Brill, humanoriginsphotos.com; (burial): Musee de l'Homme de Neandertal.

ILLUSTRATIONS

Chapter 4: Figure 4.9: Republished with permission from John Wiley & Sons, from Mark Ridley, *Evolution*, 3rd Ed., 2004; permission conveyed through Copyright Clearance Center, Inc. Figure 4.19: Jen Christiansen: Figure: Malaria Cycle, originally printed in "Tackling malaria" by Claire P. Dunavan, *Scientific American*, Vol. 293, No. 6, Dec. 2005, p. 79. Reprinted by permission.

Chapter 5: Figure 5.15: George Chaplin: Figures modified from N.G. Jablonski, *Skin: A Natural History*. 2006 © G. Chaplin. Reprinted by permission. Figure 5.22: Republished with permission of SAGE, from Eric P. Heymann and David Goldsmith, "Best approaches in the battle against Globesity? Learning lessons from our experience tackling HIV-AIDS and tobacco smoking," *JRSM Short Reports* 3(7): 1–9. Copyright © 2012, SAGE Publications. Permission conveyed through Copyright Clearance Center, Inc.

Chapter 6: Figure 6.30: Figure: "Ape and human pelvis mechanics" by Bruce Latimer. Reprinted with permission.

Chapter 8: Figure 8.21: R.H. Towner: Figure: Box 4. Constructing Chronologies from "Archaeological dendrochronology in the Southwestern U.S.," *Evolutionary Anthropology*, p. 73. Copyright © 2002, Wiley-Liss, Inc. Reprinted with permission of Wiley-Liss, Inc., a subsidiary of John Wiley & Sons, Inc. Figure 8.23a: BioArch: Figure: Amino Acid Dating from "Amino acid racemization." Reprinted by permission. Figure 8.23b: Republished with permission of McGraw-Hill Education, from Philip L. Stein and Bruce M. Rowe, *Physical Anthropology*, 9th Ed.; permission conveyed through Copyright Clearance Center, Inc.

Chapter 9: Figure 9.18: Laurie Grace: Figure: Map of Miocene Ape Fossil Localities, originally printed in "Apes" by D.R. Begun, *Scientific American*, Vol. 289, No. 2, 2003, p. 77. Reprinted by permission. Figure 9.27: Reprinted from *Current Biology* 8(16), Caro-Beth Stewart and Todd R. Disotell, "Primate evolution – In and out of Africa," 582–588. Copyright © 2002 Elsevier Science Ltd. All rights reserved. With permission from Elsevier.

Chapter 10: Figure 10.2: "Olduvai Gorge, Tanzania" from *The Human Evolution Coloring Book*, 2nd Ed. by Coloring Concepts, Inc. Copyright © 1982, 2000 by Coloring Concepts, Inc. Used by permission of HarperCollins Publishers. Figure 10.23: From Berhane Asfaw, Tim White, Owen Lovejoy, et al., "*Australopithecus garhi*: A new species of early hominid from Ethiopia," *Science* 284(5414): 629–635. Reprinted with permission from AAAS. Figure 10.28: Figure from "Did australopiths climb trees?" by Susan Larson. *Science*, Vol. 338. pp. 478–479. Copyright © 2010, The American Association for the Advancement of Science. Reprinted with permission from AAAS.

Chapter 11: Figure 11.29: Adapted by permission from Springer Nature: *Nature* News, Ewen Callaway, "Crowdsourcing digs up an early human species," Vol. 525, 2015. © 2015 Macmillan Publishers Limited. All rights reserved. Adapted from Paul HGM Dirks, Lee R. Berger, Eric M. Roberts, et al., "Geological and taphonomic context for the new hominin species *Homo naledi* from the Dinaledi Chamber, South Africa," *eLife* 4:e09561, 2015. https://doi.org/10.7554/eLife.09561.001 © 2015, Dirks et al.? This article is distributed under the terms of the Creative Commons Attribution License, which permits unrestricted use and redistribution provided that the original author and source are credited. https://creativecommons.org/licenses/by/4.0/

Chapter 12: Figure 12.29: Reprinted from *Journal of Archaeological Science* 26(6), Hervé Bocherens, Daniel Billiou, André Mariotti, et al., "Palaeoenvironmental and palaeodietary implications of isotopic biogeochemistry of last interglacial neanderthal and mammal bones in Scladina Cave (Belgium)," 599–607. Copyright © 1999 Academic Press. All rights reserved. With permission from Elsevier. Figure 12.53: Reprinted with permission of Annual Reviews, from Theodore G. Schurr, "The peopling of the new world: Perspectives from molecular anthropology," *Annual Review of Anthropology* 583(1):551–583, 2004; permission conveyed through Copyright Clearance Center, Inc.

Chapter 13: Figure 13.5B: Bruce D. Smith: Figure "The approximate time periods when plants and animals were first domesticated" from *The Emergence of Agriculture*, p. 13, 1998. Reprinted by permission. Figure 13.9: Colin Renfrew and Paul Bahn: Figure drawn by Annick Boothe. From *Archaeology: Theories, Methods and Practice*, 4th Ed. by Colin Renfrew and Paul Bahn, Thames & Hudson Inc., New York. Reprinted by permission of the publisher. Figure 13.16: Roberto Osti: Figure "Bones of the Postcontact Indians" from "Reading the bones of La Florida" by Clark S. Larsen, *Scientific American*, Vol. 282, No. 6, p. 84. Reprinted by permission of Roberto Osti Illustrations. Figure 13.20: Clark S. Larsen: Figure 3.2 "Percentage of teeth affected by dental caries in eastern North America" from *Bioarchaeology: Interpreting Behavior from the Human Skeleton*, p. 69, Cambridge University Press, 1997. © Cambridge University Press 1997. Reproduced with permission of the Licensor through PLSclear.

INDEX